5 STEPS TO A 5

AP European History

2010-2011

Jeffrey Brautigam, Ph.D.

McGraw Hill

New York   Chicago   San Francisco   Lisbon   London   Madrid   Mexico City
Milan   New Delhi   San Juan   Seoul   Singapore   Sydney   Toronto

1 2 3 4 5 6 7 8 9 10 11 12 13 14 15 16 17 18 19 20   QPD/QPD   0 9

ISBN 978-0-07-162456-5
MHID   0-07-162456-2
ISSN 2150-6388

Credits:
Public domain Soviet cartoon, page 249: Wikipedia
Public domain *Punch* cartoon, page 253: John Leech Archive

Series editor was Grace Freedson, and the project editor was Don Reis.
Series design by Jane Tenenbaum.

McGraw-Hill books are available at special quantity discounts to use as premiums and sales promotions, or for use in corporate training programs. To contact a representative, please e-mail us at bulksales@mcgraw-hill.com.

AP, *Advanced Placement Program*, and *College Board* are registered trademarks of the College Entrance Examination Board, which was not involved in the production of, and does not endorse, this product.

CONTENTS

STEP 4   Review the Knowledge You Need to Score High

Unit 1   1450 to the French Revolutionary and Napoleonic Era   45

STEP 5   Build Your Test-Taking Confidence

PREFACE

Welcome to the world of Advanced Placement (AP) European History. Whether you are, or have been, enrolled in an AP European History course at your school or are just preparing on your own, this guide will help you to move smoothly and confidently from your individual starting point through a five-step process that will bring you the level of preparation you desire. Along the way, you will be evaluating your current level of preparation, evaluating your learning strategies, reading widely, analyzing primary documents, taking practice multiple-choice tests, and writing practice essays. As you go, you will be developing the strategies and confidence you need to score a 5 on the AP European History exam.

The five-step process is described in detail in the Introduction to this guide. Here, I simply want to urge you to enter into your preparation with enthusiasm. The intricate story of European history is dramatic, fascinating, and extremely relevant to the world in which you live. The information, understanding, and skills that you learn by working through this guide will help you to do well on the AP European History exam, but they will also help you to excel in college and to become a well-informed, critically thinking human being.

As you begin, it is important that you not think of this guide as some large book to "get through." This guide is a tool and, like many tools, it can be used in a number of different ways. You can follow it through from beginning to end or you can jump around, using the information and exercises contained in it in any way that suits you best. So take some time to familiarize yourself with the contents of this guide; get a feel for how it "works." Then, when you are ready, read Chapters 1 and 2; they will help you to choose the mode of preparation that is right for you.

Good luck and enjoy your journey!

ACKNOWLEDGMENTS

I would like to thank Eric Dodge for putting me in touch with Grace Freedson, and Grace Freedson for connecting me with McGraw-Hill. I would also like to thank all those who assisted me in the preparation of this book: Ruth Mills for her superior editing of the first edition and Del Franz for his efforts on the second; Robyn Ryle for her critical reading and support; and my daughter, Grace Brautigam, for all the times she patiently waited for daddy to "finish his book."

ABOUT THE AUTHOR

JEFFREY BRAUTIGAM is Associate Professor and Chair of the Department of History at Hanover College in Hanover, Indiana, where he evaluates all requests for AP college credit and placement in history. A recipient of a Ph.D. in history from the University of Florida, he has taught European History at the college level for 15 years. He is the coauthor of *A Student Introduction to Charles Darwin* (Kendall/Hunt, 1999, ISBN 0-7872-6311-7). Professor Brautigam is a historian who writes for students and general audiences. He is a member of the American Historical Association and the Association of Core Texts and Courses.

INTRODUCTION: THE FIVE-STEP PROGRAM

The Basics

If you are looking at this book, it is because you are considering taking the AP European History exam. Maybe you are enrolled in an AP European History class in your high school, or maybe you are planning a course of study on your own. Either way, you need some help and you have come to a bookstore or are shopping online to find it. Right now, there are a number of guides either on the shelf or on the screen in front of you, and you are wondering about the differences between them. The fact is, all the guides in front of you are similar in a number of ways: Each is written by an experienced history instructor who is intimately familiar with the AP European History exam; each contains a concise review of the material you will need to master in order to do well on the exam; and each contains a number of practice exams and exercises to assist you in that preparation.

There is, however, one crucial difference: This book is based upon the highly successful "5 Steps to a 5" program. If you are like the thousands of students who have used the *5 Steps to a 5* program to successfully prepare for AP exams, it is a difference worth exploring.

Introducing the Five-Step Preparation Program

This book is organized as a five-step program to prepare you for success on the AP European History exam. These steps are designed to provide you with the skills and strategies vital to the exam and the practice that can lead you to that perfect 5. Here are the five steps:

Step 1: Set Up Your Study Program

In this step, you will read a brief overview of the AP European History exam and be guided through a process to help determine which of the following preparation programs is right for you:

- full school year: September through May
- one semester: January through May
- six weeks: basic training for the exam

This is covered in Chapters 1 and 2.

Step 2: Determine Your Test Readiness

In this step, you will work through a series of diagnostic exercises and questions that will evaluate your current level of preparation and help you to devise new strategies for success.

- Go through each diagnostic exercise step-by-step and question-by-question to build your confidence level.
- Review the correct answers and explanations so that you see what you do and do not yet fully understand.
- Evaluate your level of preparation and your current preparation strategies.

All of this is provided in Chapter 3.

Step 3: Develop Strategies for Success

In this step, you will learn strategies that will help you do your best on the exam. These strategies cover both the multiple-choice and free-response sections of the exam:

- Learn to read multiple-choice questions: see Chapter 4.
- Learn how to answer multiple-choice questions, including whether or not to guess: see Chapter 4.
- Learn how to plan and write the free-response questions, which include both document-based questions, covered in Chapter 5, and the thematic essay questions, which are covered in Chapter 6.

Step 4: Review the Knowledge You Need to Score High

In this step, you will learn or review the material you need to know for the test. This review section takes up the bulk of this book and covers the material covered on the AP European History exam:

- 1450 to the French Revolutionary and Napoleonic Era: see Chapters 7–14 and the Unit I summary
- the Napoleonic Era to the present: see Chapters 15–22 and the Unit 2 summary

At first glance, it may look like there is a lot of material to cover, enough to summarize a yearlong experience in an AP European History course. Some AP courses will have covered more material than yours, some will have covered less, but the bottom line is that if you thoroughly review this material, you will have studied the great majority of the material that is tested on the exam, and you will have significantly increased your chances of scoring well. But even more important, you will have developed successful strategies for testing well in the field of history that will help you on both the exam and in your future college history classes.

Step 5: Build Your Test-Taking Confidence

In this step, you will complete your preparation by testing yourself on practice exams. This guide contains *two* complete exams in European History, each with full answers and explanations for the multiple-choice questions and suggestions and possible outlines for answers to the free-response essay questions. Be aware that these practice exams are *not* reproduced questions from actual AP European History exam, but they mirror both the material tested by AP and the way in which it is tested.

Appendixes of Other Helpful Information

Finally, at the end of this book, you will find additional resources to aid your preparation:

- a glossary of key terms you are likely to encounter in your reading and on the AP European History exam
- a list of Web sites related to the AP European History exam
- a brief bibliography

Introduction to the Graphics Used in This Book

To emphasize particular skills and strategies, several icons are used throughout this book. An icon in the margin will alert you that you should pay particular attention to the accompanying text. The three icons are:

This icon indicates a very important concept or fact that you should not pass over.

This icon calls your attention to something you might want to try when attempting to answer a particular type of question.

This icon indicates other useful information you might want to keep in mind about the exam.

Finally, *italic* words indicate terms that are included in the glossary at the end of this book.

STEP 1

Set Up Your Study Program

CHAPTER 1

What You Need to Know About the AP European History Exam

IN THIS CHAPTER

Summary: Familiarize yourself with the exam and get answers to frequently asked questions.

Key Ideas

✪ The AP European History exam offers high school students the opportunity to earn college credit.

✪ You should check with the colleges you are considering for their AP-credit policies.

✪ The AP coordinator at your school is your contact person for the exam.

✪ The exam is divided into multiple-choice and free-response sections; each is worth 50 percent of the total grade.

✪ The free-response section consists of three essays: a document-based question and two thematic questions.

Background Information

The Advanced Placement Program is overseen by an organization known as the College Board, which is involved in many facets of the college admissions process. The program offers highly motivated high school students the opportunity to take college-level courses while still in high school, and the opportunity to earn credit or advanced standing at college or university by taking the Advanced Placement exams. Since its inception in 1955, the Advanced Placement Program has grown to 37 courses and gives exams across 22 subject areas. The European History program is just one of many offered in the social studies area.

Frequently Asked Questions About the AP European History Exam

Why Take the AP European History Exam?

Most students take the exam with the hope of earning college credit. Most schools will give you college credit for a score of 4 or 5, and some will give credit for a 3. However, the policies of individual colleges and universities will vary, so you should check with the schools you are interested in attending for their specific policies.

One advantage of having a college credit in European History is that you are one class closer to graduation, but there are a couple of other good reasons to take the exam:

- First, getting a college credit for AP European History will mean that you will be able to opt out of either a required, introductory course in European History or an elective course. Either way, you will have greater flexibility in choosing your courses and you will be able to move on to the more advanced and specific courses (either in history or in some other field) that interest you.
- Second, having AP credit on your transcript can increase your chances of getting into the school you want because it tells college admissions officers that you are a serious student who has some experience with college-level work.

Do I Have to Take an AP European History Class to Take the Exam?

No. Taking an AP European History class at your high school is a great way to prepare, but it is not required. The College Board simply urges students to study the kinds of skills and subjects outlined in the AP European History Course Description. The Course Description is available online from the College Board (www.collegeboard.com). The McGraw-Hill five-step program is based on both the College Board Course Description for AP European History and the Exam Guidelines, so working through this guide will help you both to develop the relevant skills and to familiarize yourself with the relevant subject material.

Who Writes and Grades the AP European History Exam?

The exam is written by a team of college and high school history instructors called the AP European History Test Development Committee. The Committee is constantly evaluating the test and field-testing potential questions. The exam is graded by a much larger group of college and high school teachers who meet at a central location in early June to evaluate and score exams that were completed by students the previous month.

What Is on the Exam?

The format of the AP European History exam is shown in Table 1.1. The multiple-choice questions cover European history from the High Renaissance period to the present. About half of the questions cover the period from 1450 to the French Revolutionary and Napoleonic era, with

Table 1.1 AP European History Exam Format

SECTION	TEST ITEMS	TIME LIMIT	PERCENTAGE OF TOTAL GRADE
Multiple-choice	80 questions	55 minutes	50%
		15-minute Break	
Free-response	3 essays	130 minutes	50%

Table 1.2 The Free-Response Section

PART	TEST ITEM	SUGGESTED TIME LIMIT
A	Document-Based Question (DBQ)	60 minutes (includes 15-minute reading period)
B	First Thematic Essay Question	35 minutes
C	Second Thematic Essay Question	35 minutes

the second half covering the French Revolutionary and Napoleonic era to the present. Within the 80 questions, there is a thematic breakdown:

- about one-third of the questions cover cultural and intellectual themes
- about one-third cover political and diplomatic themes
- about one-third cover social and economic themes

We will discuss strategies for doing well on the multiple-choice section in Chapter 4. The free-response section is composed of three parts, as shown in Table 1.2. The document-based question (DBQ) requires you to read a series of excerpts from historical documents and respond to a question about them. The thematic essay questions each ask you to choose one question from each of two groups of three questions. Once the 15-minute reading period for the DBQ is over, you are free to use the rest of the 130-minute time period any way you wish.

We will discuss strategies for doing well on the DBQ in Chapter 5, and on the thematic essays in Chapter 6.

How Is the Exam Evaluated and Scored?

The multiple-choice section, worth 50 percent of the total grade, is scored by computer. The three essays that make up the free-response section are, together, worth 50 percent of the total score. The DBQ essay is worth 45 percent of the free-response score; the two thematic essays together contribute 55 percent of the free-response score. All free-response essays are scored by "readers" (the college and high school teachers who are hired to do the job), who have been trained to score the responses in accordance with a set of guidelines. The scoring guidelines for each question are drawn up by a team of the most experienced readers. (We will discuss what kinds of things the guidelines tell the readers to look for in Chapters 5 and 6.) Evaluation and scoring are monitored by the chief reader and table leaders and periodically analyzed for consistency.

The scores for the multiple-choice and free-response sections are combined into composite scores; the Chief Faculty Consultant then converts the range of composite scores to the 5-point scale of the AP grades:

- Grade 5 is the highest possible grade; it indicates that you are extremely well qualified to receive college credit.
- Grade 4 indicates that you are well qualified.
- Grade 3 indicates that you are qualified.
- Grade 2 indicates that you are possibly qualified.
- Grade 1 indicates that you are not qualified to receive college credit.

How Do I Register?

Whether you are enrolled in a high school AP course or preparing for the test on your own, the best thing to do is see your guidance counselor. He or she will direct you to the AP coordinator for your school. You will need the coordinator because that is the person who collects your money and dispenses information about the exact location and date of the test. If for some reason your school does not have an AP coordinator, you can test through another school. To find out which schools in your area offer the test and to find a coordinator, you can check with the College Board's website (www.collegeboard.com). You should visit the site, even if your school has an AP coordinator, as it will always have the latest and most up-to-date information.

It currently costs $86 to take the AP European History exam. Students who demonstrate financial need may receive a $22 refund to help offset the cost of testing. There are also several optional fees that must be paid if you want your scores rushed to you or if you wish to receive multiple grade reports.

What Should I Bring to the AP Exam?

There are several things that are either required or a good idea to have with you. They include:

- a good supply of no. 2 pencils with erasers that do not smudge (for the multiple-choice section)
- several black or blue colored ink pens (for the free-response essays)
- a watch so that you can monitor your time (you never know if the exam room will have a clock and you will not have a cell phone or other electronic devices; be sure to turn any alarms or chimes off)
- your photo ID and social security number

What Should I NOT Bring to the Exam?

There are a number of things that you are not allowed to use during the exam and that you should, therefore, *not* bring with you. They include:

- reference books of any kind—notebooks, dictionaries, encyclopedias, etc.
- a laptop computer
- electronic devices like cell phones, PDAs, pagers, or walkie-talkies
- portable music of any kind, such as CD players, MP3 players, or iPods

How to Plan Your Time

IN THIS CHAPTER

Summary: The right preparation plan for you depends on your study habits and the amount of time you have before the test.

Key Ideas

✪ Choose the plan that is right for you.

✪ Use this guide in combination with your AP class (if you are currently taking one) and your outside readings in European history.

✪ Following the plan will help you build expertise and confidence.

Three Approaches to Preparing for AP Exams

What kind of preparation program for the AP exam should you follow? The answer depends on two things: how much time you have and what kind of student you are. Obviously, if you only have one semester or four to six weeks before you intend to take the exam, you cannot choose the full-year program. So first decide how much time you have. Then consider what kind of preparation works best for you. No one knows your study habits and learning style better than you do. Consider the three profiles below to see which one most closely describes you and your situation. Then, choose one of the three programs of preparation.

Full-Year Preparation: Plan A

You are a full-year prep student (and should follow Plan A) if:

1. You are leaning strongly towards history as a college major.
2. You like detailed planning and preparation.
3. You feel more comfortable and confident when you feel thoroughly prepared.

4. You cannot wait to get started.
5. You have been successful with this approach in the past.

One-Semester Preparation: Plan B

You are a one-semester prep student (and should follow Plan B) if:

1. You are fairly interested in history.
2. You like to plan but feel there is such a thing as being overprepared.
3. You feel comfortable and confident when you feel you have prepared sufficiently.
4. You have more than one exam you are preparing for and feel one semester is enough time.
5. You have been successful with this approach in the past.

Four- to Six-Week Preparation: Plan C

You are a four- to six-week prep student (and should follow Plan C) if:

1. You are only fairly interested in history, or you are interested only in the exam.
2. You feel like you get stale if you prepare too far in advance.
3. You feel well-prepared already and are just looking to sharpen your focus.
4. You are prepping for several exams and this is your lowest priority.
5. You have been successful with this approach in the past.

Table 2.1 Three Different Study Plans

MONTH	PLAN A: FULL SCHOOL YEAR	PLAN B: ONE SEMESTER	PLAN C: SIX WEEKS
September–October	Introduction, Chapters 1–6		
November	Chapters 7–10		
December	Chapters 11–14		
January	Chapters 15–18	Introduction, Chapters 1–6	
February–March	Chapters 19–22, Unit Summaries	Chapters 7–14	
April	Review Chapters 4–6, Practice Test 1	Chapters 15–22, Unit Summaries, Practice Test 1	Chapters 1–22, Practice Test 1
May	Final Review, Practice Test 2	Final Review, Practice Test 2	Final Review, Practice Test 2

Detailed Calendar for Each Plan

Plan A: You Have a Full School Year to Prepare

September–October (check off the activities as you complete them)
— Read the Introduction and become familiar with the five-step program.
— Read Chapter 1 and become familiar with the AP European History exam and procedures.
— Become familiar with the College Board AP website.
— Read Chapter 2 and choose the full-year, one-semester, or four- to-six week preparation program.
— Confer with your AP European History teacher about your preparation program.
— Take a leisurely, low-stress look at this guide and begin to use it as a resource.
— Read Chapters 3–6 and do the diagnostic exercises (and, if you feel ready, Practice Test 1) to determine your current strengths, areas that need work, and whether you need to develop some new strategies.

November
— Read Chapters 7–10 of this guide, along with relevant outside readings and course materials.
— Do the chapter review questions for each, checking the answers and explanations.
— Review the chapters where you had trouble with the review questions and focus your outside reading there.

December
— Read Chapters 11–14 of this guide, along with relevant outside readings and course materials.
— Do the chapter review questions for each, checking the answers and explanations.
— Review the chapters where you had trouble with the review questions and focus your outside reading there.

January
— Read Chapters 15–18 of this guide, along with relevant outside readings and course materials.
— Do the chapter review questions for each, checking the answers and explanations.
— Review the chapters where you had trouble with the review questions and focus your outside reading there.

February–March
— Read Chapters 19–22 of this guide, along with relevant outside readings and course materials.
— Do the chapter review questions for each, checking the answers and explanations.
— Review the chapters where you had trouble with the review questions and focus your outside reading there.
— Review the two unit summaries.

April
— Review Chapters 4–6 of this guide, then take Practice Test 1.
— Evaluate your strengths and weaknesses based on your performance on Practice Test 1.
— Study the appropriate chapters and readings to address the areas you still feel shaky on.

May—First Two Weeks
— Make a list of topics you still feel shaky about and ask your instructor or study group to help you focus on them.
— Take Practice Test 2.
— Evaluate your performance.
— Review the incorrect answers.
— Get a good night's sleep before the exam; you are well prepared.
— Go to the exam feeling confident; you have prepared well.

GOOD LUCK!

Plan B: You Have One Semester to Prepare

January (check off the activities as you complete them)
— Read the Introduction and become familiar with the five-step program.
— Read Chapter 1 and become familiar with the AP European History exam and procedures.
— Become familiar with the College Board AP website.
— Read Chapter 2 and choose the one-semester or four- to six-week preparation program.
— Confer with your AP European History teacher about your preparation program.
— Take a leisurely, low-stress look at this guide and begin to use it as a resource.

February–March
— Read Chapters 3–6 and do the diagnostic exercises (and, if you feel ready, Practice Test 1) to determine your current strengths, areas that need work, and whether you need to develop some new strategies.
— Read Chapters 7–14 of this guide, along with relevant outside readings and course materials.
— Do the chapter review questions for each, checking the answers and explanations.
— Review the chapters where you had trouble with the review questions and focus your outside reading there.

April
— Read Chapters 15–22 of this guide, along with relevant outside readings and course materials.
— Do the chapter review questions for each, checking the answers and explanations.
— Review the chapters where you had trouble with the review questions and focus your outside reading there.
— Review the two unit summaries.
— Review Chapters 4–6 of this guide, then take Practice Test 1.
— Evaluate your strengths and weaknesses based on your performance on Practice Test 1.
— Study the appropriate chapters and readings to address the areas you still feel shaky on.

May—First Two Weeks
— Make a list of topics you still feel shaky about and ask your instructor or study group to help you focus on them.
— Take Practice Test 2.
— Evaluate your performance.
— Review the incorrect answers.
— Get a good night's sleep before the exam; you are well prepared.
— Go to the exam feeling confident; you have prepared well.

GOOD LUCK!

Plan C: You Have Six Weeks to Prepare

April (check off the activities as you complete them)
— Read Chapters 1–22 of this guide.
— Take Practice Test 1.
— Evaluate your performance and review as needed.

May—First Two Weeks
— Take Practice Test 2.
— Evaluate your performance.
— Review the incorrect answers.
— Get a good night's sleep before the exam.

GOOD LUCK!

STEP **2**

Determine Your Test Readiness

CHAPTER **3** Diagnostic Exercises

Diagnostic Exercises

IN THIS CHAPTER

Summary: Diagnose your level of preparation for the exam in order to focus your program of preparation.

Key Ideas

✪ Multiple-choice questions test passive knowledge; there are several useful processes of elimination you can use.

✪ The Document-Based Question tests your ability to analyze and discuss primary source documents.

✪ The Thematic Essay Questions test your ability to use your knowledge of European history to make a historical argument.

Introduction

In order to prepare well for the AP European History exam, it is useful to gain some sense of your own strengths and weaknesses, and to become conscious of the processes you use to approach various kinds of questions. This chapter is designed to both give you a sense of your level of readiness for the AP European History exam and help you evaluate the effectiveness of the strategies you currently use when you tackle the sorts of questions that will appear on the exam.

The Multiple-Choice Questions

Below you will find a Multiple-Choice Questions Exercise, consisting of exercise multiple-choice questions like the ones you will encounter on the AP European History exam.

When you get to the end of this section, answer them. *Do not study and do not stress.* You can check the answers afterwards, but the main point here is to learn something about the way you normally approach multiple-choice questions and determine whether or not you need to develop some new strategies. So answer them just as you would on any multiple-choice exam, writing your answers down on a separate sheet of paper. But as you answer them, think about *how* you are arriving at your choice and jot down some notes describing the process. For example, say the question is:

1. An unprecedented era of exploration and discovery in the late-fifteenth and early-sixteenth centuries was spurred by
   (A) the desire for precious metals and competition for the spice trade
   (B) the need for markets to sell manufactured goods
   (C) the need to find space for an expanding population
   (D) the missionary work of the Church
   (E) the Hundred Years War

Let us say you chose A. How did you arrive at the answer? Perhaps it was: "Oh. I know this one; my teacher emphasized that the people who financed the voyages of exploration wanted silver, gold, and spice." Or maybe you did not recall covering this specifically, but you used a process of elimination that went something like this: "I do not know much about this, but I do know that the Hundred Years War happened much earlier and did not do much good for the economy; so E is out. The other four are possible, but I remember that the big population explosion in Europe was related to *eighteenth-century* agriculture and the beginnings of manufacturing; so I will eliminate B and C. That leaves precious metal and spices versus missionary work; I know there were missionaries on those voyages, but I am betting that the bottom line for the people who paid for them was profit. I am choosing A." In both cases, the correct answer has been reached, but by two very different processes.

OK, your turn. Answer the following on a sheet of paper and jot down some notes describing *your* reasoning processes. Then, compare your answers and reasoning processes with the Answers and Explanations section given at the end. *Remember: If you do not do well, do not panic. Chapter 4 will teach you how to do better.* If you did very well and want to test your readiness more broadly, go to the back of the guide and take the multiple-choice section of Practice Test 1. You can check your answers against the Answers and Explanations section that follows it.

› Multiple-Choice Questions Exercise

Directions: Choose the best answer for each question. Circle the answer of your choice. As you choose, make notes about the process of elimination you used to arrive at your answer. When you are finished, compare your answers and your reasoning with the Answers and Explanations section that follows.

1. Which of the following were effects of the Hundred Years War on England and France?
   (A) It disrupted agriculture, causing famine, disease, and a significant decrease in the population.
   (B) It created an enormous tax burden that led to a series of peasant rebellions.
   (C) It left France an economically devastated but more politically unified kingdom.
   (D) It weakened England economically but led to the beginning of a textile industry upon which it would rebuild its economic strength.
   (E) All of the above.

2. The goal of the Conciliar Movement was
   (A) the end of the Hundred Years War
   (B) to heal the rift between Catholics and Protestants
   (C) to select a new pope
   (D) to reform, reunite, and reinvigorate the Church
   (E) to allow secular governments to gain some measure of control of the Church in their kingdoms

3. In the fifteenth century, which of the following were increasing their power?
   (A) the Church
   (B) secular monarchs
   (C) the nobility
   (D) the peasantry
   (E) artisans

4. An unprecedented era of exploration and discovery in the late-fifteenth and early-sixteenth centuries was spurred by
   (A) the desire for precious metals and competition for the spice trade
   (B) the need for markets to sell manufactured goods
   (C) the need to find space for an expanding population
   (D) the missionary work of the Church
   (E) the Hundred Years War

5. The most outstanding characteristic of Renaissance Italian society was
   (A) the strength of the monarchy
   (B) the power of the traditional nobility
   (C) the degree to which it was urban
   (D) the freedom allowed to women
   (E) the development of cash-crop agriculture

6. "Humanism," in early-Renaissance Italy, refers primarily to
   (A) renewed interest in the scientific method
   (B) scholarly interest in and the study of classical cultures of Greece and Rome
   (C) an anti-Christian attitude
   (D) a focus on the qualities and strategies necessary for attaining and holding power
   (E) the study of the works of Aristotle

7. Giotto is often referred to as a transition figure between medieval art and the Renaissance style because
   (A) his subject matter was secular
   (B) of the scale of his *David*
   (C) his works were commissioned by patrons
   (D) his subject matter was religious but his concern was for the human experience
   (E) he specialized in nudes

8. Nineteenth-century conservatism tended to be supported by
   (A) traditional, landed aristocracy
   (B) the merchant class
   (C) industrial barons
   (D) the working class
   (E) women

❯ Answers and Explanations

1. **E.** All of the above are correct. Choice A is correct because the continual fighting made it difficult for peasant farmers to cultivate the land, resulting in frequent famine. Famine and the many corpses lying around led to disease; famine and disease combined to decrease the population. Choice B is correct because money had to be raised to field armies; the nobility and Church were largely exempt so the burden fell on the peasants, who frequently rebelled. Choice C is correct because the war brought economic devastation, but that devastation broke the power of regional nobility, allowing the king to politically unify the kingdom. Choice D is correct because the war similarly weakened England economically, but the difficulty of keeping trade lines open led the English to begin producing textiles for clothing.

2. **D.** The goal of the Conciliar Movement of the fifteenth century, led by various councils of cardinals, was to reform, reunite and reinvigorate the Church, which was deeply divided by the Avignon Papacy (1309–1377) and the Great Schism (1378–1417). Choice A is incorrect because the Conciliar Movement was not related in any direct way to the Hundred Years War. Choice B is incorrect because the Conciliar movement predated the Reformation and the creation of a Protestant movement. Choice C is incorrect because the Conciliar Movement was concerned with reforming the Church, not selecting a pope. Choice E is incorrect because the gains secular governments made over the Church in their kingdoms were a result of the Conciliar Movement, not a goal.

3. **B.** Secular monarchs, such as Isabella and Ferdinand of Spain, were increasing their power in the fifteenth century because traditional institutions seemed powerless in the face of calamities such as the Hundred Years War and the Black Death. Choices A and C are incorrect because the Church and the nobility were traditional institutions whose power had been weakened; the Church was additionally weakened by internal divisions. Choices D and E are incorrect because both the peasantry and the artisans still lacked any basis for political power in the fifteenth century.

4. **A.** It was the desire for precious metals and the competition for the spice trade that led the monarchies of Spain and Portugal to invest large sums of capital in voyages of exploration. Choice B is incorrect because manufacturing in Europe had not yet reached a stage that demanded new markets. Choice C is incorrect because the population of Europe was still recovering from the plague and was not large enough to create pressure for new land. Choice D is incorrect because, while it is true that missionaries accompanied the voyages, the monarchies would not have invested huge sums without hope of financial return. Choice E is incorrect because the Hundred Years War preceded the era of great voyages.

5. **C.** Renaissance Italy was uniquely urban. By 1500, seven of the ten largest cities in Europe were in Italy. Choice A is incorrect because unlike the majority of Western Europe, which was characterized by large kingdoms with powerful monarchs, the Italian peninsula was made up of numerous independent city-states, such as Milan, Florence, Padua, and Genoa. Choice B is incorrect because the urban nature of Renaissance Italy meant that the traditional landed nobility were less powerful than elsewhere in Europe. Choice D is incorrect because the social conventions of Renaissance Italy were as restrictive as elsewhere in Europe. Choice E is incorrect because cash-crop agriculture did not develop to any significant degree in Renaissance Italy.

6. **B.** Early-Renaissance humanism is best understood as a scholarly interest in and the study of classical Greece and Rome for the purpose of learning how to succeed in life and live a good life. Choice A is incorrect because the notion of a scientific method is a seventeenth-century invention. Choice C is incorrect because humanism was never anti-Christian. Choice D is incorrect because a focus on the qualities and strategies necessary for attaining and holding power was a characteristic of the "princely ideal" of *late*-Renaissance humanism. Choice E is

incorrect because the myopic focus on the works of Aristotle was a characteristic of medieval scholasticism.

7. **D**. The combination of a concern for the human experience with a religious subject matter that characterizes the transitional nature of Giotto's work can be seen in his frescos depicting the life of St. Francis, where the human characters are depicted in realistic detail and with clear concern for their psychological reaction to the saint's life. Choice A is incorrect because Giotto's subject matter was not secular, but religious. Choice B is incorrect because Giotto did not do a version of *David*. Choice C is incorrect because both medieval and Renaissance Italian art was commissioned by patrons. Choice E is incorrect because Giotto did not specialize in nudes.

8. **A**. Conservatism was the ideology that asserted that tradition is the only trustworthy guide to social and political action, and held that the monarchy, the hierarchical class system, and the Church were crucial institutions. Accordingly, they drew their support from the traditional elites of Europe, the landed aristocracy and the Church. Choices B and C are incorrect because the merchant class and industrial barons, who did not have a comfortable place in the traditional hierarchy, tended to support liberalism and its platform of reform. Choice D is incorrect because the working classes of the nineteenth century looked first to liberalism and then, increasingly, to socialism as the best hope for representation of their interests. There were women who supported conservatism, though not in a political sense, since they were excluded from political participation. But women who supported the women's rights movements tended to support the notions of individual liberty promoted by liberalism; thus, choice A is a better answer.

The Document-Based Question

The second part of the AP European History exam is the document-based question, also known as the DBQ. The DBQ is simply an essay question about primary sources. It asks you to respond to a question by interpreting a set of excerpts (typically 10–12) from documents that were written in a particular historical period. The set of excerpts will come from sources like newspaper articles or editorials, classic texts, pamphlets, speeches, diaries, letters, and other similar sources. The DBQ will also give you a paragraph of information that identifies the historical context that connects the documents.

Below you will find a DBQ of the sort that might appear on the AP European History exam, giving the question, the historical background, and a set of excerpted documents (for this exercise, we will start with five instead of the usual 10–12). If you have written essays like this before, take a shot at writing one here. Time yourself the way you will be timed in the exam, giving yourself 15 minutes to read the question and the documents (you may not write during this period) and then writing for no more than 45 minutes (the amount of time suggested by the exam). When you are finished, compare your essay with the Suggestions and Possible Outline of a Response to the DBQ Exercise at the end of this section.

If you have not written many essays of this type, then simply construct an outline of a possible answer to the question. As you do so, make some notes about your thought processes. How did you begin? What did you do with the documents? Then, compare your outline and notes with the Suggestions and Possible Outline that appear at the end of this section. *If you struggle or do not get very far in your attempts to make an outline, do not worry; Chapter 5 will teach you how to develop strategies for doing this quickly, efficiently, and well.* If you feel good about your essay or outline, you may want to go to the back of this guide and take the DBQ section of Practice Test 1. Then compare your essay with the outline and comments that appear at the end of the test.

Document-Based Question Exercise

Directions

A. Give yourself 15 minutes to read the question, historical background, and documents. Then, on separate sheets of paper, write an essay that responds to the question (take no more than 45 minutes). When you are finished, compare your essay with the Suggestions and Possible Outline that follow. If you wish, proceed to the DBQ section of Practice Test 1.

or

B. Read the question and, historical, background, and documents. Then, on a separate sheet of paper, make an outline of an essay that responds to the question and take some notes about your thought processes. When you are finished, compare your essay with the Suggestions and Possible Outline that follow.

1. Discuss the competing notions concerning the origin and nature of political sovereignty and the proper role of government that were developed in the seventeenth and eighteenth centuries.

Historical Background: Throughout the seventeenth and eighteenth centuries, European political philosophers argued about the origin and nature of political sovereignty and the proper role of government. In seventeenth-century Britain, the argument became part of a civil war and revolution that pitted the Stuart monarchy and its supporters against the forces of Parliament. In eighteenth-century France, the Bourbon monarchy, the aristocracy, and the Church all found themselves faced with an increasingly radical revolution.

Document 1

Source: James I, speech to the English Parliament, 1610.
The state of monarchy is the supremest thing upon the earth: for kings are not only God's lieutenants upon earth and sit upon God's throne, but even by God himself they are called gods . . . In the Scriptures kings are called gods, and so their power after a certain relation compared to the Divine power. Kings are also compared with fathers of families; for a king is truly *parens patriae* [parent of the country], the politic father of his people. And lastly, kings are compared to the head of this microcosm of the body of man.

Document 2

Source: Thomas Hobbes, *Leviathan*, London, 1651.
The only way to erect such common power, as may be able to defend them from the invasion of foreigners, and the injuries of one another, and thereby to secure them in such sort, as that by their own industry, and by the fruits of the earth, they may nourish themselves and live contentedly, is to confer all their power and strength upon one man, or upon one assembly of men, that may reduce all their wills, by plurality of voices, unto one will . . . This is more than consent or concord; it is a real unity of them all, in one and the same person, made by covenant of every man . . .

Document 3

Source: John Locke, *The Second Treatise of Government*, London, 1690.
The only way whereby anyone divests himself of his natural liberty and puts on the bonds of civil society, is by agreeing with other men to join and unite into a community for their comfortable, safe and peaceable living one among another, in a secure enjoyment of their

properties, and a greater security against any that are not of it ... And thus every man, by consenting with others to make one body politic under one government, puts himself under obligation to every one of that society to submit to the determination of the majority, and to be concluded by it ... [But]When the governor, however entitled, makes not the law but his will the rule, and his commands and actions are not directed to the preservation of the properties of his people, but the satisfaction of his own ambition, revenge, covetousness, or any other irregular passion, ... there it presently becomes tyranny.

Document 4

Source: M. de Montesquieu, *Spirit of the Laws*, Paris, 1748.
Law in general is human reason, inasmuch as it govern all the inhabitants of the earth; the political and civil laws of each nation ought to be only the particular cases in which human reason is applied ... Democratic and aristocratic states are not in their own nature free. Political liberty is to be found only in moderate governments; and even in these it is not always found. It is there only when there is no abuse of power ... To prevent this abuse, it is necessary, from the very nature of things, power should be a check to power. A government must be so constituted as no man shall be compelled to do things to which the law does not oblige him, nor forced to abstain from things which the law permits.

Document 5

Source: Emmanuel Joseph Sieyès, *What Is the Third Estate?* Paris, 1789.
Public functions may be classified equally well, in the present state of affairs, under four recognized heads: the sword, the robe, the church, and the administration. It would be superfluous to take them up one by one, for the purpose of showing that everywhere the Third Estate attends to nineteen-twentieths of them, with this distinction; that it is laden with all that which is really painful, with all the burdens which the privileged classes refuse to carry ... Who then shall dare to say that the Third Estate has not within itself all that is necessary for the formation of a complete nation?

Suggestions and Possible Outline of a Response to the DBQ Exercise

Suggestions

Begin by finding a way to group the documents. Notice that James I and Thomas Hobbes believed in an all-powerful ruler, while Locke and Montesquieu argued for a more limited government. On the issue of origins, note that James I believed in Divine Right Monarchy. Hobbes actually agreed with Locke and Montesquieu that power is derived from the people, but rejected the notion of "consent" introduced by Locke. Notice how Sieyès places sovereignty in the "nation" at all times.

Next, address the relationship between the groups of documents; here it would be a good idea to see them as an evolution from notions of an all-powerful, Divine Right monarch to the more modern notion of a nation. Topic sentences should make clear claims about that evolution.

The body of the essay's paragraphs must present historical evidence that supports and illustrates the topic sentences and, therefore, the thesis. An outline of such an essay might look like this.

Outline

Thesis: The documents, taken in chronological order, reflect an evolution of political thought from Divine Right Monarchy to the notion of a sovereign nation.

Topic sentence A: Documents 1 and 2 both argue for a sovereign with unlimited power, but demonstrate a shift away from Divine Right Monarchy.

Specific examples: James I, who was attempting to reestablish Divine Right Monarchy in England, is lecturing an uppity Parliament. He emphasizes: scripture, kings as gods, paternalism, and the king as head of the body politic. Hobbes, who supported the monarchy in the English Civil War, is arguing the necessity an all-powerful ruler. He allows that a ruler is chosen by the people, but he emphasizes "real unity" and a covenant, not consent. The meaning of *Leviathan* summarizes his point.

Topic sentence B: Documents 3 and 4 argue for limited government, by consent, according to the laws of reason.

Specific examples: Locke, a supporter of Parliament and writing immediately after the Glorious Revolution in England, emphasizes "natural liberty"; indicates consent as the origin of legitimate power; and gives a definition of tyranny (it does not exist in Hobbes) that must be opposed. Montesquieu, of the Enlightenment period, argues from a notion of natural law. He argues that power is always limited by reason. The meaning of "spirit of the laws" summarizes his point.

Topic sentence C: Document 5 illustrates the new concept of a "nation" as the home of sovereignty.

Specific examples: Sieyès, leader of the moderate phase of the French Revolution, is justifying the revolt of the Third Estate. He argues that "Third Estate" (define) executes the functions of administration; the burden of administration equals the right to rule.

Conclusion (if time): There was a clear evolution of political thought from Divine Right Monarchy to the notion of a sovereign nation.

The Thematic Essay Questions

The thematic essay questions make up the remainder of the 130-minute, free-response section of the AP European History exam. You will be presented with two groups of three questions (six total). The first group will present questions that ask about the period from roughly 1450 to the Napoleonic Era and the second group will present three questions that ask about the period from the Napoleonic Era to the present. You must respond to one question from each group. Remember that the exam instructions recommend that you divide your time as follows:

- Part A (the DBQ)—15 minutes reading time, 45 minutes writing time
- Part B (first thematic essay)—35 minutes writing time
- Part C (second thematic essay)—35 minutes writing time

Your goal is to quickly choose the two questions you will answer and construct a short history essay of high quality in the approximately 35 minutes allotted for each. Below you will find a thematic essay question similar to the ones that appear on the AP European History exam. If you have written essays like this before, take a shot at writing one that answers the question. Time yourself the way you will be timed in the exam, giving yourself 35 minutes to compose and write your essay. When you are finished, compare your essay with the Suggestions and Possible Outline of a Response to the Thematic Essay Questions Exercise at the end of this section.

If you have not written many of these kinds of essays, then begin by constructing an outline of a possible answer to the question and taking some notes about your thought processes. How did you begin? How did you organize your thoughts? Then, compare your outline and notes with the outline and comments that appear at the end of this section. *If you struggle or do not get very far in your attempts to make an outline, do not worry; Chapter 6 will teach you how to develop strategies for doing this quickly, efficiently, and well.* If you feel good about your essay or outline, you may want to go to the back of this guide and complete the thematic essay questions section of Practice Test 1. Then compare your essays with the Suggestions and Possible Outline that appear at the end of the test.

Thematic Essay Question Exercise

Directions

A. Write an essay that responds to the question (take no more than 35 minutes). Write your essay on separate sheets of paper. When you are finished, compare your essay with the Suggestions and Possible Outline that follow. If you want to, proceed to the thematic essay questions section of Practice Test 1.

or

B. Read the question and make an outline of an essay that responds to the question, and take some notes about your thought processes. Write your outline and notes on a separate sheet of paper. When you are finished, compare your essay with the Suggestions and Possible Outline that follow.

1. Analyze the factors that led to World War I and determine which were decisive.

Suggestions and Possible Outline of a Response to the Thematic Essay Question Exercise

Suggestions

Make a quick list of the "causes" of World War I as they were covered in your class and your readings. Rank them in order of importance and select one or two as "decisive" (i.e., most directly responsible for the outbreak of war). Compose a thesis stating clearly your argument for ranking them the way you do. Write three topic sentences making three clear points that add up to your thesis. Underneath each of the topic sentences, list specific examples that illustrate and support your topic sentences. From that outline write a clear, concise essay.

Outline

Thesis: The determination of Germany to expand and the requirements of the Schlieffen Plan were the most decisive factors in bringing about World War I.

Topic sentence A: Since unification in 1871, Imperial Germany was fearful of encirclement and determined to gain *lebensraum* (room to live).

Specific examples: German unification was itself expansionist in nature; the concept of *lebensraum* was prevalent in German culture; the fear of encirclement led to the German belief that war was inevitable and, thus, to the drawing up of the Schlieffen Plan, a plan to win a two-front war.

Topic sentence B: The Anglo-German rivalry, the Nationalities Problem in the Hapsburg Empire, and the Alliance System were all factors, but none was decisive.

Specific examples: Britain and Germany engaged in an arms race in the decades before the war; but they were also each other's largest trading partners; past examples of ethnic-nationalist agitation inside the Hapsburg Empire were handled without war; details of the alliance system did restrict diplomatic options and seemed to guarantee military response, but such alliances were broken when necessary, e.g., Italy's initial neutrality.

Topic sentence C: The assassination of the Archduke Franz Ferdinand was the fuse, but the Schlieffen Plan, born of Germany's belief that war was inevitable, was a more decisive factor.

Specific examples: Serbia agreed to the Hapsburg ultimatum, but Austrian aggression was spurred on by Germany's "blank check"; Russian troop mobilization was a standard "show of support"; the Schlieffen Plan's existence shows Germany's preparation for war (no other country was thus prepared), and its logic guaranteed large-scale military movement at the first sign of Russian mobilization.

Conclusion (if time): Of the many factors that led to World War I, Germany's determination to expand and the iron logic of the Schlieffen Plan were decisive.

STEP 3

Develop Strategies for Success

CHAPTER 4

The Multiple-Choice Questions

IN THIS CHAPTER

Summary: Develop a successful strategy for the multiple-choice section.

Key Ideas
✪ Multiple-choice questions test passive knowledge.
✪ The question always provides clues to the answer.
✪ The key is to quickly devise a process of elimination.

Introduction

Section I of the AP European History exam consists of 80 multiple-choice questions. The directions are straightforward and they resemble the directions for every multiple-choice test you have ever taken. They read:

Directions: Each of the questions or incomplete statements below is followed by five suggested answers or completions. Select the one that is best in each case and then fill in the corresponding oval on the answer sheet.

So, you know the drill; you select the best answer of the five and fill in your choice. And you have probably taken enough multiple-choice tests to know that there is an important question you should ask: "If I am not sure of the best answer, should I guess?" The answer is: "It depends," but we will get to that in a minute. Right now, ask yourself a few more questions: What does a multiple-choice question test? How did the authors of the exam come up with the 80 questions? Are there different kinds of multiple-choice question? How did they decide what order to put them in? Knowing the answers to these questions can help you develop a successful strategy for approaching them.

Passive Knowledge and the Premise

All multiple-choice exams test *passive knowledge*. The multiple-choice section of the AP European History exam will test your passive knowledge of European history from roughly 1450 to the present. That is, it will test your ability to *recognize* the best answer out of a group of possible answers to a specific historical question. The word "best" is important. It means that all multiple-choice questions are answered through a *process of elimination*; you begin by eliminating the one that is most clearly not the "best" and continue until you have a "survivor."

Additionally, a multiple-choice question and its answer try to say something meaningful about history in a single sentence. That is a very difficult thing to do. In order to do it, the question creates a *premise* which the test taker must accept. For example, look at the following question:

1. The most outstanding characteristic of Renaissance Italian society was
   (A) the strength of the monarchy
   (B) the power of the traditional nobility
   (C) the degree to which it was urban
   (D) the freedom allowed to women
   (E) the development of cash-crop agriculture

The question proceeds from the premise that there was a single most outstanding characteristic of Renaissance Italian society. That is a debatable premise (was there really one that was more "outstanding" or noteworthy than all the other characteristics?), and a sophisticated student of history could debate (and indeed write a doctoral dissertation debating) the merits of several possible answers. Doing so would make you seem very sophisticated and knowledgeable, but it would be both silly and counterproductive on an exam.

The people who wrote the question realize that the premise is debatable, but they have constructed the question so that, *if* you accept the premise (and for the purpose of the exam, they insist that you do), there is an internal, historical logic that will lead you to the *best* answer, provided you have some knowledge of the significant aspects of Renaissance Italian history (and that is what the question tests).

Organizational Keys

How did they come up with the 80 questions? The high school and college teachers who created the AP European History exam followed these organizational principles:

1. The questions are broken down by era:
   - Forty questions cover the era from roughly 1450 to 1815.
   - Forty questions cover the era from 1815 to the present.

2. The questions are also broken down by general subject:
   - Roughly 30–40 percent (or 24–32 questions) cover political and diplomatic themes.
   - Roughly 20–30 percent (or 16–24 questions) cover cultural and intellectual themes.
   - Roughly 30–40 percent (or 24–32 questions) cover social and economic themes.

Knowing these two organizing principles of the exam only helps you in a general sense; they let you know that you have to devote about equal preparation time for the questions on the period from 1450 to 1815 and that from 1815 to the present, and about equal time for the three thematic categories. But knowing some other guiding principles can actually help you to answer specific questions.

3. The questions test basic principles and general trends, *not* memorization and trivia. Knowing that the exam seeks to test basic principles and general trends tells you that you do not need to memorize loads of dates and facts; rather you can use your knowledge to reason your way to the best answer. It also tells you that the best answer will *not* be an exception or an obscure fact, but rather an illustration of the basic principle or general trend.

4. The questions appear in groups of four to seven questions that are in chronological order. You should be able to tell where the breaks between groups are. When, for example, you see a question about World War I followed by a question about the Renaissance, you have come upon a break between groups. Identifying the groups of questions can be helpful; if you come upon a question that lies between a question about the Renaissance and one about the Scientific Revolution, you know that the event or process that it asks about occurred between those two eras.

5. The questions get progressively more difficult. Therefore the early questions have easy, straightforward answers. Do not read too much complexity into the early questions. Choose the most obvious answers.

The Kinds of Questions

There are several kinds of multiple-choice questions on the AP European History exam. Most of the questions are straightforward, find-the-best-answer questions like the one about the outstanding characteristic of the Renaissance above. However, there are two other types worth watching out for:

- There are questions that include the words NOT or EXCEPT. These questions give you five choices and ask you to pick the one that is not true or, following the premise of the question, the worst answer. In these questions, the words NOT or EXCEPT are always capitalized, so you will not miss them. Just be sure to remember that you are looking for the worst answer when you analyze the choices.

- Once in a while, there are questions that ask you to interpret an *illustration*. The illustration may be a map, a graph, a chart, or perhaps a poster or cartoon from a particular period of history. You will almost certainly not have seen the illustration before, and the authors of the exam do not expect you to have seen it. What they are looking for is your ability to "get" the illustration based on your knowledge of the period.

About Guessing

Should you guess? This is what the AP European History exam says about guessing:

Many candidates wonder whether or not they should guess the answers to questions about which they are not certain. In this section of the examination, as a correction for haphazard guessing, one-quarter of the number of questions you answer incorrectly will be subtracted from the number of questions you answer correctly. It is improbable, therefore, that mere guessing will improve your score significantly; it may even lower your score, and it does take time. If, however, you are not sure of the best answer but have some knowledge of the question and are able to eliminate one or more of the answer choices as wrong, your chance of getting the right answer is improved, and it may be to your advantage to answer such a question.

In other words, there is a guessing penalty, but it is small. A good guideline is: If you understand the premise of the question and can eliminate one or two of the answers, then guess. If you do not even understand the premise of the question, skip it.

Developing a Strategy

OK. Let us put what we have learned into practice to answer that question about the Renaissance.

1. The most outstanding characteristic of Renaissance Italian society was
    (A) the strength of the monarchy
    (B) the power of the traditional nobility
    (C) the degree to which it was urban
    (D) the freedom allowed to women
    (E) the development of cash-crop agriculture

Step 1: Identify the context

In this case, that is easy. The question tells us it is about Renaissance Italy. If the question were about a specific document, say Pico's *Oration on the Dignity of Man*, we could figure out that the context was Renaissance Italy by remembering that Renaissance humanism stressed the dignity of man, or by noticing that the question started a chronological "group" of questions and was followed by a question about the Reformation.

Step 2: Identify the premise

As we noted earlier, the premise of this question is that there was one social characteristic of Renaissance Italian society that stood out more prominently than the rest.

Step 3: Decide whether you are working from a good knowledge base or a weak one, and begin the process of elimination

When you read the question was your reaction something like: "Excellent, I know the Renaissance"? Or was it more like, "Aargh! I should have studied the Renaissance"?

If you had the "Excellent" reaction, then you are working from a good knowledge base and your process of elimination would work something like this: "I know that Renaissance Italy, unlike the rest of Europe, was organized into independent *city*-states rather than large kingdoms, so the best answer is probably choice C, 'the degree to which it was urban,' because urban means lots of *cities*." All that is left to do now is quickly scan the other answers to make sure there are no other contenders: "I know choices A and B are no good because strong monarchies and powerful traditional nobility are the characteristics of the rest of Europe at this time. Choice E is no good because agriculture is a rural characteristic and Renaissance society is urban. And choice D is out because Renaissance women were no better off than women anywhere else in Europe. My first instinct was correct, the answer is choice C."

If you had the "Aargh!" reaction, you will have to operate something like this: "OK, I know zip about the Renaissance, but I am throwing out choices A and B because I am pretty sure there were lots of strong kings and powerful nobility. How about choice D? Were women better off in Renaissance Italy? I have no idea, but I do remember that women were still fighting for equal rights in the twentieth century, so it is not very likely that they had it great in the Renaissance. That leaves choices C and E, which are opposites; either Renaissance Italy was really urban or it was on the cutting edge of agricultural development. Urban? Hmmmm. Rome, Venice, yeah, Italy has lots of famous cities with a lot of famous old buildings; I am going with choice C."

Both processes of elimination produce the same, correct answer. The outstanding characteristic of Renaissance Italy was the degree to which it was urban. Now, before you go on to the next chapter, look at your notes regarding the processes of elimination you used to answer the multiple-choice questions in Chapter 3. For the ones you got wrong, construct a process of elimination that leads to the right answer. If you feel ready, go to the back of the guide and do the multiple-choice section of Practice Test 1.

STEP 4

Review the Knowledge You Need to Score High

UNIT 1

1450 to the French Revolutionary and Napoleonic Era

CHAPTER 7

Recovery and Expansion, 1300–1600

IN THIS CHAPTER

Summary: Beginning in the mid-fifteenth century, Europe recovered from a series of calamities and, under stronger, more secular monarchies, expanded its reach to Africa, the Americas, and the East.

Key Ideas

✪ By the middle of the fifteenth century, Europe had recovered socially and economically from the effects of the Hundred Years War, the Black Death, and a divided Church.

✪ Secular monarchs took advantage of the weakness of the Church and the nobility to consolidate and centralize power.

✪ The desire for precious metals and competition for the spice trade combined to produce an unprecedented era of exploration and discovery.

✪ Spain became the most powerful economic and military force in Europe.

Key Terms

Hundred Years War	Court of the Star Chamber	Inquisition
Black Death	Holy Roman Emperor	spice trade
Conciliar Movement	*Reichstag*	New Spain
War of the Roses	city-states	*haciendas*
		plantations

Introduction

Around the middle of the fifteenth century, European civilization began to recover from a series of calamities that had destroyed much of the culture that characterized the High Middle Ages. What emerged was a more secular, ambitious culture that began to explore and exploit new areas of the globe, including Africa, the Americas, and the East. The influx of trade, wealth, and new cultural influences put severe stress on the traditional economic and social organization of Europe.

Effects of the Hundred Years War

The dynastic conflict known as the *Hundred Years War* had begun in 1337, pitting the armies and resources of the Norman kings of England and the Capetian kings of France against one another. By 1453, the reorganized French had managed to push the English out of all of France except for the coastal town of Calais, and both sides agreed to end the conflict.

The Hundred Years War had several transformative effects on the kingdoms of England and France:

- It disrupted agriculture, causing famine, disease, and a significant decrease in the population.
- It created an enormous tax burden that led to a series of peasant rebellions.
- It left France an economically devastated but more politically unified kingdom.
- It weakened England economically, but (due to the difficulty of keeping trade lines open) it also led to the beginning of a textile industry upon which it would rebuild its economic strength.

Disappearance of the Black Death

The plague known as the Black Death had first appeared in Europe in 1347. Numerous outbreaks occurred in the following decades. In 1352, it disappeared as mysteriously as it had appeared. It is estimated that between one-quarter and one-third of the population of Europe died during the plague years. The virulence and unpredictability of the Black Death had several lasting effects on European society:

- The isolation that resulted from the fear of contagion weakened the traditional social bonds of society.
- The inability of the traditional authorities like the Church and the nobility to do anything about the plague weakened respect for them among the lower classes.
- The shortage of labor in some areas helped to spur the creation of a textile industry as some land owners abandoned agricultural production in favor of sheep farming, thus producing greatly increased quantities of wool.

A Weakened Papacy

The fourteenth-century Church was a deeply divided one. During the Avignon Papacy (1309–1377), the papacy had been under French influence. Attempts to break that influence led to the Great Schism (1378–1417), in which there were competing popes. In the fifteenth century, there were considerable attempts to reform, reunite, and reinvigorate the Church.

The movement, which came to be known as the *Conciliar Movement*, was led by various councils of cardinals and peaked in 1449 with the collapse of the Council of Basel. Although it failed to accomplish its reformist goals, the Conciliar Movement did have two lasting consequences:

- It articulated and spread a belief that the Church must not neglect the needs of the faithful in pursuit of worldly power.
- It allowed secular governments—kings in England and France and local magistrates in Italian, German, and Swiss cities—to gain some measure of control over the churches in their lands.

The Revival of Monarchy

The weakened papacy coincided with the revival, after 1450, of unified national monarchies. In the early part of the fifteenth century, European monarchs shared power with their noble vassals in the countryside and with local magistrates in the urban towns and cities. After 1450, the monarchs began to award royal administrative offices to high-ranking town officials rather than nobles. This marked the beginnings of an alliance between the monarchs and an emerging middle class of merchants and professionals that would make the creation of a modern, sovereign nation state possible.

European monarchs also began to create national armies in the fifteenth century. These new armies differed from their predecessors in several ways:

- Monarchs hired mercenary soldiers rather than relying on the nobility to raise troops.
- The armies became "professional," in that they fought for pay and spoils rather than honor and feudal obligation.
- The cavalry, usually composed of nobles, became less important than artillery and infantry.
- Larger professional armies increased costs, creating an even greater need for taxes.

The degree to which fifteenth-century European monarchs were able to consolidate power varied.

Power Struggles Within the English Monarchy

In the aftermath of the Hundred Years War, the English monarchy was subject to an internal power struggle between two rival branches of the royal family, the House of Lancaster and the House of York. The open warfare between the two houses has come to be known as the *War of the Roses* (1455–1485). Accordingly, the process of centralizing power did not begin in England until the reign of the House of Tudor, which began when Henry Tudor defeated the forces of Richard III at the Battle of Bosworth Field in August of 1485. Henry Tudor, who reigned as Henry VII, began to curb the power of the nobility, whose wealth and influence had put them above the law, by creating the *Court of the Star Chamber*, where the king's councillors judged cases brought against nobles.

A More Powerful Monarchy in France

In France, the cornerstones of a more powerful monarchy were built during the Hundred Years War. The English invasion of France did the work of curbing the power of French nobles, allowing the ministers of Charles VII to create a professional army and a strong governmental bureaucracy loyal to the king. Charles's successor, Louis XI, used that army and bureaucracy to defeat the last of his rivals, the Duke of Burgundy, in 1477. Once free of rivals, Louis brought the nobility into line, and he used the bureaucracy to further cultivate trade and industry, particularly silk production based in the city of Lyon.

Decentralized Power in Germany

The process of centralization was less successful in Germany and Italy. The German principalities were nominally ruled by the *Holy Roman Emperor* who, since 1356, had been elected by a seven-member council consisting of the archbishops of Mainz, Trier, and Cologne, the Duke of Saxony, the Margrave of Brandenburg, the Count Palatine, and the King of Bohemia. Under this setup, the ability of the emperor to centralize authority and power was severely limited. In the fifteenth century, further limits on the executive power of the emperor were instituted with the creation of a *Reichstag*, a kind of legislative body that included the seven electors, the remaining princes, and representatives of 65 important free cities.

Fragmented Power in Italy

On the Italian peninsula, which was organized into independent *city-states*, political power was even more decentralized as the traditional nobility gave way in power and importance to merchants made wealthy by the revival of trade in the Mediterranean. This unique political organization would be a crucial factor in the advent of the Renaissance.

The Rise of Spain

The most successful example of the rise of the monarchy and the centralization of power occurred in Spain in the second half of the fifteenth century. The marriage of Isabella of Castile and Ferdinand of Aragon in 1469 united two previously unruly kingdoms. With the resources of the joint kingdoms at their disposal, Isabella and Ferdinand were able to subdue aristocratic opposition from within, conquer the Moors in Grenada, and annex Naples. Asserting complete control over the Church in their kingdom, they used the Church as an instrument to consolidate power and build national unity. They ended a period of toleration of Muslims and Jews, establishing the *Inquisition* in 1479 to enforce their conversion to Christianity. In 1492, Spanish Jews were exiled and their properties were seized. In 1502, Muslims who had failed to convert to Christianity were driven out of Grenada.

Isabella and Ferdinand increased Spain's power by promoting overseas exploration. They sponsored the voyages of the Genoese explorer Christopher Columbus who, sailing west in 1492 in search of a shorter route to the spice markets of the Far East, reached the Caribbean, thereby "discovering" a "New World" for Europeans, and setting in motion a chain of events that would lead to the establishment of a Spanish Empire in Mexico and Peru.

Exploration and Expansion

Spain was not alone in the fifteenth century in sponsoring seafaring exploration. The Portuguese Prince, Henry the Navigator, sponsored Portuguese exploration of the African coast. By the end of the fifteenth century, Portuguese trading ships were bringing in gold from Guinea. Soon, European powers came to understand that there was also gold to be had in the selling of spices imported from India that were used to both preserve and flavor food. The search for gold and competition for the *spice trade* combined to inspire an era of daring exploration and discovery:

- In 1487, Bartholomew Dias rounded the Cape of Good Hope at the southern tip of Africa, thereby opening Portuguese trade routes in the East.

- In 1498, Vasco da Gama extended Portuguese trade by reaching the coast of India and returning with a cargo that earned his investors a 60 percent profit.
- The Portuguese formed the trading colonies in Goa and Calcutta on India's Malabar Coast.
- Amerigo Vespucci, an Italian sailing for Spain in 1499 and for Portugal in 1501, helped to show that the land discovered by Columbus was not in the Far East, but rather was a new continent that the German cartographer Martin Waldseemüller dubbed "America" in his honor.
- In 1519, a Spanish expedition led by the Portuguese sailor Ferdinand Magellan sailed west in search of a new route to the Spice Islands of the East. Rounding the tip of South America in 1520, the expedition sailed into the Pacific Ocean and arrived at the Spice Islands in 1521. In 1522, the expedition completed the first circumnavigation of the globe, returning to Spain without Magellan, who had been killed in the Philippines.

The Spanish Empire in the New World

Spain led the way in exploiting the economic opportunities of the New World. The process of exploitation got under way in 1519, when Hernán Cortés landed on the coast of what is now Mexico with 600 troops. Soon thereafter, Cortés marched on the Aztec capital of Tenochtitlán and imprisoned their leader, Montezuma. By 1521, the Aztecs were defeated and the Aztec Empire was proclaimed *New Spain*.

In 1531, Francisco Pizarro landed on the western coast of South America with 200 well-armed men and proceeded into the highlands of what is now Peru to engage the Inca civilization. By 1533, the Incas were subdued. Internal divisions with the conquering force initially made it difficult, but by the late 1560s effective control by the Spanish Crown was established.

The major economic components of the Spanish Empire in the New World were:

- mining, primarily silver from Peru and northern Mexico that was exported to Spain
- agriculture, through large landed estates called *haciendas*, which produced food and leather goods for the mining areas and urban centers of the New World, and *plantations* in the West Indies, which produced sugar for export

In both the mining and the agriculture sectors, ownership was in the hands of Spanish-born or -descended overlords, while labor was coerced from the native population.

The establishment of an exploitative foreign empire in the New World had several lasting results on the civilizations of the New World, particularly in Central and South America, including:

- the establishment of Roman Catholicism in the New World
- the establishment of economic dependence between the New World and Europe
- the establishment of a hierarchical social structure in the cultures of the New World

It also had lasting effects on Spain and, eventually, the rest of Europe, including:

- a steady rise in prices, eventually producing inflation, due to the increase in available wealth and coinage
- an eventual rise of a wealthy merchant class that sat uneasily in the traditional feudal social structure of Europe
- raised expectations for quality of life throughout the social structure of Europe

› Rapid Review

As Europe recovered from the effects of the Hundred Years War, the Black Death, and internal divisions within the Church, its monarchs attempted to consolidate and centralize political power. The most successful was the newly united monarchy of Spain, where Isabella and Ferdinand used the national Church and a strong bureaucracy to institute Catholicism as a state religion, sponsor an unprecedented era of exploration and discovery, and build a Spanish empire in the New World.

› Chapter Review Questions

1. Which of the following was NOT an effect of the Hundred Years War?
   (A) a significant decrease in the population
   (B) a series of peasant rebellions
   (C) the unification of Castile and Aragon
   (D) a more politically unified France
   (E) an economically weaker England

2. The Black Death
   (A) refers to the ruthlessness of the Norman Kings of England
   (B) refers to the outbreak of plague in Europe that killed between one-quarter and one-third of the population between 1347 and 1352
   (C) refers to the Spanish Inquisition
   (D) was a fifteenth-century phenomenon
   (E) increased the authority of traditional European institutions like the Church and the nobility

3. Fifteenth-century attempts by the cardinals to reform, reunite, and reinvigorate the Church are known collectively as
   (A) the Reformation
   (B) the Counter-Reformation
   (C) the Inquisition
   (D) the Conciliar Movement
   (E) the Court of the Star Chamber

4. Which of the following is NOT a way in which fifteenth-century armies differed from their predecessors?
   (A) They were commanded by officers of noble birth.
   (B) They were composed of mercenary soldiers.
   (C) They fought for pay and spoils rather than honor and feudal obligation.
   (D) They relied on artillery and infantry more than on cavalry.
   (E) They created a greater need for taxes.

5. Of the fifteenth-century attempts by monarchs to consolidate and centralize power, the most successful was in
   (A) England
   (B) France
   (C) Germany
   (D) Italy
   (E) Spain

6. In the fifteenth century, the Holy Roman Emperor
   (A) was another name for the pope
   (B) was dethroned in the Hundred Years War
   (C) was elected by a seven-member council of German archbishops and nobles
   (D) was Ferdinand of Aragon
   (E) sponsored the voyages of Christopher Columbus

7. The era of daring exploration and discovery at the end of the fifteenth and beginning of the sixteenth centuries was inspired by
   (A) the Reformation
   (B) the invention of the steam engine
   (C) the need to escape the Black Death
   (D) the search for gold and competition for the spice trade
   (E) the successful circumnavigation of the globe by the Magellan expedition

8. Which of the following was NOT an effect of the creation of a Spanish Empire in the New World?
   (A) inflation in the economy of Europe
   (B) the establishment of Roman Catholicism in the New World
   (C) the rise of a wealthy merchant class in Europe
   (D) the establishment of a hierarchical social structure in Europe
   (E) the establishment of a system of economic dependence between Europe and the New World

❯ Answers and Explanations

1. **C.** The unification of the Kingdoms of Castile and Aragon had nothing to do with the Hundred Years War: Castile and Aragon were unified by the marriage of Isabella and Ferdinand in 1469. The other four choices are incorrect because they *were* effects of the Hundred Years War.

2. **B.** The Black Death refers to the outbreak of plague in Europe that killed between one-quarter and one-third of the population between 1347 and 1352. Choices A and C are incorrect because the phrase *Black Death* refers specifically to the plague and, in spite of its severe name, it has nothing to do with the ruthlessness of either the Norman Kings or the Spanish Inquisition. Choice D is incorrect because the Black Death was a fourteenth-century (not a fifteenth-century) phenomenon. Choice E is incorrect because the phrase *Black Death* refers to the plague and because the plague did not *increase* but actually weakened the power of the Church and the nobility.

3. **D.** The fifteenth-century attempts by councils of cardinals to reform, reunite, and reinvigorate the Church are known collectively as the Conciliar Movement. Choice A is incorrect because, although the leaders of the movement that came to be known as the Reformation did originally have as their goal *reforming* and *reinvigorating* the Church, they were not cardinals in the Church and their movement was *not* one of *reunification*. Choice B is incorrect because, although the so-called Counter-Reformation also had reform as one of its goals, it increasingly came to be concerned with stamping out Protestantism and was also not a movement particular to the cardinals. Choice C is incorrect because the Inquisition was an instrument of the Church invented in Spain to enforce the conversion of Muslims and Jews, and later used to root out Protestants. Finally, choice E is incorrect because the Court of the Star Chamber was an instrument used by the early Tudor kings of England to curb the power of the nobility and had nothing to do with Church reform.

4. **A.** The commanding of armies by men of noble birth was a continuous aspect of European armies that did not change until the nineteenth century. Choices B–E are incorrect because these are all ways in which fifteenth-century armies *did* differ from their predecessors.

5. **E.** Spain's Isabella and Ferdinand were most successful at consolidating and centralizing political power in the fifteenth century, as they were able to use their control of the Church and the combined wealth of Castile and Aragon to curb the power of the nobility and enforce uniform loyalty to the crown. Choice A is incorrect because in England the process of centralization was delayed by an internal power struggle between two rival branches of the royal family known as the War of the Roses, though some progress was made after Henry Tudor came to power in 1485. Choice B is incorrect because France did make progress in consolidating and centralizing power, second only to Spain, but French progress was delayed by the need to subdue the powerful Duke of Burgundy, which was not accomplished until 1477. Choice C is incorrect because German nobles were able to retain considerable autonomy from the Holy Roman Emperor who was an elected ruler, which obviously impeded the consolidation of power. And choice D is incorrect because the Italian peninsula still consisted of independent city-states that were ruled by powerful merchant-princes.

6. **C.** The Holy Roman Emperor was elected by a seven-member council consisting of the archbishops of Mainz, Trier, and Cologne, the Duke of Saxony, the Margrave of Brandenburg, the Count Palatine, and the King of Bohemia. Choice A is incorrect because the Holy Roman Emperor was a specific title which did not refer to the pope. Choice B is incorrect because the Hundred Years War was an English dynastic struggle that did not involve or affect the Holy Roman Emperor. Choice D is incorrect because Ferdinand of Aragon was never Holy Roman Emperor. Choice E is incorrect because the voyages of Columbus were sponsored by the Spanish monarchy.

7. **D.** It was the search for gold and competition for the spice trade between Spain and Portugal that

provided the inspiration for the era of daring exploration and discovery at the end of the fifteenth and beginning of the sixteenth centuries. Choice A is incorrect because the Reformation's focus was internal to Europe and had nothing to do with exploration outside European borders. Choice B is incorrect because the steam engine was not widely used to power ships until the nineteenth century, not in the fifteenth and sixteenth centuries. Choice C is also incorrect not only because the timing is wrong—the Black Death was a fourteenth-century phenomenon that had ended by the fifteenth- to sixteenth-century time period mentioned in the question—but also because it was a sickness that killed much of the population of Europe and crippled Europe's economy and had nothing to do with exploring the rest of the world beyond Europe. Finally, choice E is incorrect because the successful circumnavigation of the globe by the Magellan expedition was an *example* and, in some ways, *a culmination* of the era of exploration and discovery, but it was *not* its inspiration.

8. **D.** The hierarchical social structure of Europe was *not* a result of the creation of a Spanish Empire in the New World; that social structure dates back to the early medieval period. Choice A is incorrect because the influx of new wealth from Spain's New World Empire *did* cause inflation in Europe. Choice B is incorrect because the creation of Spain's New World Empire also involved missionaries who firmly established Christianity there. Choice C is incorrect because the wealth gained in trade with the New World Empire did lead to the rise of a wealthy merchant class. Choice E is incorrect because it *did* foster economic dependence between Europe and the New World.

CHAPTER 8

The Renaissance, 1350–1550

IN THIS CHAPTER

Summary: Between 1350 and 1550, Europe experienced a rebirth (renaissance) of commerce, interest in the classical cultures of ancient Greece and Rome, and confidence in human potential.

Key Ideas

✪ The Renaissance began on the Italian peninsula because of its location as the gateway to Eastern trade.

✪ The outstanding feature of Renaissance Italian society was the degree to which it was urban.

✪ Renaissance values were based on the revival of humanism—that is, an interest in an education program based on the languages and values of Classical Greek and Roman cultures.

✪ In the fifteenth century, Renaissance values spread northward to the rest of Europe.

Key Terms

guilds	*The Prince*	*Colloquies*
doge	neoplatonism	lay piety
humanism	Florentine Academy	*On the Fabric of the*
studia humanitas	frescos	*Human Body*
Oration on the Dignity	Michelangelo's *David*	*De Revolutionibus Orbium*
of Man	Treaty of Lodi	*Caelestum*

Introduction

The word *Renaissance* means "rebirth." Historically, it refers to a time in Western civilization (1350–1550) that was characterized by the revival of three things: commerce, interest in the Classical world, and belief in the potential of human achievement. For reasons that are both geographical and social, the Renaissance began in Italy where renewed trade with the East flowed into Europe via the Mediterranean Sea and, therefore, through the Italian peninsula. The Italian Renaissance flowered for approximately a century until, as a result of invasions from France and Great Britain, it flowed north into the rest of Western Europe.

Renaissance Italian Society

The society of the Italian peninsula between 1350 and 1550 was unique in Western civilization. The most outstanding characteristic of Italian society was the degree to which it was urban. By 1500, seven of the ten largest cities in Europe were in Italy. Whereas most of Western Europe was characterized by large kingdoms with powerful monarchs and increasingly centralized bureaucracies, the Italian peninsula was made up of numerous independent city-states, such as Milan, Florence, Padua, and Genoa. These city-states were, by virtue of their location, flourishing centers of commerce in control of reviving networks of trade with Eastern empires.

Social status within these city-states was determined primarily by occupation, rather than by birth or the ownership of land, as was common in the rest of Europe during this period. The trades were controlled by government-protected monopolies called *guilds*. Members of the manufacturing guilds, such as clothiers and metalworkers, sat at the top of the social hierarchy. The next prestigious were the professional groups that included bankers, administrators, and merchants. They were followed by skilled labor, such as the stone masons.

Because the city-states of Italy developed as commercial centers, wealth was not based on the control of land as it was in the rest of Europe during this period. Instead, wealth was in the form of capital, and power was the ability to lend it. Accordingly, the traditional landed aristocracy of the Italian peninsula was not as politically powerful as their other European counterparts. Rather, powerful merchant families dominated socially and politically. Their status as the holders of capital also made the commercial elites of Italy powerful throughout Europe as the monarchs of the more traditional kingdoms had to come to them when seeking loans to finance their wars of territorial expansion.

The city-states of Renaissance Italy were set up along a variety of models. Some, like Naples, were ruled by hereditary monarchs; others were ruled by powerful families, such as the Medicis of Florence; still others, like Venice, were controlled by a military strongman known as a *doge*.

Renaissance Values

Prior to the Renaissance, the values of European civilization were based on the codes of honor and chivalry that reflected the social relations of the traditional feudal hierarchy. During the Renaissance, these traditional values were transformed to reflect both the ambition and the pride of the commercial class that dominated Renaissance Italian society. In contrast to traditional European noblemen, who competed for prestige on the battlefield or in jousting and fencing tournaments, successful Renaissance men competed with displays of civic duty that included patronage of philosophy and arts.

At the center of the Renaissance system of values was *humanism*. Renaissance humanism combined an admiration for Classical Greek and Roman literature with a new-found confidence in what modern men could achieve. Accordingly, Renaissance humanism was characterized by the *studia humanitas*, an educational program founded on knowledge of the Classical Latin and Greek languages. Once these languages had been mastered, the Renaissance humanist could read deeply in the Classical works of the ancient Greek and Roman authors, absorbing what the philosophers of the last great Western civilization had to teach them about how to succeed in life and how to live a good life.

To the Renaissance humanist, the ancient Greek and Roman philosophers were guides, but guides whose achievements could be equaled and eventually improved upon. The ultimate goal of the Renaissance humanist program was the truly well-rounded citizen, one who excelled in grammar, rhetoric, poetry, history, politics, and moral philosophy. These scholarly achievements were valued in their own right, as a testament to the dignity and ability of man, but also for the way in which they contributed to the glory of the city-state.

Prime examples of early Renaissance humanism were Petrarch, who celebrated the glory of ancient Rome in his *Letters to the Ancient Dead*, and Boccaccio, who compiled an encyclopedia of Greek and Roman mythology. The best articulation of the belief in the dignity and potential of man that characterized Renaissance humanism was Pico della Mirandola's *Oration on the Dignity of Man* (1486). In the *Oration*, Pico argued that God endowed man with the ability to shape his own being, and that man has the obligation to become all that he can be.

By the late Renaissance, humanism lost some of its ideal character, where scholarly achievements were valued for their own sake, and took on a more cynical quality that promoted only individual success. This shift is sometimes characterized as a shift from a "civic ideal" to a "princely ideal," as texts like Castiglione's *The Book of the Courtier* (1513–1518) and Machiavelli's *The Prince* (1513) focused on the qualities and strategies necessary for attaining and holding social and political power.

Neoplatonism

Another aspect of Renaissance thought that had profound implications for the intellectual development of Western civilization was neoplatonism. At the core of Renaissance neoplatonism is a rediscovery and reinterpretation of the works of the ancient Greek philosopher Plato. Medieval scholastics had found the world view of the ancient Greek philosopher Aristotle to be most compatible with Christianity. Accordingly, they made his philosophy the centerpiece of medieval scholasticism. After the fall of Constantinople in 1453, however, ancient Greek manuscripts and accompanying Greek scholars flowed into Italy. Led by the Florentine humanist Marsilio Ficino, Renaissance scholars translated the works of Plato and made a version of his thought central to their own philosophy.

Plato's writings distinguished between a changeless and eternal realm of being or form and the temporary and perishable world we experience. Crucially for Renaissance humanists, Plato contended that both human reason and love belonged to the world of forms. The implication for the Renaissance humanists was that, by cultivating the finest qualities of their being, humans could commune with God in an eternal realm of form and soul. In order to cultivate these human qualities, Ficino persuaded the Florentine merchant-prince Cosimo de Medici to fund the *Florentine Academy*, an informal gathering of humanists devoted to the revival and teachings of Plato.

The Renaissance Artistic Achievement

The unique structure of Renaissance society and the corresponding system of Renaissance values combined to give birth to one of the most amazing bursts of artistic creativity in the history of Western civilization. The wealthy and powerful elites of Renaissance society patronized the arts for the fame and prestige that it brought them. The competitive spirit of the competing elites both within and among the Italian city-states meant that artists and craftsmen were in almost constant demand.

For example, Lorenzo de Medici, who led the ruling family of Florence from 1469 until his death in 1492, commissioned work by almost all of the great Renaissance artists. As an art patron, he was rivaled by Pope Julius II, whose patronage of the arts during his papacy (1503–1513), including the construction of St Peter's Basilica, transformed Rome into one of Europe's most beautiful cities.

The artists themselves usually hailed not from the elite class but from the class of guild craftsmen. Young men with skill were identified and apprenticed to guild shops run by master craftsmen. Accordingly, there was no separation between the "artistic" and "commercial" sides of the Renaissance art world. All works were commissioned and the artist was expected to give the patron what he ordered. The Renaissance artist demonstrated his creativity within the bounds of explicit contracts that specified all details.

Another aspect of the guild culture that contributed to the brilliant innovations of the Renaissance period was the fact that the various media, such as sculpture, painting, and architecture, were not viewed as separate disciplines; instead, the Renaissance apprentice was expected to master the techniques of each of these areas. As a result, mature Renaissance artists were able to work with a variety of materials and to apply ideas and techniques learned in one medium to projects in another.

Whereas medieval art had been characterized by religious subject matter, the Renaissance style took the human being and the human form as its subject. The transition can be seen in the series of *frescos* painted by Giotto in the fourteenth century. Although he still focused on religious subject matter (i.e., the life of St Francis), Giotto depicted the human characters in realistic detail and with a concern for their psychological reaction to the events of St Francis's life. The Renaissance artist's concern for the human form in all its complexity is illustrated by two great sculptures, each nominally depicting the biblical character of David:

- One is Donatello's version (completed in 1432), the first life-size, free-standing nude sculpture since antiquity, which depicts David in a completely naturalistic way and casts him as a young Florentine gentleman.
- The second version was sculpted by Michelangelo Buonarroti (completed in 1504) and is characteristic of the last and most heroic phase of Renaissance art. Sculpted from a single piece of marble, *Michelangelo's David* is larger than life and offers a vision of the human body and spirit that is more dramatic than real life, an effect that Michelangelo produced by making the head and hands deliberately too large for the torso. Upon its completion, the rulers of Florence originally placed Michelangelo's *David* at the entrance to the city hall as a symbol of Florentine strength.

Knowledge of the Natural World

The same spirit that produced the Renaissance's artistic achievement brought advances in Europeans' understanding of the natural world. The desire to restore what the ancients knew about the natural world led Renaissance natural philosophers to both reexamine ancient texts and observe the natural world for themselves.

During this period, great strides were made in the accurate understanding and depiction of human anatomy. In 1536, Johannes Guinther published an anatomy textbook based on a new translation of the work of the ancient Greek philosopher Galen. The new textbook, titled *Anatomical Institutions According to the Opinions of Galen for Students of Medicine*, provided accurate information, previously unknown to European physicians, about the human skeleton, muscles, cardiovascular system, and internal organs. One of Guinther's students, Andreas Vesalius, produced an exhaustive study of human anatomy that was based on first-hand dissection of human cadavers. Vesalius's *On the Fabric of the Human Body*, published in seven volumes beginning in 1543, became the standard text for medical students and greatly improved the medical profession's understanding of human anatomy.

The Renaissance spirit of inquiry also produced new knowledge in the field of natural history. Georg Bauer, who published under the pen name Agricola, published *On the Nature of Fossils* in 1546. In addition to providing valuable summaries of what the ancient philosophers knew about fossils, Agricola's text classified fossils according to their physical properties.

The greatest scientific achievement of the Renaissance came in the field of astronomy. The need to produce a more accurate calendar led to both a reexamination of ancient astronomical tables and new observations of the regular movements of the stars and planets. The culmination of this effort was the publication of Nicolas Copernicus's *De Revolutionibus Orbium Caelestum (On the Revolutions of the Heavenly Spheres)* in 1543. Copernicus's *De Rev* (as it is often called) proposed the shift from a geocentric (earth-centered) model of the cosmos to a heliocentric (sun-centered) model. While Copernicus's work was known only among the educated elite during the Renaissance, his theories would become a touchstone of the Scientific Revolution in the seventeenth century.

The Spread of the Renaissance

In the late-fifteenth and sixteenth centuries, the Renaissance spread to France, Germany, England, and Spain. The catalyst for this spread was the breakup of the equilibrium that characterized the politics of the Italian peninsula. An internal balance of power had been established by the *Treaty of Lodi* (1454–1455), which brought Milan, Naples, and Florence into an alliance to check the power of Venice and its frequent ally, the Papal States. The balance of power was shattered in 1494 when Naples, supported by both Florence and the pope, prepared to attack Milan. The Milanese despot, Ludovico il Moro, appealed to King Charles VIII of France for help, inviting him to lead French troops into Italy and to revive his old dynastic claims to Naples, which the French had ruled from 1266 to 1435. French troops invaded the Italian peninsula in 1494 and forced Florence, Naples, and the Papal States to make major concessions. In response, the pope and the Venetians persuaded King Ferdinand of Aragon to bring troops to Italy to help resist French aggression. From the late 1490s through most of the sixteenth century, Italy became a battleground in a war for supremacy between European monarchs.

Once the isolation of the Italian peninsula was shattered, the ideals and values of the Renaissance spread through a variety of agents:

- teachers migrating out of Italy
- students who came to study in Italy and then returned home
- European merchants whose interests now penetrated the peninsula
- various lay groups seeking to spread their message of piety

However, the major cause of the spread of Renaissance ideals and values was the printing press. Invented by Johann Gutenberg in the German city of Mainz about 1445 in response to increased demand for books from an increasingly literate public, the moveable type printing press allowed for faster, cheaper mass-produced books to be created and distributed throughout Europe. By 1500, between 15 and 20 million books were in circulation. Among the ideas that spread with the books were the thoughts and philosophies of the Renaissance humanists, which were both adopted and transformed in northern Europe.

The most important and influential of the northern humanists was Desiderius Erasmus, sometimes referred to as "the prince of the humanists." Spreading the Renaissance belief in the value of education, Erasmus made his living as an educator. He taught his students both the Latin language and lessons on how to live a good life from Latin dialogues that he wrote himself. Published under the title of *Colloquies*, Erasmus's dialogues also displayed the humanist's faith in both the power of learning and the ability of man by satirizing the old scholastic notions that the truth about God and nature could be discerned only by priests. Erasmus argued instead that, by mastering ancient languages, any man could teach himself to read the Bible and an array of ancient philosophers, thereby learning the truth about God and nature for himself.

In France, England, and Spain, the existence of strong monarchies meant that the Renaissance would be centered in the royal courts. In the smaller, independent German provinces, the characteristics of the Renaissance were absorbed into a tradition of *lay piety*, where organized groups, such as the Brethren of Common Life, promoted pious behavior and learning outside the bureaucracy of the Church. In that context, German scholars, such as Martin Luther, who were educated in a context that combined the humanistic and lay piety traditions, would be prominent in the creation of the Reformation.

› Rapid Review

The revival of commerce, interest in the Classical world, and belief in the potential of human achievement that occurred on the Italian peninsula between 1350 and 1550 is known as the Renaissance. Within the independent, urban city-states of Renaissance Italian society, the successful merchant class sought a well-rounded life of achievement and civic virtue which led them to give their patronage to scholars and artists. Accordingly, both scholarship and artistic achievement reached new heights, and new philosophies like humanism and neoplatonism were fashioned.

In 1494, mounting jealousy and mistrust between the Italian city-states caused the leaders of Milan to invite intervention by the powerful French monarchy, thereby breaking a delicate balance of power and causing the Italian peninsula to become a battleground in a war for supremacy between European monarchies. The destruction of the independence of the Italian city-states caused the spread and transformation of Renaissance ideals and values. A northern European humanism, less secular than its Italian counterpart, developed and served as the foundation of the Reformation.

› Chapter Review Questions

1. Reasons that the Renaissance originated on the Italian peninsula include all of the following EXCEPT the peninsula's
   (A) geographic location
   (B) political organization
   (C) religion
   (D) social structure
   (E) economic structure

2. Which of the following is NOT a Renaissance value?
   (A) mastery of ancient languages
   (B) patronage of the arts
   (C) scholarly achievement
   (D) proficiency in the military arts
   (E) civic duty

3. Renaissance humanism
   (A) devalued mastery of ancient languages
   (B) urged the development of a single talent to perfection
   (C) valued ancient philosophers as the final authorities on all matters
   (D) denied the existence of God
   (E) valued scholarship for its own sake and for the glory it brought the city-state

4. The belief that by cultivating the finest qualities of their beings, human beings could commune with God was a conclusion of
   (A) guildsmen
   (B) neoplatonists
   (C) the lay piety movement
   (D) the Catholic Church in Renaissance Italy
   (E) the *doge*

5. Which of the following was NOT a factor that contributed to the Renaissance artistic achievement?
   (A) the patronage of the pope
   (B) the invasion of Italy by the French
   (C) the competitive spirit of competing elites
   (D) the apprentice system
   (E) the lack of separation between artistic and commercial aspects of the Renaissance art world

6. Which of the following did NOT enable the spread of the Renaissance?
   (A) the Treaty of Lodi
   (B) Milan's invitation to Charles VIII to bring troops to Italy
   (C) the printing press
   (D) students and teachers migrating in and out of the Italian peninsula
   (E) the lay piety movement

7. Renaissance art
   (A) was characterized by the severe specialization of its artists
   (B) was characterized by religious subject matter
   (C) abandoned painting in favor of sculpture
   (D) was characterized by its concern for the human form
   (E) did not require patrons

8. Northern humanism
   (A) was less secular than Italian humanism
   (B) linked scholarship and learning with religious piety
   (C) criticized the notion that priests were required to understand the Bible
   (D) contributed to the Reformation
   (E) all of the above

› Answers and Explanations

1. **C.** The religion of Renaissance Italy, which was Catholicism, was shared by many of the European kingdoms. Choice A is incorrect because the Italian peninsula's geographical location *was* a reason the Renaissance began here: As the gateway to Europe for Eastern trade coming in through the Mediterranean Sea, Italy was the first region to benefit from economic recovery and the influx of ancient texts. Choices B, D, and E are incorrect because the fact that the Italian peninsula was organized politically into independent city-states (choice B) that competed with each other commercially (choice E) meant that the traditional nobility was less powerful and that social status was less hierarchical and based on occupation (choice D). All these factors allowed for the development of the individual ambition and civic pride that characterized Renaissance values and ideals.

2. **D.** Proficiency in the military arts had been a traditional value of the nobility of medieval Europe, but it was downplayed in the Renaissance. The other choices are values particular to the Renaissance.

3. **E.** Renaissance humanism did indeed value scholarship. In contrast, choice A is incorrect because Renaissance humanism did not *devalue* the mastery of ancient languages; in contrast, it sought to *revive and encourage* such learning of Greek and Latin, for example. Choice B is incorrect because Renaissance humanism emphasized well-roundedness, *not* just the perfection of a single talent (think of today's use of the term "Renaissance man"). Choice C is incorrect because, although Renaissance humanists *respected* the ancient philosophers, they did not view them as the final authorities but instead believed they could enter into conversation with and eventually *surpass* them. Finally, choice D is incorrect because Renaissance humanists did not *deny the existence* of God at all: In contrast, they believed that all of man's abilities were *gifts from God* that should be developed to the fullest.

4. **B.** The belief that by cultivating the finest qualities of their beings, human beings could commune with God was a conclusion of the neo-platonists. Choice A is incorrect because the term *guildsmen* refers to members of the artisan class, not to a school of philosophy. Choice C is incorrect because the lay piety movement emphasized pious behavior and learning outside the Church bureaucracy, which obviously had nothing to do with communing with God. Choice D is incorrect because the Catholic Church in Italy maintained the traditional Christian view that pride in human achievement was a sin, a view at odds with aspiring to cultivate finer qualities in oneself. Finally, a *doge* was a military leader who wielded political power in some Italian city-states and had nothing to do with this (or any other) belief about communing with God.

5. **B.** The invasion of Italy by the French triggered the spread of the Renaissance to the rest of Europe, but it did not contribute to the Renaissance artistic achievement. Choice A is incorrect because the Renaissance popes *were* motivated by Renaissance ideals to patronize the arts, so they were a factor contributing to artistic achievement. Similarly, choice C is incorrect because the popes' elite counterparts in other city-states were also motivated to patronize the arts, so they were also a factor contributing to artistic achievement. Choice D is incorrect because the apprentice system helped increase the number of artists, which therefore led to more artistic works, increased ability to mix the techniques of various artistic media (e.g., painting and sculpting), and greater artistic achievement. Finally, choice E is incorrect because the commissioning of artistic works by specific business contracts meant that there was an unprecedented call for Renaissance artists.

6. **A.** The Treaty of Lodi, signed in the mid-fifteenth century, established a balance of power that helped keep other European powers out of the Italian peninsula, which therefore inhibited rather than enabled the spread of the Renaissance. Choice B is incorrect because Milan's invitation to Charles VIII to bring troops to Italy helped shatter that balance of power and isolation at the end of the fifteenth century, which then began a series of events that *did* lead to the

spread of the Renaissance. Choice C is incorrect because the invention of the printing press *helped* spread Renaissance ideas elsewhere in Europe. Choice D is incorrect because students and teachers who migrated in and out of the Italian peninsula also helped spread Renaissance ideas. Finally, choice E is incorrect because the lay piety movement associated learning with pious behavior, which also helped spread Renaissance ideas.

7. **D**. Renaissance art was characterized by its concern for the human form. Choice A is incorrect because Renaissance artists did *not* specialize; in contrast, they were trained in *all* media. Choice B is incorrect because this focus on the human form was a move away from religious subject matter, which characterized most art before the Renaissance (for example, think of all the Medieval Madonna-and-child paintings and depictions of other biblical scenes and Church icons). Choice C is incorrect for the same reason as choice A: Again, Renaissance artists did *not* abandon painting in favor of sculpture; instead, they were trained and worked in *all* media. Finally, choice E is incorrect because Renaissance art was, in fact, a business: Patrons commissioned and paid for all Renaissance art, so they were definitely required by artists during this time.

8. **E**. All of the answer choices are true: Choices A, B, and C are accurate and constitute the ways in which northern humanism helped to bring about the Reformation, thus choice D is also true.

CHAPTER 9

The Reformation, 1500–1600

IN THIS CHAPTER

Summary: In the sixteenth century, an attempt to reform the Christian Church developed into a Protestant movement that shattered the religious unity of Europe.

Key Ideas

✪ In the second decade of the sixteenth century, a German cleric, Martin Luther, created a rival theology based on the belief that salvation was achieved by faith alone.

✪ As Luther's theology spread, it was transformed into a Protestant movement with social and political dimensions.

✪ In England, Henry VIII used the Protestant movement as an excuse to break with the papacy in Rome and to create an English national church, known as the Church of England or the Anglican Church.

✪ The Catholic Church responded to the Protestant movement with both reforms and aggressive countermeasures.

Key Terms

Papal States	95 theses	predestination
indulgences	Peace of Augsburg	the elect
millenarianism	Huguenots	Anabaptists
salvation by faith alone	Edict of Nantes	Society of Jesus
scripture alone	Anglican Church	Council of Trent
priesthood of all believers	dissenters	the Inquisition

Introduction

The Reformation in sixteenth-century Europe began as an effort to reform the Christian Church, which many believed had become too concerned with worldly matters. Soon, however, the Church found itself facing a serious challenge from a brilliant German theologian, Martin Luther, and his followers. What began as a protest evolved into a revolution with social and political overtones. By the end of the century, a Europe that had been united by a single Church was deeply divided, as the Catholic and Protestant faiths vied for the minds and hearts of the people.

The Need for a Religious Reformation

By the onset of the sixteenth century, the Christian Church of Europe was facing a serious set of interconnected problems. Concern was growing that the Church had become too worldly and corrupt in its practices. The Church, and particularly the papacy in Rome, was widely seen to be more concerned with building and retaining worldly power and wealth than in guiding souls to salvation. The pope was not only the head of a powerful Church hierarchy but also the ruler of the *Papal States*, a kingdom that encompassed much of the central portion of the Italian peninsula. He collected taxes, kept an army, and used his religious power to influence politics in every kingdom in Europe.

The selling of *indulgences* (which allowed people to be absolved from their sins, sometimes even before they committed them, by making a monetary contribution to the Church) was just one way in which the Church seemed more concerned with amassing power and wealth than with guiding the faithful to salvation. To many common people who yearned for a powerful, personal, and emotional connection with God, the Church not only failed to provide it but worked actively to discourage it by:

- protecting the power of the priesthood
- saying the mass in Latin, a language understood by only the educated elite
- refusing to allow the printing of the Bible in the vernacular

The Lutheran Revolt

Martin Luther was an unlikely candidate to lead a revolt against the Church. The son of a mine manager in eastern Germany, Luther received a humanistic education, studying law before being drawn to the Church and being ordained as a priest in 1507. Continuing his education, Luther received a doctorate of theology from the University of Wittenberg and was appointed to the faculty there in 1512.

The revolutionary ideas that would come to define Lutheran theology were a product of Luther's personal search. Luther believed that he was living in the last days of the world and that God's final judgment would soon be upon the world. This view, now referred to as *millenarianism* and widespread in sixteenth-century Europe, led Luther to be obsessed with the question of how any human being could be good enough to deserve salvation. He found his answer through the rigorous study of scripture, and he formulated three interconnected theological assertions:

- *salvation by faith alone*, which stated that salvation came only to those who had true faith
- *scripture alone*, which stated that scripture was the only source of true knowledge of God's will

- *the priesthood of all believers*, which argued that all true believers received God's grace and were, therefore, priests in God's eyes

  Each of Luther's assertions put him in direct opposition to the Church's orthodox theology:

- Salvation by faith alone contradicted the Church's assertion that salvation was gained both by having faith and by performing works of piety and charity.
- Scripture alone contradicted the Church's assertion that there were two sources of true knowledge of God: scripture and the traditions of the Church.
- The priesthood of all believers contradicted the Church's assertion that only ordained priests could read and correctly interpret scripture.

Creation and Spread of the Protestant Movement

In the autumn of 1517, Luther launched his protest by tacking *95 theses* or propositions that ran contrary to the theology and practice of the Church to the door of the Wittenberg castle church. His students quickly translated them from Latin into the German vernacular and distributed printed versions throughout the German-speaking kingdoms and provinces. With the aid of the printing press, Luther attracted many followers, but the survival of a Protestant movement was due to the political climate.

Had the papacy moved quickly to excommunicate Luther and his followers, the movement may not have survived. However, Luther found a powerful protector in Frederick of Saxony, the prince of Luther's district. Frederick was one of seven electors, the princes who elected the Holy Roman Emperor, to whom the princes of the German districts owed their allegiance. Frederick's protection caused the pope to delay Luther's excommunication until 1520. By that time, it was too late: Luther and his followers had established throughout Germany congregations for the kind of Christian worship that, after 1529, would be known as Protestant.

Luther promoted his theology to both the nobility and common people. To the nobility, he wrote an "Address to the Christian Nobility of the German Nation" (1520), which appealed to the German princes' desire for both greater unity and power and to their desire to be out from under the thumb of an Italian Pope. To the common people, he addressed "The Freedom of the Christian Man" (1520), in which he encouraged common men to obey their Christian conscience and respect those in authority who seemed to possess true Christian principles. Through this strategy, Luther offered the noble princes of Germany an opportunity to break with the Roman Church and papacy without losing the obedience of the common people. It was an opportunity that was too good to pass up. By 1555, the German princes made it clear that they would no longer bow to Rome; they signed the *Peace of Augsburg*, which established the principle of "he who rules; his religion" and signaled to Rome that the German princes would not go to war with each other over religion.

Once it gained a foothold in northern Germany, Protestantism flourished in those areas where the local rulers were either unwilling or not strong enough to enforce orthodoxy and loyalty to Rome. Accordingly, the Protestant movement spread with success to the Netherlands, Scandinavia, Scotland, and England, but it encountered more difficulty and little or no success in southern and eastern Europe. The site of the most bloodshed was France, where Protestantism was declared both heretical and illegal in 1534. Initially French Protestants, known as *Huguenots*, were tolerated, but a civil war pitting Catholics against Protestants erupted in 1562. Peaceful coexistence was briefly restored by the *Edict of Nantes* in 1598, which established the principle of religious toleration in France, but the edict would be revoked in 1685.

The English Reformation

The English Reformation was unique. England had long traditions of dissent and anticlericalism that stemmed from a humanist tradition. In that context, Protestantism grew slowly, appealing especially to the middling classes, and by 1524, illegal English-language Bibles were circulating. But as the English monarch, Henry VIII, tried to consolidate his power and his legacy, he took the existence of a Protestant movement as an opportunity to break from Rome and create a national church, the Church of England, or *Anglican Church*.

Henry needed a divorce from his wife, Catherine of Aragon, because she could not provide him with a male heir to the throne. He also needed money and land with which to buy the loyalty of existing nobles and to create new ones that would owe their position to him. In 1534, he officially broke with the Church in Rome and had himself declared the head of the new Church of England. In 1536, he dissolved the English monasteries and seized Church lands and properties, awarding them to those loyal to him. It soon became apparent, however, that the church that Henry had created was Protestant only in the sense that it had broken from Rome. In terms of the characteristics opposed by most Protestant reformers—its episcopal or hierarchical nature, the existence of priests, and the retention of the sacraments and symbols of the traditional Roman church—the Church of England was hardly Protestant at all.

For the rest of the century, the unfinished Reformation left England plagued by religious turmoil. During the reign of Edward VI, the son of Henry and Jane Seymour, England was officially Anglican, but communities of those who refused to honor it and organized themselves along more Protestant lines grew to sufficient numbers for them to be known collectively as *Dissenters*. Upon the accession of Mary I (the daughter of Henry and his first wife, Catherine of Aragon), England was returned to Catholicism and Protestants were persecuted. Under the subsequent reign of Elizabeth I (the daughter of Henry and Anne Boleyn), England was again Anglican. While Catholics were initially persecuted under Elizabeth, there emerged during her long reign a kind of equilibrium in which a modicum of religious toleration was given to all.

Calvin and Calvinism

Once the break from the Roman Church was accomplished, Protestant leaders faced the task of creating new religious communities and systematizing a theology. The most influential of the second-generation Protestant theologians was John Calvin. Converting to Protestantism around 1534, Calvin was forced to leave his native France and flee to Switzerland, whose towns were governed by strong town councils who had historically competed with the Church bishops for local power. Calvin settled in Geneva where, in 1536, the adult male population had voted to become Protestant. For the next 40 years, Calvin worked in Geneva, articulating the theology and a structure for Protestant religious communities that would come to be known as Calvinism.

Calvinism accepted both Martin Luther's contentions that salvation is gained by faith alone and that scripture is the sole source of authoritative knowledge of God's will. But on the subject of salvation, Calvin went further, developing the doctrine of *predestination*, which asserted that God has predetermined which people will be saved and which will be damned. Those that are predestined to salvation were known as *the elect* and, although their earthly behavior could not affect the status of their salvation, Calvin taught that the elect would be known by both their righteous behavior and by their prosperity, as God would bless all their earthly enterprises.

In Calvinist communities, the structure and discipline of the congregation was integrated into that of the town. In place of the hierarchical structure of the Roman Church, Calvinist churches were organized by function:

- *Pastors* preached the gospel.
- *Doctors* studied scripture and wrote commentaries.
- *Deacons* saw to the social welfare of the community.
- *Elders* governed the church and the community in moral matters and enforced discipline.

Geneva soon became the inspirational center of the Protestant movement.

Social Dimensions and the Radical Reformation

The Protestantism of Martin Luther and John Calvin appealed to the industrious and prosperous commercial and merchant classes. At these higher rungs of the social hierarchy, people could read and react to criticism of both the doctrine and practice of the orthodox Roman Church. The strict discipline of the Calvinist communities mirrored the self-discipline their own professions demanded, and the promise that God would bless the worldly endeavors of the elect provided a self-satisfying justification for the wealth and prosperity that many were enjoying. Further down the social ladder, amongst the artisan and peasant classes, a more radical reformation was shaped.

The religious beliefs of the poorer and less educated classes were always less uniform than those of the elites. Their knowledge of Christian theology tended to be superficial and wedded to older folklore that deified the forces of nature. What they cared about was that the suffering they endured in this life would be rewarded in the next. Accordingly, leaders of Protestant movements amongst the artisan and peasant classes interpreted the doctrines of justification by faith alone and predestination to mean that God would never abandon the poor and simple people who suffered, and that they could have direct knowledge of their salvation through an inner light that came to them directly from God. In some circles, this was combined with millenarian notions that the judgment day was near, to create a belief that the poor had a special mission to purge the world of evil and prepare it for the second coming of Christ.

The first and largest group of radical reformers was known as the *Anabaptists*. In 1534, proclaiming that judgment day was at hand, a group of them captured the German city of Münster, seized the property of nonbelievers, and burned all books except the Bible. To Protestant and Catholic elites alike, the Anabaptists represented a threat to the social order that could not be tolerated. Their rebellion was subsequently put down by an army led by the Lutheran Prince Philip of Hesse, and their movement was violently repressed and driven underground.

The Catholic Response

Although it was slow to believe that Protestantism could pose a threat to its power, the Roman Church—which was increasingly referred to as "catholic" (meaning one, true, and universal)—had begun to construct a response by the middle of the sixteenth century. Although sometimes referred to as the Counter-Reformation, the Catholic response actually had two dimensions: one aimed at reforming the Catholic Church and another aimed at exterminating the Protestant movement.

At the center of both dimensions was the *Society of Jesus*. Founded in 1534 by Ignatius Loyola, the Jesuits (as they came to be known) were a tightly organized order who saw themselves as soldiers in a war against Satan. Strategically, the Jesuits focused on education, building schools and universities throughout Europe. The Jesuits also served as missionaries, and they were often among the first Europeans to visit the new worlds that the age of exploration was opening up, thereby establishing a beach-head for Catholicism. Internally, they preached a new piety and pushed the Church to curb its worldly practices and to serve as a model for a selfless, holy life that could lead to salvation.

The Catholic reform movement reached its peak with the *Council of Trent*, which began its deliberations in 1545. Over many years, the Council passed reforms abolishing the worst of the abuses that had led to Protestant discontent. However, the Council of Trent also symbolized a defeat for Protestants who hoped for reconciliation, as the Council refused to compromise on any of the key theological issues and continued to insist that the Catholic Church was the final arbiter in all matters of faith.

At the heart of the Catholic Church's efforts to defeat Protestantism was the office known as the *Inquisition*. An old institution within the Church that investigated charges of heresy, its duties were revived and expanded to combat all perceived threats to orthodoxy and the Church's authority. Those who ran foul of the Inquisition ran the risk of imprisonment, torture, and execution. The Church's other main weapon in its aggressive response to the Reformation was censorship. Books that were considered unorthodox or at odds with the Church's teachings were placed on the *Index of Banned Books*.

› Rapid Review

By the sixteenth century, the Christian Church was faced with mounting criticism of its preoccupation with worldly matters and its failure to meet the emotional and spiritual needs of an increasingly literate population. In 1517, Martin Luther charged that the Church had abandoned scripture and strayed from its mission. He offered an alternative and simplified theology that asserted that salvation came by having faith alone, and that scripture alone was the source of all knowledge about salvation. In the face of the Church's opposition and prevarication, a Protestant movement grew around Luther's theology, finding followers amongst both the German princes (who wished to break with Rome) and the poor (who felt oppressed).

In England, the powerful monarch Henry VIII used the existence of a Protestant movement to break with Rome in 1524 and to confiscate the lands the Church held in his kingdom. He created the Church of England, which retained the hierarchy and trappings of the Catholic Church, thereby creating within his own kingdom a group of Dissenters, who were Protestants for whom the Church of England was not reformed enough.

By mid-century, the Protestant movement had diversified and fragmented, as second-generation Protestant theologians faced the task of articulating the specific beliefs and structure of the new churches and communities they were building. Most influential among this second generation was John Calvin, who added the theological concept of predestination to Martin Luther's theology and oversaw the creation of Calvinist communities, whose center was Geneva.

Among the poorer classes, Protestantism became mixed with millenarianism and the desire for social reform. That fact, along with the propertied classes' opposition to such reform, was illustrated by the seizure of the German city of Münster by the Anabaptists in 1534, and by the ruthlessness with which the city was liberated by the Lutheran Prince Philip of Hesse.

The Catholic response to the Protestant movement was two-pronged. The Church, under the auspices of the Council of Trent, carried out many internal reforms that addressed the grievances of the faithful; it also put into motion a Counter-Reformation program, executed by the Society of Jesus and the Inquisition, which was aimed at stamping out Protestantism.

❯ Chapter Review Questions

1. Which of the following was NOT one of the problems facing the Christian Church in the sixteenth century?
   (A) the pope's status as ruler of the Papal States
   (B) its use of Latin in the mass and in the printed Bible
   (C) an increasingly literate population
   (D) its inability to tend to the physical needs of the poor
   (E) its inability to tend to the emotional and spiritual needs of the population

2. Which of the following was part of Luther's theology?
   (A) a belief in the need to create a Protestant Church
   (B) the notion that nature could serve as a guide to salvation
   (C) the idea that salvation came only through faith
   (D) the assertion that charitable works were necessary to go to heaven
   (E) the belief that the poor should be given more social and political power

3. Which of the following was NOT a reason that a Protestant movement emerged?
   (A) the Society of Jesus took up Luther's cause
   (B) Luther enjoyed the protection of some powerful Protestant princes
   (C) Luther's students used the printing press to spread Luther's theology
   (D) peasants saw Luther's theology as a justification for their dissatisfaction
   (E) the Church was slow to excommunicate Luther and his followers

4. The Peace of Augsburg
   (A) ended the war between the Church and the Protestant princes
   (B) established Henry VIII's right to establish the Church of England
   (C) established Geneva as the stronghold of Calvinism
   (D) unified the German principalities under the Holy Roman Emperor
   (E) established the principle of "he who rules; his religion"

5. The theology of Calvin differs from Luther's in which of the following ways?
   (A) the belief that scripture alone is the guide to salvation
   (B) the belief that salvation is earned by faith alone
   (C) the belief that the church hierarchy is unwarranted and harmful
   (D) the belief that some have been predestined for salvation
   (E) the belief that the Bible should be printed in the vernacular

6. The uprising and subsequent repression of the Anabaptists illustrates all of the following EXCEPT
   (A) the poorer classes understood the teachings of Protestantism to mean that the existing social hierarchy should be overthrown
   (B) the Catholic Church still had the power to crush its opposition
   (C) property-owning Protestant reformers were not looking to reform the social order
   (D) the poorer classes linked Protestant theology with millenarianism
   (E) Protestantism was a movement that encompassed many different, and sometimes opposing, views

7. The Council of Trent
   (A) excommunicated Martin Luther
   (B) established the Inquisition
   (C) insisted that the Catholic Church was the final arbiter in all matters of faith
   (D) reconciled Protestants and Catholics
   (E) produced the Treaty of Augsburg

8. The term "Dissenters"
   (A) refers to all Protestants who deny that good works can earn salvation
   (B) refers to the Anabaptists
   (C) refers to English Protestants
   (D) refers to those who refused to sign the Peace of Augsburg
   (E) refers to English Protestants who refused to join the Church of England

› Answers and Explanations

1. **D.** Choice D is the correct answer because the Church's network of poor relief was functioning as well as it ever had and was not, therefore, the problem. Choices A–C were all problems the Church faced. Choice A is not correct because the pope's status as ruler of the Papal States meant that the Church was constantly embroiled in the politics of the peninsula, thereby alienating Italians who lived in other city-states. Choice B is not correct because the Church's use of Latin, a language that only the elite could read, angered and alienated people. Similarly, choice C is incorrect because people were increasingly able to read the vernacular, but they still could not read Latin. Finally, choice E is incorrect because the Church *was* unable to tend to the emotional and spiritual needs of the population.

2. **C.** Luther's conclusion that salvation comes only through faith rather than through grace and good works as the Church argued, is the foundation of his theology. Choice A is incorrect because Luther's goal was to reform the Church, not to break with it . Choice B is incorrect because Luther believed that only scripture could give knowledge of how to achieve salvation. Choice D is incorrect because the Roman Church held that charitable works could help gain entrance into heaven; Luther disagreed. Choice E is incorrect because Luther did not advocate a change in the social or political order and denounced the peasant revolts.

3. **A.** The Society of Jesus was founded in order to *combat* the spread of Protestantism, not to promote it. Choice B is incorrect because the Protestant princes, sensing an opportunity to break with Rome, gave Luther the protection he needed. Choice C is incorrect because Lutheranism spread quickly thanks to the efforts of Luther's students and their use of the newly invented printing press. Choice D is incorrect because the peasants did see Luther's theology, or their own version of it, as a justification for their discontent. Choice E is incorrect because the Church did hesitate in excommunicating Luther, giving the movement valuable time to spread and gain strength.

4. **E.** The Peace of Augsburg was a treaty signed by the German princes that established the principle of "he who rules; his religion," thereby guaranteeing that they would not go to war with each other over the issue of religion. Choice A is incorrect because there was no war between the Church and the Protestant princes. Choice B is incorrect because the Peace of Augsburg was an agreement between the German princes and was not connected to the English Reformation. Choice C is incorrect because Geneva became the center of Calvinism because Calvin settled there and because the male population voted to become Protestant. Choice D is incorrect because, although the Holy Roman Emperor was elected by a group of the most powerful German princes, the process had no connection to the Peace of Augsburg.

5. **D.** The doctrine of predestination, which said that only a group known as the elect would enjoy God's salvation, was a theological conviction of Calvin and his followers; Luther taught that all who came to have true faith were saved. The other four answers are all theological beliefs that were shared by Luther and Calvin.

6. **B.** The Anabaptist movement was repressed by *Protestant* princes, not the Catholic Church. Choice A is incorrect because the fact that the Anabaptists seized the German city of Münster and the property of nonbelievers illustrates that the poorer classes understood the teachings of Protestantism to mean that the existing social hierarchy should be overthrown. Choice C is incorrect because the fact that the Protestant princes came to the aid of the property-owning classes demonstrates the fact that that property-owning Protestant reformers were not looking to reform the social order. Choice D is incorrect because the fact that the Anabaptists proclaimed that judgment day was at hand illustrates the link to millenarianism. Choice E is incorrect because the fact that the Anabaptist movement was crushed by Protestant princes illustrates the way in which Protestantism encompassed many different, and sometimes opposing, views.

7. **C.** Choice C is correct because, although the Council of Trent passed many reforms that pleased Protestants, it failed to reconcile Catholics and Protestants because it insisted that the Catholic Church was the final arbiter in all matters of faith. Choice A is incorrect because the Council of Trent did not excommunicate Luther. Choice B is incorrect because the Council of Trent did not establish the Inquisition; it was established by the pope. Choice D is incorrect because the Council of Trent *failed* to reconcile Protestants and Catholics. Choice E is incorrect because the Treaty of Augsburg was a secular treaty reached by the princes of Germany.

8. **E.** The term "Dissenters" refers to English Protestants who refused to join the Church of England. Choice A is incorrect because the term "Dissenter" implies a refusal to join the Church of England, not a reference to a specific theological stance. Choice B is incorrect because Anabaptists were just one of many groups in England to whom the term "Dissenters" was applied. Choice C is incorrect because the term "Dissenters" does not refer to all English Protestants, because members of the Church of England are Protestants. Choice D is incorrect because the Peace of Augsburg is unrelated to either "Dissenters" or English history.

CHAPTER 10

The Rise of Sovereignty, 1600–1715

IN THIS CHAPTER

Summary: From 1600 to 1715, social and economic change created new opportunities for monarchs to consolidate their power at the expense of the traditional, landed nobility.

Key Ideas

- ✪ A series of bad harvests and continual warfare pushed the overtaxed peasantry to the breaking point.
- ✪ European monarchs attempted to end the tax-exempt status of the nobility, town officials, and clergy.
- ✪ In those kingdoms in which the monarchs successfully allied themselves with a rising merchant middle class, they were able to curb the power of the nobility, town officials, and clergy and create a powerful centralized state.
- ✪ Russia was exceptional in that its monarchs were able to build a powerful centralized state by increasing the power of the nobility.

Key Terms

peasantry	*St. Therese in Ecstasy*	*Second Treatise of Civil*
nobility	*The Night Watch*	*Government*
monarchs	English Civil War	*intendent*
Divine Right of Kings	the Commonwealth	Versailles
tax revolts	Restoration	Tsars
absolutism	the Glorious Revolution	Law Code of 1649
baroque	constitutional monarchy	

Introduction

In the period from 1600 to 1715, the traditional hierarchical structure of European society came under new pressures. As you recall, this structure was one in which a large class of poor agricultural laborers (the *peasantry*) supported a small and wealthy class of elites (the *nobility*). As the *monarchs* of Europe fought wars to expand their kingdoms and created larger state bureaucracies to manage them, the pressure to raise greater sums of money through taxes stretched the economies and social structures of European societies to the breaking point. Meanwhile, the continuous increase in trade and diversification of the economy was creating a new class of people: a middle class made up of merchants and professionals that did not fit comfortably into the traditional hierarchy. Changes in the social and political structure of the seventeenth century were mirrored in the evolution of artistic style.

Economic Stress and Change

A series of unusually harsh winters that characterized the "little ice age" of the 1600s led to a series of poor harvests, which, in turn, led to malnutrition and disease. In an effort to cope with increasing poverty, members of the besieged agricultural class opted to have smaller families. This combination of famine, poverty, and disease led to a significant decrease in the population during this period.

These "natural" problems that plagued the peasantry of Europe were exacerbated during this period by increasing demands from the nobility that ruled them. The endless warfare waged by the rival monarchs of Europe at this time further depleted the agricultural population by conscripting their sons into the army and taking them off to war. War also required money that the monarchs and their governments attempted to raise by increasing taxes. Because the nobility was largely exempt from taxes, the peasantry bore the brunt of this new economic burden. In many places, the peasantry resisted violently in a series of *tax revolts*, but temporary concessions won by them were quickly reversed.

Resistance to the monarchs' desire for increased power and wealth came from provincial nobles, town officials, and church leaders. The outcome of these power struggles varied from kingdom to kingdom.

Britain: The Triumph of Constitutionalism

In Britain, these tensions came to a head in the form of a struggle between the monarchs of the Stuart dynasty and the English Parliament. Already an old and important institution by 1600, the English Parliament was an assembly of elites who advised the king. However, it differed from its counterparts in the other European kingdoms in several important ways:

- Its members were elected by the property-holding people of their county or district.
- Eligibility for election was based on property ownership, so its members included wealthy merchants and professional men as well as nobles.
- Members voted individually rather than as an order or class.

As a result, the English Parliament of the seventeenth century was an alliance of nobles and well-to-do members of a thriving merchant and professional class that saw itself as a voice of the "English people," and it soon clashed with the monarch it had invited to succeed the heirless Elizabeth I.

When James Stuart, the reigning king of Scotland (known there as James VI), agreed to take the throne of England as James I (1603–1625), he was determined to rule England in the manner described by the theory of *absolutism*. Under this theory, monarchs were viewed as appointed by God (an appointment known as the *Divine Right of Kings*). As such, they were entitled to rule with absolute authority over their subjects. Despite this tension, James I's reign was characterized by a contentious but peaceful coexistence with Parliament.

A religious element was added when James's son and successor, Charles I (1625–1649), married a sister of the Catholic king of France. That, together with his insistence on waging costly wars with Spain and France, led to a confrontation with Parliament. Having provoked the Scots into invading England by threatening their religious independence, Charles I was forced to call on the English Parliament for yet more funds. Parliament responded by making funds contingent on the curbing of monarchical power. This stalemate degenerated into the *English Civil War* (1642–1646). Forces loyal to the king fought to defend the power of the monarchy, the official Church of England, and the privileges and prerogatives of the nobility; forces supporting Parliament fought to uphold the rights of Parliament, to bring an end to the notion of an official state church, and for notions of individual liberty and the rule of law.

The victory of the Parliamentary forces led to the trial and execution of Charles I for treason and to the establishment of the *Commonwealth* (1649–1660). The Commonwealth deteriorated into a fundamentalist Protestant dictatorship under the rule of the Parliamentary army's leading general, Oliver Cromwell. Upon Cromwell's death in 1658, English Parliamentarians worked to establish a *Restoration* (1660–1688) of the English monarchy, inviting the son of the king they executed to take the throne as Charles II (1660–1685).

The relative peace of the Restoration period broke down when Charles's brother, a Catholic, ascended to the throne as James II (1685–1688). James was determined to establish religious freedom for Catholics, to avenge his father, and to restore absolute monarchy to Britain. To thwart James's plans, Parliament enlisted the aid of the king's eldest daughter, Mary, the Protestant wife of William of Orange of the Netherlands. The quick, nearly bloodless uprising that coordinated Parliament-led uprisings with the invasion of a Protestant fleet and army from the Netherlands, and which led to the quick expulsion of James II in 1688, is known as the *Glorious Revolution*. The reign of William and Mary marks the clear establishment of a *constitutional monarchy*, a system by which the monarch in Britain rules within the limits of the laws passed by a legislative body. The text written by the leading legal spokesman of the Parliamentary faction, John Locke's *Second Treatise of Civil Government* (1690), is still read today as the primary argument for the establishment of natural limits to governmental authority.

France: Absolutism

Several key differences allowed for a far different outcome in France. A series of religious and dynastic wars in the sixteenth century produced a kingdom in which the religious issue had been settled firmly in favor of the Catholic majority. The lack of religious turmoil in the seventeenth century allowed the French monarchy to cement an alliance with both the clergy and the middle class, and to use the great administrative expertise of both to build a powerful centralized government. Both Louis XIII (1610–1643) and Louis XIV (1643–1715) relied on well-connected Catholic Cardinals to oversee the consolidation of royal power by transferring local authority from provincial nobility to a bureaucracy that was both efficient and trustworthy.

As chief minister to Louis XIII, Cardinal Richelieu used the royal army to disband the private armies of the great French aristocrats and to strip the autonomy granted to the few remaining Protestant towns. More significantly, he stripped provincial aristocrats and elites of their administrative power by dividing France into some 30 administrative districts and putting each under the control of an *intendent*, an administrative bureaucrat, usually chosen from the middle class, who owed his position and, therefore, his loyalty directly to Richelieu.

These policies were continued by Richelieu's successor as chief minister, Cardinal Jules Mazarin, and perfected by Louis XIV when he took full control of the government upon Mazarin's death in 1661. To the intimidation tactics practiced by Richelieu and Mazarin, Louis added bribery. Building the great palace at *Versailles*, 11 miles outside of Paris, Louis presented the nobility of France with a choice: Oppose him and face destruction or join him and be part of the most lavish court in Europe. In choosing to spend most of their time at Versailles, French nobles forfeited the advantages that made their English Parliamentary counterparts so powerful: control of both the wealth and loyalty of their local provinces and districts. As a result, Louis XIV became known as "the Sun King" because all French life seemed to revolve around him as the planets revolved around the sun.

Central and Eastern Europe: Compromise

Whereas the contests for power and sovereignty in Britain and France had clear winners and losers, similar contests in the European kingdoms further to the east resulted in a series of compromises between monarchs and rival elites.

In general, kingdoms in central and eastern Europe, such as Brandenburg–Prussia, the independent German states, Austria, and Poland, were less economically developed than their western counterparts. The economies of Britain and France in the seventeenth century were based on an agricultural system run by a free and mobile peasantry and supplemented by an increasingly prosperous middle class consisting of artisans and merchants in thriving towns. In contrast, the land-holding nobility of the kingdoms in central and eastern Europe during this period managed to retain control of vast estates worked by serfs who were bound by the land. By doing so, they were able to avoid the erosion of wealth that weakened their counterparts in Britain and France.

In both Britain and France, the power struggle between the monarch and the elites was won by the side that managed to form an alliance with the wealthy merchant and professional class. In the European kingdoms further east, however, these classes failed to gain in wealth and numbers as their counterparts in Britain and France had done. As a result, the stalemate between royal and aristocratic wealth and power remained more balanced, necessitating compromise.

Russia: Tsarist Absolutism

The seventeenth-century kingdom furthest to the east proved to be an exception to the rule, as its monarchs, the *Tsars*, managed to achieve a high degree of absolutism despite an agricultural economy based on serfdom and the lack of an alliance with a thriving middle class.

During the period beginning in 1613 and reaching its zenith with the reign of Peter the Great (1689–1725), the Romanov Tsars consolidated their power by buying the loyalty of the nobles. In return for their loyalty, the Romanov Tsars gave the nobility complete control over the classes of people below them. A prime example is the *Law Code of 1649*, which converted the legal status of groups as varied as peasants and slaves into that of a single class of serfs. Under the Romanov Tsars, the Russian nobility also enjoyed the fruit of new lands and wealth acquired by aggressive expansion of the Russian Empire eastward into Asia.

With the nobility firmly tied to the Tsar, opposition to the Tsar's power manifested itself only periodically in the form of revolts from coalitions of smaller landholders and peasants angered by the progressive loss of their wealth and rights. Such revolts, like the revolts of the Cossacks in the 1660s and early 1670s, were ruthlessly put down by the Tsar's increasingly modern military forces, and controlled thereafter by the creation of a state bureaucracy modeled on those in western Europe, and by encouraging the primacy and importance of the Russian Orthodox Church that taught that the traditional social hierarchy was mandated by God.

The Baroque Style

The dominant artistic style of the seventeenth century is known as baroque. In the most general sense, the baroque style was characterized by its emphasis on grandeur and drama. In response to the Reformation, the Catholic Church in Europe decreed that art should focus on religious themes and cultivate an environment of contemplation and holiness. The resulting artistic style, developed initially by artists of Rome, is sometimes known as Counter-Reformation Baroque. An excellent example in architecture is the Church of Sant'Andrea al Quirinale in Rome, designed by Gian Lorenzo Bernini. Bernini's *St. Theresa in Ecstasy* (1645–1652), which decorates the Cornaro Chapel in Rome, is an example of the Counter-Reformation Baroque style in sculpture, while Caravaggio's *Calling of St. Matthew* (c.1598) and *Conversion of St. Paul* (c.1602) exemplify the Counter-Reformation Baroque style in painting.

The grandeur of the baroque also appealed to the absolutist monarchs of the seventeenth century, and under their patronage the baroque evolved beyond religious subject matter. Louis XIV of France had his great Versailles Palace (1661–1668) built in the baroque style. The sculptor Bernini produced his famous portrait bust of Louis XIV in 1665. The painter Peter Paul Rubens created baroque masterpieces for many of the monarchs of Europe. Among the most renowned examples are his cycle of 21 large canvases for the walls of the Festival Gallery of Louis XIII's Luxembourg Palace, including *Henry IV Receiving the Portrait of Maria de Medici* (1622–1625).

The baroque style reached its pinnacle when it migrated away from the royal courts and flourished in the city of Amsterdam. There, Dutch masters adopted baroque style to depict the grandeur of that bustling center of trade and learning. Foremost among them was Rembrandt van Rijn (usually just known as Rembrandt), who captured the civic pride of the Dutch in such paintings as *The Night Watch* (1642) and who displayed his personal pride in his series of self-portraits.

› Rapid Review

During the period from 1600 to 1715, the dynamics of the traditional, hierarchical social structure of European kingdoms came under new pressures. As their economies underwent a transformation from a purely agricultural base to a more complex system that included expanding trade and the uneven growth of a middle class of merchants and professionals, European monarchs attempted to solidify their claims to sovereignty.

- In Britain, their attempts failed as a section of the traditional nobility (which was motivated by both self-interest and religious conviction) formed an alliance with like-minded members of the rising merchant and professional class within Parliament, creating a system of shared sovereignty known as constitutional monarchy.
- In France, the Bourbon monarchs managed to form alliances with both the French Catholic Church and the middle classes to establish a system of Royal absolutism.
- In central and eastern European kingdoms like Brandenburg–Prussia, the German States, Austria, and Poland, a less dynamic economy meant that the stalemate between monarchs and traditional nobility was harder to break, and a series of power-sharing arrangements was made.
- Furthest east, in Russia, the Romanov Tsars constructed an alliance with the grandest of the land-owning nobility at the expense of the classes below them and consolidated their power by expanding their empire and ruthlessly crushing opposition from below.
- Changes in the social and political structure were mirrored by the development of the baroque style in the arts.

» Chapter Review Questions

1. During the period from 1600 to 1715, the traditional social hierarchy of Europe came under pressure by all of the following EXCEPT
   (A) continuous warfare
   (B) climate change resulting in series of bad harvests
   (C) the rejection of religious practice by large numbers of people
   (D) increased trade and the diversification of the economy
   (E) the desire of monarchs to increase their power and authority

2. The English Parliament during the period from 1600 to 1715
   (A) was a relatively new institution
   (B) was exclusively an institution of the nobility
   (C) was an institution opposed to monarchy
   (D) was the institution in which nobles, merchants, and professionals formed an alliance to oppose the absolutist goals of the Stuart monarchs
   (E) was in favor of a one-man, one-vote system of democracy

3. In the period 1600–1715, the English had the greatest success in resisting the absolutist designs of their monarchs for all of the following reasons EXCEPT
   (A) the nobility forged an alliance with a wealthy and powerful merchant and professional class
   (B) the English nobility was the most powerful in all of Europe
   (C) the Parliament was an old and respected institution
   (D) the Stuart monarchs were perceived to have Catholic leanings and sympathies
   (E) the English economy was well-developed and diversified

4. Compared with the Romanov Tsars, the Bourbon monarchs of France in the period 1600–1715
   (A) made less use of the Church and its expertise and influence
   (B) were less reliant on the nobility for their power
   (C) were more absolutist in their style of government
   (D) sought to expand their empire to a larger extent
   (E) were more committed to the primacy of the privileges and prerogatives of the nobility

5. The single most important factor in explaining the need of central and eastern European monarchs and nobles to reach compromises on the issue of sovereignty during the period from 1600 to 1715 was
   (A) the lack of religiosity in the people
   (B) the lack of ambitious monarchs
   (C) the existence of strong peasant movements
   (D) the lack of strong armies
   (E) the lack of a well-developed middle class of merchants and professionals

6. The reign of Peter the Great of Russia (1682–1725) resulted in
   (A) the abolition of the Russian Orthodox Church
   (B) the territorial expansion of the Russian Empire
   (C) the weakening of serfdom
   (D) a decrease in the tax burden on poor peasants
   (E) the emergence of a wealthy middle class

7. Compared with their counterparts in Russia, the English peasantry of the early 1700s
   (A) bore a greater tax burden
   (B) enjoyed less freedom of movement
   (C) had a greater chance of improving their social and economic position
   (D) enjoyed less religious freedom
   (E) were more likely to live in towns

8. By the early eighteenth century, the kingdom whose political system afforded the greatest amount of self-rule to its subjects was
   (A) England
   (B) France
   (C) Brandenburg–Prussia
   (D) Austria
   (E) Russia

› Answers and Explanations

1. **C.** Nowhere in Europe during this period was there a large-scale rejection of religious practice; rather, the religious fervor that pitted Catholics against Protestants complicated the tensions created by the other four answers. Choice A is incorrect because continuous warfare put pressure on the traditional social hierarchy by disrupting the economy and increasing the demand for taxes. Choice B is incorrect because a series of bad harvests meant that there was less wealth in the economy at a time when monarchs were demanding more. Choice D is incorrect because increased trade and a more diversified economy gave birth to a class of economically powerful merchants who did not fit into the traditional social hierarchy. Choice E is incorrect because the desire of monarchs to increase their power and authority led them to wage wars of conquest, which put enormous stress on the economy.

2. **D.** The existence of Parliament as an institution that mixed traditional nobility with newly wealthy merchants and professionals allowed for an alliance between the two to form in opposition to Stuart absolutist designs. Choice A is incorrect because Parliament was, by 1600, an old and respected institution. Choice B is incorrect because Parliament's members were elected from local elites whose qualifications were based on property ownership, not noble birth. Choice C is incorrect because the Parliament was not opposed to monarchy as a form of government, but only to the notion that the monarch had absolute and unlimited power. Choice E is incorrect because Parliament's members did not, in this period, question the notion that only those who met certain property qualifications were entitled to vote.

3. **B.** The wealth and power of the English nobility as a class was in *decline* as the economy became more diversified and new forms of wealth created an economically strong middle class. Choice A is incorrect because the nobles inside Parliament did forge an alliance with a wealthy and powerful merchant and professional class to resist the absolutist designs of the Stuarts. Choice C is incorrect because the tradition of a powerful

Parliament gave the noble–merchant alliance credibility with the English people. Choice D is incorrect because the Stuart monarchs were perceived to have Catholic leanings and sympathies, which did not sit well with the English people. Choice E is incorrect because the advanced development of the English economy is what produced the merchant middle class with whom the nobles in Parliament allied.

4. **B.** The Bourbon monarchs of France built the power of their state at the expense of the nobility and, thus, did not rely on them in the way the Romanovs did. Choice A is incorrect because the Bourbons made extensive use of the clergy as they built their new administrative state. Choice C is incorrect because the Bourbons were every bit as absolutist as the Romanovs in their aims; they simply achieved the goal by different means. Choice D is incorrect because the Bourbons were *less* expansionist than the Romanovs. Choice E is incorrect because the Bourbons were, unlike the Romanovs, set on *curbing* the power and prerogatives of the nobility.

5. **E.** The key to successfully building or resisting a powerful centralized state in this period was the degree to which the monarchs or nobles could forge an alliance with and utilize the talents and wealth of a merchant middle class. Therefore, the lack of such a class forced compromise in the central and eastern kingdoms. Choice A is incorrect because all European peoples were equally religious during this period. Choice B is incorrect because the Monarchs of Europe were equally ambitious during this period. Choice C is incorrect because peasants in all the European kingdoms resisted encroachment on their rights and livelihood in the only way they could, through occasional tax and bread riots. Choice D is incorrect because all European monarchs were capable of raising sizeable armies during this period.

6. **B.** The territorial holdings of the Russian Empire were greatly expanded under Peter the Great. Choice A is incorrect because the power of the Russian Orthodox Church was *strengthened* during the reign of Peter the Great. Choice C is

incorrect because the institution of serfdom was supported, not weakened, by Peter the Great. Choice D is incorrect because the tax burden on the Russian peasantry was *increased* under Peter the Great. Choice E is incorrect because no wealthy merchant class emerged in Russia during the reign of Peter the Great.

7. **C.** The English peasantry of the early 1700s had a greater chance of improving their social and economic position because the English economy was much more developed and diverse than that of Russia, and because the English Revolution of the seventeenth century had curbed the power of the monarchy and the nobility and established the rule of law. Choice A is incorrect because the English peasantry of the early 1700s bore a *lesser* tax burden than its Russian counterparts. Choice B is incorrect because the peasantry in England, where serfdom had long been abolished, enjoyed a greater freedom of movement than their Russian counterparts who still labored under a system of serfdom. Choice D is incorrect because the English peasantry enjoyed *greater* religious freedom than their Russian counterparts. Choice E is incorrect because "peasants" are agricultural laborers and, by definition, live in the countryside rather than towns.

8. **A.** The constitutional monarchy and the rule of law that resulted from the English Revolution of the seventeenth century guaranteed its subjects the greatest amount of self-rule in Europe. Choice B is incorrect because the subjects of France lived under an absolutist regime constructed by the Bourbon monarchy. Choices C and D are incorrect because the subjects of Brandenburg–Prussia and of Austria enjoyed only a moderate amount of self-rule as the monarchs and nobility fought each other to a standoff. Choice E is incorrect because Russians lived under an absolutist regime built through an alliance between the Tsar and the Russian nobility.

CHAPTER 11

The Scientific Revolution During the Seventeenth Century

IN THIS CHAPTER

Summary: In the seventeenth century, a small, interconnected society of thinkers created both a new way of knowing the natural world and a new model of the universe.

Key Ideas

✪ The traditional view of the cosmos was a combination of ancient Greek philosophy and Christian theology.

✪ In the seventeenth century, the development of new, more secular institutions created space for a new approach to investigating the natural world.

✪ In the early part of the seventeenth century, the mathematical philosopher Galileo championed a new view of the cosmos based on empirical and mathematical investigation.

✪ Near the end of the century, Isaac Newton created a new physics based on the concept of universal gravitation.

Key Terms

terrestrial realm
celestial realm
elements
qualities
geocentric
scholasticism

hermeticism
neoplatonism
heliocentric
Copernicanism
Kepler's laws
The Starry Messenger

Dialogue on the Two Chief Systems of the World
Discourse on Method
universal gravitation
Principia Mathematica

Introduction

The Scientific Revolution is the term given to a gradual development of a way of investigating and knowing the natural world. Although it has roots that stretch back earlier, the Scientific Revolution is considered by most historians to be a seventeenth-century phenomenon, beginning with Galileo's challenge to the old Aristotelian view of the cosmos and the authority of the Catholic Church in 1610, and culminating in the creation by Isaac Newton of the concept of a "universe" held together by the single force of universal gravitation in 1687.

The Traditional View of the Cosmos

The traditional view of the cosmos in European civilization was one that it had inherited from the ancient Greek philosopher Aristotle. The Aristotelian cosmos was based on observation and common sense. Because the Earth appeared, to all of one's senses, to stand still, Aristotle made the Earth the unmoving center point of the cosmos. The moon, the planets, and the stars were conceived of as "fixed" because they do not move relative to each other, and they were also understood to move in concentric circular orbits around the Earth because that is what they appeared to do.

The Aristotelian cosmos was divided into two realms:

- the *terrestrial realm*, which contained the Earth and all matter inside the orbit of the moon
- the *celestial realm*, or the realm of the heavens that existed beyond the orbit of the moon

In the Aristotelian cosmos, there were five basic *elements*, each of which was defined by its *qualities*:

1. earth, which was heavy and tended to sink towards the center of the cosmos
2. water, which was slightly lighter and accumulated on top of solid earth
3. air, which was lighter still
4. fire, which was the lightest of all and tended to try to rise above all the others
5. the ether, perfect matter that existed only in the celestial realm and which moved in uniform circular motion

The qualities of the five types of matter served as the basis of Aristotelian physics. The motion of terrestrial matter was understood to be the result of its composition. For example, if you threw a rock, its motion described a parabola because the force of the throw gave its motion a horizontal component, while its heaviness gave it a vertical component towards the Earth. If you filled an airtight bag with air and submerged it in water, it would float to the top because the air was lighter than earth or water. The planets and stars of the celestial realm moved at a uniform rate in perfect circles around the Earth because they were composed purely of ether.

To the medieval church scholars who rediscovered and translated the writings of Aristotle, this Earth-centered, or *geocentric*, model of the cosmos not only made logical sense, it confirmed the Christian theological doctrine that the perfect kingdom of God awaited in the heavens for those humans who could transcend the corruption of the world.

Alternative Traditions of Knowledge Before the Scientific Revolution

Although the dominant tradition of knowledge in European civilization prior to the Scientific Revolution was *scholasticism*, which derived its knowledge from ancient texts like those of Aristotle, there were other alternative traditions upon which the Scientific Revolution drew.

Hermeticism

One of these was the tradition of natural magic and alchemy, which understood the natural world to be alive with latent power, just waiting to be tapped by those who could learn its secrets. One strain of magical thought drew inspiration from a corpus of texts erroneously attributed to a supposed ancient Egyptian priest, Hermes Trismegistus. *Hermeticism* taught that the world was infused with a single spirit that could be explored through mathematics as well as through magic.

Neoplatonism

The most powerful and potent of the alternative traditions was developed by Renaissance humanists who rediscovered and revered the work of the ancient Greek Philosopher Plato. *Neoplatonism* located reality in a changeless world of spirit, or forms, rather than in the physical world we experience. To the neoplatonists, mathematics was the language with which one could discover and describe the world of forms. Like the Hermetic tradition, neoplatonism taught that mathematics described the essential nature and the soul of the cosmos, a soul that was God itself.

The Platonic–Pythagorean Tradition

By the advent of the seventeenth century, these alternative traditions had fused into an approach to gaining knowledge of the natural world that has come to be known as the *Platonic–Pythagorean tradition* (after Plato and the ancient mathematically oriented school of Pythagoras), which had as its goal the identification of the fundamental mathematical laws of nature.

Development of New Institutions

Because the curricula of traditional universities were devoted to the teaching of Aristotle and other authorities in the scholastic tradition, new institutions were required for the alternative traditions to flourish. New institutions that emerged to fill that role included:

- royal courts, where kings, dukes, and other ruling nobles were determined to show off both their wealth and their virtue by patronizing not only great artists and musicians but also natural philosophers
- Royal Societies and Academies, like the Royal Society of London and the Royal Academy of Sciences in Paris, both established in the 1660s, where organized groups of natural philosophers sought and received the patronage of the crown by emphasizing both the prestige and the practical applications of their discoveries
- smaller academies under the patronage of individual nobles, like the *Accademia dei Lincei*, which formed in 1657 under the patronage of Marquess of Monticelli in Italy
- new universities, particularly in Italy, that were funded by the civic-minded merchants in the Renaissance tradition and that were outside the control of the Church

The Rise of Copernicanism

The central challenge to the traditional view of the cosmos was made in the context of the Church's own effort to reform the calendar and, therefore, the science of astronomy.

The annual changes in the position of the Sun, the moon, and the planets with respect to the constellations of stars are the means by which human beings construct calendars that keep track of time and predict seasonal climate patterns. In keeping with the philosophy of scholasticism, European Church scholars constructed calendars based on ancient astronomical tables that dated back to the ancient Greek astronomer Claudius Ptolemy. Though amazingly accurate, the multiplication over thousands of years of small errors in the Ptolemaic astronomical tables led to a situation in the early sixteenth century where the calendars were dramatically out of sync with the actual seasons.

In 1515, a church council appointed to consider calendar reform summoned the Polish churchman and astronomer Nicolas Copernicus to remedy the situation. Educated in a neoplatonic academy and a proponent of the Platonic–Pythagorean tradition, Copernicus proposed to reconcile the calendar and the actual movements of the heavens by introducing a new Sun-centered, or *heliocentric*, astronomical model of the cosmos.

Copernicus's proposal alarmed Church authorities for several reasons:

- It questioned the authority of the Aristotelian tradition on which scholasticism relied.
- It contradicted the physical principles that served as the foundation of physics.
- It destroyed the theological coherence of the cosmos.
- It required the Church to admit it had been in error.

Shortly before Copernicus's death in 1543, the Church allowed his theory to be published in a work titled *De Revolutionibus Orbium Caelestum (On the Revolutions of the Heavenly Spheres)*, provided that it be accompanied by a preface that stated that the theory was only being presented as a useful hypothetical model, and not as a true account of the physical nature of the cosmos. Because Copernicus's great work was written in Latin (which was the language of educated scholars) and because it was a highly technical work, its publication created no great stir. But slowly, over the course of the next 70 years, *Copernicanism* (as the theory came to be known) spread in circles of men educated both within the Church and in newer academies and societies.

Kepler's Laws

By the seventeenth century, a loose network of Copernicans championed the new world view as part of a new empirical and mathematical approach to the study of the natural world. One was a German mathematician working in the hermetic and neoplatonic traditions, Johannes Kepler, who devoted his life to finding the mathematical harmonies of the cosmos. Between 1609 and 1619, he developed three laws of planetary motion that would come to be known as *Kepler's laws*.

1. The first law broke with the tradition of conceiving of the planets as moving in uniform circles, suggesting that the planetary orbits took the form of an ellipse, with the Sun as one of their foci.
2. The second law abandoned the notion that planetary motion was uniform and asserted that a planet's velocity varied according to its distance from the Sun, sweeping out equal areas in equal times.
3. The third law gave a mathematical description for the physical relationship between the planets and the Sun, asserting that the squares of the orbital period of a planet are in the same ratio as the cubes of their average distance from the Sun.

Galileo and the Value of Empirical Knowledge

Although Kepler worked in obscurity, Galileo Galilei was an ambitious self-promoter. Dubbing himself a "mathematical philosopher," Galileo championed an approach to knowing the natural world that emphasized the need to apply reason to observational and mathematical data. Also, following the English philosopher Francis Bacon, Galileo combined his approach with an appeal to the practical and pragmatic value of such knowledge.

Having dismantled and analyzed a spyglass he bought from Dutch merchants, Galileo drew up schematics for a larger, more powerful version. The result was the world's first telescope and Galileo immediately turned his new invention on the heavens. In 1610, Galileo published his findings in a pamphlet titled *The Starry Messenger*. There, he announced several discoveries which, although they did not explicitly promote the Copernican theory, did implicitly call into question the veracity of the Aristotelian model. These discoveries included the following:

- the existence of countless stars previously unseen, suggesting that there was much about the cosmos that was not known
- the rugged, crater-filled surface of the moon, suggesting that it was not created of perfect celestial matter
- four moons orbiting the planet Jupiter, suggesting that it would not be so strange for the Earth to have a moon as well

Unfortunately, Galileo mistakenly believed that both his growing fame and his value to his powerful patron (the Grand Duke of Tuscany, Cosimo de Medici) would protect him from the wrath of the Catholic Church. Because of this mistaken belief, Galileo began to promote more boldly both the Copernican theory and his method of knowing nature through the application of reason to empirical observations. In 1615, he was summoned to Rome, where he narrowly escaped being branded a heretic only because he had a powerful friend, Cardinal Maffeo Barberini, who interceded on Galileo's behalf and managed to get the Church to brand the Copernican theory "erroneous" rather than "heretical." Galileo was set free with a stern warning. In 1623, Barberini became Pope Urban VIII. The following year, Galileo returned to Rome for a series of discussions with the Pope. He left having been given permission to teach Copernicanism as a theory, but not as a true account of the cosmos.

Over the next decade and a half, Galileo continued to promote his particular brand of natural philosophy. In 1632, chafing against the constrictions put upon him, Galileo effectively took his case to the public by abandoning the Latin prose of the scholarly elite for the vernacular Italian of the masses and publishing a thinly veiled attack on what he considered to be the absurdity of the Church's defense of the Aristotelian model. The book, *Dialogue on the Two Chief Systems of the World*, dismantled the arguments in favor of the traditional, Aristotelian view of the cosmos, and it presented the Copernican system as the only alternative for reasonable people. Early the following year, Galileo was summoned before the Inquisition and forced to recant. He was sentenced to spend the rest of his life under house arrest and forbidden to ever publish again. The long-term effect of Galileo's condemnation was to shift the locus of the Scientific Revolution to the Protestant countries of Europe.

Cartesian Skepticism and Deductive Reasoning

Although many of those who took the lead in the Scientific Revolution in the second half of the seventeenth century were born in Protestant countries, Rene Descartes had been a citizen of Catholic France. But upon hearing of Galileo's condemnation, Descartes relocated to the Netherlands, where he published (in 1637) a challenge to both the authority of scholasticism and to the validity of the Galilean approach. In *Discourse on Method*, Descartes began by sweeping away all previous claims to knowledge by skeptically asserting that "received knowledge"—i.e., information that you do not learn for yourself—amounted to nothing more than "opinion." But rather than proceed from observation, Descartes extended his skepticism to the senses, which he asserted could easily be fooled; instead, he sought the "clear and distinct idea"—i.e., one that could not reasonably be doubted.

The first idea that Descartes could not doubt was that he was thinking, and that if he was thinking, then he must really exist. From that famous formulation—"I think, therefore I am"— Descartes proceeded to deduce a variety of truths, including the existence of God and a cosmos made up of only two things: matter and motion. Putting the Sun in the center (as Copernicus had done), Descartes described a solar system in which the planets were simply large chunks of matter that were caught in swirling vortices of smaller matter. This cartesian approach of deducing the details of nature from a set of clearly defined general propositions appealed to those who sought an intelligible explanation of the cosmos, rather than the mathematical calculations of the Platonic–Pythagorean tradition.

Newton and Universal Gravitation

It was Isaac Newton who supplied an explanation of the cosmos that was consistent with and conducive to precise mathematical calculation. Newton was an Englishmen who was educated at Cambridge University at a time when its faculty was committed to the advancement of neoplatonism and to the rejection of Cartesianism, which they feared would become the new scholasticism. As a fellow of Trinity College, Cambridge, Newton lived a solitary life and was driven by the notion that God had left clues to his true nature in the laws that governed the natural world. Newton was, therefore, intensely focused on solving the mystery of planetary motion. Using a mathematical system of his own creation, which he called "fluxions" (and which we now refer to as calculus), and following Kepler's suggestion that the path of planetary orbits was elliptical, Newton was able to calculate the orbits of the planets precisely by assuming that each particle of matter, no matter how large or small, was drawn to every other piece of matter by a force which he called *universal gravitation*.

Newton published his results in 1687 in his great work the *Principia Mathematica* (or *The Mathematical Principles of Natural Knowledge*), where he stated: "Every particle of matter in the universe attracts every other particle with a force varying inversely as the square of the distance between them and directly proportional to the product of their masses." The *Principia* not only provided the correct calculations for planetary motion, it set out "definitions" and "laws of motion" that demonstrated how, henceforth, mathematical philosophy was to be done.

For the rest of the seventeenth century, the methods of Newton and Descartes served as competing models, with Newtonianism reigning in Great Britain and Cartesianism dominating in Continental Europe. But by the dawn of the eighteenth century, Newtonianism had won out and served as a model not just for natural philosophy but for an approach to the understanding of human society that would come to be known as the Enlightenment.

❯ Rapid Review

By the mid-sixteenth century, the spirit of Renaissance humanism fused with other reviving traditions, such as hermeticism and neoplatonism, to create a Platonic–Pythagorean tradition that sought to identify the fundamental mathematical laws of nature. Nicolas Copernicus was the first to challenge the traditional scholastic view of the cosmos by suggesting that the Sun—and not the Earth—was at the center of the system. But it was in the seventeenth century that Copernicus's successors, taking advantage of new spaces for natural philosophy, promoted new ways of knowing about nature.

- Galileo promoted both the Copernican system and an observationally based inductive method in increasingly bold ways until he was silenced by the Inquisition in 1633.
- Rene Descartes developed and promoted an alternative method that began with radical skepticism and went on to deduce knowledge about nature by seeking the clear and distinct thought.
- Towards the end of the century, the Englishman Isaac Newton developed the notion of universal gravitation and completed the Platonic–Pythagorean program by successfully calculating the force of universal gravitation that governs the motions of all objects in the universe.
- By the dawn of the eighteenth century, Newton's work served as a model not just for natural philosophy but for an approach to the understanding of human society that would come to be known as the Enlightenment.

› Chapter Review Questions

1. Medieval Christian scholars advocated the Aristotelian view of the cosmos
   (A) because Aristotle was Christian
   (B) because Aristotle was praised in the Bible
   (C) because there was an intellectual fit between the Aristotelian view and Christian theology
   (D) because they were unaware of the works of other Ancient Greek philosophers
   (E) because the pope ordered it

2. Which of the following is NOT a reason that the Church was alarmed by Copernicus's suggestion that the cosmos was heliocentric?
   (A) It destroyed the theological coherence of the cosmos.
   (B) Copernicus was a Protestant.
   (C) It questioned the authority of the Aristotelian tradition on which scholasticism relied.
   (D) It required the Church to admit it had been in error.
   (E) It contradicted the physical principles that served as the foundation of physics.

3. The seventeenth-century astronomer who first suggested that the planets' orbits were elliptical rather than circular was
   (A) Copernicus
   (B) Galileo
   (C) Kepler
   (D) Aristotle
   (E) Newton

4. The event that finally caused the Church to summon Galileo before the Inquisition was
   (A) his invention of the telescope
   (B) the publication of *The Starry Messenger*
   (C) his meeting with the pope in 1623
   (D) the publication of the *Dialogue on the Two Chief Systems of the World*
   (E) the publication of the *Principia Mathematica*

5. Which of the following was argued by Descartes in his *Discourse on Method*?
   (A) All true knowledge is based on observation.
   (B) All matter is made of up of five elements.
   (C) Nature and scripture could never disagree.
   (D) Telescopic observations should be the basis of knowledge of the heavens.
   (E) The only true statements are those one cannot possibly doubt.

6. Which of the following is the best example of Descartes' deductive method of reasoning?
   (A) A telescope reveals craters and mountains on the moon, therefore, matter in the celestial realm cannot be perfect.
   (B) The orbits of the planets can be calculated using calculus.
   (C) "I think, therefore I am."
   (D) True reality exists in the world of pure forms.
   (E) "Every particle of matter in the universe attracts every other particle with a force varying inversely as the square of the distance between them and directly proportional to the product of their masses."

7. Isaac Newton is best described as working in
   (A) the Platonic–Pythagorean tradition
   (B) the Aristotelian tradition
   (C) the scholastic tradition
   (D) the Cartesian tradition
   (E) the hermetic tradition

8. Which of the following is NOT contained in Kepler's laws of motion?
   (A) Planets' velocities vary according to their distance from the Sun, sweeping out equal areas in equal times.
   (B) The planets orbit the Sun because they are caught in swirling vortices of matter.
   (C) Planetary orbits take the form of an ellipse.
   (D) The Sun serves as one foci of the orbit of the planets.
   (E) The squares of the orbital period of a planet are in the same ratio as the cubes of their average distance from the Sun.

» Answers and Explanations

1. **C.** The Christian notion that the world was created for mankind, and that the realm of God in heaven was perfect, fit well with Aristotle's Earth-centered cosmos where the world of corrupt matter was separated from the realm of perfection by the moon. Choice A is incorrect because Aristotle was an ancient Greek, not a Christian. Choice B is incorrect because Aristotle is not mentioned in the Bible. Choice D is incorrect because, although it was true that ancient Greek texts were rare in Europe until the Renaissance, the medieval scholastics knew of and had translated others besides Aristotle. Choice E is incorrect because the Aristotelian view of the cosmos was absorbed gradually by Church scholars, not by order of the pope.

2. **B.** Copernicus was not a Protestant but an ordained clergyman in the Catholic Church. Choice A is incorrect because the suggestion that the Sun was at the center of the cosmos destroyed the distinction between the celestial and terrestrial realms, thereby destroying the coherence between the physical description of the cosmos and the theological notions of God in the heavens and man trapped in a worldly realm of corruption. Choices C and D are incorrect because suggesting that the Earth was not in the center of the cosmos was to suggest that both Aristotle and the Church had been mistaken (and to raise the question of what else they may have been wrong about). Choice E is incorrect because locating the Sun in the center also destroyed the physical explanation that celestial objects moved in perfect circles because they were made of perfect matter, while terrestrial objects moved in various ways explained by the degree to which they were composed of the four terrestrial elements.

3. **C.** Kepler first suggested that the shape of planetary orbits was elliptical in the first decade of the seventeenth century. Choices A and B are incorrect because, although both Copernicus and Galileo advocated a heliocentric system, both agreed with Aristotle that the planets moved in uniform circular orbits. Choice D is incorrect because Aristotle believed the planets to move in uniform circular orbits. Choice E is incorrect because, although Newton proposed elliptical orbits for the planets, Kepler preceded him.

4. **D.** It was the publication of the *Dialogue on the Two Chief Systems of the World*, which openly mocked the Aristotelian view of the cosmos and its defenders, and which was published in the vernacular that many common people could read, that caused the Church to summon Galileo before the Inquisition and force him to recant. Choice A is incorrect because the Church was not opposed to Galileo's invention of the telescope. Choice B is incorrect because, although the publication of his telescopic observations in *The Starry Messenger* provoked some criticism from Aristotelian philosophers and priests, the Church took no action against Galileo at that time. Choice C is incorrect because Galileo's meeting with Pope Urban VIII in 1623 went well, and Galileo left with the permission to teach the Copernican theory as a hypothesis. Choice E is incorrect because the *Principia Mathematica* was Isaac Newton's great work, not Galileo's.

5. **E.** Descartes argued that all knowledge should proceed from a "clear and distinct idea," that is, one that could not be doubted. Choice A is incorrect because Descartes argued that observations relied on the human senses, which could be fooled. Choice B is incorrect because the five elements are a basic principle of Aristotelianism, not of Descartes' system. Choice C is incorrect because Descartes argued that all received knowledge, including scripture, was mere opinion. Choice D is incorrect for the same reason that choice A is.

6. **C.** Descartes's method of deductive reasoning begins with a proposition that cannot be doubted and then draws a logical conclusion; "I think, therefore I am" is Descartes' most famous formulation of the method. Choice A is incorrect because it begins with an empirical observation which relies on sense impressions; Descartes believed one could always doubt the senses because they were easily fooled. Choice B is incorrect because it also relies on sense impressions as the calculus is applied to observations.

Choice D is incorrect because it is a basic assumption of *neoplatonism*, not of Descartes. Choice E is incorrect because it is Newton's formulation of the law of universal gravitation, not the work of Descartes.

7. **A.** Newton is best described as working in the Platonic–Pythagorean tradition because he pursued and achieved its goal of identifying the fundamental mathematical laws of nature. Choice B is incorrect because Newton rejected the Aristotelian view of the cosmos as Earth-centered and consisting of different "realms." Choice C is incorrect because the scholastic tradition relied on ancient texts for its knowledge; Newton applied mathematics to observation. Choice D is incorrect because Descartes deduced knowledge from ideas he believed to be clear and distinct; Newton applied mathematics to observations. Choice E is incorrect because, although there are elements of the hermetic tradition in some of Newton's work, the assumptions and approach of the Platonic–Pythagorean tradition are more pronounced.

8. **B.** The vortex theory belonged to Descartes, not Kepler. Choice A is incorrect because it is from Kepler's second law. Choices C and D are incorrect because both are from Kepler's first law. Choice E is incorrect because it is from Kepler's third law.

The Enlightenment: A Cultural Movement During the Eighteenth Century

IN THIS CHAPTER

Summary: In the eighteenth century, social and political thinkers built on the achievements of the Scientific Revolution to create a vision of society based on natural law and human reason.

Key Ideas

✪ Following Newton, the men and women of the Enlightenment, known as *philosophes*, argued that the natural laws that govern human behavior could be discovered.

✪ The *philosophes* originally pinned their hopes on enlightened despotism, the hope that the powerful monarchs of European civilization, once educated in the ideals of the Enlightenment, would use their power to reform and rationalize society.

✪ In new institutions like *salons* and Masonic Lodges, a more radical Enlightenment developed, which derided traditional institutions.

Key Terms

Second Treatise of Government
civil society
Spirit of the Laws

Essay Concerning Human Understanding
tabula rasa
Wealth of Nations

invisible hand
The Vindication of the Rights of Women
sacred covenant

consent

salons

philosophe

Masonic Lodges

deism

enlightened despotism

Candide

Systema Naturae

rococo

Encyclopedia

System of Nature

The Social Contract

Almanacs

"philosophical texts"

Introduction

The Enlightenment refers to an eighteenth-century cultural movement whose proponents argued that society and its laws should be based on human reason rather than on custom or tradition. Its roots can be traced to the late seventeenth century, when political writers like John Locke began suggesting that there were natural laws that govern human behavior, which could be discovered through reason. In the eighteenth century, intellectuals known as *philosophes* developed a program for reforming society along the lines of reason, which they initially hoped to implement by educating the powerful rulers, or enlightened despots, of Europe. Later in the century, when enlightened despotism seemed to have failed, Enlightenment ideals began to be applied in more revolutionary contexts.

New Ideas About Natural Law, Human Nature, and Society

Galileo had argued that God gave man two "books" to guide him in his quest for knowledge: the Bible to show him how to find salvation, and nature to teach him about the mind of God. Isaac Newton had shown that, through the rigorous application of empirical observation and reason, man could discern the laws that God had created to govern the natural world. Their eighteenth-century successors, the *philosophes*, argued that the same process could lead to knowledge of the natural laws that govern human behavior. Accordingly, the Enlightenment view of society rested upon certain assumptions about the "natural state" of human beings.

Thomas Hobbes

One assumption about human nature that was foundational to Enlightenment thought was the belief that human beings could discern and would naturally follow their own self-interest. Thomas Hobbes, the author of *Leviathan* (1651), asserted that self-interest motivated nearly all human behavior. Specifically, Hobbes argued that human beings were naturally driven to quarrel by competition, diffidence, and glory. Hobbes therefore concluded that "without a common power to keep them in awe," the natural state of man was one of war.

John Locke

More typical of Enlightenment thought about human nature were the ideas of John Locke. In his *Essay Concerning Human Understanding* (1689–1690), Locke argued that humans are born *tabula rasa* (a blank slate). This contradicted the traditional Christian notion that humans were born corrupt and sinful, and it implied that what humans become is purely a result of what they experience. Accordingly, Locke argued that an educational and social system that taught and rewarded rational behavior would produce law-abiding and peaceful citizens.

Locke shared Hobbes's belief in self-interest, and its importance in Locke's thought can be seen in his influential theory of private property that also appears in the *Second Treatise*.

Locke argued that God created the world and its abundance so that man might make it productive. To ensure that productivity, God established a natural right to property. Private property is created, Locke argued, when an individual mixes a common resource with his individual labor. For example, when an individual does the work of cutting down a tree and crafting the wood into a chair, he has mixed a common resource with his individual labor to create something that did not exist before. That creation is his private property and, therefore, his incentive to be productive.

Adam Smith

A typical eighteenth-century example of self-interest as natural law can be seen in the work of Adam Smith, who applied Enlightenment ideals to the realm of economics. In *Wealth of Nations* (1776), Smith argued that there were laws of human labor, production, and trade that stemmed from the unerring tendency of all humans to seek their own self-interest. The economic laws that Smith identified, such as the law of supply and demand, are all by-products of human self-interestedness. Smith asserted that the sum total of these natural economic laws functioned like an *invisible hand* that guided the economy. Efforts by governments to alter the natural laws of an economy, such as putting a tax or tariff on foreign products, would ultimately fail, Smith argued. Accordingly, Smith and his followers advocated a hands-off, or *Laissez-faire*, economic policy.

Mary Wollstonecraft

In 1792, the English *philosophe* Mary Wollstonecraft published *The Vindication of the Rights of Women*, in which she argued that reason was the basis of moral behavior in all human beings (not just men). From that basis she went on to assert that the subjugation of women in European society was based on irrational belief and the blind following of tradition, and she challenged all men of reason to acknowledge the equality and human rights of all men and women.

New Political Ideas

Enlightenment ideals about natural law, human nature, and society led Enlightenment thinkers to ponder the question of the origin and proper role of government. Both Locke and Hobbes wrote in the context of the English Civil War, which pitted Royalists against Parliamentarians. The Royalists supported the traditional power and privilege of the aristocracy and the king. In contrast, the Parliamentarians were seeking to limit the power and privilege of the aristocracy and the king.

Thomas Hobbes

Hobbes was a Royalist. From his point of view, the Parliamentarians had brought chaos to England by naively ignoring the fact that the natural state of humanity was war. Peace, Hobbes argued in *Leviathan*, required a government capable of simultaneously striking the fear of death in its subjects and guaranteeing that lawful subjects would attain a good quality of life. In order to accomplish the task, the government required absolute power, which they acquired by entering into an unbreakable contract, or sacred covenant, with the people.

John Locke

Locke, a Parliamentarian, agreed that men were often ruled by their passions. But in the *Second Treatise* he argued that in *civil society* men settled disputes dispassionately and effectively by creating impartial judges and communal enforcement. In such a system, the power of government came from the consent of the people and its use was limited to protecting the people's natural rights, particularly their right to property. Any government that did not use its power to protect the rights of its people was no longer legitimate and could and should be deposed.

In the eighteenth century, it was Locke's vision of government and law that came to dominate the Enlightenment. The Italian philosopher Cesare Beccaria carried Locke's line of thinking about the proper function of government further, arguing, in *Crime and Punishment* (1764), that the purpose of punishment should be to rehabilitate and reintegrate the individual into society. Accordingly, the severity of the punishment should reflect the severity of the crime.

Baron de Montesquieu

The Baron de Montesquieu was a French aristocrat and judge who expanded on Locke's theory of limited government by investigating the effects of climate and custom on human behavior. In *Spirit of the Laws* (1748), he stressed the importance of the rule of law and outlined a system where government was divided into branches in order to check and balance its power.

Thomas Jefferson

Thomas Jefferson made the notion that the only legitimate role of a government was to guarantee its citizens "unalienable" rights to "life, liberty, and the pursuit of happiness," the philosophical justification for the American Declaration of Independence from the rule of George III and Great Britain in 1776.

The *Philosophes* and Enlightened Despotism

The term *philosophe*, originally just the French word for "philosopher," came to identify a new breed of philosopher who was dedicated to educating the broader public. Many were popularizers of the ideas of others, looking to spread an ideal of a society governed by reason. To reach the broadest possible audience, they wrote in many different genres: histories, novels, plays, pamphlets, and satires, as well as the traditional philosophical treatises.

The term *enlightened despotism* referred to the hope shared by many *philosophes* that the powerful monarchs of European civilization, once educated in the ideals of the Enlightenment, would use their power to reform and rationalize society. To one degree or another, many eighteenth-century European monarchs instituted reforms, but within limits:

- *Frederick II (the Great) of Prussia* abolished serfdom, instituted a policy of religious toleration, and attracted French Protestants and dissidents such as Voltaire to his kingdom, but Prussia remained a militaristic state under an absolutist regime and Voltaire eventually became disenchanted.
- *Joseph II of Austria* legislated religious toleration for Lutherans and Calvinists, abolished serfdom, and passed laws that liberalized the rules governing the press, but when pamphlets about the French Revolution appeared, he reimposed censorship.
- *Catherine II (the Great) of Russia* read the *philosophes*, befriended Voltaire and Diderot, and called a legislative commission to study reform, but she dismissed the commission before most of it had even reported and had no intention of departing from absolutism.

In the final analysis, enlightened despotism was the use of certain Enlightenment ideals to help monarchs modernize and reform certain government and social institutions for the purpose of centralizing and strengthening their grasp on power. In the end, the interests of a ruling monarch ran counter to the more democratic and egalitarian ideals of the Enlightenment.

Salons and Lodges

The development and spread of an intellectual movement required places for people to congregate and share ideas. While *philosophes* could be found in most major European cities, the culture of the *salons* flourished in Paris, making it the center of the Enlightenment. Originally, the term *salon* had referred to the room in aristocratic homes where the family and its guests gathered for leisure activities. During the Enlightenment, however, aristocratic and, eventually, upper-middle-class women transformed such rooms (and the term) by turning them into a place where both men and women gathered to educate themselves about and discuss the new ideas of the age in privacy and safety. In the more prestigious houses, the leading *philosophes* were often invited to give informal lectures and to lead discussions.

It was through the salons that women made their most direct contribution to the Enlightenment. As hostesses, they controlled the guest list and enforced the rules of polite conversation. They were, therefore, in control of what ideas were discussed in front of which influential men, and were somewhat able to affect the reception that those ideas were given. Additionally, they controlled an extensive international correspondence network, as they decided which letters from *philosophes* in other cities were to be read, discussed, and replied to.

Another eighteenth-century home of Enlightenment thought was the *Masonic Lodge*. The lodges were established and run by Freemasons whose origins dated back to the medieval guilds of the stonemasons. By the eighteenth century, the lodges were fraternities of aristocratic and middle-class men (and occasionally women), who gathered to discuss alternatives to traditional beliefs. Following the customs of the old guilds, the Masonic fraternities were run along democratic principles, the likes of which were new to continental Europe. Linked together by membership in the Grand Lodge, the lodges formed a network of communication for new ideas and ideals that rivaled that of the salons. Some of the most influential men of the eighteenth century were Masons, including the Duke of Montagu in England, Voltaire and Mozart in France, and Benjamin Franklin in America. In Berlin, Frederick the Great cultivated the Masonic Lodges as centers of learning.

Skepticism, Religion, and Social Criticism

Skepticism, or the habit of doubting what one has not learned for one's self, was also a key element in the Scientific Revolution that was developed more widely in the Enlightenment. A particular target of Enlightenment skeptics was religion. In his *Historical and Critical Dictionary* (1697), the French religious skeptic Pierre Bayle included entries for numerous religious beliefs, illustrating why they did not, in his opinion, stand the test of reason. More generally, Bayle argued that all dogma, including that based on scripture, should be considered false if it contradicted conclusions based on clear and natural reasoning.

The most prevalent form of religious belief amongst the *philosophes* was *deism*. The deists believed that the complexity, order, and natural laws exhibited by the universe were reasonable proofs that it had been created by a God. But reason also told them that once God had created the universe and the natural laws that govern it, there would no longer be any further role for him in the universe. A typical deist tract was John Toland's *Christianity Not Mysterious* (1696). There, Toland argued that the aspects of Christianity that were not compatible with reason should be discarded and that Christians should worship an intelligible God.

Some *philosophes* went further in their skepticism. The Scottish philosopher David Hume rejected Christianity, arguing that Christianity required a belief in miracles and that the notion of miracles was contradicted by human reason. Hume also attacked the deist position, arguing that the order we perceived in the universe was probably the product of our own minds and social conventions, concluding that all religion was based on "hope and fear." In the final analysis, Hume contended that reason must be the ultimate test and that belief should be in proportion to evidence.

The most famous skeptic of the Enlightenment wrote under the pen name of Voltaire. He raised satire to an art form and used it to criticize those institutions that promoted intolerance and bigotry. For his criticism of the French monarchy, aristocracy, and the church, he was briefly imprisoned in the Bastille. While in exile in England, he became an admirer of Newton and Locke. In *Letters Concerning the English Nation* (1733), he compared the constitutional monarchy, rationalism, and toleration that he found in England with the absolutism, superstition, and bigotry of his native France. Later, he produced a sprawling satire of European culture in *Candide* (1759). For a time he lived and worked with the most accomplished female *philosophe*, Madame du Châtelet, who made the only French translation of Newton's *Principia*.

Science in the Enlightenment

The physical sciences in the late seventeenth and early eighteenth centuries were dominated by two competing systems of natural philosophy, one building on the work of Isaac Newton and the other on the work of Rene Descartes.

The Newtonian approach was characterized by "analysis." Generally, analysis was understood to refer to the breaking down of complex phenomena into simple components, in the same way that Newton had used a prism to break light into its separate colored rays. In practice, eighteenth-century Newtonian analysis took two forms:

1. Setting up experiments and observations and drawing general conclusions from them
2. Resolving mathematical problems by reducing them to equations

An eighteenth-century example of the Newtonian approach was the calculation of the exact shape of the earth by the young Frenchman Pierre-Louis Moreau de Maupertuis based on observations of longitudinal measurement and the rates of pendulums at various points on the globe.

The Cartesian approach was characterized by "intelligibility." Followers of Descartes attempted to fashion intelligible explanations of natural phenomena. In practice, that usually meant the creation of some sort of physical or mechanical analogy to explain all natural phenomena. A good example of the Cartesian approach was the work of the Dutchman Christian Huygens, who explained the propagation of light by suggesting that it "flowed" like a fluid. The notion of "subtle fluids," substances that behaved like a fluid without mass, became very popular in the eighteenth century and was used to explain phenomena such as electricity and magnetism.

One of the greatest scientific achievements of the eighteenth century was the creation of the Linnaean system for the classification of living organisms. In *Systema Naturae* (1735), Carl Linnaeus, a Swedish botanist, physician, and zoologist, created a hierarchical system for the identification and classification of plants and animals. In Linnaeus's system, species of organisms were grouped by degree of physical similarity and difference into higher categories (genera), the genera into orders, orders into classes, and classes into kingdoms. Based on this system, Linnaeus created a simplified naming scheme by designating one Latin name to indicate the genus and one as a "shorthand" name for the species. An expanded and revised version of this system, which came to be called the binomial nomenclature, is still in use today.

The Arts in the Enlightenment

The dominant artistic style of the eighteenth century prior to the French Revolution is known as *rococo*. In the same way that the grandeur of the baroque reflected the grand designs of the seventeenth-century monarchs, rococo reflected the lighter touch of their eighteenth-century counterparts. The aesthetic preference was for subtlety and charm. The rococo style was first developed in the decorative arts and was often characterized by lighter design elements, especially the use of shell-like curves. Architectural examples of the rococo style include Sanssouci, the summer palace built for the Prussian monarch, Frederick the Great, in Potsdam, and the summer palace built for Catherine the Great of Russia in the town of Tsarskoye Selo, located just to the southeast of St. Petersburg. The rococo style as it influenced the visual arts is exemplified in such works as Antoine Watteau's *Music Party* (oil on canvas, c.1719) and by Jean Honoré Fragonard's *The Swing* (oil on canvas, 1766–1769).

The eighteenth century also saw the creation of new opportunities for artists, as the rise of a wealthy middle class broke the aristocratic monopoly on artistic patronage. The tastes of middle-class or bourgeois patrons were simpler than those of their aristocratic counterparts; the art produced for them was, consequently, less grand and less stylized. The middle class particularly patronized the visual arts, producing genre paintings that depicted more realistic scenes and themes from everyday life. The paintings of William Hogarth, such as the series titled *Marriage à la Mode* (c.1744), are examples of that genre.

The Radical Enlightenment

As the monarchs and ruling regimes of Europe showed the limits of enlightened despotism, the elements of Enlightenment thought came together in increasingly radical ways. The multivolume *Encyclopedia* (1751–1772) was produced by the tireless efforts of its coeditors Denis Diderot and Jean le Rond d'Alembert. Their stated goal was to overturn the barriers of superstition and bigotry and to contribute to the progress of human knowledge. The entries of the *Encyclopedia* championed a scientific approach to knowledge and labeled anything not based on reason as superstition. Its pages were strewn with Enlightenment thought and the rhetoric of natural rights that were egalitarian and democratic. King Louis XV of France declared that the *Encyclopedia* was causing "irreparable damage to morality and religion," and twice banned its publication.

Another more radical position was that of the German-born French *philosophe* the Baron d'Holbach, whose philosophy was openly atheist and materialist. In *System of Nature* (1770), d'Holbach offered the eighteenth-century reader a view of the world as a complex system of purely material substances, acting and developing according to laws of cause and effect that were purely mechanical rather than imposed by a rational God.

Perhaps the most influential radical voice emerged at midcentury, articulating a view of human nature that differed from Locke's *tabula rasa* and which suggested different political implications. In *Emile* (1762), Jean-Jacques Rousseau argued that humans were born essentially good and virtuous but were easily corrupted by society. Accordingly, Rousseau argued that the early years of a child's education should be spent developing the senses, sensibilities, and sentiments.

Politically, Rousseau agreed with his predecessors that men come together to form a civil society and give power to their government by their consent. But where Locke and Montesquieu were content with a constitutional monarchy, Rousseau's model was the ancient

Greek city-state where citizens participated directly in the political life of the state. He expressed his discontent with the political state of affairs in *The Social Contract* (1762), where he wrote: "Man is born free; and everywhere he is in chains." Accordingly, Rousseau believed that the virtuous citizen should be willing to subordinate his own self-interest to the general good of the community, and he argued that a lawful government must be continually responsible to the general will of the people. Towards the end of the century, as the ruling regimes of Continental Europe mobilized to protect their power and privilege, it would be Rousseau's version of the Enlightenment that resonated with an increasingly discontented population.

The Other Enlightenment

The Enlightenment of the *philosophes*, with their *salons* and lodges, was primarily a cultural movement experienced by aristocrats and upper-middle-class people. But further down the social hierarchy, a version of the Enlightenment reached an increasingly literate population through:

- excerpted versions of the *Encyclopedia*
- popular *almanacs*, which incorporated much of the new scientific and rational knowledge
- "*philosophical texts*," the underground book trade's code name for banned books that included some versions of philosophical treatises, and bawdy, popularized versions of the *philosophes*' critique of the Church and the ruling classes

In these texts the most radical of Enlightenment ideals—particularly those of Rousseau and d'Holbach—together with satirical lampooning of the clergy and the ruling class, reached a broad audience and helped to undermine respect for and the legitimacy of the ruling regimes.

› Rapid Review

In the eighteenth century, writers known as *philosophes* developed and popularized a vision of society based on reason. They wrote philosophical treatises, histories, novels, plays, pamphlets, and satires critical of the traditional social and political conventions and institutions like absolute monarchy and the Church. Initially, they hoped to reform society by educating the powerful monarchs of European kingdoms. When that strategy (known as enlightened despotism) faltered, the movement found new venues such as *salons* and Masonic Lodges, and the more egalitarian and democratic aspects of Enlightenment thought came to dominate, contributing to an atmosphere of political and social revolution that flourished in modern Europe at the end of the century. The eighteenth century was also the period in which the Newtonian approach in the physical sciences triumphed over its competitors, Linnaeus created a new system of taxonomy, and rococo became the dominant artistic style.

❯ Chapter Review Questions

1. Hobbes and Locke DISAGREED in their belief that
   (A) men are created equal
   (B) men tend to follow their own self-interest
   (C) the natural state of men is one of war
   (D) a government's power comes from the people
   (E) men are often ruled by their passions

2. Locke argued that the primary aim of government is
   (A) to guarantee peace by putting the fear of death into its subjects
   (B) to follow and enact the general will of the people
   (C) to provide and protect democracy
   (D) to assure the right to property
   (E) to institute a constitutional monarchy

3. Which of the following is NOT true of the *philosophes*?
   (A) They used their positions as university professors to influence society.
   (B) They aimed to educate the public.
   (C) Their ultimate goal was a society governed by reason.
   (D) They wrote in many different genres.
   (E) They were often guests of and correspondents with the women who hosted *salons*.

4. The economic policy known as *Laissez-faire*
   (A) advocates protectionist tariffs
   (B) is based on the notion that people have a right to do anything they want
   (C) is based on the notion that human self-interest produces natural laws that govern economic behavior
   (D) argues that the government should act as an "invisible hand" to regulate the economy
   (E) was instituted by enlightened despots

5. The religious belief of the majority of the *philosophes* was
   (A) Catholicism
   (B) Lutheranism
   (C) Calvinism
   (D) Deism
   (E) Atheism

6. The style of Enlightenment literature made famous by Voltaire was
   (A) the philosophical treatise
   (B) the satire
   (C) the play
   (D) the pamphlet
   (E) the novel

7. Which of the following presented the most radical challenge to the traditional ruling regimes of eighteenth-century Europe?
   (A) Locke's notion that humans are born *tabula rasa*
   (B) Hobbes's notion that human nature requires a ruler with absolute power
   (C) Beccaria's notion that the goal of a legal system should be the rehabilitation and reintegration of the criminal to society
   (D) the concept of religious toleration
   (E) Rousseau's notion that a lawful government must be continually responsible to the general will of the people

8. Which of the following is NOT part of Rousseau's thought?
   (A) Humans are born essentially good and virtuous but are easily corrupted by society.
   (B) The early years of a child's education should be spent developing the senses, sensibilities, and sentiments.
   (C) "Man is born free; and everywhere he is in chains."
   (D) All religion is based on "hope and fear."
   (E) The virtuous citizen should be willing to subordinate his own self-interest to the general good of the community.

› Answers and Explanations

1. **C.** Locke believed that men could and did overcome their passions in civil society; Hobbes disagreed, believing that the fears and passions of men were so strong that their natural state was war and only a ruler with the power of life and death over his subjects could guarantee peace. Choices A and B are incorrect because both argued that men were created equal and tended to follow their own interest. Choice D is incorrect because both believed that a government's power came from the people. Choice E is incorrect because both believed that men were *often* ruled by their passions; they disagreed about whether those passions could be overcome.

2. **D.** Locke argued that the legitimate aim of government was the protection of individual liberty; that liberty was, for Locke, encapsulated in an individual's right to dispense with the fruits of his labor (property) freely. Choice A is incorrect because the notion that a government must be able to put the fear of death into its subjects belonged to Hobbes. Choice B is incorrect because the notion that a government has an obligation to follow and enact the general will of the people belonged to Rousseau. Choice E is incorrect because Locke, though part of a movement that instituted a constitutional monarchy in England, argued in the *Second Treatise of Government* that any form (monarchy, oligarchy, or democracy) of government could be legitimate, provided it ensured and protected the fundamental rights of its subject.

3. **A.** Universities in the eighteenth century were traditional institutions, mostly affiliated with the Church. Accordingly, very few *philosophes* held university posts. Choices B–E are incorrect because they all accurately describe the *philosophes*.

4. **C.** Adam Smith argued that human self-interest produces natural laws that govern economic behavior and, therefore, the government should refrain from legislation that tries to produce results that run counter to those laws. Choice A is incorrect because protectionist tariffs, taxes levied on foreign goods to protect the sales of domestic goods, are an example of the kind of law that Smith argued would be either futile or harmful. Choice B is incorrect because the notion of *Laissez-faire* applies only to economic behavior; it does not argue that people have a right to do anything they want. Choice D is incorrect because the "invisible hand" referred to the natural laws that Smith believed regulated the economy, not the government. Choice E is incorrect because *Laissez-faire* was not popular with or instituted by enlightened despots.

5. **D.** Most *philosophes* were deists who believed that a rational God created the world and the laws by which it was governed, but took no further active role in the universe. Choices A–C are incorrect because, for the philosophes, Catholicism, Lutheranism, and Calvinism all failed the test of reason because they were based on received knowledge taken on faith. Choice E is incorrect because most *philosophes* were not, however, atheists, who deny the existence of God, as they believed that a rational world governed by natural laws required a rational creator.

6. **B.** Voltaire is best known for his satire, as exemplified by both *Letters Concerning the English Nation* (1733) and *Candide* (1759). Choice A is incorrect because Voltaire wrote no philosophical treatises. Choices C–E are incorrect because they are not the style for which Voltaire is best known.

7. **E.** Rousseau's notion that a lawful government must be continually responsible to the general will of the people explicitly challenged the right of the privileged classes to rule, a radical and dangerous idea in the eighteenth century. Choice A is incorrect because, although Locke's notion that humans are born *tabula rasa*, or like a blank slate, challenged the traditional Christian view of humans as depraved, it did not have the direct political implications of Rousseau's "general will." Choice B is incorrect because Hobbes's notion that human nature required a ruler with absolute power was a conservative one, and most compatible with the ideology of the ruling regimes in the eighteenth century. Choice C is incorrect because Beccaria's notion that the goal of a legal system should be the rehabilitation and reintegration of the criminal to society was

reformist in nature, while Rousseau was revolutionary. Choice D is incorrect because the concept of religious toleration was sometimes absorbed into the ideology of ruling regimes in the eighteenth century.

8. **D.** The proposition that all religion was based on "hope and fear" was articulated by Hume not Rousseau. Choices A, B, C, and E are all positions articulated by Rousseau.

CHAPTER 13

Social Transformation and Statebuilding in the Eighteenth Century

IN THIS CHAPTER

Summary: In the eighteenth century, new wealth from overseas trade transformed European society and created territorial rivalries between European states.

Key Ideas

✪ The development of a triangle of trade connecting Europe, the Americas, and Africa created large amounts of new wealth in the European economy.
✪ The development of market-oriented agriculture and cottage industry broke traditional limits on European population growth and economic productivity.
✪ The increased wealth led rulers of European states to attempt to expand their territorial holdings through war and diplomacy.

Key Terms

triangle of trade	cottage industry	the Pragmatic Sanction
the Middle Passage	putting-out system	War of the Austrian
manorial system	flying shuttle	Succession
cash crops	spinning jenny	Diplomatic Revolution
enclosure	cotton gin	Seven Years War

Introduction

In the eighteenth century, Great Britain and, to a lesser extent, France surpassed Spain, Portugal, and Holland as the dominant economic powers in Europe. They did so by controlling the majority of the increasingly lucrative triangle of trade that connected Europe to Africa and the Americas. The resulting wealth and prosperity set in motion a series of innovations that radically changed European agricultural and manufacturing production, which in turn produced changes in the social structure of Europe. Competition between Britain and France, and the desire of their eastern European rivals to catch up, led to innovations in diplomacy and war, the twin processes by which eighteenth-century European rulers built and expanded their states.

The Triangle of Trade

The phrase *triangle of trade* refers to a system of interconnected trade routes that quadrupled foreign trade in both Britain and France in the eighteenth century. Here are three characteristics of the triangle of trade:

- *Manufactured goods* (primarily guns and gin) were exported from Europe to Africa.
- *Slaves* were exported to serve as labor in European colonies in North America, South America, and the Caribbean.
- *Raw materials* (especially furs, timber, tobacco, rice, cotton, indigo dye, coffee, rum, and sugar) were exported from the colonies to Europe in exchange for the slaves and manufactured goods.

Prior to the eighteenth century, the primary destination of Africans taken into slavery by their rivals had been either the Mediterranean basin or Asia. The eighteenth-century expansion of the European colonies greatly increased the demand for African slaves and reoriented the slave trade to the west. The majority of slaves were destined for the West Indies and Brazil, with about 10 percent going to colonies in North America. The transportation of African slaves across the Atlantic on European trade ships was known as the *Middle Passage*. As many as 700 slaves per ship were transported, chained below deck in horrific conditions. It is estimated that somewhere between 50,000 and 100,000 Africans were transported each year during the height of the eighteenth-century slave trade.

Breaking the Traditional Cycle of Population and Productivity

The enormous wealth generated by the British and French colonies and the triangle of trade created pressure for social change that eventually affected the whole population. The effects were felt more strongly in Britain and led to changes that, taken together, constituted the first phase of an Industrial Revolution that began in Britain and then spread eastward throughout Europe, breaking the traditional cycle of population and productivity.

The traditional cycle worked like this:

- Population and productivity rose together, as an increase in the number of people working in an agricultural economy increased the agricultural yield.
- Eventually, the agricultural yield reached the maximum amount that could be produced given the land available and the methods in use.
- For a while, population would continue to rise but eventually, as the number of people far outstripped the agricultural yield, food would become scarce and expensive.

- Scarcity and high prices would eventually cause the population to decline.
- When the population was safely below the possible productivity, the cycle would begin again.

In the eighteenth century, several developments related to new wealth combined to break the cycle:

- Agriculture became market-oriented.
- Rural manufacturing spread capital throughout the population.
- Increased demand led to technical innovation.

The new market orientation of agriculture created a shift from farming for local consumption to a reliance on imported food sold at markets. The introduction of rural manufacture put larger amounts of currency into the system and made the working population less dependent on land and agricultural cycles, thereby breaking the natural check on population growth.

Market-Oriented Agriculture

The rise in population created more mouths to feed. The existence of a vast colonial empire of trade created an increasingly wealthy merchant class who both bought land from, and affected the behavior of, traditional land-holding elites. The result was the destruction of the traditional *manorial system* in which land-owning elites (lords of the manor) held vast estates divided into small plots of arable land farmed by peasants for local consumption and vast grounds known as commons where peasants grazed their livestock. That system was slowly replaced by a market-oriented approach in which *cash crops* were grown for sale and export.

The shift to cash crops created pressure that led to the reorganization of the social structure of the countryside. The traditional land-owning elites abandoned their feudal obligations to the peasantry and adopted the attitude of the merchant class. Cash crops created a demand for larger fields. Landowners responded by instituting a process known as *enclosure* because of the hedges, fences, and walls that were built to deny the peasantry access to the commons, which were now converted to fields for cash crops. Later, the land owners extended enclosure into other arable lands, breaking traditional feudal agreements and gradually transforming much of the peasantry into wage labor. By the middle of the eighteenth century, three-quarters of the arable land in England had been enclosed informally or "by agreement" (though the peasantry had not, in fact, been given any choice); after 1750, the process continued more formally as land was enclosed via acts of Parliament.

Rural Manufacturing

The increase in population also created greater demand for the other necessities of life, particularly clothing. In the feudal system, all aspects of textile production had been under the control of guilds (which were organizations of skilled laborers, such as spinners and weavers), who enjoyed the protection of the town officials. Membership in a guild was gained only through a lengthy apprenticeship. In that way, the guilds kept competition to a minimum and controlled the supply of textiles, thereby guaranteeing that they could make a decent living. In the eighteenth century, merchants faced with an ever-expanding demand for textiles had to find a way around the guild system; the result was a system of rural manufacturing known variously as *cottage industry* or the *putting-out system*.

In the putting-out system, merchants went into the countryside and engaged the peasantry in small-scale textile production. Each month, the merchant provided raw material and rented equipment to peasant families. At the end of the month, he returned and paid the family for whatever thread or cloth they had produced. Initially, peasant families supplemented their agricultural income in this way; eventually, some of them gave up farming altogether and pooled their resources to create small textile mills in the countryside. As the system grew, the guilds of the town were unable to compete with the mills; cottage industry replaced the urban guilds as the center for textile production.

The new system of rural manufacturing went hand-in-hand with the shift to market-oriented agriculture; the destruction of the manorial system could not have been accomplished if some of the cash flowing into the economy had not found its way into the hands of the rural population. The creation of cottage industries provided the cash that enabled rural families to buy their food rather than grow it themselves.

However, the social change that accompanied the destruction of both the manorial system and the guilds also brought hardship and insecurity. The enclosure movement meant that thousands of small landholders, tenant farmers, and sharecroppers lost their land and their social status. Forced to work for wages, their lives and those of their families were now at the mercy of the marketplace. The destruction of the guilds produced similar trauma for the artisans and their families. For both the peasantry and the artisans, the economic and social changes of the eighteenth century meant the destruction of their traditional place and status in society: they were now faced with both new opportunities and great insecurity.

Technical Innovations in Agriculture and Manufacturing

It is important to remember that technical innovations are always responses to new challenges. The people of earlier centuries did not fail to innovate because they were less intelligent; they simply had no need for the innovations. The ever-growing population and demand for food and goods in the eighteenth century created a series of related demands that eventually led to technical innovations in both agriculture and manufacturing. Single innovations often created a need for further innovation in a different part of the process.

The key technical innovation in the agricultural sector in the eighteenth century was the replacement of the old three-field system, in which roughly one-third of the land was left fallow to allow the soil to replenish itself with the necessary nutrients, with new crops such as clover, turnips, and the potato, which replenished the soil while producing foodstuffs that could be used to feed livestock in winter. More and healthier livestock contributed products such as dairy and leather.

In the manufacturing sector, a number of interconnected technical innovations greatly increased the pace and output of the textile industry.

- In 1733, John Kay invented the *flying shuttle*, which doubled the speed at which cloth could be woven on a loom, creating a need to find a way to produce greater amounts of thread faster.
- In the 1760s, James Hargreaves invented the *spinning jenny*, which greatly increased the amount of thread a single spinner could produce from cotton, creating a need to speed up the harvesting of cotton.
- In 1793, the American Eli Whitney invented the *cotton gin*, which efficiently removed seed from raw cotton, thereby increasing the speed with which it could be processed and sent to the spinners.

These technical innovations greatly increased the pace and productivity of the textile industry. The need to supervise these larger, faster machines also contributed to the development of textile mills, which replaced the scattered putting-out system by the century's end.

Eastern Ambition

The prosperity and power of Britain and France caused their eastern European rivals to try to strengthen and modernize their kingdoms.

Prussia

In Prussia, Frederick William I built a strong centralized government in which the military, under the command of the nobles, played a dominant role. In 1740, his successor Frederick II (the Great) used that military to extend Prussia into lands controlled by the Hapsburgs. Challenging the right of Maria Theresa to ascend to the throne of Austria (which was a right guaranteed her by a document known as the *Pragmatic Sanction*), Frederick II marched troops into Silesia. In what came to be known as the *War of the Austrian Succession* (1740–1748), Maria Theresa was able to rally Austrian and Hungarian troops and fight Prussia and its allies, the French, Spanish, Saxons, and Bavarians, to a stand-off.

Russia

In Russia, the progress towards modernization and centralization made under Peter the Great had largely been undone in the first half of the eighteenth century. However, under the leadership of Catherine the Great, Russia defeated the Ottoman Turks in 1774, thereby extending Russia's borders as far as the Black Sea and the Balkan Peninsula. In 1775, Russia joined with Prussia and Austria to conquer Poland and divide its territories among the three of them.

War and Diplomacy

In eighteenth-century Europe, statebuilding was still primarily conducted through war and diplomacy. The competition between Britain and France in the triangle of trade meant that they would contend militarily for control of colonies in North America and the Caribbean, but the desire to weaken one another also led them to become entangled in land wars in Europe.

The expansionist aims of Frederick II of Prussia led to a shift in diplomatic alliances that is now referred to as the *Diplomatic Revolution*:

- Prussia, fearful of being isolated by its enemies, forged an alliance in 1756 with its former enemy Great Britain.
- Austria and France, previously antagonistic towards one another, were so alarmed by the alliance of Prussia and Great Britain that they forged an alliance of their own.

Colonial and continental rivalries combined to bring all of the great European powers into a conflict that came to be known as the *Seven Years War* (1756–1763). The conflict pitted France, Austrian, Russia, Saxony, Sweden, and (after 1762) Spain against Prussia, Great Britain, and the German state of Hanover. Land and sea battles were fought in North America (where it is sometimes known as the French and Indian War), Europe, and India. The European hostilities were concluded in 1763 by a peace agreement that essentially re-established prewar boundaries. The North American conflict, and particularly the fall of Quebec in 1759, shifted the balance of power in North America to the British. The British had similar success in India.

As the eighteenth century progressed, the nature of European armies and wars changed in ways that would have profound implications for the ruling regimes. The standing army was different in several ways:

- The size of the standing army increased.
- The officer corps became full-time servants of the state.
- Troops consisted of conscripts, volunteers, mercenaries, and criminals who were pressed into service.
- Discipline and training became harsher and more extensive.

Weapons and tactics changed to accommodate the new armies:

- Muskets became more efficient and accurate.
- Cannon became more mobile.
- Wars were now decided not by a decisive battle, but by superior organization of resources.
- Naval battles were now often more crucial than land battles.

› Rapid Review

In the eighteenth century, Britain and France came to dominate the lucrative triangle of trade that imported valuable raw materials from North America and the Caribbean to Europe in exchange for slaves acquired from Africa. The influx of capital generated by the colonial trade served as a spur for unchecked population growth made possible by an agricultural revolution and the creation of a system of rural manufacturing. The changes in agricultural and manufacturing production destroyed the last vestiges of an economic system (manorialism) and a social system (feudalism) that dated back to the medieval period. In that process, both the traditional European peasantry and the guildsmen were converted to wage labor.

The intensifying rivalry between Britain and France, and the growing ambition of their eastern European counterparts, led to a series of midcentury wars, including the War of the Austrian Succession and the Seven Years War. Rivalries also led to a series of innovations in diplomacy and warfare.

› Chapter Review Questions

1. Which of the following was NOT part of the triangle of trade?
   (A) timber
   (B) tobacco
   (C) cotton
   (D) silk
   (E) slaves

2. Enclosure
   (A) changed the balance of military power
   (B) refers to the shackling of slaves below deck on the Middle Passage
   (C) denied peasants access to commons and farm land in England
   (D) made mills the center of textile production
   (E) destroyed the guilds

3. Which of the following did NOT contribute to the breaking of the traditional population cycle in Europe?
   (A) the shift of agriculture to a market orientation
   (B) the three-field system
   (C) rural manufacturing
   (D) the conversion to wage labor
   (E) technical innovation

4. Cottage industry
   (A) refers to the building of cottages in the countryside for the working population
   (B) helped to reinforce the traditional checks on population growth
   (C) refers to the establishment of large-scale, factory-based industrial production
   (D) is a component of the feudal system
   (E) refers to the engagement of the rural population in small-scale textile production

5. Which of the following was a key technical innovation in agricultural production in the eighteenth century?
   (A) new crops such as clover, turnips, and the potato
   (B) the flying shuttle
   (C) the spinning jenny
   (D) the cotton gin
   (E) the three-field system

6. The most significant impact of the introduction of rural manufacturing in the eighteenth century was
   (A) improved quality of clothing
   (B) a decrease in agricultural output
   (C) the spur to the economy provided by increased production and the spread of capital throughout the population
   (D) the creation of the triangle of trade
   (E) a shift in the population from towns to the countryside.

7. Which of the following is NOT true of the War of the Austrian Succession?
   (A) It began when Frederick the Great of Prussia challenged Maria Theresa's right to ascend to the throne of Austria.
   (B) It violated the terms of the Pragmatic Sanction.
   (C) Austria allied with Prussia to hold off French ambitions.
   (D) Maria Theresa was able to rally the Hungarians to her cause.
   (E) It was essentially fought to a stand-off.

8. As a result of the Seven Years War,
   (A) the French monarchy fell
   (B) Maria Theresa ascended to the throne of Austria
   (C) Prussia was weakened
   (D) the Ottoman Turks were further weakened
   (E) Great Britain emerged as the dominant European power outside of the European continent

› Answers and Explanations

1. **D.** Although there was a silk trade between China and Europe, it was not part of the eighteenth-century triangle of trade. Choices A, B, and C are correct because tobacco, timber, and cotton were imported into Europe from the Americas. Choice E is correct because slaves were bought in Africa and sold in the Americas and West Indies.

2. **C.** Enclosure refers to the decision by English landowners to deny peasants access to both the commons and their traditional farming plots so that the lands could be converted to cash crops. Choice A is incorrect because the term *enclosure* does not refer to military organization. Choice B is incorrect because the term *enclosure* does not refer to the inhumane methods of transporting slaves. Choice D is incorrect because the term *enclosure* does not refer to textile production. Choice E is incorrect because it was the development of cottage industry, and not the enclosure movement, that destroyed the crafts guilds.

3. **B.** The three-field system, whereby one-third of the land was left fallow, was part of the traditional agricultural cycle which helped to *establish* limits on productivity and, therefore, on population increase. Choice A is incorrect because market-oriented agriculture meant a shift from farming for local consumption to a reliance on imported food sold at markets, thereby helping to break the natural limit on agricultural productivity which enforced a limit on population growth. Choice B is incorrect because the advent of rural manufacturing put cash into the pockets of the laboring class, enabling them to buy food and, therefore, helping to remove the natural constraint on population growth. Choice D is incorrect because the conversion of the agricultural workforce to wage labor also furthered the spread of capital throughout the economy. Choice E is incorrect because technical innovation in agriculture ensured a healthy economy and increased the availability of food, thereby helping to remove natural constraints on population increase.

4. **E.** *Cottage industry* is the term that denotes the development of small-scale textile production in the countryside in the eighteenth century. Choice A is incorrect because *cottage industry* does not refer to the building of cottages. Choice B is incorrect because *cottage industry* refers to the engagement of the rural population in small-scale textile production that helped to *break* the traditional checks on population growth. Choice C is incorrect because *cottage industry* does not refer to the establishment of large-scale, factory-based industrial production, which was a nineteenth-century development. Choice D is incorrect because cottage industry helped to *destroy* the remaining vestiges of the feudal system.

5. **A.** The key technical innovation in the agricultural sector in the eighteenth century was the introduction of new crops such as clover, turnips, and the potato, which replenished the soil while producing foodstuffs that could be used to feed livestock in winter. Choices B and C are incorrect because the flying shuttle and the spinning jenny were technical innovations in the *textile industry*. Choice D is incorrect because, although cotton is an agricultural product, the cotton gin did not increase its production; it increased the speed with which it could be harvested, thereby increasing the speed with which it could be supplied to the textile producers. It is, therefore, properly understood as an innovation in the textile industry. Choice E is incorrect because the three-field system was *replaced* in the eighteenth century by new crops.

6. **C.** The most significant impact of the introduction of rural manufacturing in the eighteenth century was that it acted as a spur to the economy by increasing production and spreading capital throughout the population. Choice A is incorrect because the introduction of rural manufacturing had no significant effect on the quality of clothing, though it did increase the amount produced. Choice B is incorrect because the introduction of rural manufacturing had no negative effect on agricultural output. Choice D is incorrect because rural manufacturing played no role in the creation of the triangle of trade. Choice E is incorrect because, although the economies and social fabric of towns were damaged by the destruction of the guild system that resulted from the introduction of rural

manufacturing, there was no significant shift in the population from towns to the countryside.

7. **C.** The War of the Austrian Succession (1740–1748) was fought between Prussia and its allies, the French, Spanish, Saxons, and Bavarians, and the Austrian and Hungarian troops, who supported the right of the Hapsburg heir, Maria Theresa, to ascend to the throne; French aggression was not a factor. The other four choices are all accurate statements about the War of the Austrian Succession.

8. **E.** British victories in the Americas and in India allowed it to emerge from the Seven Years War as the dominant European power beyond the boundaries of the continent. Choice A is incorrect because the French monarchy did not fall as a result of the Seven Years War, though the financial strain put on the government was a contributing cause of the French Revolution. Choice B is incorrect because Prussia was Britain's continental ally in the Seven Years War and its power was not weakened by the outcome. Choice D is incorrect because the Ottoman Turks were not directly involved in the Seven Years War; their empire was further weakened by defeat in a conflict with Russia in 1774 that was unrelated to the Seven Years War.

CHAPTER 14

The French Revolution and the Rise of Napoleon, 1789–1799

IN THIS CHAPTER

Summary: Between 1789 and 1799, the Kingdom of France experienced a revolution that challenged the social and political structure of Europe.

Key Ideas

- ✪ In 1789, the bourgeois leaders of the Third Estate attempted to force King Louis XVI to curb the power and privilege of the clergy and the nobility by withholding taxes and threatening violence.
- ✪ In 1791, the radicalized leadership of Paris's urban working class seized control of the revolution and attempted to create a more egalitarian society and a more equitable distribution of wealth.
- ✪ By 1794, the radicals had all been consumed by their own reign of terror, and the bourgeois moderates reasserted themselves.
- ✪ By 1799, the bourgeois moderates had come to rely so heavily on the military that they were powerless to stop a military coup.

Key Terms

Thermidor	Tennis Court Oath
bourgeoisie	Bastille
Ancien Régime	August Decrees
Estates General	the Great Fear
cahiers	Declaration of the Rights of Man and
National Assembly	of the Citizen

March to Versailles
the Civil Constitution of the Clergy
sans-culottes
the flight to Varennes
Girondins
Jacobins

National Convention
Law of the Maximum
Committee of Public Safety
Reign of Terror
Directory
neoclassicism

Introduction

Between 1789 and 1799, the Kingdom of France underwent a political revolution that unfolded in three phases:

- a *moderate phase (1789–1791)*, in which the politically active portions of the *bourgeoisie* or merchant class attempted to curb the power and privilege of the monarchy, the aristocracy, and the clergy, and create a limited constitutional monarchy similar to that which existed in Britain
- a *radical phase (1791–1794)*, in which the politicized urban working class of Paris seized control and attempted to create a democratic republic and a more materially and socially egalitarian society
- an *end phase known as Thermidor (1794–1799)*, in which the moderate bourgeois faction reasserted itself and concentrated simply on restoring order

By 1799, the Thermidorian government, known as the Directory, was totally dependent on the military for its ability to govern. In November of that year, a military general, Napoleon Bonaparte staged a *coup d'état*, and embarked on an ambitious campaign to create a French Empire that spanned most of Europe. Upon his defeat in 1815 by a coalition of European powers, the French monarchy was restored and the kingdom of France was returned to its traditional boundaries.

The *Ancien Régime* in Crisis

The phrase *Ancien Régime*, or Old Regime, refers to the traditional social and political hierarchy of eighteenth-century France. It was composed of three "Estates":

1. the *First Estate*, made up of the clergy, which included all ordained members of the Catholic Church in France
2. the *Second Estate*, made up of the nobility, which included all titled aristocrats
3. the *Third Estate*, made up of the citizenry, which included everyone who was neither clergy nor nobility and whose membership accounted for 96 percent of the population of France

Together, the clergy and the nobility wielded enormous power and enjoyed tremendous privilege, while the various groups that made up the Third Estate bore the tax burden.

The Catholic Church in France functioned as a branch of the government bureaucracy. It registered births, marriages, and deaths; collected certain kinds of agricultural taxes; and oversaw both education and poor relief. The Church owned approximately 10 percent of land in France but paid no taxes to the government; instead, it made an annual gift to the crown in an amount of its own choosing. The clergy who populated the hierarchical structure of the Catholic Church in France ranged from poor, simple parish priests to the powerful cardinals who were connected to the pope in Rome, and who often served as chief advisors in the government of the French king.

The nobility were the traditional land-owning elite of France, though by this period they often supplemented their fortunes through banking and commerce. They owned somewhere between 25 and 33 percent of the land in France, but were exempt from most taxes, despite the fact that they still collected various types of manorial dues from peasant farmers. Members of the nobility held most of the high offices in the French government and army, and the Church.

The citizenry can be roughly divided into three social groups:

- the *bourgeoisie*, including merchants, manufacturers, bankers, lawyers, and master craftsmen
- the *peasantry*, including all agricultural laborers ranging from very prosperous land owners to poor sharecroppers and migrant workers
- *urban laborers*, including journeymen craftsmen, mill and other small-scale manufacturing workers, and all wage laborers that populated the cities and towns of France

By 1787, the government of King Louis XVI was in financial crisis. When he took the throne in 1774, Louis XVI had inherited a huge and ever-increasing national debt, most of it incurred by borrowing money to finance wars and to maintain an army. With interest on the debt mounting and bankers refusing to lend the government more money, Louis and his ministers attempted to reform the tax system of France and to pry some of the vast wealth out of the hands of the nobility. When the nobility resisted, he was forced to do something that had not been done since 1614; he called into session the *Estates General*. The Estates General was the closest thing to a legislative assembly that existed in eighteenth-century France. Members representing each of the three Estates met to hear the problems of the realm and to hear pleas for new taxes. In return, they were allowed to present a list of their own concerns and proposals, called *cahiers*, to the Crown. When the representatives arrived in Versailles, the palace of Louis XVI, in April of 1789, the representatives of the Third Estate presented a series of proposals that were revolutionary in nature.

The Moderate Phase of the French Revolution (1789–1791)

The representatives of the Third Estate, in reality all members of the bourgeoisie, demanded that the number of representatives for the Third Estate be doubled in order to equal the number of representatives in the other two orders combined and that representatives of all three Estates meet together and vote by head rather than by Estate. These demands were designed to give the Third Estate a chance to pass resolutions by persuading a single member of the nobility or clergy to side with them. The demands of the Third Estate posed a dilemma for Louis: granting the demands would give the Third Estate unprecedented power, but that power would come at the expense of the nobility and the clergy and could perhaps be used to get the tax reforms Louis and his ministers needed to solve France's financial crisis.

Demand for a New Constitution

While Louis considered his options, the representatives of the Third Estate grew bolder. Arguing that they were the voice of the nation, they declared themselves, on 17 June 1789, to be the *National Assembly* of France. When they were locked out of their meeting hall three days later, they pushed their way into Louis's indoor tennis court and vowed that they would not disband until a new constitution had been written for France. This proclamation became known as the *Tennis Court Oath*. On 27 June Louis decided in favor of the Third Estate, decreeing that all members should join the National Assembly.

Fear Causes Parisians to Storm the Bastille

While the bourgeois leaders of the new National Assembly worked on writing a constitution for France, the uncertainty of the situation created an atmosphere of fear and mistrust. Nervous nobles began to demand that Louis break up the new Assembly, which in turn demanded an explanation for the arrival of new regiments of mercenary troops in Versailles. By July of 1789, much of the urban population of Paris, which now looked to the Assembly as its champion, believed that the nobility and, perhaps, the king intended to remove the Assembly by force. Their fears focused on the infamous *Bastille*, a prison fortress in Paris which they wrongly believed housed the guns and ammunition that would be needed for the job.

On 14 July, an angry crowd marched on the Bastille. The nervous governor of the Bastille ordered the crowd to disperse; when they refused, he had his guard fire into the crowd. The crowd responded by storming the Bastille. When it was over, 98 people had been killed and 73 wounded. The governor and his guard were killed and their heads were paraded on pikes through the city. In the aftermath, Louis's advisors urged him to flee Versailles and raise an army to crush the Assembly and restore order to Paris. Louis decided to try to soothe the city instead, and he promised to withdraw the mercenary troops.

Rural Unrest Emboldens the Assembly

While order was restored in Paris, it was disintegrating in the countryside where peasants, aware that the nobility had been weakened and fearful that they would soon reassert their power with a vengeance, seized the opportunity and raided graneries to ensure that they had affordable bread and attacked the chateaus of the local nobility in order to burn debt records. In the context of that rural unrest, sometimes known as *the Great Fear*, the Assembly passed the *August Decrees* in which most of the traditional privileges of the nobility and the clergy were renounced and abolished. In an attempt to assure all citizens of France of their intention to bring about a new, more just society, the Assembly adopted, on 27 August 1789, the "*Declaration of the Rights of Man and of the Citizen,*" a document that espoused individual rights and liberties for all citizens.

By the end of the summer of 1789, severe economic stress in the form of high bread prices and unemployment again prompted the people of Paris to take action on their own. Prompted by rumors that the nobility in Louis's court were plotting a coup, and spurred on by an active tabloid press, the people of Paris rioted on 5 October 1789. The next day, a contingent of Parisian women organized an 11-mile march from Paris to the king's palace at Versailles. Along the way, they were joined by the Paris Guards, a citizen militia, and together they forced their way into the palace and insisted that Louis accompany them back to Paris. He did; and within two weeks the National Assembly itself had relocated from Versailles to Paris. The *March to Versailles*, as it came to be known, demonstrated two important things.

First, the crowds of Paris did not yet look upon Louis XVI as their enemy; they had marched to Versailles to *retrieve* him because they believed that, if he were with them in Paris, rather than isolated in Versailles where he was surrounded by his aristocratic advisors, he would side with them and support the Assembly's efforts.

Second, the crowd of Paris, and their willingness to do violence, had become a powerful political force.

The relocation of both the king and the National Assembly to Paris, within easy reach of the Parisian crowd, set the stage for the radical phase of the revolution.

The Radical Phase of the French Revolution (1791–1794)

The October Riot marked the beginning of a two-year period of relative calm. A gradual improvement in the economy eased the tension in Paris, and the Assembly's most determined aristocratic enemies either fled to the countryside or emigrated. The Assembly used the period of relative calm to complete the constitution and to draft and pass *the Civil Constitution of the Clergy*, a piece of legislation that turned clergymen into employees of the government and turned Church property into property of the state. The Assembly soon sold off the confiscated property to pay part of the national debt, but the attack on the clergy and the Church turned many faithful Catholics against the Assembly.

When Louis XVI signed the new constitution into law on15 September 1791, the goals of the bourgeois leaders of the Assembly had been fulfilled: The power of the nobility and the Church had been broken and France was now a constitutional monarchy. Four developments conspired to send the revolution into a more radical phase, each of which is reviewed in the sections that follow this list:

- the king's attempt to secretly flee Paris in June of 1791
- the outbreak of war with Austria and Prussia in April of 1792
- the division of the National Assembly into political factions
- the rise of a politicized laboring faction, known as the *sans-culottes* because of the long work pants they wore

The King's Attempt to Secretly Flee Paris

The king's attempt to flee Paris and head north to rally supporters, an event that came to be known as *the flight to Varennes*, was disastrous. He and the royal family were apprehended and forcibly returned to Paris. He was officially forgiven by the Assembly, but he had forever lost the trust of the people of Paris.

The Outbreak of War Between France and Austria and Prussia

The war with Austria and Prussia came about partly because French aristocratic émigrés had been urging the Austrian and Prussian monarchies to come to the aid of the embattled Louis XVI. However, both Louis and the Assembly wanted the war, Louis because he believed that the country would have to turn to him to lead it in a time of war and the Assembly because they believed it would unite Frenchmen in a common cause. When the combined forces of the Austrian and Prussian Armies invaded France, the French army collapsed and the country went into a panic.

The Division of the National Assembly into Political Factions

The development of political factions within the Assembly revealed the differing opinions about the goals and aims of the revolution that had always lurked under the surface of their united front against the nobility and the clergy. An attempt, in October of 1791, to diffuse factional rivalries by dissolving the National Assembly and electing a new Legislative Assembly failed to solve the problem.

The Rise of a Politicized Laboring Faction: The *Sans-Culottes*

From the beginning, the Parisian crowd and its willingness to do violence had been a factor in the revolution, but it had been a force with essentially traditional and conservative aims, insisting that the king pay attention to and take proper care of his people. By 1792, the crowd was different; the working people (bakers, shopkeepers, artisans, and manual laborers who were characterized by their long working pants—hence, *sans-culottes*, literally without short pants) now could be seen attending meetings of political clubs and discussing the reforms that were still needed, reforms that would bring about true equality.

Once the men and women of the *sans-culottes* began to assert themselves, political power belonged to whoever they would support. This fact became evident on 10 August 1792, when a crowd stormed first the royal palace and then the hall of the Assembly. Unable to resist the crowd, the leaders of the Assembly voted to depose and imprison the king and to immediately convene a new *National Convention* to deal with the crises facing the country.

The Vote to End the French Monarchy

The membership of the National Convention, elected by universal manhood suffrage, was more radical than its predecessors. In September of 1792, it voted to abolish the monarchy and to proclaim France a republic. It also managed to reorganize the French army and push the invading Austrian and Prussian forces back across the border. When the Convention proclaimed the war an extension of the revolution and vowed to carry it anywhere where people yearned for liberty and freedom, the monarchies of Europe responded by forming a coalition to crush the revolution.

In January of 1793, the convention put Louis XVI on trial for treason. The debate that followed his conviction revealed a split between two powerful factions with the Convention. The *Girondins*, whose membership tended to come from the wealthiest of the bourgeoisie, were mostly opposed to executing him; the *Jacobins*, whose members came from the lower strata of the bourgeoisie, were adamant that he must die. The vote was close, but the Jacobins prevailed and Louis was sent to the guillotine on 21 January 1793.

A New Constitution and Robespierre's Reign of Terror

The execution of the king, combined with a decision to increase the number of men conscripted into the army, caused large anti-Convention uprisings throughout France. In Paris, the Jacobins used the revolt as an opportunity to purge the Girondins from the Convention. In June of 1793, a Jacobin-led mob occupied the Convention hall and refused to leave until the Girondins resigned. Those Girondins that refused to resign were arrested. The purged Convention then passed the *Law of the Maximum* to cap the price of bread and other essentials and drafted a new constitution that guaranteed universal manhood suffrage, universal education, and subsistence wages. In order to secure the egalitarian, democratic republic espoused by the new constitution, the Convention created a 12-man *Committee of Public Safety* and invested it with almost total power in order that it might secure the fragile Republic from its enemies. Within the Committee, a young lawyer from the provinces, Maximilien Robespierre gained control through his ability to persuade both his fellow Jacobins and the *sans-culottes* crowd to follow him.

Under Robespierre's leadership, the Committee instituted what has come to be known as the *Reign of Terror*. Arguing that, in times of revolution, terror was the necessary companion to virtue, Robespierre created tribunals in the major cities of France to try anyone suspected of being an enemy of the revolution. During the period of the Terror, between September of 1793 and July of 1794, between 200,000 and 400,000 people were sentenced to prison; between 25,000 and 50,000 of them are believed to have died, either in prison or at the guillotine.

Among the victims of the Terror were those who rivaled Robespierre for power. When, in April of 1794, Robespierre had the popular and influential Jacobin leader Georges-Jacques Danton arrested and executed for daring to suggest that it was time to reassess the Terror, he lost the support of both the Jacobins and the crowd. In July of 1794, Robespierre was arrested, tried, and executed by the same Terror machine that he had created. The execution of Robespierre marked the end of the radical phase of the revolution, as an exhausted Paris, devoid of its radical leaders, succumbed to a reassertion of power by the propertied bourgeoisie.

The Final Phase of the French Revolution: Thermidor and the Rise of Napoleon (1794–1799)

For several months following the execution of Robespierre, the revolutionary Terror was replaced by a terror of reaction as armed bands of men, hired by the wealthier bourgeois elites, roamed the cities hunting down and killing remaining Jacobins. In the Convention, the ascendant moderates wrote a new constitution that limited the right to vote for members of legislative bodies to wealthy property owners and removed price controls. The executive functions of the government were placed in the hands of a five-man board known as the *Directory*. Increasingly, the Directory relied on the military to keep order and to protect it from both the *sans-culottes*, who stormed the Convention in May of 1795, and from Royalists who attempted a coup five months later.

When the war against the European coalition began to go badly, conservative factions within the Convention conspired with the ambitious and popular army general Napoleon Bonaparte to overthrow the Directory. On 9 November 1799, the conspirators staged a successful coup and Napoleon acquired the powers necessary to govern as "first consul." By 1804, Napoleon had rid himself of his co-conspirators and had France proclaimed an "Empire" and himself emperor. He governed France with a mixture of reform and traditionalism and oversaw the military expansion of the French Empire until his defeat at the hands of coalition forces at the Battle of Waterloo in 1815.

Neoclassicism and the French Revolution

The radical break with tradition and convention ushered in by the French Revolution was also experienced in the world of art. Artists who sympathized with the democratic and nationalist philosophy of the revolution rejected the dominant rococo aesthetic in favor of a neoclassical style. The neoclassical style took its inspiration from the art of the ancient republics of Greece and Rome. *Neoclassicism* in the late eighteenth century became the dominant style of painters, who chose subjects that conveyed messages of social sacrifice and political courage. They rendered their characters in clean, strong lines that evoked ancient Greek and Roman sculpture, and they avoided decorative details or flourishes that might distract the viewer from the message of the painting. The greatest of the revolutionary era's neoclassical painters was Jacques Louis David. David's *Oath of the Horatii* (1784) is an example of the neoclassical rendering of a classic tale of the ancient world, while his *Death of Marat* (1793) illustrates the use of the neoclassical style to illustrate contemporary themes.

› Rapid Review

When Louis XVI was forced by financial difficulties to call the little-used Estates General into session in 1789, the bourgeois representatives of the Third Estate launched a revolution aimed at curbing the power and privilege of the nobility and the clergy, and they attempted to turn France into a constitutional monarchy. Supported by the Paris crowd, the leaders of the newly formed National Assembly nearly succeeded, but foreign intervention, persistent resistance from the nobility, the indecisiveness of Louis, and the development of factions within the Assembly allowed new, more radical leaders to win over the *sans-culottes* that now made up the Parisian crowd and set the revolution on a more radical course. Besieged by a coalition of the European powers and beset with factional strife, the radicals resorted to a Reign of Terror, which eventually consumed them. During the revolution, the radical break with tradition and convention was also experienced in the world of art. Artists who sympathized with the democratic and nationalist philosophy of the revolution rejected the dominant rococo aesthetic in favor of a neoclassical style.

By 1794, the propertied bourgeoisie had reasserted itself and concentrated on restoring order and repealing the gains of the radicals. In 1799, their executive organ known as the Directory was overthrown by a military general, Napoleon Bonaparte. He gradually assumed dictatorial powers and attempted to create a European-wide French Empire. Upon his defeat in 1815 by coalition forces, the French monarchy was restored, and the Kingdom of France was restored to its prerevolutionary boundaries.

› Chapter Review Questions

1. The main obstacle to solving France's financial problems was
   (A) the extravagant lifestyle of Louis XVI
   (B) the unwillingness of the Third Estate to pay more
   (C) the fact that both the nobility and clergy were exempt from most taxes
   (D) foreign wars
   (E) a bad economy

2. The significance of the storming of the Bastille was that
   (A) it put ammunition into the hands of the Paris crowd
   (B) it marked the beginning of a radical phase of the revolution
   (C) it freed important leaders from prison
   (D) it demonstrated that the crowd could be an important ally for the Assembly
   (E) it demonstrated that the crowd was tired of monarchy

3. The Great Fear of the summer of 1789
   (A) politicized the urban workers of Paris
   (B) catalyzed a European coalition against the French revolution
   (C) put greater pressure on the Assembly to enact more radical legislation
   (D) strengthened the position of the nobility
   (E) demonstrated the desperation of an over-taxed peasantry

4. The Civil Constitution of the Clergy
   (A) allied the clergy with the Assembly
   (B) curbed the power of the clergy but alienated many Catholics
   (C) brought the Assembly greater support among the Catholic population
   (D) reaffirmed the central place of the Church in the French government
   (E) made Catholicism illegal in France

5. All of the following precipitated the radical turn of the revolution EXCEPT
   (A) the rise of the *sans-culottes*
   (B) the flight of the king
   (C) the division of the Assembly into factions
   (D) the execution of the king
   (E) the outbreak of war with Austria and Prussia

6. The Reign of Terror
   (A) was necessary, according to Robespierre, to establish a democratic republic
   (B) was opposed by the Parisian crowd
   (C) was aimed only at the nobility
   (D) was anticlerical
   (E) was worst in the countryside

7. In Thermidor
   (A) the nobility reasserted its power
   (B) France was defeated by the European coalition
   (C) the French monarchy was restored
   (D) the *sans-culottes* chose to govern France directly
   (E) the moderate portion of the propertied bourgeoisie reasserted its power

8. The Directory turned to the military because
   (A) it lost the support of the *sans-culottes*
   (B) it lost the support of the nobility
   (C) it was threatened by both Jacobin and Royalist opposition
   (D) it feared it would lose the next election
   (E) it was overthrown by a general

› Answers and Explanations

1. **C.** It was the tax exempt status of the nobility and the clergy that prevented the government from gaining access to the majority of wealth in the French economy and, therefore, from solving its financial problems. Choice A is incorrect because, although Louis's lifestyle was a drain on government resources, there was sufficient wealth in France to cover its national debt. Choice B is incorrect because the various classes in the Third Estate were already taxed beyond what they could bear. Choice D is incorrect because, although Louis's foreign wars were a drain on France's finances, there was sufficient wealth in the economy to pay for them. Choice E is incorrect because there were sufficient amounts of wealth in the French economy to deal with all of France's financial difficulties.

2. **D.** The storming of the Bastille showed the members of the Assembly that the Parisian crowd could be used as a threat of further violence if its demands were not met. Choice A is incorrect because, despite its reputation, the Bastille did not contain much ammunition. Choice B is incorrect because, although the storming of the Bastille was surprisingly violent, it did not signal radical aims. Choice C is incorrect because, despite the Bastille's reputation, it did not contain many prisoners. Choice E is incorrect because the storming of the Bastille did not signify a loss of faith in the king.

3. **E.** The Great Fear was a traditional peasant uprising; the peasants protested high bread prices and burned records of taxes that they could not pay. Choice A is incorrect because the Great Fear was an uprising that took place in rural areas of France, not the urban areas. Choice B is incorrect because the Great Fear had no effect on France's foreign relations. Choice C is incorrect because, although the rural violence seems to have emboldened the Assembly, the pressure was applied to the king, Church, and nobility as the traditional sources of authority. Choice D is incorrect because the nobility's inability to deal with the financial crisis undermined their authority.

4. **B.** The Civil Constitution of the Clergy required clergy to take an oath of loyalty to the state, something that their faith prohibited them from doing.

The action alienated many French Catholics, who sided with their priests over the National Assembly. Choice A is incorrect because, although the Civil Constitution of the Clergy, in theory, made the clergy government employees and therefore subordinate to the Assembly, the conflict it caused further alienated the clergy. Choice C is incorrect because the Civil Constitution of the Clergy angered most Catholics and made them hostile to the Assembly. Choice D is incorrect because the Civil Constitution of the Clergy sought to subordinate the Church and make it less central in the government of France. Choice E is incorrect because Catholicism remained the dominant religion in France.

5. **D.** The execution of the king was an effect of the radicalization, not a precipitant or cause. Choice A is incorrect because the rise of the *sans-culottes* led to a shift to more radical aims because the *sans-culottes'* hopes of a more egalitarian and economically fair society were more radical than those of the bourgeois members of the Assembly. Choice B is incorrect because the flight of the king eroded the people's confidence in him and forced them to consider a more radical path. Choice C is incorrect because the development of factions within the Assembly meant that each faction had to compete for the support of the Paris crowd and, therefore, be more willing to listen to their radical demands. Choice E is incorrect because the war with Austria and Prussia created an air of crisis in which bolder action seemed required.

6. **A.** Robespierre justified the Terror by arguing that a virtuous, democratic republic could only be established and flourish once the tyrannical enemies of the revolution could be eliminated. Choice B is incorrect because the Reign of Terror was supported by the crowds in big cities such as Paris and Lyon. Choices C and D are incorrect because no one was safe from the accusation of being an "enemy of the revolution"; the Terror was not aimed at either the nobility or the clergy. Choice E is incorrect because the Terror was mostly an urban phenomenon.

7. **E.** In Thermidor, bourgeois moderates reasserted their power after the great leaders of the radical phase had been consumed by their own Terror

tribunals. Choice A is incorrect because the nobility were largely absent from Paris by the time of Thermidor, having had the resources to flee the Terror. Choice B is incorrect because France was not defeated by the coalition until 1815. Choice C is incorrect because the French monarchy was not restored until after the defeat of Napoleon in 1815. Choice D is incorrect because the *sans-culottes* had exhausted their energies by Thermidor and succumbed to the counter-terror of the bourgeois elites.

8. **C.** The Directory, being a government of bourgeois moderates, turned to the military to protect it from threats posed by both the more radical Jacobins and the more conservative Royalists. Choice A is incorrect because the Directory never had the support of the *sans-culottes*. Choice B is incorrect because the Directory never had the support of the nobility. Choice D is incorrect because the new constitution written by the moderates limited voting rights to the propertied classes who supported the Directory, thus they had no fear of elections. Choice E is incorrect because, although the Directory was eventually overthrown by a general, Bonaparte, they had by that time already been dependent on the military for several years.

UNIT 1 Summary: 1450 to the French Revolutionary and Napoleonic Era

Timeline

1337–1453	Hundred Years War between England and France
1350–1550	Renaissance begins on Italian Peninsula; spreads north throughout Western Europe
1453	Fall of Constantinople, Turkey
1455	Treaty of Lodi among Milan, Naples, and Florence
1455–1485	War of the Roses between Houses of York and Lancaster, England
1469	Marriage of Isabella and Ferdinand in Spain
1486	Pico's *Oration on the Dignity of Man* is published
1487	Portugal's Bartholomew Dias sails around the tip of Africa
1498	Portugal's Vasco da Gama reaches India
1504	Michelangelo's *David* sculpture completed
1513	Machiavelli's *The Prince* is published
1519–1522	Portugal's Magellan leads Spanish Expedition, circumnavigates the globe
1519–1521	Spain's Cortés conquers the Aztecs in Mexico
1534	Henry VIII is declared head of the Church of England
1534	Anabaptists capture the city of Münster, Germany
1536	Calvin's *Institutes of the Christian Religion* is published
1543	Copernicus's *On the Revolution of the Heavenly Spheres* is published
1545–1563	Catholic reform movement's Council of Trent is convened
1555	Peace of Augsburg—"whoever rules; his religion"—is signed by German princes
1598	Edict of Nantes is signed, establishing religious toleration in France
1610	Galileo's *Starry Messenger* is published
1632	Galileo's *Dialogue on the Two Chief Systems of the World* is published
1637	Descartes' *Discourse on Method* is published
1642–1646	English Civil War: Parliament tries to curb power of the monarchy, Church, nobility
1649–1660	The Commonwealth in England is established: King Charles I is executed
1651	Hobbes's *Leviathan* is published
1660–1688	The Restoration in England of the monarchy: Charles II becomes king
1685	Revocation of the Edict of Nantes in France
1687	Newton's *Principia Mathematica* is published
1688	The Glorious Revolution in England: King James II is expelled
1690	Locke's *Second Treatise of Civil Government* is published
1696	Toland's *Christianity Not Mysterious* is published
1733	Voltaire's *Letters Concerning the English Nation* are published
1733	Kay invents the flying shuttle
1740–1748	War of the Austrian Succession
1748	Montesquieu's *Spirit of the Laws* is published
1751–1772	Diderot and d'Alembert's *Encyclopedia* is published
1756–1763	Seven Years War among nine great European countries
1759	Voltaire's *Candide* is published
1762	Rousseau's *Emil* and *The Social Contract* are published
1764	Beccaria's *Crime and Punishment* is published

1770	d'Holbach's *System of Nature* is published
1776	Smith's *Wealth of Nations* is published
1789–1791	French Revolution, moderate phase
1791–1794	French Revolution, radical phase
1792	Wollstonecraft's *Vindication of the Rights of Women* is published
1793	Whitney invents the cotton gin
1794–1799	French Revolution, Thermidor, and the rise of Napoleon

Key Comparisons

1. Italian versus Northern European Renaissance values
2. Theology of Luther and Calvin
3. Nature and power of monarchies in England, France, Spain, Central Europe
4. Economic change in England versus Continental Europe
5. Enlightened despotism versus the radical Enlightenment
6. Moderate versus radical phases of the French Revolution

Thematic Change/Continuity

Economic changes
Development of triangle of trade
Creation of a Spanish Empire in the New World
Establishment of English and French colonies in North America
Shift to cash crops
Enclosure movement in England
Creation of cottage industry in Great Britain

Economic continuities
Agricultural economy with manufacturing and trade supplements

Social/cultural changes
Traditional population cycle broken
Creation and growth of a merchant class
Reformation fractures unity of the Christian Church
Creation of wage labor
Rise of scientific thinking and the Enlightenment

Social continuities
Patriarchal society
Privileges of the aristocracy
Dominance of the Catholic Church in France, Italy, and Spain
Serfdom in Russia

Political changes
Consolidation and centralization of power in the monarchy
Constitutionalism in England and Holland
Establishment of a republic in France

Political continuities
Monarchy as the normal form of government

UNIT 2

The Napoleonic Era to the Present

CHAPTER 15

Napoleonic Europe and the Post-Napoleonic Era, 1800–1848

IN THIS CHAPTER

Summary: Between 1800 and 1848, Europe was temporarily conquered and transformed by Napoleonic France before returning to the embattled rule of its traditional aristocratic houses.

Key Ideas

✪ The Napoleonic Code, with its codification of egalitarianism and meritocracy, further eroded the traditional, feudal privileges of the aristocracy and the clergy and fostered a desire for further reform.

✪ Resentment caused by Napoleon's rule, and particularly by the restrictions of the Continental System, led to the growth of a spirit of nationalism across Europe.

✪ The aristocratic leaders of the coalition that defeated Napoleon constructed "the Concert of Europe" in an attempt to secure the domination of the traditional ruling houses of Europe and to restore the balance of power between them.

✪ The conservative aims of the architects of the Concert of Europe ran counter to the growing desire for liberal, democratic reform and nationalist self-determination among the peoples of Europe; the result was a cycle of revolution and repression from 1820 to 1848.

Key Terms

the consulate
Concordat of 1801
Napoleonic Code
Treaty of Tilsit
Battle of Trafalgar

Continental System
The Third of May, 1808
Grand Army
Battle of Waterloo
Congress of Vienna

Concert of Europe
July Ordinances
Frankfurt Assembly
Arc de Triomphe

Introduction

By 1802, Napoleon had crossed the Alps, knocked Austria out of the war, made peace with Russia, and persuaded Great Britain to sign what proved to be a temporary truce in the Peace of Amiens. But by 1805, further efforts to expand the Empire again put France at war with Great Britain and a new coalition. Napoleon would fight on for another 10 years, permanently transforming some aspects of the political and social landscape of Europe, before eventually overextending his reach and meeting defeat at Waterloo. Following Napoleon's defeat, the traditional aristocratic houses of Europe worked in concert to reestablish and defend their dominance against challenges from the forces of liberalism and nationalism.

Post-Revolutionary France and the Napoleonic Code

The French Revolution effectively came to an end with Napoleon's coup d'état in November of 1799 and the establishment of *the consulate*, a three-man executive body. In 1802, Napoleon was acknowledged as the sole executive officer and given the title "first consul for life." By the time Napoleon had himself declared Emperor in 1804, he was well on his way to completing the process, begun by the revolution, of creating a strong central government and administrative uniformity in France.

To solidify his position, Napoleon took the following measures:

- He suppressed royalists and republicans through the use of spies and surprise arrests.
- He censored and controlled the press.
- He regulated what was taught in schools.
- He reconciled France with the Roman Church by signing the *Concordat of 1801*, which stipulated that French clergy would be chosen and paid by the state but consecrated by the pope.

To provide a system of uniform law and administrative policy, Napoleon created the Civil Code of 1804, more widely known as the *Napoleonic Code*. It incorporated many principles that had been espoused during the revolution, some liberal and some conservative. In accordance with liberal principles, the Code:

- safeguarded all forms of property
- upheld equality before the law
- established the right to choose a profession
- guaranteed promotion on merit for employees of the state

In accordance with conservative principles, the Code:

- upheld the ban on working men's associations
- upheld the patriarchal nature of French society by granting men extensive rights over their wives and children

As Napoleon conquered Europe, he spread the Code across the continent. The overall effect of the Code on Europe was to erode the remnants of the old feudal system by further weakening the traditional power of the nobility and clergy.

Napoleon's Empire

Between 1805 and 1810, Napoleon's forces won a series of battles that allowed France to dominate all of Continental Europe except the Balkan Peninsula. The key victories included:

- the Battle of Austerlitz (December 1805), defeating Russo-Austrian forces
- the Battle of Jena (October 1806), defeating Prussian forces
- the Battle of Friedland (June 1807), defeating Russian forces

The resulting French Empire consisted of some states that were annexed directly into the French Empire, including:

- Belgium
- Germany to the Rhine
- the German coastal regions to the western Baltic
- west-central Italy, including Rome, Genoa, and Trieste

The Empire also included five satellite kingdoms ruled by Napoleon's relatives:

- Holland, ruled by his brother Louis
- Westphalia, ruled by his brother Jérôme
- Spain, ruled by his brother Joseph
- the kingdom of Italy, ruled by his stepson Eugène
- the Kingdom of Naples, ruled by his brother-in-law Joachim Murat

The remaining portions of the Empire consisted of a series of subservient states and confederations, which included:

- the Confederation of the Rhine, eventually consisting of 18 German states that had been part of the now-defunct Holy Roman Empire
- the 19 cantons of the Swiss Confederation
- the Duchy of Warsaw, carved out of Prussia's Polish lands

Those European states that remained independent from France were reluctant allies that simply had no choice but to bow to Napoleon's power. Such states included:

- Austria, where Francis II ruled a kingdom diminished by the disintegration of the Holy Roman Empire
- Prussia, now much smaller for losing its Polish lands and some areas to the Confederation
- Russia, which, following the defeat at Friedland, signed the *Treaty of Tilsit* on 7 July 1807, recognizing France's claims in Europe
- Sweden
- Denmark

The one European nation that still threatened Napoleon was Great Britain, whose superior naval power, as exemplified by its victory over the combined French and Spanish fleets at the *Battle of Trafalgar* on 21 October 1805, made it unconquerable. In order to weaken Britain, Napoleon established what came to be known as the *Continental System*, whereby the Continental European states and kingdoms under French control were forbidden to trade with Britain.

- The further east it went, the more the government was involved (because governments feared the political and military effects of falling behind their rivals, they invested heavily in industrialization); for example, there was no government involvement in the industrialization of Britain, some in France, more in Germany, and in Russia industrialization was almost totally government driven.

Russia Lags Behind

By 1850, large-scale industrialization had spread to northeastern France, Belgium, the northern German states, and northwestern Italy. The southern, central, and eastern areas of Europe—such as Italy, Poland, and Russia—lagged behind due to insufficient natural resources and the lack of a commercialized agricultural system to allow for a mobile workforce. These areas retained their rural character.

Russia lagged behind until two successive tsars—Alexander III (1881–1894) and Nicholas II (1894–1917)—determined that Russia should become an industrial power. In 1892, Alexander III appointed Serge Witte as finance minister. Under Witte's leadership, Russia became an iron- and steel-producing nation. By the end of the nineteenth century, factories had arisen in Moscow and St Petersburg. By 1904, the construction of a trans-Siberian railroad that linked the European portion of Russia with the East was nearly completed.

Social Effects

The Second Industrial Revolution transformed European society in significant ways:

- *Urbanization* increased rapidly, as the population moved into hastily built housing in cities to be nearer to the factories.
- *Families* were separated as the place of work shifted from the home to factories.
- *Work* lost its seasonal quality, as workers were required to follow a routine schedule.
- The *pace of work*, driven by machines, increased dramatically.
- The overall *health* of the workforce declined because of the harsh and unhealthy conditions of the factories.
- The *availability of work* became unpredictable as it rose and fell with the demand for goods.
- Gradually, *women* who had first been drawn into cities to work in the factories lost their manufacturing jobs as machines decreased the demand for labor; cut off from their families, many had no other option than prostitution.
- *Artisans and craftsmen* lost their livelihoods, unable to compete with the lower cost of mass-produced goods.
- The traditional impediment to *marriage*, which was the need for land, disappeared and people began to marry younger.
- A much greater portion of the population could afford *factory-made goods.*
- There was further *change in the class structure* as industrialization created both a class of newly wealthy industrialists and a precariously situated lower middle class of managers and clerks.
- Close working and living conditions produced a sense of *class consciousness* among the working class.

Artistic Movements in the Industrial Age

Artistic expression in the industrial age was dominated by three styles: *realism, impressionism,* and *postimpressionism.*

In the middle of the nineteenth century, young painters rejected both the romantic fantasies and the glorification of the past that had interested their predecessors. The realists sought instead to accurately and honestly render the life around them in meticulous detail. A primary example of the realist movement is the work of Gustav Courbet. In his *Burial at Ornans* (1849–1850), for example, Courbet depicted the members of a small village burying one of its community members without trying to convey any particular emotion or moral message.

By the late nineteenth century, realism gave way to the impressionist movement. The impressionists desired to render not the reality of the scene but the reality of the visual experience. The visual experience, the impressionists believed, consisted of the interaction between light, color, and human perception. Accordingly, they created images that evoked the visual experience by painting with visible brush strokes and heightened color. Édouard Manet's *Impressionisme soleil levant,* or *Impressionism, Sunrise* (1872), is often cited as the work that gave impressionism its name. Other influential impressionist painters of the period were Pierre Auguste Renoir, Edgar Degas, and Claude Monet.

After about a decade, a new generation of painters began to reject the limitations imposed by the impressionist movement. The result was a movement often known as postimpressionism, which combined the visible brush strokes, heightened color, and real-life subject matter of impressionism with an emphasis on geometric form and unnatural color to create a more emotionally expressive effect. Perhaps the most famous example of postimpressionist painting is Vincent van Gogh's *Starry Night* (1889). Other influential postimpressionist painters of the late nineteenth century include Georges Seurat, Mary Cassatt, Paul Gauguin, and Paul Cézanne.

Science in the Industrial Age

Advances in gas theory and a spirit of scientific realism dominated the physical sciences in the nineteenth century. Physicists in this period concentrated on providing a scientific understanding of the processes that drove the engines of the Industrial Revolution. In the middle of the nineteenth century, physicists such as the German Rudolph Clausius and the Scotsman James Maxwell developed the *kinetic theory of gases.* Their theory envisioned gas pressure and temperature as resulting from a certain volume of molecules in motion. Such an approach allowed them to analyze, and therefore to measure and predict, pressure and temperature statistically. Later in the century, physicists such as Robert Mayer, Hermann von Helmholtz, and William Thompson pursued this kind of statistical analysis to articulate the laws of thermodynamics.

The success of the "matter in motion" models in physics created a wider philosophical movement that argued that all natural phenomena could and should be understood as the result of matter and motion. The movement, known as *materialism,* was first articulated by a trinity of German natural philosophers: Karl Vogt, Jakob Moleschott, and Ludwig Büchner. By the end of the nineteenth century, materialism had become a foundational assumption of the scientific view of the world.

The natural sciences in the nineteenth century were dominated by Charles Darwin's theory of evolution by natural selection. As a young man, Darwin had sailed around the globe as the naturalist for the H.M.S. *Beagle.* During the *Beagle's* five-year voyage, commencing 27 December 1831 and ending 2 October 1836, Darwin collected specimens for shipment home to England and made observations on the flora and fauna of the many continents he explored. Twenty-three years later, he published a book titled *On the Origin of Species by Means of Natural Selection or the Preservation of Favoured Races in the Struggle for Life.* In *Origin,* Darwin offered an explanation to the two questions at the heart of nineteenth-century natural science: why was there so much diversity among living organisms, and why did organisms seem to "fit" into the environments in which they lived? Darwin's answer, unlike earlier answers that referred to God's will and a process of creation, was materialist in nature. He argued that both the wide range of diversity and the environmental "fit" of living organisms to their environment were due to a process that he termed "natural selection." The fact that many more organisms were born than could survive led, Darwin explained, to a constant "struggle for existence" between individual living organisms. Only those individuals that survived the struggle passed their physical characteristics on to their offspring. Over millions of years, that simple process had caused populations of organisms to evolve in ways that produced both the amazing diversity and the environmental "fit."

Origin went through six editions, and Darwin's theory became the central organizing principle of the science of biology, which developed in the late nineteenth and early twentieth centuries. In 1871 Darwin published *The Descent of Man,* which explained Darwin's views on how human beings had come into being through the process of natural selection.

› Rapid Review

Between 1820 and 1900, the demand for goods on the part of a steadily increasing population was met by entrepreneurs who created the factory system. The new system standardized and increased industrial production. As the century went on, the development of four interrelated heavy industries—iron and steel, coal mining, steam power, and railroads—combined to drive Europe's economy to unprecedented heights, constituting a Second Industrial Revolution. The urbanization, standardization of work, and effects of the class system wrought by the Second Industrial Revolution significantly transformed social life in Europe.

The changes wrought by the Industrial Revolution provoked new developments in both the arts and sciences. In the arts, the three related styles of realism, impressionism, and postimpressionism developed. Progress in the physical sciences manifested itself in the development of the kinetic theory of gases, while the natural sciences were dominated by Charles Darwin's innovative theory of evolution by natural selection.

❯ Chapter Review Questions

1. Which of the following was NOT an effect of the division of labor?
   (A) It increased the supply of labor available to manufacturers.
   (B) It raised wages for manufacturing workers.
   (C) It increased the volume that manufacturers could produce.
   (D) It allowed manufacturers to sell their products more cheaply.
   (E) It allowed manufacturers to increase their profits.

2. The invention of new forms of power such as steam and electricity
   (A) led to the creation of the factory system
   (B) facilitated the invention of the automobile
   (C) decreased demand for coal
   (D) allowed manufacturers to relocate their mills away from water sources
   (E) doomed the shipping industry

3. In general, the Second Industrial Revolution in Europe
   (A) began on the Continent and spread in all directions
   (B) took place in Great Britain
   (C) took place more slowly in Eastern Europe
   (D) was stimulated by government investment in Western Europe
   (E) took place later but more rapidly in Eastern Europe

4. The railway boom of the 1830s and 1840s
   (A) increased demand for steel but decreased demand for coal
   (B) did not affect the demand for steel
   (C) increased demand for both steel and coal
   (D) increased demand for coal but decreased demand for steel
   (E) did not affect the demand for coal

5. Which of the following was an advantage enjoyed by Great Britain that helps to explain why the Second Industrial Revolution originated there?
   (A) an extensive river system
   (B) the lack of internal trade tariffs
   (C) a well-developed commercial economy
   (D) natural resources
   (E) all of the above

6. In Russia
   (A) industrialization occurred rapidly under the direction of the government
   (B) industrialization was a gradual process
   (C) textile production was crucial to the industrialization process
   (D) railway construction was deemed unnecessary for industrialization
   (E) industrialization occurred early and rapidly due to trade with the East

7. One of the ways in which the Second Industrial Revolution affected the social structure of Europe was to produce
   (A) a more even distribution of wealth
   (B) a lower middle class of managers and clerks
   (C) poor people
   (D) a merchant class
   (E) gender equity

8. As a result of the Second Industrial Revolution, the majority of skilled artisans and craftsmen
   (A) prospered
   (B) became managers in factories
   (C) lost their livelihoods
   (D) moved to towns and cities
   (E) were women

› Answers and Explanations

1. **B**. The division of labor increased the supply of labor available, thereby causing wages for manufacturing workers to fall, not increase. Choice A is incorrect because the division of labor *did* increase the supply of labor available to manufacturers by making all jobs unskilled jobs. Choice C is incorrect because the division of labor increased volume by speeding up the manufacturing process. Choices D and E are incorrect because the combination of increased productivity and cheaper labor allowed manufacturers to sell their products more cheaply and still increase their profits through increased volume.

2. **D**. The shift to steam and electrical power and away from hydropower allowed manufacturers to move away from water sources and relocate in more convenient locations. Choice A is incorrect because the factory system is a way of organizing labor; it is not dependent on a particular source of power. Choice B is incorrect because the invention of the automobile was facilitated by the invention of the internal combustion engine, not steam and electricity. Choice C is incorrect because both steam engines and electrical generators relied on coal for fuel, therefore *increasing* demand for it. Choice E is incorrect because, although the invention of the steam locomotive led to a railway boom, the application of it to ships allowed the shipping industry to prosper as well.

3. **E**. The Second Industrial Revolution originated in Britain and took place later but more rapidly in Eastern Europe, which was able to copy and purchase key industrial innovations. Choice A is incorrect because the Second Industrial Revolution originated in Great Britain and spread *eastward* across Europe, not in all directions. Choice B is incorrect because the Second Industrial Revolution was not unique to nor contained in Britain. Choice C is incorrect because the Second Industrial Revolution occurred *later* but more rapidly in Eastern Europe. Choice D is incorrect because there was more government investment involved in *Eastern* Europe where governments feared falling economically and technologically behind their Western rivals.

4. **C**. The railway boom increased demand for steel because steel was required for the manufacture of railway engines, cars, and rails; it also increased demand for coal because coal was the fuel for steam locomotives. Choices A and D are incorrect because the railway boom increased demand for *both* steel and coal. Choice B is incorrect because the railway boom did affect the demand for steel: It increased demand. Similarly, choice E is incorrect because the railway boom did affect the demand for coal: It also increased demand.

5. **E**. All of the choices are correct. Britain's extensive river system (choice A) allowed it to move raw materials and manufactured goods with relative ease. The lack of internal trade tariffs (choice B) allowed manufacturers to buy and transport materials without eating into their profit. Britain's well-developed commercial economy (choice C) provided both a merchant class and capital for investment. Finally, Britain's rich deposits of iron and coal (choice D: Britain's natural resources) provided the necessary raw materials.

6. **A**. Industrialization occurred rapidly in Russia under the direction of finance minister Serge Witte. Choice B is incorrect because Russia industrialized *later* than its European rivals but *very rapidly*, with most of the process taking place between 1892 and 1904. Choice C is incorrect because Russian industrialization was driven by its railway construction and steel production, not by its textile industry. Choice D is incorrect because the construction of the trans-Siberian railway was *very* necessary—indeed, a crucial part of Russian industrialization. Choice E is incorrect because again, Russia did *not* industrialize early; it industrialized *later* than its European counterparts.

7. **B**. The factory system that was characteristic of the Second Industrial Revolution required and produced a class of managers and clerks whose pay and status located them precariously at the lower end of the middle class. Choice A is incorrect because the Second Industrial Revolution did nothing to distribute wealth *more evenly* throughout the population; instead, it made a

relatively small number of industrialists and entre-preneurs fabulously wealthy and made some workers better off than before. Choice C is incorrect because the poor had existed before the Second Industrial Revolution. Similarly, choice D is incorrect because a merchant class existed in Europe prior to the Second Industrial Revolution. Choice E is incorrect because, although many women initially found work in the factories of the Second Industrial Revolution, they were not paid equally and were the first to be let go when increasing mechanization decreased the demand for labor.

8. **C.** Because factory-produced goods could be made in greater quantity and sold more cheaply, most skilled artisans and craftsmen were unable to compete and lost their livelihoods. Choice A is incorrect because the skilled artisans and craftsmen did *not* prosper; instead, they faced either unemployment or factory work at wages much lower than the profits they had made in their shops. Choice B is incorrect because a factory manager was a new breed whose job was to keep the factory running at peak efficiency and whose skills were unrelated to those of the old artisans and craftsmen. Choice D is incorrect because, unlike their agricultural counterparts, artisans and craftsmen had *always* located themselves in towns and cities. Choice E is incorrect because neither men nor women were being drawn into these professions during the Second Industrial Revolution.

CHAPTER 17

The Rise of New Ideologies in the Nineteenth Century

IN THIS CHAPTER

Summary: Nineteenth-century European intellectuals coped with the changes and challenges wrought by the French and Industrial Revolutions by fashioning various ideologies, which were consistent sets of beliefs that prescribed specific social and political actions.

Key Ideas

- *Conservatism* held that tradition was the only trustworthy guide to social and political action.
- *Liberalism* asserted that the task of government was to promote individual liberty.
- *Romanticism* urged the cultivation of sentiment and emotion by reconnecting with nature and with the past.
- *Nationalism* asserted that a nation was a natural, organic entity whose people shared a cultural identity and a historical destiny.
- *Anarchism* saw the modern state and its institutions as the enemy of individual freedom.
- *Socialism* sought to reorder society in ways that would end or minimize competition, foster cooperation, and allow the working classes to share in the wealth being produced by industrialization.
- *Communism* was dedicated to the creation of a class-free society through the abolition of private property.
- *Social Darwinism* asserted that competition was natural and necessary for the evolutionary progress of a society.

Key Terms

conservatism	utopian socialism	means of production
liberalism	technocratic socialism	bourgeoisie
laissez-faire	psychological socialism	proletariat
iron law of wages	industrial socialism	social Darwinism
nationalism	scientific socialism	eugenics
Romanticism	communism	anarchism

Introduction

The French Revolution had challenged Europeans' beliefs in and assumptions about society; the Second Industrial Revolution seemed to be transforming society at a dizzying pace. In order to cope with these changes, and to answer the questions posed by them, nineteenth-century European intellectuals created, or elaborated on, a variety of ideologies, each claiming to hold the key to creating the best society possible.

Conservatism

In the nineteenth century, *conservatism* was the ideology that asserted that tradition is the only trustworthy guide to social and political action. Conservatives argued that traditions were time-tested, organic solutions to social and political problems. Accordingly, nineteenth-century conservatives supported monarchy, the hierarchical class system dominated by the aristocracy, and the Church. They opposed innovation and reform, arguing that the French Revolution had demonstrated that they led directly to revolution and chaos. Supporters of the conservative position originally came from the traditional elites of Europe, the landed aristocracy.

The British writer and statesman Edmund Burke is often considered "the father of conservatism," as his *Reflections the Revolutions in France* (1790) seemed to predict the bloodshed and chaos that characterized the radical phase of the revolution. The French writer Joseph de Maistre's *Essay on the General Principle of Political Constitutions* (1814) is a prime nineteenth-century example of conservatism's opposition to constitutionalism and reform.

Liberalism

Nineteenth-century *liberalism* was the ideology that asserted that the task of government was to promote individual liberty. Liberals viewed many traditions as impediments to that freedom and, therefore, campaigned for reform. Pointing to the accomplishments of the Scientific Revolution, nineteenth-century liberals asserted that there were God-given, natural rights and laws that men could discern through the use of reason. Accordingly, they supported innovation and reform (in contrast to conservatives), arguing that many traditions were simply superstitions. They promoted constitutional monarchy over absolutism, and they campaigned for an end to the traditional privileges of the aristocracy and the Church in favor of a *meritocracy* and middle-class participation in government. Supporters of liberalism originally came from the middle class.

Two British philosophers, John Locke and Adam Smith, are usually thought of as the forefathers of liberalism. In *The Second Treatise of Government* (1690), Locke made the argument for the existence of God-given natural rights and asserted that the proper goal of government was to protect and promote individual liberty. In *Wealth of Nations* (1776), Smith made the case for the existence of economic laws which guided human behavior like an "invisible hand." Smith also promoted the notion of *laissez-faire*, which stated that governments should not try to interfere with the natural workings of an economy, a notion that became one of the basic tenets of liberalism in the nineteenth century.

Late-eighteenth- and early-nineteenth-century thinkers extended and hardened Smith's ideas. In *An Essay on the Principle of Population* (1798), Thomas Malthus asserted that free and constant competition would always be the norm in human societies because the human species would always reproduce at a greater rate than the food supply. By midcentury, liberal economic thinkers alleged that there was an *iron law of wages*, which argued that competition between workers for jobs would always, in the long run, force wages to sink to subsistence levels. The "law" is sometimes attributed to the English economist David Ricardo, but was promoted most prominently by the German sociologist Ferdinand LaSalle.

As the nineteenth century progressed, liberalism evolved. The followers of the English philosopher Jeremy Bentham espoused *utilitarianism*, which argued that all human laws and institutions ought to be judged by their usefulness in promoting "the greatest good for the greatest number" of people. Accordingly, they supported reforms to sweep away traditional institutions that failed the test and to create new institutions that would pass it. Utilitarians tended to be more supportive of government intervention than other liberals. For example, they drafted and supported new legislation to limit the hours that women and children could work in factories and to regulate the sanitary conditions of factories and mines.

Early-nineteenth-century liberals had been leery of democracy, arguing that the masses had to be educated before they could usefully contribute to the political life of the country. But by midcentury, liberals began advocating democracy, reasoning that the best way to identify the greatest good for the greatest number was to maximize the number of people voting. The best example of midcentury utilitarian thought is John Stuart Mill's *On Liberty* (1859), which argued for freedom of thought and democracy but also warned against the tyranny of the majority. Together, Mill and his companion Harriet Taylor led the liberal campaign for women's rights, Taylor publishing *The Enfranchisement of Women* (anonymously in 1851) and Mill publishing *The Subjection of Women* (1869).

Romanticism

Romanticism was a reaction to the Enlightenment and industrialization. The nineteenth-century Romantics rebelled against the Enlightenment's emphasis on reason and urged the cultivation of sentiment and emotion. Fittingly, Romantics mostly avoided political tracts and expressed themselves mostly through art and literature. Their favorite subject was nature.

The roots of Romanticism are often traced back to the works of Jean Jacques Rousseau because in *Emil* (1762), he had argued that humans were born essentially good and virtuous but were easily corrupted by society, and that the early years of a child's education should be spent developing the senses, sensibilities, and sentiments. Another source of Romanticism was the German *Sturm und Drang* (Storm and Stress) movement of the late eighteenth century, exemplified by Johann Wolfgang von Goethe's *The Sorrows of Young Werther* (1774), which glorified the "inner experience" of the sensitive individual.

In response to the rationalism of the Enlightenment (and to some degree, of liberalism) the Romantics offered the solace of nature. Good examples of this vein of nineteenth-century Romanticism are the works of the English poets William Wordsworth and Samuel Taylor Coleridge, who extolled the almost mystical qualities of the Lake District of northwest England.

Romantic painters like John Constable in England and Karl Friedrich Schinkel in Germany offered inspiring landscapes and images of a romanticized past. Beethoven, Chopin, and Wagner expressed the imaginative, intuitive spirit of Romanticism in music.

Nationalism

Nationalism, in the nineteenth century, was the ideology that asserted that a nation was a natural, organic entity whose people were bound together by shared language, customs, and history. Nationalists argued that each nation had natural boundaries, shared cultural traits, and a historical destiny to fulfill. Accordingly, nineteenth-century nationalists in existing nation states like Britain and France argued for strong, expansionist foreign policies. Nationalists in areas like Germany and Italy argued for national unification and the expulsion of foreign rulers.

In the early nineteenth century, nationalism was allied to liberalism. Both shared a spirit of optimism, believing that their goals represented the inevitable, historical progress of humankind. In the nonunified lands of Germany and Italy, occupation by Napoleonic France had help to foster a spirit of nationalism. Under Napoleon's rule, Germans and Italians came to think of their own disunity as a weakness. The best early examples of this kind of nationalism are the German writers Johann Gottlieb Fichte, whose *Addresses to German Nation* (1808) urged the German people to unite in order to fulfill their historical role in bringing about the ultimate progress of humanity, and Georg Wilhelm Friedrich Hegel, who argued that every nation had a historical role to play in the unfolding of the universe, and that Germany's time to take center stage in that drama had arrived.

Like the Romantics, early-nineteenth-century nationalists emphasized the role that environment played in shaping the character of a nation, and sentimentalized the past. A good example of Romantic nationalism is the work of Ernst Moritz Arndt, who urged Germans to unify through a shared heritage and through love of all things German. Strains of Romanticism can also be seen in the work of the great Italian nationalist of the early nineteenth century, Giuseppe Mazzini, whose nationalist movement, Young Italy, made appeals to unity based on natural affinities and a shared soul.

Anarchism

Anarchism was the nineteenth-century ideology that saw the state and its governing institutions as the ultimate enemy of individual freedom. Early anarchists drew inspiration from the writings of Pierre Joseph Proudhon, who argued that man's freedom had been progressively curtailed by industrialization and larger, more centralized governments. Anarchy had the greatest appeal in those areas of Europe where governments were most oppressive; in the nineteenth century, that meant Russia. There, Mikhail Bakunin, the son of a Russian noble, organized secret societies whose goal was to destroy the Russian state forever. Throughout Europe, nineteenth-century anarchists engaged in acts of political terrorism, particularly attempts to assassinate high-ranking government officials.

Utopian Socialism

Nineteenth-century socialism was the ideology that emphasized the collective over the individual and challenged the liberal's notion that competition was natural. Socialists sought to reorder society in ways that would end or minimize competition, foster cooperation, and allow the working classes to share in the wealth being produced by industrialization.

The earliest forms of socialism have come to be called *utopian socialism* for the way in which they envisioned, and sometimes tried to set up, ideal communities (or utopias) where work and its fruit were shared equitably. In the nineteenth century, there were three distinct forms of utopian socialism, described in the following sections.

Technocratic Socialism

This type of socialism envisioned a society run by technical experts who managed resources efficiently and in a way that was best for all. The most prominent nineteenth-century advocate of technocratic socialism was a French aristocrat, Henri Comte de Saint-Simon, who renounced his title during the French Revolution and spent his life championing the progress of technology and his vision of a society organized and run by scientifically trained managers or "technocrats."

Psychological Socialism

This type of socialism saw a conflict between the structure of society and the natural needs and tendencies of human beings. Its leading nineteenth-century advocate was Charles Fourier, who argued that the ideal society was one organized on a smaller, more human scale. He advocated the creation of self-sufficient communities, called *phalansteries*, of no more than 1,600 people, in which the inhabitants did work that suited them best.

Industrial Socialism

This type of socialism argued that it was possible to have a productive, profitable industrial enterprise without exploiting workers. Its leading advocate was a Scottish textile manufacturer, Robert Owen. Owen set out to prove his thesis by setting up industrial communities like the New Lanark cotton mill in Scotland and, later, a larger manufacturing community in New Harmony, Indiana, that paid higher wages and provided food, shelter, and clothing at reasonable prices.

Scientific Socialism and Communism

By the middle of the nineteenth century, the exploitation of European workers had grown more evident and the dreams of the utopian socialists seemed less plausible. In their place arose a form of socialism based on what its adherents claimed was a scientific analysis of society's workings. The most famous and influential of the self-proclaimed scientific socialists was the German revolutionary Karl Marx. In *The Communist Manifesto* (1848), a slim pamphlet distributed to workers throughout Europe, Marx and his collaborator Freidrich Engels argued that "all history is the history of class struggle." In the *Manifesto*, and later in the much larger *Capital* (vol. 1, 1867), Marx argued that a human being's relationship to the *means of production* gave him a social identity. In the industrial age of the nineteenth century, Marx argued, only two classes existed: the *bourgeoisie*, who controlled the means of production; and the *proletariat*, who sold their labor for wages. The key point in Marx's analysis was that the bourgeoisie exploited the proletariat because competition demanded it; if a factory owner chose to treat his workers more generously, then he would have to charge more for his goods and his competitors would drive him out of business.

Marx's analysis led him to adopt a position that came to be known as *communism*, which declared that the only way to end social exploitation was to abolish private property. If no one could claim to own the means of production, then there could be no distinction between owner and worker; all class distinctions would disappear and the workers would be free to distribute the benefits of production more equally.

Social Darwinism

The socialist notion that competition was unnatural was countered by yet another nineteenth-century ideology that came to be known as *social Darwinism*. In 1859, the British naturalist Charles Darwin published *The Origin of Species*, which argued that all living things had descended from a few simple forms. In *Origin*, Darwin described a complex process in which biological inheritance, environment, and competition for resources combined over millions of years to produce the amazing diversity in living forms that exists in the world.

The social philosopher Herbert Spencer argued that Darwin's theory proved that competition was not only natural, but necessary for the progress of a society. Spencer coined the phrase "survival of the fittest" (a phrase adopted by Darwin in the sixth and final edition of *Origin*) and argued along liberal lines that government intervention in social issues interfered with natural selection and, therefore, with progress. By the last decades of the nineteenth century, social Darwinism was being used to argue that imperialism, the competition between nations for control of the globe, was a natural and necessary step in the evolution of the human species. *Eugenics*, the notion that a progressive, scientific nation should plan and manage the biological reproduction of its population as carefully as it planned and managed its economy, also flourished in the last decades of the nineteenth century.

〉 Rapid Review

In the nineteenth century, intellectuals articulated numerous ideologies in order to make sense of a rapidly changing world. By the end of the century, a thinking person could choose from or create combinations from a spectrum of ideologies that included and can be summarized as follows:

- conservatism—championing tradition
- liberalism—urging reform
- Romanticism—encouraging the cultivation of sentiment and emotion
- nationalism—preaching cultural unity
- anarchism—scheming to bring down the state
- socialism—trying to design a more equitable society
- communism—working to abolish private property
- social Darwinism—advocating the benefits of unfettered competition

❯ Chapter Review Questions

1. In the nineteenth century, conservatives
   - (A) argued that governments should not interfere with the natural tendencies of the economy
   - (B) emphasized the development of sentiment and emotion
   - (C) favored constitutional monarchy
   - (D) supported the privileges of the aristocracy and clergy
   - (E) espoused utilitarianism

2. Nineteenth-century Romanticism can be understood as a reaction against
   - (A) conservatism
   - (B) changes wrought by the Enlightenment and industrialization
   - (C) nationalism
   - (D) social Darwinism
   - (E) scientific socialism

3. Which of the following is NOT true of nineteenth-century liberalism?
   - (A) It asserted that the task of government was to promote individual liberty.
   - (B) It opposed government intervention in the economy.
   - (C) It supported the privileges of the clergy.
   - (D) It believed in the existence of natural laws that governed human behavior.
   - (E) It drew its support primarily from the middle classes.

4. Goethe's *The Sorrows of Young Werther* is an example of
   - (A) the anarchist movement
   - (B) socialism
   - (C) early liberalism
   - (D) nationalism
   - (E) the *Sturm und Drang* movement

5. Utilitarians differed from other liberals by
   - (A) supporting government regulation of working conditions in factories
   - (B) calling for the abolition of many traditional institutions
   - (C) believing in the existence of natural laws that govern human behavior
   - (D) calling for the abolition of private property
   - (E) regarding many religious practices as mere superstitions

6. Nineteenth-century anarchists were most active in
   - (A) Britain
   - (B) France
   - (C) Russia
   - (D) Italy
   - (E) Germany

7. Industrial socialism
   - (A) advocated the abolition of private property
   - (B) sought to create a profitable industrial enterprise without exploiting workers
   - (C) called for the creation of *phalansteries*
   - (D) advocated a return to small-scale production by skilled artisans
   - (E) advocated government regulation of working conditions

8. The idea that competition was natural and necessary for social progress was promoted by
   - (A) Karl Marx
   - (B) Charles Darwin
   - (C) Charles Fourier
   - (D) Herbert Spencer
   - (E) Robert Owen

› Answers and Explanations

1. **D.** The conservatives' belief in traditions as time-tested and organic solutions to social and political problems led them to support the traditional privileges of the aristocracy and the clergy. Choice A is incorrect because the position that government should not interfere with the natural tendencies of the economy was a *liberal* position, not a conservative one, in the nineteenth century. Choice B is incorrect because it was the *Romantics* who emphasized the development of sentiment and emotion. Choice C is incorrect because conservatives' belief in the importance of tradition led them to *oppose* constitutionalism. Choice E is incorrect because utilitarianism was espoused by mid-to-late-nineteenth-century *liberals*.

2. **B.** The emphasis on sentiment and emotion by nineteenth-century Romantics can be understood as a reaction against the Enlightenment's emphasis on reason; their glorification of nature can be understood as a reaction to industrialization. Choice A is incorrect because the conservatives' belief in the importance of traditional forms of life often put them in line with, not against, the Romantics. Choice C is incorrect because early-nineteenth-century nationalists *had* Romantic tendencies, as they emphasized the role that environment played in shaping the character of a nation, and often sentimentalized the past. Choices D and E are incorrect because both social Darwinism and scientific socialism developed *after* Romanticism.

3. **C.** Nineteenth-century liberalism *opposed* the traditional privileges of the clergy as an anachronism that stood in the way of individual liberty. The other four answers are true of nineteenth-century liberalism, which believed that the task of government was to promote individual liberty (choice A), and in the existence of natural laws that governed human behavior (choice D). They opposed government intervention in the economy (choice B) because they thought it only got in the way of the operation of those natural laws. Because of their agenda for revoking the traditional privileges of the aristocracy and the clergy, liberals drew their support primarily from the middle classes (choice E) to whom such privileges were denied.

4. **E.** Johann Wolfgang von Goethe's *The Sorrows of Young Werther* (1774) is an example of the German *Sturm und Drang* (Storm and Stress) movement of the late eighteenth century. Its glorification of the "inner experience" of the sensitive individual was a forerunner of nineteenth-century Romanticism. Choice A is incorrect because, although both Goethe's *Sorrows* and anarchism share a romanticized view of preindustrial society, the anarchist movement was dedicated to the eradication of the modern nation state, a theme that is not present in *Sorrows*. Choice B is incorrect because socialists were more concerned with designing a harmonious and equitable society than with the inner life and sentimentality. Choice C is incorrect because the early liberals emphasized the reform of society based on reason, not sentiment and emotion. Choice D is incorrect because, although *Sorrows* emphasized the power of environment to shape the individual, it did not emphasize the shared cultural identity of nations.

5. **A.** The utilitarians' belief that usefulness (i.e., the creation of the greatest good for the greatest number) ought to be the test for all laws and institutions led them to depart from the standard liberal opposition to government intervention in economic matters and to advocate the regulation of working conditions. Choice B is incorrect because utilitarians *joined with* all liberals in calling for the abolition of many traditional institutions on the basis that they inhibited social progress. Similarly, choice C is incorrect because utilitarians *shared* the liberal belief in the existence of natural laws that governed human behavior and assumed that natural laws were causing some laws and institutions to be useful and others to be useless. Choice D is incorrect because *liberals* did not call for the abolition of private property; that was a *communist* position. Choice E is incorrect because the utilitarians were *in line with* other liberals in believing that many specific religious practices were mere superstitions and that society should be

organized in harmony with natural laws based on reason.

6. **C.** Because they believed that the modern nation state and its powerful government institutions were the enemies of individual freedom, anarchists dedicated themselves to carrying out terror campaigns designed to disrupt and, if possible, bring down governments. There was, therefore, a correlation between the repressive nature of government and the activity of anarchists. Because nineteenth-century Russia had the most repressive regime, it had the most active anarchist movement.

7. **B.** Industrial socialists like Robert Owen sought to create manufacturing communities that paid *higher wages* and provided a *good quality of life* for its workers while still making a profit. Choice A is incorrect because the abolition of private property was advocated only by *communists*, not by socialists. Choice C is incorrect because the creation of *phalansteries* (which were communities of no more than 1,600 people in which the inhabitants did work that suited them best) was advocated by Charles Fourier, a *psychological* socialist, rather than an *industrial* socialist.

Choice D is incorrect because industrial socialism sought to end the *exploitation* of workers, not the abandonment of industrial modes of *production*. Choice E is incorrect because industrial socialists saw the *factory owner*, not the *government*, as the proper agent of reform.

8. **D.** The idea that competition was natural and necessary for social progress was promoted by social Darwinists, whose leading advocate was Herbert Spencer. Choice A is incorrect because Karl Marx was the founder of communism, which argued against competition because the control of the means of production was the root of class conflict. Choice B is incorrect because Charles Darwin confined his speculations to the role that competition for natural resources played in creating *biological diversity* and remained skeptical about the claims of the so-called social Darwinists. Choice C is incorrect because Charles Fourier was a psychological socialist who believed that human nature was essentially *cooperative*, not competitive. Similarly, choice E is incorrect because Robert Owen was an industrial socialist who sought to build industrial communities where people labored in a spirit of *cooperation*.

CHAPTER 18

Nationalism and Statebuilding, 1848–1900

IN THIS CHAPTER

Summary: In the second half of the nineteenth century, nationalism became a tool of conservative state-builders, and Italy and Germany became unified nation states.

Key Ideas

✪ In the second half of the nineteenth century, the Romantic and conservative tendencies of nationalism came to the fore.

✪ Between 1855 and 1866, Italy was unified by the actions of the conservative statesman Count Camillo Cavour and the Romantic nationalist Giuseppe Garibaldi.

✪ The conservative Prussian aristocrat Otto von Bismarck used diplomacy and war to unify Germany under the rule of the Hohenzollern dynasty of Prussia.

✪ Nationalism was a key component in the destruction of the anachronistic Austrian-dominated Hapsburg Empire.

Key Terms

Carbonari	Junkers	Austro-Prussian War
Risorgimento	*Realpolitik*	Ems telegram
Crimean War	Schleswig–Holstein	Compromise of 1867
Treaty of Villafranca	Affair	

Introduction

In the second half of the nineteenth century, nationalism triumphed over all the other competing ideologies. In areas where people lived under foreign domination, nationalism was used by conservative statesmen to bring about the unification of Italy and Germany. In the Hapsburg Empire, the nationalist aspirations of ethnic minorities worked to undermine Austrian domination. In France and Russia, the force of nationalism was used to end the remaining dreams of liberals and to strengthen the hold of autocratic rulers.

The End of Liberal Nationalism

In the first half of the nineteenth century, liberals and nationalists tended to ally themselves against the forces of conservatism. Both believed that political sovereignty resided in the *people*, and they shared an optimistic belief that progress towards their goals was inevitable. Campaigns for liberal reform (which attempted to break the conservative aristocracy's grip on political power and to promote individual rights) tended to merge with the struggle for national rights or self-determination. Accordingly, most liberals supported in principle the idea of a free and unified nation state in Germany and Italy, the rebirth of Poland, and Greek independence; most conservatives opposed these ideas.

However, both partial victory and eventual defeat drove a wedge between liberals and nationalists. When liberals won temporary victories over conservative aristocrats between 1830 and 1838, fundamental differences between the agendas of liberal reformers and nationalists began to emerge. The emphasis on individual liberty and limited government did not mesh well with the nationalist emphasis on the collective national tribe or with the desire of nationalists for a strong national government. In short, liberals believed in promoting the rights of *all peoples*; nationalists cared only about their *own rights*.

When, in 1848, the more radical liberal agenda of democratic reform emerged, the conservative tendencies of nationalism came to the fore. Nationalists not only shared the conservatives' belief in the value of historical traditions but also tended to mythologize the past and dream of the return of an era of national glory. Ultimately, however, what drove a wedge between liberals and nationalists was the failure of liberals to hold the power they had temporarily seized. As the conservative reaction in the second half of 1848 smashed liberal movements everywhere in Europe, nationalists dreaming of a strong unified country free from foreign rule increasingly turned to conservative leaders.

The Unification of Italy

The Forces Against Unity in Italy

The settlement after the defeat of Napoleon in 1815 had greatly disappointed those hoping for an Italian nation state. The Italian peninsula consisted of separate states controlled by powerful enemies of Italian nationalism:

- The *Hapsburg Dynasty of Austria* controlled, either directly or through its vassals, Lombardy and Venetia in the north, and the duchies of Tuscany, Parma, and Modena.
- The *pope* governed an area known as the Papal States in central Italy.
- A branch of the *Bourbon dynasty* (which ruled France) controlled the Kingdom of the Two Sicilies in the south.

- An *Italian dynasty, the House of Savoy*, controlled both the Island of Sardinia in the south and Piedmont in the northwest.

In addition to political divisions and foreign interests, the Italian peninsula was also divided by economic and cultural differences:

- The northern areas of the peninsula were well developed economically and more sophisticated culturally than the still largely rural and agricultural areas of the south.
- Culturally, the people of the more developed northern region felt little connection to the poor peasants in the south, who often spoke an entirely different dialect.
- Socially and politically, the middle-class merchants and manufacturers, located mostly in the north, wanted a greater degree of unity for easier trade and tended to support liberal reforms; they were opposed by the staunchly conservative, traditional landed elites.

Italian Nationalism to 1850

Italian nationalism had been forged in opposition to Napoleon's rule. After 1815, dreams of a unified Italy were kept alive in secret societies like the *Carbonari*, secret clubs whose members came mostly from middle-class families and from the army. In 1820, the Carbonari briefly succeeded in organizing an uprising that forced King Ferdinand I of the Kingdom of the Two Sicilies to grant a constitution and a new Parliament. But Austrian troops, with the blessing of the Concert of Europe, crushed the revolt. The Austrians put down a similar revolt by Carbonari in Piedmont in 1831–1832.

In the 1840s, Giuseppe Mazzini's Young Italy had carried the banner of Italian nationalism. Both a Romantic and a liberal, Mazzini fought for the establishment of an Italian republic that would serve, as he believed ancient Rome had, as a beacon for the rest of humanity. By midcentury, Mazzini had forged a movement known as the *Risorgimento*, which was composed mostly of intellectuals and university students who shared his idealism. From 1834 to 1848, the *Risorgimento* attempted a series of popular insurrections, briefly establishing a Roman Republic in 1848 until it was crushed (like its liberal counterparts throughout Europe) by the forces of reaction. In defeat, it was evident that the *Risorgimento* had failed to win the support of the masses.

Cavour and Victory over Austria

At midcentury, a new leader of Italian nationalist hopes emerged in the person of Count Camillo Benso di Cavour, the chief minister of King Victor Emmanuel II of the Kingdom of Piedmont-Sardinia. Cavour differed from Mazzini and other previous leaders of the Italian nationalist movement in several significant ways:

- Cavour was a *conservative aristocrat* with ties to the most powerful Italian ruler on the peninsula, rather than a *middle-class intellectual*.
- Cavour advocated a *constitutional monarchy* under Victor Emmanuel II, rather than a republic.
- Cavour was a cautious and *practical* statesman, rather than an *idealist*.

Cavour's strategy was that of an opportunist: he sought to increase the amount of territory under the control of Piedmont whenever possible and to weaken the opponents of Italian unification by playing them against each other. Between 1855 and 1860, Cavour took advantage of several such opportunities and managed to unite all of northern Italy under Piedmont:

- In 1855, Cavour brought Piedmont and its army into the *Crimean War* on the side of England and France, who were fighting Russia. This resulted in no immediate gains, but the peace conference afforded Cavour an opportunity to denounce Austrian occupation of Italian lands.

- In 1858, Cavour reached a secret agreement with Napoleon III of France gaining a promise of French support should Austria attack Piedmont.
- In 1859, Cavour goaded the Austrians into attacking Piedmont by mobilizing forces and refusing an ultimatum to disarm. French and Piedmontese troops defeated the Austrians at the battles of Magenta and Solferino, driving the Austrians out of Lombardy. Further gains by Piedmont were thwarted by Napoleon III's abrupt signing of the *Treaty of Villafranca* with the Austrians.
- By 1860, inspired by the Piedmontese victory over Austria, the majority of the northern and north-central duchies shook off their Austrian rulers and voluntarily united with Piedmont.

Garibaldi and Victory in the South

The success of northern Italians in throwing off Austrian domination inspired their southern counterparts. A series of peasant revolts, tinged with anti-Bourbon sentiment, arose in the south.

Southern Italian nationalists found a different kind of leader in Giuseppe Garibaldi and, in 1860, launched a series of popular uprisings that put all of southern Italy under his control. The southern nationalist movement differed from its northern counterpart in several significant ways:

- Garibaldi was a Romantic nationalist who had been an early supporter of Mazzini.
- The southern movement was a genuine revolt of the masses rather than the political maneuverings of a single kingdom.
- Garibaldi hoped to establish an Italian republic that would respect the rights of individuals and improve the lot of the peasants and workers.

In May of 1860, Garibaldi raised an army of 1,000 red-shirted Italian patriots and landed in Sicily to aid a peasant revolt underway there. In a few short months, Garibaldi and his red-shirts provided leadership to a nationalist revolt that took control of most of southern Italy and set its sights on Rome.

The Kingdom of Italy and the Completion of Italian Unification

Cavour had publicly condemned Garibaldi's conquests but secretly aided them. When Garibaldi's troops began to threaten Rome, Cavour persuaded Napoleon III, who had sworn to protect the pope, to allow the Piedmontese army to invade the Papal States in order to head off Garibaldi. By September of 1860, Piedmont controlled the Papal States and set up a ring around Rome.

When Piedmontese forces, led by King Victor Emmanuel II himself, met Garibaldi and his forces outside Rome in September of 1860, Garibaldi submitted and presented all of southern Italy to Victor Emmanuel; in the end, Garibaldi's dream of a unified Italy was stronger than his commitment to the idea of a republic. In March of 1861, the Kingdom of Italy was formally proclaimed. It was a constitutional monarchy under Victor Emmanuel II and a parliament elected by limited suffrage. It contained all of the Italian peninsula except the city of Rome (which was still ruled by the pope and protected by French troops) and Venetia (which was still occupied by Austrian troops). The unification of Italy was completed when Venetia came into the Kingdom of Italy during the Austro-Prussian War of 1866, and Rome (with the exception of the Vatican City) followed during the Franco-Prussian War of 1870.

The Unification of Germany

Forces Against Unity in Germany

Unlike Italy, Germany in the middle of the nineteenth century was free of direct foreign domination. It existed as a loose confederation of independent states. Within that loose confederation, several forces worked against national unity:

- cultural differences between the rural, conservative, Protestant north and the urban, liberal, Catholic south
- a long history of proud independence on the part of the individual German states
- the powerful influence of Hapsburg Austria, which controlled or influenced a large portion of the German Confederation

Prussian Leadership

With the failure of the liberal Frankfort Assembly in 1848, leadership in the German nationalist movement passed to Prussia. Prussia was a strong northern kingdom ruled by the Hohenzollern dynasty and supported by a powerful class of landed aristocrats known as *Junkers.* Prussia also had the strongest military in Germany, and led the way in establishing the *Zollverein*, a large free-trade zone. This combination of military and economic power led many Germans to look to Prussia for leadership.

Bismarck and War with Denmark and Austria

In 1861, Prussia's new monarch, William I, wanted to reorganize and further strengthen the military, but the liberal legislature resisted, and a power struggle between the monarch and the legislature ensued. William turned to the conservative Junker Otto von Bismarck to be his prime minister. Bismarck forced a showdown, and it quickly became apparent that the support of the Prussian people was with the king, the army, and Bismarck. With the power of the army and the government fully established, Bismarck set out on a policy to unify Germany under the Prussian crown that has come to be known as *Realpolitik*, which asserted that the aim of Prussia policy would be to increase its power by whatever means and strategies were necessary and useful. Bismarck asserted that the unification of Germany would be accomplished by a combination of "blood and iron."

Bismarck quickly concluded that a war with Austria was inevitable, and he engineered one in an episode that has come to be known as the *Schleswig–Holstein Affair.* He began by enlisting Austria as an ally in a war with Denmark over two duchies, Schleswig and Holstein, that had a large German-speaking population. Once Denmark was forced to cede the two duchies, Bismarck provoked an argument with Austria over control of them. Bismarck's next moves were a perfect illustration of *Realpolitik* in action:

- First, Bismarck obtained Italian support for a war with Austria by promising Italy the province of Venetia.
- Next, he ensured Russian neutrality by supporting Russia's actions against its rebellious Polish subjects.
- Then, he met secretly with Napoleon III of France and persuaded him that a weakening of Austrian power was in the best interests of France.
- Finally, and only after those preparations were in place, he carried out a series of diplomatic and military maneuvers that provoked Austria into declaring war.

In the resulting *Austro-Prussian War* of 1866, Prussian troops surprised and overwhelmed a larger Austrian force, winning victory in only seven weeks. The result was that Austria was expelled from the old German Confederation and a new North German Confederation was created, which was completely under the control of Prussia.

War with France

All that remained was to draw the south German states into the new Confederation. But the south (which was predominantly Catholic and liberal) feared being absorbed by the Protestant and authoritarian Prussians. Bismarck concluded that only one thing would compel the south Germans to accept Prussian leadership: a war with a powerful foreign enemy. So he set about engineering one.

The opportunity came when both France and Prussia got involved in a dispute over the vacant throne in Spain. Bismarck, with the support of the Prussian military leadership, edited a communication between Napoleon III and William I (a communication that is now known as the *Ems telegram*) to make it seem as though they had insulted one another, and Bismarck released this telegram to the press. Tempers flared, and France declared war. The south German states rallied to aid Prussia. Combined German forces quickly routed the French troops, capturing Napoleon III, and taking Paris in January of 1871.

The Second Reich

On January 18, 1871, the unification of Germany was completed. The heads of all the German states gathered in the Hall of Mirrors in the palace of Versailles outside Paris and proclaimed William I Kaiser (emperor) of the German Empire (formally the Second Reich, honoring the old Holy Roman Empire as the first Reich). The new empire took the provinces of Alsace and Lorraine from France and billed the French 5 billion francs as a war indemnity.

Nationalism in the Hapsburg Empire

In an age of nation-building, the Hapsburg Empire, with its Austrian minority dominating an Empire consisting of Hungarians (also known as Magyars), Czechs, Serbs, Romanians, and other ethnic groups, was an anachronism. The forces of nationalism, therefore, worked to tear it apart. After Austria's defeat by Prussia in 1866, the Austrian Emperor Franz Joseph attempted to deal with what has come to be called "the nationalities problem." By agreeing to the *Compromise of 1867*, he set up the dual monarchy of Austria–Hungary, where Franz Joseph served as the ruler of both Austria and Hungary, each of which had its own parliament. This arrangement essentially set up an alliance between the Austrians and the Hungarians against the other ethnic groups in the empire.

Nationalism in France

Louis-Napoleon Bonaparte had originally been elected president of the Second Republic in 1848. When the National Assembly refused to amend the constitution to allow him to run for a second term, he staged a coup d'état on 2 December 1851. The public overwhelmingly sided with Louis-Napoleon, who granted them universal manhood suffrage. They responded, in two plebiscites, by voting to establish a Second Empire and to make Louis-Napoleon hereditary emperor.

Like his namesake, Louis-Napoleon attempted to increase his popularity by expanding the Empire, but soon his foreign adventures began to erode his popularity. By 1870, the liberal parliament had begun to reassert itself. The humiliating defeat in the Franco-Prussian War brought down both Louis-Napoleon and the Second Empire; it also set in motion a battle between monarchists and the people of Paris who, having defended Paris from the Germans while the aristocrats fled, now considered themselves to represent the nation of France.

Nationalism in Russia

At midcentury, Russia's government was the most conservative and autocratic in Europe. The peasants of Russia were still bound to the land by serfdom. The Crimean War (1853–1856), in which Russia essentially battled Britain and France for control of parts of the crumbling Ottoman Empire, damaged the reputation of both the tsar and the military. Alexander II, who ascended to the throne in 1855, was determined to strengthen Russia by reforming and modernizing it. He abolished serfdom, made the judiciary more independent, and created local political assemblies.

However, Russia was plagued by its own nationalities problem. Alexander attempted to deal with it by relaxing restrictions on the Polish population within the Russian Empire, but this fanned the flames of nationalism and led to an attempted Polish Revolution in 1863. Alexander responded with increased repression of Poles and other ethnic minorities within the Russian Empire. And after an attempt on his life in 1866, Alexander gave up all notions of liberal reform, and proceeded to turn Russia into a police state.

❯ Rapid Review

The failure of the revolutions of 1848 broke the fragile alliance between liberalism and nationalism. The unification of northern Italy under Victor Emmanuel II was accomplished through the statesmanship of the conservative Count Camillo Cavour. The Romantic nationalist Giuseppe Garibaldi led a massive popular uprising and took control of southern Italy, then presented it to Victor Emmanuel in the name of Italian unity to create the Kingdom of Italy in 1861. The remaining two areas, Venetia and Rome, came into Italy in 1866 and 1870, respectively.

Germany was unified under William I of Prussia through the machinations of the conservative Prussian statesman Otto von Bismarck. A unified German Empire, called the Second Reich, was proclaimed, following a Prussian victory in the Franco-Prussian War in 1871. The Hapsburg Empire was plagued by a nationalities problem and became Austria–Hungary in 1867. France's defeat led to the fall of the Second Empire, while Alexander II turned Russia into a police state.

› Chapter Review Questions

1. The strongest conservative element in nineteenth-century nationalism was
   - (A) the desire for a republican form of government
   - (B) its emphasis on the concept of natural borders
   - (C) its desire to resist the rule of traditional aristocratic dynasties
   - (D) its belief in the value of historical traditions
   - (E) its belief that political sovereignty rested with the people

2. Cavour was able to unite northern Italy under the Kingdom of Piedmont through a combination of
   - (A) war and diplomacy
   - (B) diplomacy and bribery
   - (C) peasant revolts and military action
   - (D) war and secret dealings with the pope
   - (E) diplomacy and royal marriage

3. Garibaldi's capitulation to King Victor Emmanuel II illustrates
   - (A) the failure of nationalism in Italy
   - (B) the triumph of liberal nationalism
   - (C) the degree to which the nationalist desire for unity had triumphed over the liberal desire for individual rights
   - (D) the power of the Hapsburg dynasty in Italy
   - (E) the power of the Bourbon dynasty in Italy

4. The Schleswig–Holstein Affair is an example of
   - (A) the *Risorgimento*
   - (B) Russian conservatism
   - (C) German liberalism
   - (D) French imperialism
   - (E) *Realpolitik*

5. Which of the following was the factor that brought south Germans into Bismarck's new German Confederation?
   - (A) their Catholicism in the face of war with France
   - (B) their liberalism in the face of war with Austria
   - (C) their nationalism in the face of war with a foreign enemy
   - (D) their desire for a strong, authoritarian central government
   - (E) the existence of a dominant aristocratic class of Junkers in south Germany

6. By agreeing to the Compromise of 1867, the Hapsburg Emperor Franz Joseph was
   - (A) acknowledging the rights of all ethnic groups within the Hapsburg Empire
   - (B) enlisting the Hungarians in an alliance against the other ethnic minorities within the Empire
   - (C) acknowledging Prussian supremacy in the German Confederation
   - (D) ending serfdom in Russia
   - (E) ending the Crimean War

7. In France, the Second Empire was brought to an end by
   - (A) France's defeat in the Franco-Prussian War
   - (B) Louis-Napoleon Bonaparte's coup d'état on 2 December 1851
   - (C) two plebiscites
   - (D) the Crimean War
   - (E) the unification of Italy

8. In Russia, Tsar Alexander II's attempts to liberalize Russia were brought to an end by
   - (A) the abolition of serfdom
   - (B) the Crimean War
   - (C) the unification of Germany
   - (D) the Russian Revolution
   - (E) the Polish Revolution of 1863 and an attempt on his life in 1866

❯ Answers and Explanations

1. **D.** The belief in the value of historical traditions was the strongest conservative element in nationalism, which tended to use a mythologized version of history as a way to create a unified national identity. Choice A is incorrect because nationalism tended to put concerns for the *strength and unity of the nation* ahead of concerns for a particular form of government. Choice B is incorrect because the emphasis on the concept of natural borders was *shared* by liberal and conservative nationalists alike. Choices C and E are incorrect because the desire to resist the rule of traditional aristocratic dynasties like the Hapsburgs and the Bourbons and their belief that political sovereignty rested with the people were *liberal* tendencies of nationalism, not *conservative* elements.

2. **A.** Cavour's successful strategy for uniting northern Italy under Piedmont worked through a combination of secret diplomatic arrangements with France and successful war with Austria. Choice B is incorrect because the smaller Kingdom of Piedmont was in no position to *bribe* the wealthier French Bourbons and Austrian Hapsburgs. Choice C is incorrect because peasant revolts were important in the unification of *southern* Italy, not northern. Choice D is incorrect because Cavour's secret dealings were with Napoleon III of France, not the pope. Choice E is incorrect because *no* royal marriages were concluded in the unification of northern Italy.

3. **C.** Garibaldi had pledged to establish an Italian republic that protected the rights of all individuals; his willingness to hand over the southern portion of the peninsula to an aristocratic monarch, therefore, illustrates the degree to which the nationalist desire for unity had triumphed over the liberal desire for individual rights. Choice A is incorrect because Garibaldi's willingness to hand the south over to King Victor Emmanuel and Piedmont guaranteed that a unified Kingdom of Italy would come into being and, therefore, illustrates the *triumph* (not the *failure*) of Italian nationalism. Choice B is incorrect because Garibaldi's willingness to forego his dream of a republic illustrates the *death* of liberal nationalism (not the *triumph*). Choice D is incorrect because the fact that the fate of Italy was being decided by two Italians demonstrates the degree to which Austrian Hapsburg's power in Italy had *declined*. Choice E is similarly incorrect because the meeting between Garibaldi and Victor Emmanuel II illustrates the *limited* ability of the French Bourbon dynasty to dictate events in Italy.

4. **E.** Bismarck's use of the Schleswig–Holstein Affair to manufacture a war with Austria is an example of his policy of *Realpolitik*, which increased Prussian territory and power by any means available. Choice A is incorrect because the *Risorgimento* refers to the mid-nineteenth-century Italian nationalist movement. Choice B is incorrect because *Russia* was only tangentially involved in the Schleswig–Holstein Affair. Choice C is incorrect because Bismarck's disregard for the rights of individuals and groups of people is the *antithesis* of liberalism. Choice D is incorrect because France had only a *minor* role in the Schleswig–Holstein Affair and did not stand to increase the size of its empire as a result.

5. **C.** Bismarck used the strong nationalist feelings of south Germans who were aroused by war with France to convince them to join his new Confederation and accept Prussian dominance. Choices A and B are incorrect because both the Catholicism and the liberalism of south Germans caused them to *fear* being dominated by the Protestant and conservative Prussians. Choice D is incorrect because the liberal south Germans had *no* desire for the strong, authoritarian central government favored by Prussians. Choice E is incorrect because the Junkers were the dominant aristocratic class in *Prussia*, not south Germany.

6. **B.** The Compromise of 1867 set up the dual monarchy of Austria–Hungary with two parliaments, each under Emperor Franz Joseph; it was done as a concession to the Hungarians in order to enlist them in an alliance against the other ethnic groups in the Empire. Choice A is incorrect because the Compromise did nothing for *any*

ethnic group other than the Hungarians. Choice C is incorrect because the Compromise did *not* acknowledge Prussian supremacy in the Confederation: The Austrians had been expelled from the Federation by the victorious Prussians following the Austro-Prussian war of 1866. Choice D is incorrect because the compromise did *not* concern Russia; serfdom in Russia was ended by Royal decree. Choice E is incorrect because the Compromise had *nothing* to do with the Crimean War, which ended in 1856.

7. **A.** The Second Empire was brought to an end by France's defeat in the Franco-Prussian War; Napoleon III was captured and the victorious Germans proclaimed the Second Empire to be dissolved. Choices B and C are incorrect because it was the Second French *Republic* (not the Second Empire) that was brought to an end by a combination of Napoleon Bonaparte's coup d'état on 2 December 1851 and two plebiscites that declared France to be an Empire and Napoleon III to be its hereditary emperor. Choice D is incorrect because, although France's involvement in the Crimean War hurt Napoleon III's popularity, it did *not* jeopardize the Second Empire. Choice E is incorrect because the unification of Italy had *no* direct bearing on the fall of the Second Empire in France.

8. **E.** Alexander II's attempts to liberalize Russia were brought to an end by the combination of the Polish Revolution of 1863 (which was sparked by his granting Polish subjects more autonomy) and an attempt on his life in 1866 (which spurred him to crack down on his enemies and to build a police state). Choice A is incorrect because the abolition of serfdom was *part* of his attempts to liberalize Russia. Similarly, choice B is incorrect because the poor performance of the Russian military in the Crimean War was *part* of his motivation for modernizing and liberalizing Russia. Choice C is incorrect because Alexander II's liberal phase was over *before* German unification in 1871. Similarly, choice D is incorrect because Alexander II's liberal phase was over *before* the Russian Revolution, which did not occur until 1917.

CHAPTER 19

Mass Politics in Europe and Imperialism in Africa and Asia, 1860–1914

IN THIS CHAPTER

Summary: Between 1860 and 1914, the development of mass politics helped to fuel an expansion of European influence and dominance across the globe that came to be called the New Imperialism.

Key Ideas

✪ The New Imperialism of the last decades of the nineteenth century was characterized by a shift to active conquest and direct political control of foreign lands by the European powers.

✪ The phrase "mass politics" refers to the participation of increasingly larger portions of the population in the political process in European nations in the second half of the nineteenth century.

✪ The British seizure of the Suez Canal in Egypt and Belgium's aggressive expansion into the Congo set off a "scramble for Africa."

✪ European imperialism in Asia was exerted through the control of local elites rather than by direct conquest.

Key Terms

Chartism	Midlothian Campaign	*Kulturkampf*
Reform Bill of 1867	Paris Commune	Russianization
Reform Bill of 1884	Boulanger Affair	Suez Canal

Berlin Conference of 1885	Opium War	Boxer Rebellion
Sepoy Rebellion of 1857	Treaty of Nanking	Meiji Restoration
Indian National Congress	Taiping Rebellion	Russo-Japanese War

Introduction

In the last decades of the nineteenth century, the European powers shifted from indirect commercial influence to active conquest and the establishment of direct political control of foreign lands around the globe, particularly in Africa and Asia. This imperial expansion of European influence and control is known as the New Imperialism.

Causes of the New Imperialism

The causes of the New Imperialism are a matter of debate among historians, but all explanations contain the following elements to some degree:

- the need for *new raw materials* in the expanding industrial economy of Europe
- the need for *new markets* to sell European manufactured goods and to invest newly created capital
- the *technological innovations in weaponry and transportation* that encouraged European military adventurism
- the *rampant nationalism* of the nineteenth century that unified European nations and gave them a sense of historical destiny
- the traditional identity of the European political elites who competed for *fame and glory through conquest*
- the need for competing European political elites to win the *support of the newly politicized and enfranchised masses*

The Development of Mass Politics

Mass politics was the participation, in increasingly aggressive yet unstable ways, of the masses in the governing of European nations. The development of mass politics took different forms in different nations, as described in the following sections.

Mass Politics in Great Britain

In 1860, Britain had already experienced mass politics. The threat of violence from the masses had provided the pressure that enabled the Liberals to force through the Great Reform Bill of 1832, enfranchising most of the adult, male middle class. But in the decades that followed, the Liberals seemed satisfied with limited reform. The rise of *Chartism* (1837–1842) demonstrated the degree to which the lower-middle and working classes desired further reform. Chartists organized massive demonstrations in favor of the People's Charter, a petition that called for:

- universal manhood suffrage
- annual Parliaments
- voting by secret ballot
- equal electoral districts
- abolition of property qualifications for Members of Parliament
- payment of Members of Parliament

If enacted into law, the People's Charter would have had the effect of creating a completely democratic House of Commons, but Parliament rejected the Charter on numerous occasions.

In 1867, the new leader of the Conservative (or Tory) Party, Benjamin Disraeli, convinced his party that further reform was inevitable, and engineered the passage of the *Reform Bill of 1867*. The bill doubled the number of people eligible to vote and extended the vote to the lower middle class for the first time. Additionally, the Conservatives passed a number of laws regulating working hours and conditions, and the sanitary conditions of working-class housing.

In 1884, the Liberals under William Gladstone again took the lead, engineering the passage of the *Reform Bill of 1884*. This bill included the following reforms:

- It extended the right to vote further down the social ladder, thereby enfranchising two-thirds of all adult males.
- It made primary education available to all.
- It made military and civil service more democratic.

The result of this move towards mass politics was competition between the Liberals and Conservatives for the newly created votes. In 1879, Gladstone embarked on the first modern political campaign, which came to be known as the *Midlothian Campaign*, riding the railway to small towns throughout his district to give speeches and win votes. Disraeli and the Conservatives countered with a three-pronged platform of "Church, Monarchy, and Empire."

Mass Politics in France

Napoleon III had granted his subjects universal manhood suffrage, but the masses did not often recognize the results of democratic elections in the period between 1870 and 1914. France's defeat in the Franco-Prussian war brought an end to Napoleon III's Second Empire. When subsequent elections resulted in a victory for the monarchists, the people of Paris refused to accept the results and set up their own democratic government that came to be known as the *Paris Commune*. The Commune ruled the city of Paris in February and March of 1871, before being crushed by the French Army.

Monarchists initially controlled the government of the new Third Republic, but they remained divided between factions. By the end of the 1870s, France was governed by a liberal government elected by universal manhood suffrage. However, in the late 1880s, conservative nationalists supported an attempted coup by General George Boulanger. The attempt—which has come to be known as the *Boulanger Affair*—failed, but it underscored the fragility of French democracy and the volatility of mass politics in France.

Mass Politics in Germany

In the newly united Germany, the constitution of the Second Reich called for universal manhood suffrage. But the masses supported the Kaiser and his Chancellor, Otto von Bismarck. In the 1870s, Bismarck appealed to the masses' strong sense of nationalism in an attack on the nation's Catholics. In what has come to be called the *Kulturkampf* (or war for civilization), Bismarck passed a number of laws restricting the religious freedom of Catholics in Germany. The ultimate result, however, was to revive and strengthen the Catholic political party, known as the Roman Catholic Center Party.

In 1878, Bismarck conceded defeat and repealed much of the anti-Catholic legislation in order to garner Catholic support for his war against socialist parties in Germany. When he was unable to stamp out the socialist parties, he tried to undermine their working-class political base by passing, between 1883 and 1889, a comprehensive system of social insurance. Ultimately, however, the socialist parties remained strong and the aging Bismarck was dismissed by the new monarch, Kaiser William II, in 1890.

Mass Politics in Austria–Hungary

In the dual monarchy of Austria–Hungary, mass politics continued to mean the competition between nationalities for greater autonomy and relative supremacy within the empire. The introduction of universal manhood suffrage in 1907 made Austria–Hungary so difficult to govern that the emperor and his advisors began bypassing the parliament and ruling by decree.

Mass Politics in Russia

In the autocratic police state built by Alexander II of Russia, mass politics took the form of terrorism. Radical groups like The People's Will carried out systematic acts of violent opposition, including the assassination of Alexander II with a bomb in 1881. His successor, Alexander III, countered by waging war on liberalism and democracy. Initiating a program of *Russianization*, he attempted to standardize language and religion throughout the Russian Empire.

The Scramble for Africa

Two developments spurred an unprecedented "scramble" on the part of the European powers to lay claim to vast areas of the African continent: the British takeover of the Suez Canal in Egypt and Belgium's aggressive expansion into the Congo.

The *Suez Canal*, connecting the Mediterranean Sea through Egypt to the Red Sea and the Indian Ocean, was built by a French company and opened in 1869. In 1875, Great Britain took advantage of the Egyptian ruler's financial distress and purchased a controlling interest in the canal. By the early 1880s, anti-British and French sentiment was building in the Egyptian army. In the summer of 1882, the British launched a preemptive strike, landing troops in Egypt, defeating Egyptian forces, and setting up a virtual occupation of Egypt. Supposedly temporary, the occupation lasted 32 years. Britain's control of Egypt led to further European expansion in Africa in two ways:

- In order to provide greater security for Egypt, Britain expanded further south.
- In return for France's acceptance of British occupation of Egypt, Britain supported French expansion into northwest Africa.

A new competition for imperial control of sub-Saharan Africa was initiated by the expansion of Belgian interests in the Congo. In 1876, King Leopold II of Belgium formed a private company and sent the explorer Henry Stanley to the Congo River Basin to establish trading outposts and sign treaties with local chiefs. Alarmed by the rate at which the Belgians were claiming land in central Africa, the French expanded their claims in western Africa and Bismarck responded with a flurry of claims for Germany in eastern Africa. This sudden burst of activity led to the *Berlin Conference of 1885*. There, representatives of the European powers established free-trade zones in the Congo River Basin and set up guidelines for the partitioning of Africa. The guidelines essentially set up two principles:

- A European nation needed to establish enough physical presence to control and develop a territory before it could claim it.
- Claimants must treat the African population humanely.

After the conference, European nations completed the scramble for Africa until nearly the entire continent was, nominally at least, under European control. Unfortunately, the principle of humane treatment of Africans was rarely followed.

Dominance in Asia

In the era of the New Imperialism, European powers also exerted control over Asia. Here, however, the general method was to rule through local elites.

India: Ruled by Great Britain

In India, the British dominated, initially through the British East India Company, a private trading company that used its economic and military power to influence local politics. Following the *Sepoy Rebellion of 1857* (sometimes known as the Sepoy Mutiny), an organized, anti-British uprising led by military units of Indians who formerly served the British, the British government took direct control and restructured the Indian economy to produce and consume products that aided the British economy.

A sense of Indian nationalism began to develop as a response to the more intrusive British influence, resulting in the establishment of the *Indian National Congress* in 1885. The Congress, though really an organization of Hindu elites, promoted the notion of a free and independent India.

Southeast Asia: Dominated by France

In Southeast Asia, the French emulated the British strategy of ruling through local elites and fostering economic dependence. During the 1880s and early 1890s, France established the Union of Indochina, effectively dominating in the areas that would become Vietnam, Laos, and Cambodia.

China: Increasing European Control

China had been infiltrated by British traders in the 1830s. The British traded opium grown in India to Chinese dealers in exchange for tea, silk, and other goods that were highly prized in Britain. When the Chinese government attempted to end the trade, Britain waged and won the *Opium War* (1839–1842) and forced the Chinese to sign the *Treaty of Nanking*. The treaty ceded Hong Kong to Britain, established several tariff-free zones for foreign trade, and exempted foreigners from Chinese law.

The humiliation of the Manchu rulers and the undermining of the Chinese economy that resulted from foreign interference led to the *Taiping Rebellion* (1850–1864). To maintain control, the Manchus became even more dependent on Western support. Chinese nationalism and resistance to foreign influence again manifested itself in the *Boxer Rebellion* (1899–1900). The combined forces of the European powers were able to suppress the rebellion, but in 1911, a revolution led by Sun Yat-sen succeeded in overthrowing the Manchu dynasty and proclaimed a Chinese republic.

Japan: Westernization

Japan had been forcibly opened to Western trade by an American fleet commanded by Commodore Matthew J. Perry in 1853. The Japanese government signed a number of treaties granting the Western powers effective control of foreign trade. The result was civil war and revolution which culminated in the *Meiji Restoration*, in which modernizers, determined to preserve Japanese independence, restored power to the emperor and reorganized Japanese society along Western lines. By 1900, Japan was an industrial and military power. In 1904, they quarreled with Russia over influence in China and stunned the world with their victory in the *Russo-Japanese War*.

❭ Rapid Review

The New Imperialism was the result of a complex set of impulses that included economic needs created by industrialization; the traditional desire of European nations to compete with one another; and the need for those political elites to find ways to win the support of a new political force, the masses. Mass politics, the participation of increasingly larger portions of the population in the political process, developed unevenly in Europe, with Britain leading the way and Russia resisting the trend. The New Imperialism resulted in the scramble for Africa, in which the European powers laid claim to the entire continent in the last two decades of the nineteenth century. In Asia, the New Imperialism took the form of indirect European control exerted through local elites.

› Chapter Review Questions

1. Which of the following was NOT a possible cause of the New Imperialism?
   (A) the need for new markets to sell European manufactured goods and to invest newly created capital
   (B) the rampant nationalism of the nineteenth century that unified European nations and gave them a sense of historical destiny
   (C) the ability of European political elites to act without worrying about public opinion
   (D) the technological innovations in weaponry and transportation that encouraged European military adventurism
   (E) the need for competing European political elites to win the support of the newly politicized and enfranchised masses

2. In Britain, the call for a completely democratic House of Commons was put forward in
   (A) the Great Reform Bill of 1832
   (B) the Reform Bill of 1867
   (C) the Reform Bill of 1884
   (D) the People's Charter
   (E) the Midlothian Campaign

3. The nation in which the development of mass politics was vigorously resisted by political elites was
   (A) Britain
   (B) Russia
   (C) Austria–Hungary
   (D) France
   (E) Germany

4. The term *Kulturkampf* describes
   (A) Gladstone's political campaign of 1879
   (B) the attempt by a French general to overthrow the Third Republic of France
   (C) Bismarck's campaign against Catholicism in Germany
   (D) the restoration of the Japanese Emperor and modernization of Japan
   (E) the war between France and Prussia in 1871

5. The Suez Canal is significant in the history of the New Imperialism because
   (A) it connected the Mediterranean Sea through Egypt to the Red Sea and the Indian Ocean, making control of it vital to European trade
   (B) the need to control it led the British to occupy Egypt in the summer of 1882
   (C) the need to protect British interests in it led Britain to expand its African holdings south from Egypt
   (D) the need for French acceptance of their control of the canal in Egypt led Britain to support French expansion in northwest Africa
   (E) all of the above

6. The most direct cause of the Berlin Conference of 1885 was
   (A) the unification of Germany following the Franco-Prussian War
   (B) the occupation of Egypt by British troops
   (C) the setting up of criteria for European claims on African territory
   (D) the establishment of the principle that European powers claiming African territory must treat the African population humanely
   (E) the rapid expansion of Belgian interests in the Congo

7. The long-term result of Western imperialism in China was
   (A) the fall of the Manchu dynasty
   (B) the Opium War
   (C) the Treaty of Nanking
   (D) the Taiping Rebellion
   (E) the Boxer Rebellion

8. The event which caused the British government to take direct control of India was
   (A) the Indian National Congress
   (B) the Sepoy Rebellion
   (C) the Berlin Conference of 1885
   (D) the passage of the Reform Bill of 1884
   (E) the Boxer Rebellion

❯ Answers and Explanations

1. **C.** The New Imperialism occurred simultaneously with the full flowering of mass politics in Europe; public opinion, therefore, was of *great concern* to political elites in Europe and a possible cause of the New Imperialism. Choice A is incorrect because industrialization did create a need for new markets to sell European manufactured goods and to invest newly created capital and was, therefore, a possible cause of the New Imperialism. Choice B is incorrect because the rampant nationalism of the nineteenth century that unified European nations and gave them a sense of historical destiny seemed to justify and require imperial expansion. Choice D is incorrect because the technological innovations in weaponry and transportation made the New Imperialism seem almost inevitable. Choice E is incorrect because the New Imperialism was one way in which European political elites appealed to the newly enfranchised masses for support.

2. **D.** The creation of a completely democratic House of Commons required Members of Parliament to be chosen from an open field by universal suffrage. Only the People's Charter came close to making those demands (and even it lacked a provision for women's suffrage). Choice A is incorrect because the Great Reform Bill of 1832 extended voting rights only to the adult, male middle class. Choice B is incorrect because the Reform Bill of 1867 extended the vote to the lower middle class but still excluded the working class. Choice C is incorrect because the Reform Bill of 1884 enfranchised only two-thirds of the adult male population. Choice E is incorrect because the Midlothian Campaign, the first modern political campaign, contained no call for reforms that would have democratized the House of Commons.

3. **B.** In Russia, Alexander II resisted calls for liberalization and democratization by constructing a police state. In response, proponents of mass politics turned to terrorism, assassinating Alexander II in 1881. His successor, Alexander III, intensified royal opposition to reform through a policy of Russianization. Choice A is incorrect because Britain *led the way* with reforms that introduced mass politics in the Reform Bills of 1832, 1867, and 1884. Choice C is incorrect because the Hapsburg emperor made *numerous* reforms culminating in the introduction of universal manhood suffrage in 1907. Choices D and E are incorrect because both France and Germany had *mixed* records with regards to mass politics. In France, Napoleon III supported it while conservative elites resisted it. In Germany, Bismarck ushered in reforms when doing so coincided with his ultimate goals of consolidating power in the Prussian monarchy.

4. **C.** The *Kulturkampf*, or war for civilization, is a term that describes Bismarck's largely unsuccessful attempt to curtail the influence and rights of Catholics in Germany in the 1870s. Choice A is incorrect because Gladstone's political campaign of 1879 is known as the Midlothian Campaign, for the region in which it was conducted. Choice B is incorrect because the attempt by the French General George Boulanger to overthrow the Third Republic in the late 1880s is known as the Boulanger Affair. Choice D is incorrect because the restoration of the Japanese Emperor and the modernization of Japan in response to Western intervention is known as the Meiji Restoration. Choice E is incorrect because the war between France and Prussia in 1871 is known as the Franco-Prussian War.

5. **E.** All of the choices are correct. The connection between the Mediterranean Sea through Egypt to the Red Sea and the Indian Ocean was vital to European trade with the East because of the time saved. Without access to the canal, goods either had to be hauled overland or shipped around Africa. Anti-Western sentiment growing in the Egyptian military in the summer of 1882 caused the British to fear a loss of access to the Canal and prompted them to stage a military occupation of Egypt. Subsequently, concerns about the security of Egypt and the Canal led the British to expand southward into the Sudan. In order to gain French acceptance of the British occupation of Egypt, the British supported the expansion of French interests in northwest Africa.

6. **E.** It was the fear of being shut out of African territories engendered by the surprisingly rapid expansion of Belgian interests in the Congo that caused the European powers to call the Berlin Conference of 1885. Choice A is incorrect because the Franco-Prussian war was concluded in 1871 and neither it nor the unification of Germany was a direct cause of the Berlin Conference of 1885. Choice B is incorrect because the British occupation of Egypt occurred in the summer of 1882, long before the Berlin Conference of 1885. Choices C and D are incorrect because the establishment of criteria for European claims to African territory and the principle of humane treatment for the African population were *goals and results* of the Berlin Conference of 1885, not causes.

7. **A.** The long-term result of Western imperialism in China was the fall of the Manchu dynasty; its inability to resist Western intrusion and influence undermined its authority until it was finally overthrown in 1911 by a rebellion led by Sun Yat-sen. Choice B is incorrect because the Opium War of 1839–1842 was not a long-term *result* of Western imperialism in China; instead, it *initiated* a new wave of Western imperialism in China. Choice C is incorrect because the Treaty of Nanking, which ceded Hong Kong to Britain, established several tariff-free zones for foreign trade, and exempted foreigners from Chinese law, was not the long-term result of Western imperialism in China, but rather a *factor that contributed* to the fall of the Manchu Dynasty. Choices D and E are incorrect because both were failed rebellions which *contributed to* the long-term result, the fall of the Manchu Dynasty.

8. **B.** The Sepoy Rebellion of 1857, a violent uprising of Indian soldiers formerly in the service of the British, caused the British government to abolish the East India Company and to take direct control of India and to restructure the Indian economy. Choice A is incorrect because the development of a sense of Indian nationalism and the resulting formation of the Indian National Congress were *results* of the more intrusive, direct control of India by the British government, not its cause. Choice C is incorrect because the Berlin Conference of 1885 was the result of Belgian expansion in Africa and was unrelated to events in India. Choice D is incorrect because the Reform Bill of 1884 was concerned with domestic voting rights in Britain, not British policy in India. Choice E is incorrect because the Boxer Rebellion was a *Chinese* nationalist response to foreign influence and was not related to events in India.

CHAPTER 20

Politics of the Extreme and World War I, 1870–1918

IN THIS CHAPTER

Summary: In the first two decades of the twentieth century, the great powers of Europe divided themselves into two armed camps and fought what came to be known as World War I, a war of attrition that transformed Europe forever.

Key Ideas

✪ At the end of the nineteenth and beginning of the twentieth centuries, the dissatisfaction of many with the pace and nature of liberal reform generated a politics of the extreme at both ends of the political spectrum.

✪ The great powers of Europe were dragged into World War I by a combination of the discontent of nationalist groups within Austria–Hungary, the creation of an alliance system that limited diplomatic options, and the aspirations and military plans of Germany.

✪ Both sides expected a short and glorious war; the reality was nearly five years of a war of attrition which exhausted the resources of the economies of Europe and nearly wiped out an entire generation of men.

✪ In 1917, the strain of the war effort led to the collapse of the oppressive but fragile Romanov dynasty in Russia; it was replaced by a government run by Marxist revolutionaries known as the Bolsheviks.

✪ The victors of World War I imposed a peace settlement that forced Germany to accept full guilt for the war and to pay unprecedented and open-ended war reparations.

Key Terms

National Trade Unions
  Congress
International Working
  Men's Association
Fabian Society
United Socialist Party
Social Democrats
International Congress of
  the Rights of Women
National Union of Women's
  Suffrage Societies
Women's Social and
  Political Union

ultranationalists
anti-Semitism
The Dreyfus Affair
Zionism
World Zionist
  Organization
nationalities problem
Triple Alliance
Triple Entente
Schlieffen Plan
First Battle of Marne
Battle of Tannenberg
Race for the Sea

First Battle of Ypres
Battle of Verdun
Battle of Somme
Bolsheviks
Treaty of Brest-Litovsk
Treaty of Versailles
Peace of Paris
theory of relativity
quantum theory of physics
uncertainty principle
expressionism
abstractionism

Introduction

By the beginning of the twentieth century more people were participating in politics than ever before, but the majority of them were not satisfied with the reforms produced by liberals. For many, the pace of reform was too slow and the nature of reform too limited. For others, the reforms were unsettling and threatened valued traditions. As a result, an antiliberal sentiment formed that led to political activism of a more extreme nature on both the left and the right.

Politics of the Extreme

Labor Unions: In Great Britain, then Spread to Other Countries

Europe's working-class population fell into the category that believed that liberal reform was too slow and too limited and turned instead to labor unions and socialist parties. In Great Britain, working men formed the *National Trade Unions Congress*, an organization that joined all the labor unions of the country together for political action, and supported the newly formed Labour Party, a political party that ran working-class candidates in British elections. The working classes of other European countries followed Britain's lead, forming unions and supporting socialist parties.

Socialist Parties: In Britain, France, and Germany

As Europe's labor movement turned political, it turned to socialists like Karl Marx for leadership. In 1864, Marx helped union organizers found the *International Working Men's Association*, often referred to as the First International. The loose coalition of unions and political parties fell apart in the 1870s, but was replaced by the Second International in 1889.

While Marx and his communist associates argued for the inevitability of a violent revolution, the character and strength of socialist organizations varied from country to country. In Britain, the socialist organization known as the *Fabian Society* counseled against revolution but argued that the cause of the working classes could be furthered through political solutions. Their ultimate goal was a society in which the parts of the economy that were crucial to people's survival and comfort, such as heat and water, should be owned by the state and regulated by experts employed by the government. In France, socialist parties banded together to join the *United Socialist Party* under the leadership of Jean Jaurès. The fortunes of the United Socialist Party in elections improved steadily in the first years of the twentieth century and by 1914 they were a major power in French politics.

In Germany the *Social Democrats*, led by August Bebel, were the most successful socialist party in Europe. The Social Democrats espoused the "revisionist socialism" of Eduard Bernstein, who urged socialist parties to cooperate with bourgeois liberals in order to earn immediate gains for the working class. By 1914, the Social Democrats were the largest political party in Germany.

Women's Suffrage Movements and Feminism

Always left out of liberal reforms and sometimes excluded from labor unions, women of the late nineteenth and early twentieth centuries formed political movements of their own. Feminist groups campaigning for women's rights united in 1878 to convene in Paris for the *International Congress of the Rights of Women*.

In Britain, the movement focused mostly on the issue of women's suffrage, or voting rights. The movement went through three distinct phases:

- a *pioneering phase* from 1866 to 1870, when suffrage agitation focused on the Reform Act of 1867 and won a number of successes at the level of local government through petitioning and pamphleteering
- a *period of relative dormancy* from 1870 to 1905
- a *period of militancy* from 1905 to 1914, when the *National Union of Women's Suffrage Societies* headed by Millicent Garrett Fawcett campaigned vigorously for women's voting rights, and the *Women's Social and Political Union* led by Emmeline Pankhurst and her daughters Christabel and Sylvia campaigned, often violently, for a broader notion of women's rights

On the Continent, feminists such as Louise Michel in France and Clara Zetkin in Germany folded their movements into the broader cause of worker's rights and politically supported socialist parties.

Anarchist Activity

People under the more oppressive regimes, where even liberal reform was resisted, turned to anarchism. Theoreticians like Mikhail Bakunin and Pyotr Kropotkin urged the elimination of any form of state authority that oppressed human freedom, and ordinary people enacted the doctrine, first through the method of the "general strike" (massive work stoppages designed to bring the economy to a halt) and later and more often through assassination attempts on the lives of government officials. Successful assassinations in the first years of the twentieth century included King Umberto I of Italy and President William McKinley of the United States.

Ultranationalists and Anti-Semites

The international quality of the socialist movement was in direct opposition to the ideology of nationalism that had dominated the second half of the nineteenth century. At the end of the nineteenth and beginning of the twentieth centuries, a harder, more extreme version of nationalism came into being. *Ultranationalists* argued that political theories and parties that put class solidarity ahead of loyalty to a nation threatened the very fabric of civilization, and they vowed to fight them to the death.

Nineteenth-century nationalism had always had a racial component, and ultranationalism quickly merged with the age-old European suspicion of Jews, known as *anti-Semitism*. The most notorious example of ultranationalist/anti-Semitic political power was the *Dreyfus Affair*. In 1894, a group of bigoted French Army officers falsely accused Alfred Dreyfus, a young Jewish captain, of treason. Dreyfus was convicted and sent to Devil's Island prison. The evidence was clearly fabricated, and liberals and socialists quickly came to Dreyfus's defense. His numerous trials (he was eventually exonerated) divided the nation, illustrating how strong ultranationalist and anti-Semitic feelings were in the French establishment.

Zionism

In the face of anti-Semitism, a movement for the creation of an independent state for Jews, known as *Zionism*, came into being. In 1896, Theodor Herzl published *The Jewish State*, a pamphlet that urged an international movement to make Palestine the Jewish homeland. A year later, the *World Zionist Organization* was formed, and by 1914 nearly 85,000 Jews, primarily from eastern Europe, had emigrated to Palestine.

Causes of World War I

The causes of World War I are still debated by historians, but all explanations include the following to varying degrees:

- The *nationalities problem*—10 distinct linguistic and ethnic groups lived within the borders of Austria–Hungary, and all were agitating for either greater autonomy or independence.
- The rise of Germany and the Alliance System—after unification in 1871, Bismarck sought security in the *Triple Alliance* (Germany, Austria–Hungary, and Italy); Britain, France, and Russia countered with the *Triple Entente*. The alliance system was supposed to make war between the major powers too costly; instead its assurance of military reprisal limited diplomatic options.
- The Anglo-German rivalry—the unification of Germany and its rise as an industrial and military power generated a heated rivalry with Great Britain.
- The assassination of the Austrian Archduke—the assassination, on 28 June 1914, of the heir to the Hapsburg throne by a young Bosnian patriot brought the nationalities problem to a crisis stage.
- German military planning—Germany was convinced that war with the Triple Entente countries was inevitable. Accordingly, it devised a strategy, known as the *Schlieffen Plan*, for a two-front war that called for a military thrust westward towards Paris at the first sign of Russian mobilization in the east. The hope was to knock the French out of the war before the Russians could effectively mobilize.

Basic Chronology, 1914–1915

- On 23 July 1914, Austria, at Germany's urging, moved to crack down on Serbian nationalism.
- On 28 July 1914, Austria declared war on Serbia. Russia began military mobilization as a show of support for Serbia; that mobilization triggered the Schlieffen Plan.
- On 4 August 1914 the German Army invaded Belgium heading for Paris. In the first 16 months of combat, France suffered roughly half of all its war casualties. Two-thirds of a million men were killed.
- Belgian resistance gave time for British troops to join the battle in late August, but they joined a retreat.

- Russian troops mobilized faster than expected and invaded Eastern Prussia. On 26 August 1914, German Commander Helmuth von Moltke transferred troops from the Western Front to the Eastern. The victory by the Germans at the *Battle of Tannenberg* led to the liberation of East Prussia and began a slow steady German advance eastward, but the timetable of the Schlieffen Plan was altered and the Germans were doomed to fight a two-front war.
- On 6 September 1914, French troops met the Germans at the *First Battle of Marne.*
- October and November 1914 saw a series of local engagements aimed at outflanking the enemy, sometimes known as the *Race for the Sea*, which extended the front line west until it reached the English Channel.
- The British determination to hold onto the entire French Coast stretched the front north through Flanders. In the *First Battle of Ypres* in October and November of 1914, the German advance was halted for good, leading to a stalemate and the beginning of trench warfare.

Total War

When war was declared in 1914 it was met with a joyous enthusiasm all across Europe. Explanations for this reaction include:

- a fascination with militarism that pervaded European culture
- feelings of fraternity or brotherhood that a war effort brought out in people who lived in an increasingly fragmented and divided society
- a sense of Romantic adventurism that cast war as an alternative to the mundane, working life of industrial Europe

Additionally, there were several shared expectations among Europeans as they went to war:

- Recent experience, such as the Franco-Prussian war of 1871, suggested that the war would be brief; most expected it to last about six weeks.
- Each side was confident of victory.
- Each side expected a war of movement, full of cavalry charges and individual heroism.

KEY IDEA

The reality was a war of nearly five years of trench warfare and the conversion of entire economies to the war effort. As both sides literally dug in, soldiers fought from a network of trenches up to 30 feet deep and often flooded with water and infested with rats and lice. Military commanders, who commanded from rear-guard positions, continued to launch offensive attacks, ordering soldiers "over the top" to the mercy of the machine guns that lined enemy trenches.

Total war also meant changes on the home front, some of which would have lasting consequences:

- Governments took direct control of industries vital to the war effort.
- Labor unions worked with businesses and government to relax regulations on working hours and conditions.
- Class lines were blurred as people from all walks of life worked side by side to aid the war effort.
- Women were drawn into the industrial workforce in greater numbers and gained access to jobs that had traditionally been reserved for men.

Basic Chronology, 1916: "The Year of Bloodletting"

In 1916 a war of attrition was fought in trenches in France and Flanders, as each side tried to exhaust the resources of the other.

- In February 1916, French troops led by Marshall Petain repulsed a German offensive at the *Battle of Verdun*; 700,000 men were killed.
- From July to November 1916, the British attempted an offensive that has come to be known as the *Battle of the Somme*; by its end, 400,000 British, 200,000 French, and 500,000 German soldiers lay dead.
- On 6 April 1917, the United States declared war on Germany. Several factors triggered the American entry, including the sinking of American vessels by German U-boats and the Zimmerman Note (a diplomatic correspondence of dubious origin, purporting to reveal a deal between Germany and Mexico).

Russian Revolution and Withdrawal

In March of 1917, food shortages and disgust with the huge loss of life exploded into a revolution that forced the tsar's abdication. The new government, dominated by a coalition of liberal reformers and moderate socialists (sometimes referred to as Mensheviks), opted to continue the war effort.

In November of 1917, a second revolution brought the *Bolsheviks* to power. A party of revolutionary Marxists, led by Vladimir Ilich Ulyanov, who went by the name of Lenin, the Bolsheviks saw the war as a battle between two segments of the bourgeoisie fighting over the power to exploit the proletariat. Accordingly, the Bolsheviks decided to abandon the war and consolidate its revolutionary gains within Russia. They signed the *Treaty of Brest-Litovsk* with Germany in March of 1918, surrendering Poland, the Ukraine, Finland, and the Baltic provinces to Germany.

Shortly after the signing of the treaty, Russia was engulfed by civil war. Anticommunist groups, generally called the Whites in contrast to the communist Reds, were led by members of the old tsarist elite intent upon defending their privileges. Both sides received support from foreign governments and for more than three years, from December 1917 to November 1920, the Bolshevik regime was engaged in a life-and-death struggle which they ultimately won.

Germany's Disintegration and the Peace Settlement

Germany launched one last great offensive in March of 1918 through the Somme towards Paris. The "Allies," as the French, British, and American coalition came to be known, responded by uniting their troops under a single commander, the French General Ferdinand Foch, for the first time. French troops were reinforced by fresh British conscripts and 600,000 American troops. By July 1918, the tide had turned in the Allies' favor for good. German forces retreated slowly along the whole Western Front. In early September, the German high command informed their government that peace had to be made at once. On 9 November 1918, the German Kaiser, Wilhelm II, abdicated and two days later representatives of a new German government agreed to terms that amounted to unconditional surrender.

Peace negotiations began in Paris in January of 1919 and were conducted by the victors; Germany was forced to accept the terms dictated to it. The French delegation was led by

Georges Clemenceau, who desired to make sure that Germany could never threaten France again. The U.S. delegation was led by President Woodrow Wilson, who approached the peace talks with bold plans for helping to build a new Europe that could embrace the notions of individual rights and liberty that he believed characterized the United States. Britain was represented by David Lloyd George, who tried to mediate between the vindictive Clemenceau and the idealistic Wilson.

The result was a series of five treaties that have collectively come to be known as the *Treaty of Versailles*. The overall settlement, sometimes referred to as the *Peace of Paris*, contained much that was unprecedented and much that sowed the seeds of further conflict. Among the more significant aspects of the settlement were the following:

- The Germans were forced to pay $5 billion annually in reparations until 1921, with no guarantee as to the total amount (the final amount was set at $33 billion in 1921).
- New independent nations were set up in eastern Europe as Hungary, Czechoslovakia, and Yugoslavia were created out of the old Austria–Hungary, while Finland, Estonia, Latvia, and Lithuania were created out of the western part of the old Russian Empire.
- Germany, in what came to be known as "the war guilt clause," was forced to accept full blame for the war.
- Germany was stripped of all its overseas colonies.
- Alsace and Lorraine, taken by Germany during the Franco-Prussian War of 1870–1871, were returned to France.
- The Allies were given the right to occupy German territories on the west bank of the Rhine River for 15 years.
- Germany's armed forces were limited to 100,000 soldiers and saddled with armament limitations.

Artistic Movements

The turbulent decades that surrounded and encompassed World War I saw the arts scene fractured into many "isms" and "schisms." The multitude of "isms" that developed in this period can be usefully grouped into two categories: *expressionism* and *abstractionism*.

The expressionists sought to depict a world of emotional and psychological states. Accordingly, they turned away from the rules of realism and naturalism to produce images with distorted outlines and exaggerated color and form. Noteworthy examples of expressionism from this period include *The Scream* (1893) by Edvard Munch and *The Violinist* (1912) by Marc Chagall.

In contrast, the abstractionists sought to "analyze" the essence of perception and experience. Abstract painters of the period developed a system of seeing the world as composed of geometrical shapes. Influential examples of abstract painting from the period include *Woman with a Guitar* (1913) by George Braque and the series of *Compositions* begun by Wassily Kandinsky in 1911.

Changes to the Scientific View of the World

At the beginning of the twentieth century, physicists conceived of experiments and produced mathematical reasoning that challenged the nineteenth-century notion of the scientist as a completely objective observer. Between 1905 and 1915, Albert Einstein articulated a *theory of relativity*, which posited that time and space are experienced differently for observers in dif-

- Britain reacted with what has been called a policy of *appeasement*, agreeing in the *Munich Agreement* of September of 1938 to allow Hitler to take the Sudentenland over Czech objections in exchange for his promise that there would be no further aggression.
- In March 1939, Hitler broke the Munich Agreement by invading Czechoslovakia.
- As Hitler threatened Poland, the hope of Soviet intervention was dashed by the surprise announcement, on 23 August 1939 of a *Nazi–Soviet Non-Aggression Pact*, guaranteeing Soviet neutrality in return for part of Poland.
- On 1 September 1939, Germany invaded Poland.
- On 3 September 1939, both France and Britain declared war on Germany.

In order to understand why Britain followed a policy of appeasement and was slow to recognize the pattern of aggressive expansion in Hitler's actions in 1938 and 1939, one has to take into account the following:

- Britain and its allies, unlike Hitler's Germany, had not begun any kind of military buildup and were in no position to back up any ultimatums they might give to Hitler.
- Unlike the Germans, many of whom thought things could get no worse and were eager to avenge the humiliation of defeat in World War I, the British public hoped that they had fought and won the "war to end all wars," and wanted no part of renewed hostilities.
- Many of the British leaders privately agreed with the Germans that the Versailles Treaty had been unprecedented and unwarranted.
- Given British public opinion, a decision to pursue a military response to Hitler's actions would have been political suicide for British leaders.

The Course of the War

Blitzkrieg and "the Phony War" (1939–1940)

As Germany invaded Poland, Britain and France were not yet in a military position to offer much help. The Poles fought bravely, but were easily overrun by the German *blitzkrieg*, or lightning war, which combined air strikes and the rapid deployment of tanks and highly mobile units. Poland fell to Germany in a month.

Meanwhile, Britain sent divisions to France and the British and French general staffs coordinated strategy. But the strategy was a purely defensive one of awaiting a German assault behind the *Maginot Line*, a vast complex of tank traps, fixed artillery sites, subterranean railways, and living quarters, which paralleled the Franco-German border but failed to protect the border between France and Belgium. Over the winter of 1939 and 1940, war was going on at sea, but on land and in the air there was a virtual stand-still that has come to be termed "the phony war." During the lull, however, the Soviet Union acted on its agreement with Hitler, annexing territories in Poland and eastern Europe, including Estonia, Latvia, and Lithuania, and invading Finland.

The Battles of France and Britain (1940)

In April of 1940, the phony war came to an abrupt end as the German *blitzkrieg* moved into Norway and Denmark to prevent Allied intervention in Scandinavia and to secure Germany's access to vital iron ore supplies, and then into Luxembourg, Belgium, and the Netherlands in preparation for an all-out attack on France.

By early June 1940, the German army was well inside France. The Maginot Line proved useless against the mobility of the German tanks, which skirted the Line by going north through the Ardennes Forest. On 14 June 1940, German troops entered Paris. Two days later the aging General Marshal Pétain, assumed control of France and signed an armistice with Germany according to which the German army, at French expense, occupied the northern half of France, including the entire Atlantic coast, while Pétain himself governed the rest from the city of Vichy. Not all of France was happy with the deal. General Charles de Gaulle escaped to Britain and declared himself head of a free French government. In France, many joined a Free-French movement that provided active resistance to German occupation throughout the remainder of the war.

In Britain, Prime Minister Neville Chamberlain, who had been the architect of Britain's appeasement policy, resigned. King George VI turned to the 65-year-old Winston Churchill, who had been nearly the lone critic of the appeasement policy. Churchill used his oratory skill throughout the war to bolster moral and strengthen the Allies' resolve. The German *blitzkrieg* now drove to the English Channel, trapping the Allied Army at the small seaport of Dunkirk. In an episode that has come to be known as "the Miracle of Dunkirk," more than 338,000 Allied troops (224,000 of them British) surrounded on all sides by advancing German units, were rescued by a motley flotilla of naval vessels, private yachts, trawlers, and motorboats. The episode buoyed British spirits, but Churchill was somber, pointing out that "wars are not won by evacuations."

Hitler, and many neutral observers, expected Britain to seek peace negations, but Churchill stood defiant. The German high command prepared for the invasion of Britain, but the invasion never came. Instead, in one of the most significant moments in the war, Hitler changed his mind and turned on the Soviet Union. Several components make up the explanation for this fateful decision:

- Hitler's racialist view of the world made him wary of the British, whom he considered to be the closest related race to the Germans.
- Hitler's staff was handicapped by both the lack of time given to them and by their relative lack of experience in mounting amphibious operations.
- A successful invasion of England required air superiority over the English Channel; a combination of daring air-fighting by the Royal Air Force and a coordinated effort of civilian defense operations all along the coast foiled German attempts to gain it.

A frustrated Hitler responded by ordering a nightly bombing of London in a two-month attempt to disrupt industrial production and to break the will of the British people. In the end, neither was achieved. In mid-October, Hitler decided to postpone the invasion, and the Battle of Britain had been won by the British.

The War in North Africa and the Balkans (1941–1942)

In 1941, the war became a global conflict as Italian forces invaded North Africa, attempting to push the British out of Egypt. However, British forces routed the Italians; Germany responded by sending troops into North Africa and the Balkans. Germany had two objectives:

- Hitler coveted the Balkans for their rich supply of raw materials, especially Romanian oil.
- He also wanted control of the Suez Canal in Egypt, which was the vital link between Britain and its resource-rich Empire.

The Germans successfully occupied the Balkans, as British efforts to make a last-ditch stand in mainland Greece and on the nearby island of Crete proved in vain. Italian regiments in Libya were reinforced by German divisions under General Erwin Rommel, and the ill-equipped British forces were driven back into Egypt.

German Invasion of the Soviet Union (June–December, 1941)

The Nazi–Soviet Non-Aggression Pact had always been a matter of convenience. Both sides knew that war would eventually come; the question was when. Hitler answered the question late in the spring of 1941, launching Operation Barbarossa and sending three million troops into the Soviet Union. Hitler's decision was influenced by several factors:

- his desire to create an empire that dominated all of Europe
- his racialist view of the world, which told him that the "Slavic" peoples of the Soviet Union were an easier target that his "Teutonic cousins," the British
- his need to feed and fuel his war machine with the wheat of the Ukraine and the oil of the Caucasus
- his hope that, once Germany dominated the continent from the English Channel to the Ural Mountains, even the British would have to come to terms and that no invasion of Britain would be necessary

Germany's eastern army succeeded in conquering those parts of the Soviet Union that produced 60 percent of its coal and steel and almost half of its grain, and by December 1, it was within striking distance of Moscow. But as the Russian winter set in, the Russian Army launched a counterattack against German forces, which were ill-supplied for a winter war. The Russian Army suffered millions of casualties, but turned back the German invasion.

Hitler's decision to attack the Soviet Union had one other great consequence: it forged the first link in what would become the *Grand Alliance* between Britain, the Soviet Union, and the United States, as Churchill (despite being a staunch anticommunist) pledged his support to the USSR. Publicly, he announced that "Any man or state that fights against Nazidom will have our aid." Privately, he remarked that if Hitler invaded Hell it would be desirable to find something friendly to say about the devil. The final link in the Grand Alliance would come through a combination of Churchill's persuasion and a Japanese attack.

The American Entry and Impact (1942)

Churchill and the American president, Franklin Roosevelt, met in August of 1941 on a battleship off the Newfoundland coast. They composed the *Atlantic Charter*, a document setting forth Anglo-American war aims. It rejected any territorial aggrandizement for either Britain or the United States, and it affirmed the right of all peoples to choose their own form of government.

By 1939, a modernized and militarized Japan had conquered the coastal area of China, and its expansionist aims led it to join Germany and Italy in what came to be known as the Axis. When war broke out, Japan occupied the part of Indochina that had been under French control and began to threaten the Dutch East Indies. The United States responded with an economic embargo on all exports to Japan. On 7 December 1941, Japanese air forces launched a surprise attack in Pearl Harbor, Hawaii, hoping to cripple the U.S. naval presence in the Pacific Ocean. The United States immediately declared war on Japan and, within a few days, Germany and Italy had declared war on the United States.

Initially, America's impact on the war was through resources rather than soldiers, but its entry provided the third and final turning point (along with the Battle of Britain and Germany's decision to invade the Soviet Union) in the war. Throughout 1942, American productive capacities were being built up, and the American military force kept growing. In the autumn of 1942, American marines landed on the island of Guadalcanal; it was to be the first of many islands to be recaptured from the Japanese at great cost of human lives.

The Holocaust

In 1941, the embattled Hitler regime embarked on the "Final Solution," the deliberate and methodical extermination of the Jews of Europe. It began when SS troops under Reinhard Heydrich and Heinrich Himmler began executing Jewish and Slavic prisoners, who had been gathered from around Europe and forced into concentration camps. At first, firing squads were used. Next, the process was speeded up through the use of mobile vans of poison gas. Eventually, large gas chambers were constructed at the camps so that thousands could be murdered at one time. In the end, an estimated six million Jews were murdered, along with an additional seven million gypsies, homosexuals, socialists, Jehovah's Witnesses, and other targeted groups.

Outside the Nazi inner circle, people and governments were slow to believe and to comprehend what was happening, and even slower to respond:

- Neighbors turned a blind eye when Jews were rounded up and put on trains.
- Collaborating governments from Vichy France to Croatia assisted in various ways with the rounding up and extermination of the Jews.
- British and American commanders refused to divert bombing missions from other targets in order to put the camps out of commission.

The Axis in Retreat (1942–1943)

In June and August of 1943, the tide turned against the Axis forces in the Soviet Union, the Mediterranean, and the Pacific. In June of 1942, the Germans resumed their offensive in the Soviet Union. By August, they were on the outskirts of Stalingrad on the Volga River. The mammoth Battle of Stalingrad lasted six months; by the time it ended in February of 1943, the greater part of a German Army had died or surrendered to the Russians, and the remainder was retreating westward.

In October 1942, the British Eighth Army under General Bernard Montgomery halted General Rommel's forces at the Battle of El Alamein, seventy miles west of Alexandria Egypt, and began a victorious drive westward. In May of 1943, Germany's Africa Korps surrendered to the Allies. In November 1943, Allied forces under General Dwight Eisenhower's command landed in Morocco and Algeria and began a drive that pushed all Axis forces in Africa into Tunisia. Seven months later, all Axis forces had been expelled from Africa.

Allied victories in Africa enabled them to advance steadily northward from the Mediterranean into Italy and precipitate the overthrow of Mussolini and the signing of an armistice by a new Italian government. Germany responded by treating its former ally as an occupied country. German resistance made the Allied campaign up the Italian peninsula a long and difficulty one.

Allied Victory (1944–1945)

On "D-Day," 6 June 1944, Allied forces under Eisenhower's command launched an audacious amphibious invasion of German-held France on the beaches of Normandy. The grand assault took the form of an armada of 4,000 ships supported by 11,000 airplanes. By the end of July, the Allied forces had broken out of Normandy and encircled the greater part of the German Army.

By late August, Paris was liberated and Hitler's forces were on the retreat. Germany seemed on the point of collapse, but German defensive lines held, and the British people were exposed to a new threat: long-range *V-2 rockets* fired from the German Ruhr rained down on them for seven months. The last gasp of the German Army came in December of 1944 with a sudden drive against thinly held American lines in the Belgian sector. In what has come to be known as the Battle of the Bulge, the Allies checked the German attack and launched a counteroffensive.

In early 1945, Allied troops finally crossed the Rhine River into Germany. In May, they successfully defeated German forces in the Battle of Berlin. On May 1, it was announced that Hitler was dead, and on May 7, the German High Command surrendered unconditionally. In the Pacific, the long and deadly task of retaking the Pacific islands was averted by the dropping of two atomic bombs on Japanese cities: one on Hiroshima on 6 August 1945, and another on the city of Nagasaki on 8 August 1945. Japan surrendered unconditionally on 2 September.

Assessment and Aftermath of World War II

World War II was even more destructive than World War I, and civilian casualties rather than military deaths made up a significant portion of the 50–60 million people who perished in the conflict. Many of Europe's great cities lay in ruins from repeated aerial bombings.

Vast numbers of Europeans were displaced and on the move. Some were trying to get back to homes they had been driven from by the war, while others whose homes had been destroyed simply had no place to go. Russian prisoners of war were compelled, many against their will, to return to the Soviet Union, where they were greeted with hostility and suspicion by Stalin's regime; many were executed or sent to labor camps. Between 12 and 13 million Germans were moving west. Some were fleeing the vengeance of Soviet troops, while others were driven from their homes in the newly reconstituted Czechoslovakia and other eastern European countries, and from parts of East Prussia that were handed over to Poland.

The war also produced a new power structure in the world. The traditional European powers of Britain, France, and Germany were exhausted. Their overseas empires disintegrated rapidly, as they no longer had the resources or the will to keep their imperial holdings against the desires of the local inhabitants. In the years immediately following the war, these countries became independent:

- India gained its independence from Britain.
- Syria and Lebanon broke away from France.
- The Dutch were dismissed from Indonesia.

Finally, it became clear that, in the new world order that emerged from World War II, the United States and the Soviet Union stood alone as great powers.

› Rapid Review

Europe in the 1920s was characterized by a fluctuating economy built on debt and speculation. With the Stock Market Crash of 1929, credit dried up and the Great Depression ensued. The economic problems added to a climate of social and cultural uncertainty and disillusionment. Political parties of the center lost support to socialists on the left and fascists on the right.

In the late 1930s, Adolf Hitler came to power in Germany and embarked on a policy of rearmament and expansion. France and Britain responded initially with a policy of appeasement, but when Hitler invaded Poland in September of 1939, World War II began.

Initial German success in the war was reversed in stages by three crucial turning points:

1. Britain's victory in the Battle of Britain in 1940
2. Hitler's decision to abandon an invasion of Britain and invade the Soviet Union instead
3. the entry of the United States into the war following the Japanese attack on Pearl Harbor on 7 December 1941

Germany surrendered on 7 May 1945, and Japan followed suit on 2 September 1945, following the dropping of two atomic bombs on the cities of Hiroshima and Nagasaki in August. In the end, between 50 and 60 million people lost their lives in World War II, including 6 million Jews who were murdered in the Holocaust, and the traditional powers of Europe, Britain, France, and Germany gave way to the new superpowers: the United States and the Soviet Union.

〉 Chapter Review Questions

1. Europe's post–World War I economy was inherently unstable because
   (A) Germany defaulted on its war reparations
   (B) the New York stock market crashed in 1929
   (C) governments tightened the money supply
   (D) it was built on a combination of U.S. loans and war reparation payments
   (E) governments were cutting expenditures

2. Which of the following was NOT a problem that contributed to the downfall of the Weimar Republic?
   (A) It was perceived to have been imposed by Germany's vengeful war enemies.
   (B) It was composed of a coalition of socialist parties that right-wing groups would never accept.
   (C) It was wrongly blamed for the humiliating nature of the Treaty of Versailles.
   (D) It was a liberal democracy, a form of government largely alien to the German people, whose allegiance had been to the Kaiser.
   (E) It was faced with insurmountable economic problems.

3. Lenin's New Economic Plan
   (A) was the first of a series of five-year plans
   (B) marked the transition to a state-managed economy
   (C) allowed peasants and small business owners to manage their own production and sell their own products
   (D) was a response to the Great Depression
   (E) was a failure

4. The end result of Stalin's purges was
   (A) the destruction of the traditional peasant culture in Russia
   (B) the abandonment of the Marxist vision of international revolution
   (C) the Hitler–Stalin Non-Aggression Pact
   (D) a culture of complete uniformity with the Communist Party vision as articulated by Stalin
   (E) Allied victory in World War II

5. The British economist John Maynard Keynes proposed that governments deal with the Great Depression by
   (A) increasing their expenditures and running temporary deficits
   (B) decreasing their expenditures
   (C) tightening the supply of money
   (D) raising tariffs on imported goods
   (E) going to war

6. Which of the following is an element of fascism?
   (A) a fanatical obedience to a charismatic leader
   (B) a professed belief in the virtues of struggle and youth
   (C) an intense form of nationalism
   (D) an expressed hatred of socialism and liberalism
   (E) all of the above

7. Support for Franco's military coup against the Spanish Republic came from
   (A) Germany
   (B) Italy
   (C) the Spanish monarchy
   (D) the Spanish Church
   (E) all of the above

8. Which of the following was a consequence of World War II?
   (A) the Treaty of Versailles
   (B) the emergence of the United States and the Soviet Union as the only world powers
   (C) the flourishing of democracy in Eastern Europe
   (D) a strengthening of the British Empire
   (E) the German invasion of Poland

› Answers and Explanations

1. **D**. The post–World War I economy was unstable because it was built on money borrowed from U.S. banks and because it counted on war reparation payments, so it was an economy dependent on money being moved around instead of constantly created wealth. Choices A and B are incorrect because Germany's default and the stock market crash brought on the *collapse* of the already unstable economy. Choices C and E are incorrect because both were measures that made the Depression *worse*, not preexisting elements that made the economy unstable.

2. **B**. The government of the Weimar Republic was not a coalition of socialist parties, but rather a coalition of liberal democrats from the center of the political spectrum. Choice A is incorrect because the liberal democratic government of the Weimar Republic was perceived by the German people to have been imposed by vengeful enemies at the Paris Peace Conference. Choice C is incorrect because the government was blamed for the humiliating nature of the Versailles Treaty when, in fact, the negotiators had no leverage with which to bargain or negotiate. Choice D is incorrect because the liberal democratic form of government was a form with which the German people had very little experience, and their loyalty was still with the Kaiser. Choice E is incorrect because the new government of the Weimar republic was faced with an economy that was dependent on U.S. loans and which needed to find a way to pay the huge sums of reparations required of it by the Versailles treaty—an impossible task.

3. **C**. Lenin's New Economic Plan, launched in the early 1920s, was a temporary relaxation of state control of production that successfully stimulated the Russian economy. Choice A is incorrect because the first of the five-year plans was launched by Stalin in 1928. Choice B is incorrect because the NEP was a relaxation of, and not the transition to, a state-managed economy. Choice D is incorrect because the NEP was launched in the early 1920s, well before the Great Depression, which began in 1929. Choice E is incorrect because the NEP was successful in its goal of stimulating the Russian economy.

4. **D**. Stalin's purges of the late 1930s removed all independent thinkers and dissenters from the party system, creating complete uniformity with Stalin's own official Communist Party vision of the world. Choice A is incorrect because the destruction of the traditional peasant culture in Russia was accomplished in the early 1930s through Stalin's program of the collectivization of agriculture, not through the purges of the late 1930s. Choice B is incorrect because the abandonment of the Marxist vision of international revolution was marked by Stalin's policy of "socialism in one country" announced in the autumn of 1924. Choice C is incorrect because the Hitler–Stalin (Nazi–Soviet) Non-Aggression Pact, signed in August of 1939, was concerned with foreign, not domestic, Soviet policy. Choice E is incorrect because the purges concerned the removal of Stalin's internal opposition and occurred before the outbreak of World War II.

5. **A**. Keynes argued that governments should deal with the depressed economy by running temporary deficits to increase their expenditures, thereby pumping money into and stimulating or "jump starting" the stagnant economy. Choices B–D are incorrect because all are traditional measures that governments initially tried, and which only made the Depression worse; Keynes was the lone voice suggesting an opposite approach. Choice E is incorrect because, although going to war did ultimately help to end the Great Depression, it was not a suggestion made by Keynes.

6. **E**. All of the choices are correct. Fascist parties displayed: a fanatical obedience to a charismatic leader (e.g., Hitler in Germany, Mussolini in Italy, and Franco in Spain); a professed belief in the virtues of struggle and youth, as illustrated in the constant reference to struggle and in the organization of youth groups in all fascist countries; an intense form of nationalism as evidenced by the uniforms and constant dialogue about the enemies of "the nation"; and an expressed hatred of socialism and liberalism, as evidenced by their opposition to the existing liberal democratic governments and their constant rhetoric and violence against socialists.

7. **E.** All of the choices are correct. Franco garnered support from Germany and Italy because of their shared fascist ideals, and because the battles of the Spanish Civil War served as a sort of field test for the new German military weapons and tactics. He was supported by the Spanish monarchy and Church, because the socialists had abolished the monarchy and banished the king, and were likely to curtail the role and privileges of the Church in Spanish society.

8. **B.** The war effort exhausted the resources of the traditional European powers, Britain, France, and Germany, and left the United States, with its vast economy, and the Soviet Union, with the largest army in the world, as the two superpowers. Choice A is incorrect because the Treaty of Versailles was the treaty that concluded World War I. Choice C is incorrect because Eastern Europe was dominated after World War II by the Soviet Union; democracy did not flourish. Choice D is incorrect because World War II marked the beginning of the breakup of the British Empire, not a strengthening of it. Choice E is incorrect because the German invasion of Poland was one of the causes of World War II, not a consequence.

CHAPTER 22

The Cold War and Beyond, 1945–Present

IN THIS CHAPTER

Summary: The Cold War waged between the United States and the Soviet Union (1945–1989) was followed by the abrupt disintegration of the Soviet Union and the Iron Curtain.

Key Ideas

✪ At the close of World War II, a division of East and West that was both strategic and ideological hardened into a Cold War between the two superpowers: the Soviet Union and the United States.

✪ In response to the Cold War, the western European nations plotted and maintained a course of economic integration that culminated in the creation of the European Union.

✪ Between 1985 and 1989, systemic economic problems and a bold attempt at reform led to the rapid disintegration of the Soviet Union, the destruction of the Iron Curtain, and the reunification of Germany.

✪ Following the collapse of the Soviet Union, two major trends affected life in Europe: the revival of nationalism and the emergence of globalization.

Key Terms

Manhattan Project	Truman Doctrine	Warsaw Pact
M.A.D.	Marshall Plan	Treaty of Rome
United Nations	Council for Mutual	Maastricht Treaty
Iron Curtain	Economic Assistance	Prague Spring
Berlin Airlift	NATO	*perestroika* and *glasnost*

Solidarity   Velvet Revolution
Civic Forum   globalization

Introduction

Following the Second World War, a Cold War developed between the two "superpowers": the Soviet Union and the United States. In response, the western European nations plotted and followed a course of economic integration that culminated in the creation of the European Union. In the decades that followed the collapse of the Soviet Union, Europe experienced both a revival of nationalism and the emergence of globalization.

The Nuclear Arms Race

In 1944, German physicists Otto Hahn and Fritz Strassmann published a paper (based on work they had done with Lise Meitner, a Jewish physicist who was forced to emigrate due to increasing anti-Semitism in Nazi Germany) that purported to show that vast amounts of energy would be released if a way could be found to split the atom. As World War II raged, the American government secretly funded an effort, known as the *Manhattan Project,* to build an atomic bomb. In 1945, the project's international team of physicists, led by American physicist Robert Oppenheimer, succeeded in building two atomic bombs. Those bombs were dropped on two Japanese cities: Hiroshima (August 6, 1945) and Nagasaki (August 9, 1945). The advent of those nuclear weapons forced Japan's unconditional surrender and created a nuclear arms race between the United States and the Soviet Union.

On August 29, 1949, the Soviet Union successfully exploded its first nuclear weapon. In the 1950s, both the United States and the Soviet Union developed ICBMs (intercontinental ballistic missiles), which assured that either superpower could deliver enough nuclear weapons to destroy the other. That situation evolved into a risky, but ultimately successful, strategy to avoid nuclear war that came to be known as mutual assured destruction.

The Cold War

The Settlement Following WWII

There was no formal treaty at the conclusion of World War II. The postwar shape of Europe was determined by agreements reached at two wartime conferences at Tehran, Iran (in December 1943) and Yalta, Crimea, which is now part of the Ukraine (in February 1945) and, where agreement could not be reached, by the realities of occupation at the war's end. These were the primary results of the eventual settlement:

- Germany was disarmed and divided into sectors, with the Western powers controlling the western sectors and the Soviet Union controlling the eastern sectors.
- Berlin, which lay in the eastern sector, was itself divided into West Berlin (controlled by the Allies) and East Berlin (controlled by the Soviet Union).
- Poland's border with Germany was pushed westward.
- The *United Nations* was created with 51 members to promote international peace and cooperation.

- Although the United States and Britain called for free elections in the eastern European nations that were physically under the control of the Soviet Army, pro-Soviet governments were quickly installed by Stalin.
- By 1946, the world was speaking of an *Iron Curtain* that had descended over eastern Europe (the phrase was first uttered by Winston Churchill in a speech given in the United States), stretching from the Baltic Sea in the north to the Adriatic Sea in the south and dividing Europe between a communist East and a capitalist West.

The Cold War in Europe

The phrase "the Cold War" refers to efforts of the ideologically opposed regimes of the United States and the Soviet Union to extend their influence and control of events around the globe, without breaking into direct military conflict with one another. The first showdown between the superpowers occurred from June 1948 to May 1949, when Soviet troops cut off all land traffic from the West into Berlin in an attempt to take control of the whole city. In response, the Western powers, led by the United States, mounted what has come to be known as the *Berlin Airlift*, supplying West Berlin and keeping it out of Soviet control. In 1949, the Western-controlled zones of Germany were formally merged to create the independent German Federal Republic. One month later, the Soviets established the German Democratic Republic in the eastern zone.

In 1947, the United States established the *Truman Doctrine*, offering military and economic aid to countries threatened by communist takeover. That same year, President Truman's Secretary of State, George Marshall, launched what has come to be known as the *Marshall Plan*, pouring billions of dollars of aid into helping the western European powers to rebuild their infrastructures and economies. The Soviet Union soon countered with the *Council for Mutual Economic Assistance*, an economic aid package for eastern European countries.

In 1949, the United States organized the North Atlantic Treaty Organization (*NATO*), uniting the Western powers in a military alliance against the Soviet Union. The Soviet Union countered with the *Warsaw Pact*, a military alliance of the communist countries of eastern Europe. The one great military imbalance of the postwar period, the United States' possession of the atomic bomb, was countered by the development of a Soviet atomic bomb in 1949. From then on, the two superpowers engaged in a nuclear arms race that saw each develop an arsenal of hydrogen bombs by 1953, followed by huge caches of nuclear warheads mounted on intercontinental ballistic missiles. The overarching strategy of nuclear weapons became appropriately known by its acronym M.A.D. (mutual assured destruction), which "reasoned" that neither side would use its nuclear weapons if its own destruction by a retaliatory blast was assured.

The Global Cold War

Once the two superpowers had done what they could to shore up their positions in Europe, their competition spread across the globe. Major events in world history that are directly connected to the Cold War include:

- the *civil war in China*, where the Soviet-backed communist forces of Mao Zedong defeated, in 1949, the nationalist forces of Jiang Jieshi supported by the United States
- the *Korean War* (1950–1953) between Soviet- and Chinese-supported North Korean communists and UN and U.S.-backed South Koreans, which produced a stalemate at the 38th parallel (the original post–World War II dividing line between North and South Korea) at the cost of some 1.5 million lives
- the *Cuban Missile Crisis* of October 1963, in which Soviet attempts to install nuclear missiles in Cuba were met with a U.S. blockade of the island, bringing the world to the brink of nuclear war until the Soviets backed down and removed the missiles

- the *Vietnam War*, in which communist forces led by Ho Chi Minh battled an authoritarian, anticommunist government, increasingly reliant on U.S. military aid for its existence, throughout the 1960s until U.S. withdrawal in 1973

Although it was less in the headlines of world news, the Cold War also had devastating effects in Latin America and Africa where, for the better part of three decades, local and regional disputes were deformed by the intervention of Soviet and U.S. money, arms, and covert operations. Many of the difficulties faced by those regions today can be traced back to the Cold War.

Détente with the West, Crackdown in the East

In the late 1960s and lasting into the 1980s, U.S.–Soviet relations entered into a new era that has come to be known as the era of Détente. In this period, both sides backed away from the notion of a struggle only one side could win. The era of Détente was characterized by a number of nuclear test-ban treaties and arms-limitation talks between the two superpowers.

However, while Soviet–U.S. relations were thawing during this period, the Soviet Union demonstrated on several occasions that it still intended to rule the Eastern Block with a firm hand. The most dramatic occurred in 1968 in an episode that has come to be known as the *Prague Spring*. Czechoslovakian communists, led by Alexander Dubcek, embarked on a process of liberalization, stimulated by public demand for greater freedom, economic progress, and equality. Under Dubcek's leadership, the reformers declared that they intended to create "socialism with a human face." Dubcek tried to proceed by balancing reforms with reassurances to the Soviet Union, but on 21 August Soviet and Warsaw Pact troops invaded and occupied the major cities of Czechoslovakia; it was the largest military operation in Europe since World War II.

The Soviet regime also continued to demand conformity from its citizens and to punish dissent. A good example was the case of Alexander Solzhenitsyn, the acclaimed author who wrote novels which attempted to tell the truth about life in the Soviet Union. For writing novels like *The Cancer Ward* (1966) and *The First Circle* (1968), Solzhenitsyn was expelled, in November 1969, from the Russian Writers' Union. Much to the irritation of the Soviet government, his work was highly acclaimed in the West and he was awarded the Nobel Prize in 1970. Following the 1973 publication of his novel *The Gulag Archipelago*, he was arrested. But in a sign that some concessions were being made to Western opinion, he was deported to West Germany rather than exiled to Siberia.

The European Union

The leaders of western Europe realized almost immediately they were going to need to function as a whole in order to rival the economic and military power of the two superpowers. Throughout the second half of the twentieth century, Europe embarked on a plan of economic integration that proceeded through several careful stages:

- In 1950, France and West Germany created the French–German Coal and Steel Authority, removing tariff barriers and jointly managing production in that industry.
- In 1952, the Authority expanded to create the six-country European Coal and Steel Community, adding Italy, Belgium, Luxembourg, and the Netherlands.
- In 1957, those six countries signed the *Treaty of Rome*, establishing the European Economic Community (EEC), sometimes referred to as the Common Market, to begin the process of eliminating tariff barriers and cutting restrictions of the flow of capital and labor.
- In 1967, the EEC merged with other European cooperative bodies to form the European Community (EC), moving toward a broader integration of public institutions.

- Between 1967 and 1986, the EC expanded to 12 countries, adding Denmark, the United Kingdom, and the Republic of Ireland (all in 1973), Greece (1981), and Portugal and Spain (both in 1986).
- In 1992, the 12 countries of the EC signed the *Maastricht Treaty*, changing the name from the EC to European Union (EU), creating the world's largest trading bloc, and moving to adopt a common currency (the euro).
- In 1995, Austria, Finland, and Sweden joined the EU.
- Following the breakup of the Soviet Union, the EU underwent a massive expansion, welcoming countries either newly freed or newly constituted. The addition of Cyprus, the Czech Republic, Estonia, Hungary, Latvia, Lithuania, Malta, Poland, Slovakia, and Slovenia in 2004, and Bulgaria and Romania in 2007, brought the total membership to 27 countries.

The Disintegration of the Iron Curtain and the Soviet Union

Between 1985 and 1989, the world was stunned as it witnessed the rapid disintegration of the Soviet Union, the destruction of the Iron Curtain, and the reunification of Germany. The causes of these dramatic events were rooted in the nature of the Soviet system, which had for decades put domestic and foreign politics ahead of the needs of its own economy and of its people. The result was an economic system that could no longer function. The trigger for its disintegration was the ascension of a new generation of Soviet leaders.

Gorbachev and the "New Man": 1985

While western Europe was creating the EC and dreaming of economic and political power that could match the superpowers, the big lie of the Soviet economy was coming home to roost. In 1985, Mikhail Gorbachev succeeded a long line of aging Stalinist leaders. At the age of 54, Gorbachev represented a younger and more sophisticated generation that had spent significant time in the West. Gorbachev believed that the Soviet Union's survival required a restructuring (*perestroika*) of both its economy and its society, and an openness (*glasnost*) to new ideas. Accordingly, Gorbachev challenged the people of the Soviet Union and its satellite countries to take on a new level of responsibility. However, such an invitation quickly fanned the fires of autonomy in satellite states.

Poland and "Solidarity": 1980–1990

There had been growing agitation in Poland since 1980, when workers under the leadership of an electrician named Lech Walesa succeeded in forming a labor union known as *Solidarity*. Pressured by numerous strikes, the Polish government recognized the union despite threats of Soviet intervention. By 1981, the movement had become more political, as some of Solidarity's more radical members began calling for free elections. As tensions grew, the Polish military, led by General Wojciech Jaruzelski, responded to the crisis by imposing martial law and a military dictatorship. However, with Gorbachev calling for reform, Jaruzelski tried, in November of 1987, to gain legitimacy for his rule through a national referendum. The majority of voters either voted against or abstained and in August of 1988, Jaruzelski ended his military dictatorship and set up a civilian government.

The new government attempted to retain the political monopoly of the Communist Party while simultaneously opening Poland up for Western business. It proved to be impossible, and Walesa and Solidarity took advantage of the new openness to push for political freedom. In January of 1989, Solidarity was legalized and, in April, the Communist Party gave up its monopoly on political power. In the first free election in Poland since before World War II, Solidarity triumphed and a noncommunist government was set up in September. In December of 1990,

Walesa was elected president, and Poland began to face the hard task of learning how to live in an unruly democratic society and to deal with the economic ups and downs of capitalism.

Czechoslovakia and the Velvet Revolution: 1989

Seeing Poland, and then Hungary (which held free elections in the summer and fall of 1989), shed their communist governments without Soviet intervention energized Czech resistance to communist rule. Student-led demonstrations in the fall of 1989 were met with tear gas and clubs by the Czech police, but the students were soon joined by workers and people from all walks of life. Leading dissidents, like the playwright Václav Havel, began a movement known as the *Civic Forum*, which sought to rebuild notions of citizenship and civic life that had been destroyed by the Soviet system. Soon Havel and other dissidents were jailed, but they became symbols of defiance and moral superiority.

What followed has come to be known as the *Velvet Revolution*. Faced with massive demonstrations in Prague (shown around the world on television) and urged by Gorbachev himself to institute democratic reform, Czechoslovakia's communist leaders resigned on 24 November. After negotiations and maneuvers by both the Communist Party and the Civic Forum, Havel was chosen as president on 25 December. Alexander Dubcek, who had led the original revolt of 1968, was brought home from exile and named chairman of the Czechoslovakian Parliament.

German Reunification: 1989–1990

West Germans had never accepted the division of Germany. The constitution of the German Federal Republic provided legal formalities for reunification. How the East Germans felt about the society of their Western relatives was hard to know. When reunification came, it came suddenly. East German dissidents organized themselves along the lines of the Civic Forum model pioneered in Czechoslovakia. In response to the pressure for reform, the communist regime rescinded its traditional order to shoot anyone trying to escape to West Berlin, and shortly thereafter issued "vacation visas" to those wishing to see their families in the West. There was little expectation of their return.

On 9 November 1989 protesters moved toward the Berlin Wall and, meeting almost no resistance from the soldiers, started to hammer it down. East Germans streamed into West Berlin where they were embraced by tearful West Germans who gleefully gave them handfuls of cash. The West German Chancellor, the Conservative Helmut Kohl, moved quickly towards reunification. It was a reunification that amounted to East Germany being annexed by the West. Completely swept away in the pace of change were the original Civic Forum leaders who were not at all sure that they wished to be reunified with West Germany and its capitalist economy.

- In March 1990, elections were held in East Germany, creating a new government ready to negotiate with West Germany.
- By 3 August, the official treaty of reunification had been drafted.
- The East German government approved it at the beginning of October and, on 3 October 1990, the Germans celebrated Reunification Day.
- On 2 December, the first unified national elections resulted in sweeping wins for Kohl, "the Reunification Chancellor," and his party.

Yugoslavia—Fragmentation: 1989

Yugoslavia had been a fragile state of six ethnically self-conscious member republics. As the communist regime began to collapse, the ethnic rivalries of Yugoslavia quickly reasserted themselves.

- Albanians in the autonomous province of Kosovo revolted against Serbian rule.
- The Slovenes and Croatians (or Croats), both western Slavs, agitated for independence from Serbia.
- In 1989, the communist regime began to collapse and the stronger republics were moving towards independence. A fragile multiparty system was put into place.

The Soviet Union Comes Apart: 1991

Caught between the hardliners who wished to slow down reform and a population that wanted it to come faster, Gorbachev's popularity began to slip. Determined to go forward, Gorbachev persuaded the Communist Party to give up its monopoly on political power and called for free elections. Sensing collapse, Party members resigned in large numbers.

The various "republics" that made up the Soviet Union now emulated the satellite states and began to agitate for independence. The Russian Republic led the way, when its president and former Gorbachev ally, Boris Yeltsin, declared its independence from the Soviet Union. Ukraine followed suit and Gorbachev was faced with a crisis. In the spring of 1991, Gorbachev proposed a compromise. He suggested that all the republics sign a "Treaty of the Union," declaring them all to be independent but also members of a loose confederation. In August of 1991, just as the Treaty was about to take effect, hardliners tried to oust Gorbachev. For three days, there was confusion about who was in charge and what the military would do. Yeltsin seized the moment, positioning himself between the parliament building and military tanks. The military backed off and the coup attempt failed, but it was Yeltsin who was now the favorite. Gorbachev resigned late in 1991 and the Soviet Union, as the world had known it, disintegrated. Most of the republics chose to join a loose confederation known as the Commonwealth of Independent States, while a few, especially the Baltic States, opted for independence.

Nationalism and Globalization

Following the collapse of the Soviet Union, nationalism, which had been driven underground, came to the surface in eastern Europe.

- In Czechoslovakia, Slavic nationalism split the country into halves, as the Slavic regions split off to form the republic of Slovakia, leaving the Czechs to form the Czech Republic.
- In Azerbaijan, Azerbaijanis and Armenians fought for dominance.
- In the Russian Republic, Chechnyans began a guerrilla war against Russian troops when their demands for independence were refused.
- In Yugoslavia, the fragile, multiparty system fell apart. Serbians and Slovenians fought over land and power; ethnic groups in Croatia, Bosnia–Herzegovina, and Macedonia followed suit as the situation degenerated into a vicious, multisided war with acts of genocide committed on both sides.

While politics in the post–Cold War era often seemed to regress, the unity of the world's economies, societies, and cultures continued to move forward. Near the end of the twentieth century, the term *globalization* became prominent to describe the increasing integration and interdependence of the economic, social, cultural, and even ecological aspects of life. The term not only refers to way in which the economies of the world affect one another, but also to the way in which the experience of everyday life is increasingly standardized by the spread of technologies which carry with them social and cultural norms.

› Rapid Review

During World War II, the American government secretly funded an effort, known as the Manhattan Project, to build an atomic bomb. In 1945, the project's international team of physicists, led by American physicist Robert Oppenheimer, succeeded in building two atomic bombs. Those bombs were dropped on two Japanese cities: Hiroshima and Nagasaki. The advent of those nuclear weapons forced Japan's unconditional surrender and subsequently created a nuclear arms race between the United States and the Soviet Union.

Following World War II, the Soviet Union solidified its control of eastern Europe, creating an Iron Curtain that divided East from West. The two superpowers, the United States and the Soviet Union, engaged in a Cold War that had global implications. Meanwhile, the western European nations plotted and followed a course of economic integration that culminated in the creation of the European Union. Between 1985 and 1989, systemic economic problems and a bold attempt at reform led to the rapid disintegration of the Soviet Union, the destruction of the Iron Curtain, and the reunification of Germany. In the decades that followed, two major trends affected life in Europe: the revival of nationalism and the emergence of globalization.

› Chapter Review Questions

1. The settlement that followed World War II is best understood as
   - (A) an implementation of Woodrow Wilson's 14-point plan
   - (B) a solidifying of the realities that existed at the end of the war
   - (C) a reconstruction of the settlement created by the Versailles Treaty
   - (D) an outgrowth of globalization
   - (E) a revival of nationalism

2. The significance of the Berlin Airlift was
   - (A) its demonstration of the commitment of the United States to defend western Europe from Soviet expansion
   - (B) its effect on Hitler, causing him to abandon the invasion of Britain
   - (C) that it signaled the end of the war in Germany
   - (D) that it led to the division of Berlin into a western and eastern sector
   - (E) that it demonstrated the resurgence of the German Airforce

3. The plan for financial assistance to rebuild western Europe after World War II was known as
   - (A) the Warsaw Pact
   - (B) the Truman Doctrine
   - (C) the Council for Mutual Economic Assistance
   - (D) the Marshall Plan
   - (E) NATO

4. The softening of U.S.–Soviet relations from the late 1960s to the 1980s which led to a series of disarmament talks and missile-limitation treaties is known as
   - (A) the Prague Spring
   - (B) the Treaty of Rome
   - (C) Détente
   - (D) Socialism with a Human Face
   - (E) globalization

5. The Maastricht Treaty, signed in 1992,
   - (A) coordinated coal and steel production in six European nations
   - (B) established the European Economic Community (EEC)
   - (C) created the European Community (EC)
   - (D) established the reunification of Germany
   - (E) brought the European Union (EU) into being

6. *Glasnost* refers to
   - (A) a social and economic restructuring
   - (B) the attempt by Czechoslovakians to humanize socialism
   - (C) the rise of nationalism in the former Soviet republics
   - (D) an openness to new ideas
   - (E) the Polish labor union which led a political revolt in the 1980s and 1990s

7. The movement that began in 1989 in Czechoslovakia and which sought to rebuild notions of citizenship and civic life that had been destroyed by the Soviet system was
   - (A) the Velvet Revolution
   - (B) the Prague Spring
   - (C) the Civic Forum
   - (D) Solidarity
   - (E) *glasnost*

8. Which of the following is an example of the revival of nationalism in eastern Europe after the disintegration of the Soviet Union?
   - (A) the war between Chechnyans and Russia
   - (B) the multisided war in Yugoslavia
   - (C) the splitting up of Czechoslovakia
   - (D) the war in Bosnia–Herzegovina
   - (E) all of the above

› Answers and Explanations

1. **B.** The post–World War II settlement, with Germany divided into zones and the eastern European countries under the domination of the Soviet Union, was a solidifying of the reality that the Soviets occupied half of Germany and militarily controlled eastern Europe. Choice A is incorrect because Wilson's 14-point plan, proposed at the conclusion of World War I, called for the growth of liberal democracy all over Europe; that did not happen behind the Iron Curtain. Choice C is incorrect because there are many differences between the settlement constructed by the Versailles Treaty and the settlement at the end of World War II, chief among them being the fate of Germany, which was shrunk and saddled with war reparations by the Versailles Treaty and divided between East and West and rapidly rebuilt by the superpowers after World War II.

2. **A.** The Berlin Airlift, in which the United States flew supplies into a Soviet-blockaded West Berlin from June 1948 to May 1949, demonstrated the commitment of the United States to defend West Berlin and all of western Europe from Soviet expansion. Choice B is incorrect because it was the Battle of Britain (not the Berlin Airlift) that caused Hitler to abandon his plan for the invasion of Britain. Choice C is incorrect because the chronology is wrong: the war had been over for nearly three years when the Berlin Airlift occurred. Choice D is incorrect because Berlin was already divided into eastern and western sectors prior to the Berlin Airlift. Choice E is incorrect because the Berlin Airlift was carried out by the United States Airforce, in aid of West Berlin (not the German Airforce, which had nothing to do with this).

3. **D.** The Marshall Plan, named after U.S. Secretary of State George Marshall, was the plan which called for pouring billions of dollars of aid into Western Europe to rebuild its infrastructure and economy. Choice A is incorrect because the Warsaw Pact was a military alliance of the communist countries of eastern Europe. Choice B is incorrect because the Truman Doctrine offered military and economic aid to countries directly threatened by communist takeover (not countries in western Europe). Choice C is incorrect because the Council for Mutual Economic Assistance was set up by the Soviet Union to counter the Marshall Plan by offering economic aid to eastern European countries (not western European countries). Choice E is incorrect because NATO, the North Atlantic Treaty Organization, united the Western powers in a *military* alliance against the Soviet Union; it had nothing to do with *financial* assistance to western Europe.

4. **C.** The French term Détente was given to the softening of U.S.–Soviet relations that led to a series of disarmament talks and missile-limitation treaties from the late 1960s to the 1980s. Choices A and D are incorrect because the "the Prague Spring" refers to attempts by Czechoslovakian communists to resist Soviet domination and bring about a relaxation of state intervention in the lives of its citizens, a goal that came to be known as "socialism with a human face." Choice B is incorrect because the Treaty of Rome, signed in 1957, established the European Economic Community (EEC). Choice E is incorrect ecause globalization was a term coined in the late 1980s to describe the way in which the experience of everyday life is increasingly standardized by the spread of technologies which carry with them social and cultural norms.

5. **E.** The Maastricht Treaty, signed by the 12 countries of the European Community in 1992, created the European Union, the world's largest trading bloc. Choice A is incorrect because it was the European Coal and Steel Community, created in 1952, that coordinated coal and steel production in the six member nations. Choice B is incorrect because it was the Treaty of Rome, signed in 1957, that established the European Economic Community (EEC), sometimes referred to as the Common Market. Choice C is incorrect because it was the merger of the EEC and other cooperative bodies in 1967 that created the European Community (EC). Choice D is incorrect because

German Reunification was accomplished by a treaty approved in October of 1990.

6. **D.** The term *glasnost* (or openness) refers to the call by Mikhail Gorbachev in the late 1980s for an openness to new ideas in Soviet society and government. Choice A is incorrect because the term for Gorbachev's call for social and economic restructuring was *perestroika*. Choice B is incorrect because the attempt by Czechoslovakians, in 1968, to humanize socialism was known as "socialism with a human face." Choice C is incorrect because the rise of nationalism in the former Soviet republics occurred as a reaction to *glasnost*. Choice E is incorrect because the Polish labor union which led a political revolt in the 1980s and 1990s was Solidarity.

7. **C.** The movement known as the Civic Forum sought to rebuild notions of citizenship and civic life that had been destroyed by the Soviet system. Choice A is incorrect because the phrase "the Velvet Revolution" refers to the entire process, of which the Civic Forum was only a part, by which civic opposition eroded the communist regime in Czechoslovakia. Choice B is incorrect because "the Prague Spring" refers to the uprisings of Czechoslovakians against Soviet domination in 1968. Choice D is incorrect because Solidarity is the name of the Polish labor union which led a revolt against Soviet oppression in Poland. Choice E is incorrect because *glasnost* refers to the openness to new ideas called for by Mikhail Gorbachev.

8. **E.** All of the choices are correct. The Chechnyan conflict arose because of Russia's refusal to accede to Chechnyan nationalist demands for independence. The multisided conflicts in Yugoslavia and in Bosnia–Herzegovina involved both ethnic tensions between and nationalist aspirations of the Serbs, Slovenes, Croats, Bosnians and several other groups. The splitting up of Czechoslovakia was the result of nationalist aspirations of the Slovaks.

UNIT 2 Summary: The Napoleonic Era to the Present

Timeline

1802	Napoleon becomes first consul for life in France
1804	Napoleon crowns himself emperor of France
1814	The Congress of Vienna creates the Concert of Europe
1815	Napoleon is defeated at Waterloo
1830	July Ordinances in France are followed by a revolution, which forces Charles X to abdicate
1839–1842	Opium War: British defeat Chinese, opening China to the West
1848	Year of revolution in Europe
June 1848	"June Days," Revolutionaries are beaten by the army in Paris
December 1848	Louis-Napoleon is elected president of the Second Republic in France
1848	Karl Marx publishes the *Communist Manifesto*
1851	Louis-Napoleon overthrows the Second Republic in France, becomes Napoleon III
1853	U.S. naval forces open Japan to the West
1857	Sepoy Rebellion: Britain replaces East India Company and governs India directly
1864	Marx founds the First International Working Men's Association
1866	Italian unification is mostly complete (Rome added in 1870)
1866	Austro-Prussian War: victorious Prussia organizes the North German Confederation
1867	Second Reform Bill passed in Britain, doubling the electorate
1869	Suez Canal opened
1870–1871	Franco-Prussian War
18 January 1871	German Unification is complete; Second Reich proclaimed
1876	Stanley sets up posts in the Congo for Leopold II of Belgium
1881	Tsar Alexander II assassinated in Russia
1882	Britain occupies Egypt
1884	Berlin Conference sets up guidelines for Africa
1884	Reform Bill in Britain grants vote to nearly all English men
1889	Second International Working Men's Association founded
1903–1905	Russo-Japanese War; victorious Japanese a modern power
28 June 1914	Archduke Franz Ferdinand of Austria assassinated at Sarajevo
4 August 1914	Germany invades Belgium
August 1914	Russians invade East Prussia and are defeated by Germans at Tannenberg
September 1914	First Battle of Marne saves Paris
February 1916	Germans fail to capture fortress town of Verdun
July–November 1916	Battle of the Somme
March 1917	Tsarist regime overthrown in Russia
6 April 1917	United States declares war on Germany
November 1917	Bolsheviks, led by Lenin, take control of Russia
March 1918	Russia signs Treaty of Brest–Litovsk, withdraws from the war
March–June 1918	Germans launch last great offensive, advance to within 56 miles of Paris
8 August 1918	British victory at Amiens

11 November 1918	Germany signs armistice, ending World War I
January 1919	Paris Peace Conference
28 June 1919	Germany signs Treaty of Paris
1921–1928	New Economic Plan in Russia
1922	Mussolini and fascists rise to power in Italy
1924	Lenin dies, succeeded by Stalin
1928	First of Stalin's five-year plans begins rapid industrialization of Russia
1929	Collectivization of agriculture in Russia
1933	Hitler becomes Chancellor of Germany
1936–1939	Spanish Civil War
March 1938	Germany annexes Austria
September 1938	Munich Agreement; Hitler allowed to annex Sudetenland
March 1939	Germany invades Czechoslovakia
September 1939	Germany invades Poland, World War II begins
22 June 1940	France surrenders
August–September 1940	Battle of Britain
June 1941	Germany launches offensive against the Soviet Union
7 December 1941	Japan attacks Pearl Harbor; United States enters the war
1941–1945	Holocaust; Nazi regime murders six million Jews
1942	Tide of battle turns in Allies' favor
September 1943	Italy surrenders
6 June 1944	D-Day, Allies land at Normandy
August 1944	Paris is liberated
January 1945	Soviet troops invade Germany
March–April 1945	Allies penetrate Germany
7 May 1945	Germany surrenders
August 1945	United States drops atomic bombs on Hiroshima and Nagasaki; Japan surrenders
1947	Cold War begins; Truman Doctrine and Marshall Plan inaugurated
1949	NATO founded; Soviet Union acquires atomic bomb
1957	European Economic Community founded
1961	Berlin Wall built
1968	Prague Spring
1985	Gorbachev becomes leader of the Soviet Union
1988	Communist dictatorship in Poland ends
1989	Year of revolution in Europe; communist regimes ousted in Eastern Europe

Key Comparisons

1. Industrialization in Great Britain and on the Continent of Europe
2. The development of mass politics in Great Britain and on the Continent of Europe
3. The unification of Italy and the unification of Germany
4. German aspirations in World Wars I and II
5. The nature of war in World Wars I and II
6. Economic and political developments in western and eastern Europe after World War II

Thematic Change/Continuity

KEY IDEA

Economic changes
The Second Industrial Revolution and growth of the middle class
The creation and expansion of the British Empire
The rise of the United States and the Soviet Union as the dominant economic forces after
  World War II
Integration of the European economy

Economic continuities
British leadership maintained (until World War II)

Social/cultural changes
Death of the belief in progress in European culture
Rise and spread of globalization

Social/cultural continuities
Anti-Semitism

Political changes
Development of mass politics
Rise of extreme nationalism
Creation of the Soviet Union and the Iron Curtain
Dominance of the United States and Soviet Union after World War II

Political continuities
Western European leadership in progress towards democratization

STEP 5

Build Your Test-Taking Confidence

AP European History Practice Test 1
AP European History Practice Test 2

AP European History
Practice Test 1—Section I

ANSWER SHEET

1 Ⓐ Ⓑ Ⓒ Ⓓ Ⓔ	31 Ⓐ Ⓑ Ⓒ Ⓓ Ⓔ	61 Ⓐ Ⓑ Ⓒ Ⓓ Ⓔ
2 Ⓐ Ⓑ Ⓒ Ⓓ Ⓔ	32 Ⓐ Ⓑ Ⓒ Ⓓ Ⓔ	62 Ⓐ Ⓑ Ⓒ Ⓓ Ⓔ
3 Ⓐ Ⓑ Ⓒ Ⓓ Ⓔ	33 Ⓐ Ⓑ Ⓒ Ⓓ Ⓔ	63 Ⓐ Ⓑ Ⓒ Ⓓ Ⓔ
4 Ⓐ Ⓑ Ⓒ Ⓓ Ⓔ	34 Ⓐ Ⓑ Ⓒ Ⓓ Ⓔ	64 Ⓐ Ⓑ Ⓒ Ⓓ Ⓔ
5 Ⓐ Ⓑ Ⓒ Ⓓ Ⓔ	35 Ⓐ Ⓑ Ⓒ Ⓓ Ⓔ	65 Ⓐ Ⓑ Ⓒ Ⓓ Ⓔ
6 Ⓐ Ⓑ Ⓒ Ⓓ Ⓔ	36 Ⓐ Ⓑ Ⓒ Ⓓ Ⓔ	66 Ⓐ Ⓑ Ⓒ Ⓓ Ⓔ
7 Ⓐ Ⓑ Ⓒ Ⓓ Ⓔ	37 Ⓐ Ⓑ Ⓒ Ⓓ Ⓔ	67 Ⓐ Ⓑ Ⓒ Ⓓ Ⓔ
8 Ⓐ Ⓑ Ⓒ Ⓓ Ⓔ	38 Ⓐ Ⓑ Ⓒ Ⓓ Ⓔ	68 Ⓐ Ⓑ Ⓒ Ⓓ Ⓔ
9 Ⓐ Ⓑ Ⓒ Ⓓ Ⓔ	39 Ⓐ Ⓑ Ⓒ Ⓓ Ⓔ	69 Ⓐ Ⓑ Ⓒ Ⓓ Ⓔ
10 Ⓐ Ⓑ Ⓒ Ⓓ Ⓔ	40 Ⓐ Ⓑ Ⓒ Ⓓ Ⓔ	70 Ⓐ Ⓑ Ⓒ Ⓓ Ⓔ
11 Ⓐ Ⓑ Ⓒ Ⓓ Ⓔ	41 Ⓐ Ⓑ Ⓒ Ⓓ Ⓔ	71 Ⓐ Ⓑ Ⓒ Ⓓ Ⓔ
12 Ⓐ Ⓑ Ⓒ Ⓓ Ⓔ	42 Ⓐ Ⓑ Ⓒ Ⓓ Ⓔ	72 Ⓐ Ⓑ Ⓒ Ⓓ Ⓔ
13 Ⓐ Ⓑ Ⓒ Ⓓ Ⓔ	43 Ⓐ Ⓑ Ⓒ Ⓓ Ⓔ	73 Ⓐ Ⓑ Ⓒ Ⓓ Ⓔ
14 Ⓐ Ⓑ Ⓒ Ⓓ Ⓔ	44 Ⓐ Ⓑ Ⓒ Ⓓ Ⓔ	74 Ⓐ Ⓑ Ⓒ Ⓓ Ⓔ
15 Ⓐ Ⓑ Ⓒ Ⓓ Ⓔ	45 Ⓐ Ⓑ Ⓒ Ⓓ Ⓔ	75 Ⓐ Ⓑ Ⓒ Ⓓ Ⓔ
16 Ⓐ Ⓑ Ⓒ Ⓓ Ⓔ	46 Ⓐ Ⓑ Ⓒ Ⓓ Ⓔ	76 Ⓐ Ⓑ Ⓒ Ⓓ Ⓔ
17 Ⓐ Ⓑ Ⓒ Ⓓ Ⓔ	47 Ⓐ Ⓑ Ⓒ Ⓓ Ⓔ	77 Ⓐ Ⓑ Ⓒ Ⓓ Ⓔ
18 Ⓐ Ⓑ Ⓒ Ⓓ Ⓔ	48 Ⓐ Ⓑ Ⓒ Ⓓ Ⓔ	78 Ⓐ Ⓑ Ⓒ Ⓓ Ⓔ
19 Ⓐ Ⓑ Ⓒ Ⓓ Ⓔ	49 Ⓐ Ⓑ Ⓒ Ⓓ Ⓔ	79 Ⓐ Ⓑ Ⓒ Ⓓ Ⓔ
20 Ⓐ Ⓑ Ⓒ Ⓓ Ⓔ	50 Ⓐ Ⓑ Ⓒ Ⓓ Ⓔ	80 Ⓐ Ⓑ Ⓒ Ⓓ Ⓔ
21 Ⓐ Ⓑ Ⓒ Ⓓ Ⓔ	51 Ⓐ Ⓑ Ⓒ Ⓓ Ⓔ	
22 Ⓐ Ⓑ Ⓒ Ⓓ Ⓔ	52 Ⓐ Ⓑ Ⓒ Ⓓ Ⓔ	
23 Ⓐ Ⓑ Ⓒ Ⓓ Ⓔ	53 Ⓐ Ⓑ Ⓒ Ⓓ Ⓔ	
24 Ⓐ Ⓑ Ⓒ Ⓓ Ⓔ	54 Ⓐ Ⓑ Ⓒ Ⓓ Ⓔ	
25 Ⓐ Ⓑ Ⓒ Ⓓ Ⓔ	55 Ⓐ Ⓑ Ⓒ Ⓓ Ⓔ	
26 Ⓐ Ⓑ Ⓒ Ⓓ Ⓔ	56 Ⓐ Ⓑ Ⓒ Ⓓ Ⓔ	
27 Ⓐ Ⓑ Ⓒ Ⓓ Ⓔ	57 Ⓐ Ⓑ Ⓒ Ⓓ Ⓔ	
28 Ⓐ Ⓑ Ⓒ Ⓓ Ⓔ	58 Ⓐ Ⓑ Ⓒ Ⓓ Ⓔ	
29 Ⓐ Ⓑ Ⓒ Ⓓ Ⓔ	59 Ⓐ Ⓑ Ⓒ Ⓓ Ⓔ	
30 Ⓐ Ⓑ Ⓒ Ⓓ Ⓔ	60 Ⓐ Ⓑ Ⓒ Ⓓ Ⓔ	

AP European History
Practice Test 1

Section I

Time—55 minutes

80 Questions

Directions: Each of the questions or incomplete statements below is followed by five suggested answers or completions. Select the one that is best in each case and fill in the circle for the letter that corresponds to your choice on the Answer Sheet supplied.

1. The most outstanding social effect of the development of a division of labor system of production was
   (A) increased volume of manufactured goods
   (B) unemployment or decreased wages for skilled craftsman
   (C) increased profits for manufacturers
   (D) increased efficiency
   (E) decreased volume of manufactured goods

2. The development of the Bessemer process was significant because it
   (A) doubled cotton production
   (B) facilitated the move away from human and water power
   (C) shifted the balance of military power in the nineteenth century
   (D) allowed for the manufacture of iron and steel more cheaply and in larger quantities
   (E) doubled the speed with which goods could be transported

3. Throughout the Industrial Revolution, the country that held the lead in innovation and industrial production was
   (A) Russia
   (B) France
   (C) Germany
   (D) Great Britain
   (E) Holland

4. Of the nineteenth-century ideologies, the one that most staunchly defended the institution of monarchy was
   (A) conservatism
   (B) liberalism
   (C) socialism
   (D) communism
   (E) anarchism

5. The doctrine of *laissez-faire*, often attributed to the Scottish philosopher Adam Smith, argued that
   (A) people should be able to do whatever they want
   (B) Scotland should be free of English rule
   (C) governments should not try to interfere with the natural workings of an economy
   (D) welfare laws would retard the evolution of human society
   (E) imperial expansion was a necessary outcome of natural laws

6. Utilitarians differed from other liberals in their
   (A) support of tradition
   (B) emphasis on individual liberty
   (C) tendency to be more supportive of government intervention
   (D) call for the abolition of private property
   (E) advocacy of violence

7. Which of the following was a tenet of Martin Luther's theology?
   (A) salvation through good works
   (B) Church tradition as a source of knowledge about God
   (C) predestination
   (D) millenarianism
   (E) salvation by faith alone

8. The greatest significance of the Council of Trent for the history of Europe was
   (A) its triumph over Protestantism
   (B) its successful reform of the Roman Church
   (C) its pledge, on the part of the German princes, not to go to war over religion
   (D) that it signified a defeat for those who wished for reconciliation between Protestants and the Roman Church
   (E) that it served as an anti-Protestant force all over the globe

GO ON TO THE NEXT PAGE

9. The relative peace of the Restoration Period in England broke down when
   (A) Oliver Cromwell died
   (B) James II ascended to the throne
   (C) Charles II ascended to the throne
   (D) Elizabeth I ascended to the throne
   (E) a Protestant fleet invaded from the Netherlands

10. The degree of absolutism achieved by the seventeenth-century Bourbon monarchy in France is best explained by
    (A) the relatively low degree of religious turmoil in seventeenth-century France
    (B) the fact that seventeenth-century France was a republic
    (C) the series of "little ice ages" that characterized the climate of the 1600s
    (D) the availability of cheap housing for the rural poor
    (E) the brilliance of Louis XIV

11. The baroque style was popular in buildings built by
    (A) the aristocratic class only
    (B) all the classes of eighteenth-century Europe
    (C) absolute monarchs of seventeenth-century Europe
    (D) the lower classes
    (E) the bourgeoisie of nineteenth-century Europe

12. In early-twentieth-century Britain, the organization that advocated a broader notion of women's rights was the
    (A) Women's Social and Political Union
    (B) Fabian Society
    (C) Social Democrats
    (D) National Union of Women's Suffrage Societies
    (E) Zionists

13. In Britain, the political party that made the largest gains in the first decade of the twentieth century was the
    (A) Conservative Party
    (B) Liberal Party
    (C) Labour Party
    (D) British Union of Fascists
    (E) Democratic Party

14. Which of the following was a serious problem faced by the government of the Weimar Republic?
    (A) Its form was largely alien to the German people.
    (B) It was perceived to have been imposed on Germany by its vengeful war enemies.
    (C) It was blamed for the humiliating nature of the Treaty of Versailles.
    (D) It was faced with insurmountable economic problems.
    (E) All of the above.

15. Lenin's plan to allow small-scale private enterprise in order to stimulate the Russian economy was known as
    (A) the five-year plan
    (B) the New Economic Plan
    (C) the Soviet Constitution of 1923
    (D) socialism in one country
    (E) the collectivization of agriculture

16. Of the following, which is true of the fascists' rise to power in Italy?
    (A) They seized power illegally through a military coup.
    (B) They appealed to the working classes by promising to abolish private property and bring about a classless society.
    (C) They gathered massive public support by opposing the socialists and giving a sense of purpose to the disillusioned and unemployed.
    (D) They were opposed by the Church.
    (E) They were opposed by industrialists who feared that the fascists would nationalize industry.

17. The settlement which followed World War II differed from that which followed World War I because
    (A) It blamed Germany for the war.
    (B) It was a settlement imposed by the victors.
    (C) It dismantled the Hapsburg Empire.
    (D) It created national boundaries that ignored significant ethnic and nationalist differences.
    (E) There was no formal treaty or series of treaties signifying formal acceptance of the settlement.

GO ON TO THE NEXT PAGE

18. The *Risorgimento* failed because
    (A) it failed to attract intellectuals
    (B) it was not sufficiently nationalist
    (C) it failed to win the support of the masses
    (D) it failed to win German support
    (E) the military was not strong enough

19. The successful nineteenth-century drive for unification in Germany differed from that in Italy in which of the following ways?
    (A) It was led by a conservative aristocrat.
    (B) It was free of direct foreign domination.
    (C) It sought to rally support around a popular monarch.
    (D) Its strategy was characterized by opportunism.
    (E) It required the provocation of war.

20. European imperialism in Asia differed from that in Africa in which of the following ways?
    (A) It lacked economic motives.
    (B) It was facilitated by technological innovations in weaponry and transportation.
    (C) It was connected to nationalism.
    (D) It was connected to the development of mass politics.
    (E) It was exerted through control of local elites.

21. The term "Détente" refers to
    (A) the efforts of Czechoslovakian communists to reform their society in 1968
    (B) the post–World War II division of Europe into a West of United States–backed Western powers and an East dominated by the Soviet Union
    (C) the 51-member international organization created to promote international peace and cooperation
    (D) the U.S. mission to fly supplies into West Berlin in response to a Soviet shutdown of supply lines
    (E) a period of U.S.–Soviet relations characterized by a number of nuclear test-ban treaties and arms-limitation talks

22. The Warsaw Pact
    (A) was a military alliance among the countries of Eastern Europe
    (B) formed a military alliance between Poland and Russia
    (C) offered economic assistance to the countries of Eastern Europe
    (D) was a military alliance between the United States and Western European powers
    (E) offered military and economic aid to countries threatened by communist takeover

23. The theory which came to be known as Copernicanism
    (A) argued that each piece of matter in the universe was attracted to every other particle of matter by a universally operating force.
    (B) promoted a geocentric model of the cosmos
    (C) declared that all matter was made up of four elements
    (D) promoted a heliocentric model of the cosmos
    (E) argued that the universe was infinite

24. Mary Wollstonecraft's criticism, in 1792, of the subjugation of women in European society on the grounds that the subjugation was irrational identifies her as
    (A) a conservative
    (B) an Enlightenment *philosophe*
    (C) a socialist
    (D) an anarchist
    (E) a suffragist

25. "Man is born free; and everywhere he is in chains." This quotation summarizes the view of human nature of
    (A) John Locke
    (B) Martin Luther
    (C) Jean-Jacques Rousseau
    (D) Voltaire
    (E) Jeremy Bentham

26. The Middle Passage refers to
    (A) Scripture
    (B) the shipping channel that connects the Mediterranean Sea and the Red Sea
    (C) the advent of rural manufacturing
    (D) the route to China that was the backbone of the silk trade
    (E) the transportation of African slaves across the Atlantic to the Americas and the West Indies

GO ON TO THE NEXT PAGE

27. Which of the following was NOT a way in which European armies changed in the eighteenth century?
    (A) They became larger.
    (B) The discipline and training became harsher and more extensive.
    (C) The officer corps became full-time servants of the state.
    (D) Troops came to consist predominantly of conscripts.
    (E) The officer corps were chosen and promoted on the basis of merit.

28. The decision by the representatives of the Third Estate to declare themselves, on 17 June 1789, to be the National Assembly of France signified
    (A) their intention to form a republic
    (B) their belief that political sovereignty belonged to the nation as a whole
    (C) their intention to overthrow the monarchy
    (D) their belief in democracy
    (E) their willingness to go to war with Germany

29. The agreement signed by Napoleon and the pope that stipulated that French clergy would be chosen and paid by the French state but consecrated by the pope is known as the
    (A) Concordat of 1801
    (B) Napoleonic Code
    (C) Consulate
    (D) Treaty of Tilsit
    (E) Continental System

30. The principle of "he who rules; his religion" was established by
    (A) the Edict of Nantes
    (B) the Papacy in Rome
    (C) the Geneva Convention
    (D) the Peace of Augsburg in 1555
    (E) the Inquisition

31. Which of the following were part of the structure of Calvinist communities?
    (A) pastors
    (B) doctors
    (C) deacons
    (D) elders
    (E) all of the above

32. The period of British history 1649–1660, in which Britain was ruled without a monarch, is known as
    (A) the Restoration
    (B) the Glorious Revolution
    (C) the Commonwealth
    (D) the English Civil War
    (E) the Norman Conquest

33. Neoplatonism was an important component of the Scientific Revolution because
    (A) it encouraged the development of a tradition of chemical experimentation
    (B) it promoted the scientific method
    (C) it argued that scientific knowledge had practical implications
    (D) it denied the existence of God
    (E) it stimulated interest in a mathematical approach to the investigation of the natural world

34. In *Crime and Punishment* (1764), the Italian philosopher Cesare Beccaria extended the Enlightenment line of thought by arguing that
    (A) the purpose of punishment should be to rehabilitate and reintegrate the individual into society
    (B) an all-powerful ruler was necessary to keep order and prevent crime
    (C) the death penalty should be abolished
    (D) the punishment for crimes should be standard in all kingdoms
    (E) society corrupts human nature, which is naturally good

35. The significance of the Masons in eighteenth-century Europe was
    (A) their impact on the architecture of the period
    (B) their plot to assassinate the pope
    (C) that they provided a home for revolutionary plots
    (D) that their lodges formed a network for the communication for new ideas and ideals
    (E) the reform of currency they carried out

36. Which of the following were factors in the breaking of the traditional population cycle in eighteenth-century Europe?
    (A) the Black Death
    (B) the Hundred Years War
    (C) the development of heavy industry
    (D) the development of rural manufacturing
    (E) the advent of steam power

GO ON TO THE NEXT PAGE

37. Which of the following helps to account for the death of the liberal–nationalist alliance in nineteenth-century Europe?
    (A) the liberals' emphasis on individual liberty
    (B) the nationalists' tendency to mythologize the past
    (C) the liberals' emphasis on limited government
    (D) the failure of the liberals to hold and use the power they had seized at the beginning of 1848
    (E) all of the above

38. Bismarck's strategy of increasing Prussia's power by whatever means and strategies were necessary and useful has come to be known as
    (A) détente
    (B) *Lebensraum*
    (C) *Realpolitik*
    (D) the Schlieffen Plan
    (E) the *Kulturkampf*

39. The radical break with tradition and convention ushered in by the French Revolution was experienced in the world of art through
    (A) the development of impressionism
    (B) a rejection of realism
    (C) the re-adoption of religious subject matter
    (D) the rejection of the dominant rococo aesthetic in favor of a neoclassical style
    (E) works like Caravaggio's *Calling of St. Matthew* and *Conversion of St. Peter*

40. Which of the following did NOT contribute to the outbreak of World War I?
    (A) the Anglo-German rivalry
    (B) the Alliance System
    (C) the rise of a unified Germany as an industrial and military power in Europe
    (D) German military planning
    (E) the remilitarization of the Rhineland

41. In late-nineteenth-century France, the Dreyfus affair illustrated
    (A) the weakness of French nationalism
    (B) the strength of ultranationalist and anti-Semitic sentiment in the French establishment
    (C) the subjugation of women in French society
    (D) France's lack of military preparation
    (E) France's desire for war with Germany

Source: Wikipedia (Public Domain Image).

42. The above propaganda poster from the period 1917–1920
    (A) depicts Germans mistreating Russian Army prisoners
    (B) illustrates Stalin's collectivization of agriculture
    (C) depicts Stalin purging his political enemies
    (D) depicts Trotsky as a Jewish devil and Bolsheviks as foreigners
    (E) illustrates the atrocities of the Holocaust

43. The most significant aspect of the social composition of the Renaissance art world was
    (A) the high degree of women's participation in it
    (B) its apprentice system
    (C) the large proportion of artists who came from the elite classes
    (D) the lack of a patronage system
    (E) the high degree of specialization that was demanded

44. In France, England, and Spain the Renaissance was centered in
    (A) the great independent city-states
    (B) the royal courts
    (C) small independent religious communities
    (D) the great universities
    (E) all of the above

GO ON TO THE NEXT PAGE

45. The Anglican Church, as created by Henry VIII, differed from other Protestant churches in that it
    (A) was congregational
    (B) remained loyal to Rome
    (C) had an episcopal structure
    (D) broke with Rome
    (E) abolished the sacraments

46. The landholding nobles of Central and Eastern Europe differed from those in Western Europe in the period 1600–1715 in that they
    (A) were drastically reduced in number
    (B) made an alliance with the middle classes
    (C) triumphed in their struggle with the monarchs
    (D) lost control of their lands
    (E) retained control of vast estates worked by serfs

47. The publication, in 1632, of the *Dialogue on the Two Chief Systems of the World* resulted in Galileo being called before the Inquisition because
    (A) it described the Copernican system
    (B) it blatantly ridiculed the Aristotelian system in the vernacular Italian
    (C) it denied the existence of God
    (D) it was a Protestant text
    (E) it claimed that the Copernican system was actually true

48. Enlightened despotism refers to
    (A) the idea that powerful rulers would act to reform and rationalize European society
    (B) Prussian militarism
    (C) the rule of law
    (D) the extensive, international correspondence network of the *philosophes*
    (E) a network of fraternities linked together by a Grand Lodge

49. The enclosure movement in Britain was most directly a result of
    (A) the development of the manorial system
    (B) the failure of mercantilism
    (C) the collectivization of agriculture
    (D) the development of the Bessemer process
    (E) the development of market-oriented agriculture

50. In the French Revolution, the March to Versailles that occurred in October of 1789 illustrates
    (A) the conservative nature of the *sans-culottes*
    (B) the power of the French army
    (C) the beginning of the radical phase of the revolution
    (D) the fact that the crowds of Paris did not yet look upon Louis XVI as their enemy
    (E) the brilliance of Napoleon as a military leader

51. The celebratory mood at the outset of World War I is best explained by
    (A) a fascination with militarism that pervaded European culture
    (B) feelings of fraternity or brotherhood that a war effort brought out in people who lived in an increasingly fragmented and divided society
    (C) a sense of romantic adventurism that cast war as an alternative to the mundane, working life of industrial Europe
    (D) expectations that the war would be short
    (E) all of the above

52. American entry into World War I was mostly triggered by
    (A) America's economic rivalry with Germany
    (B) America's desire to seize German colonies
    (C) the sinking of American vessels by German U-boats
    (D) the fall of Paris to the Germans
    (E) the Zimmerman Note

53. Abstractionist painters of the early twentieth century
    (A) sought to depict a world of emotional and psychological states
    (B) sought to accurately and honestly render the life around them in meticulous detail
    (C) sought to "analyze" the essence of perception and experience
    (D) sought to evoke the glory and power of ancient Rome
    (E) sought to reflect the grandeur of the aristocracy

GO ON TO THE NEXT PAGE

54. Which of the following helps to explain the British policy of appeasement of Germany during the 1930s?
    (A) The British public wanted no part of renewed hostilities.
    (B) Many of the British leaders privately agreed with the Germans that the Versailles Treaty had been unprecedented and unwarranted.
    (C) British leaders believed that a decision to pursue a military response to Hitler's demands was politically unwise.
    (D) Britain and her allies were not prepared militarily to back up any ultimatums they might give to Hitler.
    (E) All of the above.

55. Which of the following did NOT occur following World War II?
    (A) Germany was divided into Western and Eastern Sectors.
    (B) Germany, in what came to be known as "the war guilt clause," was forced to accept full blame for the war
    (C) Poland's border with Germany was pushed westward.
    (D) The United Nations was created.
    (E) Pro-Soviet governments were installed in Eastern Europe.

56. The treatment received by Alexander Solzhenitsyn illustrated the Soviet regime's
    (A) preference for technocratic expertise
    (B) total immunity to pressure from the West
    (C) insistence on absolute conformity
    (D) new, more democratic policies
    (E) commitment to *glasnost*

57. The main motivation of the architects of the process of European integration that has culminated in the European Union was to
    (A) stand on more equal footing with the superpowers: the United States and the Soviet Union
    (B) end communism
    (C) rebuild a war-torn economy
    (D) increase iron and steel production
    (E) all of the above

58. The most prevalent form of religious belief among the *philosophes* was
    (A) Catholicism
    (B) Lutheranism
    (C) Islam
    (D) deism
    (E) atheism

59. Which of the following was NOT a component of the triangle of trade?
    (A) guns
    (B) silk
    (C) cotton
    (D) timber
    (E) slaves

60. The cottage industry or putting-out system that had a dramatic effect on European economic and social life in the eighteenth century primarily produced
    (A) steel
    (B) iron
    (C) cotton
    (D) guns
    (E) textiles

61. During the French Revolution, Robespierre asserted that terror was necessary because
    (A) there was no God
    (B) the revolution fought against genuine tyranny
    (C) the aims of the revolution were virtuous
    (D) the people were not loyal
    (E) the king had betrayed the people

62. The Frankfort Assembly's decision in 1848 to offer Frederick William IV of Prussia the crown of a united Germany illustrates
    (A) the power of parliamentary traditions in Germany
    (B) the weakness of the Germany monarchy
    (C) the role of liberalism in the unification of Germany
    (D) the tension between liberalism and nationalism in mid-nineteenth-century Europe
    (E) the charisma of Frederick William IV

GO ON TO THE NEXT PAGE

63. The advantage of electrical power over steam power that came to be exploited towards the end of the nineteenth century was the
    (A) speed of electricity
    (B) reliability of electrical power
    (C) greater versatility and ease of transportation of electrical generators
    (D) cheaper cost of electrical power
    (E) greater energy output of electrical generators

64. Which of the following was an outgrowth of the strain of thought known as social Darwinism?
    (A) eugenics
    (B) poor relief
    (C) workhouses
    (D) child labor laws
    (E) women's suffrage

65. In order to increase the power of the newly unified Spanish monarchy, Ferdinand and Isabella
    (A) instituted liberal reforms
    (B) bought the loyalty of the Spanish nobility by strengthening the institution of serfdom
    (C) allowed Protestantism to flourish in Spain
    (D) signed an alliance with Britain and France
    (E) used the Church to build national unity

66. The work of art that both captures the emphasis on human form and illustrates the last and most heroic phase of Renaissance art is
    (A) Giotto's *Life of St. Francis*
    (B) Picasso's *Guernica*
    (C) Donatello's *David*
    (D) Michelangelo's *David*
    (E) St Peter's Basilica

67. After the publication of Newton's *Principia Mathematica* in 1687,
    (A) mathematics became the "queen of the sciences"
    (B) people spoke of a universe instead of a cosmos
    (C) it was known that Jupiter had four moons
    (D) it was understood that the cosmos was geocentric
    (E) Newton was condemned by the Catholic Church

68. The *Encyclopedia* of the late eighteenth century was considered radical because it
    (A) was printed in English rather than Latin
    (B) was the first multivolume publication
    (C) labeled anything not based on reason as superstition
    (D) called for a revolution and overthrow of the monarchy
    (E) was a Protestant encyclopedia

69. Russia participated in the expansionist trend of the late eighteenth century by
    (A) defeating the Ottoman Turks in 1774
    (B) single-handedly conquering Poland in 1775
    (C) invading Prussia in 1770
    (D) enacting the Pragmatic Sanction
    (E) invading Finland in 1774

70. The event most responsible for turning the people of Paris against Louis XVI was
    (A) his attempt to flee Paris in June of 1791
    (B) his decision to execute Robespierre
    (C) his decision to raise taxes
    (D) his decision to crush the Paris Commune
    (E) his decision to issue the Civil Constitution of the Clergy

71. The Boulanger Affair in the late 1880s
    (A) testified to the strength of anti-Semitism in France
    (B) led to the fall of the Second Republic
    (C) was evidence of the radical nature of the French working class
    (D) led to the election of a socialist popular front
    (E) underscored the fragility of French democracy and the volatility of mass politics in France

72. The Sepoy Rebellion of 1857
    (A) was a vast nationalist uprising
    (B) demonstrated anti-Western sentiment in China
    (C) drove the British from Burma
    (D) led the British government to begin to rule India directly
    (E) led the British to concentrate on bringing liberal reforms to India

GO ON TO THE NEXT PAGE

73. The Taiping Rebellion is connected to European history because
    (A) the rebels were demanding Western-style reform
    (B) it was a result of the Russo-Japanese war
    (C) Western encroachment undermined the power of the ruling dynasty
    (D) it was caused by fighting in World War II
    (E) the rebels were acting at the instigation of Westerners

74. In the interwar years, the reconstituted nations of East-Central Europe, Hungary, Poland, and Yugoslavia,
    (A) flourished economically
    (B) became satellite states of the Soviet Union
    (C) ceased to exist
    (D) came to be ruled by right-wing, authoritarian regimes
    (E) were ruled by liberal-democratic parliaments

75. The German election of 1932 was significant because
    (A) it brought a socialist coalition to power
    (B) the Nazi Party won 35 percent of the vote
    (C) Hitler was elected Chancellor of Germany
    (D) a coalition of right-wing parties was elected
    (E) it was never held; Hitler seized power in order to prevent an expected socialist victory

76. The Marshall Plan of 1947 demonstrates that the U.S. was
    (A) an imperialist country
    (B) fearful of Soviet military expansion into Western Europe
    (C) mindful of the role that economic hopelessness had played in the rise of fascism
    (D) ready to enter World War II
    (E) fearful of Germany rising again

A BRUTAL FELLOW.

Policeman. "NOW MUM! WHAT'S THE MATTER?"
Injured Female. "IF YOU PLEASE, MISTER—I WANT TO GIVE MY WHETCH OF A 'USBAND IN CHARGE. HE'S ALLVAYS A KNOCKING OF ME DOWN AND A STAMPIN' ON ME!"

Source: *Punch* (public domain), the John Leech Archive.

77. Which of the following is connoted by the cartoon above?
    (A) support for the women's suffrage movement
    (B) skepticism about claims that marriage abuses many women
    (C) the need for child labor laws
    (D) the need for the protection of abused women
    (E) the need for a larger police force

78. Which of the following accurately illustrates the reciprocal nature of innovation in the Second Industrial Revolution?
    (A) the increase in the demand for coal created by the introduction of steam power
    (B) the demand for more and improved steam engines created by the development of the iron and steel industries
    (C) the need for a railway system to transport iron and steel
    (D) the increased demand for iron and steel created by the development of the railroad
    (E) all of the above

GO ON TO THE NEXT PAGE

79. In the first decades of the twentieth century, the "nationalities problem" referred to
    (A) the absence of an international organization to coordinate diplomacy
    (B) the Anglo-German arms race
    (C) the rise of ultranationalist parties
    (D) the agitation of linguistic and ethnic minorities within the Hapsburg Empire
    (E) the agitation of southern Slavs for independence from the Russian Empire

80. Fritz Lang's film *Metropolis* (1925) illustrates
    (A) the feeling of gaiety that permeated "the Roaring Twenties"
    (B) the futuristic style of architecture that was prevalent in the interwar years
    (C) the deep anxiety over the future that existed in the 1920s
    (D) the Romantic sensibilities of the era
    (E) the year for the pastoral that characterized the films of the era

STOP. End of Section I

Section II

Part A

(Suggested writing time—45 minutes)

Directions: The following question is based on the accompanying Documents 1–10. (The documents have been edited for the purpose of this exercise.) Write your answer on the lined pages provided with the Answer Sheet.

This question is designed to test your ability to work with and understand historical documents. Write an essay that:

- has a relevant thesis and supports that thesis with evidence from the documents
- uses the majority of the documents
- addresses all parts of the question
- analyzes the documents by organizing them in as many appropriate ways as possible and does not simply summarize the documents individually
- takes into account both the sources of the documents and the authors' points of view

You may refer to relevant historical information not mentioned in the documents.

1. Compare and contrast the ideologies presented below concerning the proper form and role of government in society.

Historical background: From the late eighteenth through to the early twentieth centuries, Europe saw the development of mass politics and political parties. In response, nineteenth-century intellectuals codified their attitudes about society into ideologies which served as the basis of a political platform for their parties. Often, they were responding to each other.

Document 1

Source: Samuel Smiles, *Self-Help*, London, 1859.
Even the best institutions can give man no active aid. Perhaps the utmost they can do is to leave him free to develop himself and improve his individual condition. But in all times men have been prone to believe that their happiness and well-being were to be secured by means of institutions rather than by their own conduct. Hence the value of legislation as an agent in human advancement has always been greatly over-estimated.

Document 2

Joseph de Maistre, *Essay on the Generative Principle of Political Constitutions*, 1809.
One of the greatest errors of a century which professed them all was to believe that a political constitution could be created and written *a priori*, whereas reason and experience unite in proving that a constitution is a divine work and that precisely the most fundamental and essentially constitutional of a nation's laws could not possibly be written.

Document 3

Source: John Stuart Mill, *On Liberty*, London, 1859.
. . . the sole end for which mankind are warranted, individually or collectively, in interfering with the liberty of action of any of their number, is self-protection. That the only purpose for which power can be rightfully exercised over any member of a civilized community, against his will, is to prevent harm to others.

GO ON TO THE NEXT PAGE

Document 4

Source: Prince Clement von Metternich, Secret memorandum to Emperor Alexander I of Russia, 1820.
Presumption makes of every man the guide of his own belief, the arbiter of laws according to which he is pleased to govern himself, or to allow some one else to govern him and his neighbors; it makes him, in short, the sole judge of his own faith, his actions and the principles according to which he guides them . . . Placed beyond the passions which agitate society, it is in the days of trial chiefly that [monarchs] are called upon to despoil realities of their false appearances, and to show themselves as they are, fathers invested with the authority belonging by right to the heads of families, to prove that, in the days of mourning, they know how to be just, wise, and therefore strong, and that they will not abandon the people whom they ought to govern to be the sport of factions, to error and it consequences, which must involve the loss of society.

Document 5

Source: George Bernard Shaw, *A Manifesto*, Fabian Tract No. 2, London, 1884.
[We hold]:
That the pretensions of Capitalism to encourage Invention and to distribute its benefits in the fairest way attainable have been discredited by the experience of the nineteenth century.
That, under the existing system of leaving the National Industry to organize itself, Competition has the effect of rendering adulteration, dishonest dealing and inhumanity compulsory.

Document 6

Source: David Ricardo, *Principles of Political Economy and Taxation*, London, 1817.
It is a truth which admits not a doubt, that the comforts and well-being of the poor cannot be permanently secured without some regard on their part, or some effort on the part of the legislature, to regulate the increase of their numbers, and to render less frequent among them early and improvident marriages. The operation of the system of poor laws has been indirectly contrary to this. They have rendered restrain superfluous, and have invited imprudence, by offering it a portion of the wages of prudence and industry. . . .

Document 7

Source: Pope Leo XIII, *De Rerum Novarum* (Concerning New Issues), papal encyclical, 1891.
. . . philosophy and Christian faith agree that the administration of the State has from nature as its purpose, not the benefit of those to whom it has been entrusted, but the benefit of those who have been entrusted to it. And since the power or governing comes from God and is a participation, as it were, in His supreme sovereignty, it ought to be administered according to the example of the Divine power, which looks with paternal care to the welfare of individual creatures as well as to that of all creation.

Document 8

Source: Karl Marx and Friedrich Engels, *The Communist Manifesto*, London, 1848.
The proletariat will use its political supremacy to wrest, by degrees, all capital from the bourgeoisie, to centralize all instruments of production in the hands of the State, i.e., of the proletariat organized as the ruling class; and to increase the total productive forces as rapidly as possible.

GO ON TO THE NEXT PAGE

Document 9

Source: Eduard Bernstein, *Evolutionary Socialism*, 1909.
I set myself against the notion that we have to expect shortly a collapse of the bourgeois economy, and that social democracy should be induced by the prospect of such an imminent, great, social catastrophe to adapt its tactics to that assumption . . . [T]he conquest of political power necessitates the possession of political rights; and the most important problem of tactics which German social democracy has at this moment to solve, appears to me to be to devise the best way for the extension of the political and economic rights of the German working classes.

Document 10

Source: Peter Kropotkin, *Anarchism: Its Philosophy and Ideal*, San Francisco, 1898.
When we ask for the abolition of the State and its organs we are always told that we dream of a society composed of men better than they are in reality. But no; a thousand times no. All we ask is that men should not be made worse than they are.

GO ON TO THE NEXT PAGE

Section II

Part B

(Suggested planning and writing time—35 minutes)

Directions: You are to answer ONE question from the three questions below. Make your selection carefully, choosing the question that you are best prepared to answer thoroughly in the limited time permitted. You should spend five minutes organizing or outlining your answer. Write your answer to the question on the lined pages provided with the Answer Sheet, making sure to indicate which question you are answering by writing the appropriate question number at the top of each page.

Write an essay that:

- has a relevant thesis
- addresses all parts of the question
- supports the thesis with specific evidence
- is well organized

2. Analyze the achievement of the Renaissance art world. Discuss both specific achievements and the context that produced them.
3. Discuss the impact of the Scientific Revolution on European society and culture.
4. Discuss the revolutions of 1848 and their lasting impact.

GO ON TO THE NEXT PAGE

Section II

Part C

(Suggested planning and writing time—35 minutes)

Directions: You are to answer ONE question from the three questions below. Make your selection carefully, choosing the question that you are best prepared to answer thoroughly in the limited time permitted. You should spend five minutes organizing or outlining your answer. Write your answer to the question on the lined pages provided with the Answer Sheet, making sure to indicate which question you are answering by writing the appropriate question number at the top of each page.

Write an essay that:

- has a relevant thesis
- addresses all parts of the question
- supports the thesis with specific evidence
- is well organized

5. Discuss the relationship between the settlement which followed World War I and the causes of World War II.
6. Discuss the causes and processes of European integration and unity in the second half of the twentieth century.
7. Compare and contrast the causes and outcomes of the French Revolution (1789–1799) and the Russian Revolution (1917–1924).

STOP. End of Section II

› Answers and Explanations

1. **B**. The creation of unemployment and decreased wages for skilled craftsmen created by the division of production into simple, unskilled tasks was an outstanding social effect of the development of a division of labor system of production. Choice A is incorrect because the increased volume of manufactured goods was not, in itself, a social effect. Choice C is incorrect because the increased profit for manufacturers is not, in itself, a social effect. Choice D is incorrect because the increased efficiency is not, in itself, a social effect. Choice E is incorrect because volume was increased, not decreased, by the division of labor.

2. **D**. The Bessemer process was a new process, developed in the 1850s, for smelting iron ore that allowed for the manufacture of iron and steel more cheaply and in larger quantities. Choice A is incorrect because the Bessemer process did not affect cotton production. Choice B is incorrect because it was the steam engine that facilitated a move away from human and water power. Choice C is incorrect because the Bessemer process did not affect the military balance of power. Choice E is incorrect because the Bessemer process did not affect transportation speed.

3. **D**. The Industrial Revolution began in Great Britain and spread east throughout Europe. Great Britain, therefore, developed and maintained a lead in innovation and industrial production that was not surpassed until after World War I.

4. **A**. The basic tenet of conservatism, that traditions were time-tested, organic solutions to social and political problems, led conservatives to defend most staunchly the institution of monarchy. Choice B is incorrect because liberals' belief that the purpose of government was to protect individual liberty led them to frequently challenge the institution of monarchy. Choice C is incorrect because socialism's emphasis on class welfare led socialists to oppose the monarchy. Choice D is incorrect because communists' belief in class struggle led them to oppose the monarchy. Choice E is incorrect because anarchists' belief that the state made men worse led them to oppose all state institutions, including the monarchy.

5. **C**. Smith's doctrine of *laissez-faire* (or hands-off) argued that it is futile for governments to interfere with the natural workings of an economy, because the natural laws that govern human economic behavior will always win out in the end. Choice A is incorrect because *laissez-faire* is a doctrine that refers only to human economic behavior. Choice B is incorrect because *laissez-faire* was not concerned with political relations. Choices D and E are incorrect because they contain notions of social Darwinism, which developed long after Smith wrote and which are best attributed to Herbert Spencer.

6. **C**. Utilitarianism, which argued that all human laws and institutions ought to be judged by their usefulness in promoting "the greatest good for the greatest number" of people, tended to be more supportive of government intervention than other liberal ideologies, calling, for example, for legislation to limit the hours that women and children could work in factories. Choice A is incorrect because it was the conservatives who supported tradition. Choice B is incorrect because utilitarians tended to place *less* emphasis on individual liberty than other liberals. Choice D is incorrect because it was the communists who called for the abolition of private property. Choice E is incorrect because it was the anarchists who advocated violence.

7. **E**. The belief that salvation could not be earned, but was a gift given by God to those who had true faith was a major tenet of Luther's theology. Choices A and B are incorrect because both were tenets of the Roman Church's theology, which Luther opposed. Choice C is incorrect because predestination was a major tenet of Calvin's theology, not Luther's. Choice D is incorrect because, though there is evidence of millenarianism in Luther's thought, it was not a major tenet of his theology.

8. **D**. The Council of Trent symbolized a defeat for those who wished for reconciliation between

Protestants and the Roman Church because it continued to insist that the Roman Church was the final arbiter in all matters of faith. Choice A is incorrect because Protestantism was not "defeated" at any point in European history. Choice B is incorrect because the reforms instituted by the Council of Trent failed to significantly affect the split between Catholics and Protestants. Choice C is incorrect because it was the Peace of Augsburg that contained the pledge of the German Princes not to go to war over religion. Choice E is incorrect because it was the Society of Jesus (or Jesuits) that served as an anti-Protestant force all over the globe.

9. **B.** The relative peace of the Restoration Period in England broke down when James II, a Stuart with a Catholic wife and a desire to revenge his executed father, ascended to the throne. Choice A is incorrect because Cromwell died before the Restoration Period. Choice C is incorrect because Charles II was the first king of the Restoration Period and his restraint allowed for the period of relative peace. Choice D is incorrect because the reign of Elizabeth I predates both the civil war and the Restoration. Choice E is incorrect because the invasion of a Protestant fleet, led by William of Orange, from the Netherlands was the culmination of the new period of hostilities that broke out following James II ascending to the throne.

10. **A.** A series of religious and dynastic wars in the sixteenth century produced a kingdom in which the religious issue had been settled firmly in favor of the Catholic majority. The lack of religious turmoil in the seventeenth century allowed the French monarchy to cement an alliance with both the clergy and middle class, and to use the great administrative expertise of both to build a powerful centralized government. Choice B is incorrect because seventeenth-century France was a monarchy, not a republic. Choice C is incorrect because the "little ice ages" that characterized the climate of the 1600s had no significant affect on the construction of an absolutist regime in France. Choice D is incorrect because the struggle to impose absolutism took place between the monarch and his administrators and the provincial nobility. Choice E is incorrect

because, while Louis XIV was more capable than his predecessor, both relied heavily upon talented members of the Church and the middle classes.

11. **C.** The baroque style appealed to the absolute monarchs of seventeenth-century Europe, who believed that its inherent grandeur reflected the grandeur of their power and influence. Choice A is incorrect because the baroque also appealed to the bourgeoisie of seventeenth-century Europe, who adopted it to reflect what they saw as the grandeur of their bustling centers of trade and learning. Choice B is incorrect because it incorrectly places the baroque in the eighteenth century; baroque was the dominant artistic style of the seventeenth century. Choice D is incorrect because the lower classes did not have the wealth to build in the grand style of baroque. Choice E is incorrect because it places the baroque in the nineteenth century; baroque was the dominant artistic style of the seventeenth century.

12. **A.** The Women's Social and Political Union led by Emmeline Pankhurst and her daughters Christabel and Sylvia campaigned, often violently, for a broader notion of women's rights. Choice B is incorrect because the Fabian Society was an organization of British socialists that did not focus specifically on women's rights. Choice C is incorrect because the Social Democrats were a German socialist party. Choice D is incorrect because the National Union of Women's Suffrage Societies headed by Millicent Garrett Fawcett confined their campaign to the issue of women's voting rights. Choice E is incorrect because the Zionists advocated a homeland for Jews in Palestine.

13. **C.** The increasing participation of the working class in British politics that resulted from accumulated reforms accounted for large gains by the Labour Party in the first decade of the twentieth century. Choice A is incorrect because Conservative gains did not match those of the Labour Party. Choice B is incorrect because the Liberal Party lost support in the first decade of the twentieth century. Choice D is incorrect because the British Union of Fascists made only modest gains, and those were made during the interwar years, not during the first decade of the twentieth century. Choice E is incorrect because there was no Democratic Party in Britain.

14. **E.** All of the choices are correct. Choice A is correct because the Weimar Republic was a liberal democracy, a form of government largely alien to the German people, whose allegiance had been to the Kaiser. Choice B is correct because the leader of the Weimar Republic, the moderate Social Democrat Friedrich Ebert, had been chosen at the Peace Conference and was therefore perceived to have been imposed on Germany by its vengeful war enemies. Choice C is correct because the leaders of the Weimar Republic were wrongly blamed for the humiliating nature of the Treaty of Versailles, when in fact they had no leverage with which to negotiate. Choice D is correct because the government of the Weimar Republic was plagued by both the general economic difficulties of interwar Europe and Germany's need to pay the huge war reparations imposed on it.

15. **B.** Lenin's New Economic Plan, launched in the early 1920s, allowed rural peasants and small-business operators to manage their own land and businesses and to sell their products in order to stimulate the Russian economy. Choice A is incorrect because the five-year plan was Stalin's attempt to industrialize Russia rapidly. Choice C is incorrect because the Soviet Constitution of 1923 created a Federal State named the Union of Soviet Socialist Republics. Choice D is incorrect because the phrase "socialism in one country" refers to Stalin's abandonment of a worldwide socialist revolution and his decision to concentrate instead on making the Soviet Union a successful socialist state.

16. **C.** In Italy, the fascists, led by Mussolini, garnered massive public support by casting themselves as the party that would save the country from socialism and put everyone to work (and in uniform) by rebuilding Italy into a world power. Choice A is incorrect because, although the Fascists did engage in intimidation tactics, Mussolini was legally appointed Prime Minister of Italy. Choice B is incorrect because it was the Communist Party that appealed to the working classes by promising to abolish private property and bring about a classless society. Choices D and E are incorrect because the fascists in Italy were supported by both the Church and the industrialists, both of whom saw the socialists and communists as greater threats to their interests.

17. **E.** Unlike the settlement which followed World War I, which was formally concluded by a series of treaties known collectively as the Treaty of Versailles, the settlement which followed World War II was not concluded by formal treaties, but rather by a hardening of the postwar occupation agreements. Choice A is incorrect because Germany was formally blamed for the war in the settlement following World War I, not World War II. Choice B is incorrect because both settlements were imposed by the victors. Choice C is incorrect because the Hapsburg Empire was dismantled by the settlement following World War I, not II. Choice D is incorrect because the construction of national boundaries which ignored significant ethnic and nationalist differences certainly occurred in the settlement to World War I.

18. **C.** The mid-nineteenth-century Italian nationalist movement known as the *Risorgimento* was composed mostly of intellectuals and university students who shared the idealism of its leader, Giuseppe Mazzini. Because it failed to win the support of the masses, it was easily crushed by conservative forces. Choice A is incorrect because the *Risorgimento* did attract intellectuals. Choice B is incorrect because the *Risorgimento* was a virulently nationalist movement. Choice D is incorrect because the fate of the *Risorgimento* was not linked to German support. Choice E is incorrect because the military was a conservative tool which only mass support could have overcome.

19. **B.** While the architect of Italian unification, Count Camillo Cavour, had to deal with both Austrian and French domination of part of the Italian peninsula, his counterpart, Otto von Bismarck, did not, as the German kingdoms were free of direct foreign domination. Choice A is incorrect because both Cavour and Bismarck were conservative aristocrats. Choice C is incorrect because Cavour rallied support around King Victor Emmanuel II of Piedmont and Bismarck rallied support around King William I of Prussia. Choice D is incorrect because both Cavour and

Bismarck were opportunists. Choice E is incorrect because Cavour provoked war with the Austrians, while Bismarck provoked war with both the Austrians and the French.

20. **E**. Unlike European imperialism in Africa, which involved the direct claiming of large amounts of territory by the European powers, European imperialism in Asia was exerted through the control of local elites. Choice A is incorrect because there were ample economic motives for European imperialism in Asia. Choice B is incorrect because *both* were facilitated by technological innovations in weaponry and transportation. Choices C and D are incorrect because *both* were connected to nationalism and the development of mass politics.

21. **E**. Détente refers to the period of U.S.–Soviet relations from the late 1960s to the early 1980s that was characterized by less conflict and which produced a number of nuclear test-ban treaties and arms-limitation talks. Choice A is incorrect because the 1968 efforts of Czechoslovakians to reform their society was known as either the Prague Spring or "socialism with a human face." Choice B is incorrect because the postwar division of Europe into an East and West is referred to as either the Cold War or the Iron Curtain. Choice C is incorrect because the 51-member international organization created to promote international peace and cooperation was the United Nations. Choice D is incorrect because the U.S. mission that flew supplies into West Berlin is known as the Berlin Airlift.

22. **A**. The Warsaw Pact, created in response to the creation of NATO, was a military alliance between the countries of Soviet-dominated Eastern Europe. Choice B is incorrect because there was no military alliance between Poland and Russia. Choice C is incorrect because it was the Council for Mutual Economic Assistance, formed by the Soviet Union to counter the Marshall Plan, that promised economic aid for Eastern European countries. Choice D is incorrect because NATO was the military alliance between the U.S. and western European powers. Choice E is incorrect because it was the Truman Doctrine that offered military and economic aid to countries threatened by communist takeover.

23. **D**. Copernicanism, the theory put forward by the Polish astronomer Nicolas Copernicus, promoted a heliocentric, or Sun-centered, model of the cosmos. Choice A is incorrect because it was Isaac Newton's theory of universal gravitation that argued that all matter was affected by a universal force. Choice B is incorrect because it was the traditional view of the cosmos, which Copernicus was arguing against, that promoted a geocentric, or Earth-centered, model of the cosmos. Choice C is incorrect because it was Aristotelian physics that declared that all matter was made up of four elements. Choice E is incorrect because, in Copernicus's model, the universe is finite.

24. **B**. Both the date and her use of the criteria of reason (or lack thereof) identify her as an Enlightenment *philosophe*. Choice A is incorrect because conservatives defended the subjugation of women as a traditional and, therefore, time-tested practice. Choice C is incorrect because socialism developed in the nineteenth century and socialists concerned themselves with issues of class, not gender. Choice D is incorrect because anarchism is a nineteenth-century ideology devoted to the abolition of the state. Choice E is incorrect because the word *suffragette* was a term coined in the late nineteenth century to describe women who advocated voting rights for women.

25. **C**. The sentence, written in the *Social Contract* (1762), is Rousseau's and summarizes his view of human nature as born good but easily corrupted by society. Choice A is incorrect because Locke's view of human nature was that it was a *tabula rasa*, or a blank slate. Choice B is incorrect because Luther viewed human nature as essentially corrupted by original sin. Choice D is incorrect because Voltaire viewed all claims about human nature skeptically. Choice E is incorrect because Bentham was a utilitarian who viewed humans as motivated by the avoidance of pain.

26. **E**. The Middle Passage refers to the deadly, middle leg of the triangle of trade in which African slaves were transported from Africa (in exchange for guns and rum) across the Atlantic to the Americas and the West Indies (in exchange for raw materials). Choice A is incorrect because the Middle Passage does not refer to scriptural

passages. Choice B is incorrect because it is the Suez Canal that connects the Mediterranean Sea to the Red Sea. Choice C is incorrect because rural manufacturing was known as cottage industry or the putting-out system. Choice D is incorrect because the route to China that was the backbone of the silk trade was known as the Great Silk Road.

27. **E**. The officer corps was still chosen from the aristocracy; officers would not be chosen and promoted on merit until the middle of the nineteenth century. The other four choices correctly describe changes to European armies that occurred in the eighteenth century.

28. **B**. The term *National Assembly* explicitly rejected the notion that France was made up of three separate estates or classes of people and, thereby, signified the belief that political sovereignty belonged to the nation as a whole. Choices A and C are incorrect because the formation of a National Assembly in June of 1789 neither signified nor reflected republicanism; many within the National Assembly simply aimed at reforms that would make France a constitutional monarchy. Choice D is incorrect because the National Assembly did not call for or represent a commitment to democracy. Choice E is incorrect because the events of 1789 in France did not involve war with Germany.

29. **A**. It was the Concordat of 1801 that reconciled Napoleonic France with Rome and which stipulated that French clergy would be chosen and paid by the state but consecrated by the pope. Choice B is incorrect because the Napoleonic Code, or Civil Code, of 1804 provided a system of uniform law and administrative policy throughout Napoleon's empire; it did not concern the clergy. Choice C is incorrect because the Consulate was the three-man executive body established shortly after Napoleon's coup of 1799; Napoleon was first consul. Choice D is incorrect because the Treaty of Tilsit was signed by Napoleon and Russia in July of 1807 in which Russia recognized Napoleon's claims to his empire in Europe. Choice E is incorrect because the Continental System refers to Napoleon's edict in 1805 that the Continental countries under his control would not trade with Great Britain.

30. **D**. The agreement among the princes of the German principalities in 1555 that established the principle of "he who rules; his religion" is known as the Peace of Augsburg. Choice A is incorrect because the Edict of Nantes, issued in 1598, briefly established the principle of religious toleration in France, which was not tied to the religion of the ruler. Choice B is incorrect because the Peace of Augsburg was signed in defiance of the papacy in Rome, which wanted all princes to stamp out the heresy of Protestantism wherever they encountered it. Choice C is incorrect because the Geneva Convention is a twentieth-century international agreement that has to do with the rules of war and especially with the treatment of prisoners. Choice E is incorrect because the Inquisition was a tool of the Roman Catholic Church developed to combat Protestantism and was, therefore, opposed to any notion of toleration of Protestant religions.

31. **E**. All of the choices were parts of the structure of Calvinist communities: pastors preached the gospel; doctors studied scripture and wrote commentaries; deacons saw to the social welfare of the community; and elders governed the church and the community in moral matters and enforced discipline.

32. **C**. The period of British history immediately following the execution of Charles I in 1649 and lasting until the Restoration in 1660 is known as the Commonwealth. Choice A is incorrect because the Restoration period in British history commences with the restoration of the Stuart monarchy in 1660. Choice B is incorrect, because the Glorious Revolution refers to the expulsion of the Stuarts and the establishment of a constitutional monarchy in Britain in 1688. Choice D is incorrect because the English Civil War, fought from 1642 to 1646 preceded the Commonwealth period. Choice E is incorrect because the Norman Conquest occurred in Britain in 1066.

33. **E**. Following Plato, neoplatonism located reality in a changeless world of spirit, or forms, rather than in the physical world, and argued that it was the language of mathematics that gave one

knowledge of that spiritual world of forms. Choice A is incorrect because the development of chemical experimentation is tied to the traditions of alchemy and magic, not neoplatonism. Choice B is incorrect because there was no concept of a single scientific method in existence during the Scientific Revolution; rather there were competing traditions of knowledge. Choice C is incorrect because the promotion of scientific knowledge as a practical pursuit was mostly the work of Francis Bacon and not a significant component of neoplatonism. Choice D is incorrect because the neoplatonists did not deny the existence of God, rather they taught that mathematics described the essential nature and the soul of the cosmos, a soul that was God itself.

34. **A.** Beccaria extended the Enlightenment tradition of applying the laws of reason to human society by arguing that the rehabilitation and reintegration ought to be the purpose of punishment. Choice B is incorrect because it was Thomas Hobbes who argued, in a pre-Enlightenment tradition, that an all-powerful ruler was necessary to keep order and prevent crime. Choice C is incorrect because Beccaria did not call for the abolition of the death penalty. Choice D is incorrect because Becarria did not call for the standardization of punishment in all kingdoms. Choice E is incorrect because it was Rousseau who argued that society corrupted human nature.

35. **D.** The complex and connected network of Masonic lodges formed a network for the communication of new ideas and ideals that rivaled the salons. Choice A is incorrect because, while Masonry has its origins in the medieval stone masons guilds, eighteenth-century Masonry had no effect on architecture. Choices B and C are incorrect because, despite their reputation for mysterious plots, the eighteenth-century Masons plotted neither to assassinate the pope nor to start any revolutions. Choice E is incorrect because, despite the fact that U.S. currency contains several Masonic symbols, the eighteenth-century Masons were not in charge of currency reform.

36. **D.** The development of rural manufacturing, sometimes known as cottage industry or as the putting-out system, combined with the shift to cash crops and technical innovation to break the traditional population cycle and allow Europe's population to grow dramatically in the eighteenth century. Choices A and B are incorrect because both the Black Death and the Hundred Years War were fourteenth-century phenomena that depressed Europe's population numbers. Choices C and E are incorrect because both were nineteenth-century developments.

37. **E.** All of the above are correct: choice A is correct because the liberals' emphasis on individual liberty did not mesh well with the nationalists' emphasis on the collective, national tribe. Choice B is correct because the nationalists' tendency to mythologize the past did not mesh well with the liberals' agenda of reform. Choice C is correct because the liberals' call for limited government contradicted the nationalists' belief that a strong national government was the best guarantee of unity. Choice D is correct because the liberals' failure in 1848 turned the nationalists to the conservatives.

38. **C.** Bismarck's strategy of employing whatever means seemed necessary and useful to increase Prussian power has come to be known as *Realpolitik* (reality politics). Choice A is incorrect because Détente is the term used to describe the warmer relations between the U.S. and the Soviet Union in the late 1960s to the early 1980s. Choice B is incorrect because *Lebensraum* refers to a German cultural idea that Germany had natural borders that were greater than her political borders. Choice D is incorrect because the Schlieffen Plan was the German military plan to avoid a two-front war with the members of the Triple Entente. Choice E is incorrect because the Kulturkampf was Bismarck's campaign to weaken the power of Catholics in the southern regions of Germany; it was an *example* of *Realpolitik*.

39. **D.** Artists who sympathized with the democratic and nationalist philosophy of the revolution rejected the dominant rococo aesthetic in favor of a neoclassical style that took its inspiration from the last known democracies, the ancient republics of Greece and Rome. Choice A is incorrect because impressionism was an artistic movement of the nineteenth century. Choice B

is incorrect because the neoclassical style favored by artists of the revolutionary era included a *greater* degree of realism than the rococo style that preceded it. Choice C is incorrect because the neoclassical style favored by artists of the revolutionary era rejected religious themes in favor of more secular, civic themes. Choice E is incorrect because Caravaggio's works exemplify the Counter-Reformation baroque style in seventeenth-century painting.

40. E. The remilitarization of the Rhineland was undertaken by Hitler in 1936, prior to *World War II*. Choice A is incorrect because the Anglo-German rivalry created an arms race that did contribute to the outbreak of World War I. Choice B is incorrect because the Alliance System contributed to the outbreak of World War I by drastically limiting diplomatic options. Choice C is incorrect because the rise of a unified Germany upset the balance of power in Europe, contributing to the creation of both the Anglo-German rivalry and the Alliance System. Choice D is incorrect because the Schlieffen Plan called for Germany to attack westward at the first sign of Russian troop mobilization.

41. B. The Dreyfus Affair, in which a group of bigoted French Army officers falsely accused Alfred Dreyfus, a young Jewish captain, of treason, and the slowness of the French legal establishment to accept the evidence of Dreyfus's innocence, illustrated the strength of ultranationalism and anti-Semitism in the French establishment. Choice A is incorrect because the Dreyfus Affair illustrated the extreme character of French nationalism, not its weakness. Choice C is incorrect because the Dreyfus Affair had nothing to do with the social position of women. Choices D and E are incorrect because the Dreyfus Affair had nothing to do with France's preparation or desire for war.

42. D. The image is a Russian Civil War White Army poster depicting Trotsky as a Jewish devil and the Bolsheviks as under the influence of the Chinese. Choice A is incorrect because there are no German soldiers in the image. Choices B and C are incorrect because the star of David identifies the image as Trotsky (who was a Jew), and Stalin did not gain control until after Lenin's death in

1924. Choice E is incorrect because the Holocaust began in the 1930s.

43. B. The fact that the Renaissance art world was populated through an apprentice system, in which young men of modest means served long apprenticeships, was most significant because it meant that art was looked upon as a craft and that all media and materials had to be mastered. The end result was that mature Renaissance artists were able to work with a variety of materials and to apply ideas and techniques learned in one medium to projects in another. Choice A is incorrect because women were still largely excluded from the Renaissance art world. Choice C is incorrect because Renaissance artists did not come from the elite classes. Choice D is incorrect because the Renaissance art world relied on a large network of patronage. Choice E is incorrect because Renaissance artists were not, as noted above, trained as specialists, but as masters of all media and materials.

44. B. The existence of strong monarchies in France, England, and Spain meant that, as the ideas of the Renaissance spread out of Italy, their development was centered in the Royal Courts. Choice A is incorrect because it was in the great independent city-states of *Italy* that the Renaissance originated. Choice C is incorrect because it was in the small German principalities that the Renaissance found a home in the small, independent religious communities that comprised the lay-piety tradition. Choice D is incorrect because the great universities of Europe were controlled by the Church, which maintained the older scholastic forms of knowledge and was mostly hostile to the ideas of the Renaissance. Choice E is incorrect because choices A, C, and D are incorrect.

45. C. The Anglican Church, unlike the other Protestant churches, retained an episcopal structure, that is, it retained its hierarchy of bishops, priests, etc. Choice A is incorrect because the Anglican church was not congregational (most other Protestant churches were). Choice B is incorrect because the Anglican Church did break with Rome. Choice D is incorrect because all other Protestant churches also broke with Rome, so that is not a way in which the Anglican

Church differed from them. Choice E is incorrect because the Anglican Church did not abolish the sacraments.

46. **E.** Because the European kingdoms in central and eastern Europe were less economically developed than their western counterparts, there was no rising middle class and less new wealth in this period for the monarchies to ally with or exploit to weaken the traditional landed nobility. As a result, that nobility was able to avoid the erosion of wealth that weakened their counterparts in Britain and France. Choice A is incorrect because the traditional landed nobility was not drastically reduced in number anywhere in Europe during this period. Choice B is incorrect because the landed nobility did not make an alliance with the middle class anywhere in Europe during this period. Choice C is incorrect because it is more accurate to characterize the struggle between the monarchs and the traditional landed nobility in central and eastern Europe in this period as a stand-off that perpetuated the status quo. Choice D is incorrect because the nobility in central and eastern Europe during this period held onto their lands.

47. **B.** In the *Dialogue*, Galileo effectively took his case to the public by abandoning the Latin prose of the scholarly elite for the vernacular Italian of the masses and publishing a thinly veiled attack on what he considered to be the absurdity of the Church's defense of the Aristotelian model. Choice A is incorrect because other works had described the Copernican system; the Church did not consider description of the model heresy. Choice C is incorrect because the *Dialogue* does not deny the existence of God. Choice D is incorrect because the *Dialogue* is not a Protestant text. Choice E is incorrect because the *Dialogue* does not, technically, claim that the Copernican system is true, rather it concentrates on ridiculing the Aristotelian system.

48. **A.** The phrase "enlightened despotism" refers to the hope shared by many *philosophes* that the powerful monarchs of European civilization, once educated in the ideals of the Enlightenment, would use their power to reform and rationalize society. Choice B is incorrect because Prussian militarism was not connected to the Enlightenment. Choice C is incorrect because, although the rule of law was something the *philosophes* hoped could be accomplished by enlightened despotism, the terms are not synonymous. Choice D is incorrect because enlightened despotism does not refer to correspondence networks. Choice E is incorrect because it was Free Masonry that was a network of fraternities linked together by the Grand Lodge.

49. **E.** The development of market-oriented agriculture, where crops were sold for cash rather than grown for winter survival, most directly led to the movement on the part of landlords to "enclose" the traditional common land and family-farmed land that characterized the more traditional manorial system of agriculture. Choice B is incorrect because it was the success of the mercantilist system that made cash-crop farming attractive to land owners. Choice C is incorrect because the collectivization of agriculture was carried out in the Soviet Union under Stalin. Choice D is incorrect because the development of the Bessemer process affected iron and steel production, not agricultural production.

50. **D.** The march, organized by the women of Paris from Paris to the king's palace at Versailles for the purpose of forcing Louis XVI to come to Paris, illustrated that the crowds still looked at him as a potential patron rather than an enemy. Choice A is incorrect because the *sans-culottes*, who were not conservative, had not yet made their presence known in the revolution. Choice B is incorrect because the French Army was not directly involved in the march. Choice C is incorrect because the radical phase would not commence until 1791. Choice E is incorrect because Napoleon was not involved in the march.

51. **E.** All the choices are correct. Choice A is correct because there was a fascination with militarism that went hand in hand with the development of nationalism. Choice B is correct because Europeans during the Industrial Age lived in a society in which they had been uprooted from both family and place. Choice C is correct because war was highly Romanticized as a way to "matter" and to achieve glory. Choice D is correct because both sides predicted victory in six weeks.

52. C. The sinking of American vessels and noncombatant vessels that had American passengers, like the *Lusitania*, by German U-boats was most directly responsible for the American entry into World War I. Choice A is incorrect because America and Germany were trading partners; fear of losing that trade was a factor that kept America out of the war for so long. Choice B is incorrect because America had no designs on German colonies. Choice D is incorrect because Paris did not fall to the Germans in World War I. Choice E is incorrect because, although the so-called Zimmerman Note (a diplomatic correspondence of dubious origin, purporting to reveal a deal between Germany and Mexico) was a small factor in America entering the war, it was not as important as the sinking of American vessels.

53. C. The abstractionists of the early twentieth century, such as Georges Braque and Wassily Kandinsky, developed a system of seeing the world as composed of geometrical shapes in order to analyze the essence of perception and experience. Choice A is incorrect because the depiction of a world of emotional and psychological states was the goal of the expressionists (such as Edvard Munch) and not a defining characteristic of abstractionists. Choice B is incorrect because the accurate and honest rendering of everyday life—the goal of the realist painters of the mid-nineteenth century—was not a concern of the abstractionists. Choice D is incorrect because the abstractionists had no interest in evoking the glory and power of ancient Rome; this was the goal of the neoclassicists of the eighteenth century. Choice E is incorrect because the abstractionists had no interest in reflecting the grandeur of the aristocracy, which was the goal of a particular subgroup of rococo artists in the eighteenth century.

54. E. All of the choices are correct. Choice A is correct because, unlike the Germans who thought things could get no worse and were eager to avenge the humiliation of defeat in World War I, the British public hoped that they had fought and won the "war to end all wars" and wanted no part of renewed hostilities. Choice B is correct because many British leaders privately agreed with the Germans that many aspects of the Versailles Treaty, such as the limits on the German military and the enormous war reparations, had been unprecedented and unwarranted. Choice C is correct because, given British public opinion, a decision to pursue a military response to Hitler's actions would have been political suicide for British leaders. Choice D is correct because Britain and her allies, unlike Hitler's Germany, had not begun any kind of military buildup and were in no position to back up any ultimatums they might give to Hitler.

55. B. The famous "war guilt clause" was part of the settlement that followed *World War I*. Choice A is incorrect because the "on the ground" reality hardened into a lasting situation as Germany was divided into sectors, with the Western powers controlling the western sectors and the Soviet Union controlling the eastern sectors. Choice C is incorrect because Poland's border with Germany was pushed westward. Choice D is incorrect because the United Nations was created with 51 members to promote international peace and cooperation. Choice E is incorrect because although the United States and Britain called for free elections in the Eastern European nations that were physically under the control of the Soviet Army, pro-Soviet governments were quickly installed by Stalin.

56. C. The expulsion of Solzhenitsyn, in November 1969, from the Russian Writers' Union for publishing novels that were not approved by Soviet censors and his arrest and deportation following the 1973 publication of his novel *The Gulag Archipelago* illustrate the Soviet regime's insistence on absolute conformity to the "party line" of the state. Choice A is incorrect because Solzhenitsyn was a writer, not a technocrat. Choice B is incorrect because the fact that Solzhenitsyn, much celebrated in the West, was deported to West Germany rather than to Siberia illustrates that the Soviet regime was *not* totally immune to pressure from the West. Choice D is incorrect because there was nothing democratic in the treatment Solzhenitsyn received. Choice E is incorrect because the treatment of Solzhenitsyn illustrates the lack of openness in the Soviet Union prior to the initiation of *glasnost* (openness) by Gorbachev in the late 1980s.

57. A. The main motivation for the French and German statesmen who were the architects of the process of European integration was to make sure that Europe could one day stand on equal footing with the superpowers, in terms of both economics and world influence. Choice B is incorrect because their concern was initially for Western Europe. Choice C is incorrect because Western Europe had the Marshall Plan to help it *rebuild*; the concern for integration of Europe's economy went beyond rebuilding. Choice D is incorrect because, although the first step in European integration was the coordination of iron and steel production, its architects were always looking forward to a much larger and total integration. Choice E is incorrect because B–D are incorrect.

58. D. The most prevalent form of religious belief amongst the *philosophes* was deism, the belief that the complexity, order, and natural laws exhibited by the universe were reasonable proofs that it had been created by a God who no longer played any active role in the universe. Choices A and B are incorrect because the *philosophes* considered revelation, the kind of knowledge upon which both Catholicism and Lutheranism were based, to be unreliable compared with reason. Choice C is incorrect because there were very few Muslims in Europe in the eighteenth century. Choice E is incorrect because, despite their skepticism of traditional religious beliefs, most *philosophes* were not atheists.

59. B. Silk was imported from the Far East and was not part of what was known as the triangle of trade that operated between Europe, Africa, and the Americas/West Indies. Choice A is incorrect because guns were sent from Europe to Africa. Choices C and D are incorrect because cotton and timber went from the Americas to Europe. Choice E is incorrect because slaves went from Africa to the Americas/West Indies.

60. E. The cottage industry or putting-out system involved farming families and communities earning extra income by doing the carding, spinning, and weaving that produced textiles. Choices A and B are incorrect because steel and iron production were the backbone of the heavy phase of industrialization that occurred in the nineteenth century. Choice C is incorrect because cotton was the raw material of much of the textile industry, not its product. Choice D is incorrect because guns were not produced by cottage industry.

61. B. Robespierre argued that, in a fight against true tyranny, it is necessary to match the ruthlessness of tyranny with terror. Choice A is incorrect because Robespierre made no mention of God in his defense of the use of terror. Choice C is incorrect because Robespierre argued that the virtuous aims of the revolution provided the *justification* of terror; the necessity for terror came from the tyrannical nature of the revolution's opponents. Choice D is incorrect because Robespierre did not speak of "the people" but rather divided humanity into the virtuous and the nonvirtuous. Choice E is incorrect because Robespierre did not mention the king in his defense of terror.

62. D. The decision of the liberal Frankfort Assembly to offer the crown of a united Germany to the authoritarian king of Prussia, Frederick William IV, illustrates the tension between the liberal aspirations of the Assembly and the desire for a strong and powerful united nation of Germany. Choice A is incorrect because the Assembly's decision illustrates nothing in particular about the Parliamentary tradition in Germany, though Frederick William's refusal says something about its weakness. Choice B is incorrect because there was no German monarchy in 1848; the assembly was proposing to create one. Choice C is incorrect because German unification would not come about for another 21 years. Choice E is incorrect because it was the military power of Prussia, rather than Frederick William's charisma, that led the Assembly to offer him the crown.

63. C. Electrical generators were more versatile—they could be made small or large and powerful, and were more easily transported than steam engines; electrical generators were used to power a wide variety of small- and large-scale factories and mills. Choice A is incorrect because the "speed" of electricity was not a relevant factor in industrial production. Choice B is incorrect because early electrical generators were not necessarily more reliable than steam engines. Choice D is incorrect because the electrical power was not initially significantly cheaper than steam power. Choice E is incorrect because it was the *range* of power that could be produced by electrical generators that made the switch desirable.

64. **A.** Eugenics, the science of monitoring and planning the biological reproduction of a population or "race," was an outgrowth of social Darwinism, which argued that "races" competed with each other and that only the "fittest" races would survive. Choice B is incorrect because relief for the poor was opposed by social Darwinists on the basis that it interfered with the natural selection process. Choice C is incorrect because the workhouses, places where the unemployed were placed until they could find work, preceded the development of social Darwinism. Choice D is incorrect because laws regulating child labor were opposed by social Darwinists on the basis that it interfered with natural selection. Choice E is incorrect because social Darwinists looked at the subjugation of women as a "natural" state produced by evolution.

65. **E.** Ferdinand and Isabella asserted complete control over the Catholic Church in Spain, and used it as an instrument to consolidate their power and build national unity; in the process they created the Inquisition and ended decades of religious toleration of Muslims and Jews in Spain. Choice A is incorrect because the authoritarianism of Isabella and Ferdinand's regime was the antithesis of liberal reform. Choice B is incorrect because Isabella and Ferdinand subdued the Spanish nobility through a combination of intimidation and bribery; serfdom was not strengthened. Choice C is incorrect because Ferdinand and Isabella enforced strict Catholicism in Spain. Choice D is incorrect because no alliance with Britain and France was signed.

66. **D.** Michelangelo Buonarroti's version of *David* (completed in 1504) is most characteristic of the last and most heroic phase of Renaissance art because it offers a vision of the human body and spirit that is more dramatic than real life, an effect that Michelangelo produced by making the head and hands deliberately too large for the torso. Choice A is incorrect because Giotto's *Life of St Francis* depicts the psychological reaction or internal life of the human subject, not its form, and comes from the earliest phase of Renaissance art. Choice B is incorrect because Picasso's *Guer-*

nica is not a Renaissance work of art, but an early twentieth-century work. Choice C is incorrect because, although Donatello's version of *David* (completed in 1432) illustrates the Renaissance emphasis on human form, it does not illustrate the last and most heroic phase of Renaissance art because David is depicted in a completely naturalistic way and is cast as a young Florentine gentleman. Choice E is incorrect because the Basilica itself is not concerned with human form.

67. **B.** In the *Principia*, Newton showed that all matter behaved in accordance with one "universal" law; hence, one spoke of a "universe" rather than a cosmos composed of different "realms" inhabited by different kinds of matter. Choice A is incorrect because the phrase "the queen of the sciences" was usually reserved for physics, not mathematics, and is not directly related to the publication of Newton's *Principia*. Choice C is incorrect because the existence of Jupiter's four moons was demonstrated by Galileo in the *Starry Messenger* in 1610. Choice D is incorrect because "geocentric" means Earth-centered; Newton was a Copernican and the *Principia* helped to establish a heliocentric, or Sun-centered, model.

68. **C.** The multivolume *Encyclopedia*, produced by Denis Diderot and Jean le Rond d'Alembert between 1751 and 1772, was radical because its stated goal was to undo the barriers of superstition and bigotry; towards that end it labeled anything not based on reason as superstition. Choice A is incorrect because the *Encyclopedia* was printed originally in French. Choice B is incorrect because other multivolume publications preceded the *Encyclopedia*. Choice D is incorrect because the *Encyclopedia* was radical by its implications; it did not directly call for revolution or the overthrow of the monarchy. Choice E is incorrect because the *Encyclopedia* was anticlerical, not a Protestant text.

69. **A.** Under the leadership of Catherine the Great, Russia defeated the Ottoman Turks in 1774, thereby extending Russia's borders as far as the Black Sea and the Balkan Peninsula. Choice B is incorrect because Russia joined with Prussia and Austria to conquer Poland and divide its territories between the three of them in 1775. Choice C is incorrect because Russia did not invade

Prussia in 1770. Choice D is incorrect because the Pragmatic Sanction was a document which guaranteed Maria Theresa's right to ascend to the throne of Austria. Choice E is incorrect because Russia did not invade Finland in 1774.

70. A. Louis's attempt to flee Paris in June of 1791 and head north to rally supporters, an event that came to be known as *the flight to Varennes*, was disastrous. He and the royal family were apprehended and forcibly returned to Paris. He was officially forgiven by the Assembly, but he had forever lost the trust of the people of Paris. Choice B is incorrect because Robespierre was taken to the guillotine by his fellow revolutionaries; Louis XVI had already been executed. Choice C is incorrect because the people of Paris had remained loyal to Louis XVI and did not blame him specifically for rising taxes. Choice D is incorrect because the Paris Commune was crushed by the French Army in *1871*. Choice E is incorrect because the Civil Constitution of the Clergy, decreeing that all clergy must take an oath to the state, was issued by the National Assembly, not by Louis XVI.

71. E. The attempted coup by General George Boulanger, which was supported by conservative nationalists who refused to accept the election of a liberal government, underscored the fragility of French democracy and the volatility of mass politics in France. Choice A is incorrect because it was the Dreyfus Affair that demonstrated the strength of anti-Semitism in France. Choice B is incorrect because the Second Republic fell in 1851. Choice C is incorrect because it was the Paris Commune of 1871 that gave evidence of the radical nature of the French working class. Choice D is incorrect because a socialist popular front would not be elected in France until the 1920s.

72. D. The Sepoy Rebellion of 1857 (sometimes known as the Sepoy Mutiny) was an organized, anti-British uprising led by military units of Indians who had formerly served the British. It led the British government to abolish the East India Company and to take direct control of India and its economy. Choice A is incorrect because, although there is considerable debate over the scope and meaning of the Sepoy Rebellion, it occurred in only parts of the continent and was not "nationalist" in any meaningful sense of the word. Choices B and C are incorrect because the Sepoy Rebellion took place in India, not China or Burma. Choice E is incorrect because the period of liberal reform in India was actually *ended* by the Sepoy Rebellion.

73. C. The power and authority of the Manchu dynasty had been undermined by China's humiliation in the Opium War (1839–1842) and the resulting Treaty of Nanking, which ceded Hong Kong to Britain, created several tariff-free zones for foreign trade, and exempted foreigners from Chinese law; the Taiping Rebellion (1850–1864) was an attempt to overthrow the humiliated dynasty and free China from foreign interference. Choice A is incorrect because the rebels were trying to free China from Western influence, not imitate the West. Choice B is incorrect because the Russo-Japanese war occurred in the twentieth century. Choice D is incorrect because World War II was much later than the Taiping Rebellion. Choice E is incorrect because the West helped the Manchus ward off the rebellion.

74. D. In the years between World War I and World War II, liberal democracy failed to take root in Hungary, Poland, and Yugoslavia, as each came to be ruled by right-wing, authoritarian regimes. Choice A is incorrect because none of the countries of Europe enjoyed consistently flourishing economies in the interwar years. Choice B is incorrect because the states of East-Central Europe did not become satellite states of the Soviet Union until after World War II. Choice C is incorrect because none of the states mentioned ceased to exist in the interwar years. Choice E is incorrect because the liberal-democratic parliaments failed in those states during the interwar years.

75. B. In the elections of 1932, the Nazis won over 35 percent of the vote and refused to take part in a coalition government; the president, Paul von Hindenburg, responded by appointing Hitler Chancellor of Germany (the equivalent of prime minister). Choice A is incorrect because a socialist coalition was not brought to power in the election of 1932. Choice C is incorrect because Hitler was not elected Chancellor in 1932, but legally *appointed* by Hindenburg in the wake of the strong showing of the Nazi party. Choice D is incorrect because a coalition of right-wing

AP European History
Practice Test 2

Section I

Time—55 minutes

80 Questions

Directions: Each of the questions or incomplete statements below is followed by five suggested answers or completions. Select the one that is best in each case and fill in the circle for the letter that corresponds to your choice on the Answer Sheet supplied.

Raw cotton consumption (metric tons)

	1830	1850
Belgium	5,000	20,000
France	40,000	60,000
German states	20,000	30,000
UK	170,000	260,000

1. 1. Which of the following is the most complete conclusion that can be drawn from the chart above for the period 1830–1850?
    (A) The United Kingdom was the largest consumer of cotton in both 1830 and 1850.
    (B) Belgium had the smallest population in Europe during this period.
    (C) The United Kingdom imported the most cotton during this period.
    (D) The United Kingdom led Europe in textile production.
    (E) The United Kingdom had both the greatest consumption of cotton and the greatest rate of increase in cotton consumption.

2. Which of the following can be understood as a result of the Seven Years War?
    (A) The French Revolution began.
    (B) Maria Theresa ascended to the throne of Austria.
    (C) Britain became the dominant imperial power in the world.
    (D) The Ottoman Turks were further weakened.
    (E) Prussia was weakened.

3. Which of following did NOT contribute to the radicalization of the French Revolution?
    (A) Austria and Prussia's declaration of war on the French Republic
    (B) the flight to Varennes
    (C) factionalizing of the Assembly
    (D) the execution of Louis XVI
    (E) the rise of the *sans-culottes*

4. The most significant, long-term result of the revolutions of 1848 was
    (A) the large-scale abandonment of liberalism by the masses
    (B) Hungarian independence
    (C) the rise of communism
    (D) the unification of Italy
    (E) the triumph of democratic reform

5. Which of the following is NOT true of the Second Industrial Revolution of nineteenth-century Europe?
    (A) It began in Great Britain.
    (B) It took place later further east.
    (C) The pace slowed after an initial quick start.
    (D) It took place more quickly further east.
    (E) There was more government involvement further east.

6. Which of the following nineteenth-century ideologies stressed both individual freedom and government regulation?
    (A) socialism
    (B) utilitarianism
    (C) liberalism
    (D) conservatism
    (E) anarchism

GO ON TO THE NEXT PAGE

7. Which of the following is a combination of tactics used by both Cavour and Bismarck in their drive to unite Italy and Germany respectively?
   (A) diplomacy and royal marriage
   (B) peasant revolts and military action
   (C) diplomacy and bribery
   (D) war and secret dealings with the pope
   (E) war and diplomacy

8. Fifteenth-century attempts to centralize and consolidate power were most successful in
   (A) France
   (B) England
   (C) Italy
   (D) Spain
   (E) Germany

9. Which of the following is true of humanism as it manifested itself in northern Europe?
   (A) It was less secular than Italian Renaissance humanism.
   (B) It pursued scholarship and learning in a tradition of religious piety.
   (C) It was critical of the notion that priests were required to understand and interpret Scripture.
   (D) It formed part of the foundation for the Reformation.
   (E) All of the above.

10. Which of the following is particular to Calvinist theology?
    (A) Salvation is achieved through faith alone.
    (B) Scripture is the only reliable guide to salvation.
    (C) The Church must not be hierarchical in nature.
    (D) Some souls have been predestined for salvation.
    (E) The Bible should be printed in the vernacular.

11. Which of the following was accomplished by Peter the Great of Russia (1682–1725)?
    (A) He abolished serfdom.
    (B) He expanded the Russian Empire.
    (C) He launched the industrialization of Russia.
    (D) He curbed the power of the nobility.
    (E) He provided tax relief for the peasantry.

12. Which of the following would be advocated by a follower of Descartes?
    (A) There are four elements in the terrestrial realm.
    (B) All true knowledge is derived from observation.
    (C) Seeing is believing.
    (D) One should always proceed from a clear and distinct idea.
    (E) Telescopic observations should be the basis of knowledge of the heavens.

13. An advocate of *laissez-faire*
    (A) advocates protectionist tariffs
    (B) argues that only natural laws are legitimate
    (C) argues that the government should refrain from trying to regulate the economy
    (D) argues that the government should act as an "invisible hand" to regulate the economy
    (E) argues that a monarch rules by the command of God

14. Which of the following was a result of the development of rural manufacturing in the eighteenth century?
    (A) the spread of capital throughout the population
    (B) a decrease in total agricultural output
    (C) the enclosure movement
    (D) urbanization
    (E) the formation of a working class

15. Which of the following precipitated the fall of the Second Republic in France?
    (A) France's defeat in the Franco-Prussian War
    (B) a coup and two plebiscites
    (C) the French Revolution
    (D) the Crimean War
    (E) the unification of Italy

16. The postimpressionists of the late nineteenth century are distinguished from their predecessors, the impressionists, by
    (A) their desire to create a more emotionally expressive effect
    (B) their use of visible brush strokes
    (C) their use of heightened color
    (D) their insistence on real-life subjects
    (E) their desire to capture the reality of the visual experience

GO ON TO THE NEXT PAGE

17. The Suez Canal episode in the early 1880s illustrates which of the following aspects of the "New Imperialism"?
    (A) the underlying economic motives
    (B) the willingness of Western governments to rule imperial holdings directly
    (C) the way imperial expansion demanded further expansion
    (D) the competitive nature of European expansion
    (E) all of the above

18. In which of the following ways did the Russian revolution affect the course of World War I?
    (A) It gave the Allies a new enemy.
    (B) Russia joined the Triple Entente.
    (C) Russia withdrew from the war.
    (D) It caused the Germans to launch a new offensive in the east.
    (E) None of the above.

19. Which of the following was NOT an element of fascism?
    (A) a fanatical obedience to a charismatic leader
    (B) an egalitarianism that extended to class and gender
    (C) a professed belief in the virtues of struggle and youth
    (D) an intense form of nationalism
    (E) an expressed hatred of socialism and liberalism

20. Successful resistance to communist rule in the 1980s was led by a labor union in which of the following countries?
    (A) Czechoslovakia
    (B) East Germany
    (C) Yugoslavia
    (D) Poland
    (E) Russia

21. Galileo's discovery of craters on the surface of the moon damaged the traditional view of the cosmos because it
    (A) demonstrated that the moon was not made of perfect matter
    (B) demonstrated the power of the telescope
    (C) contradicted the notion that the Earth was at the center of the cosmos
    (D) called into question the perfection of God's creative power
    (E) all of the above

22. Which of the following was argued by John Locke in the *Second Treatise of Government*?
    (A) Peace requires an absolute ruler.
    (B) A government must follow the "general will" of the people.
    (C) Democracy is the only legitimate form of government.
    (D) The government must always protect the people's right to property.
    (E) Monarchy must always be opposed.

23. The uncertainty principle was articulated as result of
    (A) efforts to prove that all human knowledge is relative
    (B) efforts to prove the existence of the ether
    (C) efforts to disprove Einstein's theory of relativity
    (D) efforts to develop an atomic bomb
    (E) efforts to reconcile quantum physics with the classical approach to physics

24. Which of the following explains the rapid development of technology in the textile industry in the eighteenth century?
    (A) a shortage of labor
    (B) the interconnected nature of technical innovation
    (C) the triumph of reason over superstition
    (D) the cotton boom
    (E) the invention of the steam engine

25. The War for Austrian Succession (1740–1748) was caused by
    (A) Prussian expansionist aims
    (B) a revolt of Austrian nobles
    (C) the Pragmatic Sanction
    (D) French aggression
    (E) all of the above

26. The most significant impact of the Civil Constitution of the Clergy on the course of the French Revolution was
    (A) the alliance it created between the clergy and the National Assembly
    (B) that it made the clergy subservient to the state
    (C) that it alienated much of the Catholic population from the revolution
    (D) its reaffirmation of the central place of the Church in the French government
    (E) that it made Catholicism illegal in France

GO ON TO THE NEXT PAGE

27. The larger significance of the British victory at the Battle of Trafalgar was that
    (A) the British navy defeated the combined French and Spanish fleets
    (B) Napoleon's Grand Army was destroyed
    (C) Napoleon had to call a halt to the Continental System
    (D) Napoleon was captured and sent to the island of Elba
    (E) it ended the threat of a French conquest of Britain

28. The Schleswig–Holstein affair is an example of
    (A) the *Risorgimento*
    (B) Russian conservatism
    (C) German liberalism
    (D) French imperialism
    (E) *Realpolitik*

29. The formation of the Indian National Congress in 1885 demonstrates
    (A) the successful colonization of India by Britain
    (B) the scramble for Africa
    (C) the formation of nationalism as a response to Western imperialism
    (D) the beginning of the New Imperialism
    (E) all of the above

30. Which of the following extended the right to vote to the adult, male middle class in Britain?
    (A) the Great Reform Bill of 1832
    (B) the Reform Bill of 1867
    (C) the Reform Bill of 1884
    (D) the People's Charter
    (E) the Midlothian Campaign

31. The organization that campaigned for women's voting rights in Britain was
    (A) the Fabian Society
    (B) feminism
    (C) the National Union of Women's Suffrage Societies
    (D) the National Women's League
    (E) the Women's Social and Political Union

32. Of the three main negotiators at the Paris Peace Conference of 1919, which one was most concerned to make sure that Germany could never threaten again?
    (A) David Lloyd George
    (B) Woodrow Wilson
    (C) Charles de Gaulle
    (D) Georges Clemenceau
    (E) none of the above

33. Pablo Picasso's *Guernica* (1937) depicts
    (A) the Impressionist style
    (B) the bombing of the town of Guernica by German planes
    (C) the savagery of the fighting between fascists and socialists
    (D) the valiant resistance of the socialists
    (E) Hitler invading Spain

34. The agreement which allowed Hitler to take the Sudetenland in return for his promise of no further aggression was known as the
    (A) Nazi–Soviet Non-Aggression Pact
    (B) Concert of Europe
    (C) Treaty of Brest–Litovsk
    (D) Treaty of Versailles
    (E) Munich Agreement

35. The military alliance between communist countries in Eastern Europe after World War II was known as
    (A) the Warsaw Pact
    (B) the Truman Doctrine
    (C) the Council for Mutual Economic Assistance
    (D) the Marshall Plan
    (E) NATO

36. Mikhail Gorbachev's attempt to "restructure" Soviet society and its economy was known as
    (A) socialism in one country
    (B) socialism with a human face
    (C) *glasnost*
    (D) *perestroika*
    (E) the New Economic Plan

37. In the fifteenth century, the Holy Roman Emperor was
    (A) appointed by the pope
    (B) dethroned in the Hundred Years War
    (C) elected by a seven-member council of German archbishops and nobles
    (D) the pope
    (E) Henry VIII

GO ON TO THE NEXT PAGE

38. The creation of a Spanish Empire in the New World had all of the following effects EXCEPT
    (A) economic inflation in Europe
    (B) the establishment of Roman Catholicism in the New World
    (C) the rise of a wealthy merchant class in Europe
    (D) the establishment of a hierarchical social structure in Europe
    (E) the establishment of a system of economic dependence between Europe and the New World

39. A traditional institution within the Catholic Church that was transformed in the sixteenth century to fight the spread of Protestantism was
    (A) the Reformation
    (B) the Counter-Reformation
    (C) the Inquisition
    (D) the Conciliar Movement
    (E) the Court of the Star Chamber

40. Which of the following is an example of the Cartesian approach to physical science popular in the late seventeenth and early eighteenth centuries?
    (A) Maupertuis's calculation of the exact shape of the earth based on observations of longitudinal measurement
    (B) Christiaan Huygens's explanation of the propagation of light by suggesting that it "flowed" like a fluid
    (C) Galileo's telescopic observations of the moon
    (D) Copernicus's hypothesis that the earth is in the center of the cosmos
    (E) Linnaeus's creation of a system for the classification of living organisms

41. Which of the following best characterizes the Counter-Reformation?
    (A) a movement to reform the Catholic Church from within
    (B) a movement to stamp out Protestantism
    (C) a movement to create a "third theological way"
    (D) a movement to both reform from within and combat the spread of Protestantism
    (E) a movement to censure thinkers like Galileo

42. During the period from 1600 to 1715, the traditional social hierarchy of Europe came under pressure by all of the following EXCEPT
    (A) continuous warfare
    (B) climate change resulting in series of bad harvests
    (C) the rejection of religious practice by large numbers of people
    (D) increased trade and the diversification of the economy
    (E) the desire of monarchs to increase their power and authority

43. Which of the following is the best example of the method described by Descartes in his *Discourse on Method* (1637)?
    (A) True reality exists in the world of pure forms.
    (B) "I think, therefore I am."
    (C) A telescope reveals craters and mountains on the moon; therefore, matter in the celestial realm cannot be perfect.
    (D) The orbits of the planets can be calculated using calculus.
    (E) "Every particle of matter in the universe attracts every other particle with a force varying inversely as the square of the distance between them and directly proportional to the product of their masses."

44. Which of the following best explains the eventual defeat of Napoleon and his forces?
    (A) the inefficiency of the French army
    (B) flawed policies that exacerbated resistance to French rule
    (C) internal resistance by royalists and republicans
    (D) the British victory at the Battle of Trafalgar
    (E) tactical blunders

45. The source of Prussian power in the eighteenth century was
    (A) Bismarck's genius
    (B) Prussia's industrial strength
    (C) Prussia's diplomatic alliances
    (D) Prussia's geographical position
    (E) Prussia's powerful military

GO ON TO THE NEXT PAGE

46. The revolutions of 1848 are best understood as
    (A) the result of tension between liberal and nationalist aspirations of the people of Europe and the determined conservatism of their aristocratic masters
    (B) independence movements
    (C) large-scale attempts to redistribute wealth in European society
    (D) precursors to the French Revolution
    (E) democratic revolutions

47. Which of the following might be explained as a result of the introduction of steam power?
    (A) the creation of the factory system
    (B) the invention of the automobile
    (C) decreased demand for coal
    (D) an increased demand for coal
    (E) the collapse of the shipping industry

48. Conservatives opposed "constitutionalism" because they
    (A) were monarchists
    (B) believed that constitutions ignored reality
    (C) respected tradition
    (D) wanted to hold on to power
    (E) believed a government should protect private property

49. In the 1930s, Winston Churchill stood nearly alone in his
    (A) advocacy of socialism
    (B) support of the Soviet Union
    (C) opposition to the policy of appeasement
    (D) call for a coalition government
    (E) efforts to draw the United States into the war

50. Which of the following is an example of the revival of nationalist and ethnic tensions in eastern Europe after the disintegration of the Soviet Union?
    (A) the war between Chechnyans and Russia
    (B) the multisided war in Yugoslavia
    (C) the splitting up of Czechoslovakia
    (D) the war in Bosnia–Herzegovina
    (E) all of the above

51. Which of the following led an expedition that eventually circumnavigated the globe?
    (A) Vasco da Gama
    (B) Amerigo Vespucci
    (C) Martin Waldseemüller
    (D) Ferdinand Magellan
    (E) Christopher Columbus

52. All of the following help to explain why the Renaissance originated on the Italian peninsula EXCEPT
    (A) geography
    (B) political organization
    (C) religion
    (D) social structure
    (E) economic structure

53. All of the following posed difficulties for the Christian Church in Europe during the first decade of the sixteenth century EXCEPT
    (A) the pope's status as ruler of the Papal States.
    (B) the Church's use of Latin in the mass and in the printed Bible
    (C) an increasingly literate population
    (D) the Church's inability to tend to the emotional and spiritual needs of the population
    (E) the split in the Christian population caused by the Protestant movement

54. Which of the following would NOT be included in a list of the causes of the English Civil War (1642–1646)?
    (A) the religion of Charles I's wife
    (B) wars with Spain and France
    (C) the invasion of a Protestant army from the Netherlands
    (D) the invasion of England by the Scots
    (E) Parliament's refusal to fund the war with Scotland without reform

55. Which of the following is true of the Copernican model of the cosmos?
    (A) The planets orbit the Sun in uniform circular orbits.
    (B) The planets orbit the Earth in elliptical orbits with the Sun as one focus of the ellipse.
    (C) The universe is infinite.
    (D) The planets orbit the Sun in elliptical orbits with the Earth as one focus of the ellipse.
    (E) The moon orbits the Sun, not the Earth.

56. The book *System of Nature* (1770), by the Baron d'Holbach, was one of the most radical texts of the Enlightenment because of its
    (A) advocacy of revolution
    (B) materialism
    (C) liberalism
    (D) support for the French Revolution
    (E) advocacy of science

GO ON TO THE NEXT PAGE

57. The Diplomatic Revolution of the eighteenth century refers to
   (A) the invention of the "alliance"
   (B) traditional enemies becoming allies
   (C) the moderate phase of the French Revolution
   (D) the Revolutions of 1848
   (E) the Concert of Europe

My heart leaps up when I behold
  A rainbow in the sky:
So was it when my life began,
  So is it now I am a man,
So be it when I shall grow old
  Or let me die!

58. The nineteenth-century verse above is indicative of
   (A) neoplatonism
   (B) the Romantic movement
   (C) the impressionist school
   (D) conservatism
   (E) the Enlightenment

59. Charles Darwin, in *The Origin of Species* (1859), put forward the idea that
   (A) competition was natural and necessary for social progress
   (B) human nature was essentially cooperative
   (C) biological diversity was the product of a purely natural process
   (D) competition was the root of class conflict
   (E) human beings evolved from apes

60. Bismarck overcame south German reluctance to submit to Prussian leadership by
   (A) appealing to their Catholic faith
   (B) adopting their liberal reform agenda
   (C) appealing to their nationalism
   (D) appealing to their desire for a strong, authoritarian central government
   (E) allying with the Junker class

61. All of the following were effects of the Hundred Years War EXCEPT
   (A) a significant decrease in the population
   (B) a series of peasant rebellions
   (C) a more politically unified France
   (D) an economically weaker England
   (E) the rise of a Spanish Empire in the New World

62. All of the following were highly valued in the Renaissance EXCEPT
   (A) scholarly achievement
   (B) patronage of the arts
   (C) proficiency in the military arts
   (D) civic duty
   (E) study of ancient languages

63. All of the following are basic theological beliefs of Martin Luther EXCEPT
   (A) Salvation is attainable by faith alone.
   (B) Scripture is the only guide to knowledge of God.
   (C) The Church hierarchy was unwarranted and harmful.
   (D) Good works are essential to salvation.
   (E) All who have faith can and should read the Bible.

64. Which of the following is most true of the Glorious Revolution of 1688?
   (A) It represents the triumph of constitutionalism in Britain.
   (B) It brought democracy to Britain.
   (C) It began the Restoration Period in Britain.
   (D) It began the Commonwealth Period in Britain.
   (E) It ended the Commonwealth Period in Britain.

65. Isaac Newton is best described as working in
   (A) the Aristotelian tradition
   (B) the Scholastic tradition
   (C) the Hermetic tradition
   (D) the Platonic–Pythagorean tradition
   (E) the Copernican tradition

66. All of the following are examples of the philosophy of Jean-Jacques Rousseau EXCEPT
   (A) Humans are born essentially good.
   (B) The education of children should concentrate on developing the senses, sensibilities, and sentiments.
   (C) "Man is born free; and everywhere he is in chains."
   (D) The proper role of government is to protect individual property.
   (E) The virtuous citizen should be willing to subordinate his own self-interest to the general good of the community.

GO ON TO THE NEXT PAGE

67. All of the following transactions were part of the triangle of trade EXCEPT
    (A) slaves from Africa sold in the Americas and West Indies
    (B) tea from China sold in Europe
    (C) guns from Europe traded in Africa
    (D) cotton from the Americas sold in Europe
    (E) rum from the West Indies sold in Europe

68. The phase of the French Revolution known as "Thermidor" was characterized by
    (A) a reassertion of control by the nobility
    (B) the defeat of France by Austria
    (C) the restoration of the monarchy
    (D) the rule of the Committee of Public Safety
    (E) a reassertion of control by the moderate portion of the propertied bourgeoisie

69. Which of the following was an aim of the great powers represented at the Congress of Vienna in 1814?
    (A) to punish France
    (B) to divide and weaken Germany
    (C) to restore the traditional order and to create a new balance of power
    (D) to spread liberal reform more widely in Europe
    (E) to provide independent nation states for Italy, Hungary, and Czechoslovakia

70. Which of the following was a social effect of the Second Industrial Revolution?
    (A) a more even distribution of wealth
    (B) the development of a lower middle class
    (C) the creation of a class of poor people
    (D) the railway boom
    (E) gender equity

71. Which of the following is an example of the *Sturm und Drang* movement?
    (A) Michelangelo's *David*
    (B) Bismarck's *Kulturkampf*
    (C) the assassination of Franz Ferdinand
    (D) *Guernica*
    (E) *The Sorrows of Young Werther*

72. The best example of the power of nationalism in France in the mid-nineteenth century was
    (A) the two plebiscites that established the Second Empire and made Louis-Napoleon hereditary emperor
    (B) Louis-Napoleon's coup d'état on 2 December 1851
    (C) the Paris Commune
    (D) Louis-Napoleon's granting of universal manhood suffrage
    (E) the Directory

73. The Chartist movement (1837–1842) in Britain demonstrated
    (A) the power of the monarchy
    (B) the degree to which the lower middle and working classes desired further reform
    (C) the strength of nationalism
    (D) opposition to monarchy
    (E) the degree to which working people were opposed to the mechanization of industry

74. The atmosphere of "celebration" that accompanied the declarations of war in 1914 is partially explained by
    (A) feelings of brotherhood and glory
    (B) deep racial hatreds
    (C) Germany's strong desire to repudiate the humiliating conditions of the Versailles Treaty
    (D) deep resentment towards the Continental System
    (E) all of the above

75. In the context of World War I, the phrase "total war" referred to
    (A) the bombing of civilians in major cities
    (B) the total conversion of the economy to fulfill wartime needs
    (C) the refusal to take prisoners
    (D) the fighting of the war on multiple continents
    (E) all of the above

GO ON TO THE NEXT PAGE

76. Which of the following can be understood as a consequence of World War II?
   (A) the Treaty of Versailles
   (B) the emergence of the United States and the Soviet Union as the world's two greatest powers
   (C) the reunification of Germany
   (D) a strengthening of the British Empire
   (E) the German invasion of Poland

77. Following the collapse of the Soviet Union, the two major trends that most affected life in Eastern Europe were
   (A) the flourishing of individual liberty and democracy
   (B) the spread of corporate capitalism and a revival of religion
   (C) American isolationism and European integration
   (D) the revival of ethnic-nationalism and the advent of globalization
   (E) a widening gap in the distribution of wealth and increased poverty

78. Which of the following is true of the reunification of Germany?
   (A) It was the product of a long, lengthy process of negotiation and compromise.
   (B) Separate economic policies were set up to make the transition easier for East Germans.
   (C) The former East Germany was essentially annexed by the West.
   (D) It was led by East German members of the Civic Forum.
   (E) All of the above.

79. In "The Freedom of the Christian Man" (1520), Martin Luther
   (A) called for people to rise up against an unjust social system
   (B) appealed to the German princes' desire for both greater unity and power and to their desire to be free from the control of an Italian pope
   (C) established the principle of "whoever rules; his religion"
   (D) encouraged common men to obey their Christian conscience and respect those in authority who seemed to possess true Christian principles
   (E) all of the above

80. As the chief minister to Louis XIII of France, Cardinal Richelieu was able to
   (A) disband the private armies of the great French aristocrats
   (B) strip away the autonomy of the few remaining Protestant towns
   (C) build a strong administrative bureaucracy
   (D) strip provincial aristocrats and elites of their administrative power
   (E) all of the above

STOP. End of Section I

Section II

Part A

(Suggested writing time—45 minutes)

Directions: The following question is based on the accompanying Documents 1–10. (The documents have been edited for the purpose of this exercise.) Write your answer on the lined pages provided with the Answer Sheet.

This question is designed to test your ability to work with and understand historical documents. Write an essay that:

- has a relevant thesis and supports that thesis with evidence from the documents
- uses the majority of the documents
- addresses all parts of the question
- analyzes the documents by organizing them in as many appropriate ways as possible and does not simply summarize the documents individually
- takes into account both the sources of the documents and the authors' points of view

You may refer to relevant historical information not mentioned in the documents.

1. Discuss the changing attitudes and arguments regarding the basis for knowledge of the natural world in the following documents.

Historical background: Beginning in the sixteenth and culminating in the seventeenth century, an intellectual and cultural revolution took shape that has come to be known as the Scientific Revolution. At the heart of that revolution were changing attitudes and new arguments regarding the basis for knowledge of the natural world.

Document 1

Source: Nicolas Copernicus, *The Revolutions of the Heavenly Bodies*, 1543.
In the center of all rests the sun. For who would place this lamp of a very beautiful temple in another or better place than this, where from it can illuminate everything at the same time? As a matter of fact, not unhappily so some call it the lantern; others, the mind, and still others, the pilot of the world. Trismegistus calls it a "visible god"; Sophocles Electra, "that which gazes upon all things." And so the sun, as if resting on a kingly throne, governs the family of stars which wheel around.

Document 2

Source: Giambattista della Porta, *Natural Magick*, 1584.
There are two sorts of Magick, the one is infamous, and unhappy, because it has to do with foul spirits and consists of incantations and wicked curiosity; and this is called sorcery . . . The other Magick is natural; which all excellent, wise men do admit and embrace, and worship with great applause; neither is there anything more highly esteemed, or better thought of, by men of learning . . . Others have named it the practical part of natural philosophy, which produces her effects by the mutual and fit application of one natural thing to another. Magick is nothing else but the survey of whole course of nature.

GO ON TO THE NEXT PAGE

Document 3

Source: Galileo Galilei, "Letter to the Grand Duchess Christina of Tuscany," 1615.

[Copernicus] stands always upon physical conclusions pertaining to the celestial motions, and deals with them by astronomical and geometrical demonstrations, founded primarily on sense experiences and very exact observations . . . I think that in discussions of physical problems we ought to begin not from the authority of scriptural passages, but from sense-experiences and necessary demonstrations . . . Nature . . . is inexorable and immutable; she never transgresses the laws imposed upon her, or cares a whit whether her abstruse reasons and methods of operation are understandable to men.

Document 4

Source: Robert Bellarmine, "Letter on Galileo's Theories," 1615.

For to say that, assuming the earth moves and the sun stands still, all the appearances are saved better than with eccentrics and epicycles, is to speak well; there is no danger in this, and it is sufficient for mathematicians. But to want to affirm that the sun really is fixed in the center of the heavens . . . is a very dangerous thing, not only by irritating all the philosophers and scholastic theologians, but also by injuring our holy faith and rendering the Holy Scripture false.

Document 5

Source: Francis Bacon, *Novum Organum*, 1620.

There are two ways, and can only be two, of seeking and finding truth. The one, from sense and reason, takes a flight to the most general axioms, and from these principles and their truth, settled once for all, invents and judges of all intermediate axioms. The other method collects axioms from sense and particulars, ascending continuously and by degrees so that in the end it arrives at the most general axioms. This latter is the only true one, but never hitherto tried.

Document 6

Source: William Harvey, *On the Motion of the Heart and Blood in Animals*, 1628.

The heart, it is vulgarly said, is the fountain and workshop of the vital spirits, the centre from which life is dispensed to the several parts of the body. Yet it is denied that the right ventricle makes spirits, which is rather held to supply the nourishment to the lungs . . . Why, I ask, when we see that the structure of both ventricles is almost identical, there being the same apparatus of fibres, and braces, and valves, and vessels, and auricles, and both in the same way in our dissections are to found to be filled up with blood similarly black in colour, and coagulated—why, I say, should their uses be imagined to be different, when the action, motion, and pulse of both are the same?

GO ON TO THE NEXT PAGE

Document 7

Source: Rene Descartes, *Discourse Method*, 1637.
I was especially delighted with the mathematics, on account of the certitude and evidence of their reasonings; but . . . I was astonished that foundations, so strong and solid, should have had no loftier superstructure reared on them. On the other hand, I compared the disquisitions of the ancient moralists to very towering and magnificent palaces with no better foundation than sand and mud . . . I revered our theology, but . . . I thought that in order competently to undertake their examination, there was need of some special help from heaven, and of being more than a man.

Document 8

Source: Rene Descartes, *Discourse Method*, 1637.
The ground of our opinions is far more custom and example than certain knowledge . . . I was induced to seek some other method; . . . I believed that the four following [laws] would prove perfectly sufficient for me: . . . [1] carefully avoid precipitancy and prejudice, and to comprise nothing more in my judgment than what was presented to my mind so clearly and distinctly as to exclude all ground of doubt; . . . [2] divide each of the difficulties under examination into as many parts as possible; . . . [3]commencing with objects the simplest and easiest to know, . . . ascend by little and little, and, as it were, step by step, to the knowledge of the more complex; . . . [4] in every case to make enumerations so complete, and reviews so general, that I might be assured that nothing was omitted.

Document 9

Source: Johannes Agricola, *Treatise on Gold*, 1638.
All true chymists and philosophers write that common corporeal gold is of not much use in man's body if it is only ingested as such, for no metallic body can be of use if it is not previously dissolved and reduced to the prima materia. We have an example in corals. The virtue of corals is not in the stone or the body but in their red color. If the corals are to release their power, a separation must first occur through a dissolution, and the redness must be separated from the body . . . Consequently, whoever wants to do something useful in medicine must see to it that he first dissolve and open his metallic body, then extract its soul and essence, and the work will then not result in no fruit.

Document 10

Source: Isaac Newton, *Principia Mathematica*, 1687.
Rule I. We are to admit no more causes of natural things than such as are both true and sufficient to explain their appearances.
Rule II. Therefore to the same natural effects we must, as far as possible, assign the same causes.
Rule III. The qualities of bodies, which admit neither intension nor remission of degrees, and which are found to belong to all bodies within reach of our experiments, are to be esteemed as universal qualities of all bodies whatsoever.

GO ON TO THE NEXT PAGE

Section II

Part B

(Suggested planning and writing time—35 minutes)

Directions: You are to answer ONE question from the three questions below. Make your selection carefully, choosing the question that you are best prepared to answer thoroughly in the limited time permitted. You should spend five minutes organizing or outlining your answer. Write your answer to the question on the lined pages provided with the Answer Sheet, making sure to indicate which question you are answering by writing the appropriate question number at the top of each page.

Write an essay that:

- has a relevant thesis
- addresses all parts of the question
- supports the thesis with specific evidence
- is well organized

2. Discuss the relative successes and failures of seventeenth-century monarchs' attempts to consolidate political power within their kingdoms.
3. Explain why the traditional cycles of population and productivity in western Europe were broken in the eighteenth century.
4. Discuss the reasons for the changing aims and methods of the French Revolution.

GO ON TO THE NEXT PAGE

Section II

Part C

(Suggested planning and writing time—35 minutes)

Directions: You are to answer ONE question from the three questions below. Make your selection carefully, choosing the question that you are best prepared to answer thoroughly in the limited time permitted. You should spend five minutes organizing or outlining your answer. Write your answer to the question on the lined pages provided with the Answer Sheet, making sure to indicate which question you are answering by writing the appropriate question number at the top of each page.

Write an essay that:

- has a relevant thesis
- addresses all parts of the question
- supports the thesis with specific evidence
- is well organized

5. Discuss the major social effects of the Second Industrial Revolution.
6. Discuss the ways in which the development of mass politics contributed to the New Imperialism of the late nineteenth century.
7. Compare and contrast the different methods of successful opposition to Soviet dominance in eastern Europe in the 1980s and early 1990s.

STOP. End of Section II

❯ Answers and Explanations

1. **A.** From the chart it can be concluded that the United Kingdom consumed the largest amount of cotton in both 1830 and 1850. Choice B is incorrect because the chart offers no information about population. Choice C is incorrect because the chart does not yield information about cotton imports. Choice D is incorrect because the chart does not yield information about textile production. Choice E is incorrect because the rate of increase between 1830–1850 is actually greatest in Belgium.

2. **C.** At the end of the Seven Years War, Britain's victories in North America and India showed that they had clearly surpassed France as the country with the strongest grip on the largest amount of imperial territory. Choice A is incorrect because it is too much of a stretch to say that the French Revolution was a result of France's losses in the Seven Years War. However, the financial strains put on the French government could be considered a contributing cause of the French Revolution. Choice B is incorrect because the Austrian succession was not affected by the Seven Years War. Choice D is incorrect because the Ottoman Turks were not directly affected by the Seven Years War. Choice E is incorrect because Prussia, Britain's ally in the Seven Years War, was, if anything, strengthened by French losses.

3. **D.** The execution of Louis XVI was a *result* of the radicalization of the revolution, not something that contributed to it. Choice A is incorrect because the war with Austria and Prussia contributed to the radicalization of the revolution by creating an air of crisis which seemed to demand bolder action. Choice B is incorrect because Louis's ill-fated attempt to flee Paris for Varennes contributed to the radicalization of the revolution by destroying the faith which the people of Paris had in him. Choice C is incorrect because the development of factions in the Assembly meant that the factions had to compete with each other for popular support and were, therefore, moved to propose increasingly radical measures. Choice E is incorrect because the *sans-culottes*, with their hopes of a more egalitarian and economically fair society, were more radical than the bourgeois members of the Assembly.

4. **A.** The failure, in the second half of 1848, of the liberal revolutionaries to hold on to their gains and their resulting reputation for indecisiveness and weakness led to the large-scale abandonment of liberalism by the masses. Choice B is incorrect because Hungarian independence was not achieved in the revolutions of 1848. Choice C is incorrect because nothing that could be called communism was in evidence in the revolutions of 1848; indeed, Marx referred to them as "bourgeois revolutions" in the *Communist Manifesto* penned the same year. Choice D is incorrect because the unification of Italy was not achieved until 1866. Choice E is incorrect because the conservative reaction of the second half of 1848 crushed the democratic reforms gained earlier in the year.

5. **C.** The pace of the Second Industrial Revolution increased steadily throughout the nineteenth century. Choice A is incorrect because the Second Industrial Revolution did begin in Britain. Choice B is incorrect because it is true that industrialization spread eastward from Britain and, therefore, the further east one looks, the later industrialization occurred. Choice D is incorrect because it is true that the further east one looks, the more quickly industrialization occurred, owing to the fact that the later start allowed more copying and borrowing of technology that had been developed in the west. Choice E is incorrect because there was greater government involvement further east, because the late start had governments fearful of falling behind the west.

6. **B.** The Utilitarians began with a liberal emphasis on individual freedom and argued that judicious use of government regulation could produce the "greatest good for the greatest number" of individuals. Choice A is incorrect because socialism tended to understand calls for individual freedom as part of a bourgeois ideology. Choice C is incorrect because the classic liberal stance held that government interference was inef-

fective at best and probably counterproductive. Choice D is incorrect because the conservatives opposed government regulation as nontraditional and, therefore, unwise. Choice E is incorrect because the anarchists saw the government as an institution that enslaved mankind.

7. **E.** Cavour's successful strategy for uniting northern Italy under Piedmont worked through a combination of secret diplomatic arrangements with France and successful war with Austria; Bismarck's successful strategy to unite Germany under the Prussian monarchy similarly relied upon a combination of secret diplomatic arrangements with France and Austria and later provoking war with each. Choice A is incorrect because no royal marriages were directly involved in bringing about the unification of either Italy or Germany. Choice B is incorrect because peasant revolts were important in the unification of *southern* Italy by Garibaldi, and because no peasant revolts were involved in the unification of Germany. Choice C is incorrect because the smaller Kingdom of Piedmont was in no position to *bribe* the wealthier French Bourbons and Austrian Hapsburgs. Choice E is incorrect because neither Cavour nor Bismarck had secret dealings with the pope.

8. **D.** In Spain, Isabella and Ferdinand used their control of the Church and the combined wealth of Castile and Aragon to curb the power of the nobility and enforce uniform loyalty to the crown. Choice A is incorrect because, although France would eventually become the most absolutist monarchy in Europe, this would not occur until the seventeenth century. Choice B is incorrect because, in England, the process of centralization was delayed by an internal power struggle between two rival branches of the royal family that degenerated into a war known as the War of the Roses. Choice C is incorrect because the Italian peninsula still consisted of independent city-states that were ruled by powerful merchant-princes. Choice E is incorrect because German nobles were able to retain considerable autonomy from the Holy Roman Emperor, who was an elected ruler.

9. **E.** All of the choices are correct. Choices A and B are correct because the northern European humanists worked within a tradition of religious

piety that extended to lay people and were, therefore, less secular than their Italian counterparts. Choices C and D are correct because, as the humanistic confidence in the God-given ability of all human beings was applied in a context of religious piety, the notion that all men might be capable of reading the Bible naturally arose and became a foundation for the Reformation.

10. **D.** The doctrine of predestination, which asserted that only a group known as the elect would enjoy God's salvation, was particular to Calvinist theology. Choices A and B are incorrect because both are theological principles laid down by Luther and followed by most Protestant faiths. Choice C is incorrect because opposition to the Church's hierarchy was shared by most Protestant faiths. Choice E is incorrect because the desire to print the Bible in the vernacular was shared by most Protestant faiths.

11. **B.** Under Peter the Great, the Russian Empire expanded into Asia. Choice A is incorrect because the institution of serfdom was *strengthened*, not abolished, by Peter the Great. Choice C is incorrect because Russia did not industrialize to any significant degree until the twentieth century. Choices D and E are incorrect because the power of the nobility was increased at the expense of the peasantry, who were squeezed even harder for taxes.

12. **D.** Descartes argued that knowledge should be deduced from a clear and distinct idea; that is, from an idea which could not be doubted. Choice A is incorrect because Descartes asserted that the universe was filled with a single kind of matter. Choices B, C, and E are all incorrect because Descartes argued that the senses could be deceived and therefore claims to knowledge gained through observation could be doubted.

13. **C.** The doctrine of *laissez-faire* argues that human self-interest produces natural laws that govern economic behavior and, therefore, that governments should refrain from attempts to regulate the economy. Choice A is incorrect because protectionist tariffs, taxes levied on foreign goods to protect the sales of domestic goods, are an example of the kind of law that *laissez-faire* claims would be either futile or harmful. Choice B is incorrect because the doctrine of *laissez-faire*

applies only to economic behavior; it does not argue that all man-made laws are illegitimate. Choice D is incorrect because the "invisible hand" referred to by proponents of *laissez-faire* refers to the natural laws, not government action. Choice E is incorrect because it was the doctrine of the Divine Right of Kings that argued that monarchs rule by the command of God.

14. **A.** The development of rural manufacturing, in which peasants were paid for manufacturing textiles, helped to spread the new capital generated by the triangle of trade and commerce throughout the population. Choice B is incorrect because the development of rural manufacturing did not lead to a decrease in agricultural output. Choice C is incorrect because it was the shift to cash-crop agriculture that caused the enclosure movement. Choices D and E are incorrect because it was heavy, factory-based industrialization that led to urbanization and the formation of a working class.

15. **B.** The Second Republic of France was brought to an end by a combination of Napoleon Bonaparte's coup d'état on 2 December 1851 and two plebiscites that declared France to be an Empire and Napoleon III to be its hereditary emperor. Choice A is incorrect because it was the Second *Empire* that was brought to an end by France's defeat in the Franco-Prussian War. Choice C is incorrect because the French Revolution created the First Republic. Choice D is incorrect because the fall of the Second Republic preceded the Crimean War (1854–1857). Choice E is incorrect because the unification of Italy occurred after the fall of the Second Republic in France.

16. **A.** The postimpressionists of the late nineteenth century are distinguished from the impressionists by their rejection of the impressionists' insistence on limiting themselves to depicting the reality of the visual experience. The postimpressionists wished to create images that also explored and expressed the emotional aspects of experience. Choices B, C, D, and E are incorrect because they are all characteristics shared by both impressionists and postimpressionists.

17. **E.** All choices are correct. Choice A is correct because British control of the canal, which connected the Mediterranean Sea through Egypt to the Red Sea and the Indian Ocean, was necessitated by the crucial role that India played in its economy. Choice B is correct because Britain's decision to occupy Egypt in the summer of 1882 illustrates the new willingness of Western governments to rule imperial holdings directly. Choice C is correct because the need to protect occupied Egypt necessitated an expansion of British holdings to the immediate south of Egypt. Choice D is correct because the expansion of the British Empire in Egypt led France to counter by expanding their holdings in northwest Africa.

18. **C.** After the revolution of November 1917, the Russian government was controlled by the Bolsheviks, a Marxist, communist party who saw the war as a battle between two segments of the bourgeoisie. Accordingly, they removed Russia from the war. Choice A is incorrect because, although the United States supported anti-Bolshevik forces in Russia after the revolution, it is going too far to say that it gave the Allies a new enemy. Choice B is incorrect because Russia had joined the Triple Entente prior to the war. Choice D is incorrect because the Germans no longer needed an offensive in the east, having signed a peace treaty with the Russians. Choice E is incorrect because C is correct.

19. **B.** Fascism did not promote egalitarianism, was not a worker's party (despite the original name of the party in Germany), and promoted traditional, subordinate roles for women. Choice A is incorrect because fascist parties did display fanatical obedience to a charismatic leader; e.g., Hitler in Germany, Mussolini in Italy, and Franco in Spain. Choice C is incorrect because fascist parties did profess a belief in the virtues of struggle and youth, as illustrated in the constant reference to struggle and in the organization of youth groups in all fascist countries. Choice D is incorrect because all fascist parties incorporated an intense form of nationalism, as evidenced by the uniforms and constant dialogue about the enemies of "the nation." Choice E is incorrect because all fascist parties expressed a hatred of socialism and liberalism, as evidenced by their opposition to the existing liberal democratic governments and their constant rhetoric and violence against socialists.

20. **D**. Successful opposition to communist rule was led by the labor union known as Solidarity in Poland. Choices A and B are incorrect because opposition in those countries was based on a Civic Forum model. Choice C is incorrect because resistance in Yugoslavia was led by nationalist and ethnic groups. Choice E is incorrect because resistance was led there by liberal reformers within the Parliament.

21. **A**. The existence of craters on the moon demonstrated that the moon was not made of perfect matter; this damaged the traditional view of the cosmos because the moon was supposed to delineate between God's realm of perfection and the corrupt realm of the world. Choice B is incorrect because the power of the telescope did not, in itself, damage the traditional view of the cosmos. Choice C is incorrect because the existence of craters on the moon did not necessarily contradict the notion that the Earth was at the center of the cosmos. Choice D is incorrect because the existence of an imperfect moon did not mean that God could not have created a perfect moon if he had wanted to. Choice E is incorrect because choices B–D are incorrect.

22. **D**. In the *Second Treatise*, Locke argues that the only legitimate aim of a government is to protect the individual liberty of the people, a liberty that he argues can be summed up in their right to their own property. Choice A is incorrect because Locke argues for limited government. Choice B is incorrect because the notion of the primacy of the "general will" of the people was Rousseau's. Choice C is false because Locke argues that any form of government can be legitimate if it protects the rights of the people. Choice E is incorrect because Locke argues that a monarchy, or any form of government, must be opposed only when it degenerates into tyranny.

23. **E**. The uncertainty principle was articulated by Werner Heisenberg as an effort to reconcile quantum physics, which claimed that energy was released discontinuously in discrete amounts, with Newton's classical approach, which postulated the continuous flow of energy. Choice A is incorrect because the uncertainty principle neither sought to confirm nor confirms the notion that all human knowledge is relative. Choice B is incorrect because the articulation of the uncertainty principle was unrelated to experiments concerning the existence of ether. Choice C is incorrect because the uncertainty principle does not directly involve Einstein's theory, which Heisenberg accepted. Choice D is incorrect because the uncertainty principle was not related to Heisenberg's later work on the possibility of building an atomic bomb.

24. **B**. The reciprocal nature of technical innovation meant that, for example, the invention in 1733 of the flying shuttle, which doubled the speed at which cloth could be woven on a loom, created a need to produce greater amounts of thread faster. The need for more efficient thread production led to the invention of the spinning jenny, which greatly increased the amount of thread a single spinner could produce from cotton, creating a need to speed up the harvesting of cotton; that need was met by the invention of the cotton gin. Choice A is incorrect because there was no shortage of labor. Choice C is incorrect because there were no superstitions standing in the way of technical innovation in the textile industry. Choice D is incorrect because there was no "cotton boom." Choice E is incorrect because the steam engine was not significantly involved in the wave of technical innovation in the textile industry.

25. **A**. In 1740, Frederick II of Prussia attempted to expand Prussian lands by challenging the right of Maria Theresa to ascend to the throne of Austria and marching troops into Silesia. Choice B is incorrect because there was no revolt of Austrian nobles. Choice C is incorrect because the right of Maria Theresa to ascend to the throne of Austria was guaranteed by a document known as the Pragmatic Sanction, but it was the *refusal* of Prussia to recognize the document that caused the conflict. Choice D is incorrect because it was *Prussian* aggression, not French, that led to the conflict. Choice E is incorrect because choices B, C, and D are incorrect.

26. **C**. The Civil Constitution forced the clergy to take an oath of loyalty to the French state, something their religious beliefs forbid them to do (priests owe their allegiance to God and the Church); forcing them to do this and punishing

them if they did not alienated many Catholics from the revolution. Choice A is incorrect because it did not create an alliance between the clergy and the National Assembly. Choice B is incorrect because, although it made the clergy government employees and, therefore, subordinate to the Assembly, the alienation of so many Catholics from the revolution was much more significant. Choice D is incorrect because it did not reaffirm the central place of the Church in the French government; rather it made the Church subservient to the government. Choice E is incorrect because it did not make Catholicism illegal in France.

27. **E.** On 21 October 1805, a British naval fleet under the command of Lord Nelson defeated the combined fleets of France and Spain, thereby securing supremacy of the seas and ending the threat of a French invasion of Britain. Choice A is incorrect because, although it is accurate, it is not the larger significance. Choice B is incorrect because Napoleon's Grand Army was destroyed while retreating from Moscow in the winter of 1812. Choice C is incorrect because the Continental System, forbidding European nations under Napoleonic control from trading with Britain, was not ended by the British victory at Trafalgar. Choice D is incorrect because it was in November of 1813 that British and Spanish forces moved into Paris, captured Napoleon, and exiled him to Elba.

28. **E.** Bismarck's manufacturing of the Schleswig–Holstein Affair and the subsequent war with Austria is an example of the principle of *Realpolitik* (or reality politics), which sanctions any and all means for reaching national political objectives. Choice A is incorrect because the *Risorgimento* refers to the mid-nineteenth-century Italian nationalist movement. Choice B is incorrect because Russia was only tangentially involved in the Schleswig–Holstein Affair. Choice C is incorrect because Bismarck's disregard for the rights of individuals and groups of people is the *antithesis* of liberalism. Choice D is incorrect because France had only a *minor* role in the Schleswig–Holstein Affair and did not stand to increase the size of its empire as a result.

29. **C.** The British government took direct control and restructured the Indian economy to produce and consume products that aided the British economy. A sense of Indian nationalism began to develop as a response to the more intrusive British influence, resulting in the establishment of the Indian National Congress in 1885. Choice A is incorrect because the formation of the INC represented *resistance* to British colonization. Choice B is incorrect because the formation of the INC was not connected to the scramble for Africa. Choice D is incorrect because the formation of the INC represents resistance to, not the beginning of, the New Imperialism. Choice E is incorrect because choices A, B, and D are incorrect.

30. **A.** The Great Reform Bill of 1832, by both lowering and redefining property qualifications, extended voting rights to the adult, male middle class in Britain. Choice B is incorrect because the Reform Bill of 1867 went further, extending the vote to the lower middle class but still excluded the working class. Choice C is incorrect because the Reform Bill of 1884 enfranchised two-thirds of the adult male population. Choice E is incorrect because the Midlothian Campaign was the first modern political campaign and did not alter voting rights.

31. **C.** The National Union of Women's Suffrage Societies, headed by Millicent Garrett Fawcett, campaigned for voting rights for women in Britain. Choice A is incorrect because the Fabian Society was a socialist organization in Britain. Choice B is incorrect because *feminism* is a term to describe the ideology that believes in equal rights for women; it is not the name of an organization. Choice D is incorrect because there was no National Women's League. Choice E is incorrect because the Women's Social and Political Union, led by Emmeline Pankhurst and her daughters Christabel and Sylvia, campaigned, often violently, for a broader notion of women's rights in Britain.

32. **D.** The French delegation was led by Georges Clemenceau, whose desire was to make sure that Germany could never threaten France again. Choice A is incorrect because Britain was led by David Lloyd George, who tried to mediate

between the vindictive Clemenceau and the idealistic Wilson. Choice B is incorrect because the U.S. delegation was led by President Woodrow Wilson, who approached the peace talks with bold plans for helping to build a new Europe that could embrace the notions of individual rights and liberty that he believed characterized the United States. Choice C is incorrect because Charles de Gaulle was not at the Paris Peace Conference of 1919. Choice E is incorrect because choices A, B, and C are incorrect.

33. **B.** Pablo Picasso's 25-foot-long mural *Guernica* (1937) depicts the bombing of the town of Guernica by German planes during the Spanish Civil War; Hitler sent planes in aid of the fascist cause in Spain. Choice A is incorrect because Picasso was not an impressionist. Choice C is incorrect because Guernica was bombed, and so it did not host fighting between the fascist, and socialists. Choice D is incorrect because the painting does not depict valiant resistance, only hopeless suffering. Choice E is incorrect because Hitler did not invade Spain.

34. **E.** It was the *Munich Agreement* of September 1938 that allowed Hitler to take the Sudetenland over Czech objections in exchange for his promise that there would be no further aggression. Choice A is incorrect because the Nazi–Soviet Non-Aggression Pact of 1939 guaranteed Soviet neutrality in return for part of Poland. Choice B is incorrect because the Concert of Europe was the system of diplomacy put in place following the defeat of Napoleon in 1815. Choice C is incorrect because the Treaty of Brest–Litovsk was the treaty that took Russia out of World War I in 1917. Choice D is incorrect because the Treaty of Versailles is the name given to the peace settlement following World War I.

35. **A.** The Warsaw Pact was the military alliance of the communist countries of Eastern Europe created in response to the establishment of NATO. Choice B is incorrect because the Truman Doctrine offered military and economic aid to countries directly threatened by communist takeover. Choice C is incorrect because the Council for Mutual Economic Assistance was set up by the Soviet Union to counter the Marshall Plan by offering economic aid to eastern Euro-

pean countries. Choice D is incorrect because the Marshall Plan, named after U.S. Secretary of State George Marshall, was the plan which called for pouring billions of dollars of aid into western Europe to rebuild its infrastructure and economy. Choice E is incorrect because NATO, the North Atlantic Treaty Organization, united the Western powers in a military alliance against the Soviet Union, thereby prompting the formation of the Warsaw Pact.

36. **D.** *Perestroika* was the name of Gorbachev's attempt, in the early 1980s, to restructure Soviet society and its economy. Choice A is incorrect because socialism in one country was a policy of Stalin. Choice B is incorrect because socialism with a human face was the slogan of a Czech attempt at revitalizing their socialist society in 1968. Choice C is incorrect because *glasnost* was the policy of "openness" that Gorbachev proposed as a companion effort to *perestroika*. Choice E is incorrect because the New Economic Plan was the introduction of small-scale capitalism by Lenin in the 1920s.

37. **C.** The Holy Roman Emperor was elected by a seven-member council consisting of the archbishops of Mainz, Trier, and Cologne, the Duke of Saxony, the Margrave of Brandenburg, the Count Palatine, and the King of Bohemia. Choice A is incorrect because the pope did not have the power to appoint a Holy Roman Emperor of his choosing. Choice B is incorrect because the Hundred Years War did not lead to the dethroning of the Holy Roman Emperor. Choices D and E are incorrect because neither the pope nor Henry VIII was Holy Roman Emperor.

38. **D.** The hierarchical social structure of Europe was *not* a result of the creation of a Spanish Empire in the New World; Europe's hierarchical social structure dates back to the early medieval period. Choice A is incorrect because the flood of new wealth from the Spanish Empire in the New World did cause inflation in Europe's economy. Choice B is incorrect because the founding of a Spanish Empire in the New World did establish Roman Catholicism in the New World. Choice C is incorrect because the establishment of a Spanish Empire in the New World did help to

produce a wealthy merchant class in Europe. Choice E is incorrect because the establishment of a Spanish Empire in the New World did create economic dependence between Europe and the New World.

39. **C.** The Inquisition is an institution with a long history within the Catholic Church. During the sixteenth century, it was adapted to serve as a way to combat the spread of Protestant theology, which the Catholic Church considered heresy. Choice A is incorrect because the term "Reformation" refers to the period where the Protestant movement came into being and gained force. Choice B is incorrect because the phrase Counter-Reformation describes the broad efforts of the Catholic Church to both reform itself and to stamp out Protestantism. Choice D is incorrect because the Conciliar Movement was a fifteenth-century attempt by councils of cardinals to reform, reunite, and reinvigorate the Church. Choice E is incorrect because the Court of the Star Chamber was an instrument used by the early Tudor kings of England to curb the power of the nobility.

40. **B.** Huygens's explanation of the propagation of light in terms of an analogy with a fluid was an example of trying to come up with an "intelligible" explanation for physical phenomena; providing such intelligible explanations was the goal of the Cartesian approach. Choice A is incorrect because Maupertuis's method of setting up experiments and observations and drawing general conclusions from them was characteristic of the Newtonian analytical approach. Choices C and D are both incorrect because the work of Galileo and Copernicus preceded the work of Descartes. Choice E is incorrect because Linnaeus's creation of a system for the classification of living organisms does not involve the creation of an "intelligible explanation" that was key to the Cartesian approach.

41. **D.** The Counter-Reformation, the Catholic response to the Protestant movement, had two dimensions: one whose aim was to reform the Catholic Church and another aimed at exterminating the Protestant movement. Both approaches can be seen in the work of the Jesuits who, on the one hand preached a new

piety and pushed the Church to curb its worldly practices and to serve as a model for a selfless, holy life that could lead to salvation and, on the other, saw themselves as soldiers in a war against Satan. Choices A and B are incorrect because they capture only half of the character of the Counter-Reformation. Choice C is incorrect because the Catholic Church formed no "third theological way." Choice E is incorrect because, although the censuring of Galileo by the Inquisition can be understood in the context of the Counter-Reformation, it is not a good characterization of the movement as a whole.

42. **C.** Nowhere in Europe during this period was there a large-scale rejection of religious practice; rather, the religious fervor that pitted Catholics against Protestants complicated the tensions created by processes described in the other four answers. Choice A is incorrect because continuous warfare put pressure on the traditional social hierarchy by disrupting the economy and increasing the demand for taxes. Choice B is incorrect because the "little ice ages" of the period produced bad harvests which meant that there was less wealth in the economy at a time when monarchs were demanding more. Choice D is incorrect because increased trade and a more diversified economy gave birth to a class of economically powerful merchants who did not fit into the traditional social hierarchy. Choice E is incorrect because the desire of monarchs to increase their power and authority led them to wage wars of conquest, which put enormous stress on the economy.

43. **B.** Descartes proposed a method in which knowledge was built up from a clear and distinct idea that could not be doubted; other true propositions followed logically from the first idea. "I think, therefore I am" was Descartes's most famous example of the method. Choice A is incorrect because the world of forms is a basic assumption of neoplatonism, not Descartes. Choice C is incorrect because it begins with an empirical observation which relies on sense impressions; Descartes believed one could always doubt the senses because they were easily fooled. Choice D is incorrect because it also relies on

sense impressions, as the calculus is applied to observations. Choice E is incorrect because it is Newton's formulation of the law of universal gravitation and not a statement of Descartes's method.

44. **B.** Flawed policies like the decision to constantly expand the Empire and the enforcement of the Continental System (which hampered the economies of Napoleon's allies more than that of Britain) exacerbated resistance to French rule throughout the far-flung Empire, eventually leading to an opposition coalition so large that it presented tactical and strategic difficulties that were insurmountable. Choice A is incorrect because the French army was well organized and unparalleled in its logistical efficiency. Choice C is incorrect because both royalist and republican opposition to his rule had been largely subdued by 1805. Choice D is incorrect because, although the loss of the French and Spanish fleets at the Battle of Trafalgar ended Napoleon's dreams of controlling the seas and conquering the British, it did not mean defeat for Napoleon's land armies; they went on to conquer most of Europe in the subsequent decade. Choice E is incorrect because, while Napoleon was not the military genius he has sometimes been made out to be, it was insurmountable logistical problems in the face of mounting resistance that led to his defeat.

45. **E.** Prussia devoted most of its wealth to building its military and its leaders were thoroughly militarized. The resulting military power was the basis of its power in the eighteenth century. Choice A is incorrect because Bismarck and his peculiar genius was a source of Prussian power in the nineteenth century. Choice B is incorrect because Prussia was not significantly industrial in the eighteenth century. Choice C is incorrect because Prussia's alliances were useful, but not the source of the power. Choice D is incorrect because Prussia's geographical position lacked the natural defenses of Britain, for example.

46. **A.** The actual motives and goals of the revolutions of 1848 varied widely, but they can be best understood as a combination of the desire for liberal reforms that were either briefly enjoyed or envied by others during the period of the French Revolution and Napoleonic rule and the spirit of nationalism that was awakened across Europe by both the success of the united French people and resentment towards French domination. Choice B is incorrect because only some of the revolutions were independence movements; others simply sought liberal reform within existing kingdoms and states. Choice C is incorrect because only the most radical factions of the French rebellion in 1848 advocated redistribution of wealth and they were never in a position to make any "attempts" to do so. Choice D is incorrect because it contains a major chronological error: The French Revolution occurred from 1789 to 1799, and even if one includes the Napoleonic era there is no way the revolutions of 1848 could be precursors to the French Revolution. Choice E is incorrect because only some of the revolutions even came close to aiming at changes that would truly be democratic, and many of the nationalistic revolutions, like those in Italy, often pinned their hopes on the establishment of a national monarchy.

47. **D.** The main fuel for steam engines was coal; the introduction of steam engines, therefore, dramatically increased the demand for coal. Choice A is incorrect because the factory system is a way of organizing labor; it is not dependent upon a particular source of power. Choice B is incorrect because the invention of the automobile was facilitated by the invention of the internal combustion engine. Choice C is incorrect because steam engines relied upon coal for fuel, therefore *increasing* demand for it. Choice E is incorrect because, while the invention of the steam locomotive led to a railway boom, the application of it to ships allowed the shipping industry to prosper as well.

48. **B.** Conservatives derided "constitutionalism" for its belief that men could just imagine and dictate successful systems of government and ignore the reality that the only successful systems of government were those that had developed naturally over time. Choice A is incorrect because, although most conservatives were monarchists, their opposition to constitutionalism was rooted in the reason that they were monarchists, that is, they believed that monarchy was an institution

that had developed slowly in response to the realities of human life. Choice C is incorrect because, again, conservatives opposed constitutionalism for the same reason that they respected tradition and supported monarchy. Choice D is incorrect because it was not necessarily the case that they would lose power in a constitutional system. Choice E is incorrect because the sanctity of private property tended to be a liberal position, and the liberals supported constitutionalism.

49. **C.** Churchill was a lone voice in his criticism of the Chamberlain government's policy of appeasing Hitler's aggression. Choice A is incorrect because Churchill never advocated socialism. Choice B is incorrect because he was no great supporter of the Soviet Union. Choice D is incorrect because the coalition government was created when war broke out and it was done with nearly unanimous support. Choice E is incorrect because it was in the 1940s, as Prime Minister, that Churchill mounted his effort to draw the United States into the war.

50. **E.** All of the choices are examples of the revival of nationalist and ethnic tensions. The Chechnyan conflict arose because of Russia's refusal to accede to Chechnyan nationalist demands for independence. The multisided conflicts in Yugoslavia and in Bosnia–Herzegovina involved both ethnic tensions between and nationalist aspirations of the Serbs, Slovenes, Croats, Bosnians, and several other groups. The splitting up of Czechoslovakia was the result of the nationalist aspirations of the Slovaks.

51. **D.** In 1519, a Spanish expedition led by the Portuguese sailor Ferdinand Magellan sailed west in search of a new route to the Spice Islands of the East. Rounding the tip of South America in 1520, the expedition sailed into the Pacific Ocean and arrived at the Spice Islands in 1521. In 1522, the expedition completed the first circumnavigation of the globe, returning to Spain without Magellan, who had been killed in the Philippines. Choice A is incorrect because Vasco da Gama, known for extending Portuguese trade by reaching the coast of India in 1498 and returning with a cargo that earned his investors a 60 percent profit, did not lead an expedition that circumnavigated the globe. Choice B is incorrect because Amerigo Vespucci, an Italian sailing for Spain in 1499 and for Portugal in 1501, helped to show that the lands discovered by Columbus were not in the Far East, but rather a previously unknown (to Europeans) continent, and did not lead an expedition that circumnavigated the globe. Choice C is incorrect because Martin Waldseemüller was a German cartographer who named "America" after Vespucci. Choice E is incorrect because Columbus's voyages did not include a circumnavigation of the globe.

52. **C.** There was nothing unique about the religion of the Italian peninsula prior to the Reformation. Choice A is incorrect because the Italian peninsula's geographical location *was* a reason the Renaissance began there; it was the gateway to Europe for eastern trade coming into Europe through the Mediterranean Sea. Italy was therefore the first region to benefit from economic recovery and the influx of ancient texts. Choices B and D are incorrect because the political and social organization of the Italian peninsula was unique. The Italian peninsula was organized politically into independent city-states whose social hierarchy was based on occupation. This unique structure created an atmosphere in which elites competed with one another for civic accomplishments. Choice E is incorrect because the thriving commercial economy of the Italian peninsula meant that those competing elites had vast sums of money to spend on their courts, employing philosophers and artists.

53. **E.** The Christian Church in Europe was not faced with the split in the population caused by the Protestant movement in the first decade of the sixteenth century because the Protestant movement did not begin until Luther's revolt of the *second* decade of the sixteenth century. Choice A is incorrect because the pope's status as ruler of the Papal States meant that the Church was constantly embroiled in the politics of the peninsula, thereby alienating Italians who lived in other city-states. Choice B is incorrect because the Church's use of Latin, a language that only the elite could read, angered and alienated the common people. Choice C is incorrect because the fact that people were increasingly able to read

the vernacular, but unable to read Latin, increased frustration with and anger at the Church. Choice D is incorrect because the Church, an increasingly worldly institution, *was* unable to tend to the emotional and spiritual needs of the population.

54. **C.** The invasion of a Protestant army from the Netherlands led by the Prince of Orange and his English wife, Mary, occurred in 1688, well after the English Civil War. Choice A is incorrect because the decision by Charles to marry a sister of the Catholic king of France heightened the fears of the Protestant-dominated Parliament that the ruling Stuart dynasty had plans to return England to the Church of Rome. Choice B is incorrect because Charles I's insistence on waging costly wars with Spain and France brought relations with Parliament to the breaking point. Choice D is incorrect because the invasion of a Scottish army, whom Charles provoked by threatening their religious independence, forced Charles to call on the English Parliament for yet more funds, setting the stage for a showdown. Choice E is incorrect because the decision of Parliament to respond by making funds contingent on the curbing of monarchical power convinced Charles to listen to his more bellicose advisors and try to crush the Parliament.

55. **A.** In the Copernican model, the planets orbit the Sun in uniform circular orbits; Copernicus's innovation was to put the Sun at the center of the cosmos, instead of the Earth, but he did not deviate from the Aristotelian notion of uniform circular orbits for the planets. Choice B is incorrect because, in the Copernican model, the orbits of the planets are circular not elliptical; elliptical orbits were an innovation suggested by Kepler and calculated by Newton. Choice C is incorrect because the Copernican model, like its Aristotelian predecessor, presents the cosmos as bound by the sphere of fixed stars. Choice D is incorrect because the Copernican model is Sun-centered, not Earth-centered and, in the Copernican model, the planets have circular, not elliptical, orbits. Choice E is incorrect because, in the Copernican model, the moon orbits both the Earth and the Sun.

56. **B.** *System of Nature*, by the German-born French *philosophe* the Baron d'Holbach, was openly

atheist and materialist. In it, he offered the eighteenth-century reader a view of the world as a complex system of purely material substances, acting and developing according to laws of cause and effect that were purely mechanical rather than imposed by a rational God. Choice A is incorrect because the text did not advocate revolution. Choice C is incorrect because it was a book about nature, not political ideologies. Choice D is incorrect because the book preceded the French Revolution by 19 years. Choice E is incorrect because an advocacy of science was not, in itself, radical in the eighteenth century; it was the thoroughgoing materialism of the text that made it so radical.

57. **B.** In the eighteenth century, the expansionist aims of Frederick II of Prussia led to a shift in diplomatic alliances which turned old enemies into allies, hence the notion of a "Diplomatic Revolution." Prussia, having antagonized both the French and Austrians, grew fearful of being isolated and forged an alliance in 1756 with its former enemy Great Britain. In response, Austria and France, previously antagonistic towards one another, forged an alliance of their own. Choice A is incorrect because the notion of an alliance was not invented in the eighteenth century. Choices C and D are incorrect because the term *Diplomatic Revolution* does not refer to either the French Revolution or the revolutions of 1848. Choice E is incorrect because the Concert of Europe was the name for the system of diplomacy that evolved in the early nineteenth century.

58. **B.** The verse is from William Wordsworth and is an example of the emphasis on sentiment and emotion, particularly as evoked by nature, indicative of the Romantic movement. Choice A is incorrect because neoplatonism was prevalent in the fifteenth to seventeenth centuries and emphasized a mathematical understanding of the world of forms. Choice C is incorrect because impressionism was a movement in the visual arts. Choice D is incorrect because conservatism refers to a political ideology, not an artistic movement. Choice E is incorrect because the Enlightenment was an eighteenth-century cultural movement that emphasized reason.

59. **C.** In *The Origin of Species*, Darwin argued and offered evidence for the fact that all biological

diversity was and is the product of a purely natural process which he termed natural selection. Choice A is incorrect because it was the so-called social Darwinist Herbert Spencer who put forward the idea that competition was natural and necessary for social progress. Choice B is incorrect because it was the French socialist Charles Fourier who argued that human nature was essentially cooperative. Choice D is incorrect because it was the communist Karl Marx who argued that competition was the root of class conflict. Choice E is incorrect because Darwin argued that both humans and modern apes were descended from some ancient ancestor that was neither human nor ape.

60. **C.** Bismarck appealed to the nationalist feelings of the south Germans by manufacturing a war with France in 1871. Choice A is incorrect because Prussia was a Protestant state. Choice B is incorrect because, although Bismarck was not above advocating the occasional liberal reform in order to strengthen his political position, it is too much to say that he adopted a liberal reform agenda, and because the south Germans were not won over by Bismarck's liberal overtures; they only joined Prussia when war broke out with France. Choice D is incorrect because the liberal south Germans had *no* desire for the strong, authoritarian central government favored by Prussians. Choice E is incorrect because the Junkers were the dominant aristocratic class *in Prussia*, and an alliance with them had no appeal for the south Germans.

61. **E.** The Rise of a Spanish Empire in the New World was the result of sixteenth-century voyages of exploration and the work of the soldier-adventurers who led them, a process unrelated to the Hundred Years War, which raged through the fourteenth and fifteenth centuries. The other four choices are incorrect because they *were* all effects of the Hundred Years War.

62. **C.** Proficiency in the military arts was valued highly by the traditional feudal lords of Europe. Because social status in the independent city-states of the Italian peninsula was determined by occupation, proficiency in the military arts was not highly valued there. The other four choices were all highly valued in the humanistic culture of Renaissance Italy.

63. **D.** Luther disagreed with the Church's traditional belief that good works were essential to salvation, arguing instead that salvation could only be a gift from God, given to those who have true faith. The other four choices are basic theological beliefs of Martin Luther.

64. **A.** The Glorious Revolution of 1688 represents the triumph of constitutionalism in Britain because it successfully ousted James II, the last of the Stuarts who claimed the right to rule as an absolute monarch, and replaced him with a monarchy that swore to rule as a "King in Parliament," that is, as a constitutional monarch. Choice B is incorrect because democracy, the notion of one person, one vote, came gradually to Britain, culminating in the enfranchisement of women in 1918. Choice C is incorrect because the Glorious Revolution ended the Restoration Period (1660–1688). Choices D and E are incorrect because the Commonwealth Period (1649–1660), where Britain was ruled without a monarch, preceded both the Restoration and the Glorious Revolution.

65. **D.** Newton is best described as working in the Platonic–Pythagorean tradition because he pursued and achieved its goal of identifying the fundamental mathematical laws of nature. Choice A is incorrect because Newton rejected the tradition of Aristotelian physics which relied upon an Earth-centered cosmos and the existence of different kinds of matter. Choice B is incorrect because Newton rejected the scholastic notion that all valuable knowledge was found in ancient texts. Choice C is incorrect because, although there are elements of the hermetic tradition in Newton's work, the search for fundamental mathematical laws which characterizes the Platonic–Pythagorean tradition is the most pronounced aspect of Newton's work. Choice E is incorrect because, although Newton was a Copernican in the sense that he advocated a Sun-centered model, he broke with almost every other aspect of Copernicus's approach.

66. **D.** The notion that the proper role of government is to protect individual property is a fundamental tenet of John Locke's philosophy, not of Rousseau's. The other four choices are all examples of Rousseau's philosophy.

67. **B**. Tea imported from China, in exchange for opium from British India, was sold in Europe, but this transaction was not part of the "triangle of trade," which involved Europe, Africa, and the Americas/West Indies. The other four choices describe transactions that did make up the triangle of trade.

68. **E**. In Thermidor (1794–1799), the bourgeois moderates who had begun the revolution by constituting a National Assembly came out of hiding and reasserted their control over a revolution that had briefly taken a more radical turn. Choice A is incorrect because France was not defeated by Austria, and would not be defeated until 1815. Choice C is incorrect because the French monarchy was not restored until after the defeat of Napoleon in 1815. Choice D is incorrect because the rule of the Committee of Public Safety occurred during the radical phase of the revolution (1791–1794).

69. **C**. The great powers at the Congress of Vienna were represented by members of the traditional, aristocratic ruling houses of Europe. Accordingly, their aims were to restore the traditional order of a Europe that the French Revolution had challenged and to create a new balance of power that would make another Napoleon impossible. Choice A is incorrect because the aims of restoring the traditional order and establishing a balance of power meant both the restoration of the Bourbon monarchy and of a reasonable economic and military power in France; France was not, therefore, to be "punished." Choice B is incorrect because Germany was not united in 1814 and a "weakening" of Germany would have made no sense in 1814. Choice D is incorrect because the aristocratic representatives at the Congress of Vienna were directly threatened by and, therefore, *opposed* to liberal reforms. Choice E is incorrect because the nationalist hopes of the Italians, Hungarians, and Czechs ran counter to the aim of restoring the traditional order.

70. **B**. The factory system that was characteristic of the Second Industrial Revolution required and produced a class of managers and clerks whose pay and status located them precariously at the lower end of the middle class. Choice A is incor-

rect because the Second Industrial Revolution did nothing to distribute wealth *more evenly* throughout the population; instead, it made a *relatively small number* of industrialists and entrepreneurs fabulously wealthy and made some workers better off than before. Choice C is incorrect because the poor had existed before the Second Industrial Revolution. Choice D is incorrect because, although the railway boom produced social effects, it is not itself a social effect. Choice E is incorrect because, although many women initially found work in the factories of the Second Industrial Revolution, they were not paid equally and were the first to be let go when increasing mechanization decreased the demand for labor.

71. **E**. Johann Wolfgang von Goethe's *The Sorrows of Young Werther* (1774) is an example of the German *Sturm und Drang* (Storm and Stress) movement of the late eighteenth century. Its glorification of the "inner experience" of the sensitive individual was a forerunner of nineteenth-century Romanticism. Choice A is incorrect because Michelangelo's *David* is an example of the late Renaissance period. Choice B is incorrect because Bismarck's *Kulturkampf* is an example of the political philosophy known as *Realpolitik*. Choice C is incorrect because the assassination of Franz Ferdinand is an example of ethnic nationalism. Choice D is incorrect because Picasso's *Guernica* is early cubist in style and dates from the twentieth century.

72. **A**. The fact that the French voters used their newly granted privilege of universal manhood suffrage to vote for the creation of a Second Empire (replacing the Second Republic) and to make Louis-Napoleon hereditary emperor demonstrates the degree to which nationalism (the desire to have a strong and powerful nation) had triumphed over all other ideologies in mid-eighteenth-century France. Choice B is incorrect because Louis-Napoleon's coup d'état simply illustrates his willingness to use force in order to rule; it was the overwhelming approval of this action by the public in the two plebiscites that demonstrates the power of nationalism. Choice C is incorrect because the revolt of the

working classes in Paris and their brief attempt to set up a Commune illustrates a development of class consciousness, not nationalism. Choice D is incorrect because Louis-Napoleon's granting of universal manhood suffrage illustrates his belief that he had the people's support; their use of that suffrage to bring into being an empire and an emperor demonstrates their nationalism. Choice E is incorrect because the Directory was a bureaucratic entity of eighteenth-century France.

73. **B.** The rise of Chartism (1837–1842), characterized by massive demonstrations in favor of the People's Charter, a petition that called for universal manhood suffrage and a democratic Parliament, demonstrated the degree to which the classes who had not been enfranchised by the Reform Bill of 1832, the lower middle and working classes, desired further reform. Choice A is incorrect because the Charter was ignored by Parliament; the monarchy played almost no role in the drama of Chartism. Choice C is incorrect because the Chartist movement was a reform movement; it was neither intrinsically nationalist nor antinationalist. Choice D is incorrect because the Charter called for a more democratic Parliament; it was not opposed to the monarchy. Choice E is incorrect because the Chartist movement did not involve opposition to the mechanization of industry; it was Luddism that offered organized opposition to the mechanization of industry.

74. **A.** In a European society increasingly devoted to the mundane proceedings of the business world and an accompanying sense of social alienation, war seemed to offer the possibility of a "brotherhood of arms" and the opportunity to do something glorious and worthwhile. While there was a racial component to the intense nationalism of 1914, a notion of "racial hatred" was not a strong component to the celebratory mood of 1914. Choice C is incorrect because Germany's strong desire to repudiate the humiliating conditions of the Versailles Treaty was a factor in German enthusiasm for war in 1939; the Versailles Treaty did not come into existence until the conclusion of World War I in 1918. Choice D is incorrect because the Continental System was instituted by Napoleon in the early 1800s and was long gone by 1914. Choice E is incorrect because B, C, and D are incorrect.

75. **B.** In the context of World War I, the phrase "total war" refers to the marshalling of every sector of the economy to support the war effort and the abandoning the production of normal consumer goods that was required to win the war of attrition. Choice A is incorrect because the bombing of civilians in major cities was a development of World War II. Choice C is incorrect because both sides did take prisoners in World War I. Choice D is incorrect because World War I was fought in a long line of trenches in Flanders and France; war on multiple continents was a development of World War II. Choice E is incorrect because choices A, C, and D are incorrect.

76. **B.** The war effort exhausted the resources of the traditional European powers, Britain, France, and Germany, and left the United States, with its vast economy, and the Soviet Union, with the largest army in the world, as the two superpowers. Choice A is incorrect because the Treaty of Versailles was the treaty that concluded World War I. Choice C is incorrect because it was the division of Germany that was a consequence of World War II; German reunification did not come until 1990. Choice D is incorrect because World War II marked the beginning of the breakup of the British Empire, not a strengthening of it. Choice E is incorrect because the German invasion of Poland was one of the *causes* of World War II, not a consequence.

77. **D.** Following the collapse of the Soviet Union, nationalism which had been driven underground came to the surface in eastern Europe, resulting in the split of Czechoslovakia and the advent of several ethnic-nationalist wars in the former Yugoslavia and in the former republics of the Soviet Union. The absorption of eastern Europe into the European Union has brought the effects of globalization to eastern Europe. Choice A is incorrect because, although there was an undeniable increase in individual liberty following the fall of the Soviet Union, the degree to which either individual liberty or democracy has flourished in

eastern Europe in the subsequent decades is highly debatable. Choice C is incorrect because America has not become isolationist. Choice E is incorrect because the economic effects of the fall of the Soviet Union regarding the distribution of wealth and the effect on poverty varied greatly throughout eastern Europe.

78. **C.** Following the breach of the Berlin Wall in November of 1989, the West German Chancellor, the Conservative Helmut Kohl, moved quickly towards reunification. In March 1990, elections were held in East Germany to create a new government ready to negotiate with West Germany; by 3 August the official treaty of reunification was drafted; on 3 October 1990, the Germans celebrated Reunification Day. It was a reunification that amounted to East Germany being annexed by the West. Choice A is incorrect because the process happened very quickly. Choice B is incorrect because there was nothing that could be called separate economic policies that were set up to ease the transition. Choice D is incorrect because the Civic Forum leaders, who were not at all sure that they wished to be reunified with West Germany and its capitalist economy, were swept aside in the reunification process. Choice E is incorrect because choices A, B, and D are incorrect.

79. **D.** Luther's "The Freedom of the Christian Man" (1520) was his message to the common people; no social revolutionary, Luther walked a thin line between encouraging the common people to "obey their Christian conscience" and assert their individual independence from the Church in Rome, but also to respect those in authority who seemed to possess true Christian principles. Choice A is incorrect because Luther was an opponent of social upheaval and the essay was specifically designed to discourage such uprisings. Choice B is incorrect because "The Freedom of the Christian Man" was Luther's message to the common people; to the nobility, he wrote an "Address to the Christian Nobility of the German Nation" (1520), which appealed to the German princes' desire for both greater unity and power and to their desire to be out from under the thumb of an Italian pope. Choice C is incorrect because it was not Luther, but rather the German princes who established the principle of "whoever rules; his religion" by signing the Peace of Augsburg (1555), which signaled Rome that the German princes would not go to war with each other over religion. Choice E is incorrect because choices A, B, and C are incorrect.

80. **E.** All of the choices are correct. Richelieu built a powerful royal army and used it to defeat and disband the private armies of the Great French aristocrats. He then turned the royal army on the Protestant towns, stripping them of their autonomy. In addition to the royal army, Richelieu also built a strong administrative bureaucracy and used it to strip provincial aristocrats and elites of their administrative power by dividing France into some 30 administrative districts and putting each under the control of an *intendent*, an administrative bureaucrat, usually chosen from the middle class, who owed his position and therefore his loyalty directly to Richelieu.

Suggestions and Outline for the DBQ

Suggestions

Remember the five steps to a short history essay of high quality adapted to the DBQ:

Step 1: As you read the documents, decide how you are going to group them.

Step 2: Compose a thesis that explains why the documents should be grouped in the way you have chosen.

Step 3: Compose your topic sentences and make sure that they add up logically to your thesis.

Step 4: Support and illustrate your thesis with specific examples that contextualize the documents.

Step 5. *If you have time*, compose a one-paragraph conclusion that restates your thesis.

For this question, the documents display a wide array of positions; so a good strategy would be to try to identify a central dividing issue. In these documents, you can notice that all except Copernicus seem to take some sort of position on the senses and observation: some believe that all knowledge of nature must start with direct sense experience, while others argue that starting with sense experience is a mistake. Begin the essay by discussing that central divide and then see if you can form a few groups based on the similarities and differences between their approaches.

Finally, since Copernicus does not address the central issue, ignore the document. It is okay to ignore *one* document if it does not fit into your thesis, but never ignore more than one or two.

Outline

A possible outline to an answer to this DBQ looks like this:

Thesis: These documents show that arguments regarding the basis for knowledge of the natural world have often hinged on assumptions about the reliability of sense experience.

Topic sentence A: Documents 2 and 9 illustrate the faith in direct, trial-and-error experience that developed in the "alchemy" and "natural magic" traditions.

Specific examples: Della Porta's emphasis on "practical application"; Agricola's emphasis on handling the materials, making "dissolutions" and "combinations" and recording results carefully.

Topic sentence B: Documents 5 and 6 illustrate the emphasis on observation as the correct starting place for knowledge of the natural world.

Specific examples: Bacon outlines two approaches and argues for the superiority of the one that begins with observed particulars; Harvey *illustrates* how the method should work.

Topic sentence C: Documents 3 and 10 refine the process to include the goal of finding general laws.

Specific examples: Galileo—sense experiences and very exact observations; begin not from the authority of scriptural passages, but from sense experiences and necessary demonstrations; nature never transgresses the laws imposed upon her. Newton codifies the approach into "rules."

Topic sentence D: Documents 4, 7, and 8 dissent from the view that sense experience is a valid foundation for knowledge of the natural world.

Specific examples: Bellarmine: the dangers of contradicting scholastic and church authority; Descartes: the senses are easily fooled; an alternative method, proceed logically from a general distinct idea to particulars.

Conclusion: The variety of attitudes and positions regarding knowledge about the natural world depended upon the amount of faith one put in the reliability of sense experience.

Suggestions and Outlines for Answers to the Thematic Essay Questions

Suggestions

Choose one question from each group for which you can quickly write a clear thesis and three topic sentences that you can illustrate and support with several specific examples. Then follow the five-step formula to constructing a short history essay of high quality:

Step 1: Find the action words in the question and determine what it wants you to do.

Step 2: Compose a thesis that responds to the question and gives you something specific to support and illustrate.

Step 3: Compose your topic sentences and make sure that they add up logically to your thesis.

Step 4: Support and illustrate your thesis with specific examples.

Step 5: *If you have time*, compose a one-paragraph conclusion that restates your thesis.

And remember the writing guidelines:

- Avoid long sentences with multiple clauses. Your goal is to write the clearest sentence possible; most often the clearest sentence is a relatively short sentence.
- Do not get caught up in digressions. No matter how fascinating or insightful you find some idea or fact, if it does not directly support or illustrate your thesis, do not put it in.
- Skip the mystery. Do not ask a lot of rhetorical questions and do not go for a surprise ending. The readers are looking for your thesis, your argument, and your evidence; give it to them in a clear, straightforward manner.

Outlines

Part B

Question 2

Thesis: The success or failure of seventeenth-century monarchs to consolidate political power within their kingdoms rested on their ability to form an alliance with a rising commercial class.

Topic sentence A: The French monarchy built the most absolutist government by cementing an alliance with both the clergy and middle class, and by using the great administrative expertise of both to build a powerful centralized bureaucracy.

Specific examples: Richelieu divided France into 30 administrative districts, each under the control of an *intendent*, an administrative bureaucrat, usually chosen from the middle class.

Topic sentence B: In England, the Parliament successfully resisted the absolutist designs of the Stuart monarchy because the English Parliament of the seventeenth century was a pre-existing alliance of nobles and well-to-do members of a thriving merchant and professional class that saw itself as a voice of the "English people."

Specific examples: Social composition of the two camps in the English civil war—traditional landed nobility and high Church sided with the king; newer, commercial-based nobles and merchant class fought for Parliament.

Topic sentence C: In those areas where the commercial class was less developed, a political standoff between monarch and landed nobility was the norm.

Specific examples: Brandenburg–Prussia, the independent German states, Austria, and

Poland all lacked a well-developed commercial class and all had political compromise between monarchy and traditional elites.

Conclusion: The degree to which seventeenth-century European monarchs were successful in consolidating political power was directly related to their ability to build an alliance with the commercial class.

Question 3

Thesis: In the eighteenth century, a combination of the development of market-based agriculture, rural manufacturing, and increased demand shattered the traditional population and productivity cycles of western Europe.

Topic sentence A: Prior to the eighteenth century, changes in both population and productivity were cyclical and due to natural limits on agricultural productivity.

Specific examples: Population and productivity would rise together, as more hands meant more crops planted and harvested; eventually agricultural productivity would reach a maximum, causing food to become scarce and forcing population down.

Topic sentence B: In response to an increasingly commercialized economy due to trade with the colonies, eighteenth-century British land owners began to shift to cash-crop agriculture and the importation of food, removing the natural limit to agricultural productivity.

Specific examples: Shift to growing of grain and the enclosure movement.

Topic sentence C: The development of cottage textile industry spread capital throughout the economy and enabled the full-scale shift to commercial agriculture and food importation, removing the last check to population growth.

Specific examples: Development of the putting-out system; development of rural spinning, weaving, and carding industries.

Conclusion: The removal of the natural limit to agricultural production removed the limits to both productivity and population growth; increased demand led to an unprecedented era of technical innovation that continued to feed growth well into the nineteenth century.

Question 4

Thesis: The French aims and methods of the French Revolution evolved through three phases: the Moderate Phase (1789–1791), the Radical Phase (1791–1794), and Thermidor (1794–1799); the evolution can be explained by shifts in the social makeup of the Revolutionary leadership.

Topic sentence A: The revolution was launched by the bourgeois leaders of the Third Estate who wished to curb the power and privilege of the aristocracy and clergy through economic pressure and the threat of mass violence.

Specific examples: Formation of the National Assembly, *Declaration of the Rights of Man and Citizen.*

Topic sentence B: Beginning in 1791, the politicized urban working class of Paris seized control and attempted to create a democratic republic and a more materially and socially egalitarian society by whatever means necessary.

Specific examples: Rise of the *sans-culottes*, Reign of Terror.

Topic sentence C: By 1794 the bourgeois faction reasserted its leadership and focused on restoring order, a process that led eventually to military dictatorship.

Specific examples: Death of Robespierre, Counter Terror, Directory and Napoleon.

Conclusion: The aims and methods of the French Revolution went from moderate to radical and back again as the leadership of the revolution went from the bourgeoisie briefly to the working class and back again.

Part C

Question 5

Thesis: The Second Industrial Revolution produced a western European society that was more urban, less family-oriented, and filled with uncertainty.

Topic sentence A: The rise of the centralized factory system that characterized the Second Industrial Revolution produced a western European society that was much more urban.

Specific examples: In the eighteenth century, the majority of British population lived in the countryside; by the end of the nineteenth century, the majority of British population lived in cities. Rise of Manchester, Sheffield, and Birmingham from small villages to industrial cities.

Topic sentence B: The Second Industrial Revolution created a western European society that was less family-oriented.

Specific examples: Eldest sons and daughters moved to cities to seek factory work; with the rise of industrial cities came the rise of working-class slums. Husbands, wives, and children often worked in different factories.

Topic sentence C: The Second Industrial Revolution destroyed the certainties of the traditional society.

Specific examples: In the agricultural economy, there was no such thing as unemployment; as more and more machines were introduced, the demand for labor went down and unemployment became a cyclical phenomenon; the rise of the workhouses and poor houses in Britain.

Conclusion: The Second Industrial Revolution destroyed the traditional rural, family-oriented society of certainty and created a new urban, individualized society of uncertainty.

Question 6

Thesis: The development of mass politics contributed to the development of the New Imperialism in the late nineteenth century by creating a large group of nationalistic voters whose support had to be won by political elites.

Topic sentence A: The second half of the nineteenth century saw the development of a large group of new voters.

Specific examples: In Britain, reform Bills of 1867 and 1884 created nearly universal manhood suffrage. In France, Louis-Napoleon granted universal manhood suffrage in 1848. In Germany, Bismarck promised universal manhood suffrage (though he never provided it) in return for popular support of his policies.

Topic sentence B: The newly politicized masses were enthusiastically nationalist.

Specific examples: Support for Crimean War and occupation of Egypt in Britain; plebiscites for Second Empire and making Louis-Napoleon emperor in France; support for Franco-Prussian War in Germany.

Topic sentence C: Politicians discovered that imperialism appealed to the newly politicized masses.

Specific examples: Disraeli makes conservatives the party of monarchy, church, and *empire* in Britain; Louis-Napoleon's decision to end the republic and proclaim the Second Empire in France; Bismarck's "blood and iron" unification of Germany; the popularity of the Scramble for Africa.

Conclusion: The rise of a large, nationalistic constituency that politicians had to win over contributed to the New Imperialism of the late nineteenth century.

Question 7

Thesis: The methods of successful resistance to Soviet dominance in eastern Europe in the 1980s and early 1990s can be divided into three categories: unionization, the Civic Forum model, and ethnic nationalism.

Topic sentence A: One successful method relied upon the building of a strong labor union.

Specific examples: Formation and politicization of Solidarity; legalization in 1989, and triumph with Walesa presidency in 1990.

Topic sentence B: Another successful method relied upon a rebuilding of civic life through Civic Forums.

Specific examples: Civic Forum in Czechoslovakia led by dissidents like Havel; eventual triumph and Havel presidency; Civic Forum model in East Germany; its success (but irrelevancy in Western-dominated reunification).

Topic sentence C: A third "successful" method involved the reinvigoration of ethnic-nationalist identities.

Specific examples: Albanians and Serbs in Kosovo; Slovenes and Croatians; complete fragmentation (so, successful in opposing Soviet domination, but disastrous in building stable post-Soviet society).

Conclusion: There were three models that were equally successful in opposing Soviet domination, but which produced differing long-term results.

Appendixes

Glossary of Terms
Bibliography
Web sites

GLOSSARY OF TERMS

95 theses The 95 propositions or challenges to official Church theology posted by Martin Luther on the door of Wittenberg castle in the autumn of 1517.

absolutism A theory of government that contends that a rightful ruler rules with absolute power over his or her subjects.

abstractionism An artistic movement of the late nineteenth and early twentieth centuries that sought to "analyze" the essence of perception and experience. Abstract painters of the period developed a system of seeing the world as composed of geometrical shapes.

Arc de Triomphe The most famous example of neoclassical architecture executed in Napoleonic France, the arch was commissioned by Napoleon in 1806 to honor those who fought for France in the Napoleonic Wars. It was designed by Jean Francois Chalgrin and built in the center of the Place de l'Étoile (now renamed the Place Charles de Gaulle) at the western end of the Champs-Élysées.

almanacs Popular eighteenth-century texts which incorporated much of the new scientific and rational knowledge of the Enlightenment.

Anabaptists A sect of radical Protestant reformers prevalent in Europe in the sixteenth century who considered true Protestant faith to require social reform.

anarchism The nineteenth-century ideology which saw the modern state and its institutions as the enemy of individual freedom, and recommended terrorism as a way to disrupt the machinery of government.

Ancien Régime (also Old Regime) Term that refers to the traditional social and political hierarchy of eighteenth-century France.

Anglican Church The state Church of England, established by Henry VIII in the early sixteenth century when he decided to break from the Church in Rome.

Anschluss The annexation, in March of 1938, of Austria by Nazi Germany.

anti-Semitism The singling out of Jews as culturally, and sometimes racially, different for the purpose of discriminating against them.

appeasement Britain's policy, 1936–1939, of acquiescing to Hitler's demands in return for his promise of no further aggression.

Atlantic Charter A document, drawn up in August of 1941, setting forth Anglo-American aims in World War II. It rejected any territorial aggrandizement for either Britain or the United States, and it affirmed the right of all peoples to choose their own form of government.

August Decrees Decrees passed by the National Assembly of France in August of 1789 renouncing and abolishing most of the traditional privileges of the nobility and the clergy.

Austro-Prussian War of 1866 Engineered by Bismarck as part of his master plan to unify Germany under the Prussian monarchy. Prussian troops surprised and overwhelmed a larger Austrian force, winning victory in only seven weeks. The result was that Austria was expelled from the old German Confederation and a new North German Confederation, completely under the control of Prussia, was created.

baroque The dominant artistic style of the seventeenth century characterized by its emphasis on grandeur and drama.

Bastille The prison-fortress of eighteenth-century Paris which symbolized the despotic power of the *Ancien Régime*. It was stormed by a revolutionary crowd on 14 July 1789.

Battle of Tannenberg A German victory over Russian troops in August of 1914 which led to the liberation of East Prussia and began a slow, steady German advance eastward.

Battle of the Somme (July to November 1916) World War I British offensive that produced enormous casualties: 400,000 British, 200,000 French, and 500,000 German soldiers perished.

Battle of Trafalgar The naval battle in which Great Britain's fleet, led by Lord Nelson, defeated the combined French and Spanish fleets on 21 October 1805, making Britain virtually unconquerable.

Battle of Verdun (February 1916) World War I battle in which French troops, led by Marshall Petain, repulsed a German offensive; 700,000 men were killed.

Battle of Waterloo Napoleon's last stand in 1815; he was defeated in Belgium by a coalition of forces led by Britain's Duke of Wellington.

Berlin Airlift The U.S.-sponsored airlift, from June 1948 to May 1949, which brought supplies to West Berlin; it was a response to Soviet troops cutting off all land traffic from the West into Berlin in an attempt to take control of the whole city.

Berlin Conference of 1885 A conference of the European powers to establish guidelines for the partitioning of Africa.

Bessemer Process A process, invented in the 1850s by the English engineer Henry Bessemer, that allowed steel to be produced more cheaply and in larger quantities.

Black Death A plague that first appeared in Europe in 1347 and recurred numerous times until it disappeared in 1352. It is estimated that between one-quarter and one-third of the population of Europe died during the plague years.

Blackshirts (also *squadristi*) Italian fascist paramilitary groups, largely recruited from disgruntled war veterans, commanded by Mussolini and increasingly relied upon to keep order by the Italian government in the 1920s.

Bolsheviks A party of revolutionary Marxists, led by Lenin, who seized power in Russia in November 1917.

Boulanger Affair An attempted coup by the French General George Boulanger in the early 1880s; it underscored the fragility of French democracy and the volatility of mass politics in France.

bourgeoisie In eighteenth- and nineteenth-century France, a term for the merchant and commercial classes. In Marxist social critique, the class that owns the means of production and exploits wage-laborers.

Boxer Rebellion (1899–1900) An attempted rebellion by Chinese Nationalists which aimed at overthrowing the Western-dependent Manchu dynasty; it was suppressed by European powers.

cahiers The official concerns and grievances of the three Estates that composed the political orders of eighteenth-century France. Members representing each of the three Estates met in the Estates General to hear the problems of the realm and to hear pleas for new taxes. In return, they were allowed to present their cahiers.

Candide Voltaire's sprawling satire of European culture, penned in 1759; the classic example of Enlightenment-period satire.

Carbonari Secret groups of Italian nationalists active in the early part of the nineteenth century; in 1820, the Carbonari briefly succeeded in organizing an uprising that forced King Ferdinand I of the Kingdom of the Two Sicilies to grant a constitution and a new Parliament.

Cartel des Gauches A coalition of socialist parties, swept into power in France in the elections of 1924; caused an ultranationalist reaction in France.

cash crops Crops grown for sale and export in the market-oriented approach that replaced the manorial system during the Agricultural Revolution of the eighteenth century.

celestial realm The realm, in the Aristotelian view of the cosmos, above the orbit of the moon.

Chartism (1837–1842) A movement in Britain in support of the People's Charter, a petition that called for universal manhood suffrage; annual Parliaments; voting by secret ballot; equal electoral districts; abolition of property qualifications for Members of Parliament; and payment of Members of Parliament.

city-states The independent cities of the Italian Peninsula that were ruled by powerful merchant families; the unique political structure of the Italian peninsula that was a crucial factor in the advent of the Renaissance.

Civic Forum A movement in Czechoslovakia and East Germany in the 1980s, which sought to rebuild notions of citizenship and civic life that had been destroyed by the Soviet system; became an organizational and inspirational rallying point for opposition to Soviet domination.

Civil Constitution of the Clergy Legislation passed by the National Assembly of France in September of 1791 that turned clergymen into employees of the government and turned Church property into property of the state.

civil society The society formed when free men come together and surrender some of their individual power in return for greater protection.

class consciousness The sense of belonging to a "working class" that developed among European workers during the Second Industrial Revolution of the nineteenth century; a result of their working together in factories and living together in isolated slums.

collectivization of agriculture As an extension of his five-year plan (initiated in 1928), Stalin pursued a policy of destroying the culture of the peasant village and replacing it with one organized around huge collective farms. The peasants resisted and were killed, starved, or driven into Siberia in numbers that can only be estimated but which may have been as high as eight million.

Colloquies Dialogues written (beginning in 1519) by the most important and influential of the northern humanists, Desiderius Erasmus, for the purpose of teaching his students both the Latin language and how to live a good life.

Committee of Public Safety A 12-man committee created in the summer of 1793 and invested with almost total power in order that it might secure the fragile French Republic from its enemies.

Commonwealth, The (1649–1660) The period where England was ruled without a monarch, following the victory of the Parliamentary forces in the English Civil War and the subsequent execution of Charles I.

communism The ideology dedicated to the creation of a class-free society through the abolition of private property.

Compromise of 1867 The Austrian Emperor Franz Joseph's attempt, in 1866, to deal with the demands for greater autonomy from the ethnic minorities within the Hapsburg Empire. The compromise set up a dual monarchy of Austria–Hungary, where Franz Joseph served as the ruler of both Austria and Hungary, each of which had its own parliament.

Concert of Europe The alliance created in November of 1815 that required important diplomatic decisions to be made by all four great powers—Austria, Russia, Prussia, and Great Britain—"in concert" with one another.

Conciliar Movement A fifteenth-century movement, composed of various councils of cardinals, which attempted to reform, reunite, and reinvigorate the Christian Church of Europe.

Concordat of 1801 An agreement signed by Napoleon Bonaparte and the Catholic Church of Rome, reconciling France with the Catholic Church by stipulating that French clergy would be chosen and paid by the state but consecrated by the pope.

Congress of Vienna Representatives from the four major powers that had combined to defeat Napoleon—Great Britain, Russia, Prussia, and Austria—met in Paris in November of 1814 to forge a peace settlement.

conservatism The nineteenth-century ideology which held that tradition was the only trustworthy guide to social and political action.

constitutional monarchy A theory of government that contends that a rightful ruler's power is limited by an agreement with his or her subjects.

Consulate A three-man executive body, established immediately following Napoleon Bonaparte's coup d'état in November of 1799. In 1802, Napoleon was acknowledged as the sole executive officer and given the title "first consul for life."

Continental System Established by Napoleon in order to weaken Britain, the system forbade the continental European states and kingdoms under French control from trading with Britain.

Copernicanism The theory, following Nicolas Copernicus, that the Sun is at the center of the cosmos and that the Earth is the third planet from the sun.

cottage industry (also putting-out system) A system in which rural peasants engaged in small-scale textile manufacturing that developed in the eighteenth century to allow merchants, faced with an ever-expanding demand for textiles, to get around the guild system.

cotton gin Machine invented in 1793 by an American, Eli Whitney, that efficiently removed seed from raw cotton, thereby increasing the speed with which it could be processed and sent to the spinners.

Council for Mutual Economic Assistance The Soviet Union's response to the Marshall Plan, whereby the Soviet Union offered economic aid packages for eastern European countries.

Council of Trent Reform council of the Catholic Church which began its deliberations in 1545. Despite its reformist aims, it continued to insist that the Catholic Church was the final arbiter in all matters of faith.

Court of the Star Chamber A judicial innovation of Henry VII (r. 1485–1509) of England, designed to curb the independence of the nobility, whereby criminal charges brought against the nobility were judged by a court of the king's own councilors.

De Revolutionibus Orbium Caelestum Nicolas Copernicus's astronomical book published in 1543. It proposed the shift from a geocentric (Earth-centered) model of the cosmos to a heliocentric (Sun-centered) model. Its theories contributed greatly to the Scientific Revolution in the seventeenth century.

"Declaration of the Rights of Man and of the Citizen" A declaration adopted by the National Assembly of France on 27 August 1789, espousing individual rights and liberties for all citizens.

Deism The belief that the complexity, order, and natural laws exhibited by the universe were reasonable proofs that it had been created by a God who was no longer active.

Dialogue on the Two Chief Systems of the World Galileo's treatise of 1632, where he dismantled the arguments in favor of the traditional, Aristotelian view of the cosmos, and presented the Copernican system as the only alternative for reasonable people.

Diplomatic Revolution The mid-eighteenth-century shift in European alliances, whereby the expansionist aims of Frederick II of Prussia caused old enemies to become allies. Specifically, Prussia, fearful of being isolated by its enemies, forged an alliance in 1756 with its former enemy Great Britain; and Austria and France, previously antagonistic towards one another, responded by forging an alliance of their own.

Directory A five-man board created to handle the executive functions of the government during Thermidor, the third and final phase of the French Revolution (1794–1799).

Discourse on Method Rene Descartes's treatise of 1637, where he established a method of philosophical inquiry based on radical skepticism.

dissenters The collective name for Protestant groups and sects who refused to join the Anglican Church in England.

Divine Right of Kings The theory that contended that monarchs received their right to rule directly from God.

division of labor A technique whereby formerly complex tasks that required knowledge and skill were broken down into a series of simple tasks, aided by machines.

doge The Italian word that refers to the military strongmen who ruled some of the Italian city-states, such as Venice, during the Renaissance.

Dreyfus Affair The protracted prosecution, beginning in 1894, of a young Jewish officer in the French Army, Alfred Dreyfus, for treason. His numerous trials divided the French nation, illustrating how strongly ultranationalist and anti-Semitic feelings were in the French establishment.

Edict of Nantes Royal edict which established the principle of religious toleration in France; proclaimed in 1598 and revoked in 1685.

elect, the The name given in Calvinist theology to the group of people who have been predestined by God for salvation.

elements The basic components of matter in Aristotelian physics; there were five: earth, water, air, fire, and ether.

Ems Telegram A diplomatic correspondence between Napoleon III of France and William I of Prussia, edited by Bismarck to make it seem like they had insulted one another. An example of *Realpolitik*.

enclosure The building of hedges, fences, and walls to deny the peasantry access to traditional farming plots and common lands which were now converted to fields for cash crops during the Agricultural Revolution of the eighteenth century.

Encyclopedia (1751–1772) Produced by the tireless efforts of its co-editors Denis Diderot and Jean le Rond d'Alembert, the entries of the *Encyclopedia* championed a scientific approach to knowledge and labeled anything not based on reason as superstition.

English Civil War (1642–1646) Forces loyal to King Charles I fought to defend the power of the monarchy, the official Church of England, and the privileges and prerogatives of the nobility; forces supporting Parliament fought to uphold the rights of Parliament, to bring an end to the notion of an official state Church, and for notions of individual liberty and the rule of law.

enlightened despotism The hope shared by many *philosophes* that the powerful monarchs of European civilization, once educated in the ideals of the Enlightenment, would use their power to reform and rationalize society.

Essay Concerning Human Understanding John Locke's treatise of 1689–1690, which argued that humans are born *tabula rasa* (a blank slate), contradicting the traditional Christian notion that humans are born corrupt and sinful, and implying that what humans become is purely a result of what they experience.

Estates General The representative body of eighteenth-century France. Members representing each of the three Estates met to hear the problems of the realm and to hear pleas for new taxes. In return, they were allowed to present a list of their own concerns and proposals, called cahiers, to the Crown.

eugenics A notion, first developed in the nineteenth century, that a progressive, scientific nation should plan and manage the biological reproduction of its population.

expressionism An artistic movement of the late nineteenth and early twentieth centuries that sought to depict a world of emotional and psychological states. Accordingly, expressionists turned away from the rules of realism and naturalism to produce images with distorted outlines and exaggerated color and form.

Fabian Society The socialist organization in Britain, beginning in the late nineteenth century, that counseled against revolution but argued that the cause of the working classes could be furthered through political solutions.

factory system A system of production created in order to better supervise labor. In the factory system, workers came to a central location and worked with the machines under the supervision of managers.

First Battle of Marne (6 September 1914) A victory won by French troops that stopped the initial German advance in World War I.

First Battle of Ypres (October and November of 1914) Allied troops ended all hopes of a German advance, leading to a stalemate and the beginning of trench warfare.

five-year plans A series of plans initiated by Stalin, beginning in 1928, which rejected all notions of private enterprise and initiated the building of state-owned factories and power stations throughout the Soviet Union.

flight to Varennes Louis XVI's attempt to flee Paris in June of 1791 and head north to rally supporters.

Florentine Academy An informal gathering of humanists devoted to the revival and teachings of Plato, founded in 1462 under the leadership of Marsilio Ficino and the patronage of Cosimo de Medici.

flying shuttle Machine invented in 1733 by John Kay that doubled the speed at which cloth could be woven on a loom, creating a need to find a way to produce greater amounts of thread faster.

Frankfort Assembly Legislative body formed during the brief success of liberal reformers in Germany in 1848; they failed in their attempt to form a German nation.

Freikorps Regiments of German World War I veterans, commanded by old imperial army officers, that were used by the government of the Weimar Republic to defeat Marxist revolutionaries in the 1920s.

fresco Paintings done either on wet or dry plaster; an important medium of art during the Renaissance.

geocentric Earth-centered; the Aristotelian model of the cosmos.

Girondins Faction within the National Convention of France, during the French Revolution, whose membership tended to come from the wealthiest of the bourgeoisie; they opposed the execution of Louis XVI.

glasnost Russian term that refers to a new "openness" that Soviet premier Mikhail Gorbachev believed was required for the survival of the Soviet Union. Introduced in 1985, the concept of *glasnost* (along with *perestroika* or "restructuring") quickly fanned the fires of reform and autonomy throughout the Soviet Union and its satellite states.

globalization A term that refers to the increasing integration and interdependence of the economic, social, cultural, and even ecological aspects of life in the late twentieth and early twenty-first centuries. The term not only refers to the way in which the economies of the world affect one another, but also to the way that the experience of everyday life is increasingly standardized by the spread of technologies which carry with them social and cultural norms.

Glorious Revolution, The (1688) The quick, nearly bloodless uprising that coordinated Parliament-led uprisings in England with the invasion of a Protestant fleet and army from the Netherlands, and which led to the expulsion of James II and the institution of a constitutional monarchy in England under William and Mary.

Grand Alliance The alliance between Britain, the Soviet Union, and the United States to oppose the Axis powers of Nazi Germany, Italy, and Japan. Hitler's decision to attack the Soviet Union in June of 1941 forged the first link, allying Britain and the Soviet Union; the United States joined following Japan's attack on Pearl Harbor, 7 December 1941.

Grand Army The 600,000-strong army of conscripts assembled by Napoleon to invade Russia in June of 1812; 500,000 of them perished in the effort.

Great Depression A total collapse of the economies of Europe and the United States, triggered by the American stock market crash in 1929 and lasting most of the decade of the 1930s.

Great Fear, the Atmosphere of fear created in Paris in the summer of 1789 by the violence occurring in the countryside, as peasants raided granaries to ensure that they had affordable bread and attacked the chateaus of the local nobility in order to burn debt records.

Guernica (1937) Pablo Picasso's 25-foot-long mural depicting the bombing of the town of Guernica by

German planes in 1937, poignantly illustrating the nature of the mismatch between the German-supported Spanish fascist troops and the rag-tag brigades of volunteers defending the Spanish Republic.

guilds Exclusive organizations that monopolized the skilled trades in Europe from the medieval period until they were broken by the development of cottage industry in the eighteenth century.

gulags Work camps where Stalin sent Soviet citizens whom he considered to be enemies of the state.

haciendas the large, landed estates which produced food and leather goods for the mining areas and urban centers of the Spanish Empire in the New World.

heliocentric Sun-centered; the model of the cosmos proposed by Nicolas Copernicus in 1534.

Hermeticism A tradition of knowledge which taught that the world was infused with a single spirit that could be explored through mathematics as well as through magic.

Historical and Critical Dictionary A dictionary compiled by Pierre Bayle in 1697; it included entries for numerous religious beliefs, illustrating why they did not, in his opinion, stand the test of reason.

Holy Roman Emperor The nominal ruler of the German states who, from 1356, was elected by a seven-member council consisting of the archbishops of Mainz, Trier, and Cologne, the Duke of Saxony, the Margrave of Brandenburg, the Count Palatine, and the King of Bohemia.

Huguenots The sixteenth- and seventeenth-century term for Protestants living in France.

humanism In the Renaissance, both a belief in the value of, and an educational program based on, Classical Greek and Roman languages and values.

Hundred Years War A dynastic conflict begun in 1337, pitting the armies and resources of the Norman kings of England and the Capetian kings of France against one another.

impressionism An artistic movement of the late nineteenth century. Impressionists desired to render the visual experience itself by creating images with visible brush strokes and heightened color.

Indian National Congress An organization of Hindu elites in India, established in 1885 to promote the notion of a free and independent India.

indulgences Certificates of absolution sold by the Church forgiving people for their sins, sometimes even before they committed them, in return for a monetary contribution; the selling of indulgences was one of the practices objected to by Martin Luther.

industrial socialism A variety of nineteenth-century utopian socialism which argued that it was possible to have a productive, profitable industrial enterprise without exploiting workers. Its leading advocate was a Scottish textile manufacturer, Robert Owen.

Inquisition An institution within the Catholic Church, created in 1479 to enforce the conversion of Muslims and Jews in Spain; it was revived and expanded during the Reformation to combat all perceived threats to orthodoxy and the Church's authority.

intendent An administrative bureaucrat in Absolutist France of the seventeenth century, usually chosen from the middle class, who owed his position and, therefore, his loyalty directly to the state.

internal combustion engine Developed in 1886 by two German engineers, Gottlieb Daimler and Karl Benz, it burned petroleum as fuel and, when mounted on a carriage, was used to create the automobile.

International Congress of the Rights of Women (1878) Meeting, in Paris, of the political groups which campaign for women's rights.

International Working Men's Association Founded in 1864, it was a loose coalition of unions and political parties whose aim was an international strategy for the advancement of working-class issues; the First International fell apart in the 1870s, but was replaced by the Second International in 1889.

invisible hand A phrase, penned by Adam Smith in *Wealth of Nations* (1776), to denote the way in which natural economic laws guided the economy.

Iron Curtain A phrase (first uttered by Winston Churchill in a speech given in the United States in 1946) that referred to the line which stretched from the Baltic Sea in the north to the Adriatic Sea in the south and divided Europe between a communist East and a capitalist West.

iron law of wages A theory promoted by nineteenth-century, liberal economic thinkers which argued that competition between workers for jobs would always, in the long run, force wages to sink to subsistence levels.

Jacobins A faction within the National Convention of France, during the French Revolution, whose members came from the lower strata of the bourgeoisie; they were adamant proponents of the execution of Louis XVI.

July Ordinances Issued by Charles X of France in 1830, the ordinances dissolved part of the legislative branch of the government and revoked the voting privileges of the bourgeoisie. The result was a rebellion by the bourgeoisie, students, and workers that forced Charles X to abdicate.

Junkers A powerful class of landed aristocrats in nineteenth-century Prussia who supported Bismarck's plan for the unification of Germany.

Kepler's laws Three laws of planetary motion developed by Johannes Kepler between 1609 and 1619.

kinetic theory of gases A theory developed in the mid-nineteenth century, chiefly by Rudolph Clausius and James Maxwell, that envisioned gas pressure and temperature as resulting from a certain volume of molecules in motion. Such an approach allowed them to analyze, and therefore to measure and predict, pressure and temperature statistically.

Kulturkampf Bismarck's legislative assault, in the 1870s, on the religious freedom of Catholics in Germany.

laissez-faire The notion, promoted in Adam Smith's *Wealth of Nations* (1776), that governments should not try to interfere with the natural workings of an economy; a notion that became one of the basic tenets of liberalism in the nineteenth century.

Law Code of 1649 Legislation in Russia that converted the legal status of groups as varied as peasants and slaves into that of a single class of serfs.

Law of the Maximum Law passed by the National Convention of France in the summer of 1793 to cap the price of bread and other essentials.

lay piety A tradition in the smaller, independent German provinces, flourishing in the fifteenth and sixteenth centuries, whereby organized groups promoted pious behavior and learning outside the bureaucracy of the Church.

Leviathan Thomas Hobbes's treatise of 1651, which asserted that self-interest motivated nearly all human behavior and concluded that "without a common power to keep them in awe," the natural state of man was one of war.

liberalism The eighteenth- and nineteenth-century ideology which asserted that the task of government was to promote individual liberty.

M.A.D. The acronym for the risky, but ultimately successful, strategy (mutually assured destruction) that evolved between the United States and Soviet Union to avoid nuclear war by assuring that neither side could survive one.

Maastricht Treaty The treaty, signed in 1992, creating the European Union, the world's largest trading bloc, and moving to adopt a common currency (the euro).

Maginot Line A vast complex of tank traps, fixed artillery sites, subterranean railways, and living quarters built by the French, which paralleled the Franco-German border but failed to protect the border between France and Belgium.

Manhattan Project The project, secretly funded by the American government, that successfully invented and produced two atomic bombs in 1945.

manorial system The traditional economic system of Europe, developed in the medieval period, in which land-owning elites (lords of the manor) held vast estates divided into small plots of arable land farmed by peasants for local consumption.

March to Versailles, the Following riots in Paris on 5 October 1789, a contingent of Parisian women organized an 11-mile march from Paris to the king's palace at Versailles. Along the way, they were joined by the Paris Guards, a citizen militia, and together they forced their way into the palace and insisted that Louis accompany them back to Paris.

Marshall Plan The plan, named after U.S. Secretary of State George Marshall, launched in 1947 which provided billions of dollars of aid to help the western European powers rebuild their infrastructures and economies.

Masonic Lodges Secret meeting places established and run by Freemasons whose origins dated back to the medieval guilds of the stonemasons. By the eighteenth century, the lodges were fraternities of aristocratic and middle-class men (and occasionally women) who gathered to discuss alternatives to traditional beliefs.

materialism A philosophical movement of the nineteenth century that argued that all natural phenomena could and should be understood as the result of matter and motion. First articulated by the German natural philosophers Karl Vogt, Jakob Moleschott, and Ludwig Büchner, materialism became a foundational assumption of the scientific view of the world by the end of the nineteenth century.

Meiji Restoration A successful rebellion by Japanese modernizers who were determined to preserve Japanese independence; it restored power to the emperor and reorganized Japanese society along Western lines.

Metropolis (1925) Film by Fritz Lang that depicts a world in which humans are dwarfed by an impersonal world of their own creation; illustrates the alienation and anxiety that permeated European culture in the 1920s.

Michelangelo's *David* Sculpted by Michelangelo Buonarroti (completed in 1504), this sculpture of the biblical hero is characteristic of the last and most heroic phase of Renaissance art; sculpted from a single piece of marble, it is larger than life and offers a vision of the human body and spirit that is more dramatic than real life, an effect that Michelangelo produced by making the head and hands deliberately too large for the torso.

Middle Passage, The The leg of the triangle of trade in which African slaves were transported in brutal conditions across the Atlantic on European trade ships.

Midlothian Campaign (1879) Generally acknowledged to be the first modern political campaign; British liberal candidate for Prime Minister, William Gladstone, rode the railway to small towns throughout his district (Midlothia) to give speeches and win votes.

millenarianism The belief that one is living in the last days of the world and that the judgment day is at hand (originally tied to the belief that the end would come in the year 1000 A.D.).

monarchs The hereditary rulers of traditional European society.

Munich Agreement The agreement of September of 1938 whereby Britain and France allowed Hitler to take the Sudentenland, an area of Czechoslovakia populated primarily by German speakers, over the objections of the Czechoslovakian government, in exchange for his promise that there would be no further aggression; in March of 1939, Hitler broke the Munich Agreement by invading Czechoslovakia.

Napoleonic Code (also known as the Civil Code of 1804) A system of uniform law and administrative policy Napoleon created for the empire he was building in Europe.

National Assembly Name taken by the representatives of the Third Estate on 17 June 1789, declaring themselves to be the legislative body of France; often seen as the beginning of the French Revolution's moderate phase.

nationalism The nineteenth-century ideology which asserted that a nation was a natural, organic entity whose people shared a cultural identity and a historical destiny.

nationalities problem The name given to the conflict between the 10 distinct linguistic and ethnic groups that lived within the borders of Austria–Hungary and their German-speaking rulers.

National Socialist German Workers' Party (NSDAP, or the Nazi Party) German political party that began as a small right-wing group and one of the more than 70 extremist paramilitary organizations that sprang up in postwar Germany. It was neither socialist nor did it attract many workers; it was a party initially made up of war veterans and misfits. The man responsible for its rise to power in Germany was Adolf Hitler.

National Trade Unions Congress The late-nineteenth-century British organization that joined all the labor unions of the country together for political action, and which supported the newly formed Labour Party, a political party that ran working-class candidates in British elections.

National Union of Women's Suffrage Societies An organization, headed by Millicent Garrett Fawcett, that campaigned vigorously for women's voting rights in Britain during the period 1905–1914.

NATO (North Atlantic Treaty Organization) A military alliance, formed in 1949, uniting the Western powers against the Soviet Union.

Nazi–Soviet Non-Aggression Pact The agreement, reached on 23 August of 1939, guaranteeing Soviet neutrality in World War II in return for parts of Poland.

neoclassicism The dominant artistic style of the late eighteenth and early nineteenth centuries that took its inspiration from the art of the ancient republics of Greece and Rome. Neoclassicism was characterized by subject matter that conveyed messages of social sacrifice and political courage and by a style that avoided decorative details or flourishes.

neoplatonism In the Renaissance and Early-Modern period, a philosophy based on that of Plato which contended that reality was located in a changeless world of forms and which, accordingly, spurred the study of mathematics.

New Economic Plan (NEP) A plan instituted by Lenin in the early 1920s which allowed rural peasants and small business operators to manage their own land and businesses and to sell their products; a temporary compromise with capitalism that worked well enough to get the Russian economy functioning again.

New Spain The name given to the area in Mexico controlled by the Spanish upon conquering the Aztec Empire in 1521.

The Night Watch The Rembrandt painting (1642) that exemplifies the baroque style of painting as it was practiced by the Dutch masters of the seventeenth century.

nobility Originally the warrior class, the class of privileged landowners in traditional European society.

On the Fabric of the Human Body Andreas Vesalius's textbook published in seven volumes beginning in 1543. It became the standard text for medical students and greatly improved the medical profession's understanding of human anatomy.

Opium War (1839–1942) A war launched by the British when the Chinese government tried to prevent the British from trading opium grown in India to Chinese dealers in exchange for tea, silk, and other goods that were highly prized in Britain. The victorious British forced the Chinese to sign the Treaty of Nanking which ceded Hong Kong to Britain, established several tariff-free zones for foreign trade, and exempted foreigners from Chinese law.

Oration on the Dignity of Man The best articulation of the belief in the dignity and potential of man that characterized Renaissance humanism; authored by Pico della Mirandola in 1486.

Papal States A kingdom in central Italy, ruled directly by the pope until Italian unification (1866–1870).

Paris Commune Working-class uprising in Paris, in February and March of 1871; having defended the city against a German invasion, the Parisian working class refused to accept the results of an election won by monarchists (who had deserted the city at the first sight of Germans). They ruled the city for two months before being crushed by the French Army.

Peace of Augsburg Signed in 1555, it established the principle of "whoever rules; his religion" and signaled Rome that the German princes would not go to war with each other over religion.

peasantry The class of rural, agricultural laborers in traditional European society.

perestroika Russian term that refers to a "restructuring" that Soviet premier Mikhail Gorbachev believed was required for the survival of the Soviet Union. Introduced in 1985, the concept of *perestroika* (along with *glasnost* or "openness") quickly fanned the fires of reform and autonomy throughout the Soviet Union and its satellite states.

philosophe Public intellectuals of the French Enlightenment who believed that society should be reformed on the basis of natural law and reason.

philosophical texts The underground book trade's code name for banned books that included some versions of philosophical treatises, and bawdy, popularized versions of the *philosophes'* critique of the Church and the ruling classes.

plantations The large, landed estates in the West Indies, which produced sugar for export to Europe.

Platonic–Pythagorean tradition A tradition of philosophy that developed in the sixteenth and seventeenth centuries which embraced the works of Plato and Pythagoras, and which had as its goal the identification of the fundamental mathematical laws of nature.

postimpressionism An artistic movement of the late nineteenth century that combined the visible brush strokes, heightened color, and real-life subject matter of impressionism with an emphasis on geometric form and unnatural color to create a more emotionally expressive effect.

Pragmatic Sanction The document that guaranteed the right of Maria Theresa to ascend to the throne of Austria, but which was challenged in 1740 by Frederick II (the Great) of Prussia.

Prague Spring An episode in 1968, when Czechoslovakian communists, led by Alexander Dubcek, embarked on a process of liberalization. Under Dubcek's leadership, the reformers declared that they intended to create "socialism with a human face." Dubcek tried to proceed by balancing reforms with reassurances to the Soviet Union, but on 21 August, Soviet and Warsaw Pact troops invaded and occupied the major cities of Czechoslovakia; it was the largest military operation in Europe since World War II.

predestination Calvinist belief that asserts that God has predetermined which people will be saved and which will be damned.

priesthood of all believers One of the central tenets of Martin Luther's theology; the belief that all who have true faith are "priests," that is, they are competent to read and understand scripture.

Prince, The The book, by Niccolo Machiavelli (1513), which marks the shift from a "civic ideal" to a "princely ideal" in Renaissance humanism; the princely ideal is focused on the qualities and strategies necessary for attaining and holding social and political power.

Principia Mathematica Isaac Newton's treatise of 1687, which became the model for the scientific approach to investigating the natural world.

proletariat A term in the Marxist critique of society that refers to the class of industrial wage-laborers.

psychological socialism A variety of nineteenth-century utopian socialism which saw a conflict between the structure of society and the natural needs and tendencies of human beings. Its leading advocate was Charles Fourier, who argued that the ideal society was one organized on a smaller, more human scale.

purges Stalin's systematic elimination, between 1935 and 1939, of all centers of independent thought and action within the Communist Party and the government in the Soviet Union. Somewhere between seven and eight million Soviet citizens were arrested; at least a million of those were executed, while the rest were sent to work camps known as gulags.

putting-out system (also cottage industry) A system in which rural peasants engaged in small-scale textile manufacturing that developed in the eighteenth century to allow merchants, faced with an ever-expanding demand for textiles, to get around the guild system.

qualities A term, in Aristotelian physics, for the tendencies of matter; that is, earth sinks; air floats, etc.

quantum theory of physics The theory developed in the first decade of the twentieth century that holds that energy does not flow evenly but is released in discrete units or "quanta."

Race for the Sea A series of local engagements aimed at outflanking the enemy in November 1914, which extended the front line of battle on the Western Front until it reached the English Channel.

railway boom The rapid development of a railway system, beginning in Britain in the 1830s. The development of railway systems further spurred the development of heavy industries, as railroads facilitated the speedy transportation of iron and steel while simultaneously consuming large quantities of both.

realism An artistic movement in mid-nineteenth century painting that rejected both romantic fantasies and glorification of the past, seeking instead to accurately and honestly render everyday life in meticulous detail.

Realpolitik A political theory made fashionable by Bismarck in the nineteenth century, which asserted that the aim of any political policy should be to increase the power of a nation by whatever means and strategies were necessary and useful.

Reform Bill of 1867 British legislation that doubled the number of people eligible to vote and extended the vote to the lower middle class for the first time.

Reform Bill of 1884 British legislation that extended the right to vote to two-thirds of all adult males.

Reichstag The legislative body for the German states, created in the fifteenth century as a check to the executive power of the Holy Roman Emperor; it included the seven electors, the remaining princes, and representatives from 65 important free cities in Germany.

Reign of Terror Instituted under Robespierre's leadership by the Committee of Public Safety during the French Revolution; Robespierre created tribunals in the major cities of France to try anyone suspected of being an enemy of the revolution. During the period of the Terror, between September of 1793 and July of 1794, between 200,000 and 400,000 people were sentenced to prison; between 25,000 and 50,000 of them are believed to have died either in prison or at the guillotine.

Restoration, The (1660–1688) The period of English history following the Commonwealth and preceding the Glorious Revolution; encompasses the reigns of Charles II (1660–1685) and James II (1685–1688).

Risorgimento The mid-nineteenth-century Italian nationalist movement composed mostly of intellectuals and university students; from 1834 to 1848, the *Risorgimento* attempted a series of popular insurrections and briefly established a Roman Republic in 1848.

rococo The dominant artistic style of the eighteenth century that reflected the lighter touch of monarchs prior to the French Revolution. First developed in the decorative arts, rococo was often characterized by lighter design elements, especially the use of shell-like curves.

Romanticism The nineteenth-century ideology which urged the cultivation of sentiment and emotion by reconnecting with nature and with the past.

Russianization Alexander III's attempt, in the 1880s, to make Russian the standard language and the Russian Orthodox Church the standard religion throughout the Russian Empire.

Russo-Japanese War A brief war in 1904 pitting Japan against Russia after they quarreled over influence in China; Japan's quick victory stunned the world and announced Japan's arrival as a modern, military, and industrial power.

St. Theresa in Ecstasy A sculpture executed between 1645 and 1652 by Bernini that exemplifies the Counter-Reformation baroque style.

salons Places where both men and women gathered, in eighteenth-century France, to educate themselves about and discuss the new ideas of the Enlightenment in privacy and safety.

salvation by faith alone One of the central tenets of Martin Luther's theology; the belief that salvation is a gift from God given to all who possess true faith.

sans-culottes The working people (bakers, shopkeepers, artisans, and manual laborers who were characterized by their long working pants—hence, *sans-culottes*, literally without short pants) who asserted their will in the radical phase of the French Revolution (1791–1794).

Schleswig–Holstein Affair Originally a dispute over the administration of two Danish duchies, Schleswig and Holstein, that had a large German-speaking population, it was used by Bismarck to engineer a war with Austria in 1866; it is a perfect illustration of *Realpolitik* in action.

Schlieffen Plan The German plan for a two-front war that called for a military thrust westward towards Paris at the first sign of Russian mobilization in the east. Its logic helped to precipitate World War I.

scholasticism A term for the pre-Renaissance system of knowledge characterized by the belief that everything worth knowing was written down in ancient texts.

scientific socialism A variety of socialism based on what its adherents claimed was a scientific analysis of society's workings. The most influential of the self-proclaimed scientific socialists was the German revolutionary Karl Marx.

scripture alone One of the central tenets of Martin Luther's theology; the belief that scripture is the only guide to knowledge of God (the Catholic Church holds that there are two guides to knowledge of God: scripture and Church tradition).

Second Industrial Revolution The second phase of industrialization, lasting from roughly 1820 to 1900, was characterized by the advent of large-scale iron and steel production, the application of the steam engine, and the development of a railway system.

Second Treatise of Civil Government (1690) Philosophical treatise by the Englishman John Locke; the primary argument for the establishment of natural limits to governmental authority.

Sepoy Rebellion of 1857 (sometimes known as the Sepoy Mutiny) An organized, anti-British uprising led by military units of Indians who had formerly served the British; it resulted in the British government taking direct control of India and restructuring the Indian economy to produce and consume products that aided the British economy.

Seven Years War (1756–1763) The conflict which pitted France, Austrian, Russia, Saxony, Sweden, and (after 1762) Spain against Prussia, Great Britain, and the German state of Hanover. Land and sea battles were fought in North America (where it is sometimes known as the French and Indian War), Europe, and India. The European hostilities were concluded in 1763 by a peace agreement that essentially reestab-

lished prewar boundaries. The North American conflict, and particularly the fall of Quebec in 1759, shifted the balance of power to the British. The British had similar success in India.

Social Contract, The Jean-Jacques Rousseau's treatise of 1762, where he wrote: "Man is born free, and everywhere he is in chains," and where he argued that virtuous citizens should be willing to subordinate their own self-interest to the general good of the community and that the government must be continually responsible to the general will of the people.

social Darwinism The nineteenth-century ideology which asserted that competition was natural and necessary for the evolutionary progress of a society.

Social Democrats By 1914, the most successful socialist party in Germany; the Social Democrats espoused the "revisionist socialism" of Eduard Bernstein, who urged socialist parties to cooperate with bourgeois liberals in order to earn immediate gains for the working class.

socialism The ideology which seeks to reorder society in ways that would end or minimize competition, foster cooperation, and allow the working classes to share in the wealth being produced by industrialization.

socialism in one country Policy adopted by Stalin in the autumn of 1924, in which the notion of a worldwide socialist revolution was abandoned in favor of making the Soviet Union a successful socialist state.

Solidarity (*Solidarnos*) The name of the Polish labor union, founded in 1980 and led by Lech Walesa, that led the eventually successful opposition to Soviet domination in Poland.

Soviet Constitution of 1923 The constitution created by Lenin for the Soviet Union in July of 1923. On paper it created a Federal State, renamed the Union of Soviet Socialist Republics but, in practice, power continued to emanate from Lenin and the city that he named the capital in 1918, Moscow.

spartacists Marsixt revolutionaries in post–World War I Germany, led by Rosa Luxemburg and Karl Leibknecht, who were dedicated to bringing a socialist revolution to Germany.

spice trade The importation of spices from Asia into Europe; revived during the Renaissance, the need to find shorter, more efficient routes gave impetus to the great voyages of exploration of the fifteenth and sixteenth centuries.

Contents

Contents

Cells and the Chemistry of Life

Have you ever had the chance to watch a pet grow from a baby to an adult? If so, you've seen the pet go through remarkable changes as it got older. Animals, plants, even you, grow in height and weight with each passing year. These changes result from an increase in the number and size of cells in the organism's body.

All living things are made up of basic units called cells. Your body contains trillions of cells. At this very minute, some of your cells are dying. But don't worry, your body constantly makes new cells to replace them. Your body also supplies its cells with the materials they need to live and removes waste products from your cells. Day after day, your body takes care of itself by carrying out these processes.

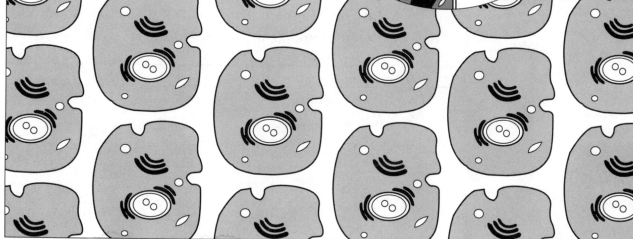

Lesson 1
The Cell Theory

Key Words

cell: basic unit of structure and function of all living things
protoplasm: living material

KEY IDEAS

The development of the microscope allowed scientists to observe traits of living things that could not be seen with the naked eye. Their observations led to the discovery of the cell. The cell is the basic unit of structure and function of all living things.

Cell biologists study the cells of living things. Cell biologists try to discover how cells work. They use complex tools to observe the life processes of cells. An understanding of the cell theory is vital to the work of cell biologists.

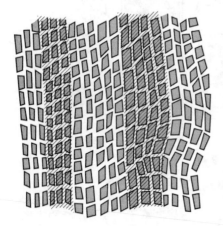

Fig. 1-1   Cork cells

Discovery of Cells.   Today we know that all organisms are made up of cells. The **cell** (sehl) is the basic unit of structure and function of all living things. It is the smallest unit that performs all life processes, such as growth, reproduction, transport, storing and using energy.

In 1665, scientist Robert Hooke used a microscope to view thin slices of cork. Hooke noticed that the cork was divided into thousands of small walled sections. He called these sections "cells." The cells Hooke observed were not living cells. Rather, Hooke observed the cell walls of dead plant cells. See Fig. 1-1. Hooke's discovery was important because it opened up the study of cells.

 1. **How did Hooke contribute to our understanding of living things?**

_____

_____

Almost 200 years later, Matthias Schleiden (mah-TEE-ahs SHLY-duhn) looked at plant parts through a microscope. He discovered that living plants are made up of cells. At about the same time, another scientist, Theodor Schwann (TAY-oh-dohr SHVAHN) used the microscope to view parts of animals. He discovered that animals also are made up of cells. As a result of these studies, scientists concluded that all living things are made up of cells.

Soon after the discoveries of Schwann and Schleiden, another scientist, Rudolf Virchow (ROO-dawlf FIHR-khoh), added to their findings. By studying microscopic organisms, Virchow showed that all cells come from other living cells. He said that this occurs when the living cells divide to form new cells.

 2. What contribution did Virchow make to the cell theory?

_____

_____

Protoplasm. At the time of the discoveries scientists called all the living substance inside a cell **protoplasm** (PROHT-oh-plaz-uhm). They believed that protoplasm was the same in all cells. As time went on, the tools people used to view cells improved. Scientists were able to see the inside of a cell more clearly. Today, we know that protoplasm is not one single substance but many different substances and structures. We also know that protoplasm contains different things in different kinds of cells. For example, special food-making structures are found in the protoplasm of plant cells but not in the protoplasm of animal cells. Now, the term protoplasm is sometimes used to describe any living material.

 3. What is protoplasm?

_____

_____

Cell Theory. Early scientists made many correct discoveries about the cell. The conclusions of these people were blended to form the modern cell theory. The cell theory states:

- All living things are made up of cells.

- Cells are the basic units of structure and function in living things.

- All cells come from other cells.

Fig. 1-2 shows the contributions that formed the cell theory.

Fig. 1-2

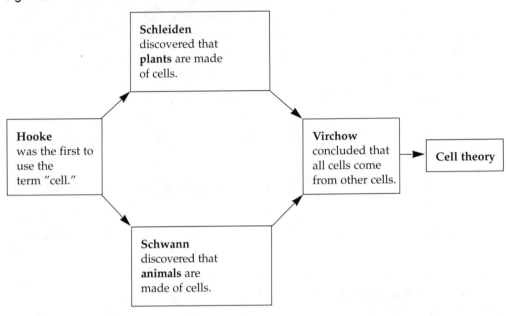

Check Your Understanding

Complete Fig. 1-3 by writing the letter of the statement that correctly explains what each scientist discovered:

a. He concluded that cells come from other living cells.

b. He discovered that living plants are made of cells.

c. He discovered that animals are made of cells.

d. He was the first to use the word "cells."

Fig. 1-3

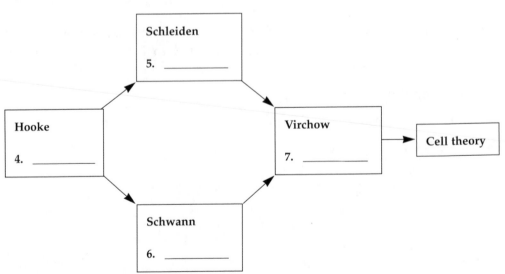

8. What is a cell? _____

_____

9. How were the discoveries of Schleiden and Schwann alike? How did they differ? _____

_____

_____

10. What is the cell theory? _____

_____

_____

_____

11. Early scientists formed an idea about cells that proved to be false. What was this idea? _____

_____

_____

12. Which is more useful, the study of dead cells or living cells? Why?

_____

_____

_____

Lesson 2

Structures of a Cell

KEY IDEAS

Most cells possess common structures. The three basic parts of most cells are the cell membrane, the nucleus, and the cytoplasm.

Fig. 2-1

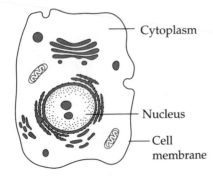

Have you ever heard the expression "a picture is worth a thousand words"? Medical artists make a career out of this saying. They create drawings to illustrate the traits of living things. Textbook publishers, hospitals, medical schools, and research companies use these drawings to help people understand scientific concepts. For example, medical artists sketch the many structures of a cell.

Cells vary in size and shape. Our own bodies contain more than 200 different kinds of cells. However, there are three cell structures common to most cells. They are the cell membrane, the nucleus, and the cytoplasm. Fig. 2-1 shows the locations of these three structures in the cell.

Cell Membrane. The thin outer covering of a cell is called the **cell membrane** (sehl MEHM-brayn). The cell membrane separates the cell from its environment. It is a flexible structure made up of lipids and proteins.

Fig. 2-2

Lipids (LIHP-ihdz) are made of substances called fatty acids. A fatty acid is a chemical compound containing carbon, hydrogen, and oxygen. **Proteins** (PROH-teenz) are chains of amino acids. An **amino acid** (uh-MEE-noh AS-ihd) is a chemical compound containing nitrogen, carbon, hydrogen, and oxygen. A cell membrane contains two layers of lipids. Proteins are scattered throughout the lipids. See Fig. 2-2.

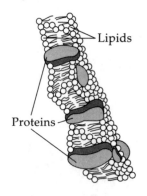

The actions of the cell membrane help the cell maintain **homeostasis** (HOH-mee-oh-STAY-sihs), a balance of substances within the cell. This balance is necessary for the cell to live. The cell membrane maintains homeostasis in three ways. First, it controls the flow of substances into and out of the cell. Substances the cell needs to carry out its life processes can enter the cell membrane. Waste products produced by the cell exit through the cell membrane. Second, it protects the cell from its surroundings. Third, it supports the cell and gives it a shape.

Nucleus. Located near the center of most cells is the nucleus. The **nucleus** (NOO-klee-uhs) is the control center of a cell. It directs most of the activities that occur within the cell. A thin membrane surrounds the nucleus. Pores in this membrane allow certain molecules to enter and leave the nucleus.

Inside the nucleus are nucleic acids and proteins. **Nucleic acids** (noo-KLEE-ihk AS-ihdz) are the materials that help direct the cell's activities. There are two kinds of nucleic acids: RNA and DNA. DNA stands for deoxyribonucleic acid. RNA stands for ribonucleic acid. Both nucleic acids guide and assist in the building of proteins. Proteins are used to build and repair cells.

Fig. 2-3

Nucleic acids are long complex chains. Each link in the chain is called a nucleotide. A **nucleotide** (NOO-klee-oh-tyd) is made up of a simple sugar, a phosphate, and a base. See Fig. 2-3. Bases are made up of nitrogen, carbon, and hydrogen. There are four kinds of bases in a nucleic acid chain. Bases are important because of their role in the genetic code. You will learn more about the genetic code in Lesson 9.

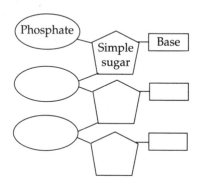

 1. What is the job of the nucleus?

_____

_____

_____

The nucleic acids and the proteins in the nucleus make up structures called **chromosomes** (KROH-muh-sohmz). The DNA of chromosomes contains hereditary information. This information is passed between parents and offspring. It determines the traits of an organism. You will learn more about chromosomes in Lesson 8.

Cytoplasm. All the material inside the cell membrane, except the nucleus, is **cytoplasm** (SYET-oh-plaz-uhm). Many important structures, called organelles, are in the cytoplasm of a cell. Since organelles vary among different types of cells, they are not considered basic cell parts. You will read more about organelles in Lesson 3.

 2. What are the three parts that make up most cells?

_____

The cell contains three main parts: the cell membrane, the cytoplasm, and the nucleus. The cell membrane surrounds the cytoplasm. The cytoplasm surrounds the nucleus. The nucleus contains the chromosomes. Fig. 2-4 shows the relationship of these structures and their functions.

Fig. 2-4

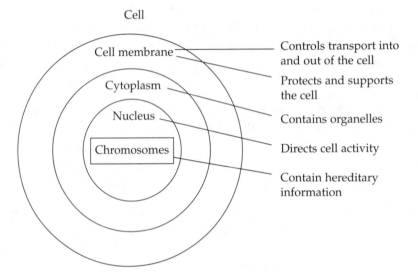

Check Your Understanding

Write a sentence explaining the connection between each pair of words.

3. cell membrane, cytoplasm _____

_____

4. lipids, proteins _____

_____

5. nucleus, DNA _____

_____

6. nucleic acids, chromosomes _____

_____

7. nucleic acid, nucleotides _____

_____

Look at Fig. 2-5. Then label the following cell parts on the lines below: *cell membrane, nucleus, cytoplasm.*

Fig. 2-5

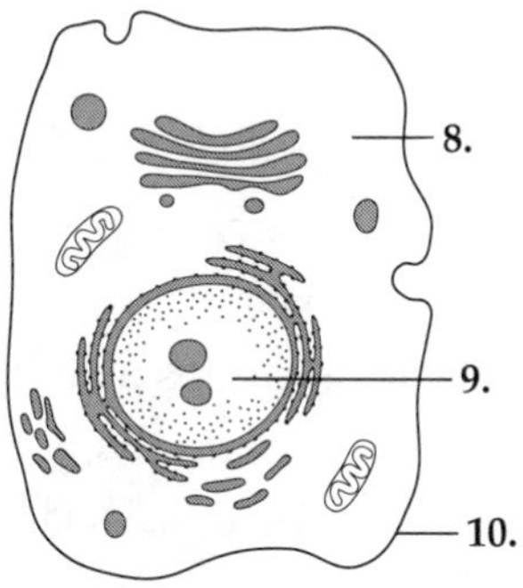

8. _____

9. _____

10. _____

8.

9.

10.

---

11. Why aren't organelles considered to be basic parts of a cell?

_____

_____

12. What are the three ways the cell membrane helps a cell stay balanced?

_____

_____

_____

13. What part of a cell would you study if you wanted to observe chromosomes? Why? _____

_____

14. Suppose the cell membrane of a certain cell allowed materials to pass into the cell but prevented materials from flowing out of the cell. Predict the effect this would have on the cell.

_____

_____

What Do You Know?

Cell Organelles

organelles:	structures located within the cell cytoplasm that perform specific jobs
mitochondria:	organelles that supply the cell with energy
carbohydrate:	substance made of carbon, hydrogen, and oxygen
endoplasmic reticulum:	network of passageways through which materials flow within a cell
ribosomes:	organelles at which proteins are made
vacuoles:	organelles that store food, other materials needed by the cell, and wastes

KEY IDEAS

The cytoplasm of a cell contains small structures called organelles. Each organelle performs a specific task. Together, the organelles carry out the life processes of a cell.

Scientists believe that certain structures in the body cells were once separate organisms. These cell structures are called mitochondria (singular, mitochondrion). For a number of reasons, scientists think that mitochondria evolved from a kind of bacteria. For example, mitochondria have bits of their own DNA. The structure of the DNA molecules is similar to that of bacteria. Mitochondria also contain many of the same enzymes found in bacteria. However, mitochondria do need the DNA found in the body to help it function. In this lesson, you'll learn how these structures and others work together to carry out the life processes of a cell.

The small structures within a cell's cytoplasm are called **organelles** (awr-guh-NEHLZ). Each type of organelle performs a special job. The organelles help carry out the life processes of the cell.

Mitochondria. All living things need energy. Since a cell is a living thing, it too needs energy. **Mitochondria** (meyet-oh-KAHN-dree-uh) are rod-shaped organelles that provide the cell with energy. They are sometimes called the "powerhouses" of a cell. Mitochondria release the chemical energy stored in carbohydrates for the cell to use. A **carbohydrate** (kahr-boh-HEYE-drayt) is made of carbon, hydrogen, and oxygen. Carbohydrates may be simple sugars or chains of sugars called starches or cellulose.

The mitochondria change carbohydrates into water and carbon dioxide. Large amounts of energy are released by this change. The energy is stored in high-energy molecules. The cell uses these energy-rich molecules to carry out life processes. You will learn more about these molecules in Lesson 6.

Endoplasmic Reticulum. You have already discovered that materials move into and out of a cell through the cell membrane. But how do materials move within a cell? The **endoplasmic reticulum** (ehn-doh-PLAZ-mihk rih-TIHK-yuh-luhm) is a network of passageways within the cytoplasm. Materials move from one organelle to another through this folded membrane. You can see some of these folds in the diagram of the cell in Fig. 3-1.

Fig. 3-1

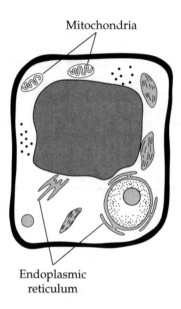

Mitochondria

Endoplasmic
reticulum

 1. What is the endoplasmic reticulum?

_____

_____

Ribosomes. The organelles at which proteins are made are the **ribosomes** (REYE-buh-sohmz). The cell needs these proteins to carry out its processes. Many ribosomes are attached to the endoplasmic reticulum. Some ribosomes float freely in the cytoplasm.

Vacuoles. Another type of organelle found in cells are vacuoles. **Vacuoles** (VAK-yoo-ohlz) are sacs that store materials for the cell. Water, food, or waste products can be stored in a vacuole. Fig. 3-2 shows the cell's ribosomes and vacuole.

Fig. 3-2

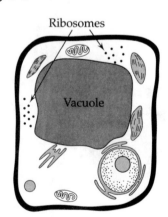

Ribosomes

Vacuole

 2. How do ribosomes help the cell carry out life processes?

_____

_____

Fig. 3-3 shows the different types of organelles and their functions.

Fig. 3-3

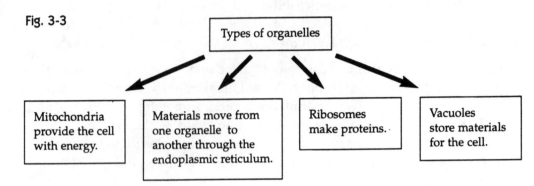

Types of organelles

Mitochondria provide the cell with energy.

Materials move from one organelle to another through the endoplasmic reticulum.

Ribosomes make proteins.

Vacuoles store materials for the cell.

Check Your Understanding

Write a sentence explaining the connection between each pair of words.

3. carbohydrate, mitochondria _____

    _____

4. endoplasmic reticulum, ribosomes _____

    _____

5. vacuoles, organelles _____

    _____

Label the cell parts on Fig. 3-4. Use the following terms: *mitochondrion, endoplasmic reticulum, ribosome, vacuole.*

Fig. 3-4

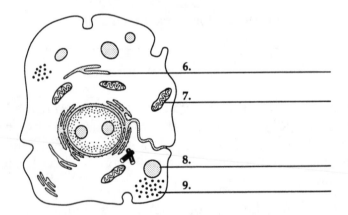

6. _____

7. _____

8. _____

9. _____

10. What are organelles? _____

_____

_____

11. Why do you think mitochondria are sometimes called the "powerhouses"
of a cell? _____

_____

_____

12. How do vacuoles help a cell survive? _____

_____

_____

13. Suppose the endoplasmic reticulum of a cell was damaged. What effect
do you think this would have on the other organelles in the cell?

_____

_____

_____

14. Different kinds of cells have different numbers of mitochondria. Which
do you think would contain more mitochondria: a very active cell or a
barely active cell? Why?

_____

_____

_____

Lesson 4

Types of Cells

Key Words

prokaryotic cells: cells that lack a nucleus

eukaryotic cells: cells that have a nucleus

cell wall: rigid structure that surrounds the cell membrane of plant cells

chloroplasts: organelles in a plant cell in which light energy is changed into chemical energy

KEY IDEAS

Many cells share common traits. However, there are some differences among cells. For example, some cells possess a nucleus, while others do not. Plant cells contain structures not found in animal cells. In both plants and animals, cells become specialized to perform certain jobs.

An animal technician assists a veterinarian in the care and treatment of animals. The duties of an animal technician include collecting specimens, performing tests, gathering data, and caring for the animals. Understanding the nature of animal cells is vital to the work of an animal technician.

Fig. 4-1

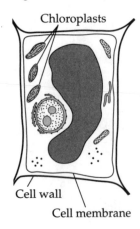

Chloroplasts

Cell wall

Cell membrane

Differences in Cells. In Lesson 2, you learned about the cell nucleus. Most cells have a nucleus, but some do not. The cells of bacteria, for example, lack a nucleus. Bacteria are **prokaryotic cells** (PROH-kar-ee-YAH-tik sehlz). Cells that have a nucleus are called **eukaryotic cells** (YOO-kar-ee-YAH-tik sehlz). Eukaryotic cells include plant cells and animal cells. In addition to a nucleus, plant cells and animal cells both have a cell membrane and cytoplasm. However, plant cells have a number of structures not found in animal cells.

Plant Cells. Unlike animal cells, plant cells have a cell wall. The **cell wall** (sehl WAHL) is a rigid structure that surrounds the cell membrane. See Fig. 4-1. The cell wall is made up mostly of cellulose. Cellulose is a long chain of sugar molecules. It is a kind of carbohydrate. The rigid cell wall protects the plant cell and gives it support. Even though the cell wall is tough and rigid, water and other material needed by the cell can pass through it.

Chloroplasts are another structure found in plant cells. These are also shown in Fig. 4-1. **Chloroplasts** (KLAWR-uh-plasts) are green, oval organelles that trap the light energy necessary for photosynthesis. Photosynthesis occurs in the chloroplasts of leaves as light energy from the sun is changed into chemical energy. You'll learn more about photosynthesis in Lesson 7.

1. How are chloroplasts used in photosynthesis?

_____

_____

Specialized Cells.   All cells are not alike. In both plants and animals, cells become specialized to do certain jobs. For example, some kinds of cells provide support. Bone cells in humans have special structures that make bone. The human skeleton is made up of bone, which supports the body. In plant cells, support is given to the cell by the cellulose of the cell wall. Some plants also have special cells that make tough fibers for support. For example, stem fibers provide support to certain plants.

Plants and animals also contain cells that are specialized for absorbing and transporting nutrients. Many plants have root cells that absorb water and nutrients from soil into the plant. Specialized cells form transport vessels in plants so that nutrients and water can move up from the soil to the leaves. In humans, cells in the intestines absorb food. Blood vessels, which are made of specialized cells, transport nutrients throughout the body.

Many plants have specialized cells that make up the parts of the flower. These cells are specialized to make sperm and ova for reproduction. Similarly, specialized cells in humans make sperm and eggs for reproduction.

Animal Cells.   Most animals have cells not found in plants that perform special functions. For example, animals have nerve cells. These cells send and receive messages to and from the brain. Animals also have muscle cells that allow them to move about in their environment. When you study the human body in Unit 9, you'll learn more about the systems that use specialized cells.

2. What are two kinds of specialized cells that most animals have that plants do not have? _____

_____

TAKE ANOTHER LOOK

Fig. 4-2 compares special cell functions of plants and humans.

Fig. 4-2

Cell Functions	Plants	Humans
Make food	Leaf cells	None
Provide support	Stem fibers	Bone cells
Absorb nutrients	Root cells	Specialized cells in intestines
Transport nutrients	Specialized cells that make transport vessels	Blood vessel cells
Reproduction	Specialized cells that make sperm and ova	Specialized cells that make sperm and eggs
Allow movement	None	Muscle cells
Send and receive messages to and from the brain	None	Nerve cells

Check Your Understanding

Write a sentence explaining the connection between each pair of words.

3. plant cell, cell wall _____

_____

4. human cells, reproduction _____

_____

5. What is the difference between a eukaryotic cell and a prokaryotic cell?

_____

_____

6. What structures are found in plant cells but not in animal cells?

_____

_____

7. How do chloroplasts help a plant carry out its life processes?

_____

_____

8. Give an example of special plant cells and special human cells that absorb nutrients. _____

_____

_____

9. What function do nerve cells perform in animals?

_____

_____

10. What function do muscle cells perform in animals?

_____

_____

Passive Transport

Key Words

diffusion:	the movement of molecules from areas of greater concentration to areas of lesser concentration
concentration:	amount of a substance in a given area
osmosis:	diffusion of water across a membrane
passive transport:	movement of molecules across a cell membrane without the use of energy
carrier protein:	protein in the cell membrane that moves large molecules through the membrane

KEY IDEAS

Passive transport is the movement of molecules across a cell membrane without the use of energy. The constant motion of molecules causes them to move by diffusion from areas of greater concentration to areas of lesser concentration. Water moves in or out of a cell by a special kind of diffusion called osmosis. Other molecules move in or out of a cell with the help of carrier proteins.

Have you ever been in a supermarket's produce aisle when suddenly a mist of water shot out over the fruits and vegetables? You might have wondered why plants that have already been picked need water. The reason for misting the produce is to keep it from wilting. The water droplets land on the produce and pass into the plant's cells.

A cell must take in water to carry out its life processes. A cell also must take in certain other substances. These substances enter the cell through the cell membrane. A cell must also rid itself of waste products to work properly. Wastes leave the cell by passing through the cell membrane.

Recall that the cell membrane controls the flow of substances into and out of the cell. Not every substance can pass through the cell membrane. The cell membrane is selectively permeable. It allows only certain materials to pass into the cell and certain others to pass out. For example, the cell membrane allows food and oxygen molecules to enter the cell. It allows only waste products such as carbon dioxide to leave the cell.

Diffusion.   Molecules move across the cell membrane in several ways. Some kinds of molecules, such as oxygen and carbon dioxide, pass through the cell membrane by diffusion.   **Diffusion** (dih-FYOO-zhuhn) is the movement of molecules from an area of greater concentration to an area of lesser concentration. **Concentration** (KAHN-sen-TRAY-shuhn) is the amount of a substance in a given area.

Carbon dioxide is constantly made by cells as they use energy. Therefore, the concentration of carbon dioxide inside the cell is higher than that outside the cell. This causes the carbon dioxide to diffuse out of the cell. On the other hand, the cell constantly uses oxygen to perform its life processes, so the concentration of oxygen outside the cell is higher than it is inside the cell. This causes the oxygen molecules to diffuse through the cell membrane into the cell. The diffusion of molecules continues until equal amounts of the molecules lie on both sides of the cell membrane. Fig. 5-1 shows how a substance moves into or out of a cell by diffusion.

Fig. 5-1

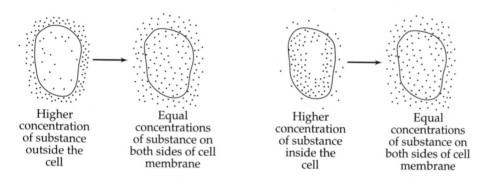

Higher concentration of substance outside the cell

Equal concentrations of substance on both sides of cell membrane

Higher concentration of substance inside the cell

Equal concentrations of substance on both sides of cell membrane

Diffusion occurs because molecules are constantly in motion. The moving molecules collide and spread out in all directions. As they spread out, molecules tend to move into and out of the cell. Small molecules such as water and oxygen are able to pass through spaces between the lipids that make up the cell membrane.

Osmosis.   The diffusion of water across a membrane is called **osmosis** (ahs-MOH-sihs). Water molecules move into or out of a cell by osmosis. In osmosis, water molecules diffuse across the cell membrane until they are in equal concentration on both sides. The misting of produce in a supermarket is an attempt to trigger osmosis. Since the plant parts were removed from the live plant, they have no water supply. The cells begin to wilt.   By misting the produce, osmosis can occur.   The water can pass into the produce and keep it crisp.

Diffusion and osmosis occur without the use of energy. For this reason, they are said to be forms of **passive transport** (PAS-ihv TRANS-port).

Carrier Proteins. Another type of passive transport is a form of diffusion that involves carrier proteins. **Carrier proteins** (KA-ree-yer PROH-teenz) are in the double layer of lipids that form the cell membrane. Most types of molecules are too large to pass through the spaces between lipids in a cell membrane. Carrier proteins move these large molecules across the cell membrane and into or out of the cell. See Fig. 5-2.

Fig. 5-2

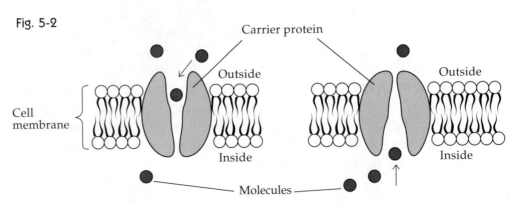

Passive transport always moves molecules from a place of higher concentration to a place of lower concentration. For example, a cell uses up glucose molecules soon after they enter the cell. So the concentration of glucose molecules inside the cell is often lower than outside it. Carrier proteins move glucose molecules into the cell faster than they could move without carrier proteins.

Fig. 5-3 shows the different forms of passive transport.

Fig. 5-3

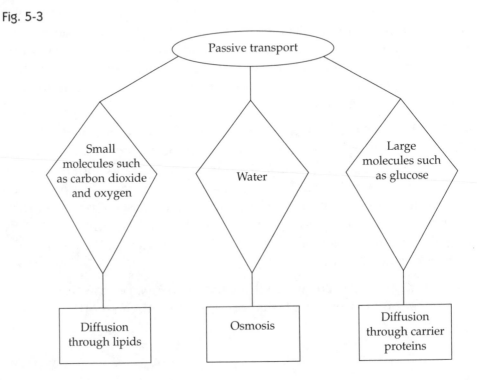

1. Explain the relationship between diffusion and osmosis.

   _____

   _____

Complete the paragraph with the following terms: *diffusion, higher, lipids, lower, osmosis, passive transport, carrier proteins, selectively permeable.*

The cell membrane is made up of a double layer of **(2)**_____.

Buried in these layers are **(3)**_____. Only certain substances

can move into or out of the cell through the cell membrane. It is said to be

(4)_____. In the process of **(5)**_____,

molecules move from an area of **(6)**_____ concentration to

an area of **(7)**_____ concentration. Water diffuses across the

cell membrane by **(8)**_____. Both diffusion and osmosis are

forms of **(9)**_____.

---

10. Why are osmosis and diffusion called passive transport?

    _____

    _____

11. How does the motion of molecules trigger diffusion?

    _____

    _____

12. How do carrier proteins help substances enter the cell?

    _____

    _____

13. While conducting an experiment, you discover a certain substance passing out of a cell by diffusion. What might you conclude about the concentration of this substance?

    _____

    _____

    _____

What Do You Know?

Lesson 6

Cell Energy Transport and Use

KEY IDEAS

Active transport is the use of energy to move substances across the cell membrane. Cellular respiration and fermentation are two processes that supply cells with the energy needed for active transport.

Have you ever baked bread? If so, you probably added yeast to the bread dough. After some time passed, you may have noticed that the dough had risen. Did you wonder why this happened? If you thought the yeast caused the change, you were correct. Yeast breaks down a sugar in the flour. As the sugar breaks down, it releases gas bubbles into the dough. The gas bubbles cause the dough to expand, or rise. In this lesson, you will find out more about processes that release energy from food.

You may recall that diffusion is a process in which molecules move from an area of higher concentration to an area of lower concentration. Sometimes molecules need to move in the opposite direction. They need to get from an area of lower concentration to an area of higher concentration. In such cases, energy is needed to move the molecules across the cell membrane. Processes in which energy is used to move a substance across the cell membrane are called **active transport** (AK-tihv TRANS-port). There are two types of active transport.

In one type of active transport, molecules are carried across the cell membrane. Energy is used to change the shape of the membrane and pull the molecules through it. This kind of active transport is used to move molecules both into and out of the cell.

Fig. 6-1 shows one way molecules are moved through the cell membrane by active transport. This type of transport is similar to passive transport through carrier proteins. However, in this type of active transport, molecules move from an area of low concentration to an area of high concentration.

Fig. 6-1

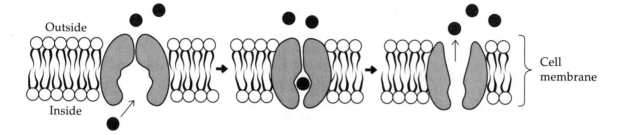

Another type of active transport is used to take large molecules into a cell. The cell membrane forms a sac around the molecule. Once the molecule is surrounded, the sac breaks away from the cell membrane and moves into the cytoplasm. The sac forms a vacuole. The vacuole stores the molecule for use by the cell. This process is shown in Fig. 6-2.

Fig. 6-2

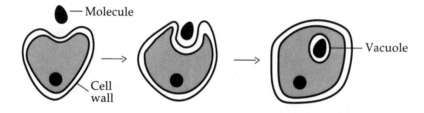

The cell can take in liquids through a similar type of active transport. As shown in Fig. 6-3, the cell membrane forms tiny sacs. These sacs fill up with liquids in the environment outside the cell. Once full, the sacs move into the cytoplasm and form a vacuole. The vacuole stores the liquids for use by the cell.

Fig. 6-3

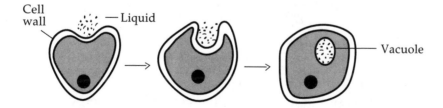

1. What is active transport? _____

_____

Materials can exit a cell in a similar manner. The cell stores its waste materials in a vacuole. The sac of wastes attaches to the cell membrane. Once the sac is joined to the membrane, its contents are released from the cell. The steps of this kind of transport are shown in Fig. 6-4.

Fig. 6-4

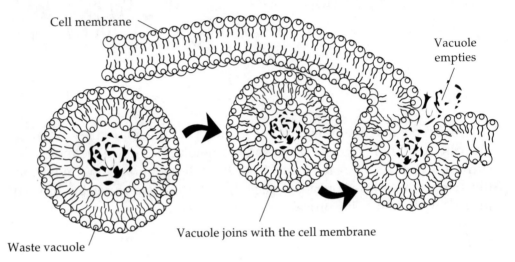

Cell membrane

Vacuole empties

Vacuole joins with the cell membrane

Waste vacuole

Cellular Respiration. In each process of active transport, the cell uses energy. Cells get the energy needed for active transport through cellular respiration. **Cellular respiration** (SEHL-yoo-luhr rehs-pih-RAY-shuhn) is the process by which glucose is broken down with the help of oxygen. Glucose is a type of sugar found in food. Plants and a few other organisms make their own glucose. Animals obtain glucose from the organisms they eat. All organisms need to break down glucose to gain energy. This process of cellular respiration occurs in the mitochondria of a cell. Recall from Lesson 3 that mitochondria are organelles that supply the cell with energy.

During cellular respiration, oxygen combines with glucose. Through a series of steps, the glucose is broken down. Water and carbon dioxide are released as waste products. The energy that is released forms high-energy molecules called ATP. The cell can directly use the energy in the ATP.

$$\text{glucose} + \text{oxygen} \longrightarrow \text{carbon dioxide} + \text{water} + \text{energy}$$
$$C_6H_{12}O_6 \quad 6\,O_2 \qquad\qquad 6\,CO_2 \qquad 6\,H_2O \qquad ATP$$

Fermentation. Sometimes, oxygen is not available to the cell. Yet, the cell still needs energy. In such cases, the cell obtains energy by fermentation. **Fermentation** (FER-mehn-TAY-shuhn) is the process by which glucose is broken down without the help of oxygen. Fermentation occurs in the cytoplasm of a cell. During fermentation, a compound called lactic acid is released as a waste product. Energy is also released. As with cellular respiration, energy-rich molecules of ATP are produced. However, fermentation produces fewer ATP molecules than cellular respiration does.

When you observe bread dough rise, you are seeing the result of fermentation. The yeast breaks down the glucose in the dough. Bubbles of carbon dioxide are released into the dough, causing it to expand.

 2. What is fermentation? _____

_____

 3. How do the waste products of fermentation differ from those of cellular respiration? _____

_____

Cellular respiration and fermentation are processes that release energy from glucose. ATP is a molecule that carries the energy until the cell needs it. Fig. 6-5 compares how cellular respiration and fermentation produce ATP molecules.

TAKE ANOTHER **LOOK**

Fig. 6-5

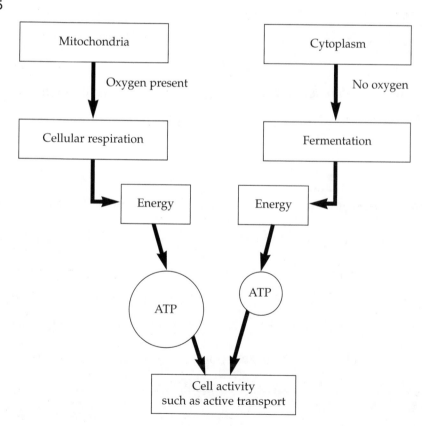

Check Your Understanding

Write a sentence explaining the connection between each pair of words.

4. active transport, cellular respiration _____

_____

5. cellular respiration, fermentation _____

_____

Complete the passage with the following terms: *active transport, ATP, cellular respiration, cytoplasm, energy, fermentation, less than, sac.* You may need to use some of the terms more than once.

The process in which energy is used to transfer a substance through the cell membrane is called **(6)**_____. Sometimes, **(7)**_____ is used to change the shape of the cell membrane. Then, the cell uses energy to form an **(8)**_____ around a molecule. The molecule is then drawn into the **(9)**_____ of the cell for future use.

Cellular respiration and fermentation are processes that supply a cell with the energy needed for active transport. In **(10)**_____, glucose is broken down in the presence of oxygen. Energy-rich molecules of **(11)**_____ are formed by this process. If oxygen is not present, a cell can obtain energy by **(12)**_____. However, the amount of ATP formed by **(13)**_____ is less than the amount formed by **(14)**_____.

What Do You Know?

15. When is energy needed to move substances across the cell membrane?

_____

_____

_____

16. Describe a form of active transport similar to the work of carrier proteins.

_____

_____

_____

17. How can materials exit a cell by active transport? _____

_____

_____

_____

18. How does cellular respiration help organisms carry out their life processes? _____

_____

_____

19. How are cellular respiration and fermentation alike? How are they different? _____

_____

_____

_____

_____

KEY IDEAS

Producers are organisms that can make their own food. The process by which producers change energy from the sun into chemical energy is called photosynthesis. Photosynthesis occurs in chloroplasts.

If you've ever visited a plant nursery, you've probably seen all kinds of plants for sale. Have you ever wondered whose job it was to keep the plants healthy? It's the job of the nursery manager. The manager oversees the growth of plants from seeds or cuttings. The manager also makes sure that the plants get all the things they need to stay healthy.

Photosynthesis. Organisms that can make their own food are called **producers** (pro-DOO-surhz). Plants and blue-green bacteria are two kinds of producers. They make food through photosynthesis. **Photosynthesis** (foht-oh-SIHN-thuh-sihs) is the process by which producers change energy from the sun into chemical energy.

Recall from Lesson 4 that plant cells contain organelles called chloroplasts. These large, oval structures, shown in Fig. 7-1 are located in the cytoplasm of the cell. Inside the chloroplasts is a green pigment called chlorophyll. **Chlorophyll** (KLAWR-uh-fihl) traps the light energy necessary for photosynthesis.

Chloroplasts and chlorophyll are not the only things needed for photosynthesis. The plant also needs sunlight, water, and carbon dioxide from the air.

Fig. 7-1

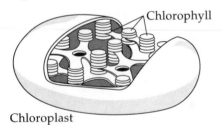

Chlorophyll

Chloroplast

Photosynthesis occurs in two stages. The first stage is the light reactions and the second stage is the dark reactions. Light reactions begin when sunlight is absorbed by chlorophyll. The sun's energy is used to split water molecules into hydrogen and oxygen. The oxygen is released as a waste product.

Dark reactions begin when the hydrogen formed in the light reaction combines with carbon dioxide. These combined substances produce glucose, a simple sugar. Glucose is the food made by producers. Glucose gives the plant the chemical energy it needs to carry out its life processes. Fig. 7-2 show how photosynthesis occurs in a leaf.

Fig. 7-2

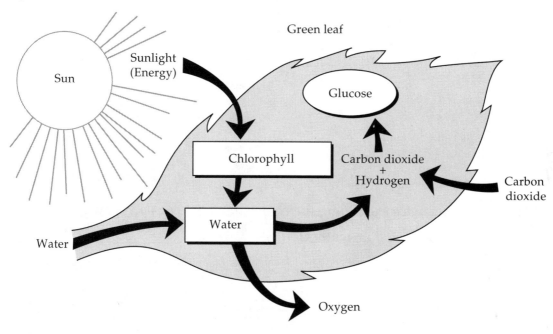

 1. **During which stage of photosynthesis does water split into hydrogen and oxygen?** _____

_____

The following equation shows the chemical changes that occur when plants convert sunlight into chemical energy.

$$\text{Carbon dioxide} + \text{Water} \xrightarrow{} \text{glucose} + \text{oxygen}$$
$$6\,CO_2 + 6\,H_2O \xrightarrow{\text{sunlight}} C_6H_{12}O_6 + 6\,O_2$$

Producers need chlorophyll, sunlight, water, and carbon dioxide for photosynthesis. Fig. 7-3 shows the light reactions and dark reactions that take place during photosynthesis.

Fig. 7-3

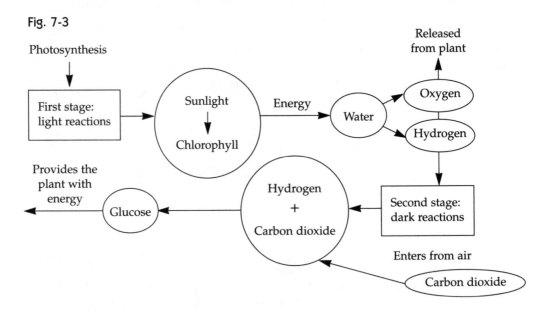

Check Your Understanding

Write a sentence explaining the connection between each pair of words.

2. producers, photosynthesis _____

_____

3. chlorophyll, chloroplasts _____

_____

Complete the passage with the following terms: *chlorophyll, chloroplasts, dark reactions, glucose, light reactions, oxygen, photosynthesis, producers, water.*

Organisms that can make their own food are (4)_____. The

process by which most producers make food is called (5)_____.

Photosynthesis occurs in the (6)_____ of a plant cell. The

(7)_____ begin when sunlight is trapped by (8)_____.

This energy is used to split (9)_____ into hydrogen and oxygen.

The (10)_____ is released from the cell. The (11)_____

begin when the hydrogen combines with carbon dioxide. (12)_____

is produced, which supplies the cell with energy.

13. What is the role of chlorophyll in photosynthesis? _____

_____

_____

14. What three things do plants need for photosynthesis to occur?

_____

_____

_____

15. What occurs during the light reactions of photosynthesis?

_____

_____

_____

_____

16. What occurs during the dark reactions of photosynthesis?

_____

_____

_____

_____

17. Where does a plant get the carbon dioxide it needs for photosynthesis?

_____

_____

18. Animal cells do not contain chloroplasts. Do you think animal cells are able to produce glucose through photosynthesis? Explain.

_____

_____

_____

_____

8 DNA and Cell Division

Key Words

cell cycle:	process by which a cell grows, prepares for division, and divides to form two daughter cells
interphase:	part of the cell cycle during which a cell grows and copies its chromosomes
chromosomes:	cell structures made of DNA and proteins that contain hereditary information
mitosis:	part of the cell cycle during which a parent cell distributes its chromosomes to two daughter cells

KEY IDEAS

The cell cycle is the continuous process by which cells grow, prepare for division, and divide into two daughter cells. The daughter cells inherit chromosomes from the parent cell. The process of distributing chromosomes during cell division is called mitosis.

If you look at a picture of yourself as a toddler, you'll find that your body has changed dramatically since then. Your height and weight increased as you got older. Did you ever wonder why this happened? You grow partly because the number of cells that make up your body increases.

The Cell Cycle. Even as you read these words, the cells in your body are growing. Materials that flow into the cell cause it to increase in size. As a cell gets larger, substances have more difficulty moving through it. Yet, to function properly, the cell must be able to transport materials throughout itself. Every cell has a size limit, or a point at which it can no longer transport materials throughout itself. When the cell reaches this limit, it divides, forming two new cells. The term **cell cycle** (sehl SY-kuhl) is used to describe the continuous process by which cells grow, prepare for division, and divide into new cells called daughter cells.

Interphase. The stage of the cell cycle during which the cell grows and copies its chromosomes is called **interphase** (IHN-tuhr-fayz). This is the longest stage of the cell cycle. It is an active time before cell division.

Near the end of interphase, the cell makes a copy of its chromosomes. For example, a cell that contains 12 chromosomes before interphase would contain 24 chromosomes after interphase. **Chromosomes** (KROH-muh-sohmz) are large, threadlike structures located in the cell nucleus. Chromosomes contain hereditary information that is passed on to new cells. This hereditary information is carried on DNA molecules found inside each chromosome.

Mitosis. When a cell divides, it passes on copies of its DNA to its offspring through mitosis. **Mitosis** (my-TOH-sihs) is the process of the cell cycle in which chromosomes are distributed to two daughter cells. There are four stages of mitosis. Fig. 8-1 shows these stages in animal cells.

Fig. 8-1

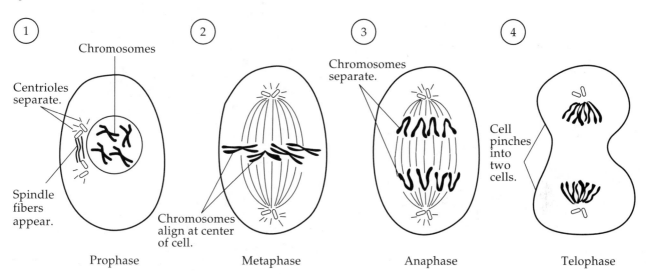

Prophase   Metaphase   Anaphase   Telophase

Prophase: Organelles called centrioles help to separate the duplicated chromosomes. Two pairs of centrioles are found outside the nucleus in the cytoplasm. The centriole pairs move apart. As they separate, fine threads of protein called spindle fibers form between the centriole pairs. By the end of prophase, the centriole pairs are at opposite ends of the cell. The nuclear membrane disappears. The spindle fibers align between the centriole pairs.

Metaphase: In the second stage of mitosis, the chromosome pairs line up across the center of the cell. Each chromosome pair is attached to a spindle fiber.

Anaphase: During the third stage of mitosis, each chromosome pair separates to form two single chromosomes. The spindle fibers pull one chromosome from each pair to opposite ends of the cell. This forms two sets of single chromosomes.

Telophase: In the last stage of mitosis, a nuclear membrane forms around each set of chromosomes. The spindle fibers disappear. Mitosis ends when the cell membrane begins to pinch the cell in two. This causes the cytoplasm to divide, forming two identical daughter cells.

 1. **How do spindle fibers help distribute chromosomes to daughter cells?**

_____

_____

TAKE ANOTHER LOOK

Fig. 8-2 summarizes the cell cycle.

Fig. 8-2

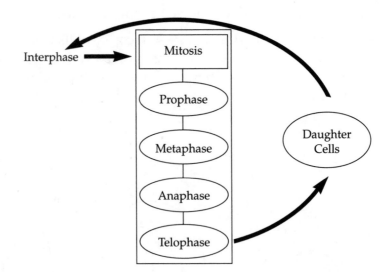

Check Your Understanding

Write a sentence explaining the connection between each pair of words.

2. chromosomes, interphase _____

_____

3. cell cycle, mitosis _____

_____

4. Fig. 8-3 shows each of the four stages of mitosis. On each line, write the name of the stage shown. Then write the letters in the correct order of their occurrence.

Fig. 8-3

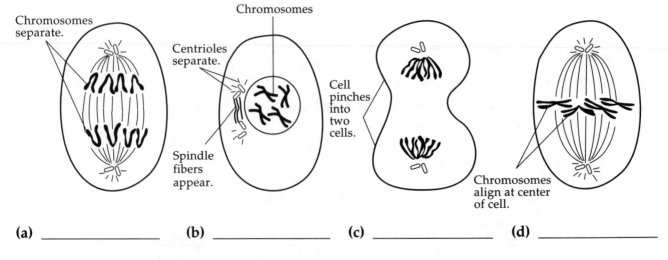

(a) _____ **(b)** _____ **(c)** _____ **(d)** _____

(e) Correct order of occurrence: _____

5. What is the cell cycle? _____

_____

_____

6. What causes cells to divide? _____

_____

_____

7. How is hereditary information passed from a parent cell to daughter

cells? _____

_____

_____

8. What are the four stages of mitosis? _____

_____

_____

_____

9. What is interphase? _____

_____

_____

10. If a parent cell contains eight chromosomes, how many chromosomes
are present after interphase? Why?

_____

_____

_____

_____

Summary

- Scientists made their first discoveries about cells through the use of microscopes. These discoveries led to the formation of the cell theory.

- The cell theory states the following: All living things are made up of cells. The cell is the basic unit of structure and function in all living things. All cells come from other cells.

- Most cells contain a cell membrane, a nucleus, and cytoplasm. Organelles are cell structures with specific jobs. Organelles are located in the cytoplasm of most cells.

- Eukaryotic cells contain a nucleus. Prokaryotic cells lack a nucleus. Plant cells and animal cells are eukaryotic cells. Plant cells contain a cell wall and chloroplasts.

- The cell membrane controls the flow of materials into and out of the cell. Many substances move across a cell by diffusion. Water moves into or out of a cell by osmosis. Since neither process uses energy, diffusion and osmosis are types of passive transport.

- Sometimes energy is needed to move substances across a cell membrane. Such processes are called active transport. Cells get the energy needed for active transport through cellular respiration and fermentation.

- Photosynthesis is the process by which producers change energy from the sun into chemical energy. Photosynthesis occurs in the chloroplasts of plant cells.

- The cell cycle is the continuous process by which cells grow, prepare for division, and divide into new cells. The new cells are called daughter cells.

- Mitosis is the process of distributing chromosomes from a parent cell to each daughter cell during cell division. The four steps of mitosis are prophase, metaphase, anaphase, and telophase.

For Your Portfolio

1. With a group of classmates, design a skit in which an animal cell and a plant cell meet. Topics the cells might "discuss" include their unique structures and the processes by which they get energy. Perform your skit for the class.

2. Suppose you were asked to explain diffusion to some of your classmates. Design an activity to illustrate the process. For example, you could use an open bottle of perfume to demonstrate the process.

3. Draw a cartoon that shows how a molecule enters a cell through active transport. Include captions to describe what the molecule is "thinking" on its "trip" into the cell.

4. Make a flow chart to illustrate the process of photosynthesis. Do not show it to your classmates. Then draw different parts of your flow chart on separate pieces of paper. Exchange your papers with those of another student. Try to organize the parts of your classmate's flow chart in the correct order. Your classmate will try to organize yours. Compare your results with the original charts.

5. Use paper plates, small squares of paper, rubber bands, and strips of yarn to show how chromosomes are distributed during mitosis. Tie together two rubber bands. Repeat this three more times. The rubber band pairs represent four pairs of chromosomes. Use single rubber bands to show single chromosomes. The paper plates represent the cell. The squares of paper are the centrioles. The yarn strips are the spindle fibers. Work in groups of four. On a stiff poster board, make four diagrams using the materials described above to show the four stages of mitosis. All members of the group may work together on all the stages or each member can design one stage for the poster.

Match the correct letter from Fig. PT-1 with each of the following parts of a cell. Write the letter in the space provided.

Fig. PT-1

_____ 1. cell membrane   _____ 6. mitochondrion

_____ 2. cell wall   _____ 7. nuclear membrane

_____ 3. chloroplasts

_____ 4. cytoplasm   _____ 8. nucleus

_____ 5. endoplasmic reticulum   _____ 9. ribosomes

_____ 10. vacuoles

Answer each of the following questions about Fig. PT-1.

11. Is the cell shown in the diagram a plant cell or an animal cell? Explain your answer.

_____

_____

12. Is the cell shown in the diagram a eukaryotic cell or prokaryotic cell? Explain your answer. _____

_____

13. Explain the process by which the cell shown in the diagram obtains energy.

_____

_____

14. How could the cell shown in the diagram obtain water without using energy?

_____

_____

15. How are the chloroplasts of a plant cell similar to the mitochondria of an animal cell?

_____

_____

Answer one of the following questions.

16. Make a sketch to show why the two daughter cells formed by mitosis are identical to their parent cell. Or, write an essay to explain why this occurs.

17. A certain substance has a higher concentration inside the cell than outside. But the cell needs even more of the substances inside. What kind of transport is needed? Draw a diagram or write an essay to describe the relationship between the concentration of the substance and the type of transport needed.

Genetics and Heredity

Do you resemble one of your parents? Do people sometimes say you look just like another member of your family? Do you know anyone who is adopted? Does he or she look very different from his or her adoptive parents?

It is not by chance that children often look like their biological parents. Parents pass copies of their genetic material to their offspring. This genetic material controls the way people look and how their bodies work.

Sometimes copying errors happen when cells replicate. If an error is passed on to a child, the child can inherit a disorder. Using technology, doctors can sometimes find out if the genetic material of the parents contains errors. This information can help parents know in advance what the chances are of having a child with a certain disorder.

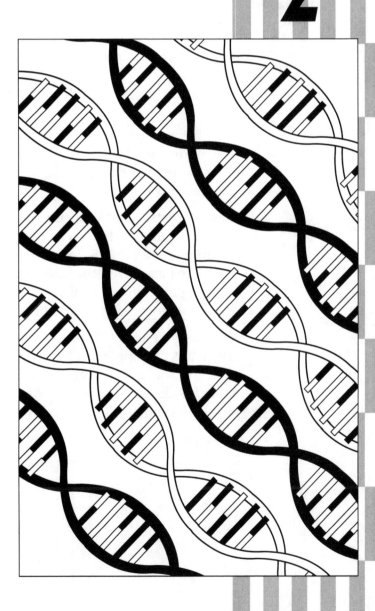

Lesson 9

The Chemistry of Genes

Key Words

base triplet:	group of three bases on a strand of DNA
gene:	portion of DNA that contains the information needed to make a specific protein
trait:	characteristic or property
protein synthesis:	the process by which proteins form

KEY IDEAS

DNA is responsible for the production of proteins. DNA contains a genetic code for forming proteins. The kinds and amounts of proteins present in an organism determine its traits.

Genetics counselors advise people about whether they are carriers of a genetic disease. They consult with people about the possibilities of passing the traits on to their children. To do this, genetics counselors must understand the chemistry of genes.

Base Triplets. DNA consists of two strands of nucleotides attached to each other. Recall from Lesson 2 that there are four kinds of bases in DNA. They are represented by the letters *A, T, C,* and *G.* The bases on one strand of DNA are paired with the bases on the other strand in a consistant pattern. *A* always pairs with *T*; *C* always pairs with *G.* The bases on either strand of DNA are arranged in groups of three called **base triplets** (bays TRIHP-lihts).

The base triplets of DNA can consist of any combination of the four bases. The bases can appear in any order along the strand. The triplets *AGC* and *GTC* are shown on strand *1* of the DNA molecule in Fig. 9-1. The DNA strand is divided into segments called genes. A **gene** (jeen) is a portion of DNA that contains the information needed to make a specific protein.

Fig. 9-1

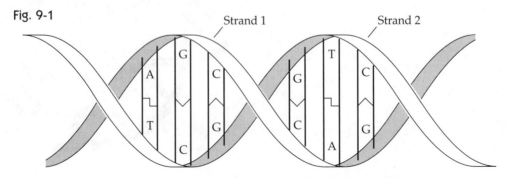

Strand 1   Strand 2

A **trait** (trayt) is a characteristic or a property. One example of a trait is eye color. Genes control the traits that are passed from parents to offspring. Each kind of gene is different from every other kind of gene in its DNA molecule. The DNA in the genes of a simple virus consists of thousands of bases. The DNA contained in a human's genes consists of about *10 billion* bases.

There are an endless number of base combinations which can form an infinite number of genes. This explains how it is possible for so many different types of organisms to exist. It also explains why so much variety exists among organisms of the same species.

1. What is a base triplet? _____

    _____

2. What is a gene?_____

    _____

Formation of Protein. Genes control an organism's traits by controlling the formation of proteins. The kinds and amounts of proteins present in an organism determine its traits. Each kind of protein is made from a different arrangement of amino acids. Organisms contain twenty kinds of amino acids. If the order or kinds of amino acids in a chain change, a different protein is made.

A gene's DNA contains the code for forming proteins. This is a process called **protein synthesis** (PROH-teen SIHN-thuh-sihs). The code is in the sequence of the bases in the DNA molecule. The triplets in a gene determine which proteins it is coded to synthesize. Protein synthesis occurs in the cytoplasm at the organelles called ribosomes. However, DNA is found mainly in a cell's nucleus. The DNA cannot leave the nucleus.

RNA. RNA is a chemical that can move in and out of the nucleus. RNA acts as a messenger to bring the code from the nucleus to the cytoplasm. This type of RNA is appropriately called messenger RNA (mRNA).

The base sequence of a DNA strand is a code for the sequencing of bases on the messenger RNA. The bases of the mRNA line up in a sequence that corresponds to the sequence of bases on a strand of DNA. For example, where the DNA has base G, the RNA matches it with base C. See Fig. 9-2. However, RNA does not contain base T. So RNA produces a different base, U, to match base A. Like the bases in DNA, the RNA bases also form triplets.

Fig. 9-2

DNA		RNA
A	~	U
T	~	A
C	~	G
G	~	C

3. What RNA triplet would match the DNA triplet GTA?

    _____

Once it is coded, mRNA moves through the cytoplasm to a ribosome. The end of the mRNA attaches to the ribosome. Meanwhile, another kind of RNA called transfer RNA (tRNA) is at work. The tRNA grabs onto an amino acid in the cytoplasm. The base triplet at the end of the tRNA strand determines the kind of amino acid to which it attaches.

A number of tRNA strands bring their amino acids to the mRNA strand attached to the ribosome. A triplet in the middle of each tRNA pairs with a triplet on the mRNA. In this way, the tRNA line up their amino acids along the mRNA.

Each amino acid bonds to the amino acid next to it. The result is a bonded chain of specific kinds of amino acids arranged in a specific order. This chain results in a newly formed protein. When a chemical signal is received, the protein separates from the RNA. The protein is then ready to perform its special function in the organism.

 4. What is the difference between mRNA and tRNA?

_____

_____

TAKE ANOTHER LOOK

Study the relationship between DNA and RNA shown in Fig. 9-3.

Fig. 9-3

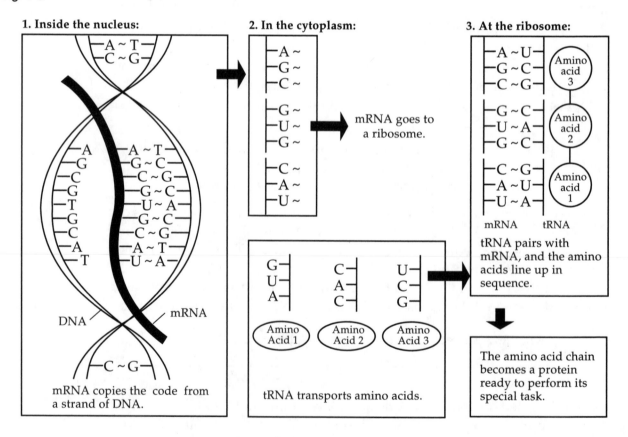

1. Inside the nucleus:

—A ~ T—
—C ~ G—

—A   —A ~ T—
—G   —G ~ C—
—C   —C ~ G—
—G   —G ~ C—
—T   —U ~ A—
—G   —G ~ C—
—C   —C ~ G—
—A   —A ~ T—
—T   —U ~ A—

DNA   mRNA

—C ~ G—

mRNA copies the code from a strand of DNA.

2. In the cytoplasm:

—A ~
—G ~
—C ~

—G ~
—U ~
—G ~

—C ~
—A ~
—U ~

mRNA goes to a ribosome.

G—   C—   U—
U—   A—   C—
A—   C—   G—

Amino Acid 1   Amino Acid 2   Amino Acid 3

tRNA transports amino acids.

3. At the ribosome:

—A ~ U—   Amino acid 3
—G ~ C—
—C ~ G—

—G ~ C—   Amino acid 2
—U ~ A—
—G ~ C—

—C ~ G—   Amino acid 1
—A ~ U—
—U ~ A—

mRNA   tRNA

tRNA pairs with mRNA, and the amino acids line up in sequence.

The amino acid chain becomes a protein ready to perform its special task.

Write a sentence explaining the connection between each pair of words.

5. amino acid, protein _____

_____

6. cytoplasm, ribosome _____

_____

7. gene, DNA _____

_____

8. base triplet, code _____

_____

For each numbered box in the mRNA strand shown in Fig. 9-4, write the letter
of the missing base that matches the DNA base.

9. _____

10. _____

11. _____

12. _____

13. _____

14. _____

15. _____

Fig. 9-4

DNA	mRNA		DNA	mRNA
A ~	U		G ~	12
G ~	9		C ~	13
C ~	G		T ~	G
T ~	10		A ~	14
C ~	G		A ~	15
A ~	11		T ~	A

On each numbered line in Fig. 9-5, write the letter of the base on the tRNA
that pairs with the base on the mRNA.

Fig. 9-5

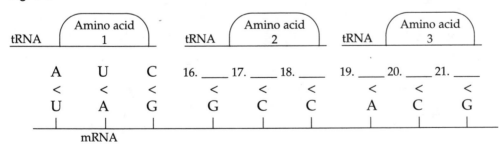

Amino acid 1   Amino acid 2   Amino acid 3

tRNA   tRNA   tRNA

A   U   C   16. ___ 17. ___ 18. ___   19. ___ 20. ___ 21. ___
<   <   <   <   <   <   <   <   <
U   A   G   G   C   C   A   C   G

mRNA

Fill in the blanks in the sentences with the proper term from the list below. You will use two of the terms twice.

DNA   mRNA   tRNA   protein

In the nucleus, the mRNA bases align in a sequence that corresponds to the sequence of bases on the (22)_____. The (23)_____ carries the code to the ribosomes. In the cytoplasm, (24)_____ attaches to a specific amino acid. At the ribosomes, the (25)_____ carrying the amino acids attaches to the (26)_____. The amino acids line up to form a chain. This chain of amino acids is called a (27)_____.

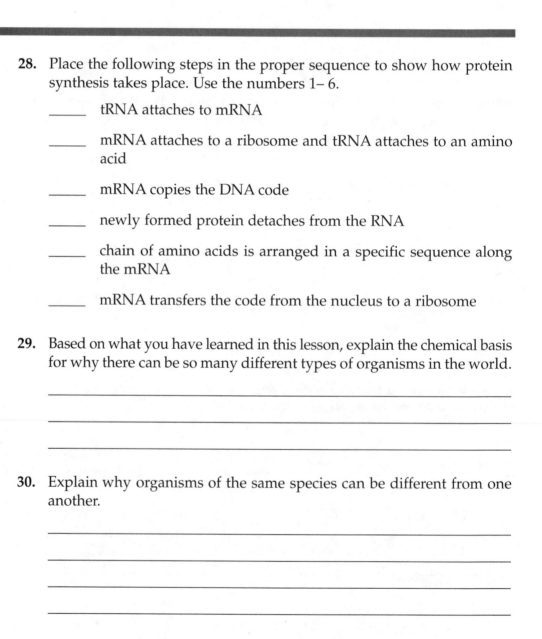

What Do You Know?

28. Place the following steps in the proper sequence to show how protein synthesis takes place. Use the numbers 1– 6.

_____ tRNA attaches to mRNA

_____ mRNA attaches to a ribosome and tRNA attaches to an amino acid

_____ mRNA copies the DNA code

_____ newly formed protein detaches from the RNA

_____ chain of amino acids is arranged in a specific sequence along the mRNA

_____ mRNA transfers the code from the nucleus to a ribosome

29. Based on what you have learned in this lesson, explain the chemical basis for why there can be so many different types of organisms in the world.

_____

_____

_____

30. Explain why organisms of the same species can be different from one another.

_____

_____

_____

_____

31. Suppose scientists found parts of the DNA from a dinosaur. What information would this discovery provide to the scientists? What information would it not give them?

_____

_____

_____

_____

32. Imagine that an unknown base triplet is missing from the gene for the height of an animal. Suppose scientists were able to correct the code. What information would they need before they could do this? How could they find this information?

_____

_____

_____

_____

10 Sex Cells and Meiosis

gametes:	sex cells
egg:	female sex cell
sperm:	male sex cell
haploid number:	number of chromosomes found in a gamete
diploid number:	number of chromosomes found in the body cells of an organism
meiosis:	type of cell division that produces gametes

KEY IDEAS

During sexual reproduction, two sex cells join. Each sex cell contains half the number of chromosomes found in the body cells of the parents. The process in which the number of chromosomes in a cell is reduced by half is called meiosis.

Our bodies consist of millions of cells. However, all humans begin life as only one cell. The one cell is formed by the joining of two sex cells: one from the mother and one from the father. After 36 hours, the cell divides to form two cells. Five days after the first cell formed, it has divided enough times to produce 120 cells.

Sex Cells. All organisms that reproduce sexually produce sex cells called **gametes** (GAM-eets). Female gametes are called **egg** (ehg) cells. Male gametes are called **sperm** (sperm) cells. Each gamete contains half the number of chromosomes as the body cells of the organism. The number of chromosomes in a gamete is described as the **haploid number** (HAP-loid NUM-buhr).

A single body cell from a particular organism contains a certain number of chromosomes. For example, human body cells contain 46 chromosomes each. The body cells of a dog contain 78 chromosomes each. An earthworm's body cells hold 36 chromosomes. The number of chromosomes in a single body cell of an organism is called the **diploid number** (DIHP-loid NUM-buhr). Since the body cell of a spider plant contains 24 chromosomes, its diploid number is 24.

1. How do gametes differ from body cells? _____

_____

_____

Meiosis and Chromosomes. The kind of cell division by which diploid cells produce haploid gametes is called **meiosis** (my-OH-sihs). Meiosis occurs in two stages. The first stage resembles mitosis. In this stage, the chromosomes in the parent cell duplicate, or make exact copies of each other. When this cell divides, each of the two resulting daughter cells contains the same number of chromosomes as the original parent cell.

Fig. 10-1 Meiosis in a human cell

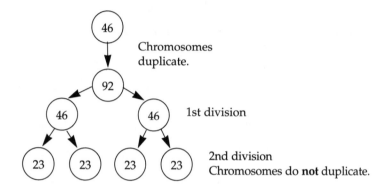

In the second stage of meiosis, each daughter cell divides a second time. Unlike mitosis, this second cell division does not begin with duplicating the chromosomes. Thus, when the daughter cells divide, each of the four cells produced has half as many chromosomes as the original parent cell. Fig. 10-1 shows meoisis in a human cell.

By dividing twice, the original diploid cell produces haploid gametes. When two such gametes join during sexual reproduction, they form a single cell that again has a diploid number.

Sperm and Eggs. During meiosis, a single cell divides twice to form four daughter cells. In males, meiosis produces four sperm cells of almost equal size. In females, meiosis produces four cells of varying size. One cell receives most of the cytoplasm, making it much larger than the other three cells. The large cell becomes the female gamete, or egg cell. The three smaller cells are called polar bodies. Polar bodies are not involved in sexual reproduction.

Occasionally, something goes wrong during meiosis. The parent cell does not separate evenly, causing a daughter cell to have an abnormal number of chromosomes. If this gamete joins with a normal gamete during sexual reproduction, the new cell that forms lacks the diploid number. An organism that develops from this cell will have a genetic disorder.

Fig. 10-2 shows the differences that occur in the formation of sperm and eggs.

TAKE ANOTHER LOOK

Fig. 10-2

A.
○ 1st division
○ ○ 2nd division
○ ○ ○ ○
🜃 🜃 🜃 🜃 Sperm

B.
○ 1st division
○ ○ 2nd division
○ ○ ○ ○
Polar bodies
○ Egg

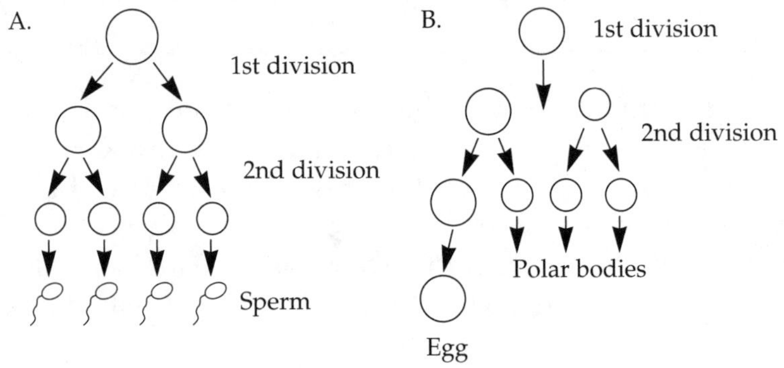

Check Your Understanding

Write a sentence explaining the connection among each group of words.

2. gametes, egg cell, sperm cell _____

_____

3. diploid, haploid, meiosis _____

_____

_____

Complete the following passage using words from the list below.

divisions   diploid number   egg   four   gamete
haploid number   meiosis   polar bodies   two

The **(4)**_____ of an organism is twice its **(5)**_____.
A **(6)**_____ contains half the number of chromosomes found in the
body cells of an organism. Gametes are formed through **(7)**_____.
In this process, a parent cell undergoes two **(8)**_____. The first
stage of meiosis produces **(9)**_____ daughter cells. In males,
the second stage of meiosis results in **(10)**_____ sperm cells. In
females, one **(11)**_____ cell and three **(12)**_____
are formed.

Complete exercises 13 – 17 by adding the correct number to the sentences.
Using the fruit fly as an example.

13. If the body cell of a fruit fly contains 8 chromosomes, its diploid number
is _____.

14. The haploid number of a fruit fly is _____.

15. When a body cell doubles its chromosome number to begin meiosis, it contains _____ chromosomes.

16. Cells produced by the first division of meiosis contain _____ chromosomes.

17. Cells produced by the second division of meiosis contain _____ chromosomes.

---

18. Explain the difference between a body cell and a sex cell.

_____

_____

_____

19. If the body cell of a grasshopper contains 24 chromosomes, how many chromosomes does the egg cell of a female grasshopper contain? Explain how you determined your answer.

_____

_____

_____

20. How is the number of sperm cells and egg cells produced by meiosis different? _____

_____

_____

21. Explain how mitosis and meiosis are alike.

_____

_____

_____

22. Explain how mitosis and meiosis are different.

_____

_____

_____

11
Traits, Heredity, and Gene Expression

KEY IDEAS

Genes control the traits passed from generation to generation. More than one form of a gene may exist for a particular trait. By understanding how genes interact, it is possible to predict the inheritance of certain traits.

Blood type is just one of many traits passed from parents to their offspring. Certain tests performed by blood laboratory technicians indicate the blood type of an individual. This information is useful when giving blood transfusions. Blood typing can even help solve crimes.

Traits and Heredity. Gametes join to form a single cell through sexual reproduction. The new cell contains chromosomes from each parent. These chromosomes are made up of a series of genes. Genes determine which traits, or characteristics, the new organism will inherit from its parents. The passing of traits from parent to offspring is known as **heredity** (huh-REHD-ih-tee).

Some traits are controlled by two genes, or a *gene pair*. One gene is inherited from each parent. If one gene in the pair is **dominant** (DAHM-uh-nuhnt), that gene will mask the traits carried by the other gene. The organism will show the trait of the dominant gene. The gene whose traits are masked is said to be **recessive** (rih-SEHS-ihv). In some gene pairs, neither trait masks the other. The genes blend, showing a trait that is a combination of the two.

A **homozygous** (hoh-moh-ZY-guhs) organism has two genes that are alike for a particular trait. They can be either two dominant genes or two recessive genes. A **heterozygous** (heht-er-oh-ZY-guhs) organism has two genes that are different for a trait, one dominant and one recessive. A heterozygous organism shows the dominant form of the trait.

1. How are heterozygous and homozygous organisms alike? How are they different? _____

_____

Predicting Traits. You can predict the traits an organism might inherit if you know what gene pairs its parents have. A Punnett square is a diagram that helps you make such predictions. Let's consider the trait for hair texture in humans. The gene for curly hair is dominant. The gene for straight hair is the recessive. A capital letter is always used to represent the dominant gene; a lower case letter is used to represent the recessive gene. In this case, **C** stands for curly hair and **c** stands for straight hair.

Assume that in our example, the mother is homozygous recessive for hair texture. Her genes are represented as **cc**.

Step 1: We write the first gene, **c**, of the mother's gene pair above the top left-hand square. The second **c** is written above the top right-hand square. In this example, the father is heterozygous for this trait. His genes are represented as **Cc**. We show this by writing **C** to the side of the upper left-hand square and **c** to the side of the lower left-hand square. See Fig. 11-1.

Next, we find the different combinations of genes that can be inherited by their child.

Step 2: In each square, we write the gene from the side of the square next to the gene from above the square. See Fig. 11-2. To the side of the top left-hand square is the first gene from the father's gene pair, **C**. Above the square is the first gene of the mother's gene pair, **c**. So, we write **Cc** in the top left-hand box.

Step 3: In the top right-hand box, we write the first gene from the father's pair and the second gene from the mother's pair. We write **Cc** in that square. See Fig. 11-3.

Step 4: To fill in the bottom left-hand box, we match the second gene of the pair from the square's side, **c**, with the first gene of the pair above, **c**. See Fig. 11-4

Step 5: To complete the square, we pair the second gene of the pair to the square's side, **c**, with the second gene from the pair above the square, **c**. See Fig. 11-5.

Fig. 11-1   Step 1

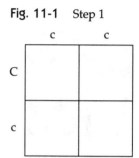

Fig. 11-2   Step 2

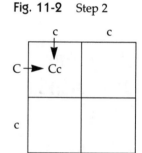

Fig. 11-3   Step 3

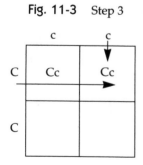

Fig. 11-4   Step 4

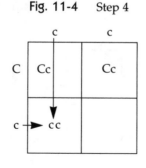

Fig. 11-5   Step 5

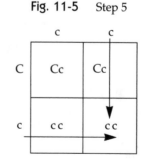

By using a Punnett square, you find that two gene combinations can result from these two parents. The offspring will either be heterozygous (Cc) or homozygous recessive (cc) for the trait of hair texture. The heterozygous person will have curly hair. The homozygous person will have straight hair.

Some traits are controlled by more than one gene pair. For example, a mix of four different gene pairs controls a person's skin color. Another human trait, gender, is determined by the absence or presence of a Y chromosome. All female gametes contain an X chromosome. Male gametes may contain either an X chromosome or a Y chromosome. If a female gamete joins with a male gamete containing an X chromosome, the offspring will be female (XX). If a female gamete joins with a male gamete containing a Y chromosome, the offspring will be male (XY).

The process of sex, or gender, determination is shown in Fig. 11-6.

Fig. 11-6

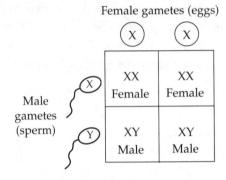

Check Your Understanding

Write a sentence explaining the connection between each pair of words.

2. traits, heredity _____

_____

3. dominant, recessive _____

_____

4. The gene for brown eyes (B) is dominant over the gene for blue eyes (b). Draw a completed Punnett square to show all possible gene combinations that may result from two parents who are heterozygous (Bb) for eye color.

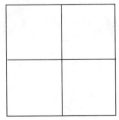

Fill in the numbered blanks with a term from the list below.

dominant   homozygous   heterozygous
Punnett square   recessive

A **(5)**_____ is a diagram that shows the possible gene combinations an offspring can inherit from its parents. A capital or upper case letter represents the **(6)**_____ gene. A lower case letter represents the **(7)**_____ gene. A gene pair represented by two capital letters shows the offspring is **(8)**_____ dominant for the trait. An uppercase and lowercase letter shows the offspring is **(9)**_____ for the trait.

What Do You Know?

10. Why do children often have traits similar to those of their parents?

_____

_____

_____

11. In pea plants, green peas are a recessive trait and yellow peas are a dominant trait. Explain how two plants with yellow peas can produce offspring with green peas. _____

_____

_____

12. How is the gender of an organism determined?

_____

_____

_____

13. Could a person with curly hair and a person with straight hair both be homozygous for the hair type trait? Explain.

_____

_____

_____

12 Mutations

Key Words

mutation:	a change in form
gene mutation:	permanent change in the DNA of a gene
chromosome mutation:	permanent change in the number or structure of chromosomes of a cell
carrier:	person who has a recessive gene for a trait but does not show the trait
sex-linked mutation:	mutation carried on either the X or Y chromosome

KEY IDEAS

The genetic code is passed from parents to offspring through gene replication and cell division. A change in a gene or chromosome can occur during either of these processes. Either type of change can change the genetic code of a cell. If the changed cell is a gamete, then all cells formed from the gamete will differ from the original parent cell.

Technology has provided methods for making changes to the genetic code of an organism. Plant breeders use these methods to develop useful traits in plants. They change the genetic code of the parent plant's cells to produce helpful mutations. Through experiments and field study, plant breeders "create" new plants. These plants can be made to be more resistant to disease, to produce more offspring, or to taste better than the plants from which they came. Many of the tomatoes you buy at the supermarket have been altered in these ways.

Mutation. In mitosis, DNA contained in the nucleus of a parent cell makes copies of itself. This process, called replication, ensures that the resulting daughter cells will contain the same genetic code as the parent cell.

A **mutation** (myoo-TAY-shuhn) is a change in something's form. An error can occur during replication that changes DNA. A permanent change in the DNA of a gene is called **gene mutation** (jeen myoo-TAY-shuhn). Sickle cell anemia is a deadly blood disorder. The disease is the result of a change in one base of a base triplet in the DNA molecule.

Mistakes that occur during cell division may cause a **chromosome mutation** (KROH-muh-sohm myoo-TAY-shun). Sometimes an error occurs when a chromosome copies itself. The chromosomes in the resulting daughter cells are then different from the parent cell.

In some cases, a portion of a chromosome may not be copied. People who are missing a small part of chromosome 11 have a condition called aniridia. Aniridia is the absence of the iris of the eye. Other times, the cell does not divide evenly. This results in daughter cells with a different number of chromosomes from the parent cell. Down syndrome is an example of this type of mutation.

If a mutation occurs in a gamete, the changed gene or chromosome is passed to the offspring. All cells formed from the gamete contain the mutation. Many types of mutations have little or no harmful effect on the resulting organism. Some mutations can be helpful to an organism. They also add variety to a species.

 1. How are gene mutations and chromosome mutations alike?

_____

_____

_____

Mutation and Disease. Mutations can be harmful. They can reduce an organism's chances of survival. For example, genetic disorders in humans are caused by mutations.

Down syndrome is a genetic disorder caused by chromosome mutation. During meiosis, a chromosome pair fails to separate. One of the resulting gametes contains an extra chromosome. The other gamete lacks the chromosome. The gamete with the extra chromosome may join a normal gamete during fertilization. The resulting offspring inherits Down syndrome.

Other genetic disorders are caused by gene mutations. Sickle cell anemia results from a gene mutation. The mutation causes the wrong amino acid to join a protein. The changed protein causes cells to be sickle shaped instead of round. The sickle cells cause blood clots and deprive the body's organs of needed oxygen.

Fig. 12-1 shows the genes involved in sickle cell anemia. A person with the sickle cell trait must inherit a mutated gene from both parents. A person who inherits one normal gene and one altered gene is a carrier of the disorder. A **carrier** (KAR-ee-uhr) has the recessive gene for a trait but does not actually show the trait. Carriers of the sickle cell trait produce both normal and sickle-shaped cells. Because the carriers have enough normal cells, they do not get the disease.

Fig. 12-1

	S	S
A	AS	AS
S	SS	SS

A = normal gene
S = gene for sickle cell

Sex-linked Mutation. In humans, certain genes are carried on either the X or Y chromosomes. A change in the DNA of these genes produces a **sex-linked mutation** (sehks-lihngkt myoo-TAY-shuhn). For example, the trait of colorblindness is a sex-linked mutation. The genes for color vision are carried on the X chromosome. The trait for normal color vision is dominant. The gene for colorblindness is recessive.

Fig. 12-2

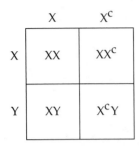

A female who is homozygous dominant has normal color vision. A female who is heterozygous has normal color vision, but is a carrier of the trait. However, a male will be colorblind only if his mother is a carrier of the trait. There is no gene for color vision on the Y chromosome. The inheritance of colorblindness is shown in Fig. 12-2. X^c shows the X chromosome with the gene for colorblindness.

 2. **What is a sex-linked mutation?** _____

_____

Fig. 12-3 shows how mutations can occur during mitosis and meiosis.

Fig. 12-3

```
          ┌─────────┐                      ┌─────────┐
          │ Meiosis │                      │ Mitosis │
          └─────────┘                      └─────────┘

        ( Cell division )              ( DNA replication )

              │ Error                         │ Error

        ( Chromosome )     Sex-linked ( Gene mutation )
        ( mutation   )     mutation

        ( Down syndrome )  ( Colorblindness )  ( Sickle cell anemia )
```

Check Your Understanding

Complete each sentence with a term from the list below.

cell division   chromosome mutation   Down syndrome   DNA
gene   gene mutation   sickle cell anemia

During replication, **(3)**_____ in the nucleus of a parent cell duplicates. If an error occurs during this process, the resulting **(4)**_____ is changed. A permanent change in the DNA of a gene is called a **(5)**_____. One genetic disorder caused by a gene mutation is **(6)**_____. Errors can also occur during

(7)_____. If a parent cell does not divide evenly a
(8)_____ may occur. One genetic disorder caused by a
chromosome mutation is (9)_____ .

10. What is a gene mutation and how is it caused?

_____

_____

_____

11. What is a chromosome mutation and how is it caused?

_____

_____

_____

12. How could a mutation help a species?

_____

_____

_____

13. Does a carrier for sickle cell anemia show the trait? Explain.

_____

_____

_____

14. How are sex-linked mutations and gene mutations alike? How are
they different?

_____

_____

_____

15. Why are most colorblind people male?

_____

_____

_____

Summary

- Genetics is the branch of science that studies heredity. Heredity is the passing of traits from parents to offspring. To understand heredity, you need to understand the chemistry of genes.

- Organisms are made mostly of protein. Therefore, protein determines what traits an organism will have. DNA holds the code that tells how amino acids should be arranged to make a protein.

- mRNA carries the information in the DNA code from the nucleus to the ribosomes.

- The mRNA and tRNA come together at the ribosomes to arrange amino acids in a particular order. The order and kinds of amino acids determine the types of proteins made.

- Genes are passed from parents to offspring. Meiosis is the first step in this process. Meiosis is a type of cell division that produces sex cells, or gametes. As a result of meiosis, gametes contain half the number of chromosomes of the body cells of an organism.

- During sexual reproduction, two gametes join. The resulting cell contains the same number of chromosomes as were present in the body cells of the parent organisms. Genes contained on these chromosomes are copies of the parents' genes.

- By understanding how a pair of genes interact, you can predict the inheritance of certain traits.

- Errors can occur when genetic information is passed from parent to offspring. These errors, called mutations, can occur either during cell division or during DNA replication.

- A mutation is a permanent change to a gene or chromosome. If the changed cell is a gamete, an organism formed from the cell may inherit a genetic disorder.

For Your Portfolio

1. Make a labeled model of DNA showing 9 base pairs. Show and label the strand of RNA that would match the strand of your DNA.

2. Along with other students in your class, put on a play that demonstrates how protein is synthesized. You will need to have people play the following roles: two base triplets on a DNA molecule; two matching triplets on a piece of mRNA; two amino acids; a ribosome; and two pieces of tRNA.

3. There are 20 important kinds of amino acids. There are 61 base triplets that "code" them. Use a biology textbook or an encyclopedia to find out which base triplets code each kind of amino acid. Make a chart showing the amino acids in one column and the base triplets that "code" them in a second column. Use your chart to explain to the class why there are so many different kinds of proteins.

4. Imagine you are a chromosome in a parent cell. Write a diary entry that describes what happens to you during the process of meiosis.

5. Use reference texts to identify five different human traits controlled by a single gene pair. Make a chart that identifies the traits and the dominant and recessive forms of the gene.

6. With a group of classmates, role-play a situation in which you are a group of pet store owners trying to breed a goldfish with iridescent scales. You know that iridescent scales in goldfish are recessive. Discuss what your plan would be to breed the goldfish.

7. With a group of classmates, role-play a situation in which a married couple is informed that they both carry the gene for sickle cell anemia. Professionals must explain to the couple that while neither of them show the disease, it is likely their offspring will have the sickle cell trait.

Match the terms in Column A with their definitions in Column B.

Column A

_____ 1. amino acid

_____ 2. chromosome mutation

_____ 3. cytoplasm

_____ 4. gametes

_____ 5. gene mutation

_____ 6. heredity

Column B

a. passing of traits from parent to offspring

b. living material inside a cell *not* including the nucleus

c. type of chemical used to build protein found in the cytoplasm

d. permanent change in the DNA of a gene

e. sex cells

f. change in the number or structure of chromosomes in a cell

Fill in the blanks.

7. Protein synthesis occurs at the _____.

8. A type of cell division that produces gametes is _____.

9. A chain of amino acids arranged in a particular order is a _____.

10. A _____ is altered genetic information carried on the X or Y chromosome.

Write a brief answer in the space provided.

11. What is the difference in the types of bases found in DNA and RNA?

_____

12. What is the difference between diploid number and haploid number? _____

_____

13. Would a carrier for sickle cell anemia show the disorder? Explain why or why not.

_____

Answer one of the following questions.

14. Explain why colorblindness occurs mainly in males. Draw a Punnet square to support your answer.

15. What role does meiosis play in the passing of genetic information from parent to offspring? Use a drawing or sentences to answer the question.

Evolution

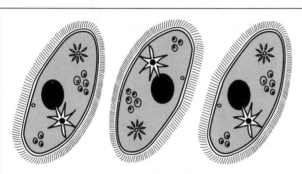

Many movies have been made about dinosaurs. A recent movie, Jurassic Park, presents information about dinosaurs that seems very believable. Although some of the "science" of the movie is purely fictional, some of the ideas presented are based on scientific theories.

By studying the bones of dinosaurs, scientists have made hypotheses about the physical appearance of dinosaurs. For example, whether a dinosaur is a meat-eater or a plant-eater can be determined by studying its teeth. The height and weight of these huge animals can also be estimated from their preserved bones.

Why did dinosaurs become extinct? Although many theories have been suggested, none have been proved. One popular theory is that a huge meteor from space struck the earth, creating thick clouds of dust that blocked out sunlight for months. This would have caused a major change in the climate which may have caused the dinosaurs to die off very rapidly.

13 Natural Selection

species:	a group of closely related living things whose members can mate and produce young for generations.
adaptation:	process by which a species becomes better suited to a change in its environment
survival of the fittest:	another term for natural selection
natural selection:	process by which the best adapted species survive and reproduce

KEY IDEAS

Many differences, or variations, exist among the individuals of any single species. Some variations may make an organism better suited to its environment. A species that is the best suited to its environment will survive and reproduce.

Over time, scientists have realized how much can be learned from studying differences among species. One of the first people to see the importance of slight variations among species was Charles Darwin. Darwin was an English scientist who lived more than 100 years ago.

Darwin's Studies. On a long voyage around the world, Darwin stopped at several small islands in the Pacific Ocean. While there, he noticed slight variations in the traits of the animals that lived on each island.

Darwin observed that one type of bird, a finch, lived on all the islands. But the finches living on each island had slightly different beaks. On one island, the finches had heavy beaks. The finches on another island had thinner, more pointed beaks. Darwin also noticed differences among the islands themselves. Some islands were covered with trees and bushes. Others were rocky and had only a few plants. After careful study, Darwin concluded that the finches' beaks had adapted to the type of food available on each island.

A **species** (SPEE-sheez) is a group of closely related living things with a common ancestor. Members of the group can mate with one another and produce young for generations.

Darwin suggested that many slight variations in traits existed within any single species. For example, an individual bird might be slightly smaller or a bit lighter in color than other birds of the same species.

Adaptation. Sometimes conditions in an environment change. The change may be sudden, such as that caused by a fire or a storm. Or the changes may be slow, such as the wearing down of mountains. If members of a species are not suited to the new, changed environment, the species may not survive. To survive, the species must either change or move away. But such changes occur slowly. They happen over long periods of time and over many generations.

Sometimes, an organism has a trait that allows it to survive. If this trait is passed on to its offspring, the offspring also have a better chance of survival. The process by which a species becomes better suited to a change in its environment is called **adaptation** (ad-uhp-TAY-shuhn).

 1. What is adaptation? _____

_____

_____ Fig. 13-1

Darwin wrote that the differences in the finches' beaks were variations. See Fig. 13-1. On an island that had many plants with large seeds, the finches had large, heavy beaks. This trait allowed them to crack open the seeds. Because these birds had plenty to eat, they would be healthy, and would be likely to find a mate and produce young.

Small seed-eating finch

In contrast, a finch with a smaller beak would have a hard time cracking open and eating the large seeds. This bird might not get enough to eat. As a result, it would not be as healthy as other well-fed finches. The hungry bird might not find a mate, and it might even die. Thus, it would not pass traits to a new generation of offspring.

Insect-eating finch

Darwin suggested that only the better adapted finches would be healthy enough to survive and produce young. He called this process **survival of the fittest** (suhr-VY-vuhl uhv thuh FIHT-uhst). In this process, organisms that survived produced young that inherited the traits they needed to adapt to their environment. These helpful variations were passed from one generation to the next.

Cactus-feeding finch

Natural Selection. Darwin realized that survival of the fittest also happened in species other than finches. He suggested that all species compete for survival. He also noted that species that are best adapted to their environment survive longer and reproduce more. Darwin called this process **natural selection** (NACH-uhr-uhl suh-LEHK-shuhn). The terms *survival of the fittest* and *natural selection* are both used to describe the process in which organisms with the best adaptations survive and reproduce.

Large seed-eating finch

 2. What is natural selection? _____

_____

_____

Fig. 13-2 shows an example of natural selection in moths. Imagine two different traits for wing color in moths. One trait is for light-colored wings. The second trait is for dark-colored wings. Because dark-colored moths are easy to see on tree trunks, predators capture many of them. Most of the moths that remain have light-colored wings.

Then the environment changes. Pollution darkens most of the tree trunks. Now dark-colored moths have the advantage because they are hard to find. They become more common as predators capture more of the light-colored moths.

Fig. 13-2

Check Your Understanding

Write a sentence explaining the connection between each pair of words.

3. adaptation, trait _____

_____

_____

4. natural selection, survival _____

_____

_____

5. survival of the fittest, reproduce _____

_____

_____

Complete the concept map shown in Fig. 13-3. Use the following terms:

young   move away   adapts

Fig. 13-3

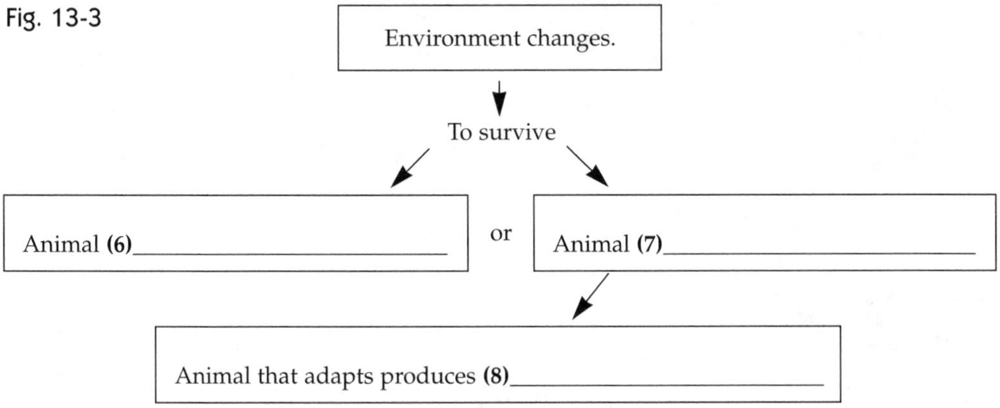

```
                    ┌─────────────────────────┐
                    │   Environment changes.  │
                    └─────────────────────────┘
                                │
                                ▼
                            To survive
                        ↙              ↘
┌────────────────────────────────┐   or   ┌────────────────────────────────┐
│                                │        │                                │
│ Animal (6)_____    │        │ Animal (7)_____    │
└────────────────────────────────┘        └────────────────────────────────┘
                                                    ↙
              ┌──────────────────────────────────────────────┐
              │ Animal that adapts produces (8)_____  │
              └──────────────────────────────────────────────┘
```

Fill in the blanks.

9. Another term for natural selection is _____.

10. Species that are best _____ to their environment survive longer and produce more young.

11. The process by which a species with the best adaptations survive and reproduce is called _____.

---

12. Within any group of species, there are variations of traits. How are these variations helpful to the group?_____
   _____
   _____

13. How did Darwin's finches adapt to the different environments of the islands? _____
   _____
   _____

14. Are all different types of traits the result of adaptation? Explain.
   _____
   _____
   _____

What Do You Know?

14 Evolution of Species

Key Words

evolution: the process by which living things change over time

KEY IDEAS

Over time, single-celled organisms have evolved into multicellular living things. As a result of natural selection, groups of living things can change so much that they become new species.

Evolution. Over a long period of time, a species of living things can change into a different species. **Evolution** (ehv-uh-LOO-shuhn) is the process by which living things change over time.

Life on earth has evolved from the earliest one-celled organisms into the many different multicellular organisms around us today. The first living things appeared on earth about 3.8 billion years ago. They were single cells that could not make their own food. Instead they took in organic chemicals from their surroundings to get energy. They lacked cell organelles.

Sometime between 3 and 3.8 billion years ago, some of the early organisms evolved ways to make their own food through photosynthesis. These cells may have been the first photosynthetic bacteria.

Later, single cells with complex organelles and membranes evolved. This was an important step, for it led to the type of cell found in modern plants and animals. Between 3 billion and 1 billion years ago, various species of single-celled organisms evolved. Some of them began to live in groups or colonies. Species of multicellular organisms appeared on the earth less than 1 billion years ago.

 1. What is evolution? _____

_____

Evolution of Species. New species continue to evolve today. One way in which a new species can evolve is through separation of groups within one species. The groups may be isolated by barriers such as an ocean, a mountain range, or other physical features.

Once the organisms of a species are isolated, each group adapts to its own environment. If the traits don't vary too much, organisms from the two groups might still be able to mate and produce offspring. They are still the same species. But as more time passes and variations between the groups become greater, the two groups become more different. They can no longer mate and produce young. They have developed into two new species. This concept is shown in Fig. 14-1.

Fig. 14-1

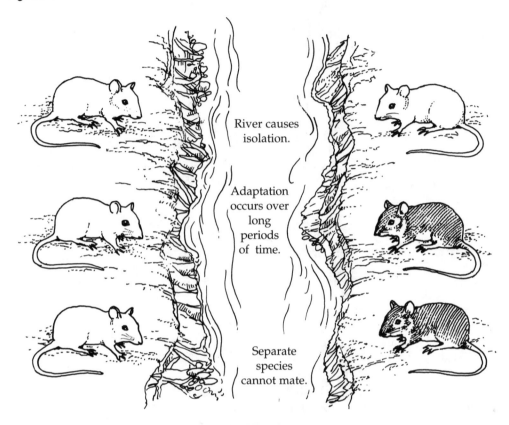

River causes isolation.

Adaptation occurs over long periods of time.

Separate species cannot mate.

Natural selection causes living things to change over time. Darwin's finches changed as they adapted to their islands. Because each group of birds lived on a separate island, they did not mate. Instead, the birds on each island changed in different ways as they adapted. In time, the finches became different species.

Darwin showed how groups of animals could adapt to their environment. He used the finch example and others to explain that all living things evolved from earlier species.

Genes Influence Evolution. Modern scientists explain evolution by studying genes. Recall that genes control the traits of each cell in the body and make living things the way they are. Genes from each parent come together in the young, making a new mix of genes for that individual. This new mix makes each living thing slightly different from all others.

Genes control the production of many chemicals in the body of an animal. Scientists have discovered that studying these chemicals helps them follow the chain of evolution. If certain chemicals of the same type are found in different species, this suggests that the different species may have evolved from the same species.

A summary of how organisms have changed over time is shown in Fig. 14-2.

Fig. 14-2

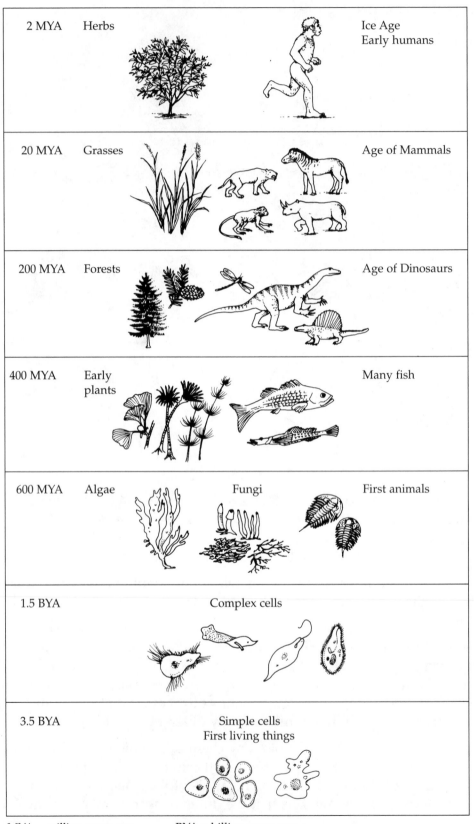

2 MYA	Herbs	Ice Age / Early humans
20 MYA	Grasses	Age of Mammals
200 MYA	Forests	Age of Dinosaurs
400 MYA	Early plants	Many fish
600 MYA	Algae / Fungi	First animals
1.5 BYA	Complex cells	
3.5 BYA	Simple cells / First living things	

MYA = million years ago   BYA = billion years ago

Complete the concept map shown in Fig. 14-3. Use the following terms:
bacteria   plants   complex cells

Fig. 14-3

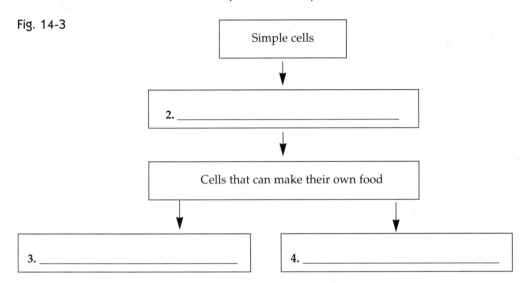

Simple cells

2. _____

Cells that can make their own food

3. _____

4. _____

What Do You Know?

5. Why does a group of living things change over time?

_____

_____

_____

6. What was one of the most important steps in the evolution of early living things? _____

_____

_____

7. Explain how a new species can evolve from an older, existing species.

_____

_____

_____

Lesson 15
Evidence of Evolution

KEY IDEAS

Scientists can learn about living things of the past by studying fossils. From fossils, scientists can learn how living things of the past evolved and how they compare to living things of today. By comparing living things of the present, scientists can also find evidence of common ancestors.

Fossils.   When most living things die, they decay. They die without leaving any trace of their passing. Occasionally, however, the remains of an organism last for a very long time. For example, sometimes an insect becomes trapped in the sap that runs down a tree. A larger animal might become trapped in a tar pit and die. Sometimes, an animal is buried in ice. In each of these cases, the animal is preserved, or kept from decaying. The animal or other living thing becomes a fossil. A **fossil** (FAHS-uhl) is the preserved remains or traces of a once-living thing.

Most fossils are not complete. They are usually made up of only the hard parts of an organism such as the bones, the shells, or the teeth. Often when an animal dies, its soft parts quickly decay or are eaten by another organism. The hard parts may be covered by dust or soil. In time, more and more soil is layered on top of the remains. These layers of soil press down upon each other and harden to form rock. Sometimes, the remains themselves turn into rock. Most fossils are formed in this way. See Fig. 15-1.

 1.   **What is a fossil?** _____

_____

From animal fossils, scientists can learn where the animal lived and what it might have eaten. From plant fossils, scientists can learn what the weather was like millions of years ago. But even more important, by studying fossils scientists can find out how different living species of today have evolved.

Fig. 15-1

HOW FOSSILS FORM

Animal dies.

Soft parts of animal are eaten or decay. Bones remain.

Bones are covered by dust and soil.

Bones are buried in layers of soil.

Layers of soil turn to stone.
Remains of animal turn to stone and form fossil.

Ancestors and Descendants. By looking at fossil bones, scientists can see that many species living today have common ancestors. An **ancestor** (AN-sehs-tuhr) is a species of the past, from which another living species has evolved. The living thing that has evolved from an ancestor is called a **descendant** (dee-SEHN-duhnt). For example, the ancestor of the modern horse lived about 60 million years ago. From its leg bones and skull, scientists can tell that the modern horse evolved from an earlier horse that was about the size of a dog. Today's horse is the descendant of the earlier horse.

Ancestors themselves do not change into modern forms. Instead, they pass traits onto their offspring from one generation to another. Occasionally, an individual offspring has a trait that helps it adapt to its environment. That offspring passes the trait onto its offspring. Eventually, over a long time and many generations, a new species with the trait evolves. The new species is better adapted to its environment than the original ancestor.

 2. What is the difference between an ancestor and a decendant?

_____

_____

Scientists can tell that animals living today are related to each other by looking at similar structures. Look at Fig. 15-2. You will see that the limbs of all these animals have a similar shape, or structure. Although they are used in different ways, the hand of a human, the flipper of a whale, the wing of a bird, and the foot of a lizard all share a common structure. The common structure of these body parts shows that these very different animals all evolved from the same ancestor.

Fig. 15-2

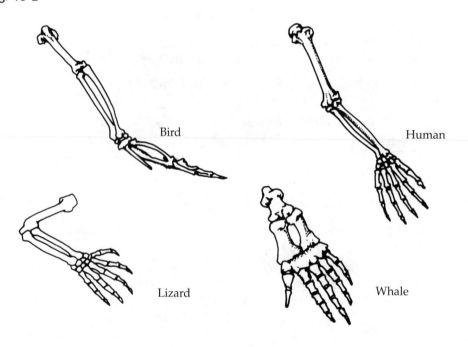

Study Fig. 15-3. Notice how the sizes of the leg bone and skull of the modern horse differ from those of its ancestors.

Fig. 15-3

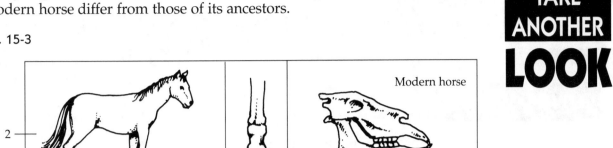

millions of years ago

Modern horse

One-toed horse

Early horse

2

12

26

40

60

Fill in the blanks.

The preserved remains or traces of a once-living thing is called an **(3)**_____.

They are usually made up of the hard parts of an organism, such as teeth,

(4)_____, and **(5)**_____. Scientists study similar structures to

help them understand which species evolved from **(6)**_____.

7. The most common animal fossils are shells, bones, and teeth. Why?

    _____

8. Explain how scientists can learn about the evolution of horses from fossils.

    _____

The Beginning of Life

Key Words

compounds:	chemicals that join together in consistent ways
organic compounds:	compounds that contain carbon

KEY IDEAS

People have long wondered how life began. Some scientists have shown that gases found on the early earth may have combined to form the compounds that make up living things.

Miller's Experiment.   In 1953, a scientist named Stanley Miller set up an experiment to try to find out how life on the earth began. In his experiment, Miller attempted to duplicate the climate and conditions of the early earth. He filled a chamber with water that contained methane, ammonia, water vapor, and hydrogen. Miller then heated the water and added energy in the form of electricity to his system. See Fig. 16-1. Energy, like the lightning of the early earth, is needed to make simple compounds into more complex compounds.

Fig. 16-1

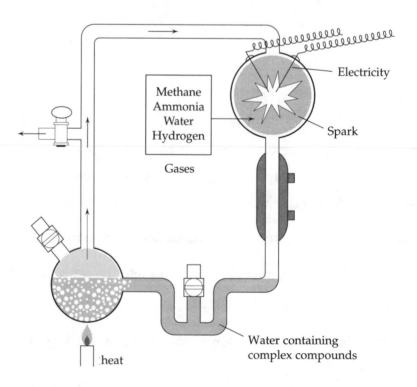

Methane
Ammonia
Water
Hydrogen

Gases

Electricity

Spark

heat

Water containing
complex compounds

Compounds (KAHM-powndz) are chemicals that join together in certain, consistent ways. Many different compounds make up the cells of all living things. **Organic compounds** (awr-GAN-ihk KAHM-powndz) are compounds that contain carbon.

Miller waited to see what happened to his experiment. At the end of one week, he discovered organic compounds called amino acids in the water. Amino acids are complex compounds that serve as the building blocks of proteins. Miller's experiment showed that complex compounds found in living things could sometimes be made outside of cells.

1. What did Miller's experiment show? _____

_____

_____

After Miller showed that complex compounds found in living cells could be made in the lab, other scientists tried to duplicate his results. In other laboratory experiments, scientists were able to produce other organic compounds, including sugars and fatty acids. They did this by combining the four main elements found in the atmosphere of the early earth: carbon, hydrogen, oxygen, and nitrogen. Scientists also showed that some of these large organic compounds react with each other to make still larger compounds. This process is similar to what happens inside cells.

The Early Earth. Most scientists agree that the early earth was much different from the earth today. Most of the compounds found in living things were not present when the earth and solar system formed. The early earth was covered with water warmed by the earth itself and by the sun. Steam from the seas formed clouds, which in turn produced violent thunderstorms. The atmosphere of the early earth was made up of ammonia, water vapor, hydrogen, and methane. These gases were also dissolved in the ocean.

Origins of Life. Some scientists think that lightning from the violent storms of the early earth provided energy to split the molecules of ammonia, water vapor, hydrogen, and methane, in the early earth's atmosphere. The divided molecules recombined to form small organic compounds. These compounds collected in shallow pools, forming a kind of "organic soup." Some of the simple compounds in the "soup" reacted with other compounds to form larger organic compounds. Eventually these large organic compounds began to replicate. The ability of molecules to copy themselves is necessary for life as we know it.

Some of the first simple cells on the earth gave off oxygen and carbon dioxide that collected in the atmosphere. Once these gases were available, living things began to evolve rapidly.

2. What was the early earth like? _____

_____

TAKE ANOTHER LOOK

Study Fig. 16-2 to see how Miller's experiment reflected conditions on the early earth.

Fig. 16-2

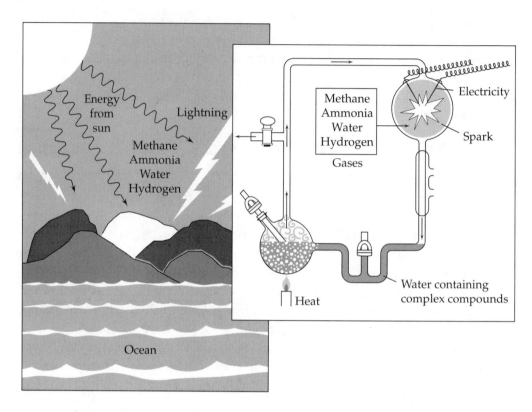

Check Your Understanding

3. In your own words, write a paragraph describing Miller's experiment. Explain how each part of the experiment modeled conditions of the early earth.

_____

_____

_____

_____

_____

_____

_____

_____

_____

_____

What Do You Know?

4. In one or two sentences, explain how life on the earth might have begun.

_____

_____

_____

_____

5. Miller showed that complex compounds might have been formed in the early ocean. How could these compounds form cells?

_____

_____

_____

_____

6. Imagine that humans could travel back in time to the early earth. Would they be able to survive? Why or why not?

_____

_____

_____

_____

Summary

- Differences which make an organism better suited to its environment may help the organism survive and reproduce. This process is called natural selection or survival of the fittest.

- Darwin suggested that as a result of natural selection, a group of living things can change so much that they evolve into a new species.

- One way scientists learn about living things from the past is by studying fossils. Fossil studies support the idea that species of today have common ancestors.

- Scientists have long wondered how life began. Experiments which combined gases that could have been found on the earth billions of years ago have shown that these gases may have formed the compounds needed to make the cells of living things.

For Your Portfolio

1. Recently, the remains of a human who lived thousands of years ago were found buried in a glacier near the borders of Austria and Italy. This fossil is special because it is of a complete human, not just a few bones. It is the most complete fossil of an ancient human ever found. This fossil is referred to as the Ice Man. The Ice Man was protected from the movement of the glacier because he was wedged between rocks while the glacier flowed above him. Find out how the Ice Man was discovered and what scientists have learned from this early human. Look up information about the Ice Man and get pictures to share with your class. Find out about the tools he used, the clothes he wore, and other details about his daily life. Give an oral report of your findings.

2. Go to a museum of natural history. Look at the displays of animals from the last Ice Age. Do any of these ancient animals remind you of animals that are alive today? Find out what kinds of ancient animals used to live in your part of the country. Report your findings to the class.

3. Make a survey of ten dinosaurs. Create one or more posters showing the differences among them. On your poster, write their scientific names, the places where their remains have been found, and the time period when they lived.

4. Different theories have been developed about why dinosaurs died so quickly after living on the earth for millions of years. Research each theory. Then explain to the class which theory you most strongly support and the reasons for your decision.

5. Make a time line of evolutionary time periods. Show the evolution of life, from when life first appeared on the earth to the present. Use books from the library containing evolution charts to help you make your time line.

6. Learn more about the experiment performed by Stanley Miller. Make a poster that includes a picture which shows how gases and energy might have produced the first compounds that make up life.

7. Comparative anatomy is the study of the structures of living things. Find a book on comparative anatomy. Write a report about how mammals of different species are similar to each other. Include a discussion of the animals that are believed to be the ancestors of mammals.

Match the terms in Column A with their definition in Column B.

Column A

_____ 1. a living thing of the past, from which other living things evolved

_____ 2. development of traits that make an organism better able to live in its environment

_____ 3. chemicals joined together in a specific, consistent way

_____ 4. group of living things that can mate with each other and produce young that can also produce young

_____ 5. process by which organisms with certain traits survive and reproduce

_____ 6. the preserved remains or traces of a once-living thing

_____ 7. process by which living things change over time

Column B

a. adaptation

b. natural selection

c. species

d. evolution

e. fossil

f. ancestor

g. compounds

Fill in the blanks.

8. The members of a population have many different traits. The traits that are the most helpful are _____ .

9. Another term for natural selection is _____.

10. In general, life evolved from very _____ living things to those that are more complex.

11. As a population of living things becomes different from others of the same kind, it may evolve into a new _____.

12. Because living things decay after they die, fossils are often made of only the remaining _____ parts.

13. Scientists can tell if different animals are related by looking at _____ structures in animals.

Answer one of the following questions.

14. In a paragraph, describe the events that take place in natural selection.

15. Describe how the compounds that make up living things may have appeared on the earth.

Microbes and Fungi

Have you ever walked through a forest and noticed mushrooms growing on the forest floor? Have you ever found mushrooms growing in your yard after a big rainstorm? You might have even seen mushrooms growing in a flower pot at home. Have you ever asked yourself what a mushroom is? Why do they grow in such damp areas?

Mushrooms belong to a group of living things called fungi. Fungi grow almost everywhere: on plants and animals, in soil, and even in water.

Many kinds of fungi are helpful. For example, fungi are often eaten as food. You've probably eaten mushrooms on a pizza. Fungi are also used to make breads and some kinds of cheeses. Some fungi are used to make medicine. Fungi are very important to the environment. They are decomposers. They break down dead organisms into materials that can be reused by other living things.

Lesson 17 Viruses

People often visit a doctor when they have a sore throat. The nurse may take a throat culture to find out what is causing the throat to become red and sore. The culture is then grown in a medical lab. If the culture shows that a virus is causing the sore throat, not much can be done to make it better. Viruses cause illnesses such as colds, flu, sore throat, mumps, and chicken pox.

Viruses. A **virus** (VY-ruhs) is a noncellular organism that is made up of genetic material and protein. Some scientists think that viruses evolved from cell organelles that may have found a way to live and reproduce outside of cells.

Fig. 17-1

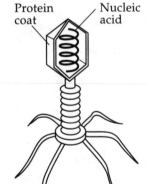

Protein coat   Nucleic acid

Fig. 17-1 shows that viruses are made up of two main parts. A protein coat makes an outer shell. Inside the shell is a nucleic acid, DNA, or RNA. The nucleic acid contains instructions for making more viruses. The protein coat surrounding the nucleic acid protects the virus.

 1. What is a virus? _____

_____

_____

Scientists have a difficult time classifying viruses. Viruses have some, but not all, of the traits of other living organisms. For example, viruses are made up of proteins and nucleic acids, two substances found in all living cells. All living organisms are made up of one or more cells. Viruses, however, do not have a cell structure. For example, they lack a cell membrane and a nucleus.

Viral reproduction. Viruses can reproduce only when inside the cells of living organisms. **Reproduction** (ree-pruh-DUK-shun) is the process of making more of the same kind.

To reproduce, a virus must first contact a living cell. The virus attaches itself to the cell wall. The virus then produces a chemical that breaks down the cell wall. The nucleic acid of the virus invades the cell through the cell wall. The virus leaves behind its empty protein coat. Inside the cell, the viral nucleic acid directs the cell to make new viruses. The cell eventually bursts open and releases the new viruses. As many as 300 viruses may be produced inside one cell. Fig. 17-2 shows how a virus reproduces.

Fig. 17-2

(1) Virus attaches itself to cell wall.

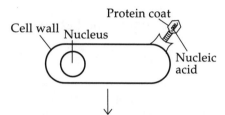

(2) Nucleic acid from the virus enters cell.

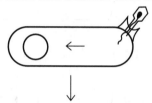

(3) Nucleic acid of virus directs cell to make new virus parts.

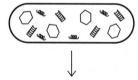

(4) Virus parts are put together, making copies of the virus.

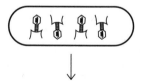

(5) Cell bursts open and viruses are released.

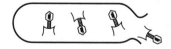

Fig. 17-3 shows the traits of viruses and other living things. The portion of the circles that overlap show the traits viruses share with other living things.

Fig. 17-3

- Lack a cell structure
- Do not grow
- Do not use energy
- Can reproduce only when inside living cells

- Contain nucleic acid and protein
- Respond to the environment
- Evolve

- Composed of one or more cells
- Grow
- Use energy
- Reproduce

Traits of viruses   **Traits of other living things**

Check Your Understanding

Write a sentence explaining the connection between each pair of words.

2. virus, nucleus _____

_____

3. viral reproduction, living cell _____

_____

4. Use numbers 1–5 to put the following steps of viral reproduction in the correct order.

_____ Nucleic acid from the virus enters the cell.

_____ Cell bursts open and viruses are released.

_____ Virus attaches itself to cell wall.

_____ Nucleic acid of virus directs cell to make new virus parts.

_____ Virus parts are put together, making many copies of the virus.

5. In the space below, draw the steps showing reproduction of a virus.

Fill in the blanks with the correct word.

6. A virus, unlike other living things, is not made up of one or more

   _____.

7. The trait that a virus shares with other living things is the ability to

   _____.

---

8. What are the two main parts of a virus? _____

   _____

9. Describe how viruses differ from other living things. _____

   _____

   _____

   _____

10. Describe how viruses are like other living things. _____

    _____

    _____

    _____

11. What is one way viruses are harmful to people? _____

    _____

12. Biology is the study of living things. Why do you think viruses are

    discussed in biology books? _____

    _____

    _____

    _____

What Do You Know?

Key Words

bacteria:	single-celled living things that do not have a nucleus
nucleus:	cell structure that controls most cells and that is not present in bacteria
capsule:	layer outside the cell wall that protects the bacteria
flagella:	long, whiplike fibers that help some types of cells move
microbes:	organisms that can be seen only through a microscope
hosts:	organisms that contain other organisms inside them
blue-green bacteria:	bacteria that make their own food by photosynthesis

KEY IDEAS

Bacteria are the simplest types of living things. All bacteria are made up of a single cell. Bacteria do not have structures that are found in other types of cells. For example, a bacterial cell does not have a nucleus.

Bacteria were the first types of cells to evolve billions of years ago. Today, there are more bacteria on the earth than any other types of living things. Bacteria live almost everywhere: in water, in air, and in soil. In fact, a tiny speck of soil can hold billions of bacteria. Bacteria also live in your mouth, on your hands, and on other parts of your body.

Fig. 18-1

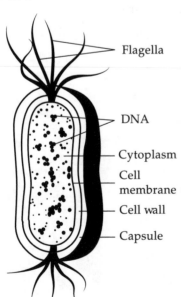

Flagella

DNA

Cytoplasm

Cell membrane

Cell wall

Capsule

Structure of Bacteria. Bacteria (bak-TIR-ee-uh) are single-celled living things. Unlike other types of cells, a bacterium has no **nucleus** (NOO-klee-uhs), the structure that controls a cell. In most cells, DNA is located inside the nucleus. In bacteria, DNA is scattered throughout the cell.

Most bacteria have the same structure. Their cytoplasm is surrounded by a cell membrane. The cell membrane is surrounded on the outside by a cell wall that holds the bacterium together and gives it shape. The cell wall is made up of amino acids and sugars. Some bacteria have another layer outside their cell wall. This layer is called the capsule. Usually made up of a thick jelly-like material, the **capsule** (KAP-suhl) protects the bacteria. Many bacteria also have long, whiplike fibers called **flagella** (fla-JEHL-uh) that help them move. Find each of these structures in Fig. 18-1.

1. What are bacteria? _____

_____

Size and Shape of Bacteria. Bacteria are so small that more than 300,000 of them would fit on the period at the end of this sentence. Very small organisms, like bacteria, are called **microbes** because they can be seen only through a microscope. The bacterium in Fig. 18-1 is about 15,000 times its actual size.

Bacteria have three basic shapes: ball, rod, and spiral. The three shapes are shown in Fig. 18-2.

Fig. 18-2

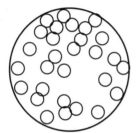 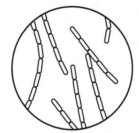 

Ball-shaped bacteria   Rod-shaped bacteria   Spiral-shaped bacteria

Sometimes bacterial cells group together. Ball-shaped bacteria often form pairs or clumps. Rod-shaped bacteria usually link up end-to-end, forming long chains. Spiral-shaped bacteria may be hundreds of times larger than other types of bacteria. They do not usually group together.

 2. What are the three shapes of bacteria? _____

_____

Kinds of Bacteria. There are many different species of bacteria. Bacteria may be classified by their shape and by the way they get energy. Most bacteria cannot make their own food. They must break down other matter to get food. Bacteria that break down dead organisms are one type of bacteria that cannot make their own food. Many of these kinds of bacteria live in soil. Other bacteria live inside animals and plants and get their food from their hosts. **Hosts** (hohsts) are organisms that contain other organisms inside them.

Some kinds of bacteria can make their own food. Like plants, **blue-green bacteria** (BLOO-GREEN bak-TIR-ee-uh) make their own food by a process called photosynthesis. Blue-green bacteria grow almost anywhere there is water: in ponds, in the ocean, and in moist soil. You may have seen blue-green bacteria floating at the top of a still pond.

3. How do blue-green bacteria differ from other types of bacteria?

_____

_____

Bacteria are very small single-celled living things, but viruses are even smaller. Fig. 18-3 shows the size difference between a cell nucleus, a bacterium, and a virus. Each of these structures is really much smaller than shown.

Fig. 18-3

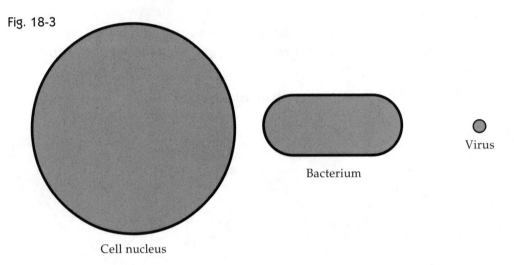

Cell nucleus

Bacterium

Virus

Check Your Understanding

Write a sentence explaining the connection between each pair of words.

4. bacteria, nucleus _____

_____

5. cell wall, capsule _____

_____

6. blue-green bacteria, plants _____

_____

Fig. 18-4

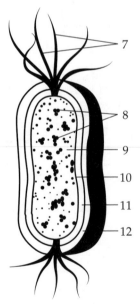

On the lines provided write the names of the bacterial cell structures shown in Fig. 18-4.

7. _____   **10.** _____

8. _____   **11.** _____

9. _____   **12.** _____

13. In the space below, draw and label the three main shapes of bacterial cells.

What Do You Know?

14. How is a bacterial cell different from other types of cells?

_____

_____

_____

15. What are two ways in which bacteria are classified?

_____

_____

_____

16. What is one way in which bacteria get energy?

_____

_____

_____

17. Bacteria were the first living things on the earth. Today, there are more bacteria on the earth than any other type of living thing. Why do you think there are so many bacteria?

_____

_____

_____

19 The Importance of Viruses and Bacteria

Key Words

decomposer:	living thing that breaks down organisms into materials that can be reused by other living things
nitrogen-fixing bacteria:	bacteria that take nitrogen from the air and form nitrogen compounds
antibiotic:	drug used to treat diseases caused by bacteria
vaccine:	drug that helps the body protect itself from disease

Key Ideas

Viruses and bacteria can impact other organisms because viruses and bacteria can cause disease. But some types of bacteria are so important that other living things could not survive without them.

What do you think of when you hear the word bacteria? Many people think of germs and illness. Many types of bacteria do cause disease or even death. But some types of bacteria are so important that other living things would die without them. One kind of bacteria lives inside your body and helps you digest food. Other kinds of bacteria are also useful. For example, certain foods, such as yogurt, are made using bacteria.

Helpful Bacteria. One of the most important jobs of bacteria is to break down dead organisms. Some bacteria are decomposers. A **decomposer** (dee-kuhm-POHS-er) is a living thing that breaks down dead organisms into materials that can be reused by other living things. Think about walking through a forest. Leaves, branches, and other plant matter cover the ground. Without bacteria and other decomposers, there would be so much dead matter piled up that you would not be able to walk between the trees.

 1. What is a decomposer? _____

_____

Another type of bacteria allows plants to grow. Plants need nitrogen to grow. Although nitrogen is present in the air, it is not in a form that plants can use. Plants can use only nitrogen compounds. **Nitrogen-fixing bacteria** (NY-truh-juhn-FIKS-ing bak-TIR-ee-uh) form nitrogen compounds from nitrogen in the air. These nitrogen-fixing bacteria live in soil and in the roots of some types of plants. See Fig.19-1.

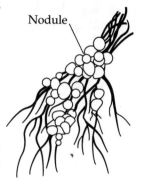

 2. How do nitrogen-fixing bacteria help plants to grow?

_____

_____

Harmful Bacteria. While some kinds of bacteria are helpful, others are harmful. Some types of bacteria cause food poisoning. These bacteria can live in food that has not been correctly prepared or stored.

Other kinds of bacteria can cause serious diseases such as tetanus, scarlet fever, whooping cough, strep throat, or tuberculosis. These diseases easily spread from person to person. In the past, diseases caused by bacteria were hard to prevent and treat. But today drugs called **antibiotics** (an-ty-by-AHT-ihks) are used to treat many diseases caused by bacteria. Most antibiotics work by keeping the bacteria from growing. Some prevent the bacterial cell wall from forming.

 3. What is an antibiotic? _____

_____

Viral Disease. Some viruses also cause disease. Viral diseases include the common cold, flu, measles, mumps, and chicken pox. Compared to diseases caused by bacteria, those caused by viruses are much harder to prevent and treat. Antibiotics do not work against viral diseases. But many medicines and vaccines have been developed that do control viral diseases. A **vaccine** (vak-SEEN) is a drug that helps the body protect itself from infection by a virus. However, some viral diseases, such as AIDS, currently have no vaccine nor effective treatment.

Viruses cause disease in two ways. First, when the nucleic acid of a virus gets inside a cell, it takes over the cell. The cell can no longer do what it is supposed to. Instead, it follows the directions of the virus. The second way a virus causes disease is by reproducing. After many new copies of a virus form inside a cell, the new viruses burst out of the cell, and the cell is destroyed.

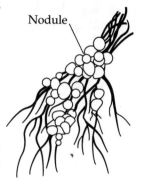
Fig. 19-1

Nitrogen-fixing bacteria live in nodules on the roots of some plants.

Nodule

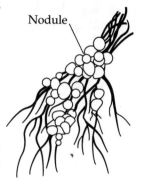

Nitrogen-fixing bacteria change nitrogen from the air into a form plants can use. When plants die, the nitrogen stays in their cells. Decomposers break down the plant cells and release the nitrogen into the air and soil. Two different types of bacteria, nitrogen-fixing bacteria and decomposers, make nitrogen available to plants. Together these bacteria recycle nitrogen, as shown in Fig. 19-2.

Fig. 19-2

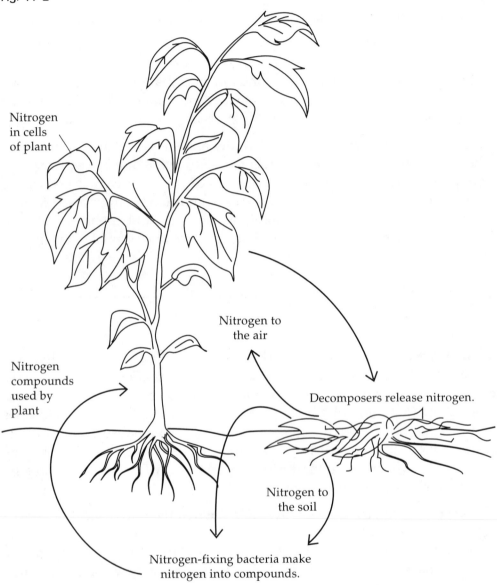

Nitrogen in cells of plant

Nitrogen to the air

Nitrogen compounds used by plant

Decomposers release nitrogen.

Nitrogen to the soil

Nitrogen-fixing bacteria make nitrogen into compounds.

Complete the paragraph by adding the correct words.

One way bacteria are helpful is by breaking down dead organisms. Bacteria that do this are called **(4)**_____. Nitrogen-fixing bacteria form nitrogen compounds that can be used by **(5)**_____. Harmful bacteria can cause **(6)**_____. Drugs used to treat bacterial infections are called **(7)**_____. A **(8)**_____ is a drug used to protect against infection by a virus.

What Do You Know?

9. What are two ways in which bacteria are helpful? _____
    _____
    _____
    _____

10. Why are decomposers important? _____
    _____
    _____

11. What do nitrogen-fixing bacteria do? _____
    _____
    _____

12. What does a vaccine do? _____
    _____
    _____

13. What can antibiotics do? What can they not do?
    _____
    _____

14. Explain two ways viruses cause diseases._____
    _____
    _____
    _____

Key Words

protist:	single-celled living thing that is more complex than a bacteria
chloroplast:	structure in which a plant or protist cell uses light energy and matter to make food
euglena:	plantlike protist that moves with a flagellum
paramecium:	animal-like protist that moves with cilia
cilia:	tiny "hairs" on the outside of some cells that push the cell through water
amoeba:	animal-like protist that moves by changing its shape

KEY IDEAS

Like bacteria, most protists are microbes that are made up of only one cell. The cells of protists are more complex and varied than bacterial cells.

Bacteria and viruses are not the only causes of disease. Diseases are also caused by some protists.

Protists. A **protist** (PROH-tist) is a single-celled living thing that is more complex than a bacterium. The first protists evolved from bacteria more than one billion years ago. Long ago, some bacterial cells may have taken in other bacteria. These bacteria eventually became structures within the larger bacterial cell. Over time, this bacterial cell and its structures evolved into a protist.

For example, a bacterium may have surrounded the cell of a blue-green bacterium. The blue-green bacterium, in turn, evolved into a chloroplast. A **chloroplast** (KLAWR-oh-plast) is a cell structure in which light energy and matter are used to make food. Chloroplasts are found in food-making protists and plant cells. Chloroplasts and other cell structures make protists more complex than bacteria.

 1. What is a chloroplast? _____

_____

Protists can be divided into two main groups. One group makes its own food, while the other group does not. These two groups are sometimes called plantlike protists and animal-like protists.

Plantlike Protists. The **euglena** (yoo-GLEH-nah) is a plantlike protist. See Fig. 20-1. The nucleus of the euglena directs the cell. Chloroplasts make food, which is stored in starch granules.

The euglena is called a plantlike protist because it can make food. However, it also has animal traits. It can move from place to place. The flagellum is a long, whiplike structure that helps the euglena move. The euglena has a sense organ called an eye-spot. An eye-spot senses light and dark. Light is needed to make food, so it is important for the euglena to be in an area with light. It also lacks the cell wall found in plant cells.

Fig. 20-1

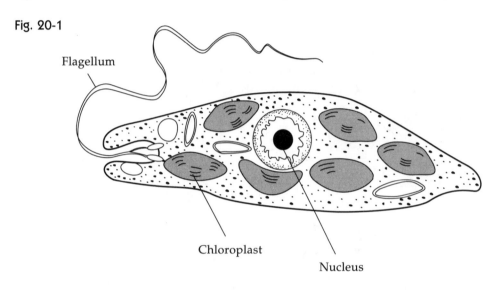

Flagellum

Chloroplast

Nucleus

 2. How does a euglena find and move into an area with light?

_____

_____

_____

Animal-like protists. Animal-like protists do not have chloroplasts. Therefore, they cannot make their own food. One type of animal-like protist is the **paramecium** (pa-ruh-MEE-see-uhm), shown in Fig. 20-2. Notice the tiny "hairs" on the outside of the paramecium. Like oars on a rowboat, these tiny hairs, or **cilia** (SIL-ee-uh), push the cell through water.

The paramecium moves from place to place and takes in food as it goes. Food enters an oral groove and is carried through the cell in bubbles called food vacuoles. Food moves out of the cell through an anal pore.

One type of animal-like protist that does not have a flagellum nor cilia is an **amoeba** (uh-MEE-buh), shown in Fig 20-3. This protist moves by changing its shape and flowing from place to place.

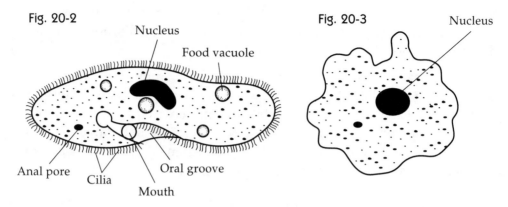

Fig. 20-2

Nucleus

Food vacuole

Anal pore

Cilia

Mouth

Oral groove

Fig. 20-3

Nucleus

Fig. 20-4 shows how more than one type of bacteria evolved into protists, and how protists evolved into many different types.

Fig. 20-4

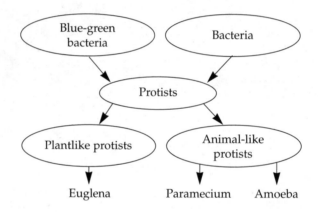

Blue-green bacteria

Bacteria

Protists

Plantlike protists

Animal-like protists

Euglena

Paramecium

Amoeba

Check Your Understanding

Write a sentence explaining the connection between each group of words.

3. protist, complex _____

_____

4. chloroplast, food _____

_____

5. cilia, flagellum _____

_____

6. paramecium, euglena, amoeba _____

_____

_____

Label the structures of the euglena shown in Fig. 20-5.

Fig. 20-5

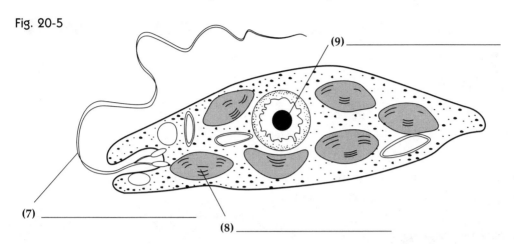

(9) _____

(7) _____

(8) _____

What Do You Know?

10. In your own words, describe a protist. How do protists differ from bacteria? _____
_____
_____

11. What is one way plantlike protists differ from animal-like protists?
_____
_____

12. In what ways is a euglena both plantlike and animal-like?
_____
_____
_____
_____

13. How does a paramecium differ from a euglena?
_____
_____
_____
_____

Fungi

Key Words

fungi:	living things that absorb food from living or dead things
hyphae:	branching tubes that often grow in a tangled mass and make up the main part of fungi
fruiting body:	part of fungi used in reproduction; often the only part of fungi that can be seen

KEY IDEAS

Fungi are a group of living things that share traits with both plants and animals. Although we may not be aware of their presence, fungi are as common as plants and animals.

You may have seen or eaten fungi and not have known it. Fungi include mushrooms, molds, and yeasts. For thousands of years, people have been using yeasts to make bread and to brew beer.

Traits of fungi. Fungi (FUN-geye) are living things that absorb food from living or dead things. You may have seen tiny mushrooms in damp earth after a rain shower. Like plants, some fungi grow in the ground and do not move from place to place. Fungi are like plants in another way. The cells of fungi have cell walls. For these reasons, fungi were once classified as plants. But fungi do not share the main trait of plants. Unlike plants, fungi cannot make their own food.

Like animals, fungi must take in and break down food. However, fungi differ from most animals because fungi break down their food before they absorb it. For example, fungi living on bread digest the bread and then absorb the digested food. Fungi are so different from other types of living things that they are now classified in their own kingdom.

 1. Why are fungi no longer classified as plants? _____

_____

Structure of Fungi. There are many types of fungi. Some are tiny single-celled organisms. Others are large organisms, such as the mushrooms used in cooking But all fungi share some common traits. Most fungi are made up of branching tubes called **hyphae** (HY-fee). The hyphae often grow tangled together in a mass that makes up the largest part of fungi. Sometimes you can see a mass of hyphae growing on the surface of a food. In other cases, hyphae are hidden under the food's surface.

Often, the only part of the fungi you can see are fruiting bodies. **Fruiting bodies** (FROOT-ihng BAHD-ees) are the parts of fungi used in reproduction. Look at the structure of two types of fungi shown in Fig. 21-1. Find the hyphae and fruiting body in each.

Helpful Fungi. Many fungi are helpful. Along with bacteria, fungi are important decomposers. Decomposers break down dead things and release matter that can be used by other living things.

Some fungi, such as mushrooms, are an important source of food. Mushrooms are a good source of vitamins and minerals. Other types of fungi are used as medicines. For example, the type of fungus that grows on the skin of an orange is used to make the antibiotic penicillin. Penicillin is used to treat many diseases caused by bacteria.

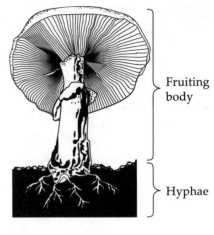

Fruiting body

Hyphae

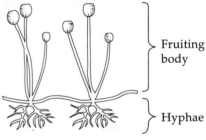

Fruiting body

Hyphae

Fig. 21-1

For thousands of years, people have been using yeast, a tiny one-celled fungus, to make bread. Yeast takes in sugar as energy. As yeast uses sugar, the yeast gives off carbon dioxide gas that makes bread dough rise. Yeasts are also used to make beer and some kinds of cheese.

 2. What are some examples of helpful fungi? _____

_____

_____

Harmful Fungi. Many types of fungi are harmful. Fungi can cause diseases in humans. One type of fungus causes athlete's foot, a disease in which the skin of the feet becomes itchy and red. Athlete's foot is easy to get if your feet stay damp. Fungi that cause athlete's foot and other diseases often live where it is warm, damp, and dark.

Fungi are harmful in other ways, too. Some mushrooms, for example, are poisonous. If you eat a poisonous mushroom, you could become very ill. Some fungi, such as those that cause Dutch elm disease, attack and kill plants. Before Dutch elm disease spread and destroyed many of these plants, elm trees were common in most parts of the United States.

Many kinds of fungi grow on foods such as fruits, vegetables, cheeses, and breads. Such fungi change the taste and smell of the food and eventually cause the food to rot.

Fig. 21-2 shows the traits that fungi share along with plants, animals, and protists.

Fig. 21-2

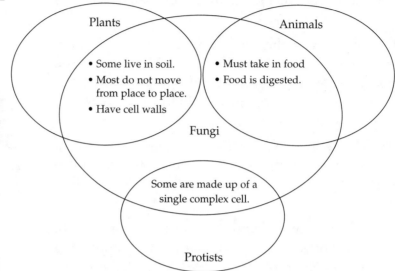

Check Your Understanding

Write a sentence explaining the connection between each pair of words.

3. fungi, absorb _____

_____

4. hyphae, tubes _____

_____

5. fruiting body, reproduction _____

_____

6. In the space below, draw and label two main parts of any kind of fungus.

7. In what ways are fungi like plants? In what ways are they different?

_____

_____

_____

_____

8. In what ways are fungi like animals? _____

_____

_____

9. Describe some harmful fungi. _____

_____

_____

10. Explain why yeasts are important. _____

_____

_____

_____

_____

11. Think about a forest from which all fungi have been removed. Describe how the forest will change without fungi. _____

_____

_____

_____

_____

Summary

- Viruses are made up of a nucleic acid and a protein. Viruses are not made up of cells.

- Viruses can reproduce. However, viruses can reproduce only when inside other living things.

- Bacteria are made up of a single cell with only a few of the structures found in more complex cells.

- Blue-green bacteria differ from most other bacteria because blue-green bacteria can make their own food.

- Viruses and bacteria affect other living things. Many cause diseases.

- Other living things could not survive without some types of bacteria. Decomposers break down dead organisms. Nitrogen-fixing bacteria make nitrogen into a form that plants can use.

- Protists are mostly single-celled living things that evolved from bacteria and blue-green bacteria.

- Protists have a complex cell structure, much like the cells of plants or animals.

- Protists may have traits of plants, of animals, or of both.

- Fungi are living things that share some traits with plants, animals, and protists.

- Some fungi can have harmful effects. Other fungi are very helpful and are used to make certain foods and medicines.

For Your Portfolio

1. Have you ever left a glass of milk on the kitchen counter? The milk may have turned into a solid. What caused this change? Look up a recipe for yogurt. Follow the recipe. Why do you think milk is one of the ingredients in the recipe?

2. Go to the library and find books about how cheese is made. Make a poster that shows the steps in the process. Get your teacher's and your parents' permission to bring samples of different types of cheeses to class. Tell your classmates how each kind of cheese was made.

3. What is pasteurization? Why is it important? On whose name is this word based? Use reference books to find out about the history of pasteurization. Share your results with your class.

4. Go to the library or the school nurse to find out about common diseases that are caused by viruses, bacteria, or protists. Find out as much as you can about one of the diseases. Make a poster about the disease and share your results with your classmates.

5. Go to your library or to a local health clinic to find out as much as you can about HIV. What is HIV? How does it spread? What can be done to prevent its spread? What is AIDS, and who can get it? What is the relationship between HIV and AIDS? Why is AIDS such a difficult disease to control? Report your findings to your class.

6. Find out about drug-resistant tuberculosis. Why do some diseases become drug resistant? What can be done to solve the problem? Go to the library and find articles in magazines and newspapers that discuss the issue. Report your findings to your class.

7. Go to the produce section of a large grocery store in your town. Find the mushrooms. What kinds of mushrooms are there? Use a key about fungi to learn the scientific name of each mushroom you observed. Display the mushrooms for your class.

8. Experiment with yeast. Add some yeast to warm water, set it aside, and watch what happens. If you have someone to help you, try making bread with dry yeast. Make many small batches of dough. Compare the results when you change the temperature at which you prepare the yeast. Which temperature works best? Why?

In the space provided, write the letter of the correct term for each definition below.

_____ 1. noncellular organisms made up of genetic material and protein

_____ 2. process of making more of the same kind

_____ 3. single-celled living things that lack a nucleus

_____ 4. cell structure that controls most cells and is not present in bacteria

_____ 5. bacteria that make their own food, similar to the way in which plants make food

_____ 6. living things that break down dead matter into simpler materials that can be reused by other living things

_____ 7. bacteria that take nitrogen from the air and form nitrogen compounds that can be used by plants

_____ 8. a living thing made up of a single cell that is more complex than a bacterial cell.

_____ 9. plantlike protist that moves with a flagellum

_____ 10. long, whiplike structure that helps some types of cells move from place to place

_____ 11. tiny "hairs" on the outside of some cells that push the cell through water

_____ 12. animal-like protist that moves by changing its shape

_____ 13. part of fungi used in reproduction and often the only part that can be seen

a. cilia

b. fruiting body

c. virus

d. decomposers

e. nucleus

f. protist

g. flagellum

h. blue-green bacteria

i. reproduction

j. nitrogen-fixing bacteria

k. bacteria

l. euglena

m. amoeba

Complete the following sentences.

14. Viruses can _____ only when inside the cells of living organisms.

15. Compared to bacteria, protists have a _____ cell structure.

16. Fungi share traits with _____.

Answer one of the following questions.

17. In a short essay, name two kinds of decomposers and explain why decomposers are important.

18. Draw a paramecium and label its main parts.

Plant Life

Have you ever wondered what plant part you are eating when you eat a salad? The main ingredient in most salads is lettuce. The part of the lettuce plant you eat is the leaf. Other foods you eat for their leaves include cabbage and spinach. The leaves make food by the process of photosynthesis.

Sometimes a salad might contain carrots, tomatoes, and celery. Carrots are roots. Roots anchor a plant in the soil and take water and other nutrients needed by the plant from the soil. Beets and radishes are other foods that are roots.

What about the tomato? You might think of a tomato as a vegetable, but it is really a fruit. A fruit is a special plant structure that protects one or more seeds. Seeds contain tiny plants and their food inside a protective outer coat. Can you think of other fruits most people consider to be vegetables? You might have guessed cucumbers, zucchini, pumpkins, and other kinds of squash.

The celery in your salad is a plant stem. The stem carries water and other nutrients to and from the roots and leaves of a plant. Another kind of stem you eat is an underground stem—the potato.

The leaves, roots, stems, seeds, and fruits of a plant are all eaten as food. They also help the plant grow and survive in its environment.

Ferns and Mosses

Key Words

moss:	type of plant that reproduces by spores and does not have a vascular system or true roots
vascular system:	system of tubes that carries water and other materials throughout a plant
fern:	type of plant that reproduces by spores and has a vascular system, true roots, and true leaves
spores:	special cells with which some living things, such as mosses and ferns, reproduce

KEY IDEAS

Mosses are plants that lack a vascular system and other structures found in higher plants. A fern is a type of higher plant that has a vascular system, true roots, and true leaves. Mosses and ferns reproduce by spores.

Have you ever noticed small, fuzzy green plants growing in damp, shady areas? The plants may have looked more like a green mat than a clump of plants growing together. Most likely, the plants were mosses. Mosses often live in shady areas on the sides of trees, on rocks and fallen logs, or between sidewalk cracks.

Mosses. A **moss** (maws) is a type of plant that does not have a vascular system. A **vascular system** (VAS-kyuh-luhr SIHS-tuhm) is a system of tissue, or tubes, that transports water and other materials throughout a plant. In mosses, water flows directly and slowly from cell to cell by diffusion. Water cannot travel very far or very fast in this way. Because water moves directly from cell to cell, most mosses grow only a few inches tall.

Mosses lack many structures found in other plants. For example, mosses do not have roots that reach down into the soil and bring water up to the plant. Because they lack roots, most mosses live in moist areas. Mosses also need a constant supply of water to reproduce.

 1. Why do mosses live in moist, damp areas?

_____

_____

Ferns. A **fern** (fern) is a type of plant that reproduces by spores and has a vascular system, true roots, and true leaves. Because it has a vascular system, a fern is considered to be a higher plant. Ferns can grow taller than mosses because a fern's vascular system carries nutrients and water quickly from the soil to the leaves. In fact, during the time of the dinosaurs when the earth's climate was warm and wet, ferns grew as tall as trees. Fern forests covered the earth. In warm, tropical jungles where there is plenty of rain, ferns still grow to be very large.

 2. How do ferns differ from mosses? _____

_____

_____

Reproduction. Ferns and mosses both reproduce, or make young, with spores. **Spores** (spohrz) are special cells from which new plants can grow. If you look on the underside of a fern leaf, you may see rows of black or brown dots. These dots are spore cases. Hundreds of spores may be contained in a single spore case. See Fig. 22-1. When the spores are ready, the cases split open. The tiny spores spill out and the wind carries them away. When a spore lands in a suitable place, it can grow into a new plant.

Fig. 22-1

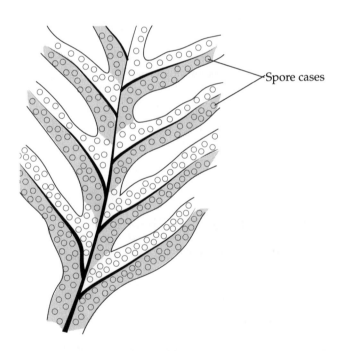

Spore cases

The new fern plant does not look like the plant that released the spores. Instead it looks like a tiny, heart-shaped leaf. This tiny plant releases male sex cells, or sperm, that join with female sex cells, or eggs, to form a new fern plant. The new fern looks just like the one that released the spores. When the new plant has grown, it releases spores that start the cycle again.

Fig. 22-2 shows the structure of a fern and the stages of fern reproduction.

Fig. 22-2

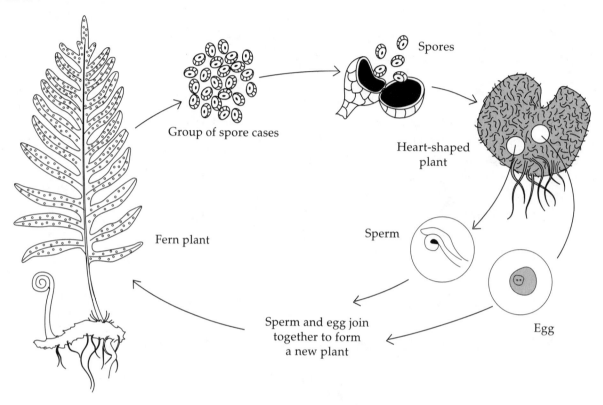

Group of spore cases

Spores

Heart-shaped plant

Sperm

Fern plant

Sperm and egg join together to form a new plant

Egg

Check Your Understanding

Write a sentence explaining the connection between each pair of words.

3. moss, damp environment _____

_____

4. fern, vascular system _____

_____

5. vascular system, water _____

_____

6. spores, reproduce _____

_____

7. Write the letters of the steps of fern reproduction in the correct order. _____ _____ _____ _____

   a. sperm and egg join together   b. spores form
   c. large fern plant grows   d. heart-shaped plant grows

8. In the margin, make a simple drawing of a fern plant. Show where the spores are found.

What Do You Know?

9. What trait do mosses and ferns have in common?

   _____

   _____

10. Why do moss plants usually grow to be only a few inches tall?

    _____

    _____

    _____

11. How does not having roots affect a moss plant?

    _____

    _____

12. What is a major difference between mosses and ferns?

    _____

    _____

13. In your own words, describe what spores do.

    _____

    _____

    _____

14. What do you think are some possible reasons that the earth is no longer covered with giant fern forests?

    _____

    _____

    _____

    _____

Structure and Function of Higher Plants

Key Words

phloem: vascular tissue that carries food made in the leaves to all other parts of the plant

xylem: vascular tissue that carries water and nutrients up from the roots through the stem to the leaves

stomata: pores in leaves through which excess water is released

flowers: special reproductive structures in which seeds form

pollen: grains in which male sex cells, or sperm, form in flowers

ovary: structure of flowers in which egg cells form

fertilization: the joining of sperm and egg

embryo: a developing plant formed through fertilization

seed: special reproductive structure of a plant that contains an embryo and its food

fruit: structure that protects one or more seeds

KEY IDEAS

As plants become more complex, different structures help the plant make food, reproduce, and move materials into, out of, and through the plant.

Fig. 23-1

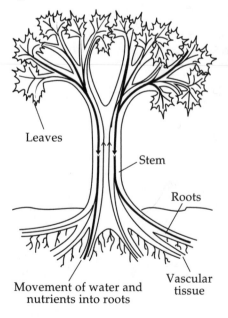

Leaves

Stem

Roots

Vascular tissue

Movement of water and nutrients into roots

If you have ever tried to grow plants indoors, you may have found that they have special needs. Some plants do well in warm rooms with little water; others die when they get too warm or too dry. Each type of plant is best adapted to a certain amount of light, heat, and water. Special structures of a plant help it function in its own environment. These structures help the plant make food, reproduce, and move materials into, out of, and through the plant.

Roots, Leaves, and Stems. All higher plants have roots, leaves, and stems. See Fig. 23-1. Each of these parts has a main function, or job. Roots anchor the plant in soil and bring water and other needed materials to the plant.

Leaves make food for the plant. Food may also be made in other green parts of a plant. However, making food is the main function of leaves.

The stem holds leaves up to the light and connects the leaves to the roots. Vascular tissue in the stem moves materials back and forth from the roots to the leaves. Some plants, such as trees, have woody stems. Other plants have soft stems. The basic function of stems is the same in any type of plant.

 1. What are the three main parts of a higher plant?

_____

_____

Transport. Notice in Fig. 23-1 that the roots, stem, and leaves are connected by the vascular system. This system is made up of tubes that carry materials throughout the plant. One type of tube is made up of phloem. **Phloem** (flohm) is vascular tissue that carries food made in the leaves to other parts of the plant to be used or stored.

Another type of tissue, **xylem** (ZY-luhm), carries water and nutrients up from the roots, through the stem, and into the leaves. The leaves need a large amount of water to make food.

The cells that make up xylem have thick cell walls. When xylem cells die, their cell walls remain in place. New cells form in a circle around the dead cells. Woody stems are made up of many layers of xylem cells. If you have ever looked at the rings in a tree trunk, you were looking at layers of xylem cells. Each year a new ring is made as a new layer of xylem tissue forms. Fig. 23-2 shows xylem and phloem in a stem.

Fig. 23-2

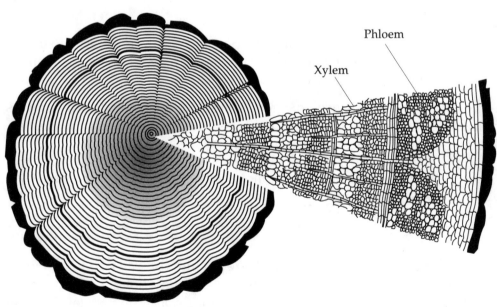

 2. What does phloem do? What does xylem do?

_____

_____

3. How do tree rings form? _____

_____

Photosynthesis. The main function of leaves is to make food. Although plants differ in many ways, they all make their own food. Recall from Unit 1 that plants make food by the process of photosynthesis.

In photosynthesis, the plant takes in water from the soil, carbon dioxide from the air, and energy from sunlight. The plant gives off food and oxygen. Animals depend on the food made by plants. The food made by photosynthesis is a simple sugar that can either be used or stored by the plant. Often the sugar is changed to starch before it is stored. Fig. 23-3 shows the process of photosynthesis.

Fig. 23-3

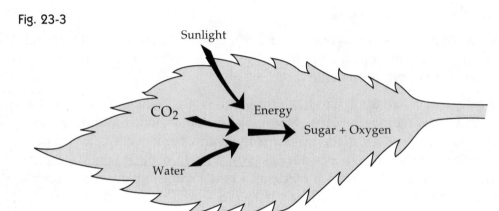

Oxygen is a product of photosynthesis. Some oxygen is released into the air by the plant's leaves. If it were not for plants, there would be no oxygen for humans and other animals to breathe.

Almost all living things need oxygen. Cells take in oxygen for the process called respiration, in which food is broken down and energy is released. Respiration is the opposite of photosynthesis.

 4. What do plants take in for photosynthesis? What do they make by photosynthesis? _____

_____

During photosynthesis, a plant pulls large amounts of water up to its leaves. Excess water exits the leaves through pores, or tiny holes, called **stomata** (STOH-mah-tah). See Fig. 23-4. Stomata (sing., *stoma*) do not stay open all the time. A stoma is opened and closed by two guard cells, one on each side.

When the guard cells are full of water, they swell up and change shape, causing a hole to form between them. When the guard cells lose water, they get limp and the hole disappears. The opening and closing of the stomata allows the plant to give off excess water during photosynthesis and to save water at other times.

Fig. 23-4

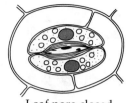

Leaf pore closed

Leaf pore open

Reproduction. Most plants have special structures for reproduction called **flowers** (FLOW-uhrz). In seed plants, the male sex cells, or sperm, are found in **pollen** (PAHL-uhn) grains. Female sex cells, or eggs, are formed in the **ovary** (OH-vuh-ree). The sperm cells inside the pollen grains travel down to the ovary, allowing the sperm and egg to come together. The joining of sperm and egg is called **fertilization** (fuhrt-uhl-ih-ZAY-shuhn). An **embryo** (EHM-bree-oh) is a developing plant that is formed through fertilization.

A **seed** (seed) is a reproductive structure of a plant that contains the embryo and its food. After seeds have formed inside the flower, the flower petals fall off and the ovary becomes larger.

In time the ovary grows into a fruit. The fruit stays attached to the plant until the fruit is ripe. See Fig. 23-5. The **fruit** protects one or more seeds. In order for new plants to grow, seeds must be released from the fruit. When the seeds are released and land in a new location, they may form a new plant.

Fig. 23-5

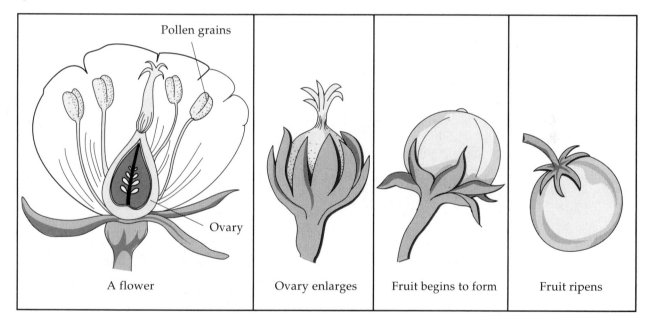

Pollen grains

Ovary

A flower

Ovary enlarges

Fruit begins to form

Fruit ripens

5. How do flowering plants reproduce? _____

_____

_____

TAKE ANOTHER LOOK

In photosynthesis, plants take in carbon dioxide and energy. They make food and oxygen. In respiration, cells take in oxygen and some type of food, most often a sugar. The cells break down food and release energy. Photosynthesis and respiration are summarized in Fig. 23-6.

Fig. 23-6

	CO_2	Water	Sugar	Oxygen	Energy
Photosynthesis	uses	uses	makes	makes	uses light energy
Respiration	makes	makes	uses	uses	releases energy

Check Your Understanding

6. In the spaces on the right, write the letters of the steps of plant reproduction in the correct order.

    a. fruit forms   _____

    b. seeds land in new location   _____

    c. flower forms   _____

    d. embryo forms in ovary   _____

    e. new plant begins to grow   _____

    f. pollen moves to ovary of plant   _____

    g. seeds are released from fruit   _____

    h. petals fall, and ovary gets larger   _____

    i. seed forms in flower   _____

Write a sentence explaining the connection between each pair of words.

7. phloem, xylem _____

    _____

8. photosynthesis, respiration _____

    _____

9. stomata, water _____

    _____

10. pollen, ovary _____

_____

11. flower, fruit _____

_____

What Do You Know?

12. List the three main parts of a higher plant. Describe the main function of each part. _____

_____

_____

13. Describe how stomata open and close. _____

_____

_____

_____

14. Imagine a plant whose stomata could not close. What do you think might happen to this plant?

_____

_____

_____

Gymnosperms and Angiosperms

Key Words

gymnosperms: seed plants whose seeds are usually found inside a cone

conifers: cone-bearing plants with needle-shaped leaves

angiosperms: seed plants whose seeds form inside flowers and are protected by fruits

KEY IDEAS

Gymnosperms and angiosperms are seed plants. Seed plants are the most common type of plant because seeds enable them to reproduce successfully.

Almost everywhere you look, you see plants. From the grass on a baseball field to vegetables in a garden, our world is filled with plants. But what do these plants have in common? They reproduce by seeds. Seed plants are found in so many places because seeds are the best adaptation for plant reproduction.

Seeds. Recall from Lesson 23 that a seed is a special reproductive structure of a plant. Because a seed is quite small, you may think it is very simple. But even the smallest seed holds a young plant and its food. Seeds are wrapped in a hard coat that protects the young plant inside from damage or drying out before the plant starts to grow. Almost everything the young plant needs to start life is inside the seed, as shown in Fig. 24-1.

Fig. 24-1

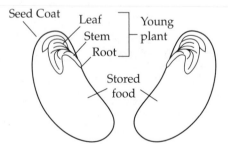

 1. What is inside a seed? _____

 2. Why are seeds the best adaptation for plant reproduction?

_____

Gymnosperms. There are two main types of seed plants. The seed plants that evolved first are called gymnosperms. **Gymnosperms** (JIHM-noh-spermz) are seed plants whose seeds are usually found inside a cone, instead of a flower. The word "gymnosperm" means "naked seed," because the seeds inside a cone are not protected by a fruit.

Most gymnosperms are conifers. **Conifers** (KAHN-uh-fuhrz) are cone-bearing plants with needle-shaped leaves. See Fig. 24-2. Conifers include pine, fir, and spruce trees, and are commonly called evergreens. Some conifers, such as giant redwood trees, are the oldest and largest living things on the earth.

Conifers are well-adapted to live in cold or dry areas. Their leaves are needle-shaped, rather than flat and broad. The special needle shape keeps conifer leaves from drying out. Conifer leaves are also protected by a hard, waxy coating.

Fig. 24-2

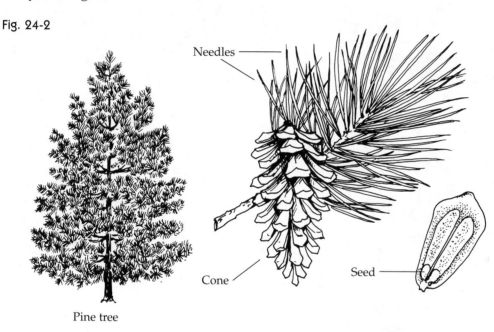

Needles

Cone

Seed

Pine tree

Angiosperms. The most common type of seed plants are the flowering plants, or **angiosperms** (AN-jee-oh-spermz). Their seeds form inside a special reproductive structure called a flower. You may recognize flowering plants, such as roses and daisies, by their large, pretty flowers. But did you know that grasses, oak trees, and clover are also flowering plants? These plants and many others have flowers that are very small. Recall from Lesson 23 that the flower develops into a fruit, which protects one or more seeds. The fruit's protection of the seed is one reason why angiosperms are better adapted to reproduce than gymnosperms. Fruits include apples, pears, tomatoes, and cucumbers. They all contain seeds.

3. **Why are angiosperms better adapted to reproduce than gymnosperms?** _____

_____

Fig. 24-3 shows a variety of the two main types of seed plants: gymnosperms and angiosperms.

Fig. 24-3

Seed Plants

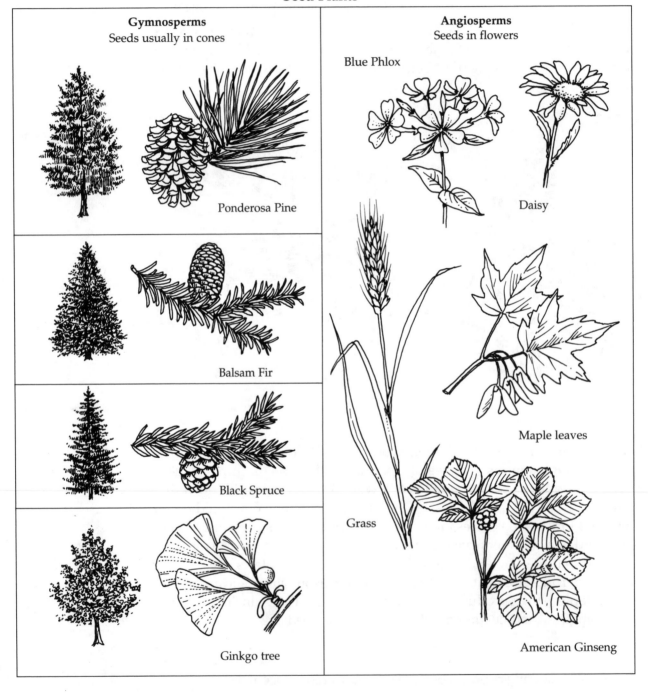

Gymnosperms
Seeds usually in cones

Ponderosa Pine

Balsam Fir

Black Spruce

Ginkgo tree

Angiosperms
Seeds in flowers

Blue Phlox

Daisy

Maple leaves

Grass

American Ginseng

Write a sentence explaining the connection between each pair of words.

4. gymnosperm, angiosperm _____

_____

5. conifer, cone _____

_____

6. cone, flower _____

_____

What Do You Know?

7. How do seeds help seed plants reproduce successfully?

_____

_____

_____

8. Why is the term "naked seed" a good name for a gymnosperm?

_____

_____

9. Why are conifers well-adapted to live in cold or dry areas?

_____

_____

10. Why are there more angiosperms than gymnosperms?

_____

_____

_____

_____

Summary

- A moss is a type of plant that does not have structures to carry water or other materials throughout the plant. As a result, mosses are small and usually live in damp areas.

- Ferns are plants that have a vascular system. A vascular system consists of tubes that carry water and nutrients throughout a plant.

- Ferns and mosses reproduce with special cells called spores.

- Higher plants have three main parts: roots, stems, and leaves.

- Xylem carries water and nutrients up from the roots to other parts of a plant. Phloem carries food from the leaves to other parts of a plant.

- Roots anchor a plant in soil and take in other materials needed by the plant. Stems connect roots to leaves. Leaves make food by photosynthesis.

- Stomata are pores in leaves. Stomata open and close, allowing water to escape or to be held in the plant.

- Sperm and egg cells come together in a flower to form seeds.

- Seed plants are the most common types of plants and are the best adapted for reproduction.

- A seed contains a young plant and its food and provides a protective outer covering.

- Gymnosperms are said to have "naked seeds" because their seeds are not protected by a fruit. Most gymnosperms living today are conifers.

- Angiosperms are the most common types of seed plants. In angiosperms, seeds develop in a flower and are later protected by a fruit.

For Your Portfolio

1. Go to a grocery store with some of your classmates. Find examples of at least 20 foods that are made from different types of plants. Write a list of the foods. What type of plant is each food? How many foods are flowering plants? What examples can you find of foods that are other types of plants?

2. Go to the library and look up different cultures that depend on grains as their main source of food. Grains, such as wheat, are certain types of flowering plants that are grown primarily for food. Look up Egyptian, Greek, Mexican, and Chinese civilizations. Report your findings to your class.

3. With a few of your classmates, conduct an experiment with house plants. Get several small inexpensive plants, such as African violets. Place each one in the same environment, but change one factor. For example, place one plant in a bright, cool spot and give it a moderate amount of water. Keep another plant in the same area but give it very little water. Give a third plant extra water. Continue the experiment for at least three weeks. Which plant grows the most? How would you explain your results?

4. Watch seeds sprout. You'll need these supplies: radish, bean, pea, or other fast germinating seeds; paper towel; a small self-sealing plastic bag; water. Fold the paper towel so that it is just slightly smaller than the plastic bag. Wet the towel and squeeze out the excess water. The towel should be damp, but not dripping wet. Place the towel in the bag. Place the seeds in a row on top of the towel so that you can see them through the bag. Seal the bag. Place the bag in a dark area such as inside a drawer. Observe the seeds each day for two weeks. Keep notes on the seedlings. Record when they start to sprout. Measure them as they grow.

5. Go to the library to find out about peat moss. What is it made of? How is it used for gardening? Explain how it helps other plants. How has peat been used as a fuel? Where has it been used this way? Report your findings to your class.

In the space provided, write the letter of the correct term for each definition.

_____ 1. system of tubes that carries water and nutrients throughout a plant

_____ 2. process by which plants make food

_____ 3. pores in leaves through which excess water is released

_____ 4. vascular tissue that carries food made in the leaves to all other parts of the plant

_____ 5. special cells with which some living things such as mosses and ferns reproduce

_____ 6. vascular tissue that carries water up from the roots through the stem to the leaves

_____ 7. type of plant that does not have vascular tissue

_____ 8. process in which living things break down food and release energy

_____ 9. cone-bearing plant with needle-shaped leaves

_____ 10. type of plant that has a vascular system and reproduces by spores

_____ 11. most common types of seed plants whose seeds form in a flower and are protected by a fruit

_____ 12. type of seed plant whose seeds are usually found inside a cone

a. phloem

b. xylem

c. photosynthesis

d. respiration

e. stomata

f. moss

g. fern

h. vascular system

i. spores

j. angiosperms

k. gymnosperm

l. conifer

Give a brief answer for each of the following.

13. What trait do ferns have that mosses do not have? What trait do mosses and ferns share?

_____

_____

14. What is an important difference between angiosperms and gymnosperms?

_____

_____

Answer one of the following questions.

15. Write an essay to explain why angiosperms are better adapted to reproduce than gymnosperms?

16. Compare the processes of photosynthesis and respiration. Make a chart or write an essay to describe the differences between the two processes.

Invertebrates

Can you guess which animals lived thousands of years ago and are still around today? If you guessed roaches, you're right! In ancient Egypt, animals very similar to roaches, called scarabs, were used as charms. Golden scarabs studded with jewels were buried along with Egyptian royalty.

Today nobody wants these pests around, but roaches show up anyway. Roaches are so common because they eat many different kinds of food and can live almost anywhere. They also have relatives that live in the few places that roaches don't.

Roaches and their many relatives make up the largest group of animals—the arthropods. These armored animals belong to a larger group of animals called invertebrates. Invertebrates are animals without backbones. Other animals, including humans, have backbones. Animals with backbones are called vertebrates.

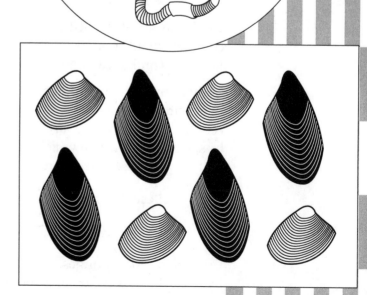

Lesson 25 Sponges and Cnidarians

Key Words

sponges:	simple invertebrates that live on the ocean floor
cnidarians:	simple invertebrates that have a mouth and a large central cavity
tentacles:	long flexible appendages that surround the mouth of a cnidarian
asexual reproduction:	reproduction that requires only one parent to produce offspring

KEY IDEAS

Two types of invertebrates are sponges and cnidarians. Both live in water and have large central cavities. Sponges and cnidarians reproduce both sexually and asexually.

Have you ever used a "natural" sponge? These tan-colored, odd-shaped sponges are often sold in bath shops. A natural sponge is the part of a sponge that remains after the sponge has died.

Sponges and Cnidarians. The simplest kinds of invertebrates are **sponges** (SPUNJ-uhz). All sponges live in water; most live in the ocean. In the past, many people thought sponges were plants. Unlike most animals, adult sponges do not move from place to place. Sponges grow attached to rocks on the ocean floor. However, unlike plants, sponges cannot make their own food.

Cnidarians (nih-DEHR-ee-uhnz) are simple invertebrates that are more complex than sponges. They live in both salt water and fresh water. Jellyfish, corals, sea anemones, and hydras are types of cnidarians.

Body Form. Sponges have hollow, saclike bodies made up of two layers of cells with a jellylike layer between them. See Fig. 25-1. The body has a central cavity with one large opening at the top. The central cavity is lined by special cells, each of which has a flagellum. The body walls have hundreds of tiny openings called pores.

 1. Describe the body form of a sponge. _____

_____

Cnidarians, like sponges, have bodies made up of two cell layers separated by a jellylike layer. Unlike sponges, cnidarians have three types of tissues

Fig. 25-1   Sponge

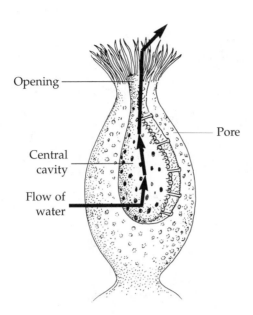

located in three different layers—an inner layer, a middle layer, and an outer layer. Like sponges, cnidarians have a large central cavity. However, in cnidarians, this cavity is a digestive cavity. The cavity has one opening—a mouth surrounded by tentacles. These **tentacles** (TEHN-tuh-kuhlz) are long flexible appendages that contain special stinging cells.

Cnidarians have one of two main body shapes, as shown in Fig. 25-2. Some cnidarians have tubelike bodies and do not move from place to place. Others have bell-shaped bodies and can move from place to place.

Reproduction. Sponges and cnidarians can both reproduce by either sexual or asexual reproduction. **Asexual reproduction** (ay-SEHK-shoo-uhl ree-pruh-DUK-shuhn) is a type of reproduction that requires only one parent to produce offspring.

When sexual reproduction occurs in sponges, a single sponge produces both male and female sex cells. Sperm cells float from one sponge to another. When they reach another sponge, the sperm cells join with egg cells to form new sponges.

Fig. 25-2   Cnidarians

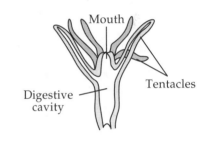

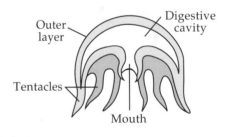

Sometimes sponges reproduce asexually by fragmenting. In this process, a piece of a sponge breaks off and eventually grows into a new sponge. Sponges also reproduce asexually by budding. In this process, a group of cells, called a bud, forms on the outer wall of a sponge's body. The bud grows larger and eventually breaks off from the parent to form a new sponge.

Cnidarians also reproduce sexually and asexually. An adult bell-shaped female produces egg cells. An adult bell-shaped male produces sperm. The sperm swim to and join with the egg to form a new tube-shaped organism that attaches itself to the ocean bottom. During asexual reproduction, this tube-shaped cnidarian produces many small bell-shaped offspring. These offspring eventually break apart and grow into male or female adults. The sexual and asexual life cycle of a cnidarian is shown in Fig. 25-3.

Fig. 25-3   Reproduction of cnidarians

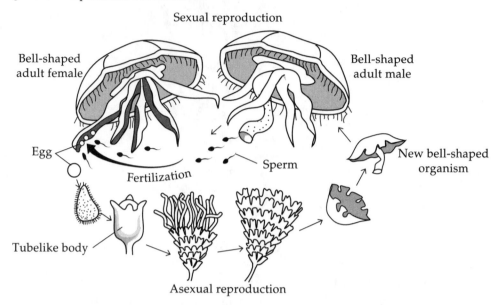

Sexual reproduction

Bell-shaped
adult female

Bell-shaped
adult male

Egg

Fertilization

Sperm

New bell-shaped
organism

Tubelike body

Asexual reproduction

 2. What is asexual reproduction? _____

_____

Feeding.   Sponges cannot move from one place to another to get their food. Instead, they are filter feeders. Water flows into the sponge's main body cavity through pores in the body wall. Flagella filter tiny food particles, such as bacteria and protists, from the water. The food is digested in the individual cells of the sponge's body. Any undigested food exits the sponge's body through the opening of the central cavity. Look back at Fig. 25-1 to see the direction in which water flows through a sponge.

Cnidarians feed in a much different way than sponges do. Tentacles surround prey such as small shrimp. The stinging cells in the tentacles sting and paralyze the prey. The tentacles direct the food through the mouth into the digestive cavity. There, special chemicals begin to digest the food. The partially digested food then enters the cells where digestion is completed. Undigested food leaves the body of the cnidarian through its mouth.

 3. How do sponges feed? _____

_____

Fig. 25-4 lists some traits of sponges and cnidarians.

Fig. 25-4

Traits of Sponges	Traits of Cnidarians
Reproduce sexually and asexually	Reproduce sexually and asexually
Adults cannot move from place to place	Some types can move, others cannot
Filter feed	Feed by catching prey

Write a sentence explaining the connection between each pair of words.

4. sponge, cnidarian _____

_____

5. tentacles, mouth _____

_____

6. Draw arrows on Fig. 25-5 to show the direction water flows through a sponge.

Fig. 25-5

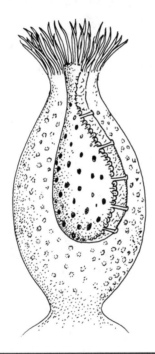

7. Describe two ways sponges reproduce asexually. _____

_____

_____

What Do You Know?

8. Describe how cnidarians feed. _____

_____

_____

9. What do you think might be some drawbacks of humans using natural

sponges instead of artificial sponges? _____

_____

_____

Lesson 26 Worms

Key Words

flatworms:	worms that have a flat body and a distinct head and tail
parasite:	organism that lives on or in a host and harms it
roundworms:	smooth, tube-shaped worms that are pointed at both ends
segmented worms:	complex worms with bodies made up of many segments
fission:	type of asexual reproduction in which an organism splits into two parts
regeneration:	process by which an organism grows new parts to replace lost ones

KEY IDEAS

Worms are invertebrates that live in many different environments. Many worms are parasites. Three types of worms are flatworms, roundworms, and segmented worms.

Fig. 26-1 Flatworm

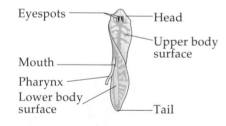

Eyespots — Head
— Upper body surface
Mouth —
Pharynx —
Lower body surface — Tail

Fig. 26-2 Roundworm

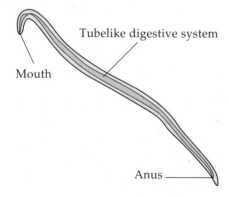

Tubelike digestive system
Mouth
Anus

Worms are invertebrates that are classified into three large groups: flatworms, roundworms, and segmented worms. Compared to sponges and cnidarians, all worms are complex. All worms have three layers of tissue and an organ system.

Body Form. Worms that have a flat body and a distinct head and tail are called **flatworms** (FLAT-wurmz). They have a digestive cavity with only one opening at the end of the pharynx. See Fig. 26-1. Flatworms are the simplest type of worms. Most flatworms are parasites. A **parasite** (PAR-uh-seyet) is an organism that lives on or in another organism, called a host, and causes the host harm. Some flatworms are free-living. They are nonparasitic and live in fresh water or in the ocean.

Roundworms (ROUND-wurmz) are smooth, thin, tube-shaped worms that are pointed at both ends. Roundworms have a digestive cavity, or tube, that is open on both ends. The mouth is at one end of the tube; the anus is at the other. See Fig. 26-2. Roundworms also have muscles that run the length of their bodies. Roundworms are the most common worms on the earth. Many live in soil and are free-living. Other roundworms are parasites that can harm humans.

1. How do the body forms of flatworms and roundworms differ?

_____

_____

Segmented worms (SEHG-mehnt-uhd wurmz) are the most complex worms. Their bodies are made up of many segments, or parts, that can be seen on the outside of the body. See Fig. 26-3. Each segment has hairlike bristles. Like roundworms, their digestive system has openings at both ends. However, segmented worms are different from flatworms and roundworms because they have a tube-within-a-tube body plan. Segmented worms also have sets of muscles, and circulatory, respiratory, and nervous systems that are more complex than those of other worms. Most segmented worms are free-living and live in the ocean. Others live in fresh water. The best known segmented worm—the earthworm—lives in soil.

Feeding. The three different types of worms feed in different ways. Flatworms, such as the planarian, feed on dead or slow-moving animals. The worm secretes enzymes through a special structure in its mouth and partially digests its food outside its body. The food is then brought into the body where it is further digested. Wastes leave the body through the mouth.

Roundworms take in food through their mouths. Food is absorbed by the body from the digestive tube. Undigested food leaves the body through the anus.

One kind of segmented worm, the earthworm, feeds as it moves through soil. As an earthworm moves forward, it swallows soil that passes through the worm's digestive system. The earthworm removes the food from the soil. The remaining soil leaves the worm through the anus. The earthworm's wastes enrich the soil, and its movement loosens the dirt, making the area better for plant growth.

Reproduction. Each of the three kinds of worms reproduces in a different way. Flatworms, such as planarians, reproduce asexually by fission. **Fission** is the process in which an organism splits into two. See Fig. 26-4. Planarians, for example, split in half between their head and tail end. One half then grows a new head. The other half grows a new tail. This process of growing new parts to replace lost ones is called **regeneration**. Planarians can also regenerate if they are cut into pieces.

Flatworms also reproduce sexually. Each adult flatworm contains both male and female sex organs and produces both sperm and eggs. Sperm from one flatworm generally fertilize the eggs of another flatworm.

Fig. 26-3 Segmented Worm

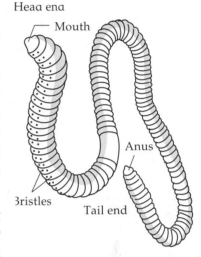

Head end
— Mouth
Anus
Bristles
Tail end

Fig. 26-4 Fission

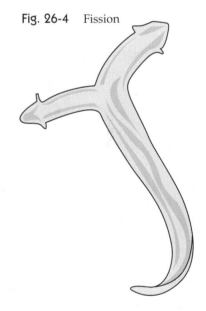

2. How does a flatworm reproduce asexually?

_____

_____

An *ascaris* is a common type of roundworm. It is a parasite and reproduces inside a host. Male and female adult worms live inside the host's intestine. The female produces eggs; the male produces sperm. Fertilized eggs pass out of the host's intestine with body wastes. The eggs eventually enter a new host's body, where they hatch when they reach the new host's intestine.

Like flatworms, segmented worms such as the earthworm have both male and female sex organs. They produce both sperm and eggs. Like flatworms, the sperm from one segmented worm fertilize the eggs of a different worm.

Fig. 26-5 shows the different traits of flatworms, roundworms, and segmented worms.

Fig. 26-5

Flatworms	Roundworms	Segmented worms
Flat body with distinct head and tail	Smooth, thin, tube-body	Segmented body with bristles on each segment
Asexual reproduction by fission; sexual reproduction, adult produces both egg and sperm	Sexual reproduction, with separate male and female adults	Sexual reproduction, adult produces both eggs and sperm
Some are free-living in water. Most are parasites.	Free-living in water and soil; some parasites	Free-living in water or soil; few parasites
Simplest type of worm	Most common worm	Most complex worm

Check Your Understanding

Write a sentence explaining the connection between each pair of words.

3. flatworms, roundworms _____

_____

4. segmented worms, tube _____

_____

Complete the following paragraphs by adding the correct words.

Flatworms are worms with a **(5)**_____ body and a **(6)**_____ structure. They have a distinct **(7)**_____ and **(8)**_____. Most flatworms are **(9)**_____. Some flatworms reproduce asexually by the process called **(10)**_____.

Roundworms are smooth, thin, tube-shaped worms that are **(11)**_____ at both ends. Roundworms are the **(12)**_____ common worms on the earth. Some roundworms reproduce inside their host's **(13)**_____.

Segmented worms are the most **(14)**_____ type of worm. Their bodies are made up of many **(15)**_____. The best-known segmented worm is the **(16)**_____. When it reproduces, each earthworm produces **(17)**_____ and **(18)**_____.

19. In what way is the reproduction of a flatworm and that of a segmented worm similar? _____

_____

_____

20. How does soil pass through an earthworm as an earthworm moves?

_____

_____

_____

What Do You Know?

Mollusks

Key Words

mollusk:	invertebrate with a soft body, which is usually covered by one or more hard shells
visceral mass:	part of a mollusk body that contains the reproductive, digestive, and excretory organs
mantle:	fold of skin that wraps around and protects the visceral mass of a mollusk
bivalves:	mollusks that have two shells hinged together
univalves:	mollusks that usually have a single coiled shell
cephalopods:	mollusks that have either no shell or a small shell inside the body

KEY IDEAS

Mollusks are soft-bodied vertebrates that are usually covered by a shell. Although many mollusks live in water, some types live on land.

Mollusks make up the second largest group of animals. They live in fresh water, in the ocean, or on land. A **mollusk** (MAHL-uhsk) is an invertebrate with a soft body that is usually covered by one or more hard shells. The mollusk body has four main parts: a muscular foot used for movement; a head that contains the mouth and sense organs, the visceral mass, and the mantle. The **visceral mass** (VIHS-uhr-uhl mas) contains the reproductive, digestive, and excretory organs. The **mantle** (MAN-tuhl) is a fold of skin that wraps around and protects the visceral mass. The mantle also produces the shell in those mollusks that have a shell.

Depending on the type of mollusk, the head may be separate or absent. The foot can be different shapes. Mollusks are classified by the shape of their foot and the number of shells that cover their body.

 1. What are the four body parts of a mollusk?

_____

_____

Body Form. Mollusks that have two shells that are hinged together are called **bivalves** (BEYE-valvz). They have a wedge-shaped foot that they use to pull themselves forward or to dig holes in sand or mud. Unlike other mollusks, bivalves do not have a head. However, they do have sense organs that are normally found in the heads of other animals. Look at the row of dots on the scallop in Fig. 27-1. Each dot is a simple eye. Other bivalves include oysters, clams, and mussels.

Univalves make up the largest group of mollusks. **Univalves** (YOON-uh-valvz) are mollusks that usually have a single coiled shell, like a snail shell. Some univalves, such as the slug, have no shell. A univalve has a large flat foot that ripples as the animal creeps forward. Univalves have a distinct head with two pairs of tentacles. One pair of tentacles is used by the univalve to feel its way around. A simple eye is at the end of each of the other two tentacles.

 2. What are three differences between univalves and bivalves?

_____

_____

Cephalopods (SEHF-uh-loh-pahdz) are mollusks that have either no shell or a small shell inside their body. They are the largest, most complex, and most active mollusks. Examples of cephalopods are the giant squid and the octopus. All cephalopods live in the ocean. A cephalopod has a large head and brain. Its foot is divided into long tentacles that are used for grabbing and pulling prey into its mouth. A cephalopod moves by squirting water out of its body.

Fig. 27-1

| Scallop | Snail | Octopus |
| Bivalve | Univalve | Cephalopod |

Feeding. Each kind of mollusk feeds in a different way. Bivalves such as clams are filter feeders. Water passing through a bivalve's body carries small particles of food. The food is removed by cilia and sticky surfaces within the visceral mass. Univalves such as snails have a mouth and a well-developed digestive system. They feed on plants. Ocean-dwelling cephalopods such as the octopus feed on fish and other mollusks. The tentacles surrounding the cephalopod's mouth catch and hold the prey. The tentacles then move the food into the mouth where it is crushed by powerful jaws.

Reproduction. Most mollusks have separate sexes. A male produces sperm and a female produces eggs. The sperm and egg join to form the offspring. Most mollusks have a distinct kind of larva that looks like two cones placed on top of one another. See Fig. 27-2. A band of cilia separates the two cones in the middle. The larva is free-swimming.

Fig. 27-2 Mollusk larva

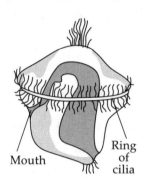

Mouth

Ring of cilia

TAKE ANOTHER LOOK

Fig. 27-3 shows the different traits of the three main groups of mollusks.

Fig. 27-3

Class	Characteristics	Examples
Bivalves	Body with no head, wedge-shaped foot for digging, two-part hinged shell, filter feeder	Clams, oysters scallops
Univalves	Head with eyes and tentacles, large flat foot for movement, coiled one-part shell often present, feeds on plants	Snails, slugs
Cephalopods	Head with eyes; foot divided into arms or tentacles; shell may be internal, external, or absent; feeds on fish or other mollusks	Octopus, squid

Check Your Understanding

Write a sentence explaining the connection between each pair of words.

3. bivalve, two _____

_____

4. univalve, one _____

_____

5. cephalopod, shell _____

_____

Complete the following sentences.

6. The _____ are mollusks that do not have a head.

7. A _____ creeps forward as its large foot ripples.

8. A univalve has two pairs of _____ on its head.

9. The largest and most complex mollusks are the _____.

Label each mollusk in Fig. 27-4. Choose from *univalve*, *bivalve*, or *cephalopod*.

Fig. 27-4

10. _____   11. _____   12. _____

13. Describe the differences in body forms of bivalves, univalves, and cephalopods. _____

_____

_____

_____

14. Although slugs have no shells, they are classified as univalves? Why do you think they are classified this way? _____

_____

_____

What Do You Know?

Arthropod Characteristics

Key Words

arthropods:	animals with segmented bodies that have hard outer coverings and jointed legs
exoskeleton:	hard outer covering of an arthropod that protects and supports the animal
molt:	to shed an old exoskeleton

KEY IDEAS

Arthropods make up the largest group of animals. All arthropods share the following traits: segmented bodies, jointed legs, and hard outer coverings.

Arthropods (AHR-throh-pahdz) are animals with segmented bodies, jointed legs, and hard outer coverings. They make up the largest group of animals. There are more species of arthropods than all other types of animals combined. Arthropods include huge lobsters that live at the bottom of the ocean and mites that are tiny enough to be parasites of wasps. Each species of arthropods differs from the others as it has adapted to its own environment. As a result, arthropods have many adaptations of a basic body plan.

 1. What is an arthropod? _____

_____

Body Form. The body of an arthropod is divided into segments, or parts. Most arthropods have three main body parts: a head, a thorax, and an abdomen. The head contains the mouth and sense organs. Jointed legs are attached to the thorax, or middle part. The last part, the abdomen, contains the reproductive and digestive systems. Other anthropods have only two segments: a head and thorax that are fused together, and an abdomen.

Like all invertebrates, arthropods have no bones. Instead, they have a hard outer covering called an **exoskeleton** (ehks-oh-SKEHL-uh-tuhn). The exoskeleton protects and supports the soft inner parts of the animal in many ways. The exoskeleton protects arthropods from drying out and allows them to live in dry areas as well as in water. The exoskeleton also protects the arthropod from injury.

An exoskeleton has some drawbacks. It is heavy to carry around. Unlike the skeleton inside your body, an exoskeleton cannot grow. When an arthropod grows, it must **molt** (mohlt), or shed its old exoskeleton, and grow a new one. The old skeleton splits open, and the animal wriggles out. Because it has no protection, the animal usually hides while its new exoskeleton grows.

 2. What are three functions of an exoskeleton?

_____

_____

All arthropods have pairs of jointed legs. The joints, or places where the legs bend, allow the legs to move. The legs may be used for walking, swimming, hopping, or grabbing food. The number and type of legs depends on the type of arthropod.

Reproduction. Arthropods reproduce sexually. Separate male and female adults produce sperm and eggs that join to form fertilized eggs. Some arthropods reproduce in the water.

Feeding. Arthropods eat almost anything, including plants, other animals, wood, and paper. They have strong jaws used for chewing and specialized appendages such as claws used for capturing food.

A Typical Arthropod? Because there are so many different species of arthropods, there is no typical arthropod. Fig. 28-1 shows the structure of a crayfish, an arthropod that lives in water. This animal has four pairs of walking legs attached to a fused head and thorax. A much larger pair of legs are adapted as claws that are used to grab food. Smaller legs that are used for swimming are tucked under segments of the abdomen.

Fig. 28-1 Crayfish

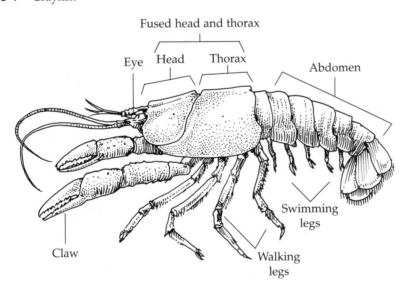

TAKE ANOTHER LOOK

Fig. 28-2 shows how arthropods differ from other invertebrates.

Fig. 28-2

	Sponges and cnidarians	Worms	Mollusks	Arthropods
Body form	Soft bodies made of two layers surrounding central cavity; no organs or organ systems	Soft bodies with three tissue layers; organs and organ systems	Soft bodies often with one or more hard shells; organs and organ systems	Segmented body; jointed legs; exoskeleton; organs and organ system
Reproduction	Reproduce sexually and asexually by fragmentation and budding	Reproduce sexually and asexually by fission; Some adults have both male and female sex organs	Reproduce sexually; separate sexes	Reproduce sexually; separate sexes
Movement	Some do not move from place to place; others do	Most move; some parasites stay attached to host	Some do not move; others do	Except for some stages, move from place to place; some fly
Feeding	Many are filter feeders; some capture prey	Some are parasites, others vary	Many are filter feeders; others capture prey	Many different food sources

Check Your Understanding

Write a sentence explaining the connection between each pair of words.

3.   arthropod, segmented body _____

_____

4.   exoskeleton, protection _____

_____

5.   exoskeleton, molt _____

_____

Complete the following sentences.

The three main parts of most arthropods are the **(6)**_____,

(7)_____, and **(8)**_____. After an arthropod

(9)_____, it often hides. At this time, its body has little or

no **(10)**_____.

Fig. 28-3 shows a different view of the same arthropod that is shown in
Fig. 28-1. Label its main parts.

Fig. 28-3

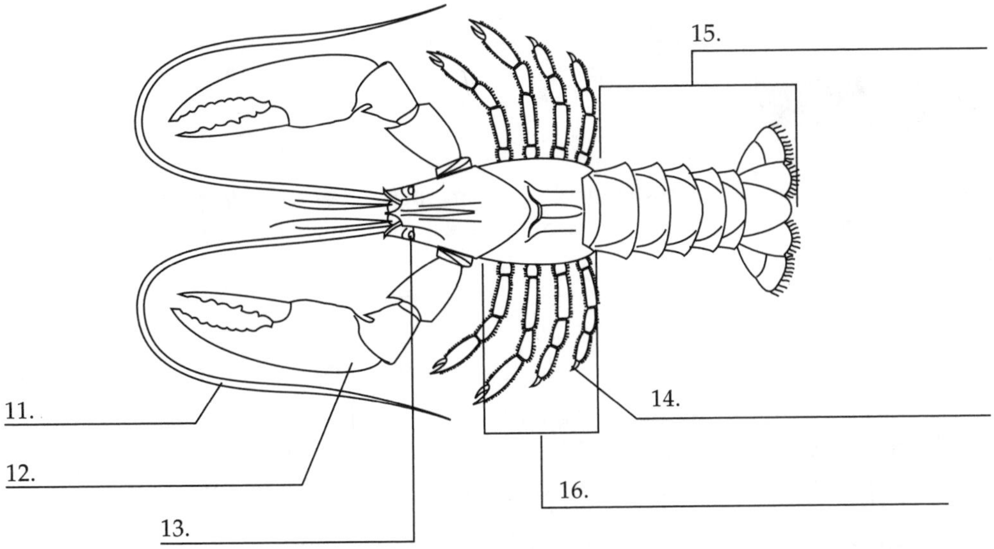

15._____

11._____

12._____

13._____

14._____

16._____

17. Why do arthropods live in so many different places?

_____

_____

18. What are two disadvantages of an exoskeleton? _____

_____

19. Sometimes many different arthropods live close together but have
    different adaptations. As a result, they may not eat the same things
    and do not compete for food. How do you think this might affect
    arthropods as a group?

_____

_____

_____

What
Do You
Know?

Lesson 29 Insects

Key Words

insects: arthropods with three pairs of jointed legs
compound eyes: eyes made up of many tiny lenses that can sense movement
simple eyes: eyes that can sense only light and dark and cannot form images

KEY IDEAS

Insects are the most successful class of arthropods. They are a large and diverse group. Most insects can fly, have compound eyes, and produce large numbers of offspring.

Mosquitoes bite. Wasps sting. Moths eat wool. Some insects are harmful to humans. Others are helpful. For example, most flowering plants are pollinated by bees. If bees did not pollinate flowers, they would not produce seeds and fruit. As a result, we would have little fruit to eat.

The arthropods are made up of several classes of animals. The largest class is the insects. **Insects** (IHN-sehkts) are arthropods with three pairs of jointed legs. Insects vary in size and structure, in the type of food they eat, and in the places they live. Because there is so much variety, many different kinds of insects can live in a small area without competing for food or space.

In general, most insects are small. Because they are small they need little space and little food. Because both space and food can be limited, the small size of insects helps them survive and thrive.

 1. **What is an insect?** _____

_____

Body Form. All insects have the same basic body form and parts. An insect has three body parts: the head, the thorax, and the abdomen. All insects have three pairs of jointed legs. In some insects, the legs may have special adaptations. In a grasshopper, for example, the third pair of legs is large and strong. These legs are well adapted for jumping. See Fig. 29-1.

Insects also have antennae (sing. *antenna*) on their heads. In most insects, the antennae can sense touch and smell. In others insects, the antennae may also sense taste and aid in hearing.

Fig. 29-1   Grasshopper

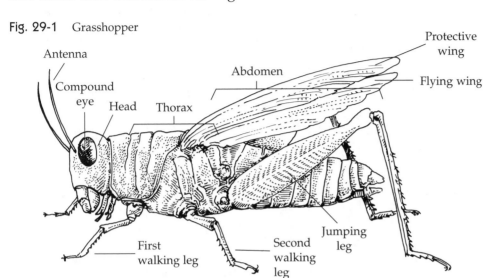

Most insects have large **compound eyes** (KAHM-pound eyez) that are made up of many tiny lenses. Each lens sees only part of the world around the insect. Together, the lenses make up the whole picture. A compound eye is very good at sensing movement. This eye helps insects catch prey and keeps the insects safe. Most insects also have **simple eyes** (SIHM-puhl eyez) that do not form images, but sense only light and dark.

Most adult insects have wings. However, some insects, such as certain types of ants, do not have wings. Mosquitoes and flies have only one pair of wings. Other insects, such as butterflies, bees, and dragonflies, have two pairs. In some insects, such as beetles, the first pair of wings covers and protects a more fragile second pair of wings that is used for flight.

Insects are the only arthropods, and the only invertebrates, that can fly. This adaptation helps insects survive. By being able to fly, insects can travel long distances in search of food and can quickly escape danger.

 2. What are three traits of insects? _____

_____

Feeding.   Insects feed on a wide variety of plants, animals, and other materials. They have special mouth parts adapted for the kinds of food they eat. Butterflies, for example, have long tubes in their mouths that enable them to suck nectar from flowers. A mosquito has piercing mouth parts that allow it to puncture the skin of an animal and suck its blood.

Reproduction.   Another reason insects thrive is their ability to reproduce. Although the life span of an individual insect may be very short, the insect makes up for it by the large number of offspring it produces. In most cases, the female lays hundreds of eggs that later develop into adults. Between the stages of egg and adult, the insect may go through one or two other stages, depending on the type of insect.

Fig. 29-2 shows a variety in insect traits.

Fig. 29-2

Insect	Mouthparts	Wings	Other characteristics
Flies (houseflies, black flies, mosquitoes midges, gnats, horseflies)	Sucking	1 pair	Some feed on plants, others are parasites, and still others feed on insects. Some damage plants, some transmit animal diseases.
Mayflies	No real mouthparts	2 pairs	Found in and around ponds and streams. Adults live only a day or so, and do not eat.
Bugs (water bugs, water striders, bedbugs, assassin bugs, stinkbugs)	Sucking	None or 2 pairs	Very large group. Most live on land; some live in water; few parasitic. Some feed on plants, others prey on insects.
Bees, wasps, ants, sawflies	Bees: sucking Wasps, ants, and sawflies: chewing	None or 2 pairs	Live mainly on flowers, and on the ground. Some are parasites of other insects. Ants and some wasps and bees live in colonies.
Butterflies and moths	Sucking, with coiled sucking tube	Usually 2 pairs	Found on vegetation. The young are caterpillars, which feed on plants. Silk is produced by silkworm moths.

Write a sentence explaining the connection between each pair of words.

3. insect, arthropod _____

_____

4. compound eye, lenses _____

_____

5. simple eye, light _____

_____

Complete the following sentences.

6. One way to identify insects from other arthropods is by counting their legs. Insects have _____ pairs of legs.

7. Because of the _____ size of most insects, they need little space and little food.

8. The _____ of insects can often sense touch and smell, and in some insects it can also sense taste and aid in hearing.

9. Insects are the only invertebrates that can _____ .

10. Most female insects lay _____ eggs.

11. Describe at least one way in which insects are helpful to people.

_____

_____

What Do You Know?

12. Give at least three reasons that explain why insects thrive so successfully.

_____

_____

_____

30 Other Arthropods

Key Words

arachnids: arthropods that have four pairs of jointed legs

crustaceans: arthropods that have five pairs of jointed legs

centipedes: arthropods that have one pair of jointed legs attached to most of their body segments

millipedes: arthropods that have two pairs of jointed legs attached to most of their body segments

KEY IDEAS

Insects are just one of many classes of arthropods. Other classes include arachnids, crustaceans, centipedes, and millipedes.

In addition to insects, arthropods include many other invertebrates. Among them are spiders, lobsters, crabs, centipedes, and millipedes. Like other arthropods, all these arthropods have segmented bodies, jointed legs, and exoskeletons.

Arachnids. Arthropods that have four pairs of jointed legs are **arachnids** (uh-RAK-nihdz). Unlike insects, arachnids do not have wings or antennae. While insects have three body segments, arachnids have only two—a fused head and thorax and an abdomen. See Fig. 30-1.

The most common arachnids are spiders. There are thousands of kinds of spiders. Some are as tiny as the head of a pin. Others are larger than your hand. Spiders make silk from a special gland in their bodies. Most spiders spin the silk into complex webs which they use to catch their prey. Spiders feed mostly on insects. They capture their food by hunting or trapping the prey in webs. Once a spider catches its prey, the spider injects poisons into it. The poison paralyzes the prey.

Other kinds of arachnids are ticks, mites, and scorpions. Ticks and mites are very tiny and are often parasites. Ticks may affect dogs, deer, mice, and other animals. Many ticks carry disease from one animal to another. Two diseases that affect humans—Rocky Mountain spotted fever and Lyme disease—are carried by ticks. Scorpions are large arachnids that have a stinger at the end of their abdomens. Their sting is painful, but usually not fatal.

Fig. 30-1   Arachnids

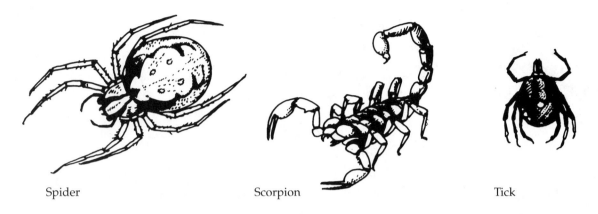

Spider   Scorpion   Tick

1. **What are three ways in which arachnids differ from insects?**

_____

_____

_____

Crustaceans.   Arthropods that have five pairs of jointed legs are **crustaceans** (kruhs-TAY-shuhnz).   Many crustaceans have a fused head and thorax. Unlike insects, crustaceans do not have wings. However, they do have two pairs of antennae. The first pair of walking legs are often adapted as claws that are used to get food and for defense. Smaller legs, called swimmerets, are attached to each segment of the abdomen. See Fig. 30-2.

Fig. 30-2   Crustaceans

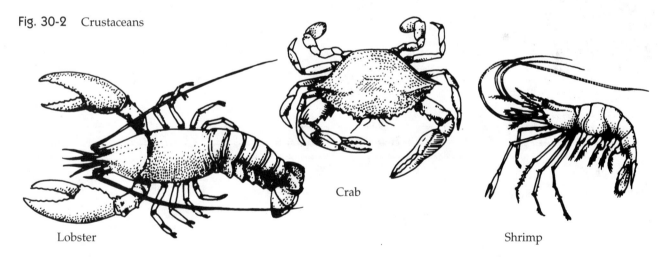

Crab

Lobster   Shrimp

Although insects outnumber all other arthropods on land, crustaceans "rule" the waters. Some crustaceans that live in the oceans, such as lobsters, grow very large and have heavy exoskeletons. Other crustaceans, such as shrimp, are tiny and are important as food for larger animals.

Fig. 30-3

Centipede

Millipede

Crustaceans eat by grinding up their food with their powerful jaws. The ground up food then passes into the mouth and through the digestive system. Crustaceans feed mostly on smaller arthropods.

Crustaceans have separate male and female adults that produce sperm and eggs. The sperm and egg join to form a fertilized egg that hatches several weeks later. Crayfish are a type of crustacean. In crayfish, the female lays the eggs before they are fertilized by the sperm.

Centipedes and millipedes. Some arthropods—centipedes and millipedes—look like armored worms. They are longer and thinner than most arthropods in other classes. Their many body segments are not clearly grouped into a head, thorax, and abdomen. See Fig. 30-3.

Centipedes (SEHN-tuh-peedz) have one pair of legs on most of their body segments. A pair of poison claws is attached to the first segment below the head. These claws are used to catch insects, worms, and other small animals. Even though the name *centipede* means "having 100 legs," most centipedes have only 30 legs.

Millipedes (MIHL-ih-peedz) have two pairs of jointed legs attached to most of their body segments. Millipedes mostly eat dead plants.

TAKE ANOTHER LOOK

Fig. 30-4 lists the traits of different classes of arthropods.

Fig. 30-4

	Insects	Crustaceans	Arachnids	Centipedes	Millipedes
Number of pairs of legs	3	5	4	1 per body segment	2 per body segment
Number of body segments	3	Usually 2	2	Many	Many
Habitat	Land, air, water	Fresh water and salt water	Land	Land	Land
Food	Wide variety including plants, wood, blood	Other crustaceans and small mollusks	Prey on small animals including insects	Small animals including insects	Dead plants and insects
Special features	Most have wings and can fly	Main arthropod in ocean	Make silk and spin webs	Look like segmented worms	Look like segmented worms

Write a sentence explaining the connection between each pair of words.

2. arachnids, four _____

_____

3. crustaceans, five _____

_____

4. centipedes, one _____

_____

5. millipedes, two _____

_____

Complete the following outline.

I. The "ruling" class of arthropods in the water are the (6)_____.

   A. Crustaceans have (7)_____ pairs of legs.

   B. Crustaceans have (8)_____ pairs of antennae.

II. Arthropods in the (9)_____ class make silk and spin webs.

   A. Arachnids have (10)_____ pairs of legs.

   B. Arachnids have (11)_____ body parts.

III. The (12)_____ and (13)_____ look more like worms than like other arthropods.

   A. Centipedes have (14)_____ pair of legs attached to most segments.

   B. Millipedes have (15)_____ pairs of legs attached to most segments.

16. How do spiders catch their prey? _____

_____

_____

17. Describe the difference between centipedes and millipedes.

_____

_____

What Do You Know?

31 Echinoderms

Key Words

echinoderms:	spiny-skinned invertebrates that live in the ocean
radial symmetry:	body plan in which body parts repeat around an imaginary line drawn through a central area
tube feet:	water-filled suction cups that are used in movement and in feeding

KEY IDEAS

Echinoderms are complex invertebrates that live in the ocean. Unlike most other animals, echinoderms have radial symmetry.

Have you ever walked along a beach and found a starfish? Despite the name, starfish are not really fish. That is why starfish are sometimes called sea stars. Starfish are **echinoderms** (ee-KEYE-noh-dermz), spiny-skinned invertebrates that live in the ocean.

Body Form. The first thing you probably notice about an echinoderm is its overall shape. Unlike arthropods and most other animals, most adult echinoderms do not have left-right symmetry. Instead, an adult echinoderm has radial symmetry. **Radial symmetry** (RAY-dee-uhl SIHM-uh-tree) is a body plan in which body parts repeat around an imaginary line drawn through a central area. Imagine drawing a line down the center of your body. There is only one way that you could draw this line to form mirror images of the two halves of your body. This is left-right symmetry. But if you were to draw a line through an animal with radial symmetry, such as a starfish, there are many different places you could form mirror images. See Fig. 31-1.

Fig. 31-1   Left-right symmetry   Radial symmetry

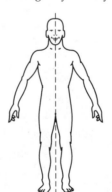 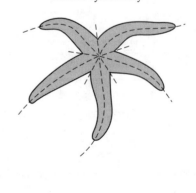

1. How does the symmetry in an adult echinoderm differ from that of most other animals?_____

_____

The word *echinoderm* means "spiny skin." Most echinoderms are covered with spines that help protect the animal. These spines stick out from the skeleton beneath the echinoderm's skin. Unlike arthropods, echinoderms have an internal skeleton.

On the underside of each of the five arms of a starfish are tiny tube feet. **Tube feet** (toob feet) are water-filled suction cups that are used in movement and in feeding. See Fig. 31-2. Water-filled tubes run throughout the echinoderm's body and connect to the tube feet. When water moves within these tubes, the tube feet become longer or shorter and function as suction cups. By stretching out and attaching to surfaces, the tube feet can pull the animal forward.

Fig. 31-2

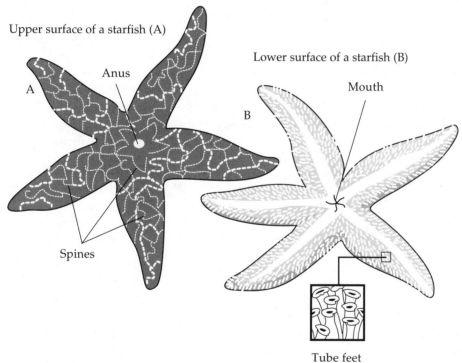

2. What are tube feet? _____

_____

Feeding. Echinoderms have several ways of feeding. For example, a starfish feeds by wrapping its arms around a clam and attaching its tube feet to both of the clam's shells. The tube feet pull against the shells and tire the clam, which uses its strong muscles to keep its shells closed. In the end, the clam loses the "tug of war" and its shells open slightly. The starfish then turns its stomach inside out through its mouth and pushes it into the clam. Once the stomach is inside the clam, it digests the soft body of the clam. Later the stomach and partly digested clam are sucked back into the starfish.

Reproduction.   Echinoderms reproduce sexually. Most often the eggs of females are fertilized by sperm of males in open water. Some echinoderms can also reproduce asexually by regeneration. For example, if a starfish loses one of its arms, it can grow a new one. In the same way, if a starfish is cut into many pieces, each piece can grow into a whole new animal. However, each piece must contain a portion of the central part of the body for regeneration to occur.

Fig. 31-3 shows the traits of some echinoderms.

Fig. 31-3

	Starfish (sea star)	Sea cucumber	Sea urchin and sand dollar
Body form	A central disk with several arms growing from it; has radial symmetry; spiny skin; internal skeleton	Resembles a cucumber; does not have arms; only echinoderm which does not have radial symmetry; leathery small skin; internal skeleton	Disk-shaped or sphere-shaped bodies with no arms, have radial symmetry; have a solid internal shell-like skeleton; body covered with moveable spines
Movement	Uses tube feet with suction cups to pull itself along; moves about freely	Three rows of tube feet on bottom of body; moves about freely	Can use spines for movement; sea urchins can also use tube feet; sea urchins usually attach to rock or coral; sand dollars crawl in sand and burrow
Feeding	Mouth in underside of body; sucks partly digested food through stomach which can be pushed out through mouth opening	Mouth at one end of body surrounded by tube feet; tube feet help gather food into the mouth	Have a mouth surrounded by tooth-like structures; tube feet sometimes used to push food toward mouth
Reproduction	Sexual; eggs are fertilized by sperm; sexes are separate; can regenerate	Sexual; sexes can be separate or both sexes in same animal; can regenerate	Sexual; sexes are separate; can regenerate

Write a sentence explaining the connection between each pair of words.

3. echinoderm, spiny _____

_____

4. radial symmetry, body plan _____

_____

5. tube feet, food _____

_____

Complete the following sentences.

6. Echinoderms live in the _____.

7. Unlike arthropods, echinoderms have an _____ skeleton.

8. Tube feet are used in both _____ and _____.

What Do You Know?

9. What is the difference between left-right symmetry and radial symmetry?

_____

_____

_____

_____

10. Because starfish eat clams, some people have tried to get rid of starfish in certain areas. People have cut up all the starfish they have caught, and have thrown the pieces back in the water. What do you think happened next? Did the number of starfish increase or decrease? Did the number of clams increase or decrease? Explain.

_____

_____

_____

_____

Summary

- An invertebrate is an animal that does not have a backbone.

- Sponges and cnidarians are invertebrates that have bodies made up of two cell layers separated by jellylike layers.

- An adult sponge remains in one spot and filter-feeds by bringing water through pores in its body wall into a central cavity.

- Cnidarians have stinging cells at the ends of their tentacles that they use to stun their prey.

- Worms are more complex than sponges or cnidarians.

- There are three large groups of worms—flatworms, roundworms, and segmented worms.

- Flatworms have a digestive cavity with only one opening. Many flatworms are parasites; others are free-living.

- Roundworms have long thin bodies with pointed ends and a digestive tube with two openings—a mouth and an anus.

- Segmented worms have complex organ systems. The earthworm is a common segmented worm that improves soil for plant growth.

- A mollusk is an invertebrate with a soft body that is usually covered by one or more hard shells.

- Many mollusks live in water. A few live on land.

- Mollusks are sometimes classified by their number of shells or by the shape of their muscular foot.

- The four main parts of a mollusk are the head, the visceral mass, the mantle, and the foot.

- An arthropod is an invertebrate that has a segmented body with a hard outer covering and jointed legs.

- An arthropod's exoskeleton protects its body, but cannot grow along with the animal. When the animal grows, the exoskeleton is molted.

- Insects are a large and diverse group of arthropods. Most insects can fly, produce a large number of offspring, and have compound eyes.

- Other classes of arthropods include crustaceans, arachnids, centipedes, and millipedes.

- Echinoderms are complex invertebrates that have radial symmetry. Unlike arthropods, echinoderms have internal skeletons.

For Your Portfolio

1. Set up an ant farm. You may be able to find a pre-made ant farm in a hobby shop, toy store, or craft shop. You can also make your own by placing a sealed, empty glass jar into a slightly larger glass jar. Fill the space between the two jars with sandy soil. Add ants and food scraps, such as small pieces of lettuce and fruit. Sprinkle the added materials with water. Make holes in the lid and close the larger jar. You may want to place a piece of screen over the lid on the outside. Observe the ants as they tunnel through the soil. Record in a journal the ants' activities for a few weeks. Release the ants into a suitable environment after you have completed your observations.

2. If you live in an area close to the ocean, visit a tide pool. Tide pools are small bodies of water that remain when the tide goes out. You can see many different types of invertebrates living together in tide pools. Sketch the animals you see. Look in library books to identify the animals you observe. Be sure to just observe—and not touch—the animals!

3. If you do not live near an ocean, you may be able to visit an aquarium. Although aquariums usually focus on large ocean animals, including fish and mammals, many aquariums also have exhibits on invertebrates. Some even have tide pools where you can touch animals such as starfish. Learn all you can about the animals at the aquarium and report your findings to your class.

4. Do library research on one of the invertebrates you have learned about in this unit. For example, you may wish to learn all you can about butterflies. Find out where the monarch butterfly lives, what it eats, and how it moves. Make a poster of the animal you have researched.

5. Adopt a hermit crab. Hermit crabs are very small crabs that live in mollusk shells. They stay inside their chosen shell until they grow too large; then they find a new shell. Anywhere the crab goes, it carries its new home with it. The shell gives extra protection to the little crab. You can get hermit crabs in pet shops. Find out what foods your hermit crab needs and set it up in a terrarium. Observe its actions and give a report to your class.

6. Order meal worms from a biological supply catalog or buy them from a pet shop. Observe the meal worms when you get them. Place them in meal. Then dig them up every few days. What changes do you see? Report your findings to your class.

7. Find out about complete and incomplete metamorphosis. How do these two processes differ? Which insects go through complete metamorphosis? Make a poster showing the differences in the stages of the two processes. If you can, observe insects that go through the two different types of metamorphosis. Report your findings to your class.

Complete the following statements.

1. Animals that do not have a backbone are called _____.

2. The simplest invertebrates are _____.

3. Sponges reproduce asexually by _____ or _____.

4. _____ may have a tube-shaped body or they may have the shape of an upside-down bell surrounded by tentacles.

5. The simplest worms are _____.

6. Many worms live on or in another living thing and cause it harm. These worms are _____.

7. The most complex worms are _____.

8. A type of segmented worm that lives in and improves soil is the _____

9. Invertebrates with a segmented body, a hard body covering, and pairs of jointed legs are called _____ .

10. The hard body covering of an arthropod is called a(n) _____.

11. _____ differ from other arthropods and from all other invertebrates because they can fly.

12. A _____ is made up of many tiny lenses.

13. Spiders are one type of _____.

14. _____ outnumber insects in the water.

15. _____ have one pair of legs on most of the segments of their body.

16. _____ use their tube feet for movement and feeding.

Answer each of the following questions.

17. What is the main way in which the body form of an echinoderm differs from most other animals? _____

18. What is the difference between flatworms, roundworms, and segmented worms?

    _____

    _____

Answer one of the following questions.

19. Insects have many traits that help them to thrive. Give three traits of insects that help them to thrive and explain the role of each trait.

20. Write an essay in which you describe an imaginary arthropod. The imaginary animal must have all the traits of an arthropod: a segmented body, a hard body covering, and pairs of jointed legs. Where does your imaginary arthropod live? What does it eat? How does it move? How does it reproduce? Draw a picture of your arthropod.

Vertebrates

Imagine a group of animals that live on land, in water, and move through the air. Animals in this group have bodies covered with scales, hair, feathers, and mucus. These animals live almost everywhere. They live in hot dry deserts, in tropical forests and jungles, on snow-capped mountains, in grassy fields, and in rivers and oceans. Some of these animals swim, others fly, and many run or walk on either two or four legs. An important trait of some of these animals is that they can live on land. They have adapted from life in the water by having different ways to breathe, reproduce, and move.

What are all of these animals? The animals in this very large group are called vertebrates. Unlike invertebrates, vertebrates have a backbone. In this unit, you will learn more about the traits of vertebrates.

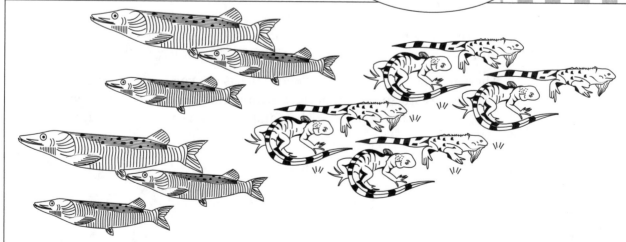

Lesson 32 Vertebrate Characteristics

Key Words

chordates: animals that have a thin, flexible rod that supports three features: the body, gill slits, and a nerve cord. The three features are present either throughout the animal's life or at some stage of its development.

vertebrates: animals with a strong, flexible backbone

endoskeleton: skeleton inside the body that provides support and protection

vertebrae: bones that make up the backbone

KEY IDEAS

Vertebrates are the most complex of all animals. They range in size from the tiny hummingbird to the giant blue whale. Vertebrates all have strong, flexible backbones.

You may already be familiar with the main characteristic of a vertebrate. Have you ever felt the ridge down the back of a dog or cat when you petted it? That bony ridge is the animal's backbone. The backbone of a hummingbird is only about 5 cm long. The backbone of a blue whale is about 18 m long.

Chordates. Animals with backbones belong to a large group of animals called chordates. **Chordates** (KAWR-dayts) are animals that have a thin, flexible rod that supports three features: the body, gill slits, and a nerve cord. Gill slits are a pair of structures behind the mouth that function in breathing. For an animal to be classified as a chordate, the three features supported by the thin rod must be present at some stage during an animal's development. For example, humans are chordates. But humans have gill slits only when they are young embryos. Chordates are classified into three groups. Two of the groups contain animals that live in the ocean.

The third and largest group of chordates is the **vertebrates** (VER-tuh-brihts). Vertebrates are animals that have strong, flexible backbones. There are five main groups of vertebrates: fishes, amphibians, reptiles, birds, and mammals.

Characteristics of Vertebrates. Vertebrates share several common characteristics which make them more complex than invertebrates. Vertebrates all have strong, flexible backbones and a complex body plan. Most vertebrates have two pairs of limbs such as arms, legs, wings, or fins. Most also have eyes, ears, a nose, and a mouth located on the head. All vertebrates have a large central body cavity containing a number of vital organs, such as the heart, lungs, and liver. Vertebrates also have an endoskeleton. An **endoskeleton** (ehn-doh-SKEHL-uh-tuhn) is a skeleton inside the body that provides support and protection. The brain of a vertebrate is complex and covered by the bones of the skull.

 1. **What are the five main groups of vertebrates?**

_____

_____

_____

Vertebrate Endoskeleton. The main feature of the endoskeleton is the backbone. The backbone is the characteristic that separates vertebrates from all other animals. The backbone is made up of small bones stacked on top of one another. These bones are called **vertebrae** (VER-tuh-bray). The backbone protects and supports the main nerve of a vertebrate called the spinal cord.

The other main parts of a vertebrate's skeleton are the skull, the rib cage, and two areas called girdles, where the limbs are attached. One girdle is located at the shoulders, where the arms, or forelimbs, are attached. The other is located at the hips, where the legs, or hindlimbs, are attached. Fig. 32-1 shows the main parts of a cat's skeleton.

Fig. 32-1

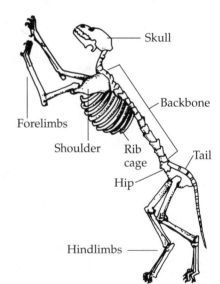

 2. **What characteristic distinguishes a vertebrate from all other animals?** _____

_____

_____

Vertebrate Organ Systems. All vertebrates have highly organized and specialized organ systems. The endoskeleton makes up the skeletal system. Other systems are the nervous system, a closed circulatory system, the digestive system, the respiratory system, the excretory system, and the reproductive system. Fig. 32-2 shows the organ systems of a cat. The cat represents a typical vertebrate.

Fig. 32-2

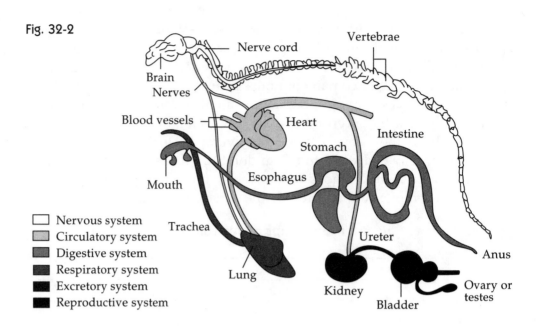

Nerve cord
Vertebrae
Brain
Nerves
Blood vessels
Heart
Intestine
Stomach
Esophagus
Mouth
Trachea
Ureter
Anus
Lung
Kidney
Bladder
Ovary or testes

☐ Nervous system
▨ Circulatory system
▧ Digestive system
▨ Respiratory system
▨ Excretory system
■ Reproductive system

TAKE
ANOTHER
LOOK

Fig. 32-3 shows the functions of the seven main organ systems of a vertebrate.

Fig. 32-3

Vertebrate Organ System		
System	**Main Parts**	**Function**
Skeletal	Bones, cartilage	Offers support and protection
Digestive	Mouth, stomach, intestines	Prepares food for use, removes undigested food
Excretory	Kidneys, bladder	Removes liquid wastes
Respiratory	Gills or lungs	Allows gas exchange between animal and its environment
Circulatory	Heart, blood vessels	Carries blood from heart to rest of body
Nervous	Brain, spinal cord, nerves	Controls and coordinates body functions
Reproductive	Male and female reproductive organs	Produces sperm and eggs for fertilization

Write a sentence explaining the connection between each pair of words.

3. chordate, vertebrate _____

_____

4. vertebrate, vertebrae _____

_____

Fill in the blanks in the following paragraph.

Animals with backbones are called **(5)**_____. They belong

to a larger group of animals called **(6)**_____. These animals

have an internal skeleton called a(n) **(7)**_____. Animals with

backbones are divided into five main groups. They are **(8)**_____,

(9)_____, **(10)**_____, **(11)**_____,

and **(12)**_____.

13. List the seven main organ systems of a vertebrate.

_____

_____

_____

_____

14. Why are vertebrates considered complex animals?

_____

_____

_____

_____

What Do You Know?

Key Words

fishes:	vertebrates that live in the water and breathe with gills
gills:	respiratory structures that allow fishes to breathe in water
ectothermic:	having a body temperature that changes with the temperature of the environment
jawless fishes:	fishes with a smooth, round body and no jaw
cartilaginous fishes:	fishes with hinged jaws and skeletons made of cartilage
cartilage:	tough, flexible tissue of the skeletal system
bony fishes:	fishes with hinged jaws, scaly skin, and skeletons made of bone

KEY IDEAS

Fishes are vertebrates that live in the water and breathe with gills. They are classified into three groups depending on the structure of their skeleton.

Imagine walking into the schoolyard and finding a live dinosaur. That's just how scientists felt with the discovery of the coelacanth. The coelacanth is a fish thought to be extinct for *60 million* years. Then in 1938, a live coelacanth was caught in the ocean off the coast of South Africa. Since then, about 200 coelacanths have been found living near some islands off the eastern coast of Africa. Scientists hope that studies of this fish can give them clues to the evolution of all fishes and, perhaps, of humans.

Fishes are a large group of vertebrates that live only in water. Sharks, tuna, eels, and colorful clown fish are some types of fishes that live in the ocean. Bass and trout are just a few of the fishes that live in freshwater streams, rivers, ponds, and lakes.

Characteristics of Fishes. Vertebrates that live in the water and breathe with gills are **fishes** (FIHSH-ehz). The **gills** (gihlz) are respiratory structures that allow a fish to breathe in the water. All fishes are **ectothermic** (EHK-toh-thuhr-mihk) animals. Their body temperature changes with the temperature of the environment.

A fish's body has three distinct parts: a head, a tail, and a trunk. Most fishes have fins, membranes that extend out from the body and help the fish swim. Fins are supported by bones that are part of the skeleton. Most fishes also have scales covering their bodies. Like other vertebrates, fishes have well-developed organ systems such as the digestive, circulatory, and nervous systems. All fishes have a heart with only two chambers.

 1. What is an ectothermic animal? _____

_____

Classification of Fishes. Fishes are classified into three groups. The simplest group is the jawless fishes. **Jawless fishes** (JAW-lehs FIHSH-ehz) have round mouths and no jaws. They have wormlike bodies that are covered with mucus. Jawless fishes do not have teeth or scales. They have soft backbones. The two kinds of jawless fishes, hagfish and lampreys, are shown in Fig. 33-1. Hagfish are scavengers that live in the ocean. Lampreys live in both fresh water and salt water.

Fig. 33-1

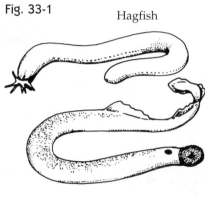

Hagfish

Lamprey

Sharks and rays belong to the group of fishes called cartilaginous fishes. **Cartilaginous fishes** (kahrt-uhl-AJ-uh-nuhs FIHSH-ehz) have soft, flexible skeletons made up of cartilage. **Cartilage** (KAHRT-uhl-ihj) is a tough, flexible tissue found in the skeletons of most vertebrates. Cartilage is not hard like bone. Unlike jawless fishes, cartilaginous fishes have both jaws and scales. They also have pairs of fins on their bodies. Sharks have long bodies covered with tiny, smooth scales. Rays have flat bodies with winglike fins. All sharks and rays live in the ocean. See Fig. 33-2.

Fig. 33-2

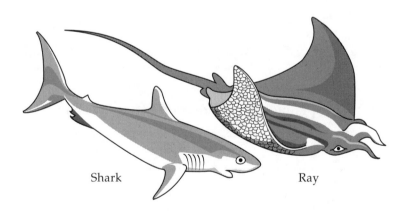

Shark   Ray

The third and largest group of fishes is the **bony fishes** (BOH-nee FIHSH-ehz). As their name suggests, these fishes have skeletons made up of hard bone. There are more than 30,000 species of bony fishes. That's more than all other species of vertebrates combined. Bony fishes live in salt water and fresh water. Fig. 33-3 shows the main body parts of a perch. The perch is a typical bony fish.

Fig. 33-3

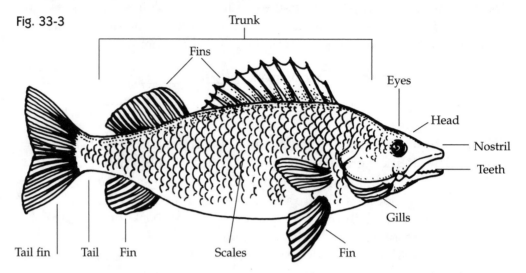

Fig. 33-4 shows the characteristics of the three groups of fishes.

Fig. 33-4

Characteristics of Fishes			
	Jawless	**Cartilaginous**	**Bony**
Habitat	Fresh water or salt water	Salt water	Fresh water or salt water
Skeleton	Cartilage	Cartilage	Bone
Jaws	No	Yes	Yes
Scales	No	Yes	Yes
Teeth	No	Yes	Yes
Fins	No	Yes	Yes

Check Your Understanding

Write a sentence explaining the connection between each pair of words.

2. fishes, gills _____

   _____

3. jawless fishes, cartilaginous fishes _____

   _____

4. cartilaginous fishes, cartilage _____

   _____

On the figure below, label the main parts of a bony fish.

Fig. 33-5

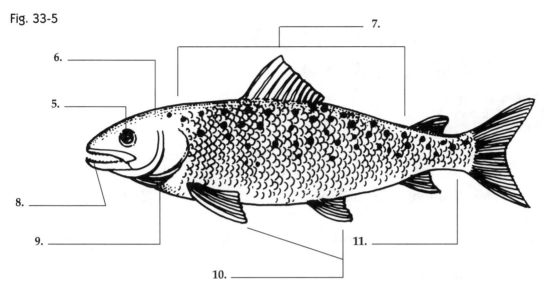

6. _____

5. _____

7. _____

8. _____

9. _____

10. _____

11. _____

12. What are three characteristics of a fish? _____

_____

_____

13. What is the primary difference between jawless fishes and other kinds

of fishes? _____

_____

_____

14. What is the primary difference between a cartilaginous fish and a bony

fish? _____

_____

_____

15. Tropical fishes must have a high body temperature to live. Why
wouldn't you put tropical fishes in a tank full of cool water?

_____

_____

_____

_____

Evolution of Land Vertebrates

Key Words

lungs:	primary internal organs of the respiratory system of land vertebrates
external fertilization:	fertilization that takes place outside a female animal's body, usually in water
internal fertilization:	fertilization that takes place inside a female animal's body
endothermic:	having an internal body temperature that stays constant regardless of the temperature of the environment

KEY IDEAS

One of the greatest changes in the kinds of animals on the earth occurred when vertebrates moved from the water onto land. This movement to life on land required major changes in vertebrates' structures and ways of living.

Scientists have a number of ideas about which vertebrates were the first to live on land. One idea is that the first land vertebrates were fishes that developed lungs and strong front fins. When the water in which the fishes lived was low in oxygen, they could rise to the surface and gulp air. These adaptations were successful because they allowed the fishes to move to new sources of water. The lungs and fins also helped the fishes move onto land located between pools of water. The fact that these adaptations helped vertebrates to survive on land proved to be an advantage.

Benefits of Life on Land. Scientists believe the move of vertebrates from life in the water to life on land occurred more than 350 million years ago. Living on land offered many advantages over living in the water. The land provided many new sources of food and places to live. Air has at least 200 times more oxygen to breathe than an equal volume of water. Land also has more protection and shelter in which to raise offspring.

1. What are three benefits to life on land? _____

_____

Adaptations to Life on Land. In addition to offering many benefits, living on land also has many problems. Life on land is very harsh compared to life in the water. Animals need water, or moisture, for breathing and reproduction. Different kinds of vertebrates developed different adaptations to life on land. Some vertebrates developed internal lungs for breathing instead of external gills. **Lungs** (luhngz) are the primary internal organs of the respiratory system of land vertebrates. The liquids inside a vertebrate's body keep its lungs moist. Vertebrates that breathe with lungs include amphibians, reptiles, birds, and mammals.

 2. What are lungs? _____

_____

Reproduction. Some vertebrates that moved to land changed the way they reproduced. Most vertebrates that live in or near water have external fertilization. Recall that fertilization is the joining of sperm and egg. **External fertilization** (ehks-TER-nuhl fuhrt-uhl-ih-ZAY-shuhn) is fertilization that takes place outside a female's body. In this process, the sperm moves through water to join with the eggs.

Most land vertebrates adapted a different way to reproduce. They developed internal fertilization. **Internal fertilization** (ihn-TER-nuhl fuhrt-uhl-ih-ZAY-shuhn) takes place inside a female's body. Water is not needed to move the sperm to the egg. Instead, the sperm moves through moist mucus inside the female's body to the egg.

In some land vertebrates, the young develop inside the mother's body. Other vertebrates lay eggs. Many vertebrates that live in or near the water lay their eggs in the water. These eggs do not dry out. However, eggs laid on land will dry out. An adaptation of land vertebrates is an egg with a leathery or hard outer shell. These kinds of shells protect the eggs from drying out.

Skin Protection. Land vertebrates also face the problem of their bodies drying out. These vertebrates evolved ways to prevent their bodies from losing water. Amphibians, for example, have special glands in their skin that produce a slimy substance called mucus to keep their skin moist. Reptiles are protected from drying by a covering of tough outer scales.

Body Support. Another problem of life on land is that air provides less support to the body than water. Vertebrates that moved to land evolved to have strong skeletons to support their bodies. Land vertebrates also evolved to have legs, instead of fins, to allow for better movement on land.

✓ 3. Why did vertebrates that moved to land need a strong skeleton?

_____

Body Temperature. Another difference between water and land environments is the temperature. On land, temperatures change more frequently than in water. Water environments have a nearly constant temperature from day to night. There are only slight temperature changes from one season to another. On land, the temperature can change greatly from day to night and from season to season.

Recall that most vertebrates that live in the water are ectothermic. Their body temperatures change with the temperature of the water. Many vertebrates that live on land are endothermic. **Endothermic** (ehn-doh-THUHR-mihk) animals maintain a constant internal body temperature regardless of the temperature of their environment. Unlike ectothermic vertebrates, endothermic vertebrates do not need to absorb heat from their surroundings. Thus, endotherms can survive greater changes in temperature than ectotherms. Of all the vertebrates, only birds and mammals are endothermic.

TAKE ANOTHER LOOK

Fig. 34-1 compares the characteristics of some vertebrates that live in water to some of those that live on land.

Fig. 34-1

Characteristics	Vertebrates that live in water	Vertebrates that live on land
Fertilization	External fertilization	Internal fertilization
Eggs	Jelly-like eggs	Eggs with a hard outer shell
Skin protection	Skin protected by water, mucus, and/or scales	Skin protection includes mucus and hard scales
Breathing structure	Gills	Lungs
Body temperature	Most ectothermic	Endothermic, ectothermic
Limbs	Fins or flippers	Strong skeleton with legs

Check Your Understanding

Write a sentence explaining the connection between each pair of words.

4. external fertilization, internal fertilization _____

_____

5. endothermic, ectothermic _____

_____

Fill in the blanks in the paragraph using the following terms:
food, lungs, oxygen, shelter, skeletons, endothermic, water

Life on land offered new sources of **(6)**_____ and **(7)**_____.
The air also has more **(8)**_____ than water. Vertebrates that moved
to live on land developed **(9)**_____ for breathing and strong
(10)_____ to support their body weight. **(11)**_____ land
vertebrates have a constant internal body temperature.

---

12. What are two ways that some land vertebrates keep their bodies from
drying out?_____

_____

_____

13. In what two ways did the reproduction of many land vertebrates
change from that of vertebrates that live in water?_____

_____

_____

14. You have just read about how vertebrates evolved to live on land.
Imagine that in the future, humans were forced to live in water. How
would the human body have to change for humans to be able to live in
water? _____

_____

_____

_____

_____

What
Do You
Know?

Amphibians

KEY IDEAS

Amphibians were the first vertebrates to adapt to life on land. When they are young, most amphibians have gills and live in water. As adults, most amphibians breathe through lungs and live on land.

Have you ever opened your eyes under water while swimming? If so, you know how irritated your eyes can get from the water. Now imagine being a frog. Frogs live most of their lives under water. But they need to be able to see where they're going. Frogs have special eyelids. These eyelids are clear so that the frog can see through them. Yet the lids cover the eyes to keep water from bothering them.

Like other amphibians, frogs are adapted to life both in and out of the water. **Amphibians** (am-FIHB-ee-uhnz) are vertebrates that usually have gills and live in water when they are young, and have lungs and live on land as adults. Amphibians include familiar animals such as frogs, toads, and salamanders.

Characteristics of Amphibians. Many characteristics of amphibians are adaptations to life on land. Most adult amphibians have internal lungs rather than gills. The lungs are kept moist by fluids inside the body. Another adaptation amphibians have are mucus glands in the skin. **Mucus glands** (MYOO-kuhs glandz) secrete a slimy substance called mucus that covers the skin and prevents water loss. The skin of amphibians is smooth and thin. Amphibians also have bony skeletons that are strong enough to support their weight. Most amphibians have two pairs of legs with clawless toes.

Amphibians are only partially adapted to life on land. For example, almost all amphibians must return to the water for at least part of their reproductive cycle. Most amphibians have webbed feet for swimming. Like fishes, amphibians have external fertilization and are ectothermic. Unlike fishes, adult amphibians have a heart with three chambers. Fish hearts have only two chambers.

1. What is an adaptation of amphibians that prevents water loss?

_____

_____

Classification of Amphibians. Most amphibians are classified into two groups. The first group is made up of amphibians without tails. These include frogs and toads. Frogs are the most common amphibians. They have short, wide bodies with two pairs of legs—small front legs and large, powerful back legs used for jumping. The back feet of frogs are large and webbed. Frogs also have large, protruding eyes that allow them to see above the water when they are swimming. Another feature of a frog is its large, external ears. See Fig. 35-1.

Fig. 35-1   Frog

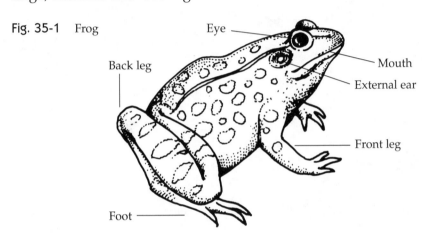

The second group of amphibians has tails. Salamanders, shown in Fig. 35-2, are in this group. Salamanders live in moist places near water. They have two pairs of legs that stick straight out from the body.

Fig. 35-2   Salamander

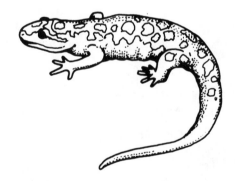

Reproduction in Frogs.   There are both male and female adult frogs. During reproduction, the female frog lays eggs in water. The male frog then releases sperm cells and spreads them over the eggs. Recall that reproduction in which sperm fertilizes the eggs outside the body is called external fertilization. The fertilized eggs then grow and develop. They eventually hatch into tadpoles.

Life Cycle of Frogs. A **tadpole** (TAD-pohl) is the immature stage of a frog. The tadpole lives in water and goes through a series of changes as it develops. Fig. 35-3 shows the series of changes in the frog life cycle. The young tadpole has a tail, breathes through gills, and eats plants. The tadpole gradually grows legs, and the tail disappears. Gills are replaced by lungs. The young frog can now survive on land. Unlike tadpoles, adult frogs eat other animals, mostly insects.

Fig. 35-3

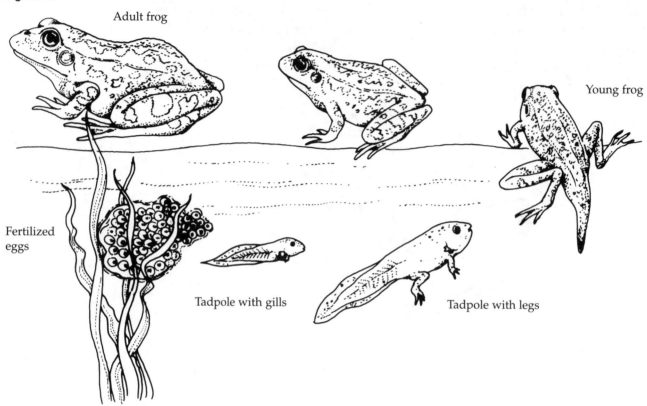

Adult frog

Young frog

Fertilized eggs

Tadpole with gills

Tadpole with legs

Fig. 35-4 summarizes the differences between fishes and amphibians.

Fig. 35-4

Characteristics	Amphibians	Fishes
Habitat	On land or in water	Only in water
Fertilization	External	External
Skin protection	Mucus	Scales and mucus
Breathing structure	Gills when young, internal lungs as adult	Internal gills
Body temperature	Ectothermic	Ectothermic
Limbs	Two pairs of legs	Fins
Heart	Three chambers	Two chambers

Write a sentence explaining the connection between each pair of words.

2. amphibian, lungs _____

_____

3. tadpole, frog _____

_____

Fill in the blanks to complete the following paragraph.

Amphibians are **(4)**_____ that usually live part of their life

on **(5)**_____ and part of their life in the **(6)**_____.

Mature frogs have internal **(7)**_____ rather than external

(8)_____. To keep their skin from drying out, amphibians

have **(9)**_____. Frogs reproduce by **(10)**_____

fertilization. Immature frogs are called **(11)**_____.

What
Do You
Know?

12. What are the two main kinds of amphibians? _____

_____

13. What are three adaptations amphibians have for life on land?

_____

_____

14. How are amphibians different from fishes? _____

_____

_____

_____

_____

15. How are tadpoles different from adult frogs? _____

_____

_____

_____

_____

reptiles: vertebrates with scaly skin that lay their eggs on land

amniotic egg: reptile egg that has a fluid-filled sac enclosed by a protective shell

KEY IDEAS

Reptiles were the first vertebrates to live completely out of the water. They have special characteristics that allow them to live on land. Reptiles include snakes, lizards, crocodiles, and turtles.

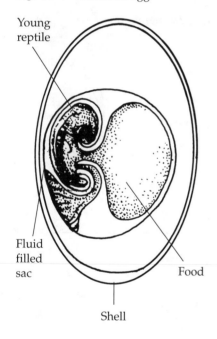

Fig. 36-1 Amniotic egg

Young reptile

Fluid filled sac

Food

Shell

Dinosaurs were giant reptiles that lived on the earth from about 200 million years ago until about 65 million years ago. Dinosaurs ranged from the size of a chicken to the giant Brachiosaurus, which was 25 meters long and weighed 50 tons. Scientists are not sure why dinosaurs became extinct. Some believe that the climate became too dry and cold for the dinosaur to survive. However, some reptiles similar to the dinosaur were able to survive. These animals evolved into today's reptiles.

Reptiles (REHP-teyelz) are vertebrates with scaly skin that lay their eggs on land. The first vertebrates to live completely on land were reptiles. On land they had little competition from other animals for food and territory.

Characteristics of Reptiles. Many of the traits of reptiles are adaptations to their life on land. Unlike amphibians, reptiles do not need water to reproduce. Reptiles reproduce by internal fertilization. Recall that internal fertilization means that the sperm fertilizes the egg inside the female's body. Internal fertilization does not require water to carry the sperm to the egg.

Reptiles have amniotic eggs, which they lay on land. The **amniotic egg** (am-nee-AHT-ihk ehg) has a fluid-filled sac enclosed in a protective shell, as shown in Fig. 36-1. This leathery, flexible shell prevents the developing young from drying out.

Reptiles have skin that keeps them from drying out. Unlike the soft, thin skin of amphibians, reptiles have thick skin covered with scales. The scales make the skin both hard and waterproof.

Like amphibians, most reptiles have two pairs of limbs and are ectotherms. They also have well-developed organ systems and a three-chambered heart.

 1. **What are three characteristics of reptiles that allow them to live completely on land?** _____

_____

Classification of Reptiles. Modern reptiles can be classified into four main groups. The smallest group has only one species—the tuatara. This reptile has a long tail and a scaly crest that runs down its back and neck. All tuataras in the wild live on an island off the coast of New Zealand.

Turtles and tortoises belong to another group of reptiles. Turtles generally live in the water. Tortoises most often live on land. Both turtles and tortoises have a two-part shell that they use for protection from predators. A turtle shell is shown in Fig. 36-2. Turtles do not have teeth. Instead, they have hard beaks with which they eat both plants and animals.

Fig. 36-2 Turtle shell

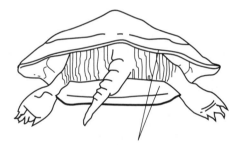

Two-part shell

Another group of reptiles contains alligators and crocodiles. Both alligators and crocodiles have strong tails to help them swim. Strong jaws and teeth help them capture and eat food. These reptiles spend most of their time in the water, where they hunt for food. Because they are ectothermic, they spend their time on land sunning themselves to keep warm. They also go on the land to lay their eggs.

Snakes and lizards make up the fourth group of reptiles. Snakes are reptiles with long, thin bodies and no limbs. They have a large number of ribs and a very long backbone. The greatest difference between snakes and lizards is that lizards have two pairs of legs. Both snakes and lizards live in a variety of environments and eat many different kinds of food. Some kinds of snakes and lizards have poisonous venom, which they inject into their prey.

Fig. 36-3 shows similarities and differences between amphibians and reptiles.

Fig. 36-3

Characteristics	Reptiles	Amphibians
Habitat	On land or in water	On land or in water
Fertilization	Internal	External
Eggs	Amniotic egg laid on land	Eggs laid in water
Skin protection	Scales	Mucus glands
Body temperature	Ectothermic	Ectothermic
Limbs	Two pairs	Two pairs
Heart	Three chambers	Three chambers

Check Your Understanding

Write a sentence explaining the connection between each pair of words.

2. reptile, amniotic egg _____

_____

3. reptile, internal fertilization _____

_____

Fill in the blanks in the following outline.

I. Reptiles are (4)_____ that lay their eggs on (5)_____.

   A. Reptiles reproduce by (6)_____ fertilization.

   B. Reptiles have a special kind of egg called an (7)_____ egg.

   C. Reptiles have thick scales that keep their skin from (8)_____.

II. Reptiles can be classified into (9)_____ main groups.

   A. Only one species of (10)_____ is still alive today.

   B. (11)_____ and (12)_____ have protective shells.

   C. (13)_____ and (14)_____ have strong jaws with large teeth.

   D. (15)_____ have legs and tails, (16)_____ do not.

17. What is the main difference between a snake and a lizard?

_____

_____

_____

18. Identify three different kinds of reptiles. Explain how they differ from

one another. _____

_____

_____

_____

_____

_____

19. Describe three ways that reptiles and amphibians are similar. Describe

three ways they are different. _____

_____

_____

_____

_____

_____

_____

Lesson 37 Birds

Key Words

birds: endothermic vertebrates that have feathers and wings
feathers: modified scales adapted for flight and conserving body heat

KEY IDEAS

Birds are vertebrates that have feathers and wings. They have special characteristics, such as feathers and lightweight bones, that allow them to fly.

The oldest bird fossil ever found is of the *Archaeopteryx* (ahr-kee-AHP-tuhr-ihks). The *Archaeopteryx* had wings and feathers like today's birds. It also had teeth and three clawed fingers on its wings. Birds today do not have teeth. The Hoatzin (hoh-AT-sihn), found in South America, is one of the few birds with claws on its wings. However, the Hoatzin only has claws while it is young. The claws disappear as the bird matures.

Characteristics of Birds. **Birds** (berdz) are endothermic vertebrates that have feathers and wings. The most obvious characteristic of birds is that they can fly. Insects can fly, but they are not vertebrates. Bats are vertebrates that can fly, but they do not have feathers. Feathers are the characteristic that makes birds different from all other vertebrates. **Feathers** (FEHTH-uhrz) are modified scales adapted for flight and for conserving body heat.

Many characteristics of birds are also adaptations for flight. They have hollow, lightweight bones that are filled with air. Birds have air sacs throughout their bodies that help them breathe more easily during flight. Their front limbs are modified into wings.

Another characteristic of birds are hind legs that can be used for perching, jumping, and swimming. Birds also have hard beaks rather than teeth.

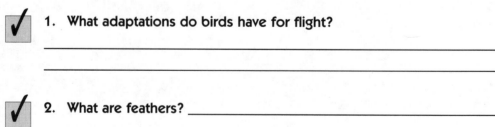

1. **What adaptations do birds have for flight?**

_____

_____

2. **What are feathers?** _____

_____

Like reptiles, birds reproduce by internal fertilization and have an amniotic egg. However, the amniotic egg of a bird has a hard shell. Unlike reptiles and amphibians, birds have a heart with four chambers and are endothermic. Recall that endotherms have a constant internal body temperature.

Types of Feathers. Birds have different kinds of feathers that perform different functions. Soft, fluffy feathers, called down, help keep the bird warm and maintain its body temperature. Streamlined feathers, called contour feathers, form a smooth surface to ease the bird's movement through the air. They also help keep the bird warm. Special contour feathers on the wings and tail help the bird fly. Fig. 37-1 shows these two different types of feathers.

Skeleton. A bird's skeleton has many adaptations for flight, as you can see in Fig. 37-2. The bones are lightweight and filled with air. The most noticeable difference between birds and other vertebrates is the shape of their breast bone. You may have noticed this bone while eating chicken or turkey. The muscles used for flapping are attached to this large bone.

Classification of Birds. Birds are classified into 27 groups according to their physical characteristics. These characteristics include beaks, feet, and feathers. Scientists have also classified birds according to their behavior and song. One group of birds is water birds. These birds have feet like paddles for swimming or long legs for wading. Water birds include ducks, sandpipers, and gulls. Another group of birds cannot fly. Flightless birds include penguins and ostriches.

Fig. 37-1

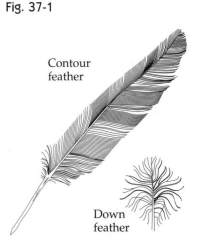

Contour feather

Down feather

Fig. 37-2

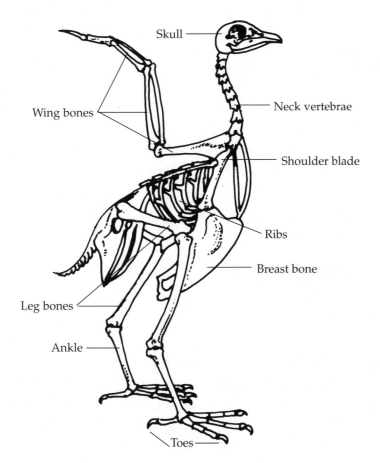

Skull

Wing bones

Neck vertebrae

Shoulder blade

Ribs

Breast bone

Leg bones

Ankle

Toes

Fig. 37-3 shows the characteristics of four common groups of birds.

Fig. 37-3

Type	Examples	Type of feet	Types of beaks
Flightless birds 	Penguins, rheas, ostriches	Adapted for running 	(Beaks vary) 
Water birds 	Ducks, swans, geese	Webbed 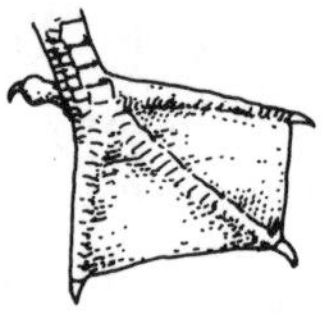	Broad and flat for filtering 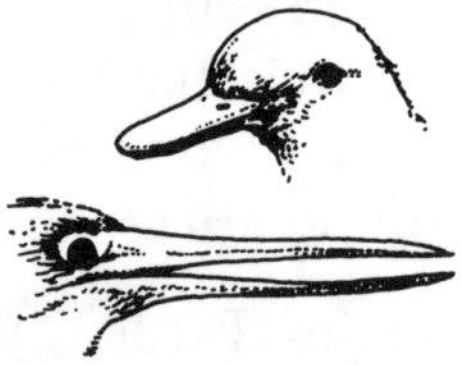 Long and pointed for fishing
Perching birds 	Sparrows, robins, other songbirds	Toes cling to branches 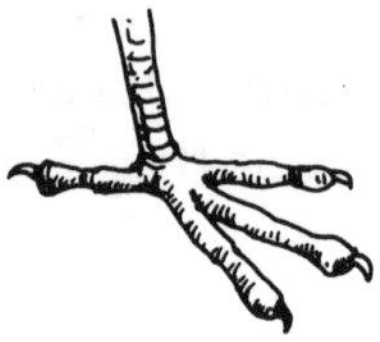	Short, thick, strong (seed eaters)  Long and slender for probing (insect eaters)
Birds of prey 	Hawks, eagles, owls	Sharp, curving claws 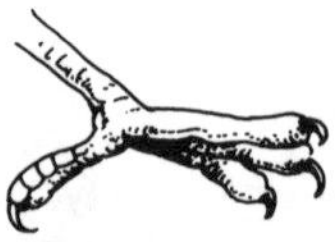	Tearing beaks 

Fig. 37-4 compares the characteristics of birds and reptiles.

TAKE ANOTHER LOOK

Fig. 37-4

Characteristics	Birds	Reptiles
Habitat	On land, in the air, or in water	On land or in water
Flight	Can fly	Cannot fly
Fertilization	Internal	Internal
Eggs	Amniotic eggs	Amniotic eggs
Body protection	Feathers	Scales
Body temperature	Endothermic	Ectothermic
Heart	Four chambers	Three chambers

Write a sentence explaining the connection between each pair of words.

3. bird, endothermic _____

_____

4. bird, feathers _____

_____

Complete the following paragraph by filling in the blanks.

Birds are endothermic vertebrates that have **(5)**_____ and **(6)**_____. Endothermic means having a **(7)**_____ internal body temperature. Birds are like reptiles in that they have **(8)**_____ fertilization and **(9)**_____ eggs. They are different from reptiles because birds have a **(10)**_____-chambered heart and they are **(11)**_____. Birds have special characteristics that allow them to fly. These traits include **(12)**_____, **(13)**_____, and **(14)**_____ bones.

What Do You Know?

15. What are two functions of feathers? _____

_____

_____

_____

16. Name four common groups of birds. Give an example of each.

_____

_____

_____

_____

17. In what two ways are birds different from most other vertebrates?

_____

_____

_____

_____

38 Mammals

Key Words

mammals:	vertebrates that have mammary glands, and hair; most give birth
mammary glands:	special glands in the female that produce milk to feed to the young
placenta:	special organ that connects the unborn young to the mother inside the mother's body

KEY IDEAS

Mammals are the most complex and successful of the vertebrates. They give birth to live young and then take care of the young for long periods of time.

Mammals are the most complex and the most successful of all vertebrates. Mammals have adapted to live almost anywhere—in oceans, in desert sands, in tropical forests and snow-capped mountains, and even in the air. Mammals range in size from the tiniest mouse to humans to the giant blue whale. The blue whale is the largest animal to ever live on the earth. Living in the water helps the whale support its immense weight.

Characteristics of Mammals. Vertebrates that have hair and mammary glands are **mammals** (MAM-uhlz). Most mammals give birth. Birth occurs when a young animal leaves its mother's body in which it has been growing. **Mammary glands** (MAM-uh-ree glandz) are special glands in the female that produce milk to feed to the young soon after it is born. Most young mammals go through a long period of development after they are born. Their parents care for them during this time.

Mammals are the only animals that have hair on their bodies. Some mammals have more hair than others. A furry black bear, for example, has more hair than an elephant. Hair has two functions: it protects the skin from injury and helps keep the body warm.

Mammals have well-developed organ systems. Like birds, mammals are endothermic and have four-chambered hearts. Mammals also have large and well-developed brains. Their brains help them adapt to changes and direct many kinds of complex behavior.

 1. What is a mammal? _____
_____

 2. What are two functions of hair? _____
_____

Classification of Mammals. Mammals are classified into three groups based on how they reproduce. The three groups are egg-laying mammals, pouched mammals, and placental mammals.

Only two kinds of egg-laying mammals live on the earth. They are the duck-billed platypus and the spiny anteater. Both of these animals live in Australia. These mammals have mammary glands and hair. But unlike most mammals, they do not give birth. Instead, these mammals lay eggs. After the eggs hatch, the young mammals drink the mother's milk and are cared for by their parents.

Pouched mammals include kangaroos, opossums, and koalas. Most of these mammals live in Australia, but a few live elsewhere. These animals give birth to live, undeveloped young. The young mammals complete their development inside their mother's protective pouch.

The most common mammals are the placental mammals. These mammals have a special organ called a placenta. The **placenta** (phuh-SEHN-tuh) connects the unborn young to the mother inside the mother's body. The young grows and develops inside the mother's body. At birth, the young must be large and developed enough to survive in the outside world. After they are born, young placental mammals need their parents to care for them.

 3. How is a duck-billed platypus different from most other mammals?
_____

 4. What is the placenta? _____
_____
_____

Fig. 38-1 lists the characteristics of some mammals.

Fig. 38-1

Type of Mammal	Characteristics	Examples
Egg-laying mammals	Mothers lay eggs	Platypus, spiny anteater
Pouched mammals	Young poorly developed at birth; remain in mother's pouch until fully developed	Kangaroo, koala, opossum
Placental mammals: Hand-winged	Only flying mammal; active at night; sharp teeth; large ears	Bat
Odd-numbered toes	Odd number of toes; plant eaters	Horse, rhinoceros
Trunk-nosed	Has a trunk, tusks, and massive legs; plant eater; large size	Elephant
Flesh eaters	Meat and/or plant eaters; sharp teeth and claws; powerful legs; predators	Bear, cat, dog, seal
Whales	Marine animals; streamlined bodies; paddlelike front limbs; no hind limbs	Whale, dolphin, porpoise
Gnawers	Small; one pair of upper incisors used for gnawing	Squirrel, mouse, rat, beaver, porcupine
Primates	Most are tree dwellers; have opposable thumbs; most have eyes in front; capable of standing upright	lemur, monkey, ape, human

Check Your Understanding

Write a sentence explaining the connection between each pair of words.

5.   mammal, mammary glands _____

_____

6.   mammal, bird _____

_____

Complete the concept map using the following words and phrases: *egg-laying, human, inside the mother's pouch, attached to the placenta, kangaroo, laying eggs, placental, spiny anteater.*

Fig. 38-2

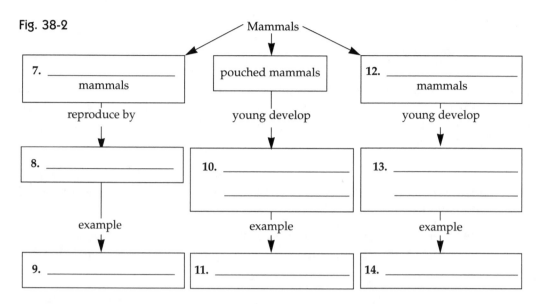

7. _____ mammals

reproduce by

8. _____

example

9. _____

Mammals

pouched mammals

young develop

10. _____ _____

example

11. _____

12. _____ mammals

young develop

13. _____ _____

example

14. _____

15. What are three characteristics of mammals that make them different from other vertebrates? _____
_____

16. What is the advantage to a mammal of having a well-developed brain?
_____
_____

17. Describe the differences in reproduction among the three groups of mammals. _____
_____
_____
_____

Summary

- A chordate is an animal that has a thin, flexible rod that supports three features: body, gill slits, and nerve chord. All chordates have these three features at some time during their life. A vertebrate is one kind of chordate.

- A vertebrate has a backbone, a complex body plan with well-developed organ systems, sense organs located on the head, a large central body, and an endoskeleton.

- Fishes are ectothermic vertebrates that live in water and breathe with gills. Fishes are classified into three groups: jawless fishes, cartilaginous fishes, and bony fishes.

- Life on land offered vertebrates many advantages. These advantages included new sources of food, more oxygen to breathe, and more places for shelter.

- Life on land involved many adaptations. Lungs replaced gills as the main organs of the respiratory system. Some land vertebrates have mucus glands or hard scales covering their skin. These structures prevent their skin from drying out. Land vertebrates reproduce by internal fertilization. Their eggs have hard or leathery shells that prevent drying.

- Amphibians are ectothermic vertebrates that usually have gills and live in water when they are young, and have lungs and live on land as adults. Amphibians reproduce in the water by external fertilization.

- Reptiles are ectothermic vertebrates that have scaly skin and lay their eggs on land. Reptiles have internal lungs, an amniotic egg, and scales that prevent water loss.

- Birds are endothermic vertebrates. Most birds can fly. Their adaptations for flight include wings, feathers, lightweight bones, and air sacs in the body.

- Mammals are the most complex vertebrates. They give birth and have mammary glands and hair. Mammals are classified into three groups: egg-laying mammals, pouched mammals, and placental mammals. The placenta is a special organ that connects the unborn young to the mother inside the mother's body.

For Your Portfolio

1. Make a list of some of the vertebrates you see living near your school. After you have completed the list, classify the animals as fishes, reptiles, amphibians, birds, or mammals. Make a chart of all the vertebrates you identified. Include their names, classification, and where they live.

2. Go to the library and do research on fish that are commonly eaten by people. How important is fish in the diets of people of different cultures? For example, how much and what kinds of fish are eaten by the Japanese, Chinese, Greenlanders, people of the United States, and other cultures? What is the nutritional value of fish in the human diet? Report your findings to your classmates. If possible, you may want to sample some different kinds of fish eaten by different cultures.

3. Go to the library and borrow a field guide of birds in your area. For several days, observe the birds around you. If possible, use a pair of binoculars. Except in the coldest part of winter, you should see many different kinds of birds. Try to identify all the birds you see. Make a list of the birds you see. Keep a journal that tells when and where you saw the bird, what the weather was like, and what the bird was doing. You may even want to include a drawing of the bird.

4. Use library resources to find out about John James Audubon. What is Audubon famous for? You might also want to find out about the National Audubon Society. What are the society's functions and goals? Share your findings with your class. If possible, invite a member of your local Audubon Society to speak to your class.

5. Visit a local aquarium or tropical fish store. Look at as many fishes as you can. How are the fishes different? How are they the same? What do they eat? How big are they? Make drawings of five of your favorite fishes and label the main parts. Share your drawings with your classmates.

6. Visit a natural history museum in your area. Look at the dinosaur skeletons and fossil dinosaur bones. If possible, talk to a paleontologist— a scientist who studies ancient animals—at the museum. You may want to call ahead and make an appointment. Ask the paleontologist where the dinosaurs came from, what they ate, and when they lived. Share your findings with your class.

Complete the following statements.

1. A chordate with a strong, flexible backbone is called a _____.

2. _____ are ectothermic vertebrates that live in the water.

3. The three kinds of fishes are _____, _____, and _____.

4. An animal whose body temperature changes with the environment is _____.

5. A vertebrate with scaly skin that lays eggs on land is a _____.

6. Reptiles have a kind of egg called an _____ egg that protects the offspring from drying out.

7. Before birth, the organ that connects a young mammal to the inside of its mother's body is the _____.

Answer the following questions.

8. Describe three characteristics of all vertebrates. _____

    _____

    _____

9. Describe three differences between fishes and birds._____

    _____

    _____

10. Describe three differences between amphibians and reptiles. _____

    _____

    _____

    _____

Answer one of the following questions.

11. Mammals have many traits that help them survive and reproduce in their environment. Describe three traits of mammals that help them survive and explain the role of each.

12. Make a chart comparing the characteristics of fishes, reptiles, amphibians, birds, and mammals. Include information about body temperature, type of heart, type of fertilization, type of skeleton, type of breathing organ, and habitat.

Ecology

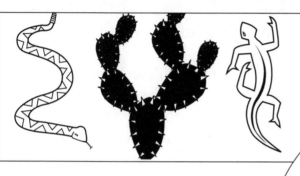

During the 1950's and 1960's, populations of ospreys, bald eagles, and other large fish-eating birds fell drastically. Scientists noticed that large amounts of a pesticide, DDT, were present in the birds' bodies. They decided to study the feeding relationships in the birds' environment to find out why.

Scientists found that the DDT sprayed on crops would run off into lakes and streams. Tiny organisms in the water absorbed the DDT. Small fish ate the tiny organisms. Larger fish ate the small fish. Birds ate the large fish.

Each time one organism ate another, the DDT was passed on. The DDT that the birds were eating had made them ill. The DDT made the shells of their eggs thinner, too. The thin shells broke easily, and the chicks died. Once the scientists knew what was harming the birds, they could fix the problem. The use of DDT was banned in the United States. This is just one example of why it's important to understand the relationships between all the organisms in a single environment.

Ecosystem Interactions

Key Words

ecosystem:	organisms that interact with one another and with their nonliving environment
community:	the living part of an ecosystem
population:	group of the same type of organism, or species, living together in a particular area
competition:	the struggle among living things to obtain what they need to survive
predation:	relationship in which one organism kills and eats another
commensalism:	relationship between organisms in which only one organism benefits
mutualism:	relationship between organisms in which both organisms benefit

Key Ideas

An ecosystem is made up of all the living and nonliving things in an area that interact with one another. Some relationships in an ecosystem help an organism. Other relationships may harm it. A change in one relationship can affect other parts of the ecosystem. By studying the relationships in an ecosystem, we can predict how a change will affect the ecosystem.

Landscape designers are responsible for the health of the plant life growing in a particular area. They do far more than make the plants and trees "look good." Landscape designers identify the specific needs of every plant growing in an area. They ensure that the plants are able to meet their needs. Understanding how different types of organisms interact while sharing a common area is an important part of a landscape designer's job.

Ecosystems. Organisms interacting with one another and with their nonliving environment make up an **ecosystem** (EE-koh-SIHS-tuhm). An ecosystem may be as small as a drop of pond water or as large as a forest. The living part of an ecosystem is a **community** (kuh-MYOO-nuh-tee). A forest community may include deer, trees, and mushrooms. A pond community may include fish, insects, and plants.

A **population** (PAHP-yoo-LAY-shun) is all the members of a particular species that live in the same area. The members of a population can reproduce among themselves. One population of a forest community might be all the oak trees that grow there. Another population in the same forest community could be all the termites that live on the trees.

 1. What is the difference between a community and a population?

_____

_____

Ecosystem Relationships. Each organism in a community carries out its own unique role. A large part of an organism's role is obtaining resources, or the things it needs to survive. Often, the amounts of these resources are limited. As a result, competition occurs. **Competition** (KAM-puh-TISH-uhn) is a relationship in which living things struggle with each another to obtain limited resources.

Another type of limiting relationship in an ecosystem is predation. **Predation** (preh-DAY-shun) occurs when one organism kills and eats another. A predator is the organism that eats another. The prey is the organism that is eaten. The graph in Fig. 39-1 shows the connection between populations of predators and prey.

Fig. 39-1

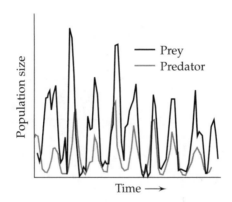

Some relationships in an ecosystem are helpful to one or both organisms involved. **Commensalism** (kuh-MEHN-suhl-izm) is a relationship in which one organism benefits. The other organism in the partnership is unaffected. An example of commensalism exists between tropical orchid plants and the trees on which they grow. By resting in the tree's branches, the orchids obtain the sunlight they need to survive. The tree is unaffected by the presence of the plants.

Mutualism is another helpful relationship between organisms. In **mutualism** (MYOO-chu-wuhl-ihsm), both organisms benefit. The relationship of hummingbirds and flowers is an example of mutualism. When the hummingbird drinks nectar from a flower, it obtains nutrients it needs to live. As the bird moves from flower to flower, it transfers pollen. By pollinating the flowers, the hummingbird makes it possible for the plants to reproduce.

Fig. 39-2 shows the various types of relationships that exist in communities of an ecosystem.

Fig. 39-2

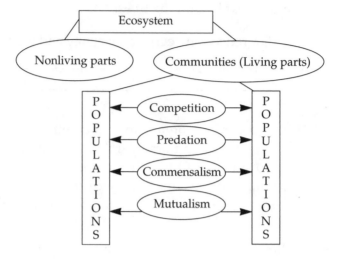

Check Your Understanding

Write a sentence explaining the connection between each pair of words.

2. ecosystem, community _____

_____

3. community, population _____

_____

4. competition, predation _____

_____

Complete the passage with a term listed below.

commensalism   community   competition   ecosystem
mutualism   populations   predation

All the living and nonliving things with which an organism interacts make up a(n) **(5)**_____. The living part of an ecosystem is a(n) **(6)**_____. A community may contain many different **(7)**_____. They interact, or have relationships, with one another. **(8)**_____ is a relationship in which one organism kills and eats another. **(9)**_____ is a relationship in which organisms struggle with each other to meet their needs. **(10)**_____ is a relationship in which one organism benefits while the other is unaffected. **(11)**_____ is a relationship which benefits both organisms.

12. What is an ecosystem? _____

_____

_____

13. What is predation? _____

_____

_____

14. What is competition? _____

_____

_____

15. Compare commensalism and mutualism. _____

_____

_____

16. Two hawks notice a rabbit on the ground below them. Both swoop down to grab the rabbit. Only one hawk catches and eats the rabbit. Explain how this situation is an example of competition and predation.

_____

_____

_____

_____

_____

17. The relationship that exists between the lynx and the snowshoe hare is an example of predation. Lynx are predators that feed on snowshoe hares. Explain what might happen to a lynx population if there was a sudden drop in a snowshoe hare population.

_____

_____

_____

_____

_____

Energy Flow in Ecosystems

producers:	organisms that are able to make their own food
consumers:	organisms that obtain energy by eating other organisms
decomposers:	organisms that obtain energy by breaking down dead organisms
food chain:	a model that shows the flow of energy through the organisms in an ecosystem
food web:	a model that shows how food chains overlap in an ecosystem
energy pyramid:	a model that shows how energy is transferred and lost in a food chain

KEY IDEAS

For populations to survive, energy must constantly flow through an ecosystem. The sun is the primary source of energy for living things. Feeding patterns within an ecosystem allow for the transfer of energy to all its organisms. By studying the feeding patterns of the organisms, we discover how energy flows through an ecosystem.

Many types of insects feed on farm crops to obtain their energy. Farmers often spray pesticides to kill the insects. However, pesticides poison drinking water and may harm helpful animals. Recently, farmers have begun to use feeding relationships to control crop-eating insects. They release insects into the environment that feed on the crop-eating insects. For example, in Nigeria, cassava farmers release wasps into the environment to feed on the mealy bugs that feed on the cassava plants.

Obtaining Energy. All organisms need energy to live. The primary source of energy for all organisms is the sun. Energy from the sun enters the ecosystem and is trapped by producers. **Producers** (pruh-DOOS-erz) are organisms that use the sun's energy to make their own food. The food is made through the process of photosynthesis. In photosynthesis, plants make complex molecules from simple ones.

Producers use some of their food to carry out their life processes. The producer stores any extra food. The stored food makes the producer a source of energy for organisms that feed on the producer. Plants, some protists, and blue-green bacteria are examples of producers.

All organisms that are not producers are consumers. **Consumers** (kuhn-SOO-merz) are organisms that obtain energy by feeding on other organisms. Some consumers eat only producers. Some consumers eat only other consumers. Still other consumers eat both producers and consumers. Humans are consumers. Most people eat both consumers and producers.

 1. What is the difference between a producer and a consumer?

_____

_____

_____

Another type of organism in an ecosystem is a decomposer. **Decomposers** (dee-kuhm-POHZ-erz) feed on dead organisms. A decomposer obtains its energy by breaking down dead organic matter. Mushrooms are an example of decomposers and are often found growing on dead trees.

In its feeding process, a decomposer returns some nutrients to the ecosystem. Producers use these nutrients to carry out life processes, such as photosynthesis.

Energy Relationships. Energy moves through an ecosystem by the feeding relationships of its organisms. A **food chain** (food chayn) is a model that shows an ecosystem's feeding relationships. An example of a food chain is:

$$\text{SUN} \succ \text{GRASS} \succ \text{MOUSE} \succ \text{SNAKE} \succ \text{HAWK}$$

An ecosystem contains many different, overlapping food chains. A **food web** (food wehb) is a model that shows the connections among food chains. In an example of a food web, grasshoppers, rabbits, and mice all eat the producer, grass. Snakes and hawks both feed on rabbits and mice. However, a snake can be eaten by a hawk.

It is important to remember that a food chain shows how energy is transferred through an ecosystem. Energy enters the ecosystem through producers. Some of the energy is passed along to consumers that eat the producers. However, a great amount of energy is lost to the ecosystem in the form of heat.

An **energy pyramid** (EHN-er-jee PIHR-uh-mihd) is a model that shows how energy is transferred and lost in a food chain. Look at Fig. 40-1. You can see that energy is transferred from the grass to the mice to the snake to the hawk. Note that the shape of the pyramid shows that each level contains less energy than the level below. There is more energy to support life in the beginning of a food chain than in the end of a food chain.

Fig. 40-1

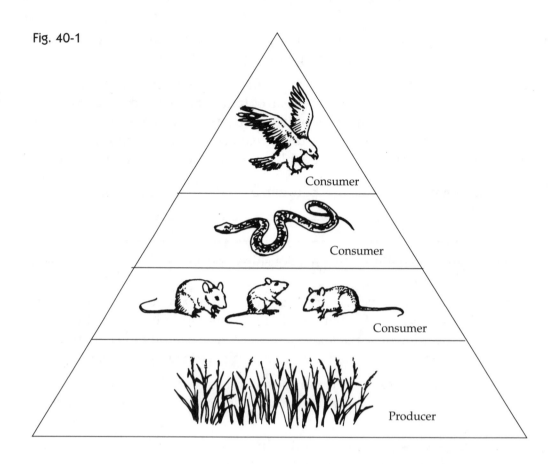

Consumer

Consumer

Consumer

Producer

TAKE ANOTHER LOOK

Fig. 40-2 is a model of a food web that shows the connections among food chains.

Fig. 40-2

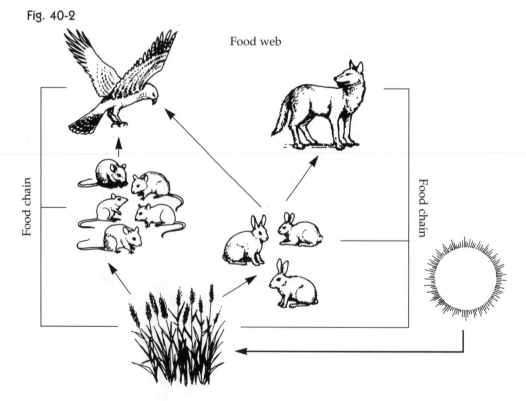

Food web

Food chain

Food chain

Complete the following outline by adding the correct word.

All organisms need **(2)**_____ to carry out life processes. Organisms that can make their own food are **(3)**_____. Organisms that obtain energy by eating other living things are **(4)**_____. **(5)**_____ feed on dead organisms. The feeding relationships that exist in a(n) **(6)**_____ allow for the flow of energy throughout the system. A(n) **(7)**_____ is a model that shows these feeding relationships. A(n) **(8)**_____ is a model that shows how food chains are connected. A(n) **(9)**_____ is a model that shows how energy is lost in a food chain.

What Do You Know?

10. Could a food chain ever begin with a consumer? Explain.

_____

_____

_____

11. How do decomposers help energy flow through an ecosystem?

_____

_____

_____

12. Why is the amount of energy present at the upper levels of an energy pyramid less than the amount of energy present at the lower levels?

_____

_____

_____

13. Why are there usually more organisms at the bottom level of an energy pyramid than at the top level? _____

_____

_____

_____

Lesson 41 Biomes

Key Words

biome:	large geographic area with a certain climate and specific types of communities
tundra:	extremely cold and dry land biome
taiga:	biome dominated by large forests of cone-bearing trees
littoral zone:	area that runs along the shore and is affected by the tides
sublittoral zone:	area that lies just beyond the littoral zone through which sunlight passes to the ocean floor
pelagic zone:	the open ocean past the sublittoral zone

KEY IDEAS

Each population of organisms is adapted to a particular environment. It is no coincidence that regions of the earth that have a similar climate also have similar communities. A biome is a large geographic area with a certain climate and specific types of communities.

More than half of all the species on the earth live in the tropical rain forests. The many different kinds of species found in the rain forests are helpful to humans. Many foods and ingredients in the medicines we use come from the rain forests. For example, many plants that have chemicals which fight cancer come from the tropical rain forests. Unfortunately, the rain forests are being destroyed by human activities. They are being cut down for timber, mining, farming, and grazing. Most rain forest organisms are adapted to a very specific environment. Once their home is destroyed, they become extinct. People worldwide are working hard to preserve the rain forests.

The tropical rain forest is an example of a biome. A **biome** (BY-ohm) is a large region of the earth with a certain climate and specific plant and animal species. There are two major types of biomes: land biomes and water biomes. Most land biomes are named for the plant life that dominate the area. Climate affects the plant life of land biomes. Fig. 41-1 compares rainfall and temperature among the earth's six major land biomes.

Fig. 41-1

Land Biome Climates		
Biome	Average yearly rainfall	Average yearly temperature range
Tundra	less than 25 cm	–25°C – 4° C
Taiga	25–100cm	–10°C –14 °C
Deciduous forests	75–125cm	6°C –28° C
Tropical rain forests	200–450cm	25°C –28° C
Grasslands	25–75 cm	0°C –25° C
Deserts	less than 25cm	15°C –40° C

The kinds of populations found in each biome depend on the amount of energy the biome receives. Recall that the main source of energy for all the earth's organisms is the sun. Some regions of the earth receive much energy from the sun all year. The more energy that is available in an area, the more diverse are its populations. The tropical rain forest is such a place. In other places, the amount of energy varies with the seasons. A limited amount of energy, in turn, limits the kinds of species that can be supported by an area.

1. **What is a biome?** _____

_____

Tropical Rain Forest Biome. Near the equator is the tropical rain forest biome. Rain forests receive more than 200 centimeters of rain each year. Temperatures in this biome stay warm all year. The energy flow in tropical rain forests is generally constant. The plentiful energy allows for greater diversity in the populations. The populations are not limited by the amount of water or energy. As a result, more species of plants and animals live in the tropical rain forests than in any other biome.

The organisms live where they can receive the energy they need. Most of the animals live in trees high above the floor of the rain forest. The thick covering of trees prevents the sun's energy from reaching much of the lower part of the forest.

Deciduous Forest Biome. In the deciduous forest biome, average rainfall is more than 75 centimeters each year. This amount of rainfall helps the plant life flourish. The dominant plant life is deciduous trees. Deciduous trees have broad, flat leaves, which they lose in autumn. Examples of deciduous trees are oaks, maples, and birches. The trees are suited to the cold winters and warm summers of the region. The supply of energy in the winter is less than in the summer. The populations must be able to cope with the energy difference. This change limits the number of species that can live in the deciduous forest biome.

Many populations of animals live in the deciduous forest. They include squirrels, deer, rabbits, and wolves. During the summer when energy is plentiful, the plants and animals take in energy and reproduce. During the winters, when little energy is available, the trees and many of the animals become inactive. This allows them to conserve their energy. A large variety of birds spend summers in the deciduous forest. However, the lower energy in the winter forces many bird species to fly to a warmer climate.

 2. Why are plants and animals in the deciduous forest biome inactive in winter? _____

_____

Tundra Biome. The **tundra** (TUN-druh) is a very cold and very dry land biome. Temperatures in this biome are below freezing most of the year. Plants such as mosses, grasses, and low shrubs sprout in the tundra during summer. The plants must grow and reproduce quickly. They have to use the sun's energy when it is available during the short summer. Because there is so little energy available, only one percent of all the earth's plants live in the tundra biome. Only a few animal species with small populations can survive in the tundra. Animals such as caribou and reindeer feed on the sparse plants that appear in summer.

Taiga Biome. The **taiga** (TY-guh) biome is dominated by large forests of coniferous, or cone-bearing, trees. Conifers such as fir, pine, and spruce trees thrive in the taiga. The needle-shaped leaves hold in heat and water to survive the long, cold, dry winters. Many types of animals are also adapted to this environment. Moose, black bears, and elk inhabit the taiga year round. During the summer, birds such as ducks and geese migrate to the coniferous forests. They feed on the many insect populations that thrive during the warm, moist summer.

Desert Biome. In the desert biome, rain might fall only once every few years. To survive, desert plants, such as sagebrush and cacti, must be able to store water. Desert organisms must also be able to survive the very hot days and very cool nights of this biome. Many desert animals, such as owls and coyotes, are active mainly at night.

Grassland Biome. The grassland biome is generally found in the interior parts of the continents. The biome does not receive enough rainfall to support much tree growth. However, the hot, dry summers and cold, snowy winters are ideal for wheat, corn, and other grasses. Grazing animals such as antelope, cattle, and sheep thrive in this biome.

The six land biomes you have just read about cover vast areas of the earth. But more than 75 percent of the earth's surface is covered by water. This water surface is divided into two biomes: freshwater biomes and marine biomes.

Freshwater Biome. Rivers, streams, swamps, and lakes make up freshwater biomes. These bodies of water contain little or no salt. Some freshwater biomes, such as lakes and ponds, contain standing water. Other freshwater biomes, such as rivers and streams, contain running water. The types of organisms found in a freshwater biome are determined by temperature, water speed, food sources, sunlight, and the amount of oxygen and particles in the water. Algae, trout, crayfish, and bass are examples of populations suited to this biome.

Marine Biome. The other type of water biome is the marine, or ocean, biome. The marine biome is larger than all other biomes combined. This biome consists of bodies of salt water such as the earth's oceans. Because it is so vast, scientists divide the marine biome into three different zones, or areas.

The **littoral zone** (LIHT-er-ul ZOHN) is the area of the ocean that runs along the shore. It is affected mostly by the tides, or the rise and fall of water. Organisms that live in the littoral zone must be able to stand the force of waves hitting the shore. They must also be adapted to changes in water level and temperature. Sea stars, mussels, and crabs are organisms that live in the littoral zone.

Farther out to sea, just past the littoral zone is the **sublittoral zone** (suhb-LIHT-er-uhl ZOHN). The sublittoral zone is shallow. This zone receives a large amount of energy from sunlight. Sunlight passes through the shallow salt water to the ocean bottom. This energy and the large supply of nutrients make the sublittoral zone the most populated place in the ocean. In fact, about 90 percent of all the ocean's species live in the littoral and sublittoral zones.

 3. Why is the sublittoral zone the most populated place in the ocean?

_____

_____

Beyond the sublittoral zone lies the open ocean, or **pelagic zone** (puh-LAJ-ihk ZOHN). Sunlight passes through only the top 200 meters of this zone. The ocean is 15,000 meters deep in some parts. This means that all the energy is concentrated in a very small portion of the zone. Water at depths below 200 meters is dark and cold. Water pressure is very high. Thus very few organisms live in the ocean below 200 meters. The organisms that do live there cannot get energy directly from the sun. They must depend on eating organisms that live in the sunlit zone to obtain energy.

Organisms living in the pelagic zone below 200 meters must be adapted to its unique environment. Often, the organisms have keen sense organs that help them find food in the dark. The flashlight fish, for example, produces light that helps it find prey.

Fig. 41-2 shows the 6 major land biomes and the 2 water biomes.

Fig. 41-2

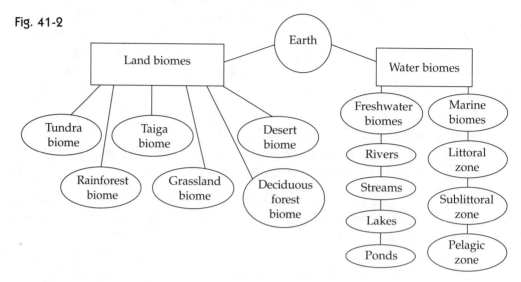

Check Your Understanding

Label Fig. 41-3 with the names of the three zones of a marine biome.

Fig. 41-3

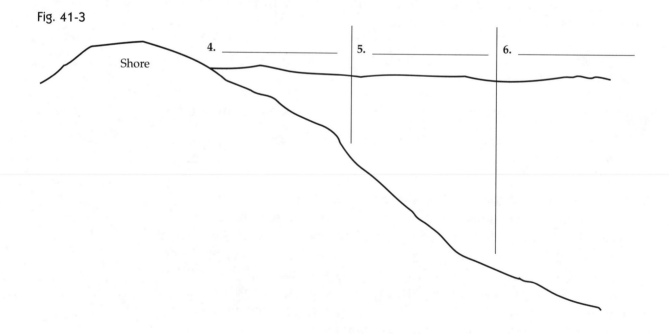

Shore

4. _____

5. _____

6. _____

7. What are the six land biomes?

_____

_____

8. Why do certain populations live in a particular biome?

_____

_____

9. Why are there are so many different species living in the tropical rain

forest biome? _____

_____

_____

10. Why do organisms living in the pelagic zone below 200 meters depend
on organisms living above that depth to supply their energy?

_____

_____

_____

_____

Human Impact on Ecosystems

natural resources:	materials in the environment that are used by people
renewable resources:	natural resources that can be replaced
non-renewable resources:	natural resources that cannot be replaced by nature
pollution:	any harmful substance released into the environment
conservation:	the wise use of natural resources

KEY IDEAS

Humans use the earth's resources to meet their needs and maintain their lifestyles. As the human population grows, the demands placed on the earth's resources also grow. To preserve the earth's ecosystems, the amount of resources used by humans must be reduced.

The world's supply of fresh water is becoming scarce. To make more water available for drinking, people are looking for ways to cut down on the amount of fresh water used for crops. One way this might be done is to use wastewater to water crops. The water left over from treated sewage is high in nutrients. The nutrients in it would help the plants to grow better.

Natural Resources. Materials in the environment that humans use are **natural resources** (NACH-er-uhl REE-sawrs-ehz). A natural resource that is replaced by natural processes is a **renewable resource** (ree-NOO-uh-buhl REE-sawrs). Trees are an example of a renewable resource. When trees are cut down for use, new trees can grow in their place.

Natural resources that cannot be replaced naturally are **non-renewable resources** (NAHN-ree-NOO-uh-buhl REE-sawrs-ehz). Oil and coal are two types of non-renewable resources. Non-renewable resources take millions of years to form. Once they are used, they cannot be replaced.

Pollution. As the human population has grown, the demand for natural resources has greatly increased. One result of the increased use of natural resource is pollution. **Pollution** (puh-LOO-shuhn) is any harmful substance released into the environment. Pollution can destroy the habitats of many types of organisms.

Air pollution occurs when harmful substances are released into the air. Burning fuel for heat, electricity, and transportation causes air pollution. Sulfur dioxide, nitrogen oxide, carbon monoxide, and soot are given off through burning fuel.

One serious problem caused by air pollution is smog. Smog is a mixture of smoke, gases, and fog. Another harmful result of air pollution is acid rain. Acid rain occurs when certain gases from burning fuel mix with water in the air to form acids. The acids fall back to the earth in raindrops. Acid rain damages soil, crops, and forests. Acid rain also pollutes lakes and streams. The acids are harmful to many of the organisms living in lakes and streams.

Other harmful substances released into water ecosystems cause pollution. Sewage, fertilizers, and pesticides used in farming, and chemical wastes from factories are all sources of water pollution. These substances can poison water supplies, killing plants and animals.

Human Activity. Certain human activities have destroyed many ecosystems. For example, forests are cut down for timber. New trees can be grown to replace them. However, it takes decades for the new trees to reach the size of the old ones. During that time, damage to the environment occurs.

The tiny roots of the new trees cannot hold the soil in place. Much soil is washed away by the rain. Nutrients are also washed out of the soil. With fewer nutrients, the new trees and other plants won't grow as well. Also, many organisms depend on the old forests for their food. With the forest cut down, many of the organisms that lived there die or move away from the area.

All the earth's ecosystems depend on natural resources. To preserve ecosystems, humans must take steps to decrease their use of the earth's resources. This can be done through conservation. **Conservation** (KAHN-ser-VAY-shuhn) is the wise use of natural resources.

Conservation includes reducing the amount of pollution we release into the environment. Many countries have set aside nature parks where nothing can be built or destroyed. People also can recycle, or reuse, resources to make new products. For example, the more paper we recycle, the fewer trees we will have to cut down. By thinking about the effect our actions have on the environment, we can help protect all the earth's ecosystems.

Fig. 42-1 summarizes the relationship between human actions and the earth's natural resources.

Fig. 42-1

Recycling → Natural resources ← Conservation

Renewable resources   Non-renewable resources

Human action

Burning fuel   Water pollution   Growth of human population

Air pollution   Sewage   Destruction of ecosystems

Smog   Pesticides   Endangered species

Acid rain   Kills living organisms   Extinct species

Check Your Understanding

Write a sentence explaining the connection between each pair of words.

1. natural resources, conservation _____

_____

2. renewable resources, non-renewable resources _____

_____

Complete the paragraphs by adding the correct words.

Materials in the environment that can be used by living things are

(3)_____. (4)_____ resources can be replaced.

(5)_____ resources cannot be replaced once they are used.

Air pollution occurs when (6)_____ substances are released

into the air. (7)_____ is a mixture of smoke, fog, and gases in

the air. The mixing of gases with water in the air to form acids causes

(8)_____. Fertilizers and (9)_____ used in farming

can pollute water. Chemical wastes from (10)_____ are another

source of water pollution.

To save the environment, humans must change the way they use

(11)_____. (12)_____ means using resources wisely.

(13)_____ means reusing resources to make new products.

14. What is the difference between renewable natural resources and non-renewable natural resources? _____

_____

_____

_____

15. Give two ways that the human population has affected resources.

_____

_____

_____

_____

16. What are the main sources of air pollution? _____

_____

_____

_____

17. What causes acid rain? _____

_____

_____

18. How does acid rain affect water ecosystems? _____

_____

_____

_____

19. What is conservation? _____

_____

_____

20. What are two ways that humans can help preserve natural resources?

_____

_____

_____

_____

Summary

- Organisms that interact with one another and with their nonliving environment make up an ecosystem. All the organisms that live in an ecosystem make up a community. A population is all the organisms of the same species that live in a community.

- All living things need energy to survive. Organisms get their energy from food.

- Organisms that can make their own food are producers. Organisms that obtain energy by eating other organisms are consumers. Organisms that feed on dead matter are decomposers.

- Energy flows through an ecosystem by the feeding relationships of its populations. A food chain is a model of feeding relationships in an ecosystem. A food web shows how food chains are connected. An energy pyramid shows how energy flows through an ecosystem.

- A large geographic region with a certain climate and specific communities is a biome. The six land biomes are the tundra, taiga, deciduous forest, rain forest, desert, and grassland biomes. The two water biomes are the freshwater and the marine biomes.

- The kinds of populations found in each biome depend on the amount of energy the biome receives. The more energy a biome receives, the more diverse are its populations.

- Natural resources are materials in an environment used by people. Some natural resources can be replaced. These are called renewable resources. Resources that cannot be replaced are called non-renewable resources.

- As the human population has grown, the demands for resources has increased. Pollution and destruction of ecosystems are two effects of the increased use of natural resources. Conservation and recycling are two ways humans can preserve natural resources.

For Your Portfolio

1. Think of an ecosystem that you have observed, such as a pond ecosystem or a forest ecosystem. You can use library resources to find out more about this ecosystem. List a minimum of five organisms that live in the ecosystem. Then, draw a food chain to show a feeding relationship in the ecosystem.

2. Make a travel brochure for people traveling to a biome other than the one in which you live. Identify locations on earth where travelers will find this biome. In your brochure, give the travelers some tips on the type of clothing they should pack. Also inform them of plant and animal populations they may observe.

3. Suppose you were a display designer at a local zoo. Choose an animal, and research the habitat of that animal. Then sketch out a display using graph paper. Be sure that your design includes as many elements as possible from the animal's natural surroundings. This can include the plants they use, the organisms they eat, what they use for shelter, and so on. Draw the display to scale.

4. Work with classmates to create a skit in which different organisms try to persuade humans to take greater care of the earth. You may want to be one of the following endangered species: California condor, white rhino, giant panda, snow leopard, black-footed ferret, or black lace cactus.

5. The dodo bird is an example of an organism that has become extinct because of human interference with an ecosystem. Use reference texts to learn more about the dodo bird. Write a report that explains how humans caused the extinction of this organism.

Match the terms on the left with the definitions on the right.

_____ 1. biome   a. eats other organisms

_____ 2. community   b. materials from the earth used by people

_____ 3. conservation   c. an area with a certain climate and specific communities

_____ 4. consumer   d. organisms in an ecosystem

_____ 5. decomposer   e. one species in an ecosystem

_____ 6. ecosystem   f. using resources wisely

_____ 7. natural resource   g. can make its own food

_____ 8. population   h. eats dead organisms

_____ 9. producer   i. communities interacting with the environment

Give a brief answer for each of the following.

10. Explain the relationship among populations, communities, and ecosystems.

   _____

   _____

   _____

11. How does energy enter an ecosystem? _____

   _____

   _____

12. Explain the difference between renewable and non-renewable natural resources. Give
    an example of each. _____

   _____

   _____

Answer one of the following questions.

13. Can an organism exist in any type of biome? Explain your answer in a short essay.

14. What are some ways that people have harmed the earth's ecosystems? What are
    some of the ways people can help preserve the earth's ecosystems?

Human Biology

Have you ever played softball or baseball? Think about the motions your body makes when you play. Before your turn at bat, you loosen up with a few practice swings. Then, you walk up to the plate. As you take your batting stance, you bend your knees, raise your arms, and flex your muscles. As the pitcher throws the ball, your eyes track its movement toward you. At just the right moment, you swing. The ball sails toward the outfield. You drop the bat and run full speed toward first base.

Some movements, such as hitting a baseball, require hundreds of parts of the body to work together. The human body can perform these and many other actions with very little thought. The human body consists of a number of different systems. All these systems work together to make the body perform simple and complex tasks.

Bone, Muscle, and Skin

cartilage:	tough, flexible tissue from which many bones form
joint:	place where two or more bones meet
ligaments:	strips of connective tissue that join bones together
tendons:	bands of tissue that connects skeletal muscles to bones
epidermis:	outer layer of skin
dermis:	inner layer of skin

KEY IDEAS

Bones protect and support the body. They also provide a system of levers on which muscles work to move the body. Together, the skeletal and muscular systems control the body's movements.

An important part of any professional sports team is an athletic trainer. Athletic trainers help prepare athletes for competition. They design exercise programs that will keep the athletes' muscles strong. They create warm-up programs to protect the athletes from injury. The job of an athletic trainer requires an understanding of how bones and muscles work together.

The Skeletal System. Think of all the different ways you have moved your body since you woke up today. The combined work of your bones and muscles make all these movements possible. The 206 bones in your body are part of your skeletal system. The skeletal system is made up of bones, cartilage, tendons, and ligaments.

In addition to helping you move, your skeletal system provides your body with shape and support. It protects your internal organs. Certain kinds of bones make blood cells. Your body even stores minerals in your bones.

Cartilage and Bone. When you were a baby, most of your skeleton was made of cartilage. **Cartilage** (KAHRT-uhl-ihj) is a tough, flexible tissue. Over time, bone cells replaced the cartilage by forming mineral deposits. However, even as an adult, parts of your skeletal system will still contain cartilage.

Joints. All movement occurs at the joints. A **joint** (joint) is the place where two or more bones meet. Strips of tough connective tissue, called **ligaments** (LIHG-uh-muhnt), hold bones together at a joint. As ligaments stretch, the bones move.

Different kinds of joints permit different kinds of movement. Your shoulder contains a ball-and-socket joint. This joint allows your arm to move in all directions. At your elbow, you have a hinge joint. A hinge joint allows bones to only move back and forth.

 1. What are ligaments? _____

_____

Muscles. Your muscles work with the skeletal system to move your body. Muscles are specialized tissues that contract, or shorten. Your body contains three types of muscle: cardiac muscle, smooth muscle, and skeletal muscle. Your heart is made up of cardiac muscle. Your stomach and other organs contain some smooth muscle. Since you do not think about controlling the actions of cardiac muscles or smooth muscles, they are called involuntary muscles.

Your skeletal muscles are called voluntary muscles because you do think about controlling their motion. Skeletal muscles are attached to bones by bands of tissue called **tendons** (TEHN-duhnz). Skeletal muscles work in pairs to move bones at a joint. The brain sends a signal for one muscle of the pair to contract. As it contracts, the muscle pulls on tendons. The tendons pull on bones, which move with the muscle. At the same time, the other muscle of the pair relaxes. You can see in Fig. 43-1 that the bicep and tricep work as a pair to move the arm at the elbow joint.

Fig. 43-1

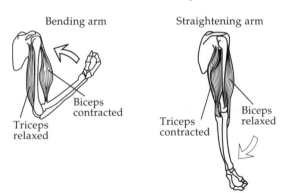

Muscles need energy to contract. Muscle cells get most of this energy through cellular respiration. However, the body sometimes uses up the oxygen needed for cellular respiration. When this occurs, the muscles get their energy from fermentation. Recall that fermentation gives cells energy from glucose when oxygen is not available.

Skin. The surface of the body is covered with skin. Skin protects the internal organs from the outside world. It also provides the body with support. Skin is made up of two layers. The outer layer of skin is the **epidermis** (ehp-uh-DER-mihs). The epidermis is a thin barrier that helps prevent water loss. It also protects the body from germs.

The inner layer of skin is the **dermis** (DER-mihs). Nerves, blood vessels, hair follicles, oil glands, and sweat glands are located in the dermis. Waste products and water are eliminated from the body through the sweat glands. The release of water through the skin helps the body maintain a certain temperature.

Fig. 43-2 summarizes the relationship among the parts of the skeletal and muscular systems.

Fig. 43-2

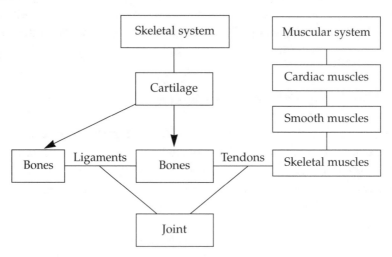

Check Your Understanding

Write a sentence explaining the connection between each pair of words.

2. cartilage, bones _____

_____

3. tendons, muscles _____

_____

4. dermis, epidermis _____

_____

Complete the following paragraph.

Skeletal (5)_____ work in pairs to move the (6)_____ that meet at the (7)_____. The brain sends a signal for one muscle to (8)_____. As it shortens, the muscle pulls on (9)_____. The tendons pull on a bone, causing it to (10)_____. In order to do this work, muscle cells and bone cells need (11)_____. The cells get energy through (12)_____ and fermentation.

What Do You Know?

13. What are five jobs of the skeletal system?

    _____

    _____

14. How do ligaments help you move? _____

    _____

15. What is the difference between a ligament and a tendon?

    _____

    _____

16. What is the difference between a hinge joint and a ball-and-socket joint?

    _____

    _____

17. What is the difference between voluntary and involuntary muscles? Give an example of each. _____

    _____

18. How do skeletal muscles move bones? _____

    _____

19. Describe the importance of the epidermis and the dermis.

    _____

    _____

The Brain. The messages carried by neurons are called **impulses** (IHM-pul-sehz). Impulses are carried from nerves to the brain or from the brain to nerves. The brain is called the control center of the body because it makes the body respond to all the impulses.

The brain has three main parts which are shown in Fig. 46-2. The large, upper part of the brain is the **cerebrum** (SEHR-uh-brum). The cerebrum controls all voluntary activities of the body. It controls movement, speech, memory, and emotions. The cerebrum also identifies the impulses it receives from the senses. The cerebrum controls activities such as learning, reasoning, problem solving, and decision making.

Fig. 46-2

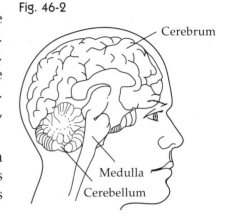

Near the back of the head, beneath the cerebrum, is the **cerebellum** (sehr-uh-BEHL-um). The cerebellum coordinates and balances the actions of the voluntary muscles. It makes your muscles move smoothly and helps you keep your balance.

Bundles of nerves from the cerebrum and cerebellum come together at the base of the brain. They form the brainstem. The lowest part of the brainstem is the **medulla** (mih-DUL-uh). The medulla controls involuntary actions such as breathing, heart rate, and digestion.

The Spinal Cord. The brainstem continues into the spinal cord. The spinal cord is a part of the nervous system. The **spinal cord** (SPY-nuhl KORD) is a long bundle of nerve fibers surrounded by the backbone. It connects the brain with the neurons in all parts of the body.

The Senses. The nervous system receives messages about the environment and then responds to the messages. Some of the messages go through the spinal cord to the brain. Other messages go only to and from the spinal cord. The brain and spinal cord get the messages from the sense organs. The sense organs are the eyes, ears, skin, tongue, and nose. Each sense organ is associated with a specific sense: vision, hearing, touch, taste, or smell. Special cells in the sense organs detect energy. The energy can be light, heat, sound, chemical, or even pressure. Fig. 46-3 shows which organ senses each kind of energy.

Fig. 46-3

Organ	Sense	Energy
(eye) →	Sight →	Light
(ear) →	Hearing →	Sound
(hand) →	Touch →	Heat, pressure
(tongue) →	Taste →	Chemical
(nose) →	Smell →	Chemical

The sense organs and nervous system work together to help the body respond to its environment. When the cells sense energy, they send an impulse through neurons. Certain kinds of impulses require quick responses. These impulses travel only to the spinal cord. The spinal cord sends another impulse back to the neurons in the body part that needs to respond. For example, if you touch a very hot pan, nerves in the skin of your fingers sense the heat. The heat impulse travels through neurons to the spinal cord. The spinal cord instantly sends back an impulse that makes your hand pull back. This is an automatic response that takes less than one second. At the same time, a slower impulse travels to your brain. Soon after you've responded, your brain knows what happened.

Other impulses do not cause automatic responses. The neurons in your sense organs relay these impulses through the spinal cord to the brain. The brain then decides what the impulse means. For example, when you hear a friend call your name, neurons in your ears carry the sound impulse to your brain. The brain understands the meaning of the words and tells you who spoke.

You can then decide if you want to respond. The brain sends an impulse through the spinal cord to the part of the body that you want to move. For example, you decide to turn your head toward your friend, and your neck moves. This response is not automatic. Instead, you respond consciously, or think about how to respond.

Fig. 46-4 shows how nerve impulses reach the brain and the different ways the body responds.

Fig. 46-4

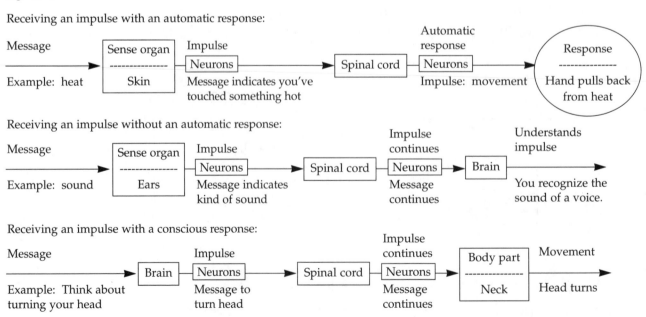

Receiving an impulse with an automatic response:

Receiving an impulse without an automatic response:

Receiving an impulse with a conscious response:

Complete the following paragraph with the correct terms.

The nervous system is made up of billions of **(2)**_____. Neurons carry **(3)**_____ throughout the body. **(4)**_____ organs send messages about the environment. The **(5)**_____ tells the body how to respond to these messages. The **(6)**_____ is the part of the brain that controls all voluntary activities. The **(7)**_____ coordinates and balances the actions of the voluntary muscles. Involuntary actions are controlled by the **(8)**_____.

What Do You Know?

9. What does the nervous system do? _____

_____

_____

10. How do dendrites differ from axons? _____

_____

_____

_____

11. Why is the brain called the control center of the body?

_____

_____

_____

12. What form of energy do the ears detect? _____

_____

_____

13. How do sense organs relay information about the environment to the brain? _____

_____

_____

_____

Reproduction and Development

Key Words

testes:	primary reproductive organs of the male where sperm are produced
hormones:	chemicals that direct body activities
ovaries:	primary reproductive organs of the female where eggs are produced
ovulation:	monthly release of a mature egg from an ovary
menstrual cycle:	monthly cycle during which an egg matures and is released from an ovary while the uterus prepares to receive a fertilized egg
zygote:	fertilized egg
embryo:	offspring that develops inside the uterus
placenta:	organ that supplies the embryo with nutrients and oxygen and eliminates carbon dioxide and wastes
umbilical cord:	tissue that connects the embryo with the placenta and that carries nutrients and oxygen from the mother to the embryo

KEY IDEAS

The reproductive system produces, stores, and releases specialized sex cells called gametes. Male gametes, called sperm, are produced in the testes. Female gametes, called eggs, are produced in the ovaries. Human development begins when an egg is fertilized by a sperm.

Think about how much you have changed since you were born. Now think about how different you will be when you are 35. These changes occur as you pass through various stages of growth and development. For example, puberty is a time when the body gains the ability to reproduce sexually.

Fig. 47-1

The reproductive system is different in males and females. However, the *function* of the reproductive system is the same in both females and males. Both male and female reproductive systems produce, store, and release specialized sex cells called gametes.

Male Reproductive System. Male gametes are called sperm. Sperm are single cells with a head and a tail, as shown in Fig. 47-1. The head contains genetic information. The tail aids in movement.

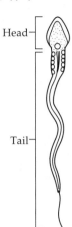

Sperm are produced in the **testes** (TEHS-teez) (sing. *testis*). The testes are the primary reproductive organs of the male. The testes lie outside the body cavity in a sac called the scrotum. This location makes the temperature of the testes slightly lower than that of the body. The cooler temperature is necessary for sperm production.

Sperm production begins at puberty when hormones are released in the testes. **Hormones** (HAWR-mohnz) are chemicals that direct body activities. One kind of hormone triggers the production of sperm.

Sperm travel from the testes through a network of tubes. The urethra is the tube that leads out of the body through the penis. During ejaculation, sperm exit the reproductive system through the penis. The male reproductive system is shown in Fig. 47-2.

Fig. 47-2

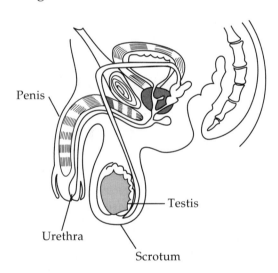

Female Reproductive System. The primary reproductive organs of the female are the **ovaries** (OH-vuh-reez). The ovaries are two egg-shaped structures located inside the female's body cavity. When a female reaches puberty, hormones are produced in the ovaries. These hormones trigger the production of female gametes, or eggs. About once a month, a mature egg is released from an ovary. This process is called **ovulation** (ahv-yoo-LAY-shun).

Located near the ovaries are two fallopian tubes. The fallopian tubes lead to the uterus. As a mature egg leaves an ovary, it travels through one of the fallopian tubes to the uterus. The uterus is a hollow organ where a fertilized egg develops. The narrow end of the uterus connects to the cervix. The cervix leads to the vagina, or birth canal. The offspring leaves the female's body by passing through the vagina. The female reproductive system is shown in Fig. 47-3.

Fig. 47-3

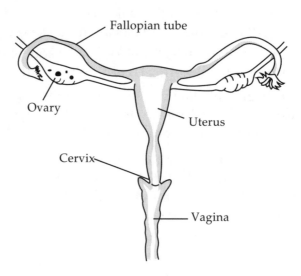

 1. **What are the primary organs of the male and female reproductive systems?** _____

_____

The Menstrual Cycle. Once a female reaches puberty, her reproductive system undergoes a monthly cycle of changes called the **menstrual cycle** (MEHN-struhl SY-kuhl). The menstrual cycle involves the development and release of an egg for fertilization. It also involves the preparation of the uterus to receive a fertilized egg. This cycle of change occurs in four stages over a period of one month.

The menstrual cycle begins with the release of a hormone. The hormone causes an egg in an ovary to mature. The ovary then releases another hormone. This causes the walls of the uterus to thicken. About halfway through the cycle, ovulation occurs. The mature egg moves through one of the fallopian tubes.

If sperm are not present in the fallopian tube, the egg is not fertilized. However, the unfertilized egg still moves into the uterus. The walls of the uterus, which had thickened in preparation for a fertilized egg, begin to break apart. Cells from the uterus and the unfertilized egg pass from the vagina during a process called menstruation. Menstruation lasts an average of four days. As menstruation ends, a new menstrual cycle begins.

2. What happens during menstruation? _____

_____

Fertilization. If sperm are present in the fallopian tube during ovulation, then fertilization can occur. Recall that fertilization is the joining of an egg cell and a sperm cell. The fertilized egg, or **zygote** (ZY-goht), moves to the uterus. The zygote undergoes a series of cell divisions to form a hollow ball of cells. This ball of cells attaches to the thick wall of the uterus. When this occurs, the developing offspring is called an **embryo** (EHM-bree-yoh).

Tissues in the uterus develop into the placenta. The **placenta** (pluh-SEHN-tuh) supplies the embryo with nutrients and oxygen and eliminates carbon dioxide and wastes. The **umbilical cord** (uhm-BIHL-uh-kuhl KORD) connects the embryo with the placenta. Blood vessels in the umbilical cord carry nutrients and oxygen to the embryo. Other vessels carry carbon dioxide and wastes from the embryo to the mother. The mother releases these wastes with those of her own body.

 3. What does the umbilical cord do? _____

_____

The embryo develops inside the mother's uterus for about nine months. During this time, the embryo is surrounded by a clear sac filled with fluids. This sac cushions and protects the embryo.

Birth. Birth occurs when the baby leaves the mother's body. Birth begins when hormones trigger contractions of the uterus. The contractions cause the amniotic sac to break. They also push the baby out of the uterus and out of the mother's body through the vagina.

At birth, the offspring enters the first stage of its life cycle. A life cycle is the series of stages of growth and development that an organism passes through. Stages in the human life cycle include infancy, childhood, adolescence, adulthood, and old age. Each stage has its own unique traits.

Fig. 47-4 summarizes the relationship between the male and female reproductive systems.

Fig. 47-4

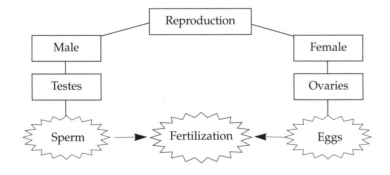

Check Your Understanding

Write a sentence explaining the connection between each pair of words.

4. sperm, testes _____

_____

5. ovaries, eggs _____

_____

6. ovulation, menstrual cycle _____

_____

7. zygote, fertilization _____

_____

8. Label the diagrams in Fig. 47-5 with the following words: *cervix, ovary, fallopian tube, scrotum, penis, testes, urethra, uterus, vagina.*

Fig. 47-5

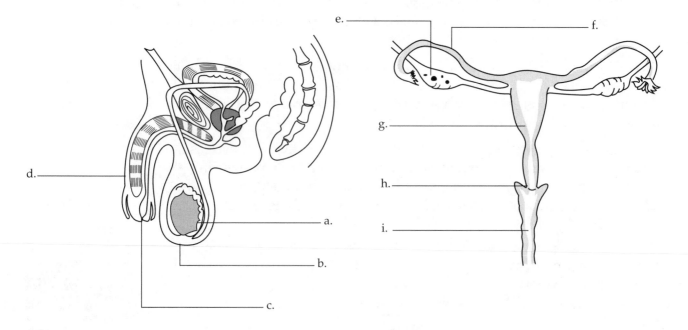

9. What is the job of the reproductive system?

_____

_____

10. How does the location of the scrotum help sperm to produce?

_____

_____

11. Describe the path an unfertilized mature egg takes as it leaves an ovary.

_____

_____

_____

12. Describe the changes that the uterus undergoes during the menstrual cycle. _____

_____

_____

13. Can fertilization occur before ovulation? Explain why.

_____

_____

14. How does an embryo receive nutrients and oxygen?

_____

_____

15. What are the stages of the human life cycle?

_____

_____

Immune System

pathogens:	substances that cause disease
inflammatory response:	process in which special white blood cells move into the tissue where the pathogen lies and destroy the invading pathogen.
antigens:	proteins or chemicals that are foreign to the body
antibodies:	proteins produced by the body to fight off specific pathogens
T-cells:	special white blood cells that fight off specific pathogens

KEY IDEAS

The immune system protects the body from disease. The system uses both nonspecific and specific defenses for destroying disease-causing substances. If the immune system does not work well, the body is not protected.

Have you ever canned vegetables? If so, you probably followed a very specific set of directions to ensure that your vegetables did not contain bacteria that cause disease. Some of the steps you followed, such as boiling the container, kill bacteria. The human body also has ways of killing these disease-causing organisms.

Right now, pathogens surround your body. **Pathogens** (PATH-uh-juhnz) are substances that cause disease. Your body works to fight off these pathogens. The constant struggle to protect the body from disease is the job of the immune system.

Nonspecific Defenses. The immune system consists of both nonspecific and specific defenses. Nonspecific defenses are not directed at a particular type of pathogen. They guard against all disease-causing substances. Nonspecific defenses are the first to protect you from disease-causing substances that enter your body.

The skin is part of the first line of nonspecific defenses. Very few pathogens can get through this barrier. Natural openings to the body, such as the mouth and nose, contain other nonspecific defenses. Mucus and hairs that line the inside of your nose trap pathogens. This keeps the pathogens from moving into the body.

Cilia and mucus in other parts of the respiratory system also trap pathogens. Recall that cilia are tiny hairs.

Digestive juices in the stomach break apart pathogens that enter the digestive system. Body secretions, such as tears, saliva, and sweat, also contain enzymes that break down pathogens.

Inflammatory Response. Despite these defenses, pathogens do get into the body. When this occurs, the body's second line of nonspecific defenses attacks the pathogen. This type of defense is called the inflammatory response. The **inflammatory response** (in-FLAM-uh-toh-ree ree-SPAHNS) is a process in which special white blood cells move from the blood into the tissue where the pathogen lies. The white blood cells then surround and destroy the pathogen. This causes swelling, or inflammation, in the area of the attack.

 1. **List five nonspecific defenses that help protect the body from pathogens.** _____

_____

Antigens and Antibodies. Sometimes, a pathogen is able to survive both the first and second line of nonspecific defenses. If this occurs, chemicals on the surface of the pathogen then alert the immune system to begin a specific defense. A specific defense is a response of the immune system to a specific pathogen. The surface of a pathogen has chemicals that the body recognizes as foreign. These foreign chemicals are called **antigens** (AN-tuh-juhnz). The body reacts to the presence of antigens by producing antibodies. **Antibodies** (AN-tih-bahd-eez) are special proteins that fight off pathogens.

Fig. 48-1

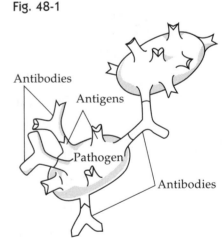

One pathogen can have a number of different antigens on its surface. Each kind of antibody works against only one kind of antigen. The body recognizes the antigen and produces the proper antibody. Sites on the antibody are shaped to fit together with sites on a certain antigen. As Fig. 48-1 shows, the antibodies bond with the antigens. Once the antibodies bond with the antigen, they can help destroy the pathogen.

T-cells. The immune system fights some pathogens with another specific defense called T-cells. **T-cells** (TEE-sehlz) are special white blood cells. Some T-cells directly attack the cells of pathogens. The T-cells transfer proteins directly into the cell membrane of the pathogen. This causes the pathogen cell to burst and die. Other T-cells search for and identify pathogens. The T-cells then alert the immune system, which sends antibodies to attack the pathogen. T-cells also help control the immune system so that the system responds only when necessary.

AIDS. AIDS is a disease in which the immune system cannot protect the body from infection. A virus, called HIV, causes this deadly disease. HIV attacks the immune system. Once it enters the body, HIV virus destroys white blood cells that identify antigens, produce antibodies, or destroy invading antigens. As the virus takes over the cells of the immune system, the infected person is no longer able to fight disease. Diseases that the body normally can fight off become deadly.

 2. **What causes AIDS?** _____

_____

Fig. 48-2 summarizes the relationship among the nonspecific and specific defenses of the immune system.

Fig. 48-2

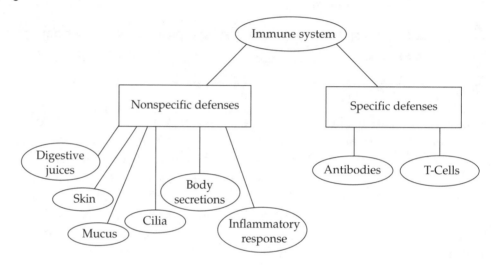

Check Your Understanding

Complete the paragraph with the following terms: *antibodies, antigens, HIV virus, immune system, nonspecific, pathogens, skin, specific.*

Substances that cause disease are called **(3)**_____. The **(4)**_____ protects the body from these substances. There are two types of defense mechanisms that work against pathogens. **(5)**_____ defenses guard against all types of pathogens. The **(6)**_____ belongs to this line of defense. **(7)**_____ defenses attack certain types of pathogens. This reaction is triggered when the body detects a foreign chemical or **(8)**_____. The immune system reacts by producing special proteins called **(9)**_____. The antibodies bond with the antigens to destroy the pathogen.

10. What is the difference between the nonspecific defenses and specific
defenses of the immune system? _____

_____

_____

_____

11. Why are tears considered to be a nonspecific mechanism of the immune
system? _____

_____

_____

_____

12. What is the inflammatory response? _____

_____

_____

_____

13. How do T-cells help fight disease? _____

_____

_____

_____

14. What effect does HIV have on the immune system?

_____

_____

_____

_____

15. Why is a common disease, such as a cold, extremely dangerous for a
person with AIDS? _____

_____

_____

_____

Summary

- The skeletal system is made up of bones, cartilage, tendons, and ligaments. The skeletal system provides a framework for the body. It supports and protects the body.

- The muscular system works with the skeletal system to enable the body to move. Muscles are specialized tissue that contract to cause movement.

- The circulatory system consists of the heart and blood vessels. The circulatory system transports nutrients and oxygen to all cells of the body. It also carries wastes to the excretory and respiratory systems.

- The main organ of the respiratory system is the lungs. The respiratory system takes oxygen into and removes carbon dioxide from the body.

- The digestive system consists of the mouth, pharynx, esophagus, stomach, small intestine, and large intestine. The digestive system changes food into a form that the body can use.

- The main organ of the excretory system is the kidneys. Wastes are released from the body by the actions of the excretory system.

- All actions of the body are controlled by the nervous system. The brain is the command center of the nervous system. Messages are transmitted between the body and brain by a network of nerves.

- The reproductive system enables a person to produce offspring. This is the only organ system whose structure differs in males and females. However, both male and female reproductive systems produce, store, and release specialized sex cells called gametes.

- The immune system protects the body from disease. The system has both nonspecific and specific defenses to fight disease. The nonspecific defenses include the skin, mucus, digestive juices, and body secretions. Specific defenses include antibodies and T-cells.

For Your Portfolio

1. Pretend you were able to become very small and travel inside a human body. Think about the trip you would take through one of the following body systems: respiratory, digestive, circulatory, or nervous. Write an essay that describes your trip. Be sure to visit all the parts of the system. Include how you enter and exit the system.

2. Draw a series of pictures to show what happens to a slice of pizza as it enters your mouth and moves through your digestive system.

3. With a group of classmates, create a skit that explains what occurs in the nervous system of a person who accidentally places his hand on a hot stove. You will need the following characters: neurons, impulses, and the brain. Be sure the skit shows how messages are transmitted throughout the person's body.

4. Suppose you had to teach a group of your classmates about the skeletal and muscular systems. Work in groups of four to write a plan that describes how you would teach the lesson. Include a demonstration to show how a joint moves or how muscles work in pairs. You may want to create a series of diagrams to help with the instruction.

5. Make an outline or flowchart of the reproductive system. Include information on the parts of the system in both males and females, the menstrual cycle, and the steps involved in fertilization.

Match each body system in Column I with its function in Column II.

		Column I		Column II
_____	1.	circulatory	a.	protects against disease
_____	2.	respiratory	b.	transmits messages in the body
_____	3.	digestive	c.	gives the body shape and support
_____	4.	reproductive	d.	brings oxygen into the body
_____	5.	immune	e.	produces offspring
_____	6.	nervous	f.	moves blood through the body
_____	7.	skeletal	g.	helps bones move the body
_____	8.	muscular	h.	changes food into a usable form

Answer each question in the space provided.

9. How do the skeletal and muscular systems work together to move the body?

   _____

   _____

10. How do the respiratory and circulatory systems work together to remove waste products from body cells? _____

    _____

11. What role does the stomach play in the digestive and immune systems?

    _____

    _____

    _____

12. How are the testes and the ovaries alike? _____

    _____

    _____

Answer one of the following questions.

13. Make a series of sketches that show how the fertilization and development of an egg occurs. Or, write an essay that explains this process.

14. Make sketches that show what happens when a pathogen enters the body. Show both a nonspecific and specific defense at work. Or, write an essay that explains what happens.

Glossary/Index

A

active transport   process in which energy is used to transport materials across the cell membrane   *22*

adaptation   process by which an organism becomes better suited to changes in its environment   *63*

amino acid   chemical compound containing nitrogen, carbon, hydrogen, and oxygen   *7*

amniotic egg   egg that has a fluid-filled sac enclosed by a protective shell   *172*

amoeba   animal-like protist that moves by changing its shape   *96*

amphibian   vertebrate that usually has gills and lives in water when it is young, and has lungs and lives on land as an adult   *168*

ancestor   species of the past, from which other living species have evolved   *72*

angiosperm   most common type of seed plant; plants whose seeds form in a flower and are protected by a fruit   *117*

antibiotic   drug used to treat diseases caused by bacteria   *91*

antibody   (plural, *antibodies*) proteins produced by the body to fight off pathogens   *235*

antigen   protein or chemical that is foreign to the body   *235*

arachnid   arthropod that has four pairs of jointed legs   *144*

arthropod   animal with a segmented body, a hard outer covering, and jointed legs   *136*

asexual reproduction   reproduction that requires only one parent   *125*

atrium   (plural, *atria*) upper chamber of the heart   *215*

B

bacteria   (sing., *bacterium*) single-celled living things that do not have a nucleus   *86*

biome   large geographic area with a similar climate and communities   *196*

bird   endothermic vertebrate that has feathers and wings   *176*

bivalve   mollusk that has two shells hinged together   *132*

blue-green bacteria   bacteria that make food through photosynthesis   *87*

bony fish   fish with a hinged jaw, scaly skin, and a skeleton made of bone   *161*

C

capillary   tiny, thin-walled blood vessels through which the exchange of substances between blood and body cells takes place   *215*

capsule   protective layer surrounding the cell wall of bacteria   *86*

carbohydrate   substance made of carbon, hydrogen, and oxygen   *10*

carrier   person who has a recessive gene for a trait but does not show the trait   *55*

carrier protein   protein in the cell membrane that moves large molecules through the membrane   *20*

cartilage   tough, flexible tissue of the skeletal system from which many bones form   *161, 210*

cartilaginous fish   fish with a hinged jaw and a skeleton made of cartilage   *161*

cell   basic unit of structure and function of all living things   *2*

cell cycle   process by which a cell grows, prepares for division, and divides to form two daughter cells   *32*

cell membrane   outer covering of the cell that controls the passage of substances into and out of the cell   *6*

cell wall   rigid structure that surrounds the cell membranes of plant cells and some bacterial cells   *14*

cellular respiration   process in which glucose is broken down in the presence of oxygen to supply a cell with energy   *24*

centipede   arthropod that has one pair of jointed legs attached to most of its body segments   *146*

cephalopod   mollusk that has either no shell or a small shell inside the body   *133*

cerebellum   part of the brain that coordinates and balances the actions of the voluntary muscles   *225*

cerebrum   part of the brain that controls all voluntary activities of the body   *225*

chemical digestion   the breaking down of food into simple molecules by enzymes   *220*

chlorophyll   green pigment contained in chloroplasts that traps light energy   *28*

chloroplast   structure in a plant cell in which light energy is changed into chemical energy for the purpose of making food   *15, 94*

chordate   animal that has a thin, flexible rod that supports three features: the body, gill slits, and a nerve cord. The three features are either present throughout the animal's life or at some stage of its development   *156*

chromosome mutation   permanent change in the number or structure of chromosomes of a cell   *54*

chromosome   cell structure made of DNA and proteins that contains the hereditary information   *7, 32*

cilia   (sing., *cilium*) tiny "hairs" on the outside of some cells that push the cell through water   *95*

circulation   movement of blood through the body   *214*

cnidarian   simple invertebrate with a mouth and a large central cavity   *124*

commensalism   relationship in which only one organism benefits   *189*

community   living part of an ecosystem   *188*

competition   struggle between living things to obtain what they need to survive   *189*

compound eye   eye made up of many tiny lenses that can sense movement   *141*

compounds   chemicals joined together in certain ways, some of which make up the cells of living things   *75*

concentration   amount of a substance in a given area   *19*

conifer   cone-bearing plant with needle-shaped leaves   *117*

conservation   wise use of natural resources   *203*

consumer   organism that obtains energy by eating other organisms   *193*

crustacean   arthropod that has five pairs of jointed legs   *145*

cytoplasm   living substance of a cell located between the nucleus and cell membrane   *7*

D

decomposer   living thing that breaks down the remains of dead organisms into materials that can be reused by other things   *90, 193*

dermis   inner layer of skin   *212*

descendant   living species that has evolved from an ancestor   *72*

diaphragm   large flat muscle at the bottom of the rib cage that assists breathing   *217*

diffusion   movement of molecules from areas of greater concentration to areas of lesser concentration.   *19*

diploid number   number of chromosomes found in a single body cell of an organism   *46*

dominant   gene or trait that dominates, or masks, another gene or trait   *50*

E

echinoderm   spiny-skinned invertebrate that lives in the ocean   *148*

ecosystem   organisms interacting with one another and with their nonliving environment   *188*

ectothermic   having a body temperature that changes with the temperature of its environment   *160*

egg   female sex cell   *46, 230*

embryo   offspring that is developing inside the uterus   *231*

endoplasmic reticulum   network of passageways through which materials flow within a cell   *11*

endoskeleton   skeleton inside the body that provides support and protection   *157*

endothermic   having an internal body temperature that stays constant regardless of the temperature of the environment   *166*

energy pyramid   model that shows how energy is lost in a food chain   *193*

epidermis   outer layer of skin   *212*

euglena   plant-like protist that moves by means of a flagellum   *95*

eukaryotic cell   cell that has a nucleus   *14*

evolution   process by which living things change over time   *66*

exoskeleton   hard outer covering of an arthropod that protects and supports the animal   *136*

external fertilization   fertilization that takes place outside the body of an organism, usually in the water   *165*

F

feathers   modified scales adapted for flight and conserving body heat   *176*

fermentation   process in which glucose is broken down in the absence of oxygen to supply a cell with energy   *24*

fern   type of complex plant that has a vascular system and reproduces by means of spores   *107*

fertilization   joining of an egg and a sperm   *231*

fish   vertebrate that lives in the water and breathes with gills   *160*

fission   type of asexual reproduction in which an organism splits into two   *129*

flagellum   long, whiplike structure that helps some types of cells move   *95*

flatworm   worm that has a flat body and a simple structure   *128*

flower   special reproductive structure in which seeds form   *113*

food chain   model that shows the flow of energy through organisms in an ecosystem   *193*

food web   model that shows how food chains overlap   *193*

fossil   preserved remains or traces of a once-living thing   *70*

fruit   structure that protects one or more seeds   *113*

fruiting body   part of fungi that is used in reproduction; often the only part of fungi that can be seen   *99*

fungi   (sing., *fungus*) living things that absorb food from living or dead things   *98*

G

gamete   sex cell   *46*

gene   portion of DNA that contains the information needed to make a specific protein   *40*

gene mutation   permanent change in the DNA of a gene   *54*

gills   respiratory structures that allow fishes to breathe in water   *160*

gymnosperm   type of seed plant whose seeds are usually found inside a cone, not inside a flower   *117*

H

haploid number number of chromosomes found in a gamete *46*

heredity passing of traits from parents to offspring *50*

heterozygous organism that has two different genes for a particular trait *50*

homeostasis balance of substances within a cell *7*

homozygous organism that has two identical genes for a particular trait *50*

hormones chemicals that direct body activities *229*

hyphae (sing., *hypha*) branching tubes that often grow in a tangled mass and make up the main part of fungi *98*

I

impulse message carried by neurons *225*

inflammatory response process in which special white blood cells move from the blood and into the tissue where the pathogen lies in order to surround and destroy the invading pathogen *235*

insect arthropod with three pairs of jointed legs *140*

internal fertilization fertilization that takes place inside the body of an organism *165*

interphase part of the cell cycle during which a cell grows and copies its chromosomes *32*

J

jawless fish fish with a smooth, round body and no jaw *161*

joint place where two or more bones meet *211*

L

ligament strip of tissue that joins bones together *211*

lipids chains of fatty acids *7*

littoral zone area that runs along the shore and is affected by the tide *199*

lungs primary internal organs of the respiratory systems of land vertebrates *165*

M

mammal vertebrate that has mammary glands and a body covered with hair; most give birth *180*

mammary glands special glands of female mammals that produce milk to feed to the young *180*

mantle fold of skin that wraps around and protects the visceral mass of a mollusk *132*

mechanical digestion breaking down of food into smaller pieces by physical means *220*

medulla part of the brain that controls involuntary actions *225*

meiosis type of cell division that produces gametes *47*

menstrual cycle cycle during which an egg matures and is released from an ovary while the uterus prepares to receive a fertilized egg *230*

millipede arthropod that has two pairs of jointed legs attached to most of its body segments *146*

mitochondria (sing., *mitochondrion*) organelles that supply the cell with energy *10*

mitosis process by which a parent cell distributes its chromosomes to two daughter cells *33*

mollusk invertebrate with a soft body, which is usually covered by one or more hard shells *132*

molt to shed an old exoskeleton before a new one grows *137*

moss type of simple plant that does not have tissue to transport water and other materials throughout its body *106*

mucus glands glands in the skin which produce a slimy substance that keeps the skin from drying out *168*

mutation change in form *54*

mutualism relationship in which both organisms benefit *189*

N

natural resource material in the environment that is used by people *202*

natural selection process by which the best adapted organism survives and reproduces *63*

neuron   nerve cell that carries messages throughout the body   *224*

nitrogen-fixing bacteria   bacteria that take nitrogen from the air and form nitrogen compounds that can be used by plants   *91*

nonrenewable resource   natural resource that cannot be replaced by nature   *202*

nucleic acid   chains of nucleotides that direct a cell's activities   *7*

nucleotide   chemical made of a simple sugar, a phosphate, and a base   *7*

nucleus   part of a cell that controls most of the activities that occur within the cell; not present in bacteria   *7, 86*

O

organelle   structure located within the cytoplasm that performs a specific job   *10*

organic compound   compound that contains carbon   *75*

osmosis   diffusion of water across a membrane   *19*

ovary   primary reproductive organ of female plants and animals where eggs are produced   *229*

ovulation   release of a mature egg from an ovary   *229*

P

paramecium   (plural, *paramecia*) animal-like protist that moves by means of cilia   *95*

parasite   organism that lives on or in a host and harms it   *128*

passive transport   movement of molecules across a cell membrane without the use of energy   *19*

pathogen   substance that causes disease   *234*

pelagic zone   open ocean past the sublittoral zone   *199*

phloem   vascular tissue that carries food made in the leaves to all other parts of the plant where the food is used or stored   *111*

photosynthesis   process by which producers change radiant energy into chemical energy for the purpose of making food   *28, 112*

placenta   organ that connects the unborn to the mother inside the mother's body and supplies the unborn with nutrients and oxygen   *181, 230*

plasma   liquid part of blood made mostly of water that contains minerals, vitamins, and wastes   *215*

pollen grains found in flowers in which male sex cells, or sperm, form *113*

pollution any harmful substance released into the environment *203*

population group of the same type of organism, or species, living together in a particular area *189*

predation relationship in which one organism kills and eats another *189*

producer organism that is able to make its own food *28, 192*

prokaryotic cell cell that lacks a nucleus *14*

protein chain of amino acids arranged in a specific order *7*

protein synthesis process of forming protein *41*

protist single-celled living thing that is more complex than a bacteria *94*

protoplasm living material *3*

puberty time during which the body becomes sexually mature *228*

R

radial symmetry body plan in which body parts are arranged in a circle around a central area *148*

recessive gene or trait that is not expressed when paired with a dominant gene *50*

regeneration process by which an organism grows new parts to replace lost ones *129*

renewable resource natural resource that can be replaced *202*

reproduction process of making more of the same kind *83*

reptile vertebrate with scaly skin that lays its eggs on land *172*

respiration process by which living things break down food and release energy; process of taking oxygen into and removing carbon dioxide from the body *112, 216*

ribosome organelle inside which proteins are made *11*

roundworm smooth, tube-shaped worm that is pointed at both ends *128*

S

seed special reproductive structure of a plant that contains a young plant and its food *113*

segmented worm complex worm with a body made up of many segments *129*

U

umbilical cord   tissue that connects the embryo with the placenta and carries nutrients and oxygen from the mother to the embryo   *231*

univalve   mollusk that usually has a single coiled shell   *133*

V

vaccine   drug that helps the body protect itself from infection by a virus   *91*

vacuole   sac that stores food, wastes, and other materials needed by the cell   *11*

vascular system   system of tubes that carry water and other materials throughout a plant   *106*

vein   blood vessel that carries blood to the heart   *215*

ventricle   lower chamber of the heart   *215*

vertebrae   (sing., *vertebra*) bones that make up the backbone   *157*

vertebrate   animal with a strong, flexible backbone   *156*

virus   very simple particle made up of genetic material and a protein   *82*

visceral mass   part of a mollusk body that contains the reproductive, digestive, and excretory organs   *132*

X

xylem   vascular tissue that carries water up from the roots through the stem to the leaves   *111*

Z

zygote   fertilized egg   *231*